★ TASTING FREEDOM ★

MEN OF COLOR

To Arms! To Arms!

NOW OR NEVER

This is our golden moment! The Government of the United States calls for every Able-bodied Colored Man to enter the Army for the

THREE YEARS' SERVICE!

AND JOIN IN FIGHTING THE

BATTLES OF LIBERTY AND THE UNION

A new era is open to us. For generations we have suffered under the horrors of slavery, outrage and wrong; our manhood has been denied, our citizenship blotted out, our souls seared and burned, our spirits cowed and crushed, and the hopes of the future of our race involved in doubt and darkness. But now our relations to the white race are changed. Now, therefore, is our most precious moment. Let us rush to arms!

FAIL NOW, & OUR RACE IS DOOMED

on this the soil of our birth. We must now awake, arise, or be forever fallen. If we value liberty, if we wish to be free in this land, if we love our country, if we love our families, our children, our home, we must strike now while the country calls; we must rise up in the dignity of our manhood, and show by our own right arms that we are worthy to be freemen. Our enemies have said that the country between them are an enslaved, cowardly, servile and, without and without-stood, without the spirit of soldiers. Shall we die with this stigma resting upon our genius? Shall we leave this inheritance of shame to our children? No! A thousand times No! WE WILL Rise! This alternative happens us. Let us embrace the freemens fate live or let slaves... What is life without liberty? We say that we have manhood; now is the time to prove it. A nation or a people that cannot fight may be pitied, but cannot be respected. If we would be regarded men, if we would forever

SILENCE THE TONGUE OF CALUMNY

Of Prejudice and Hate, let us Rise Now and Fly to Arms! We have seen what

VALOR AND HEROISM

OUR BROTHERS DISPLAYED AT

PORT HUDSON AND MILLIKEN'S BEND,

Though they are just from the galling, poisoning grasp of Slavery, they have startled the World by the most exalted heroism. If they have proved themselves heroes, cannot WE PROVE OURSELVES MEN?

ARE FREEMEN LESS BRAVE THAN SLAVES

More than a Million White Men have left Comfortable Homes and joined the Armies of the Union to save their Country. Cannot we leave ours and swell the Hosts of the Union, to save our liberties, Vindicate our manhood, and deserve well of our Country. MEN OF COLOR! the Englishman, the Irishman, the Frenchman, the German, the American, have been called to assert their right to freedom and a manly character, by an appeal to the sword. The day that has seen an enslaved race in arms, in all history, seen their last trial. We are men now.

OUR LAST OPPORTUNITY HAS COME

If we are not lower in the scale of humanity than Englishmen, Irishmen, White Americans, and other Races, we can show it now.

MEN OF COLOR, BROTHERS AND FATHERS!

WE APPEAL TO YOU!

By all your concern for yourselves and your liberties, by all your regard for God and humanity, by all your desire for Citizenship and Equality before the law, by all your love for the Country, to stop at no subterfuge, listen to nothing that shall deter you from rallying for the Army. Come Forward, and at once Enroll your Names for the Three Years' Service.

STRIKE NOW!

And you are henceforth and forever FREEMEN!

E. D. Bassett,	Rev. J. Underdue,	Frederick Douglass,	Rev. J. C. Gibbs,	Elijah J. Davis,	James Needham,	Daniel Colley,
Wm. Whipper,	John W. Price,	P. J. Armstrong,	Daniel George,	John P. Burr,	Rev. Elisha Weaver,	J. C. White, Jr.,
D. D. Turner,	Augustus Dorsey,	J. W. Simpson,	Robert M. Adger,	Robert Jones,	Ebenezer Black,	Rev. J. P. Campbell,
Jos. McCreanuell,	William D. Forten,	Rev. J. B. Trusty,	Henry M. Cropper,	O. V. Catto,	Rev. William T. Catto,	Rev. W. J. Alston,
A. S. Cassey,	Rev. Stephen Smith,	S. Morgan Smith,	Rev. J. B. Reeve,	Thos. J. Dorsey,	James R. Gordon,	J. P. Johnson,
A. M. Green,	N. W. Depee,	William G. Gipson,	Mrs. J. A. Williams,	I. D. Cliff,	Samuel Stewart,	Franklin Turner,
J. W. Page,	Dr. J. H. Wilson,	Rev. J. Boulden,	Rev. A. L. Stanford,	Jacob C. White,	David B. Bowser,	Jesse E. Glasgow,
J. R. Seymour,	J. W. Cassey,	Rev. A. Asher,	Thomas J. Bowers,	Morris Hall,	Henry Minton,	

U. S. Steam-Power Book and Job Printing Establishment, Ledger Buildings, Third and Chestnut Streets, Philadelphia.

DANIEL R. BIDDLE
MURRAY DUBIN

TASTING FREEDOM

★ ★ ★ ★ ★

OCTAVIUS CATTO

and the Battle for Equality
in Civil War America

TEMPLE UNIVERSITY PRESS PHILADELPHIA

TEMPLE UNIVERSITY PRESS
Philadelphia, Pennsylvania 19122
www.temple.edu/tempress

Frontispiece: Negro leaders had been divided about whether their young men should enter the war. In June 1863, fifty-five black men, including Octavius and William Catto, said it was time to fight and signed their names to this eight-foot-high broadside. (Courtesy of The Library Company of Philadelphia.)

Paperback edition published 2017
Hardcover edition published 2010

Library of Congress Cataloging-in-Publication Data

Biddle, Daniel R.
    Tasting freedom : Octavius Catto and the battle for equality in Civil War America / Daniel R. Biddle and Murray Dubin.
        p.   cm.
    Includes bibliographical references and index.
    ISBN 978-1-59213-465-6 (hardcover : alk. paper)
    ISBN 978-1-59213-467-0 (e-book)
    1. Catto, Octavius V., 1839–1871. 2. Free African Americans—Pennsylvania—Philadelphia—Biography. 3. African American political activists—Pennsylvania—Philadelphia—Biography. 4. African American teachers—Pennsylvania—Philadelphia—Biography. 5. African American baseball players—Pennsylvania—Philadelphia—Biography. 6. African Americans—Civil rights—Pennsylvania—Philadelphia—History—19th century. 7. Civil rights movements—Pennsylvania—Philadelphia—History—19th century. 8. McMullen, William, 1824–1901. 9. Racism—Pennsylvania—Philadelphia—History—19th century. 10. Philadelphia (Pa.)—Race relations—History—19th century. I. Dubin, Murray. II. Title.
    F158.44.C36B53 2010
    323.092—dc22
    [B]

                                                                                    2009049276

    ISBN 978-1-59213-466-3 (papercover : alk. paper)

♾ The paper used in this publication meets the requirements of the American National Standard for Information Sciences—Permanence of Paper for Printed Library Materials, ANSI Z39.48-1992

Printed in the United States of America

    4   6   8   9   7   5   3

For
Cindy, Libby,
Alex, Minna, and Ellery

Temple University Press gratefully acknowledges the contribution made by the College of Education of Temple University and the Bernard C. Watson Chair in Urban Education in supporting the publication of this book.

★ CONTENTS ★

October 10, 1871

THE YOUNG WHITE MAN had the number 27 tattooed on his hand and a bandage around his head when he began shooting at a colored man named John Fawcett. He missed. Fawcett, a hod carrier from the Philadelphia neighborhood of Frankford, ran up South Street to escape. Joined by a crowd, the bandaged man chased him.

Fawcett saw a cellar door in front of a store in the middle of the block. Before he could dive in, a white boy stuck out a foot and tripped him. Fawcett scrambled to his feet, and the bandaged man fired again.

That same afternoon, about a mile away, another Negro, a schoolteacher with the Roman-sounding name of Octavius Valentine Catto, left a pawnshop on Third Street and began walking home. People on the street knew who he was—an orator who shared stages with Frederick Douglass, a second baseman on the city's best black baseball team, a teacher at a black school of national renown, and an activist who had fought in the state capital and on the streets for equal rights. He was thirty-two.

It was election day 1871, and the busy South Street area—the institutional and emotional heart of the black community—had been rocked by violence since the night before. Was it all the Squire's doing? White policemen and Democrats who answered to him were attacking black voters, and scores had gone to the hospital. Catto had sent his pupils home early. Rather than going directly to his boardinghouse, he chose a safer route—up Lombard to Ninth Street, near his fiancée's home, and then down to South Street. He lived at 814.

Catto walked with an assured, athletic gait, as if his right to the pavement were guaranteed. Which it was—but only lately. Memories of slavery haunted every colored home. Generations of men and women had risked their lives to claim the simplest of rights—to learn in a schoolhouse, serve in the army, ride the railways, cast a ballot. Now those rights were being tested. Catto turned onto South Street at the moment when, in W.E.B. Du Bois's words, Americans of color "were first tasting freedom."

As Catto walked east, the bandaged man was looking for more Negroes to hurt, more Negroes who would not be able to vote that day. He passed Catto nonchalantly, but once he was five steps beyond, the bandaged man turned and crouched. A young girl at 822 South shouted to Catto, "Look out for that man!"

The bandaged man was pulling out his gun.

★ TASTING FREEDOM ★

"A Hundred O. V. Cattos"

SAY THE WORDS *civil rights movement* and the conversation veers to Selma and Birmingham and what people remember reading or seeing on small black-and-white televisions—sit-ins on buses and at lunch counters, Rosa Parks and Dr. Martin Luther King Jr., Governor George Wallace and Sheriff Bull Connor. It was all so very long ago, the 1950s and 1960s.

There are few memories before that.

It is difficult to point to a moment when a movement began or ended or emerged as distinct from another. But the civil rights movement in the mid-twentieth century was the second or third organized effort by African Americans to be treated as the equals of white persons.

This book is about the first civil rights movement, about its heroes, villains, and battles. Not the Civil War battles at Antietam or Bull Run but the street wars—pogroms, as the historian Roger Lane says—of whites against blacks in Washington, New York, Cincinnati, and Philadelphia. The heroes from the 1800s have not had highways named after them, or commendations from a thankful nation. So the stories of Henry Highland Garnet, Caroline Le Count, and Octavius Valentine Catto are a new way for us to see an old century and an older problem. The nineteenth century had its charismatic racial villains as well—this time, another "Bull," William "Bull" McMullen, also known as the Squire.

This is a book about the North, about "free" blacks whose freedom was in name only. For the most part, they could not vote, testify, or participate in their community's July 4 celebration. Black people in the mid-nineteenth-century North were threatened not with whippings by slaveholders but with insults, brickbats, torches, and gunfire. They lived in a time when mob violence was so common that the word *mobbed* was a verb. African Americans were routinely assailed in the public square, in the courts and the legislatures, even in the privacy of their churches, schools, and homes. Their assailants? Everyone—from the resentful Irish poor to some of the nation's most powerful men.

Octavius Catto, his father, and his friends and allies fought a street battle for equal rights in Northern cities before, during, and after the Civil War. The men and women of Catto's generation presaged the better-known civil rights era, sitting down as Rosa Parks did, challenging baseball's color line as Jackie Robinson did, marching for the right to vote as Martin Luther King Jr. did. But they did all these things a century before. Think about that for a moment—Caroline Le Count did almost the same thing as Rosa Parks did, but her streetcar in 1867 was powered by a horse.

So while ending slavery and bringing fugitive slaves to freedom through the Underground Railroad captured the hearts and minds of abolitionists, black and white alike, we write, instead, about the peril and prejudice felt in New York and Boston and Detroit among African Americans. They had libraries, Odd Fellow lodges, choral societies, and ladies clubs but never the freedom to walk down the street safe from white boys attacking them, or, at the very least, spitting out the word *Nigger*.

And speaking of that vile word: It will appear often in these pages. At the risk of offending readers, we chose to include this and other racist words in an effort to depict accurately the talk of those days. For similar reasons we chose to use *Negro* and *colored*, the latter being a term many nineteenth-century African Americans accepted and preferred.

The man at the center of our story, O. V. Catto—who electrified a biracial audience in 1864 when he said, "There must come a change"—was a charmer of ladies, a hard-hitting second baseman, a talented teacher, and a Renaissance man of equal rights whom one historian likens to Dr. King and another to George Steinbrenner.

Catto spent too much money on clothes, ate too well at banquets, and reveled in late-summer parties at the New Jersey shore. He wrote poetry and fell in love—and now we are getting ahead of the story.

Catto, with a group of other African Americans who called themselves a "band of brothers," challenged one injustice after another. His story— their story—begins in lesser-known corners of our history, in Charleston, South Carolina, where people of color owned slaves and where teaching blacks to read was a crime punished by whipping, and ends in Philadelphia, where police used billy clubs on Negro voters and where business leaders condoned arson to break up an abolitionist convention within sight of Independence Hall.

This first civil rights movement did not begin or end with Catto. No, he stood on the shoulders of older heroes—Richard Allen, Frederick Douglass, Harriet Tubman, Lucretia Mott. Catto's generation, in turn, left footsteps for twentieth-century men and women to follow.

As the Catto family descendant Leonard Smith says today, "There were a hundred O. V. Cattos." Their stories need telling.

We begin with the earliest Cattos, and their story starts in Charleston.

CHAPTER 1

Charleston

O N NOVEMBER 24, 1800, as Thomas Jefferson rode from Monticello in an open four-wheeled phaeton to conclude his campaign for president, Octavius Catto's grandmother was being dragooned into slavery in South Carolina.

This indignity gave poor Fanny Shields the distinction of having been enslaved twice. So says a document two centuries old: Her owner had freed her, but he was dead by 1800, and another slaveholder seized Fanny and her daughter "with force & Arms" to use them as his slaves.

It was a peril well-known to the mulattoes, mechanics, Indians, dockhands, and former slaves who made up the city of Charleston's free colored population. *Free* was how the tax code defined their world. But somewhere on the high fence of caveats and contradictions around that world, this much was clear: You could be bullied into bondage at almost any time. Reclaiming your freedom, flimsy as it was, depended on having a white "guardian" vouch for you. He could do so by filing a claim of "ravishment of ward." Those words are scrawled on the document that records the freedom of Fanny Shields and the moment of her re-enslavement.

★ ★ ★

FOUNDED IN 1670, Charleston was the first English city in North America to be born with slavery as part of its initial breath. The city's collective first fears were attacks—from the Spanish two hundred miles away in

St. Augustine and from slaves rising up inside the city. Worries about the Spanish would end before the Revolutionary War. Fear of slave violence would last a hundred years beyond that.

Ninety-three passengers were on the *Carolina*, the three-masted frigate that arrived in Charleston that first April, seven months after leaving England. Twenty-nine were men of property and free; sixty-three were indentured white servants who would serve two to seven years to repay their passage. One man on board, his name lost to history, was a black slave. That September, a ship from Bermuda arrived with all manner of cargo aboard, including white servants and the first black slaves whose names we know: John, Elizabeth, and John Jr. The African slave trade into Charleston had begun.

Immigrants came from France and England and throughout Europe to the bustling port city with the palmettos and the giant oaks covered in Spanish moss. South Carolina's eight British proprietors, or landowners, paid for advertising circulars in Europe promoting the healthful air that made men "more lightsome" and women "very Fruitful." Not mentioned was the hot, humid climate, the malaria and yellow fever. Each settler was to get 150 acres of free land. By the end of the 1600s, Charleston had about a thousand residents and four broad municipal thoroughfares, streets sixty feet wide filled with Indians carrying venison, planters hailing from Barbados, and pirates trading gold and silver for supplies. Along the waterfront, furs were loaded on ships to England while meat and lumber filled ships headed to the West Indies in exchange for rum and sugar.

Rice soon became a larger export crop—resulting in the need for more slaves for planting, hoeing, and husking. And more exports attracted more piracy. So ships were sent out to rid the waters of pirates and to bring in more slaves from the West Indies. In 1696, copying from a slave code in Barbados, the Carolina General Assembly enacted its first major legislation concerning black slaves and their "barbarous, wild, savage Natures." The new law provided for the "policing of slaves and the trials of miscreant slaves."

A year later, three black slaves fled to Spanish Florida and what they hoped was freedom. Instead they were caught, returned to Charleston, and emasculated. One slave died, and his owner was paid sixty-five dollars for *his* loss of property.

Early in the new century, Charleston joined Philadelphia, Boston, and New York as a principal city in British North America. With a pop-

ulation of 8,270 and a Negro community that exceeded 3,200, peninsu-
lar Charleston was about to become the only colony in North America
with more blacks than whites. The assembly passed curfews for blacks
and empowered town constables to arrest any black "who had no good reason" to be out at night "and lock him up until morning, have him whipped
'severely,' & return him to his owners after a fine was paid."

South Carolina beat back real and imagined uprisings of African
slaves, torturing and killing those involved and passing one slave law after
another, each more restrictive than the last. There was no sham or pretext
to these legislative acts. A 1741 law said its purpose was to make sure that
slaves "be kept in due subjection & obedience." That same law noted that
for anyone who became too physical with a slave, perhaps taking out an eye
or scalding with boiling water, punishment was swift—there was a fine.

Fear drove the attitudes and actions of whites toward slaves. So too
did money. By mid-decade, five hundred ocean-going ships and countless
smaller vessels were loading and off-loading merchandise, foodstuffs, and
slaves each year. On Sundays, slaves from plantations came into Charleston on their day of rest, frightening white residents with their sheer numbers and leading the state to raise the import duty on slaves. But a howl
went up from local brokers who marketed the slaves to plantations for field
work and to city homeowners for domestic labor, so lawmakers relented
and lowered the fees. This debate, pitting fear against greed, went back
and forth throughout the century.

★ ★ ★

RACE REVERBERATED THROUGH much of Charleston conversation
in the 1700s and beyond: There was talk of sex, of firearms, and of how
much freedom to confer on free persons of color.

Visitors to the eighteenth-century city often observed the cruelty that
marked a slave's life, including parents' occasionally offering children
their own black slaves to abuse. Slave owners' mulatto children were not
shunned, nor was conversation about masters making sexual use of slave
women. Charleston was the only English city in North America where
that issue was openly discussed.

Visiting ministers accused Carolina masters of being "white Sodom-
ites." One visitor in the 1770s wrote, "The enjoyment of a negro or a
mulatto woman is spoken of as quite a common thing." Sixty years later,
the Scottish traveler James Stuart wrote of an overnight stagecoach ride

into Charleston. Stuart heard a wealthy passenger explain that he considered himself "first husband" to his plantation's half dozen slave girls, that "he was frequently waited upon at table by his own [mulatto] children, and had actually sent some of them to the public market to be sold as slaves." This talk sparked "merriment" among the other travelers as the stage rattled across the low country. A doctor on board said he, too, made use of his slave girls.

Not everyone took these relationships quite so calmly, especially the slave owners' wives. Mary Boykin Chesnut wrote: "Our men live all in one house with their wives and concubines; and the mulattoes one sees in every family partly resemble the white children. Any lady is ready to tell you the father of all the mulatto children in everybody's household but her own."

As for male slaves, South Carolina did not want to arm them, even when requested to do so by the fledgling federal government. "We are much disgusted here at the Congress recommending us to arm our slaves," the Charleston leader Christopher Gadsden wrote in the Revolutionary War. He said the recommendation "was received with great resentment as a very dangerous and impolitic step." South Carolina did enlist slaves to be laborers, to build defenses around Charleston, but it wanted no part of a slave militia.

★ ★ ★

THE NATION'S FIRST federal census in 1790 counted Charleston's population as 8,089 whites, 8,831 slaves, and 600 free Negroes. Many of the 600 had bought their freedom after being permitted to "hire out" their work for a wage, often divided between master and slave. Some were freed because of their service in the war.

This free population grew into a demi-monde, a layer squeezed between white Charleston and black slavery. By 1790 they formed a fraternal order. Many owned slaves.

This is the confusing, cruel, and changing world into which Octavius Catto's father was born and in which his grandmother was twice enslaved.

Catto's mother had been owned by Matthew Shields, a Charleston man. Before his death, he freed Fanny and her daughter, Mary Shields. It is unclear whether Shields was Mary's last name because Matthew Shields owned her or fathered her or both. Slave owners sometimes freed women they had impregnated and children they had fathered.

Fanny and Mary Shields came to the court's attention when James Pring, a white overseer on a rice plantation, swore out a summons for a slaveholder named Francis Mulligan. Pring accused Mulligan of forcing Fanny and Mary to become his slaves. Court documents describe both Fanny and Mary as free and mulatto.

Proving one's freedom in court was a daunting task, making the bogeyman of kidnapping loom all the larger to free Negroes, North and South. But a judge named John Faucheraud Grimké, who had slaves of his own, ordered Mulligan to court. (Grimké signed his name; the illiterate Pring drew an X.) A jury convicted Mulligan. For stealing two Negroes' freedom, he paid court costs and a fine of four dollars—or about sixty-two dollars today. Pring, at his request, was declared guardian of Fanny and Mary Shields.

To be sure, a judge upholding two Negroes' limited liberties in 1801 was hardly a sign that Charleston was reconsidering slavery as a new century began. That year, a mob mistook a visiting minister for an abolitionist—not at all the sort of tourist Charleston embraced. He was dragged from a pulpit and held beneath a pump. A plucky woman saved him from drowning, using her shawl to stop the pump while a man moved the crowd back by waving a sword. If anything, Charleston seemed to be looking backward.

★ ★ ★

FANNY WAS FREE when she bore a son, William Catto, in about 1810.

By now, South Carolina was a state well versed in forced servitude. Since 1670, the Port of Charleston had taken in more than 100,000 slaves and a hundred local firms had processed and sold them. Slavery flourished even as Northern states began to outlaw it. Fanny's son was born in Charleston at a time when its 11,568 slaves and 1,472 free people of color were 53 percent of the city.

Tracing black ancestry in the antebellum South is fraught with difficulty. As one famous former slave said, "Genealogical trees do not flourish among the slaves." William's last name was *Catto*, but his father's identity is a mystery. *Cato* was a common name in South Carolina, seen in records of Scotsmen and slaves alike. But *Catto* with a double *t* was unusual. On occasion, the two spellings were interchangeable.

Who was William Catto's father? He may have been a slave, Francis Catto, whose age was given as sixty when he died in Charleston in 1836.

Perhaps he bore a scar from the Revolutionary War: According to the family story passed down through generations of Catto descendants, William's father suffered a minor wound but won his freedom, as some Negroes did, by serving as a driver or a laborer in that war. Archival records say a Negro named Catto was a "wagoner" for George Washington's troops.

We can offer one other theory about William Catto's last name.

Free blacks in South Carolina could not testify, even to attest to their freedom. So in 1819, a white man named Patrick McGann swore in court that young William Thomas Catto was not a slave. McGann said Fanny was free when her son was born. Because freedom was usually determined by the mother's status, McGann's oath was crucial.

But how was he certain that she was free? And why was he in court in the first place?

McGann, born in Ireland, was a Charleston silversmith and watchmaker. He owned a mulatto woman, Barsheba Cattle, whose name was spelled many ways. He acquired her in 1798, but records suggest she was less slave than lover and business partner. She bought and sold slaves with him from 1805 on and appears to have been the moving force in those transactions.

Barsheba becomes important because she died seven months before McGann's 1819 court appearance. In her will, she called herself "a free person of color" and asked that her slave, Bob, be sold and the proceeds shared by "my friend, Patrick McGann, and my daughter, Jane Rebecca McGann." She bequeathed to Jane her linens, blankets, a featherbed, and "6 silver teaspoons."

Fanny Shields needed a white man to vouch for her son's liberty. Since she asked McGann, it makes sense that she knew Barsheba as well. When free Negroes came of age, say at fifteen or sixteen, their white guardians attested to their freedom—their "free papers." The fact that McGann went to court when William Catto was about nine, and soon after Barsheba Cattle's death, suggests that, in an age of rampant spelling inconsistency, the spelling of Catto was Fanny's attempt to honor the name and memory of a friend.

★ ★ ★

SO IN 1819, William Catto, son of a mulatto mother, was now officially a free person of color. His skin was brown, and free brown men in Charleston distanced themselves from darker men. Brown, as historians have written, "marked a Negro as someone whites had to watch." Slaves were property and owners maintained that property with food and shelter. Free Negroes fended for themselves, causing chronic uneasiness in white Charleston. They were, in one white man's view, "a bad example" to black domestics, "and a growing evil to our State."

Nor did being free and brown endear young William to the slaves. One free man, Michael Eggart, said "our people"—Charleston's free mulattoes—must close ranks to survive on the middle ground, between "the prejudice of the white man" and "the deeper hate of our more sable brethren."

Eggart said the only balm for such hate and prejudice was education, "our life, our sun, our shield." But who taught William Catto? South Carolina had outlawed teaching slaves to read, and in 1801 barred free Negro meetings devoted to "mental faculties." Even so, by the time William was in his early twenties, his vocabulary was flowery, his penmanship precise.

Perhaps he learned from Thomas Bonneau, "the most popular schoolmaster" among Charleston mulattoes. Bonneau taught reading, writing, and "ciphering" to Daniel Payne, a mulatto boy William came to know. Bonneau and a few other colored teachers held classes in churchyards or in their homes.

Payne's boyhood in Charleston roughly paralleled William's. Payne, too, grew up hearing stories of white kidnappers—of how his freeborn father, as "a mere lad" in Virginia, had been lured onto a boat by a promise of cakes—then smuggled off to Charleston and sold into slavery for years before he could buy his freedom back.

Being apprenticed to a carpenter at the age of twelve did not stop young Payne from learning.

"I resolved to devote every moment of leisure to the study of books, and every cent to the purchase of them. I raised money by making tables, benches, clothes-horses, and 'corset-bones,' which I sold on Saturday night in the public market. During my apprenticeship I would eat my meals in a few minutes and spend the remainder of the hour allowed me at breakfast and dinner in reading. After the day's work was done I perused my books till nearly 12 o'clock; and then, keeping a tinder-box, flint, steel, and candle at my bedside, I would awake at 4, strike a light, and study till 6, when my daily labors began."

But the time of such teaching was coming to an end, and a former slave with the memorable name of Denmark Vesey was one reason why.

What is known has melded with what is supposed about Vesey. Born in 1767, he may have come from St. Thomas in the West Indies, his first name likely an Anglicization of Telemaque. From about age fourteen, he was the ship captain Joseph Vesey's personal slave. But in 1800, he won fifteen hundred dollars in a Charleston lottery, bought his freedom for six hundred dollars, opened a carpentry shop, bought property, joined the new African Church of Charleston (it had begun in 1818), married more than once, and became a well-known figure among slaves and free blacks. He was handsome, could read and write, and hated slavery.

What happened next remains a matter of debate—was it a carefully planned slave revolt or a white overreaction? Vesey and his trusted lieutenants either spent as many as four years actively planning an insurrection involving thousands of slaves, or they bragged, groused, and wondered what would happen *if we did this.*

Whichever it was, it sounded serious. Peter Desverneys, a mulatto slave, said he was asked to join a plot to kill many whites. He quietly sought the counsel of a man he trusted, William Penceel, a free mulatto who owned slaves. Penceel said tell your master. In other words, betray the plotters.

The "plot" was exposed on June 14, 1822. Vesey was caught eight days later and hanged on July 2. In all, 131 were arrested, 30 deported, 1 whipped, 1 banished from South Carolina, 35 executed. Did young William Catto see them die? Nearly everyone in Charleston did. John Bailey Adger, a white boy his age, remembered: "I saw distinctly from the third-story window of my father's house . . . a long gallows erected . . . and on it 22 negroes hanged at one time. I might say the whole city turned out for this occasion."

On December 25, Desverneys, the mulatto slave whose concern about killing whites led to the killings of the Vesey plotters, was officially cleared of wrongdoing. He was not shunned by the mulatto elite in Charleston. In fact, the opposite occurred. He married a woman whose brother belonged to the Brown Fellowship Society, the exclusive fraternal group for the city's brown-skinned men. By 1840, Desverneys owned eight slaves.

The fears that followed Vesey led white South Carolina leaders to reconsider their attitudes and actions toward free blacks and slaves and to wonder whether too much leniency had been shown. Congressman Thomas Pinckney wrote in 1822 that new laws should be used to curb "the indulgences which have so pampered the enormous number of domestics." He blamed "public inattention" to the existing laws and warned that Negroes in the city must be stopped from obtaining any more of "the dangerous instrument of learning which many of them have acquired."

The Vesey insurrection, as it would come to be known, besides causing thirty-five people to die, killed the black church in Charleston and strangled the throat of education for free blacks.

Vesey and the men around him belonged to the new African church in town, which, after the one in Philadelphia, was the largest African Methodist Episcopal (A.M.E.) church. Its minister, Morris Brown, had no role in the plot, but Charleston's white leaders believed that the church was Vesey's Trojan horse, that Brown had at least nourished the plotters' minds. And there had long been talk that Northern abolitionist money had paid for the church building.

After all, Brown had been to Philadelphia. There he had been ordained into the newborn A.M.E.'s ministry by Richard Allen himself. That was in 1816. Two years later, in Charleston, police had arrested Brown and 140 worshippers for "unlawful assembly"—a Sunday prayer meeting. The court said Brown could leave Charleston forever or serve a month in jail. A model for every minister who ever engaged in civil disobedience in the name of civil rights, Brown had chosen jail.

Now, the Vesey terror gave authorities another chance to banish him. A judge ordered Brown to leave Charleston. The City Council ordered his church demolished—though a mob burned it first. Brown and his family headed to Philadelphia.

Vesey had become the "savage," the free Negro carpenter who had won white customers' respect even as he plotted to see their city "wrapped in flames," as his judges wrote. After Vesey, the idea of a black church was unthinkable. Aspiring black clergymen left town. Black congregants, slave and free, moved to white Methodist, Presbyterian, and Baptist houses of worship, drastically changing the color configuration of the church on a Sunday. Slaves sat separately from whites, in the galleries or in the back. Where free persons of color sat was a contentious issue.

Three Methodist churches offered "a few seats on the lower floor behind those used by whites," separated by a "dividing panel near the doors for the aged and disabled colored members." But often there was not enough room for all the mulatto congregants back there. On occasion, "a few free persons of color were allowed to use some [white] seats beyond the dividing line. . . . Others followed, until the matter became annoying to the whites, especially when congregations were full."

In addition to opening their doors to Negroes, the Methodist clergy strove to bring God's word to slaves on plantations near Charleston. By the 1830s, these two policies stuck firmly in the craw of the churches' whites. "This care over the colored people, & the multitudes of them attending our services, had hindered our work with the whites," a white minister recalled. "Methodism was, by some, condemned as 'the negro church.' . . . But the Negro was a man with a soul to save, one for whom little care was shown."

The missionary work was begun by young Southern clergy, among them the Methodist William Capers and the Presbyterian Charles Colcock Jones, who, a biographer wrote, "shared an uneasy dissatisfaction with the slave system and the way in which it brutalized people." As a young seminarian in the North, Jones called slavery "a violation of all the Laws of God and man." He went back south and became devoted to the mission, but not as an end to slavery. The mission aimed to "change blacks' behavior and beliefs so that they would share the same world view as white Evangelicals."

One way to do that was to teach the lessons of the Bible, but in most instances it meant teaching the uneducated how to read the Bible, and before too long, teaching reading to Negroes would be illegal in South Carolina. So clergymen like Jones and Capers focused on oral lessons and tailored their catechisms to oral teaching.

Mission leaders thought the slavery debate would change because their teachings would change the Negroes, slave and free, by uplifting them from what Jones called their "heathen" and "degraded" state. Their plan was grandiose and naïve. Because of an "almost hysterical Southern sensitivity" to openly discussing slavery, the mission movement had little impact on a debate that few in the South wanted to have.

Before the name Vesey could slip from white memories, a bloody 1831 slave revolt in Virginia brought it back. States enacted new curbs. In Alabama, five slaveholders had to be present before a colored man could preach. In Georgia, no Negro could preach to more than seven people unless three white ministers approved. Churches with Negro lay preachers or "exhorters" running Sabbath school classes had these men's characters "thoroughly investigated." Some Southern states simply expelled all free blacks.

South Carolina decreed that owners could no longer free their slaves—
only the legislature could, if properly petitioned. The state required free
Negroes over age fifteen to have a white guardian, or risk being sold into
slavery. One law gave a formal South Carolina farewell to free Negroes
exiting the state. Once they left, they could not return.

A law enacted after Vesey required visiting Negro sailors to be jailed
in South Carolina ports and not freed until their ship's departure. If a
ship captain failed to pay the costs of this custody, the sailor could be
auctioned into slavery. The state's lawyer likened this law to quarantining
yellow fever victims: "In South Carolina, we think the presence of a free
negro, fresh from the lectures of an Abolition Society, equally dangerous."

A federal judge ruled the Negro Seamen's Act unconstitutional. (More
than a century later, a black lawyer, Thurgood Marshall, cited this decision as he argued before the Supreme Court in *Brown v. Board of Education*.) But South Carolina ignored the judge, and federal marshals did not
intervene on behalf of colored sailors.

White men could enter meetings of Negroes at any time and demand
each person's "free papers." A man caught without them faced twenty
lashes or a return to bondage. After 1818, if a Negro prayer meeting was
held in secret, after sunset, or behind a locked door, municipal patrolmen
were authorized to smash the windows and break down the doors.

Enforcement of such laws ebbed and flowed, easing as the terror of
Vesey slowly gave way to fledgling academies in the rooms of men like
Payne and Bonneau; in the 1830s, tightening up again.

Free Negroes could not meet in groups of more than seven or be on
the streets after 9:00 P.M. or be found without their papers in Charleston
Neck, the section north of the city where many free Negroes lived. Yet
some managed to learn and teach. At Payne's little Sabbath school, conducted with Capers's blessing, the free colored teachers were carpenters,
tailors, smiths, and millwrights such as William Catto.

★ ★ ★

BY 1830, WILLIAM CATTO had acquired a trade. In an economy dependent on rice mills, Catto and a few other free Negroes became millwrights.

Low-country planters sent slaves to grow rice, a many-handed task
performed in the watery provinces of thousand-acre empires. West Africans brought centuries' know-how in cultivating and preparing rice on a
small scale. But white planters had little use for small. Each September,

from dawn until dark, thousands of slave men and women swung sickles to cut down the rice stalks, then bundled them on flatboats that eased down the canals and rivers to Charleston, Beaufort, and Savannah. There, the mills took over.

As cotton depended on Eli Whitney's gin, rice required mills—thrashing mills to strip the grain from its golden stalk, pounding mills to crack the brown husk off the kernel in the manner of mortar and pestle—gently, lest kernels crack and lose value at market. The thrashing mill was three stories of bands, flanges, flywheels, and metal teeth that stripped the stalks—*trashed* them, people said. It ran on water, horse power, and eventually steam and was such an investment that owners brought in partners or charged for thrashing other planters' rice. The mill required constant tinkering by swift-handed millwrights like Catto, who made himself indispensable before he turned twenty-one.

Another Negro probably trained him. On the Weston plantation, near Charleston, a millwright named Anthony was so valued that his owner bequeathed him his freedom and a few dollars to open a shop. Other planters came to rely on "Toney" Weston. A colored author in the North ranked him among the race's pioneers for getting a mill to thrash a thousand bushels of rice a day. That author, Martin Delany, said Weston "improved" on the work of a younger Negro, who had coaxed the daily yield to five hundred bushels by 1831. Delany identified the younger millwright as William Thomas Catto.

Because he was a Negro, any schooling he received was informal—"in the shade," as Jones put it. Had Toney Weston trained the boy? Had the silversmith Patrick McGann, who knew his mother, set him on this course? Or his mother's guardian, James Pring, an overseer in the Bull Island rice fields? Catto became so skilled that owners entrusted to him, as they had to Weston, the care of a machine on which an economy relied. A slave economy—in which Catto and Weston were among the few Negroes paid for their labor.

A British visitor to a low-country thrashing mill found himself impressed with how the free Negro millwrights carried themselves: "When these mechanics come to consult [the owner] on business, their manner of speaking to him is quite as independent as that of English artisans to their employers. Their aptitude for the practice of such mechanical arts may encourage every philanthropist who has had misgivings in regard to the progressive powers of the race."

* * *

TO THE EXTENT that colored tradesmen could prosper in 1830s Charleston, William Catto prospered. He taught in Payne's Sabbath school. He joined a Negro fraternal society and rented a room on Boundary Street, close enough to hear the morning reveilles of the troops stationed in Charleston "out of fear of the Negroes." He lived near the market, with its oranges from Florida and pineapples from Cuba, its nuts and cabbages and beets red and white. He walked among slaves darker than himself, men with numbered badges who roasted oysters in the market as turkey buzzards watched from rooftops, waiting to feed on the scraps. Killing one—a buzzard, not an oyster seller—was a five-dollar fine. And if a seller forgot his slave badge, city law called for "20 stripes on the bare back," delivered right there in the market.

A longer walk from Catto's room was the city workhouse, nicknamed the Sugar House, where errant slaves could be heard getting "a little sugar," as people said. The main work of the workhouse was a treadmill where men and women were flogged.

Catto might have heard distant sounds of heavy construction and federal engineers at work. He could look across the harbor to see the building of a new fort, called Sumter.

The Cumberland Street Sabbath school, where he taught the Bible, was run by Payne, and its teachers were persons of color. The school operated with the approval of two white clergymen, James O. Andrew and William Capers, the latter so active in the mission movement. The other teachers—Richard Holloway, Samuel Weston, William Boone Clark, and Anthony Weston—had become an important part of Catto's life, a tight circle. They were all free persons of color, brown men, successful men. Some, like Weston, were becoming well-to-do. Some—though not Catto or Payne—bought and sold slaves. Even Bonneau, the teacher everyone respected, owned slaves. In the North, black leaders railed against slavery. In Charleston, many brown men and women took advantage of the practice.

Some scholars have argued that black slave owners possessed a certain benevolence, that they frequently purchased family members and friends in order to free them. But some trafficked in slaves for profit. Understand that the Holloways and Bonneaus were seen as upright and charitable men, respected by their peers. Their values and choices were rooted in their time, not ours. We would like to say William Catto did not own slaves because he found that choice morally repugnant. His actions and words later in life support that view. But in the 1830s, perhaps he just never was able to afford the price.

In 1830, 474 mulattoes owned nearly 2,800 slaves in the state, with most of those owners in Charleston. When legislators considered outlawing Negro slave-owning, the editors of the *Charleston Courier* wrote that the Negro's "right to hold slaves gives him a stake in the institution of slavery and makes it in his interest as well as his duty to uphold it. It identifies his interests and his feelings . . . with those of the white population."

* * *

SOME NEGRO SLAVE OWNERS joined the city's most exclusive club for mulattoes, the Brown Fellowship Society, which barred men if their skin was too dark, a prerequisite that later generations called the "grocery bag rule." Other Negro fraternal groups were less choosy. In 1831, Catto joined the Friendly Union Society, as did his friend William Boone Clark and Peter Desverneys, whose name was forever linked to Vesey's. Samuel Weston, a fellow Sabbath school teacher, joined, along with Thomas Bonneau.

The society's preamble explained its reason for existence. "[We believe] it to be an essential duty of mankind to contribute as liberally as possible towards relieving the wants of those who are in distress, and promoting the welfare and happiness of each other. We . . . declare ourselves a society for mutual aid in time of distress."

The societies were hothouses of parliamentary procedure, tiny clubs of tradesmen, tailors, and mechanics gathering in this man's room or that man's yard, making motions, taking votes, electing corresponding secretaries, writing bylaws. Some promoted "literary improvement," others separated themselves from the currents of the day—the Brown Fellowship Society bylaws banned discussion of politics. All sought to give their dues-paying members something white Charleston would not: a burial ground.

But none of what happened inside the clubs protected these men from numerous prohibitions that governed their public behavior. The laws, for example, forbade Negroes from lighting a cigar or pipe or carrying a cane, unless the carrier was blind or lame. A white man snatched Daniel Payne's walking stick and struck him with it. Payne was jailed for striking back.

Stuart, the Scotsman visiting South Carolina in 1830, wrote of horse-racing week in Charleston, an event so popular that he had trouble securing a hotel room. The homes were "real palazzos," with verandas shaded by orange trees and magnolias and gardens abloom in March with jonquils and early roses. He found the streets deserted at night—and learned that the colored populace was not allowed out after nine. Returning to his hotel, he saw slaves asleep in the hall. "They neither get beds nor bedding here," he wrote, "and you may kick them or tread upon them . . . with impunity."

Before breakfast, Stuart saw his landlady give a slave "such a blow behind the ear as made him reel." "It was her daily and hourly practice," he noted, "to beat her servants." The colored cook told Stuart he had seen his wife and children sold in the market two years earlier.

Stuart toured a rice mill and dined on turtle soup, fish, venison, mutton, turkey, "two boiled salted tongues, two tame ducks, two wild ducks," West Indies fruits, "iced-cream in profusion," claret and Madeira, and champagne and lemonade, served by slaves in livery. At the racetrack, he saw "the nobility" arrive in coaches emblazoned with coats-of-arms to watch colored jockeys compete. But when a free Negro wandered close to the course, a track steward in high boots and white corduroys "struck him with his horse-whip."

Stuart wrote, "No wonder these people thirst for vengeance."

★ ★ ★

IN AUGUST 1831, a slave preacher in Virginia set out to slake that thirst. Nat Turner led some forty other men on a two-day rampage against plantation owners, axing and bludgeoning nearly sixty whites to death in the nation's bloodiest slave revolt. In response, local whites executed as many as two hundred blacks. Turner believed a solar eclipse was God's signal to launch the uprising; white Southerners suspected the real signal was the *Liberator*, the paper the Boston abolitionist William Lloyd Garrison had launched that year. Southern states enacted a new wave of curbs on black preaching, teaching, and assembling. South Carolina prohibited schools for blacks and, for that matter, the teaching of reading and writing.

Charleston's city fathers posted a one-thousand-dollar reward for the arrest and conviction of anyone distributing abolitionist writings. On the morning of July 30, 1835, the *Charleston Courier* reported that the city post office had received a bundle of antislavery pamphlets from the North, intended for the colored population. After midnight, a mob stormed the post office and burned the pamphlets. The rioters were not "any ignorant or infuriated rabble," the postmaster reported. "The excitement . . . had evidently taken possession of men of all parties and of every grade of society."

A committee of leading citizens announced that the postmaster would bar delivery of all other "incendiary documents." In Washington, President Andrew Jackson so loudly condemned the antislavery mailings that South Carolina's legislature thanked him.

City and state officials enacted measure after measure to take away the "dangerous instrument of learning" from Catto's world—above all, to stop the ears and shutter the eyes of Negroes to the words being spoken and published by Garrison and other abolitionists. The objective was to cut off black Charleston from the antislavery arguments that, in the 1830s, were raging across the North and across the Atlantic. In 1833, the British Empire officially ended slavery.

★ ★ ★

WILLIAM CATTO'S EARLIEST known writing is dated September 6, 1833. He was inviting Richard Holloway to join a society of mulattoes, "Formed for the purpose of Obtaining further progress in Literary Improvement," and named for their beloved teacher who had died two years before. The Bonneau Literary Society was meeting on Wednesday evening in Daniel Payne's rented room. Would the carpenter Holloway do them the honor of attending?

Payne, Holloway, and Catto all taught Sabbath school. Their little society elected Catto its corresponding secretary. He wrote with a flourish, finishing words such as "accepting" and "honorary" with a confident leftward swoop.

About this time Catto came to know a young woman of some means. Her name was Sarah Isabella Cain, and her lineage amounted to mulatto aristocracy in Charleston. Cain men fished the waters off Charleston in two boats that they owned. Their wealthier cousins, the Dereefs, ran a lumberyard. No newspaper followed Sarah and William's courtship, and no church bulletin recorded them gaily dancing. No surviving city or church document marked this union, but a newspaper article many years later said that William wed a woman of "fervent piety and great nobility of character," when he married Sarah Cain. She already had a son named John.

The patriarch of her family was Richard Edward Dereef. He had so astutely run his "wood factorage" as it was called, that by the 1830s the dock at the end of Chapel Street was known as Dereef's Wharf. He was a longtime member of the Brown Fellowship. He and his cousin, the fisherman John Cain, had gone to court in 1823 and persuaded a magistrate that the Dereefs and Cains were descended from the same Indian woman and therefore exempt from the state free-Negro tax. That saved two dollars a year (the equivalent of about forty dollars today) on themselves and each of their kin. It added up.

In a portrait, Dereef's high collar and piercing gaze suggest a discerning businessman. He dealt in lumber—and in slaves. He owned as many as sixteen or twenty people at a time, and while these numbers did not rival the hundreds enslaved on plantations outside Charleston, it made him one of the largest slaveholders of color in the United States. A generation later, when a white abolitionist remarked what a blessing the Civil War's outcome had been, Dereef muttered that it had not been a blessing for everyone.

William and Sarah became parents in 1835, when Catherine was born. The family was living at 7 Wall Street. They moved to nearby Henrietta Street before the birth of their first son, William S., in 1837. Henrietta Street was in Charleston Neck, where black and white children sometimes played together. It was a neighborhood just north of Boundary Street, just beyond the reach of Charleston's stricter laws.

In those same 1830s, white churches in Charleston were having a terrible time determining where free Negro worshippers should sit. Meetings were called and pamphlets written, compromises arrived at and dissolved. Methodist conference minutes are filled with page after page on the seating schism.

Young white men angrily threw mulatto men, women, and children out of churches when they would not give up their seats on the main floor. Ministers criticized the actions of the white congregants, and those congregants responded angrily, charging that the clergy cared too much about the Negroes. As many as 150 white Trinity members resigned in protest. Capers asked his flock to behave with "charity and kindness for the people of color." It didn't work. He was losing white congregants, and many of those who stayed took offense at his policy of seating "coloured persons . . . among the whites."

Catto was a member of Trinity Methodist Episcopal Church, and by 1834 his name was known to Capers. The pastor had qualities in common with clergymen such as Charles Colcock Jones; Capers was committed to converting slaves to Christianity but not to freeing them. He thought it important for free blacks to sit with whites but that slaves sit separately. Slavery troubled him, yet he defended it.

Though mulattoes had sat on the main floor behind the whites for more than a decade, the Methodist conference yielded to white complaints, recommending that Trinity rearrange itself to prevent Negroes from "intermixing with whites." Free persons of color began leaving the church. Catto stayed.

Capers showed a sense of humor by thanking his critics for calling him names normally not heard in church but never calling him an abolitionist. In the end, he acquiesced to his white congregants and forced Catto and other free persons of color to sit upstairs in the gallery, already crowded with slaves.

★ ★ ★

IN 1835, THE LAW came crashing down on the little Sabbath school that Daniel Payne was running for Negro children "in the shade" on Cumberland Street. The South Carolina legislature, imagining "the dangerous instrument" in the hands of the next Denmark Vesey or Nat Turner, outlawed the teaching of reading and writing to Negroes and decreed that persons of color breaking this 1835 law would face a whipping "not exceeding 50 lashes." Negroes teaching Negroes—that was all that Payne and his clutch of teachers wanted to do. And now the state made it a crime.

Payne, an endlessly curious scholar who had nearly blinded himself by staring at a solar eclipse, saw the law as aimed straight down at his little school. He went sleepless for days. Then he wrote a rather long poem about what the legislators had done. He wrote that if "tears of blood" would change their minds,

> I at their feet the crimson tide would pour,
> Till potent justice swayed the senate floor.

If South Carolina prevented him from teaching Negro children, he would have to go someplace where he could. Then he dreamed of soaring. "I was lifted up from the earth . . . flying south of the chain of lakes which separate the United States from Canada. To and fro along this line I was still flying in my teaching robes, till I awoke and found myself still in Charleston, but greatly comforted in the midst of my troubles."

Capers gave Payne letters of introduction to Northern churchmen. He received wise counsel and warm clothing from his mulatto compatriot Samuel Weston, "a venerable, intelligent, holy man."

Leaving the South in 1835 would not take Payne beyond slavery's reach. Kidnappings of free Northern blacks had been so commonplace that Negro children in Philadelphia grew up knowing the name of the city's most feared "slave catcher." A Negro leader in New York City exposed judges' and policemen's involvement in a kidnapping ring and published their names and addresses in a "slaveholder's directory."

But Payne knew little of that. He was ready to say good-bye to the strange and anxious world of Charleston's brown men.

★ ★ ★

CATTO AND HIS mulatto friends decided they had had enough of sitting with the slaves in the balcony of Trinity Methodist Episcopal Church. The slaves had made it intolerable.

On behalf of his fellow congregants, among them men who had taught with him at Payne's school—William Boone Clark, Richard Holloway, and Samuel Weston—Catto wrote a four-page letter to Capers and Methodist officials on February 11, 1836. Weston and Holloway were older, wealthier, and better known—but they turned, instead, to the twenty-six-year-old to speak their minds. Seven signed with Catto. He wrote beside their signatures, "Committee in behalf of the Free people of Color."

The letter is a voyage in distinctive handwriting, first rising on waves of respect and acknowledgment of the goodness of the Methodist clergymen before landing in the shoals of the problem with "our dark brethren."

"And here, most Rev. Sirs, we would not in the least exaggerate our lamentable situation. . . . We . . . humbly beg you in behalf of ourselves, our families, our children, and our friends to give us a patient hearing. . . .

"You are aware . . . that some time back, say two years ago, a portion of the Free People of Color, was driven from their seats . . . on the lower floor of all the Churches to take their seats in the gallery. Since that time, many of our brethren have left the church . . . wandering like lonely exiles from their father's home."

Catto writes that he and his friends have remained loyal and uncomplaining, until now. The letter describes the treatment they and their families received in the balcony: "From many of our dark brethren . . . our very children have been very often lifted from their seats and made to stand until the services are over . . . and in many instances called by opprobrious names disgraceful to a Christian's ear. . . . Our wives have often been made to weep at the manner in which they have been treated by our dark brethren."

When the church was full, those darker worshippers would push the women "from their seats and many times sit in their laps regardless of their state (which Sirs has in one instance prov'd fatal) and when spoken to, they say you are driven from downstairs and now you come to take our seats."

"Sirs," Catto asks in the letter, "what shall we do?"

He points out that all the free people of color want is to sit in peace in the seats they once sat in, "but we are not permitted." He says the parents passionately want their children to learn the "Love of God . . . in the Methodist Church" but the current situation makes that exceedingly difficult.

"Our object is not for disunion with our dark brethren—God forbid! It is that many of [the] dark brethren will not let us rest in peace, that we would implore you to grant us a place to rest in peace where we can be at ease as formerly."

And though he says that he did not separate himself from his dark brethren, that is exactly what he did. Catto writes of drunken slaves, of his friends' hats found with a gift inside, "a lump of tobacco freshly chewed that has saliva in large quantities."

The letter was written in an outpouring of emotion, as if these good brown Methodists were receiving a punishment they neither deserved nor understood—first from whites, who had thrown them out, and then from the blacks, already squeezed together on the upstairs benches. The agitation had even "prov'd fatal" for a pregnant woman or her baby. The letter implores, Why have you abandoned us?

Yet the writer's words never spill over the banks of respect for the white clergy.

The clergymen had other concerns in that first week of February 1836. Capers and the others were meeting in Columbia, inland from Charleston, to take stock of their mission work among plantation slaves—how many

converted, baptized, proselytized, saved? Amid these details, the preachers took pains to make clear what they were not.

They scorned abolitionism, conceding only that slavery's excesses—
severe beatings or withholding food—needed curbing. "Our missionaries inculcate the duties of servants to their masters," the ministers
reported. "We hold that a Christian slave must be submissive, faithful,
and obedient."

These were the men to whom Catto had written. The plea failed; free
persons of color were not allowed back downstairs. Catto's 1836 letter is in
Methodist records in South Carolina, files that contain no reply. A century
and a half would pass before the downstairs of Trinity Church integrated.

So Catto, a naturally restless soul, found himself in difficulty. The
state would not let his children learn in school; the church would not let
his family worship in peace. And that family was growing. On February
22, 1839, Sarah gave birth to their third child, a baby boy, Octavius.

Some of his neighbors were signing up for voyages to Liberia. The
handbills of the American Colonization Society promised a new life for
free Negroes on the fertile African coast. Others were looking north. His
friend Payne had followed Morris Brown's footsteps and settled in Philadelphia, where colored churches were said to thrive within sight of the
Hall of Independence.

William Catto needed to make a move.

CHAPTER 2

Arm in Arm

O N A MAY Monday in 1838, the prince and princess of the American fight for abolition were married in Philadelphia. They joined hands in a nation already spilling blood on the issue of slavery, more than two decades before swords were officially crossed. By the end of that week in May, the cobblestone streets of Philadelphia would be a battleground.

Forces fighting for an end to slavery throughout the North also came to the city that week for meetings in a new, well-lit hall that people were already calling a "temple of freedom." The city was abuzz—this was surely the antislavery union of the year, love and politics embracing in the same place where organized American abolitionism was born with the founding of the Pennsylvania Abolition Society in 1775. And the city— no, the nation—had not seen such an extraordinary edifice created for such a purpose. Two new beginnings. Abolition leaders intended both events to attract notice to their cause, and in this they succeeded beyond expectation.

★   ★   ★

THE SPLENDID GAS LAMPS of Pennsylvania Hall were being lit for the first time to illuminate a rare scene. Antislavery orators would stand at the polished walnut rail of the speaker's platform in the three-thousand-seat main salon and address both sexes, seated in mixed rows—"promiscuous" audiences, the saying went. There were even female speakers.

Angelina Grimké, "the pretty Quakeress," as one newspaper called her, changed her wedding date in order to attend the antislavery meetings. She asked only that she not be married "in such a hurry as to attend a meeting that same evening." The tall, ill-shaven groom, Theodore Weld, renounced the law of a wife as "chattel" when he said his vows. He said little else that day—by age thirty-four he was hoarse from giving antislavery speeches over hecklers' shouts. The wedding cake was baked with "free sugar," not derived from the unrecompensed labor of slaves.

The leading light of both events was Angelina Grimké. She was the child of Charleston slaveholders; her father was John Faucheraud Grimké the same judge who had long ago freed Fanny Shields. As adults, Angelina, thirty-three, and her sister Sarah, forty-five, had not only turned against the slavery system; they had set out to destroy it. They had toured New England giving speeches in sixty-seven towns to forty thousand people. After they spoke, volunteers came forward. New antislavery societies sprang up. The movement was getting stronger, and its enemies took notice.

White men looked at the Grimkés and saw women associating themselves with black men. "Why are all the old hens abolitionists?" a New England paper asked. "Because not being able to obtain husbands they think they may stand some chance for a negro, if they can only make amalgamation fashionable."

Angelina Grimké had broken precedent in February 1838 by delivering an antislavery speech to the Massachusetts legislature. One newspaper's correspondent said her prettiness and eloquence that day "made me 19/20 of an abolitionist." Another noted the crowds on hand for "the extraordinary phenomenon of a *woman talking!*"

She spoke "in excellent off-hand style, as if she were only engaged at the spinning wheel—as she ought to have been," the *Boston Post* said. When, at first, legislators barred her from the rostrum, she balanced the pages of her speech on two men's hats.

★　★　★

SHE WORE A simple brown wedding dress. Her groom, a stranger to tailors, took up her suggestion of a matching brown jacket and a vest of gleaming white.

Soon after they met, she asked how he'd come by his abolitionism. He explained that at age six or seven, growing up in Connecticut, he'd seen his teacher and schoolmates so mercilessly ridicule the only colored pupil that he, Weld, had gotten permission to sit beside the boy every day. The ridicule stopped—and the course of Weld's life was set.

By the time of the wedding, Weld's speeches and the crowds that jeered him had won him the sobriquet "most mobbed man" in America. He was breaking a vow by marrying, because he and a poet friend had pledged to stay bachelors until American slavery ended. The friend, John Greenleaf Whittier, declared Weld a worse turncoat than Benedict Arnold in a comic poem that saluted his choice of Miss Grimké as a bride.

The couple prepared an invitation with a sketch of a slave girl and the words, "Am I Not Thy Sister?" He was a Presbyterian and she a convert to Quakerism, so they improvised a ceremony. A third Grimké sister, the widow Anna Frost, hosted the wedding at her house near Broad Street, in a part of Philadelphia as yet more country than city. She had freed her two slaves but was no abolitionist, preferring the popular sentiment that Africans should be sent back to Africa.

Presiding was the great abolitionist William Lloyd Garrison, a man described as "slight and tidy" with "rimless spectacles," a bald head, and a skin condition that irritated him, a precise man who seemed more a "country school teacher than a fiery agitator."

Hoarse as he was, Weld spoke his vows "in a solemn and tender manner," an onlooker wrote, and foreswore "the unrighteous power vested in a husband . . . over the person and property of his wife." The bride promised "to prefer him above herself, to love him with a pure heart fervently." A black clergyman and a white clergyman spoke. All knelt and prayed.

Garrison read the wedding certificate aloud and laid it out for guests to sign. Thus was formed a galaxy in pen and ink of abolition names from the Northern states and Canada: Burleigh, Stanton, Dresser, Wright, men who had been chased nearly as often as Garrison and Weld. Amos Dresser had been whipped twenty times in Nashville's main square for carrying, along with his bibles, abolition pamphlets.

Then came the names Sarah Mapps Douglass and her mother, Grace—colored Quakers, friends of the Grimké sisters', officers of the city's Female Anti-Slavery Society—and Elizabeth Dawson and her daughter. The Dawsons were free people, liberated by Angelina's sister Anna. In South Carolina, they had been Grimké family slaves.

"What a motley crew did you assemble," the bride's mother wrote. But that was the point, Sarah Grimké said. Her sister's wedding was "our testimony against the horrible prejudice against colored persons, and the equally awful prejudice against the poor."

By the next day, the people of Philadelphia, a city with one leg in the North and one in the South, heard the story of the wedding and began to embellish it.

There were "six whites and six blacks for groomsmen and bridesmaids," and five hundred blacks and whites were seen "promenading on Chestnut Street" near the new abolition hall, which had opened on the same day. The word *amalgamation* was used. People stopped in front of homes of abolitionists and peered in the windows. A colored child peered back. Lucretia Mott's daughter wrote of seeing the boy "perched by the parlor window, watching the passersby who were shocked at all their prophesies of amalgamation appearing to be thus fulfilled."

It was Monday, May 14, 1838. A visiting British abolitionist, J. J. Gurney, wrote that as the week progressed, events took on "a more frightful and violent character."

★ ★ ★

ABOUT NINETEEN THOUSAND of Philadelphia's quarter of a million residents—one of every thirteen—were Negroes, more than in any other Northern city. Most were poor and getting pushed out of work on the Schuylkill and Delaware river docks by the growing Irish population. But the Negro community was rising in other ways. It had during this time fifteen churches, thirty-four clergymen, twenty-one day schools, seventeen Sabbath schools, five literary societies (two for men, three for women), three debating societies, eighty mutual relief or benefit organizations, one moral reform group, four temperance societies, and one library.

The colored population lived all over the county but was centered in the South Street corridor, from Pine south to Shippen, the Delaware west to Eleventh—where free people of color lived in narrow streets and attended houses of worship such as Mother Bethel A.M.E. The church was just a mile down Sixth Street from the new hall.

And by 1838, antislavery forces needed nothing so much as a safe meeting hall.

In the past few years, a Boston mob had tied a rope to Garrison and dragged him through the city like a bald string-puppet. Another mob slew an abolitionist editor, Elijah Lovejoy, in front of his press in Alton, Illinois. Still another had stormed the Charleston post office to burn newly arrived abolition pamphlets. On one city's wharves, a thousand-throated cheer went up as men seized a box of antislavery tracts intended for the mails, and with the mayor looking on approvingly, dumped the box in the river that linked the city to the world. That city was Philadelphia.

The South "was Philadelphia's best customer," the city's commissioned historian writes. Independence Hall was half a day's carriage ride to a slave state, Delaware. And in 1838, the South drew closer: A railroad, offering Southern shippers a cheaper tonnage fee than its New York and Boston competitors, opened a new terminus on Market Street.

The mayor's son-in-law owned slaves. In summer, slaveholding families filled Cape May beaches and Philadelphia hotels. In fall, their sons attended the city's renowned medical schools. Southern printers used Philadelphia type, Southern preachers studied Philadelphia bibles, and "every Southern belle considered Philadelphia-made boots as a necessity."

Amid all that, "there stood, almost alone, the conscience of the Society of Friends, which was either passively or actively arrayed, upon moral grounds, against slavery."

But even a leading Quaker antislavery man, James Mott, brokered Southern cotton to Philadelphia textile mills—until his antislavery wife persuaded him to deal in wool instead. If Angelina Grimké Weld was the princess of the abolition movement, its queen was Lucretia Mott—a woman who enjoyed calling her husband's trade "wool-gathering." Few of the city's Quakers stood as firm as the Motts in their antislavery zeal—fewer, still, when it came to questions of color prejudice and equal rights.

The schoolteacher Sarah Douglass, the Grimké sisters' colored friend, had attended the thousand-member Arch Street Meeting. It had a separate "colored bench"—with a Friend posted at each end to shoo off whites. Douglass said she routinely heard, "This bench is for the black people, this is for the colored people." "And oftentimes I wept," she said, "at other times I felt indignant and queried in my own mind, are these people Christians?" After she stopped attending, her mother, Grace, often had "a whole long bench to herself."

When the Grimké sisters learned of this in 1837, they took to joining the Douglasses on the colored bench—attracting publicity and a reprimand from the meeting's elders.

Another woman who helped raise money for the new abolition hall was Sarah Louisa Forten, daughter of the city's best-known colored merchant. In 1837, Angelina Grimké, preparing a treatise on prejudice, asked her to describe its effect. Sarah Forten, who at twenty-three was writing under pen names for Garrison's *Liberator*, seemed almost to apologize.

"In reply to your question—of the 'effect of Prejudice'—on myself, I must acknowledge that it has often embittered my feelings, particularly when I recollect that we are the innocent victims of it—for you are aware that it originates from dislike to the color of the skin, as much as the degradation of slavery. . . . [I]t has often engendered feelings of discontent & mortification in my breast when I saw that many were preferred before me, who by education—birth—or worldly circumstances were no better than myself—their sole claim to notice depending on the superior advantage of being white."

Then her words took wing, carrying her reader to schoolhouse doors, lecture halls, the churches, and the highways.

"It can be seen in the exclusion of the Colored people from their Churches, or placing them in obscure corners," she wrote, "the colored people . . . may not avail themselves of the right to drink at the fountain of learning—or gain an insight into the arts and science of our favored land. . . . Even our professed friends have not yet rid themselves of it—to some of them it clings like a dark mantle obscuring their many virtues."

As for her family—her father's sailmaking shop had served the shipyards since Benjamin Franklin's time—"We feel it, but in a slight degree compared with many others. We are not much dependent upon the tender mercies of our enemies."

Sometimes those enemies came through the door. It had been only a decade since young white men had crept into Mother Bethel Church during a Sunday night service and put cayenne pepper in the stove. The smoke had sent hundreds of coughing and gagging worshippers running for the door. Two were trampled to death.

The men who administered the pepper had been admonished by church ushers for smoking cigars while entering the sanctuary.

Even the Fortens avoided the streets. "We never travel far from home & seldom go to public places unless quite sure that admission [is] free to all," Sarah Forten wrote. "[T]herefore, we meet with none of those mortifications which might otherwise ensue."

★ ★ ★

IT MADE SENSE, then, if colored men and women were to feel welcome, to locate the new abolition hall in a relatively sympathetic part of town.

The site was on Sixth Street, where well-to-do Quakers owned brick houses on leafy lanes. The Motts, with their wondrous garden and a front parlor that they made into a kind of abolition headquarters, were nearby on Ninth Street. The hall was a good distance from the traffic of the Delaware docks, and if protection should be needed, it was near at hand. The mayor commanded 160 police from his office just three squares south—in the State House, which had come to be known for its gloried past as Independence Hall.

As the new building neared completion, there were mutterings of trouble.

Less than three years had passed since Mayor John White Swift had condoned the dumping of the abolitionist mail. But he was an old soldier, a big man who preferred order and who had used his ample size to wade into howling mobs and make arrests personally. Now, the hall's managers reported, he "boastingly assured us that the abolitionists should never be molested while *he* was Mayor."

Sarah Forten and the hall committee had taken two years to raise forty thousand dollars. They had sold shares for twenty dollars apiece, to affluent Friends but also to working men and women.

Joseph Eaton placed stones cut by the quarryman, Alexander Scott. Caleb Clothier laid bricks fired in John Bosler's kiln. Charles Thorne constructed tall windows with protective shutters of wooden plank. William French applied the plaster, Thomas Armitage forged the ironwork, Harned & Elliott stamped the tin plate, and Daniel Smith dug the cellar.

The result was a hall of gaudy splendor. People said it was the best they'd ever seen—sixty-two feet wide, one hundred feet deep, four stories high. Its front was a classical colonnade. The first-floor lecture room could hold three hundred people. The second-floor salon, three thousand.

Braces of gas lamps lit the salon. Gilded ventilators fanned the air. A reporter described the "very judiciously inclined plane" of the floor sloping down to the speaker's platform, lest a full house leave anyone unable to see the orators. The platform's desks and chairs were polished black walnut from Pennsylvania forests. Ionic columns flanked the stage, and overhead a soaring, flowered arch was inscribed, "Virtue, Liberty, And Independence," painted in letters of gold.

Three stairwells led to the main salon, each seven feet wide—designed for crowds. Downstairs were smaller "committee rooms" and offices for two young editors: Benjamin Lundy, whose journal was *The Genius of Universal Emancipation*, and Whittier, who besides writing poetry edited the weekly *Pennsylvania Freeman*. He had moved his books and papers in and wrote 152 lines of verse for the grand opening.

> This fair hall to truth and freedom given,
> Pledged to the right before all earth and heaven;
> A free arena for the strife of mind,
> To caste or sect or color unconfined.

The proximity to Independence Hall became fresh rhetorical fuel. What better place for a "Temple of Liberty," as the legislator Thaddeus Stevens called it? Weld, declining the managers' speaking invitation— he was too hoarse—wrote that antislavery speakers everywhere had been "banished from our halls of legislation and of justice, from our churches and our pulpits." He said the city of Ben Franklin was a fitting place for abolition's "hunted exiles" to find a home.

To colored Philadelphians, however, one aspect of the State House stood for ground recently lost.

On election days, men lined up to vote at the State House's first-floor windows. That right had belonged to both races. Voting was perilous for Negroes; white toughs routinely sauntered up to yank them from the lines. But some, at least, voted—until 1838.

The Pennsylvania General Assembly had passed the first state abolition law in 1780. But in the 1800s—especially after Nat Turner's uprising—the legislators considered one measure after another to constrict colored rights: by sealing off the borders from new Negro arrivals, by expelling blacks altogether, and by starting a system of registry books.

In early 1838, even as workmen put the final touches on the new hall, the Reform Convention was meeting in the State House to draft changes in the state constitution. The convention agreed to submit to a statewide referendum a proposal to take the vote away from colored men. The "reformers" took their cue from a recent state court decision.

Gurney, the visiting Briton, happened to arrive in the city just then. A "gradualist" on abolition, Gurney nonetheless professed a belief in universal rights. He watched aghast as state officeholders prepared to snatch the ballot from colored men's hands.

"By the introduction of that single word, '*white*,' the whole coloured population, 40,000 in number, were at once deprived of their citizenship. This affecting act of degradation was received by the coloured people with deep sorrow," Gurney wrote. "I was told that a white boy was observed seizing the marbles of a coloured boy in one of the streets, with the words, 'you have no rights now.'

"The coloured boy submitted in silence."

★ ★ ★

MUCH WAS MADE of the new hall's being open "to any purpose not of an immoral character." Some of the first lectures were on temperance and the plight of the American Indian. During one of the temperance speeches, someone outside threw a rock, smashing one of the windows.

But everyone from passersby to presidents knew the hall's true purpose.

"I learnt with great satisfaction," John Quincy Adams wrote to the managers, "that the Pennsylvania Hall Association have erected a large building . . . wherein liberty and equality of civil rights can be freely discussed, and the evils of slavery fearlessly portrayed." The need was desperate—debate on slavery "is banished from one-half the states," the former president said, and "*suspended* in both houses of Congress."

Two years earlier, Congress had placed a "gag" on all slavery debate. The Panic of 1837 had made matters worse—credit was tightened, debts went unpaid, New York had bread riots, and men in every city were thrown out of work. Northern congressmen reasoned that slavery questions could wait, and on December 21, 1837, the House of Representatives renewed its "gag rule," requiring that petitions or bills relating to the selling and transporting of slaves be "laid upon the table"—which was to say, silenced.

Abolitionists noted that this step was taken on the winter solstice, the year's darkest day. They began gathering more signatures, and by the time the new hall opened in Philadelphia, the antislavery petitions "laid upon the table" in Washington filled a twenty-by-forty-foot room to the ceiling. But no amount of lobbying by Adams and others could sway Northern congressmen who favored the gag. "Sold, bargained off for Southern votes," Whittier wrote in a poem. "A passive herd of Northern mules."

Even so, a hopeful excitement was in the spring air. "They are working with all speed to finish the Hall," Lucretia Mott, a tiny, dyspeptic hurricane of abolition zeal, reported. "The Grimkes are doing a noble part in this great work," she wrote, exulting in Angelina's address before the Massachusetts legislature.

Two black abolitionists, the aging James Forten and his young son-in-law, Robert Purvis, huddled in Second African Presbyterian Church and wrote *Appeal of 40,000 disfranchised citizens of Pa. to their fellow citizens against the decision of the Reform Convention.* Whittier, invited to hear this "appeal" read aloud, was so impressed that he printed it in the *Freeman.* The poet-editor predicted great things for the third week in May: "We advise our friends to hold themselves free from engagements on those days, as it is the intention of the managers and stockholders of the [hall] to furnish a rich treat, an intellectual banquet . . . such as is seldom enjoyed in this or any other city."

★ ★ ★

ON MONDAY, MAY 14, opening day, the hall was full. Two policemen were on hand at the managers' request. The abolitionist David Paul Brown spoke.

"Liberty is like life, to be enjoyed, not be defined," he said, ". . . the more general it is, the more perfect. . . . The Supreme Court of Pennsylvania has recently decided that the words 'every freeman' in the old Constitution signified every *white* freeman. . . . It is a subject of deep regret that so highly elevated, honorable, and dignified a tribunal . . . should be betrayed into so gross and lamentable an error."

The next day, Philadelphians awoke to discover placards posted in the streets. Handwritten, the placards were in a language as formal as a lawyer's:

> Whereas a convention for the avowed purpose of effecting the immediate abolition of slavery in the Union is now in session in this city, it behooves all citizens, who entertain a proper respect for the right of property, and the Constitution of these states to interfere, forcibly if they must, and prevent the violation of pledges heretofore held sacred.

We therefore propose that all persons so disposed meet at Pennsylvania Hall on 6th st between Arch and Race tomorrow morning, Wednesday, May 16, and demand the immediate dispersion of said Convention.

The placards were signed, "Several Citizens."

★ ★ ★

TUESDAY, MAY 15, was the first day of the second Anti-Slavery Convention of American Women. The names of those assembled in the hall's smaller lecture room have an antique, rickety sound: Hetty Burr, Thankful Southwick, Mary Grew, Hetty Reckless, Sarah Mapps Douglass, Huldah Justice, Lucretia Coffin Mott. They were pioneers; before the week was out, women would address both sexes on political matters—an unheard-of occurrence in 1838.

Harriet Purvis, who helped start the Philadelphia Female Anti-Slavery Society four years earlier, was one of the delegates. Her husband, Robert, at age twenty-seven, was an anomaly for 1838, a Negro who possessed inherited wealth. He was much lighter than his wife and was regularly taken for white. One writer claimed Purvis *pretended* to be a Negro.

He could have lived in ease on his farm northeast of Philadelphia. Instead, he agitated for abolition and equal rights, sometimes making ammunition of his oft-mistaken color. He liked to tell of the Virginian who forced a ship's captain to bar Purvis from a trans-Atlantic voyage because of his race. The Virginian befriended Purvis on a later voyage, thinking he was a white man.

The Purvises rode down that day to the city in their carriage. At the hall's colonnaded front, a curious crowd watched Purvis, tall and elegant, climb out and offer his arm to his wife.

About that time, more rumors began—a black man walking with two "pretty white girls," and of white men and negresses "arm in arm." A man in the crowd grabbed a chimney sweep's arm and made the sooty little man promenade back and forth, arm in arm, directly in front of the hall. It made a kind of human cartoon, as if to say, *See now! black and white, arm in arm, that's what they do inside.*

What they were actually doing inside was listening to speaker after speaker rail against the Southern Slave Power, as abolitionists called it, and its tendrils in the North.

Garrison was watching from the back of the main salon when the crowd began calling out for him. Before the thunder of applause subsided, he was thundering against his hosts for not inviting a "single colored brother" to the speaker's platform. "Why is this? It cannot be because there is no one present, who, on the score of intellectual and moral worth, is entitled to such respectful treatment. . . . I fear this exclusion may be traced to a wicked prejudice, or to a fear of giving public offense."

★ ★ ★

THE DAY AND HOUR of the meeting announced in the "Several Citizens" placards came and went without disturbance, raising hopes in the hall that the placards were merely the "wickedness of a few, or perhaps a single person." But women at Wednesday morning's antislavery meetings noticed something unusual: "From 20 to 50 persons [were] prowling about the doors, examining the gas pipes, and talking in an incendiary manner. . . . Some of them ventured to hiss during the discussion that morning [and] continued to hang about the Hall through the day, at times crowding into the Anti-Slavery Office, & creating an excitement by their violent & abusive language."

Meanwhile, the women's convention was adding Angelina Grimké—now Mrs. Weld—to the evening's list of speakers. She was the biggest attraction of the week. Everyone, male and female, colored and white, wanted to hear this Joan of Arc from Charleston.

As the main salon began to fill, the crowd outside grew. People heard a murmur of threats from men on the corners.

Juliana Tappan took the floor. She had been at the wedding on Monday; her father, Lewis, was a New York abolition leader. She offered a condemnation of Congress's "gag rule." "*Resolved* . . . that we will maintain practically the right of petition, until the slave shall go free, or our energies, like Lovejoy's, are paralyzed in death. . . . That for every petition rejected by the National Legislature . . . we will endeavor to send five."

Inside the main salon, a few speakers were making the case for gradual abolition. Frederick Plummer, an evangelist known as "Elder" to his rural flock, was bracing the audience to contemplate questions much like those the placards had raised.

Jefferson had said it: The nation had a wolf by the ears.

Shall the nation "deprive the slaveholder of what he has honestly inherited?" Plummer asked. "Shall we resort to force? . . . [L]et us pause, *sol-*

emnly pause, before we make any attempt which will jeopardize our union, the life of the master and that of the slave."

Others spoke up for "colonization," the campaign to move the colored race back to Africa. The Douglasses, Purvises, and Motts scorned this scheme; Sarah Forten had called it "the offspring of prejudice." The *Colored American* newspaper lampooned its white backers: "Why is colonization necessary?—Only because we hate colored people."

In truth, the colonization movement was complicated. It encompassed a few abolitionists of both races, many wealthy slaveholders, and a lustrous list of founders—among them James Monroe, Thomas Jefferson, Henry Clay, and Francis Scott Key. Fear of slave rebellions such as Haiti's played a part; so did Christian evangelism. "Every emigrant to Africa is a missionary . . . in the holy cause of civilization, religion and free institutions," Clay declared. (Jefferson, perhaps not thinking of the children he had fathered with his slave Sally Hemings, wished to jettison free Negroes whose "amalgamation with the other color produces a degradation to which no lover of his country . . . can innocently consent.")

Over the next half century, as many as fifteen thousand free Negroes would sail for Liberia on ships financed by the American Colonization Society. But the society was barely a month old when the sailmaker James Forten and other merchants and ministers of colored Philadelphia convened a meeting in a blacksmith shop that had been converted into a church known as Bethel. Three thousand Negroes attended. Historians see this 1817 event as one of the first protests organized by Americans of color. The assembly drafted, debated, and approved resolutions protesting colonization.

> WHEREAS our ancestors (not of choice) were the first successful cultivators of America, we . . . feel ourselves entitled to participate in the blessings of her luxuriant soil, which their blood and sweat manured. . . . Resolved, that we will never separate ourselves voluntarily from the slave population of this country; they are our brethren by the ties of consanguinity, of suffering, and of wrong; and we feel that there is more virtue in suffering privations with them, than enjoying fancied advantages for a season.

The ministers who led this protest brought a luster of their own. Absalom Jones had founded the city's African Episcopal Church of St. Thomas in 1795. Richard Allen, humiliated by ushers who caught him kneeling to pray in a Methodist church's white section and pulled him to his feet, had gone on to found the African Methodist Episcopal Church—right there, in "Mother Bethel," as worshippers came to know it. Colonization had run up against another great movement: the rise of the black church.

Many a white abolitionist still supported colonization by the time Pennsylvania Hall's doors opened.

Anna Grimké Frost helped direct the Ladies Liberia School Association, much to her sisters' chagrin. Elliot Cresson, one of the city's leading Quaker merchants, had crisscrossed England raising funds for colonization—Garrison nipping at his heels, making speeches against him, until Cresson called him "a Bedlamite." Cresson had helped finance a Liberian outpost and named it Port Cresson (that is, until the local Bassa people overran it and renamed it Bassa Cove).

In the hall, Garrison said he had seen the campaign's handbills in the city. "There is too much colonizationism here," he said. "Can it be possible that any man at this day will have the audacity to come forward, publicly, as an advocate for that wicked scheme?"

A shout came back: "I am that man!"

Garrison responded, "Then I blush for him as a man, as a Christian."

A colored man in the hall called out, "He is not an American!"

That was true. The shouter was W. W. Sleigh, a London surgeon who had become a writer of sensational books with such titles as *The Christian's Defensive Dictionary Against Infidelity.* Sleigh was about to publish a forty-page pamphlet with a fifty-two-word title that began, *Abolitionism exposed! Proving that the principles of abolitionism are injurious to the slaves.*

Beneath the much-complimented gas lamps, radical ideas took shape. Whether antislavery efforts were "appropriate fields for the exertion of the influence of woman" was debated. So was the stance favored by the Grimkés and Motts: that in order to defeat prejudice, white abolitionists must walk, ride, pray, and visit with free people of color.

But seating them on the speakers' platform was ticklish matter. Someone had invited three Negroes to sit in the polished walnut seats. The managers asked them to leave, explaining that even some of the hall shareholders had been denied these coveted seats.

By late Wednesday afternoon, the main salon was filling to its three-thousand-person capacity. "A daughter of Carolina, too well known to need a repetition here, was announced among those of the expected speakers." Hundreds of ticket seekers were turned away.

Speakers began alluding to the hostile crowd outside. Garrison said abolitionists should rejoice, for the cause would succeed only if it "brings down upon it a shower of brickbats and rotten eggs, and is threatened with a coat of tar and feathers." Whittier, parceling his time between the *Freeman's* first-floor office and the second-floor salon, tinkered with a resolution supporting political candidates who favored "immediate abolition." He wanted to add: candidates who favored colored voting rights and who opposed "mob law."

As the evening session began, the hall managers sent a plea to the mayor for more police. He replied that the four officers already at the hall were the only ones available.

★ ★ ★

LAURA H. LOVELL, a delegate to the women's convention from Fall River, Massachusetts, arrived Wednesday night to find a "noisy throng about the door."

Lovell, a schoolteacher, had promised a written report to Fall River's Female Anti-Slavery Society. She lined up early on May 16 and secured a seat near the front. "The platform was occupied by the most eminent abolitionists of both sexes," Lovell wrote. "It was a heart-thrilling spectacle."

When Garrison rose to speak, "the mob without became very riotous."

The audience heard rocks and brickbats strike the walls. Garrison, who had seen worse, kept talking. He lambasted "that proud, implacable and hypocritical association, the Colonization Society." He mocked the argument for "gradual" abolition: "Let it come *in time*, a thousand years hence—before the earth is destroyed and the whole human race swept into eternity. . . . The slaveholders would agree to that."

Garrison finished, but the noise outside grew louder and more stones and brickbats were hurled against the windows. These missiles were easily obtained. Less than three squares away, sewer work was tearing up Chestnut Street in front of the State House.

The hall's wooden shutters spared the audience from being struck, but the noise drowned out the next speaker, the New England abolitionist Maria Chapman. Men were trying to shove their way through the door. Someone shouted, "Fire!" The hall's president, Daniel Neall, tall and stately—"Like some gray rock from which the waves are tossed," Whittier wrote—stepped to the rail of the platform.

Neall, accustomed to pro-slavery crowds in his native Delaware, said police would arrest any miscreants. (Lovell wrote that while she was "new to mobs," she wondered why the police stood idle as men heaved stones at the hall.) Neall held a hand out over the audience. "It is very important that we keep ourselves calm," he said. Then he introduced Angelina Grimké Weld.

A calmness came to her, as it had in the Massachusetts legislature. She raised her voice just enough to be heard above the din.

"What is a mob?" she said. "What would the breaking of every window be? What would the leveling of this hall be? Any evidence that we are wrong, or that slavery is a good and wholesome institution? What if the mob should now burst in upon us, break up our meeting and commit violence upon our persons—would this be any thing compared with what the slaves endure? No, no."

The transcript of her speech that night was laced with brackets such as these:

[Just then stones were thrown at the window,—a great noise without. . . .]

Those voices without tell us that the spirit of slavery is *here*, and has been roused to wrath by our abolition speeches and conventions. . . . This opposition shows that slavery has done its deadliest work in the hearts of our citizens. Do you ask then, "what has the North to do?" I answer, cast out first the spirit of slavery from your own hearts, and then lend your aid to convert the South.

[a great noise without, and commotion within.]

Laura Lovell was awed by the speaker's demeanor—"perfectly calm, unmindful of the mob, except that she alluded to it once by saying, 'We are sometimes told that slavery has no influence in the North.'"

Pointing to the windows, Weld said, "Hear it, hear it."

Garrison, too, sat spellbound. "As the tumult from without increased," he wrote afterward, "and the brickbats fell thick and fast . . . her eloquence kindled, her eye flashed, and her cheeks glowed, as she devoutly thanked the Lord that the stupid repose of that city had at length been disturbed by the force of truth."

Lovell said the speech was only twenty minutes or so. Garrison put it at nearly an hour. The speech rose on the words *what is a mob*, again on *Hear it, hear it*; yet again on the words *I have seen it*.

"As a Southerner I feel it is my duty to stand up here tonight and bear testimony against slavery," Weld said. "I have seen it—I have seen it. I know it has horrors that can never be described."

★ ★ ★

SHE *HAD* SEEN IT. She had seen a Charleston couple hide its slaves from company because beatings had so disfigured them; she had seen healthy Negroes return crippled from the Charleston Workhouse. She had seen two white boys pulling a woman toward the workhouse—and when the woman cried out, "Missis!" Angelina Grimké remained silent, and forever blamed herself. "If I could only be the means of . . . 'bringing to light the hidden things of darkness,'" she wrote in her diary in 1829, quoting a psalm.

At age twenty-three, she heard her brother Henry, a lawyer and plantation owner, inflict a night of whipping on a slave boy named John; the sounds "went like daggers to my heart." John ran away, and Angelina confronted her brother. He called her a meddler and said he meant to whip John "until he could not stand." But when John was found, Henry did not whip him, much to his sister's relief.

Her words had made a difference. Now, she had found her voice.

"Every Southern breeze wafted to me the discordant tones of weeping and wailing, shrieks and groans," she told the audience in Pennsylvania Hall. "But how different do I feel now! . . . I will lift up my voice like a trumpet."

Before she sat down, Weld made a special plea to women in the hall to send more petitions to Congress. "Do you say, 'It does no good?' The South already turns pale at the number sent." She looked around the main salon one last time and remarked that she was "gratified to see so few *ladies*, and so many *women*." Such a cheer went up as she left the platform that, for a moment, no one could hear the mob outside.

Now it was time to face that mob. The three thousand inside the hall moved slowly down the stairs and through the massive wooden doors into a crowd that hated them, a frightening, intimidating mass of shouting mouths and angry eyes. But "no violence was offered, and all reached their homes in safety." So said the first reports.

★ ★ ★

ON THURSDAY MORNING, May 17, Colonel Augustus J. Pleasonton of the Pennsylvania Militia was in the midst of a busy week. A young bachelor with boyish cheeks and dense side-whiskers, Pleasonton had attended a Wednesday night lecture on the peoples and produce of Palestine. He wrote in his diary that he had learned the basis of the phrase *land of milk and honey*, had been favored by his friend Kate with kisses of "finest silk velvet," had conveyed orders to his militiamen, and had paid four dollars to get his sword repaired when a neighbor rushed in with news: Last night, at the new abolition hall, a mob of nearly two thousand "broke the windows and pommeled the negroes as they came out."

The colonel set out to investigate.

A more complicated picture of Wednesday night began to emerge. Most of the audience had left the hall safely, and the ranks of shouters and stone throwers had thinned. But some stayed "all night, assaulting every belated colored man who came along." Black men leaving the hall were "brutally assaulted" and "severely injured," the managers reported. The mob had spared the colored women but singled out the men.

Thursday morning's *Freeman* described one Negro "dreadfully wounded by a brick-bat upon his head." A New York delegate, Sarah T. Smith, said she'd gotten a short distance from the hall that night when a black man ran into her at full speed. Smith was startled by "such rudeness in one of that race." Then she realized he was "escaping from the mob, having already received a deep gash from which the blood was freely flowing." Her dress was sprinkled with his blood.

Laura Lovell, returning to the hall on Thursday morning, "was surprised to find a noisy crowd of miserable looking people still around the house." Other witnesses said a large number of "respectable" people were in the mob as well.

Inside, the women convened in a downstairs room and prepared expressions of sympathy "with the city's colored population, towards whom the fury of the mob seemed last evening particularly directed." Mott, running the session, called on everyone in the room "to be steadfast and solemn in . . . the business for which they are assembled."

True, she said, the women had been "a *little* disturbed last evening by the tumultuous sea of human passions around us." Mott, a mother of five, predicted that after a night's sleep the mob would, like a squalling infant, "soon rock itself to rest."

But a new rumor circulated—the mob intended to set the hall afire. A newspaper said shipwrights were seen hauling supplies up from the docks to the hall's vicinity—axes, crowbars, turpentine, and tar.

Neall and the other managers sent out formal pleas for help to Mayor Swift and the county sheriff, John G. Watmough, explaining that on Wednesday night the mob had "disturbed the meeting very much, by yelling, stamping, and throwing brick-bats and other missiles through the windows." The mob had seemed to take direction from one man, and the managers offered, in a peculiarly Quaker turn of phrase, to "furnish thee with the name of the ringleader."

The mayor said he would check the law and the liabilities. The sheriff said "it was the mayor's business." Watmough said if he had the mayor's 160 men, he would have suppressed the mob the first night. But he had only three deputies. Watmough, who got around the county on horseback, promised to be at the hall that night.

Mayor Swift's history gave the abolitionists hope. He had commanded an army regiment; as mayor, in 1834, he led a wedge of officers against the young whites whose attack on blacks at a South Street carousel was dubbed the Flying Horses riot. True, that riot had raged two days before he acted; and he had overseen the dumping of abolition mails into the river. But he had also deployed his police to squelch the threat of attacks on the banks in the Panic of 1837. He gave the abolitionists his word—they would be safe.

He met with the managers at the hall—and quickly impressed them by arresting a fellow who was outside haranguing the crowd. Swift explained that his city solicitor had *ordered* police to make no arrests the night before. He said that if the managers would close the hall for one night and hand him the keys, he would make sure it was protected. An agreement was reached. As part of it, he promised to address the crowd.

Swift also remarked to the abolitionists, "It is public opinion makes mobs! And 99 out of a hundred of those with whom I converse are against you."

★ ★ ★

NOW A ONE-DAY VETERAN of mob watching, Lovell went back to the
hall for a 4:00 P.M. session, saw "the number and noise of the mob much
increased." Inside, she counted fewer colored women than before. The
meeting dealt with boycotting slave produce and shunning churches with
ties to slaveholders. But it was hard to get anything done. The work was
"very much interrupted by the swearing and hallooing without. Sometimes
the voice of the speaker was lost in the horrid din."

Mott conveyed the hall managers' request that the women's convention discourage its Negro members from attending the evening's session—
because "the mob seemed to direct their malice particularly towards the
colored people." Mott said she disagreed with this request and hoped
nobody "would be alarmed by a little appearance of danger." A colored
New York delegate picked up the call: It would be selfish and cowardly
for her people to shrink in this hour of danger, she said. "Our friends have
suffered much for us, and shall we fear to suffer a little for ourselves?"

It was said that this New York woman had, by her own labor, raised
enough money to buy the freedom of eleven slaves. Lovell marveled at the
"many bright streams of happiness" this one woman had unearthed.

The antislavery men made a calculation. Believing the mob would
not burn a hall filled with women, they asked whether the women would
stay in session from afternoon to evening, despite the "perilous surroundings."

Mary Grew recorded their reaction: "A few minutes of solemn delib-
eration; a few moments' listening to the loud madness surging against the
outer walls; a moment's unvoiced prayer for wisdom and strength, and the
answer came: 'We will;' and the business of the meeting proceeded."

Someone announced the agreement with the mayor. The hall would
close for the night; the women would adjourn until Friday. A minister's
speech on slavery's evils was postponed. As a cautionary step, the nearby
Temperance Hall was rented for the women's next session. The managers asked the women to leave through back doors for their own safety.
The women declined. Instead, Angelina Grimké Weld suggested a tactic that had worked before with a New England mob. The women needed
to march out the front of the hall two at a time, and "we should, as far
as possible, protect our colored sisters . . . by taking each one of them by
the arm."

The hall committee's report described the scene outside. "The doors were blocked up by the crowd, and the streets almost impassable from the multitude of fellows of the baser sort." By every account, there were many "gentlemen" as well. Estimates put the crowd at anywhere from two thousand to seventeen thousand.

Women like Thankful Southwick, Mary Grew, Abby Kelly, and Juliana Tappan stood up and linked arms with women like Grace Douglass, Sarah Douglass, Hetty Burr, and Harriet Forten Purvis. The hall's heavy wooden doors swung open and the double line saw the scowls of the men screaming at them.

Lovell wrote: "We passed out through a mob of two or three thousand, fierce, vile-looking men and large boys. They allowed us just room to walk, two abreast. We heard the worst language, and saw the most hideous countenances." But no women in the line suffered serious attack.

The Fall River teacher also wrote: "This was a new, and unexpected scene to me."

★ ★ ★

IT WAS NEARLY DARK outside the hall when the mayor addressed the mob.

"There will be no meeting here this evening. The house has been given up to me," Swift said. "The Managers had the right to hold their meeting; but as good citizens they have, at my request, suspended their meeting for the evening. We never call out the military here! We do not need such measures. Indeed, I would, fellow citizens, look upon you as my police! . . . and I trust you will abide by the laws, and keep order. I now bid you farewell for the night."

The crowd gave him three cheers and he headed back to his post in the State House. Within a few minutes, men began extinguishing gas lamps along the street. Others hoisted a great wooden beam and lugged it toward the hall's main doors.

The women's convention had already dispersed, and Swift, in the relative peace of the State House, began "to entertain a lively hope that all would pass off quietly."

But messengers brought word "that large collections of persons coming in from the northern districts had reinforced the mob." Sixth Street alongside the hall was reported to be so packed with people that no cart or carriage could pass. The city solicitor arrived with word that the gaslights were out. Others rushed in to say the mob was battering down the hall's main doors.

What happened next was a matter of ferocious dispute. The mayor and the sheriff said they battled mightily to protect the hall. The managers accused the city fathers of winking at the mob and looking away.

Swift marched his 160 policemen three squares north toward the hall but found "the crowd very dense in Cherry Street." He sounded the alarm, winding a police "rattle" that gave off an ear-splitting clack. For a moment, the crowd quieted.

"Shame!" Swift shouted. "Is there nobody here to support the law?" No answer came. People started shouting again and swarmed Swift's police. It was 160 against thousands, and the mayor and his men fell back. In front of the hall, cheers went up as the doors began to give way.

By now, Laura Lovell and other delegates were huddled in a private home awaiting news. A New England abolitionist, Arnold Buffum, was telling them how forty large men had surrounded him in the street that day and demanded to know whether his wife was a Negro.

This sort of talk had spread all week. Letters in newspapers as far away as Louisiana and Georgia described couples of mixed race "promenading arm and arm" outside the Philadelphia hall. Buffum—whose only speech that week had been on temperance—assured the men that his wife was white.

They asked whether he favored whites and Negroes amalgamating. He explained that he did not. Did he have daughters? He did. Did he wish them to marry Negroes? He did not.

With that, he told Lovell's group, the largest of the men declared him a good fellow and sent him on his way!

As Buffum got to the end of his story, someone ran into the room with the news that Pennsylvania Hall was burning.

★ ★ ★

THE ONLY MAN still in a position to defend the hall was a captain of police, Thomas Hayes. Mayor Swift had handed the hall's brass keys to this experienced officer. As other police retreated and the mob surged into the hall, Captain Hayes grabbed Officer Miller, a man he trusted, and together they waded through the crowd until they were inside the hall's passageways.

They got through a door, closed it behind them—and found themselves in complete darkness, feeling their way up one of the grand stairwells. They reached a door to the main salon but found it locked from within. More surprises followed. They descended the staircase, raced around to the Haines Street doors, and ran up another stairs. On their way up, they heard the footsteps of a dozen or more men running down.

Finally they entered the main salon and found three small fires burning.

Hayes and Miller were trying to smother the fires when a dozen men and boys ran in. Hayes did not recognize them, but they seemed to know his name. It became clear to him that they'd doubled back to this room when they realized the two officers were alone.

Stop putting the fires out! Hayes and Miller refused. The men leaped upon them and pulled them to the floor. Hayes sensed that they didn't want to hurt him. He and Miller scrambled away, stumbling down to Haines Street. By now, the fire was spreading in the hall, and outside, Hayes saw a nonsensical sight: firemen turning hoses away from a fire.

They were playing the hoses, instead, on neighboring buildings. Hayes could hear the crowd admonishing the firemen—you'd better let the hall burn.

★ ★ ★

WHITE PHILADELPHIA MOBS had attacked blacks before—in the Flying Horses riot, for one. Young "roughs" made Independence Square on July 4 so perilous for colored families that they had taken to doing their celebrating on July 5. But those mobs had consisted mainly of wild young men who earned too little and drank too much. By Thursday afternoon, the crowd outside Pennsylvania Hall was a different mix. The sheriff observed many "respectable citizens . . . [and] a few noisy boys in the street." It was "a mob of well dressed persons," Sidney George Fisher, himself a well-dressed Philadelphian, wrote.

The hall managers described "citizens of other states, slaveholders actual & slaveholders expectant, mingled in the mass. . . . Men of standing & respectability, substantial merchants, & influential citizens . . . either looked on in cold indifference, or, as was in many instances the case, expressed both in language & action their unequivocal approbation & encouragement."

Colonel Pleasonton detected another difference in these rioters: They seemed to have a plan. "The perfect order and system which prevailed throughout these proceedings, by the mob, proved that there was a complete organization for this especial purpose."

Inside the main salon, men hammered the nearest gas pipes loose and turned them toward the flames. They piled up papers on the platform. They went through Whittier's and Lundy's first-floor offices, pulling out armfuls of papers and books.

Whittier was visiting with another abolitionist, Dr. John Parrish, when he heard the hall was burning. A shy man who shunned public speaking, Whittier got to his feet, shouting that the next day's *Freeman* was in peril. He disguised himself in the doctor's coat and wig and rushed into the hall. He was able to retrieve enough material to publish the next day's edition.

The fire moved quickly. Flames "rolled upward along the walls, & roared & crackled in the fresh night breeze." The spire of the State House reddened in the glow. When the roof of Pennsylvania Hall collapsed, the crowd let out a "fiend-like cry."

★ ★ ★

ON FRIDAY MORNING, a hundred or so shaken delegates to the women's convention arrived to meet in the Temperance Hall. They found it locked. Its managers explained that they could not chance their hall's getting destroyed. A Philadelphia delegate offered them the schoolhouse she ran in another part of the city.

The mob, now appearing to consist of fewer "gentlemen" and more of the lowly, shouted insults as the little parade of respectable women from New England and New York walked past.

The walk was "a long way," Lovell reported, describing an almost medieval scene. "We were advised to separate ourselves into small companies, that we might not attract attention. . . . As we passed through some lanes, several low-looking women, who I should think be fit companions for the leaders of the mob, actually came out of their huts to jeer at us; pointing the finger of scorn, distorting their faces to express contempt, and saying. . . . 'you had better stay at home and mind your own business, than to come here making such a fuss.'"

The schoolhouse meeting lasted six hours. "Many were in tears," Lovell wrote. The women got word of the mob's approach but kept working.

They passed resolution after resolution—Thankful Southwick's, for aboli-tionist families to buy "products of *free labor*, so that their hands may be clean," and Mary Grew's, to shun any church financed by slaveholders. Five women dissented, saying efforts must be made to enlist those congre-gations in the cause.

Sarah Grimké wrote two resolutions. One blamed the pro-slavery "spirit" for the mob that burned the hall and the efforts to take the vote away from Pennsylvania Negroes. The other, which set off the loudest de-bate, asked abolitionists to wage a daily war against color prejudice as well as slavery and declared the two inextricably linked. "Resolved, That prej-udice against color is the very spirit of slavery . . . and is the fire which is consuming the happiness and energies of the free people of color."

Her next words evoked scenes past—Robert Purvis standing alone on a dock, Grace Douglass alone on a Friends' bench, Sarah Forten's testa-ment on public "mortification":

"That it is, therefore, the duty of abolitionists to identify themselves with these oppressed Americans by sitting with them in places of worship, by appearing with them in our streets, by giving them our countenance in steam-boats and stages, by visiting them at their homes and encouraging them to visit us, receiving them as we do our white fellow citizens."

Finally, they mourned the loss of the hall, "our beautiful house."

* * *

FOR TWO MORE DAYS, the mob was an octopus slithering through the streets. It threatened homes of abolitionists and attacked presses, colored churches, even the new black orphanage that the Quakers were building.

It might have targeted Garrison, too, had he not managed to slip out of town with the help of Purvis, two other men, and a covered carriage that came in the middle of the night. Safely back in Boston, he exulted to a relative, "Awful as this occurrence in Philadelphia, it will do incalculable good to our cause!"

A few squares south down Sixth Street, the mob stoned Mother Bethel A.M.E.—the church Richard Allen had founded, the spot where he and Absalom Jones and James Forten and three thousand others had met in protest. The city recorder, Samuel Rush, a son of Benjamin Rush, the Phil-adelphia physician who signed the Declaration of Independence, stood in the doorway and warned the crowd that to stone Mother Bethel they would have to stone him first.

By then the police were regaining their resolve—they quietly led away a man who had exhorted them to help "down the nigger church."

The Friday morning minutes of the Requited Labor Convention put it starkly: "Held at the *ruins* of the Pa. Hall, at 10 o'clock A.M. On motion, adjourned to James Mott's, North 9th St." The swarm of abolitionists regrouped in the Motts' parlor.

Then came word that the mob was approaching.

The family quickly moved some possessions to a neighbor's house. Thomas Mott, age fourteen, sat on the front step and watched for crowds. Lucretia Mott was trying to calm her guests when her son ran in and shouted, "They're coming!"

Men were running down Race Street's paving stones, a half-square away.

As the sound grew closer, Mott realized she was about to be injured. "It was a searching time. I have often thought how I should sustain myself if called to pass such an ordeal. . . . I believe I was strengthened of God. I felt at the moment that I was willing to suffer whatever the cause required."

The men ran past Ninth Street without stopping. People said some secret friend had slipped into the crowd and shouted "On to Mott's!"—but directed the crowd elsewhere.

The rioters kept going until they were at Thirteenth Street and the new orphanage. It was set afire—but this time a fire company, the Good Will ("Our name is our motto"), fought both fire and mob successfully. A future mayor, Good Will chief Morton McMichael was credited with persuading his fellow firemen to save the building.

Sheriff Watmough said he had arrested a dozen men when the hall was attacked, including "a sturdy blackguard engaged in forcing the doors with a log of wood, and a youth with a brand of fire in his hands"—only to see the men to whom he had entrusted these miscreants turn them loose instead. "Prejudice and madness held sovereign sway," Watmough wrote. "The laws were trampled in the dust."

Crowds formed in the streets just south of the city in Southwark and Moyamensing, where immigrants from Ireland lived across narrow alleys from free people of color. The sheriff told Colonel Pleasonton that the mob was vowing to lay waste Negro churches. The rioters were a different populace now. Poor men and out-of-work laborers filled the street. Police arrested a dozen with Irish-sounding names.

The sheriff rode north to the Liberties and south to Moyamensing, plunging his horse into unruly crowds. Fresh rumors circulated that the abolitionists' homes were threatened. Men surrounded David Paul Brown's house and readied tar and feathers.

Targeted, too, was the *Public Ledger*'s office. The newspaper had condemned the fire as far worse than the regrettable sight of black promenading with white. *Ledger* employees, mindful that an Illinois mob had killed an antislavery editor the year before, sent Pleasonton a request for a dozen muskets. The colonel's diary does not include his reply but says the mob moved on after discovering that *Ledger* employees had firearms.

Pleasonton also wrote down his idea for preventing such civil strife in the future: Expel all Negroes from the state.

★　★　★

BY SUNDAY MORNING, Swift's 160 policemen and Watmough's three deputies regained control of the streets. Philadelphians began to inventory the damage.

"To be sure there was great provocation," the diarist Fisher wrote. "Black & white men & women sat promiscuously together, & walked about arm in arm. Such are the excesses of enthusiasm. There will be more trouble yet, I doubt not. . . . Such is the hatred of abolition here, that many respectable persons, tho' they do not defend these outrages, blame them faintly & excuse them."

Evil had come "to our very doors," a young minister, William H. Furness, told his Unitarian congregants that Sunday morning. "The whole city has been illuminated by the glare of the incendiary's torch. And what is the state of the public mind? . . . Why, with a few faint professions of regret at the manner in which that Hall has been destroyed, are mingled words of hearty satisfaction and triumph over its ruins. 'We are sorry that it was done in such a way, but we are glad it is done.' This is what we hear on all sides.'"

Whittier said the fire would be condemned "from Georgia to Maine." But many writers blamed what a St. Louis paper called the "parade of black and white amalgamation." A "Southerner and An Eyewitness" praised the firemen's inaction in a letter to a New Orleans paper. A letter signed "A," dated May 17 and purporting to have been mailed from Philadelphia, offered readers of an Augusta, Georgia, paper this street-corner view:

> Yesterday, in the broad light of day, I saw many pairs and trios of different hues, From "jetty black to snowy white," arm in arm, emerge from its spacious halls. There, sir, was the descendant of Ham or of Africa linked, side by side, with some of the fairest and wealthiest daughters of Philadelphia. . . . One pretty woman (white) was seen seated between two black fellows with wooly heads. Men were gallanting black women to and from the hall.

The writer's next letter boasted that he'd helped to burn the building.

From the other side came vows to rebuild the cause, if not the building. As secretary of the Philadelphia Female Anti-Slavery Society, Sarah Douglass published this notice in the Freeman:

> Resolved, that the state of public feeling as manifested by the burning of Pennsylvania Hall by a mob, countenanced by a large number of citizens, and unopposed by the civil authorities, because the principles of the 'Declaration of Independence' were there advocated and maintained, call upon us for redoubled efforts. . . . That in the denunciations . . . so liberally heaped upon us, we find new calls upon our fortitude to endure, our firmness to withstand.

Lucretia Mott insisted the week of meetings had been a "rich feast . . . not seriously interrupted even by the burning of the Hall." She was more upset about efforts by "pseudo-Abolitionists" to kill the antiprejudice resolution. To her dismay, Parrish—her physician—had "left no means untried to induce us to expunge from our minutes [the] resolution relating to social intercourse with our colored brethren."

The resolution had set off a "wonderful hubbub," as Sarah Douglass put it, and had panicked Parrish, a leader of the state abolition society. Parrish believed walking with Negroes and "visiting them at their homes" would merely offend the white public. He even called a meeting of "respectable" Negroes—at the home of Sarah Douglass's father—and urged them to "issue a disclaimer." No such disclaimer was issued.

All of which merely stiffened Sarah Douglass's resolve. The fire transformed "the language of my soul," the young teacher wrote to the Colored

American, in a letter signed "S." "Great efforts were made by those who call themselves our friends, to suppress that resolution for fear the 'poor colored people' would have to suffer. Out upon such sympathy say I."

★ ★ ★

THE COUNTY CONVENED a grand jury to investigate the fire. Its foreman was the colonizationist Elliot Cresson. In September, his grand jury concluded that two men who were in the mob should be charged with arson but that abolitionists shared in the blame for having brought white and black "into close and familiar intercourse."

Five days later, the state Reform Convention's proposal to disfranchise black men was approved by a margin of 1,212 votes, out of 225,000 cast statewide.

The women's antislavery convention returned to Philadelphia the following year. But in the fire's wake, no landlord would rent them a hall; neither would the churches or any of the city's seven Quaker meetings.

The new mayor, Isaac Roach, paid a visit to Mott. He did not object to the convention's being held again in his city. He only wished to avoid chaos. He suggested Mott and the other women help by avoiding "unnecessary walking with colored people."

Whereupon Mott told the mayor off. First, she said, they had "never made a parade, as charged upon us, of walking with colored people." Second, the women had been walking with colored people "as occasion offered" and would continue to do so.

The women eventually held their 1839 antislavery meetings in an old riding school with a barn roof. Mary Grew, a lifelong loyalist to the cause, later reflected on that time, when much had seemed possible, even after the fire. "How readily and hopefully, in the beginning of our work, we turned for help to the churches and religious societies of the land, and how slowly and painfully we learned their real character."

Such setbacks, however, became points of pride and reminiscence. Women such as Grew, Mott, Sarah Douglass, the Grimkés, and Harriet Forten Purvis, who marched out of Pennsylvania Hall arm in arm, black and white, remained at the barricades of abolition and equal rights. Their alliances bridged the color line, the Mason-Dixon Line, and the Atlantic. As young Americans of another era told of being changed forever by the Freedom Rides, so did a few men and women point back to that week in 1838. James Mott wrote, "The color prejudice lurking within me was entirely destroyed by the night of Pennsylvania Hall."

Sarah Douglass went on to teach generations of children as Philadelphia became a hub of intellectual activity for nineteenth-century black America. John Greenleaf Whittier bragged of his coat-and-wig exploits until his dying day. He wrote antislavery poems, including fourteen stanzas titled "The Relic," named for a gift he had received—a cane fashioned from the charred wood of Pennsylvania Hall. He directed his harshest verses at Northerners who

> Outdo the [South] in their readiness
> To roast a negro, or to mob a press.

Robert Purvis, twenty-seven when the hall burned, testified a few years later about the fire's origins. The hall managers had sued the county for the loss of the building. The trial was "painful and ludicrous," Purvis wrote a friend. The county's lawyers argued that "promiscuous intermingling" of the races had provoked the riot. Jurors heard a white witness testify in excruciating detail of having seen "a negress" step from a carriage to be escorted into the hall on the arm of a white gentleman.

Purvis testified next. He confirmed each detail of the previous man's testimony, except one. Purvis said *he* was the gentleman who'd escorted the negress—his wife, Harriet. Offering his arm to her "seemed so natural," Purvis deadpanned.

Laughter began, and swelled to fill the courtroom.

Purvis started spending more time on his farm in Byberry. He constructed hiding places on his land, as part of the broader network that was secreting fugitives into the North and Canada. In his old age, Purvis would tally his recollections and determine that he and his Philadelphia associates had helped men, women, and children ride this Underground Railroad at the rate of one person a day.

For those who had been inside Pennsylvania Hall, Angelina Grimké Weld's "I have seen it" speech was an unforgettable moment—and her last great speech. An illness caused her to give up lecture tours, so she made herself heard in other ways. In the year after the fire, she, her husband, and her sister Sarah collected Southern newspapers and culled their words—Theodore Weld said he stopped counting at twenty thousand articles—and in 1839 they published a 210-page report entitled *American Slavery as It Is.*

The book told of men and women whipped until their backs retained few islands of unscarred skin; of slaves beaten at the Charleston Workhouse until crippled; of pronged iron collars designed to deprive the wearer of sleep; of parents running away—not north to freedom, but *south*, to search for children who had been sold away. It named names and was read across the North. It was a fiery polemical tract, one still cited by twenty-first-century historians, a meticulous record of broken limbs and broken hearts.

★ ★ ★

RIOTS IN PHILADELPHIA had preceded the burning of Pennsylvania Hall and more would follow, often coinciding with the worst economic times. White mobs swept through black sections of Moyamensing and Southwark to avenge an insult, a rumor, a mistaken phrase. They chased black citizens out of homes, setting fire to bed linens in the street. (Purvis wrote after a riot in 1842, "I am convinced of our utter and complete nothingness in public estimation.") They attacked colored churches and schools. They bedeviled Negro life in Northern cities for the next three decades and beyond. These events were less riots than pogroms, less a clash between equals than organized attacks against the defenseless.

Reacting to the 1842 riot, Whittier's newspaper said the city's elite had all but licensed future mobs by letting the hall burn in 1838. The fire "was applauded by a large portion of the merchants of the city," the *Freeman* said. "One of them went so far as to issue his card or advertisement, with a picture on it of Pennsylvania Hall in flames, thinking thereby to conciliate the slaveholding merchants of the South."

The burning hall thus became an enduring symbol for both sides—an announcement that Philadelphia would not tolerate meetings "from which buck negroes walked home with white women," as a Southern minister put it twenty years later; and a caution against any undue exuberance, say, on the part of a runaway slave arriving in the city, or a free family of color, coming North from Charleston's "middle ground."

Later in the nineteenth century, Frederick Douglass would remind audiences of the fire, as would W.E.B. Du Bois in the early twentieth.

Pennsylvania Hall proved what Northern Negroes already knew—a malevolence lurked out there, a capacity for terror that could be channeled and directed in the same way the incendiarists had bent the gas pipes.

A despairing Daniel Neall wrote to an ally named John Priestly. The hall they had built was "nothing but a pile of smoking ruins," he wrote. "Where is our Country, John?"

The ruins stood for many years, reproaching all who passed.

CHAPTER 3

"Keep the Flame Burning..."

ON A JANUARY DAY in 1844, the nation's secretary of state described the condition of colored America. The 1840 Census showed that free Negroes in the North were dissolute and degraded, and prone to illness, lunacy, and suicide. The cause was clear, John C. Calhoun, who hailed from Charleston, said. Freedom made Negroes crazy.

Calhoun, the young nation's emissary to an increasingly antislavery world, said the South's 2.7 million slaves lived better than their 171,000 free Northern counterparts: Slaveholders provided shelter, a meal on the table, and a moral life. Statisticians doubted his claim. A black physician, James McCune Smith, said the census showed free Negroes outliving slaves by an average of seven years. Calhoun brushed these critics aside, insisting that Northern Negroes led lives of "vice and pauperism."

As Calhoun spoke, a black son of Charleston was embarking on a course that pointed north. William Catto's journey began with finding a new place to sit.

On January 5, Catto joined Second Presbyterian Church, an immense white-columned building completed in 1811 for the substantial price of one hundred thousand dollars. People called Charleston the Holy City for its eminent clergy and soaring spires. Second Presbyterian was built of brick with white stucco and topped by an octagonal belfry. At sunset, the belfry of the church without a spire cast its shadow on Henrietta Street.

The minister in 1844 was Rev. Thomas Smyth. Born in Belfast, schooled in Great Britain, and trained at the Princeton Theological Seminary, Smyth at age thirty-seven was already a luminary among Presbyterian clergy.

Smyth's new Negro congregant made a good impression. The long-hand entry for January 5 in the church's minute books says, "William T. Catto, free coloured man . . . presented himself & after a very full & satisfactory examination was admitted a member & appointed a Leader with Mr. Howard of a Free Coloured Class."

The class leaders performed a delicate function. They were racial go-betweens, screened and selected by Second Presbyterian's very white ministry to instruct the very black people who squeezed into the second-floor galleries. The church had in the years since Vesey and Turner seen the same surge in colored congregants as Trinity Methodist. Once again, they were sent upstairs. "Color'd members were main support of [the] Church," one of them wrote later, and "in return they were crowded in galleries."

As at Trinity, older, more influential men of Second Presbyterian turned to Catto, now in his thirties. This time the men were white.

In the church's lecture room on Monday evening, March 8, 1845, "Views were exchanged as to the arrangements of the classes for the coloured people & the appointment of leaders." Among those invited to present his views was Catto.

That spring, Charleston clergymen—Charles Colcock Jones, William Capers, Smyth, and others—met for three days to thrash out how best to teach religion to blacks. Smyth, who already had decided to appoint a handful of Negro congregants as "colored leaders," would have been especially attentive to Jones, a fellow Presbyterian, who advocated a greater role and more attention to black members. Preaching to them, Jones said, could not be just an afterthought: "They are good judges of a good sermon. They . . . like to be treated with some consideration, and are as fond of an able ministry as are any other people. He who preaches to the Negroes, should study just as profoundly, and as extensively, as he who preaches to whites." Jones, too, favored using "coloured helpers."

Charleston church leaders also wrestled with how best to be spiritually supportive of slavery. For some, this task was not so difficult. James Henley Thornwell went to Cincinnati for an 1845 meeting of the Presbyterian Church's National General Assembly. On May 19, he wrote enthusiastically to his wife that the assembly was about to come out strongly against abolitionism. And, he predicted, there would soon be a pronounce-ment that "will declare slavery not to be sinful, will assert that it is sanc-tioned by the word of God."

While this larger conversation was going on, inside the Second Pres-byterian lecture room candidates "for leaders over the coloured people ap-peared." Two weeks later, at another Monday night meeting, Catto and eight other men were "further examined as to their knowledge and belief of our Confession and standards."

It was decided that there would be four classes in addition to a prayer meeting. Two candidates were rejected. The remaining seven were divided into three pairs. Only Catto was asked to lead a class by himself. He and another man were also chosen to lead the prayer meeting for free persons of color.

The task before them was like climbing a ladder with bound hands. They had to lift the minds of their classes using scripture and the appro-priate catechisms without entering the forbidden, illegal territory of preaching or teaching literacy. They visited class members at home, set-tled arguments, and spoke for colored congregants before the church hier-archy. When a death occurred in a class member's family, Catto performed the "graveside duties"—after Smyth conducted the service.

Perhaps those experiences helped Catto when his turn came to grieve.

His wife, Sarah, died in 1845, a year after the birth of their fourth child, Francis. A legal document named William the children's guardian and said her oldest child, John Dewees, would get a share of her estate, which was less than ninety dollars. It listed her Catto children—Cathe-rine, Francis, William, and Octavius, who was six when his mother died.

So now William Catto had four children to rear, and a more compli-cated future. In 1846, he decided his calling was no longer refurbishing machinery but saving souls.

He must have considered the difficulties involved. The Presbyterians' written rules required a "learned ministry," tested in the arts and sciences, ecclesiastical history, Latin translations, and explication of sacred texts. The unwritten rules said white Charleston would never ordain a man of color. Even so, Catto was intent on finding a way.

He married anew, to a free Charleston mulatto, Mary B. Anderson. And he had an idea: He would go overseas as a missionary. He could serve God and leave the shackling prejudices of Charleston. The Presbyterians had missions in Liberia, a place that in the 1840s attracted as many as one in five of Charleston's free Negroes, on American Colonization Society ships. He found a sponsor in Smyth.

Just two years older than Catto, Smyth, the pastor of Second Presbyterian, was frail and suffered debilitating headaches that made public speaking painful. Yet he spoke and wrote prodigiously and owned twenty thousand books. His sermons after the deaths of two of his nine children were published as *Solace for Bereaved Parents*. In his 404-page *Unity of the Human Races*, he defended the humanity of Africans. But he opposed abolition. Along with John Bailey Adger, Thornwell, and Jones, he viewed the master-slave relationship as a millwright might regard a mill: in need of constant repair. Though Smyth owned no slaves, slaveholders filled his pews and loaded his collection plates.

In 1844, when the new Free Church of Scotland needed money for its missions to the poor, Smyth led the American response, raising two thousand dollars of the nine thousand dollars donated by Southern churches. But when he went to the British Isles in 1846 for a speaking tour, Smyth discovered that a black abolitionist from the United States had gotten there first.

In Britain, which had outlawed slavery thirteen years earlier, people were calling on the Free Church to shun the "bloodstained money" of American slaveholders. The protesters sided with a visiting Negro whose lectures in Dublin and Edinburgh had caused a sensation. Britons were buying his book and using his slogan, "Send back the money!" He called it out to audiences in London, and they roared it back. Soon, white urchins were shouting it to the tall brown-skinned visitor, Frederick Douglass, as he strode down Edinburgh's streets.

Barely seven years had passed since Frederick Bailey had fled slavery in Maryland and changed his name to Douglass. He had found work in New Bedford hauling casks of whale oil, work requiring "good wind and muscle"—of which he had both. He studied a primer on oratory, began speaking in church, and was invited to address a Quaker antislavery meeting on Nantucket, where he stammered at first to find his voice.

Then he began telling his story and felt his words flow "with considerable ease." He so electrified his audience that William Lloyd Garrison and other abolitionists in the room arranged to bring him on lecture tours across the North. (Douglass bristled at being typecast—"It was said to me, 'Better have a *little* of the plantation manner of speech than not; 'tis not best that you seem too learned.'") But his handlers also encouraged him to write. By the time Smyth ran afoul of him in Britain in 1846, the *Narrative of the Life of Frederick Douglass, an American Slave, Written by Himself* was selling on two continents, and thousands of Americans had heard the voice that a biographer called "one of the great instruments of the 19th Century."

To this day, he is the exception, the rare black political leader from that earlier time whose name is widely known to modern Americans. (The list is absurdly, misleadingly short: Sojourner Truth, Harriet Tubman, Douglass, the *Amistad* mutineers, the soldiers of *Glory*, and there it ends.) Even now, in this story, we exploit him: Douglass's much-studied life illuminates lives around him, and fortunately for our purposes, those lives included the Cattos.

★ ★ ★

TRIPS TO BRITAIN to rally support and raise money were as much a staple for Garrison's abolitionists as for church leaders such as Thomas Smyth. For the abolitionists, sending Douglass kept him conveniently beyond the reach of any slave catchers his Maryland owners might hire. And British audiences embraced him.

In his late twenties, Douglass was muscular and handsome; his baritone sizzled with sarcasm and boomed reproach. In an era when even revolutionists tended to drape a sentence in Victorian doilies and passive verbs, his speeches thumped with the language of the street. He told of his own slavery and escape; he elicited gasps by reading from the Weld and Grimké book and its inventory of slavery's toolshed—"the gag, the thumb-screw, cat-hauling." (In this last punishment, a cat was placed on a slave's back and slowly dragged off, digging in with its claws.)

In his 1845–1846 British Isles tour, Douglass became a celebrity, a human terminal in whom currents of abolitionism, feminism, Irish nationalism, and worker's rights met and merged. A Scotsman wrote him into a ballad about the Free Church's money. Two antislavery women ventured out one night to help him carve "Send back the money" in the sod of an Edinburgh park. He shook the aging hand of Thomas Clarkson, father of British abolitionism, who had battled slavery for fifty years and bade Douglass keep up the fight. He visited a home for the blind.

A young teacher had invited Douglass; she had read his *Narrative* to her blind pupils. Now they greeted the author with "much shaking of hands."

In the first pages of his book, Douglass tells of a woman who was taken from him in infancy. She often walked twelve miles to visit him after her day's work and faced a whipping if she was not back in the field at sunrise. She died when he was seven. It is worth imagining the sound of Douglass's words as the teacher read them aloud: "I do not recollect of ever seeing my mother by the light of day. She was with me in the night. She would lie down with me, and get me to sleep, but long before I waked she was gone."

★ ★ ★

THE FIRST WAVES of famine were hitting Ireland when a friend took Douglass to hear Daniel O'Connell speak in Dublin's Conciliation Hall on September 29, 1845. Douglass found himself awed by "the ample person and musical voice" of the hero of Irish nationalism, especially when O'Connell reminded his audience of another fight.

"He said, with an earnestness which I shall never forget, 'I have been assailed for attacking the American institution, as it is called—Negro slavery. I am not ashamed of that attack. . . . My sympathy with distress is not confined within the narrow bounds of my own green island. . . . My heart walks abroad, and wherever the miserable are to be succored, or the slave to be set free, there my spirit is at home, and I delight to dwell.'"

As other speakers took their turn, Douglass's friend took him to the platform to meet O'Connell. The man the Irish called the Liberator lumbered over, grasped Douglass's hand, and insisted he, too, give a speech. "I scarce knew what to say," Douglass wrote.

O'Connell had shaken colored hands before. Robert Purvis, who urged blacks to support the Irish cause, had met him, as had the Massachusetts orator Charles Lenox Remond. (O'Connell initially mistook the pale Purvis for a slaveholder and refused his hand.) O'Connell's was the first of sixty thousand names on an 1840 broadside asking Irish immigrants to "treat the colored people as your equals, as brethren," and to "cling by the abolitionists." Remond lugged this "Address" across the sea and unrolled it down the aisles of meetings so Americans could see O'Connell's signature. Now, the Liberator stood with Frederick Douglass before a clapping Irish audience. "Playfully," as Douglass put it, O'Connell introduced him as "the Black O'Connell of the United States!"

Douglass wrote that though he had no speech prepared, "I managed to say something, which was quite well received."

In America, brutalizing contests between blacks and Irish for jobs and neighborhoods had already begun. Young Irishmen outside Pennsylvania Hall had proven as likely to stone Negro abolitionists as "cling by" them. But on that September night in Dublin, as the Irish O'Connell stepped aside and the Black O'Connell rose to speak and both men looked out at the upturned faces in Conciliation Hall, it was possible to envision two pillars of a bridge that spanned the seas.

★   ★   ★

"HOW DIFFERENT HERE, from my treatment at home!" Douglass wrote to Garrison. "I am . . . received as kindly and warmly as though my skin were white." Because he was still a fugitive, British abolitionists began raising money to purchase his freedom. He heard Dublin children squeal, "There goes Dan" as he walked with the beloved O'Connell. Boys in the streets of Edinburgh shouted, "Send back that money!"

Some Britons countered with a different slogan—"Send back the nigger." So said bills posted in Belfast on the night Douglass came to speak. This was Thomas Smyth's native city and a place where he had connections. Even as the posters went up, someone circulated a rumor about Douglass. By July 1846, Douglass had two British lawyers threatening to sue Smyth for libel.

Smyth denied calling Douglass "an Infidel" who had been "seen coming out of a Brothel in Manchester." The minister had merely repeated "reports that I had heard."

Leaving his wife and children in Charleston, Smyth had come to London for an evangelical conference and a grand lecture tour. But Douglass and other abolitionists had wrecked all that, demanding debates, threatening suits, and making Smyth miserable. And they knew it. "I am playing mischief with the character of Slaveholders in this land," Douglass wrote to a friend. "The Rev. Thomas Smyth D.D. of Charleston has been kept out of every pulpit here. He is terrible mad with me for it."

★   ★   ★

THE NEGRO IN Smyth's parlor in Charleston was asking to borrow a book—"a Geography," as Mrs. Smyth put it.

Not that William Catto needed instruction in the crossing of frontiers.

He spoke with Margaret Milligan Adger Smyth on a July morning in 1846. Catto was thirty-six; Smyth had just turned thirty-seven. Both had

young children, were active in the church, and wrote well. There the sim-
ilarities ended. Margaret Smyth, whose soft smile belied an implacable
will, was the daughter of a shipping executive who had been described as
the fourth richest man in the United States. Catto was the son of a former slave.

He was seeking a book from the Smyth library, an ever-growing collection that stretched from the ancients to Milton to modern "extracts"
scissored from the newspapers, as well as Thomas Smyth's prodigious sermons and enough pictures and maps to fill the walls of three rooms. In a
time and place that by turns viewed Negro learning as either suspicious
or criminal, Catto was asking this white woman to help him become more
literate. He was even engaging her in conversation.

She meant to write her husband in Britain that morning, "but just as
I was preparing to sit down Catto called, & as he seemed in trouble I listened to his story until I found it too late."

The library was on the sweltering third floor. As their conversation
continued, the morning gave way to afternoon. But Smyth found herself in
Catto's thrall.

"I am truly sorry for the state of things as he [describes] them in the
Church," she wrote. The portion of her letter that survives does not say
what that trouble was. She would rather the church let go of all its other
Negro class leaders "to retain him: but I am afraid he has made up his
mind to go to either Liberia or Hayti."

Margaret Smyth's racial views were unmistakable. She was keeping
their nine-year-old, Adger, in school that summer lest he play with the
neighborhood's "many little negro boys"—such as Catto's sons, Octavius
and William. (Such play was forbidden in the Smyth house. Decades later,
Adger remembered his father catching him in the act and sparing him a
whipping only on condition that the boy never do it again.)

She suggested Catto write to her husband—and the next morning, he
returned with his letter for her to forward. Now, she had a tactical idea: In
his war of words with the British abolitionists, Rev. Thomas Smyth would
have a friendly letter, written in a graceful hand, to throw in the face of his
detractors and their new-found idol, Douglass.

"It will do for you to shew [Catto's letter] there as from a negro in Carolina," she wrote her husband. Catto had impressed her as too well-spoken and civilized to lump with the degraded race. "He is not a negro," she

wrote. "I don't know when I have been as much pleased with the conversation of any one as with his."

She even endorsed Catto's aspirations to go to Haiti or Liberia. "I do not know that we ought to retain him, if he will have a wider field abroad," she wrote.

It was well-known by then that free Negroes who resettled in Liberia might encounter disease or deprivation. The Colonization Society's advertisement for the voyage offered a cutaway diagram of a vessel far more accommodating than the ships that had brought their grandparents in chains to America.

At the same time, the Smyths and Thornwells and other white clerics saw a need for missionaries to teach the gospel to the heathens. Catto might have been drawn by something else as well. The Haitian slave revolt of 1803 had so captured the imaginations of Negroes in America that families began naming newborn boys for its leader, Toussaint L'Ouverture. (Whole hamlets changed their names; to this day, a section of Durham, North Carolina, is called Hayti.) On that morning in 1846, Haiti and Liberia were places where black men ruled themselves.

Margaret Smyth went into the library and got Catto the geography book he wanted—along with a copy of her husband's sermon about Sabbath school.

By the time Catto's letter crossed the Atlantic, Smyth had fended off Frederick Douglass's lawyers. There is no record of Smyth's "shewing" the letter to anyone. But Douglass would soon know Catto's name for quite different reasons.

★ ★ ★

TO BE A MISSIONARY, Catto had to be formally approved as a candidate for the ministry and then pass the examination.

And on an October day in 1846, Smyth did the unthinkable—he nominated a Negro for the ministry. He introduced Catto as a "candidate for licensure" to the Charleston Presbytery. He did so at a time when the nagging details of slavery clogged the Presbytery's agenda: Could slave men remarry after being sold away from their wives? Was it right to baptize "infant servants in the faith of believing Masters"?

The Presbytery asked the statewide synod for direction on what to do with Catto. A month later, the synod instructed: "examine the Coloured

Man, William Thomas Catto" to see whether he should be licensed "as a Preacher of the Gospel."

Now he had to prepare for the test. Presbyterian licensing rules made it clear that "no candidate, except in extraordinary cases, be licensed, unless, after his having completed the usual course of academic studies, he shall have studied divinity at least two years, under some approved divine or professor of theology." Catto did not have two years of divinity schooling—such training was unthinkable for a Negro in the South.

But knowing Smyth gave Catto access to a bottomless well of knowledge. His pastor could lend him books on nearly every subject; he could counsel him on church politics from the city Presbytery to the state synod to the national Board of Foreign Missions, where Smyth had served.

Catto was sent upstate to Columbia for instruction from the learned "divines" at the church's seminary. They groomed him only to preach the Gospel abroad. But throughout his life, Catto never confined himself to one purpose, place, or task. He was recruited to preside at a colored burial in Columbia. He wrote that people started saying "they had a man, a Presbyterian, whom they thought could talk for them."

On a spring day in 1847, as the dogwoods and azaleas bloomed, a few Negro men and women greeted him in the street and asked, "When will Brother Catto preach?"

The words so struck him that he repeated them in a letter to "my brethren" in the Charleston congregation. He told of being assigned to speak to a prayer meeting in Columbia and watching the people arrive. His ordinarily measured tone turned breathless.

"Old and young, Christians and sinners, some single, some in pairs, they throng the street" to hear Catto speak. Catto was shaken at the size of his audience and of their expectations. "I look at them [and] my heart fails [and] I feel like turning back. Something . . . told me not to fear; . . . I preached the word,—no not I, my Master did it."

On the morning of September 8, the examination of Catto occurred in a place he was familiar with—the lecture room of Second Presbyterian. Five ministers and two elders were there, as were two guests from Alabama, where brave Presbyterians had ordained a colored missionary the year before.

The clerics in the room included Smyth, Thornwell, and Adger, who had seen the Vesey hangings as a boy. Each believed "religious instruction" of Negroes could ennoble slave and slaveholder alike, making one more loyal and the other more humane. None of them was an abolitionist; still, their modest scheme for teaching Negroes put them at odds with most of white South Carolina. A Charleston publisher warned their ally, Rev. Charles Colcock Jones, that anyone "doing any thing for the Negroes, was in a ticklish situation" with the white populace. Now Catto stood before them, answered their questions, and dared them to walk farther out on that limb.

In addition to queries about theology, the examiners asked this mill-wright about the working of machines. The session lasted all day. After a recess, an evening session began in Smyth's parlor. As the roomful of white men sat and listened, Catto delivered a sermon.

When he was done, the examiners acted promptly. They wrote: "The Presbytery . . . have come to the conclusion that though the literary attain-ments are not such as the Standards require, yet the decided evidence that he gives of personal piety—of a call to the Sacred Ministry and particu-larly of the call to the work of missions in Africa—the importance and urgency of that field of labour—coupled with the fact that he has been eminently useful among the Coloured People here justify in his case a departure of the ordinary rule and authorize his licensure."

The clerics noted, lest anyone think a bold act had taken place, that they were "only acting in accordance . . . with the express instructions [or] at least with the implied direction of [the] Synod." They gave Catto a qual-ified or "probationary" ordination.

And so it was done. A pro-slavery Presbytery had given permission for William Thomas Catto, son of a former slave, to enter their minis-try. His elation must have been without bounds, his thanks to God with-out end.

The Catto family would go to a Liberian coast town, Nanna Kroo. They would first go to Baltimore to await their voyage. Much had to be done in preparation.

They were probably leaving Charleston forever. William Catto could not expect to revisit his friends, the Westons and Clark and Holloway, or correspond freely with them. The South's postmasters were known to open mail addressed to Negroes and scan it for the remotest hint of a call-to-arms, a coded phrase, a whiff of insurrection. And the Presbyteri-ans' Board of Foreign Missions had rules: Volunteers for West Africa duty returned to America only with the board's consent. Fevers notwithstand-ing, the mission work was for life.

For a black man in Charleston in late 1847, these steps of Catto's were lightning quick. He had only months ago been a "free" Negro in a slave capital, with no vote and no legal standing. He had no access to the nation's debate on slavery and could never be a participant—in fact, he was only a step or two ahead of the man stealers who had taken his mother. Now, he and his family were on the move, hurtling outward from that strange world and preparing to land in another.

★ ★ ★

THE SOUND THAT greeted William and Mary Catto and their children when they reached Baltimore in January 1848 was black men shouting and whistling.

They were hired touts for the city's hotels, purveyors of hot and cold street-corner meals, and hawkers of five daily newspapers. An old man named Moses promoted ice creams and oysters in the same breath. His skill as a whistler was said to be second only by the *Daily Telegraph* hawker, Whistling Bob.

The rest of the scene felt familiar—the forest of masts, stevedores straining at loads of grain and tobacco, ships disgorging West Indian fruits, oysters roasting, horses stamping, gulls gliding, the call and crackle of an American port in the republic's seventy-first year. Though the winter was colder and the streets steeper, the noisy city at the mouth of the Patapsco River was in most ways not so different from Charleston.

But free black voices shouting and black hands holding newspapers— that was different. A Baltimore newspaper article had helped the slave boy Frederick Bailey learn what *abolition* meant. Charleston censored such words; even as the Cattos headed north, their former city was banning a Methodist manual for its rumination on how "the great evil of slavery" might someday be "extirpated."

Not that Baltimore welcomed all writings in 1848: A semi-literate Negro was caught at the post office picking up the *Ram's Horn*, a struggling New York antislavery sheet that a friend had sent. Maryland law conferred ten years' prison for possessing or receiving "any abolition handbill, pamphlet, newspaper or pictorial representation of an inflammatory character, having a tendency to create discontent among or stir up to insurrection the people of the State."

Except in parts of its Eastern Shore, Maryland bore little resemblance to the low country's rice fields. Wheat was the cash crop, followed by cotton and tobacco. The need for labor varied with seasons, storms, and crop prices; keeping hundreds of slaves year-round made less sense here. And Maryland slaveholders emancipated more slaves than their counterparts farther south. Maybe it was the proximity to "free" Pennsylvania, or Quaker abolitionists' lectures in Baltimore and Washington. For whatever reasons, free Negroes were streaming into Baltimore by the time the Cattos arrived.

News of the Cattos' imminent voyage from Baltimore to Africa preceded them across the ocean. The Presbyterians' Board of Foreign Missions, grateful that a black man had signed up (even though his four young children seemed a risky encumbrance), sent word from its New York office that the Cattos would sail by early spring on a Liberia-bound packet. In sweltering Monrovia, a man was assigned to await the Cattos' provisions, arriving with other mission supplies on a separate brig. In shivering Baltimore, William Catto received a kind letter from the board's secretary, Walter Lowrie, about what to expect in Africa.

Lowrie had just received his own awful lesson in the perils of trying to Christianize far-off lands. Chinese pirates had stormed a boat carrying his son, a missionary. The younger Lowrie, in Shanghai to help revise a Chinese New Testament, had tried to calm things by stepping to the bow and waving a small U.S. flag. The pirates threw him overboard and he drowned.

Walter Lowrie did not mention this incident in his letter to Catto, or the desperation seen lately in mail from Liberia—a tribal war that had all but closed the mission's tiny school (eight pupils on a good day), the two-day ritual poisoning of a chief who had earned his people's "odium," the reports of prohibited contact between missionaries and natives of the opposite sex. Nor did he pass along the things being written about William Catto.

The Nanna Kroo people want white missionaries, one letter said. Why not post Catto to the capital instead? Catherine Connelly, a mission wife, wrote, "There are many at Monrovia personally acquainted with Mr Cato."

Connelly's youngest child was ailing. Her husband, who had survived a brutal fever, lamented "the long train of African sickness that [Catto] and his family would go through." Lowrie offered Catto a hopeful gloss: "As soon as you may be through the fever which we trust you will have very slightly, then you can remove with your family to Nanna Kroo. Mr & Mrs Connelly have had great experience of the best mode of breaking these fevers." When the ship made its first two landfalls on Liberia's coast, "we would strongly advise you not to sleep on shore at either place."

Lowrie said the board hoped Catto could "commence a boarding school" at Nanna Kroo and take over the Connellys' duties while they visited the United States. "This will place you at once in a station of much responsibility, and you will need to look constantly to God for directions and assistance."

On his son Octavius's ninth birthday, February 22, 1848, Catto wrote back. As he waited for the oft-delayed Liberia packet, he'd set out with "a few friends to look around for some business in which I might engage to carry out our views." He'd scrounged for work, spent a few dollars on "Bedstead, Bedding, stove, Chairs, Tables, provisions etc," and some winter clothes for his children and himself.

He turned to what he knew—teaching, preaching, fixing machines. He and his new friends "tried to get up a school" to no avail, he wrote. A local pastor offered to let him preach, but only as a fill-in until a permanent man was picked, so Catto declined. Work at the docks was scarce— in several East Coast ports, mechanics' jobs were going to new arrivals, especially Irish famine refugees. "Where a few years ago we saw nothing but Blacks, we now see nothing but Irish," an observer wrote in Philadelphia. Catto wrote to Lowrie, "I sought some mechanical employment, but in vain."

He landed a temporary helper's job at the office of the state Colonization Society. This group's efforts incensed some Maryland Negroes but meshed neatly with the Presbyterian missionaries, who split their time in Liberia between converting natives and ministering to colored "colonists" from America. Financed by well-to-do Maryland businessmen, the society paid Catto thirty dollars a month—nearly what he would earn in Liberia.

As had happened in South Carolina, he found colored worshippers imploring him to preach. "We have a crowded church every Sabbath, and the people here are very importunate for me to remain and preach for them," he wrote Lowrie, "but sir my heart is set for Africa and nothing, however flattering shall ever turn me from going there."

My heart is set for Africa. It is possible, however, to look back at the long, graceful loops of Catto's handwriting and see something else.

A white man in New York was addressing him respectfully—Lowrie began letters "Rev. Wm. Thomas Catto" and "My Dear Sir." The Colonization Society in Baltimore let Catto write from its office. Around him were free Negroes who spoke of starting schools and getting him a pulpit—men like Daniel Payne, a familiar bespectacled face from Charleston days, now an A.M.E. church leader in Baltimore and Philadelphia. This was not the "degraded" race portrayed by the Calhouns and Joneses and other learned whites of South Carolina—"*Calhoun*ia," Frederick Douglass dubbed it.

Finally, the near presence of abolitionists and the Mason-Dixon Line lent intrigue to life in Baltimore. The Underground Railroad had people here. They coded their words, and with good reason. Prison awaited anyone caught helping slaves run; treachery was commonplace. A Negro could earn a few dollars and dodge a beating if he agreed to be a spy. White wagon drivers betrayed some of the hundreds of runaways sent north from Washington and Baltimore by Charles T. Torrey, a white Congregationalist minister.

Against this background, Catto, ordinarily known for the clarity of his spoken and written words, began a strange correspondence.

★ ★ ★

AT THEIR MONTHLY MEETING, Smyth and other leaders of the Presbytery of Charleston studied an ominous report. A letter dated January 27, 1848, had been intercepted on its way to a black man in Columbia, South Carolina. The writer had apparently used the same ruse Frederick Douglass once employed: He had jumbled his initials.

My dear friend [the letter began],

Keep the flame burning among your people.

As it regards that man, who, for a few stripes, betrayed Mr. C____, it were better for him if a millstone was about his neck than for him to come North! Better for such as him to stay where they are; they don't want such characters here. You understand me. That circumstance is known here about as well as it is in Columbia.

Read this to as many as you deem proper. Use it as your judgment directs.

Your friend and brother,
W. C. T.

The return address was Baltimore.

The white clerics studied the words. *Keep the flame burning. . . . For a few stripes, betrayed Mr. C_____. . . . Read this to as many as you deem proper.* Why would a Negro as clear-spoken as Catto write this way? Why the switched initials? The reason was clear.

A statement was prepared. "Certain Papers were also laid before Presbytery regarding W.T. Catto, a coloured licentiate of this Presbytery," the minutes for April 14, 1848, read. The Presbytery had "great difficulty in licensing" Catto in the first place, and "whereas recent developments have satisfied the Presbytery that he ought not to have been licensed, this Presbytery now therefore feels solemnly bound to withdraw his license."

A report was dispatched to Lowrie at the missions board in New York. A handwritten copy of the "Flame" letter went to the board's Liberia file, along with a note. Authorities sent word to Maryland of intercepted letters that "would excite discontent and insurrection among the slaves," according to one published account. They asked that a colored man in Baltimore, William Thomas Catto, be arrested and taken south.

Catto learned of this request just hours before officers arrived.

That meant packing four children and rushing away. The roads were muddy and the April wind was blowing. But the Pennsylvania border was not far from Baltimore.

Catto "was without the means of escape, having no papers, but finally succeeded after much difficulty in getting beyond the limits of Maryland," according to an article that appeared in a Rochester, New York newspaper, the *North Star*, signed by the editor, Frederick Douglass. Somehow he had gotten his hands on a copy of Catto's letter and of the note alongside it in the mission board's file and printed both. The note read:

CAUTION TO THE PEOPLE OF THE SOUTH

That the . . . people of the South may have some idea of the means used to excite dissatisfaction and disaffection among their slave population, . . . we place before them an extract of a letter . . . written from the City of Baltimore by a colored man who passed several months in Columbia during the last year, enjoying the protection and religious instruction of some of our most worthy divines . . . preparatory to his being sent to Liberia by the Board of Foreign Missions. . . . Most of our citizens will understand his allusions, and every considerate man will draw his own conclusions.

The *North Star* said Catto had settled in Philadelphia—"and though making himself useful there, by no means fills the place for which his excellent talents and devotion to the cause of our people eminently fit him. . . . We hope yet to hear his eloquent voice uplifted . . . for the slave, and for the elevation of his people. He has the head, the heart, and the experience which would make him a powerful instrument, under God, for breaking down prejudice, and elevating the colored man in the public estimation."

CHAPTER 4

With Giants

OCTAVIUS CATTO WAS nine years old when his father said prayers with the giants. It was late on an October night, past bedtime for children in Philadelphia's most respectable colored homes—especially the children of a new-in-town, Southern-born minister, a widower with a new young wife. But Rev. W. T. Catto had already made an impression with his sermons about personal duty (we must all "contribute our something" or "be pushed aside") and his devil-may-care willingness to host antislavery meetings at a time when Philadelphia pastors of both races were still hemming and hawing. Also, the roster of visiting speakers on the night of October 3, 1848, was enough to make parents consider letting a promising child stay up late to learn something.

Two days of antislavery strategy meetings were already under way at Brick Wesley African Methodist Episcopal Church. After suppertime, people began to fill the church's wooden benches, a hut compared to the soaring pillars and segregated stairwells the Catto family had known at Second Presbyterian in Charleston. By the time Catto eased his way to the pulpit, as many as eight hundred people filled Brick Wesley. Those who could not squeeze past the doors stood in the flickering light of Lombard Street's lamps and prepared to crane their necks. Grownups said the giants of the race were coming.

Giants! Their names had a colossal ring—Charles Lenox Remond from Salem, Massachusetts, Frederick Douglass from Rochester, Dr. Martin Delany of Pittsburgh; perhaps Henry Highland Garnet, the one-legged New York preacher who had caused an uproar a few years back by proposing a slave revolt. The colored Philadelphians in the room included stalwarts of the 1838 suffrage fight, the storming of Pennsylvania Hall, and the riots of 1842. At least five of the Underground Railroad operatives were in the church: Robert and Harriet Forten Purvis; Dr. J. J. Gould Bias and his wife, Eliza Anne; John P. Burr; and more were on the way.

Douglass was due on a steamboat at 11:00 P.M. Catto asked for volunteers to escort the young sensation from the Walnut Street wharf. When Catto was finished recruiting, the greeting party numbered fifty.

This gesture was as much about safety as formality. Every colored man and woman in the church knew the risks of walking alone from the docks at night, and the added risks if the walker was the increasingly recognizable Douglass. He could not board one of the hulking horse-pulled omnibuses that plied the city streets. They were for whites.

Douglass, clean-shaven and thirty years old, bounded down the gangplank with word that Garnet was arriving later by train. This news gave the greeting committee a second assignment and sent a thrill through the dimly lit confines of Brick Wesley Church. For all of Garnet and Douglass's sparring over tactics and philosophy, their presence along with Remond and Delany meant the church was hosting a rare treat, a confluence of the antislavery, pro-equality brain trust of the free black North.

If Catto's favorite child, Octavius, could have compressed himself into a corner at the back or stood on tiptoe to peer between the adults in their dark coats, he would have glimpsed an impressive tableau. There, assembled around his father at the pulpit, were four of the race's greatest men.

Remond, Delany, Douglass, and Garnet had a quality in common with Octavius's father: All had become educated in places where Negro schooling was circumscribed by custom or by law. Douglass had learned his ABC's from carpenters' chalkings on the timbers of Chesapeake Bay boats. Delany's mother had fled Virginia after her children were caught "playing school"—evidence of her crime of teaching them at home. Garnet, a former slave, had enrolled at nineteen in a broadminded New Hampshire academy only to be driven off by white neighbors so fearful of race mixing that they had hitched up ninety oxen and pulled the school down. Remond, born free in Massachusetts, had completed all grades at a respected Salem grammar school before it expelled its Negroes, including his little sister, who remembered crying "bitter tears" when the teacher explained that her schoolwork was very fine; the problem was her color.

Yet these men were founding newspapers and writing books and petitioning legislatures. By October 1848, each had argued the case for abolition and equal rights to thousands of Americans. Each led a secret second life as an Underground Railroad operative and had been threatened, beaten, shot at, or stoned for lesser acts of defiance, ranging from sitting down in a railroad car to trying to enter college. None had yet turned forty.

To be sure, they did not all look like giants. Garnet got around on a wooden leg. Remond's voice rang "like the bugle blast," but his body was a narrow, gloomy isthmus beset by twitches and tics. Remond looked even smaller in the shadow of young Douglass, whose yellow cheekbones caught the lamplight as he strode up the aisle and grasped other speakers' hands. ("They were in full blast when we arrived," Douglass wrote.) His *North Star* co-editor, the moon-faced Delany, was black as jet and touted the purity of his African blood. So did Garnet, who claimed descent from a Mandingo chief. Garnet's hour-long sermons and transatlantic travels made people forget his leg. (Once, a white legislator, needing to point out an intelligent Negro, turned and shouted, "Stand up, Mr. Garnet!")

And there stood Octavius's father: thirty-eight years old, remarried, energized by the full house and the gravity of the meetings. He grasped the pulpit in his roughened millwright's hands and delivered the prayer, addressing God in that smooth embracing voice as the famous heads around him bowed and the Amens murmured and rumbled forth from every part of the room.

★ ★ ★

THIS MOMENT ALSO marked the distance William Catto had traveled in a year. He had somehow managed to get his family north of the Mason-Dixon Line to Pennsylvania ahead of his pursuers. He did not reveal exactly how, but several people in the church that night had been in a position to aid him. Dr. Bias and his wife knew how to get colored families out of Maryland—they had helped the white minister Charles Torrey move runaways north from Baltimore. (Perhaps the Catto brood got a checkup, too. With each arrival from the South, out came the doctor's goblet-like wooden stethoscope. In the Bias home, freedom included a free medical exam.)

The A.M.E. Church's Philadelphia conference took in Catto promptly. He and Bias and three other men were ordained as deacons on the same day, June 3, 1848. This was a quick step up for a new man—but the conference needed preachers for its fast-growing flock, and Catto was no stranger. His old Charleston friend Daniel Payne had become the conference's top Baltimore man and a fixture in Philadelphia as well. By September, Catto was pastor of a little Philadelphia church. Catto's fifth child was born that year, his first in the free North. He gave this boy the name of the best-known white abolitionist: Garrison. Now he could begin to consider the horizons of his new-found life.

It was no paradise. A colored man in Philadelphia could neither cast a ballot nor work in most trades; nor could he buy a first-class railway ticket or celebrate July 4 on Independence Square. Even walking there, as Purvis's tearful mother-in-law told a visitor, usually resulted in "a company of degraded creatures running after us in the streets and calling out, 'Nigger, nigger!'"

But certain doors were open to Catto for the first time. He could teach his children to read and write and do simple arithmetic, and he placed Octavius in a grammar school for Negroes, a short walk down Lombard Street from his church. This meant the preacher could get his boy to the little school before work, the morning sun in their faces as they walked east on Lombard toward the Delaware docks. He could write an antislavery letter or read his own name in an antislavery newspaper, in the same sentence with Remond's and Garnet's.

This was something to show his family—his name, deep in newspaper columns stuffed to their limit with six-point type: "The Convention was mainly addressed by Dr. Bias, . . . Robert Purvis, . . . Charles Lenox Remond, Henry Highland Garnet, . . . Rev. Mr. Catto, and many others." This was the North Star, Douglass's paper, just in its second year, its tone teeter-tottering from thunder to derision. But it aspired to be the movement's communication link, and a Philadelphia committee of young colored women was haranguing everyone to support it—"because it is RIGHT to do so," their letter, signed by the educator Sarah Mapps Douglass, no kin to Frederick, said. By late 1848, the North Star's ledger books began to fill with names of subscribers from across the North and as far away as Britain. One of the handwritten entries was "Rev. Wm. T. Catto."

Two inner engines now propelled Catto. One was a restlessness that sent him from one city to another, one pulpit to another, one faith to another. This inner agitation made him useful to the cause of abolition and equal rights—not as a general such as Douglass or Garnet but more like an officer on horseback, "contributing his something," as he said, in constant motion, racing up and down the battle lines from encounter to encounter. Within his first few years in the North, Catto joined in the drafting of fire-breathing broadsides—against slavery, against colonization, against any church (such as his former Charleston church) that lent comfort to slaveholders. He offered the movement a Philadelphia meeting place when other preachers would not; he drafted an appeal to white New Jersey citizens to sign petitions for black men's voting rights—"We are indeed *men* like unto yourselves."

He admonished one audience that the most vivid writings on slavery's evils "fell far short of the realities his own eyes had witnessed" in South Carolina; he advised another that the Colonization Society was a Trojan Horse—a ruse to exile free, opinionated Negroes like himself, "a large, increasing and improving free population, that [slaveholders] may hold our brethren the more quietly and safely in chains."

He exhorted other black ministers to steer the brightest children to Oberlin and the few other colleges that "open their doors to all classes, without distinction or favor." And therein was heard the roar of his other inner engine. It was so powerful as to be his personal law of physics: Every action of the authorities of South Carolina and the United States of America to bar him and his people from the subversive acts of reading and writing, teaching and learning would cause in him an equal and opposite reaction in the upbringing of his son.

Octavius would attend the best schools available to a free Negro boy, and since such schooling was limited at best, his father would track down tutors, petition school committees, and inveigle white men of influence to let his son join their academies. The same persuasive powers that had won him an endorsement and a geography book from Margaret Smyth and a semester at the feet of the Presbyterian "divines" would, from this day forward, be applied on behalf of his son.

A caring father, then. But that is not a complete picture. There is no evidence William Catto went to such lengths for any of his other children. It was more as though he were a gambler who had looked around the family table and made a cold calculation: Being Negro boys and girls in 1848, his children were fated to be waiters or drivers or domestics and to go to their graves, as Remond said, "unwept" by other Americans, "uncared for, unprayed for." So Catto placed his entire bet on his most promising child, the one most persuasive and well-spoken, most curious and unafraid.

The one most like himself.

★   ★   ★

THE MEETINGS IN October 1848 offered fresh proof of his gift for gaining the confidence of celebrated men—even men who despised each other. The learned whites examining him in Second Presbyterian's book-lined lecture room in 1847 were determined to save heathens on two continents, believing in their own power to sheath slavery's hard fists in velvet Christian gloves. The learned blacks with him just a year later in Brick Wesley's crowded confines were determined to rip apart those gloves and smash those fists.

A peculiar symmetry marked these two camps. Each knew or claimed to know the other race well. The white Charleston ministers had closely examined Negro behavior—Thomas Smyth was writing 404 pages on the unity of mankind; Charles Colcock Jones, with a plantation and a hundred slaves of his own, was dubbed "Apostle to the Slaves" for his mission work. And the black leaders gathering in Philadelphia had learned much about the behavior of whites. That knowledge, too, was hard-earned.

Charles Lenox Remond had caught the eye of white abolitionists at an early age and hired on as their first Negro lecturer in 1838. He was also the first Negro to address the Massachusetts legislature, in a losing effort to outlaw Jim Crow on rail and steamship lines. He was no beauty: In an old photograph, a bony Remond stares bug-eyed at the camera, his hair banked sharply to one side, as if he is trying to stand up in a permanent gust of wind. In 1844, employing nightmare imagery and self-effacing wit, he asked the New England Anti-Slavery Society to call on the *North* to secede from the Union.

The Union, Remond argued, was slavery's silent partner and was blind to Negro lives. "Oh, Sir!" he addressed the chairman. "Look at them as they are falling, generation after generation, beneath the sway of the Union, sinking into their ignominious graves unwept, uncared for, unprayed for, enslaved, and say what has the Union been to them?"

He asked what the Union had meant to Francis L. McIntosh, a mulatto boatman roasted alive in St. Louis for killing a deputy and wounding another in 1836. (People argued afterward—Did the fire kill McIntosh quickly or slowly? Either way, the mob's epithets make it likely that *nig-*

ger was the last word he heard.) McIntosh was chased down, chained to a tree, and in Remond's words, "burned in a slow fire!"

Remond let the image linger. "Men say to me, 'Remond, you're wild!' 'Remond, you're mad!' 'Remond, you're a revolutionist!' Sir, in view of all these things, ought not this whole assembly—this whole nation to be revolutionists, too?" The secession resolution carried, 252 to 24.

In the 1840s Remond and Douglass had ventured out from the relative safety of New England, crisscrossing Indiana and Ohio in a campaign of antislavery persuasion called the Hundred Conventions tour. Often as not, they spoke in meeting halls with angry crowds outside. Remond was chased from one meeting and warned away from another. When no landlord obliged, they lectured outdoors.

Douglass was speaking on an open-air platform in Pendleton, near Indianapolis, when "60 of the roughest characters I ever looked upon" demanded that the speeches stop or they would tear down the platform. The speakers, white and black, tried to negotiate a truce. But men began pulling the platform apart with speakers still atop it.

Douglass, trying to use a stick to fight his way out, was knocked senseless. He awoke to find his right hand—his writing hand—broken. The mob brained a white abolitionist who tried to shield him from the blows. That man, William White, lost several teeth that day. Douglass wrote to him later.

"I laugh always when I think how comic I must have looked when running before the mob, darkening the air with the mud from my feet. How I looked running you can best describe but how you looked bleeding—I shall always remember. You had left home and a life of ease and even luxury that you might do something toward breaking the fetters of the Slave and elevating the despised black man. And this too against the wishes of your father and many of your friends. . . . Dear William, from that hour you have been loved by Frederick Douglass."

★ ★ ★

BY THE SUMMER of 1848, Delany, Douglass, and Garnet exuded a shimmering confidence. They, of all people, knew better than to mistake the lurching forward of a train for progress. Yet events around the world had them babbling like evangelists.

A new coalition, the Free Soil Party, was setting out to run a candidate for president who would stop the spread of slavery into the western territories. Democratic movements were roaring to life in capitals of Europe; names of the leaders—O'Connell of Ireland, Kossuth of Hungary, and Mazzini of Italy—turned up in the *North Star* and the bigger newspapers. American workingmen soon began wearing "Kossuth hats" with high crowns and wide, shadowing brims. At the biggest meeting anyone could remember on Independence Square, speeches in four languages pledged solidarity with brothers fighting monarchs across the sea; at the crowd's urging, a black man climbed atop a dry-goods box and spoke, ignoring police admonitions. The talk of revolution reached south across the city into Moyamensing, where a writer glorified a street gang of Irish immigrants as radicals, "putting down aristocrats, monopolies and the Dollar's Misrule." He likened them to the Jacobins of France. They preferred to call themselves the Killers.

Garnet dared a New York audience: Why not educate rich and poor, black and white in the same schoolroom? "This age is a revolutionizing age," he said, "and change after change, and revolution after revolution will undoubtedly take place, until all men are placed upon equality."

At times, Garnet conjured up epitaphs for the unremembered dead. Trained in upstate New York as a Presbyterian preacher, he had studied scripture and his rhetoric and rhythms often drew upon ancient texts.

"Ye destroyers of my people draw near, and read the mournful inscription; aye, read it, until it is daguerreotyped on your souls: 'You have slain us all the day long.' . . . Legions of haggard ghosts stalk through the land. . . . Hark, hear their broken bones as they clatter together. With deep, unearthly voices, they cry, 'We come, we come, for *vengeance* we come!'"

Their cries would permeate the Capitol, Garnet prophesized, until "sworn Senators and perjured demagogues" would have to stop and listen. "The father of waters may roar in his progress to the ocean, the Niagara may thunder, but these voices from the living and the dead will rise above them all."

The news from Europe made him and Douglass gawk at a shrinking world. "Thanks to steam navigation and electric wires, we may almost hear the words uttered, and see the deeds done, as they transpire," Douglass wrote. "A revolution now cannot be confined . . . but flashes with lightning speed from heart to heart, from land to land, till it has traversed the globe. . . . The revolution of France, like a bolt of living thunder, has aroused the world from its stupor; . . . the slaveholders of America, are astonished, confused, and terrified."

Such declarations were all the more surprising in the light of what Garnet, Douglass, and Delany had encountered in their most recent American travels. In the previous September, Douglass and Garrison had been invited to speak in Harrisburg. They knew Pennsylvania was uneven antislavery ground; white boys routinely broke up black Harrisburg church services, and one creative pro-slavery citizen had ended a West Chester abolition meeting by tossing in a hornet's nest. But minds needed changing, and the countryside was also home to Thaddeus Stevens and other durable abolitionists, some of whom had made the invitation.

As the Harrisburg meeting began, uninvited local men filled the back of the hall. They listened in silence to Garrison. When Douglass rose to speak, they began bombarding the speaker's platform with cayenne pepper and dozens of rotten eggs.

The air became unbreathable and people ran for the doors. Howls went up—"Throw out the nigger!" A rock caught Douglass in the back before the melee ended. He and Garrison could hope news of such a rude attack would rally public sympathies. Instead, some editorials faulted Garrison for airing America's dirty laundry amid the war with Mexico. As for the other speaker? "Douglass is a darkey and a tool for the enemies of our country."

Garnet took a trip across New York State in late June. A few years had passed since his bad limb had been amputated, and he was moving with his usual dispatch. En route to a speaking invitation in Canada, he reached Buffalo, bought a railway ticket, clambered aboard a Tuesday morning train to Niagara, and plunked down in a seat.

Even with his high imposing forehead bent over his reading, Garnet in a car of white people was bound to draw attention—if not to his very dark skin then to the deep reverberations of his voice. A conductor came by and instructed him to move.

Garnet complied—till he realized he was being reseated in the noisy, sooty Jim Crow car, behind the locomotive. He asked whether he had offended someone. The conductor said Southern tourists, a summer staple on Northern trains, were sure to demand his removal. "This was not a sufficient reason to my mind," Garnet wrote, "and not being accustomed to yield up my rights without making at least a semblance of lawful resistance," he sat down. The conductor summoned a helper and grabbed Garnet by the throat.

His ejection followed a pattern Remond, Douglass, and others had encountered on Northern trains. If a Negro refused to give up a seat, the

conductor repeated the order. If defied, the conductor—sometimes pausing ominously to remove his coat—summoned a "tough" or two to help do
the ejecting. Passengers gasped as the Niagara conductor and the "tough"
nearly got Garnet entangled in the wheels. "I have been for many years a
cripple," he wrote. "I made no resistance further than was necessary to
save myself from injury; but nevertheless, this conductor and another person . . . continued to choke and to assault me." Battered and bruised, Garnet told his story in the *North Star*.

"Atrocious Outrage On Henry H. Garnet," the headline read. This
news spread quickly—Horace Greeley's *New York Tribune*, with its wider,
whiter audience, said a prominent cleric was "dragged from the cars" and
injured. "Reason: His forefathers were stolen from Africa." Within weeks,
an antislavery monthly in Newcastle-upon-Tyne was repeating the story
for British readers.

The news of Garnet's ejection had just hit the papers in late June 1848
when Martin Delany visited Marseilles—not France's port city, but its
namesake, a village in the cornfields of northwest Ohio. Then, as now,
local people pronounced it *Mar-SAILS*.

Delany and his Ohio contact, the light-skinned Negro abolitionist
Charles H. Langston, were riding north from a meeting in Columbus and
stopped at the hotel of a sympathizer in Marseilles. The sun was setting
and townsmen were pitching quoits in the main street. When they saw the
two Negroes climb from a carriage, the game came to a halt.

In the hotel, local men buttonholed the visitors and proposed an impromptu antislavery meeting at the schoolhouse. Would Delany and Langston agree to address the meeting? They could not say no. They washed up
and started for the schoolhouse.

As Delany and Langston walked, white men and boys, in Delany's
words, fell in "close to our heels" and followed them into the schoolhouse.
Sensing a trap, they declined to speak. The man who had invited them
shouted, "I move we adjourn and consider this a darkie burlesque." A cry
went up—"Darkie burlesque!"—and the swelling, almost festive crowd
followed them to the hotel.

Delany and Langston watched from a window as whites lit a barrel
of tar and shouted, "Rush in and take them!" "Kill the niggers!" Delany
could hear "a thousand demoniac howls," along with talk of taking him
and Langston south to sell them. A blacksmith forged handcuffs. Boys
blew horns and banged tambourines as the fire lit the night.

Delany secured a butcher knife and vowed not to be taken alive. The innkeeper and a one-armed Mexican War veteran tried to calm people down. "Didn't you hear how that black fellow talked?" the veteran said. "These are *educated* negroes." In time, the crowd's energy ebbed, and at dawn the Negroes sprinted out. They reached their carriage amid a barrage of stones and shouted promises of death if they ever returned.

Thus did a group of citizens nearly cut short Delany's career as a doctor, orator, journalist, novelist, African explorer, and soldier—and nearly deprive the world of the poetry of Langston's future grandson, who went by the name of Langston Hughes.

No black antislavery orator escaped white violence. Purvis survived Pennsylvania Hall and sat through a night of Philadelphia's 1842 riot, a rifle on his lap, as whites encircled his house. A rock hit Remond's thin frame as he spoke in rural Bucks County. Douglass, whipped as a boy and mobbed as a man, was a walking registry of scars.

But a quality these men shared was a willingness to return to harm's way. "I have been in danger of my life on more occasions than one," Remond said in 1841, "and before slavery is abolished, it is probable that I shall again."

★ ★ ★

IN SEPTEMBER 1848, Delany and Douglass revisited Ohio. The Free Soil convention in Buffalo had drawn cheering crowds, white and black, and now a "National Convention of Colored Freemen" met in Cleveland. Should Negroes support the Free Soil ticket, with its reluctance to call for immediate abolition? Could Free Soil candidates win seats in Congress, lest the aging Daniel Webster be left to stand alone against slavery's main defender in the Senate, South Carolina's Calhoun? The convention had much to consider.

Sometimes, such conventions nearly strangled on twining vines of procedure. People yawned in a warm Cleveland hall as debate slogged on and committees were named for the purpose of naming other committees. At Langston's urging, the convention guardedly endorsed the Free Soil ticket. A snippet of the proceedings reads: "The Business Committee presented Resolutions 13 to 23 for the consideration of the Convention. Resolution No. 8 was then adopted. . . . [The]11th resolution [was] taken up and adopted. . . . C.H. Langston thought the 8th and 13th resolutions conflicted."

But the conventions served a purpose. "The talent displayed, the order maintained, the demeanour of the delegates, all impress . . . the community," Samuel Ringgold Ward, a former slave, wrote. The leaders "show themselves qualified for legislative and judicial positions."

★ ★ ★

DOUGLASS WENT HOME to Rochester ebullient. His daughter, Rosetta, was nine now, and having been tutored by two abolitionist cousins of James and Lucretia Mott, she was in an elite Rochester school. But when her father asked about lessons, Rosetta broke down in tears, saying the teacher had put her alone in a room—"because I am colored."

White pupils had sided with Rosetta, shouting "By me! By me!" when asked where she could sit in class. The complainer was a white parent—a Rochester newspaper editor. His insistence on segregating Rosetta was reported in the *North Star*—along with an open letter to him: "You are in a minority of one," Douglass wrote, adding, Rosetta had already accepted an invitation to attend another equally fine school.

Letters of support for Rosetta followed in the *North Star*. One came from Scotland and was signed by the Ladies' Emancipation Society in Edinburgh, where two antislavery women had once slipped out at night to help a Negro carve a message in a park.

★ ★ ★

BY THE TIME Rev. W. T. Catto said the prayer to start the October 2–3 meetings, he was becoming known to the leaders in the room.

He and his friend Gould Bias had been in Trenton that June for their first A.M.E. convention. The *North Star* had published the tale of Catto's disillusionment with his Presbyterian handlers and their view of "degraded" Northern negroes; the same article included the drama of his sudden flight from Maryland.

Douglass—ever-willing to use his paper as a shaming tool—took to publishing names of Philadelphia churches that refused to host antislavery meetings. Within one such list, he saluted the exception: "Little Wesley, presided over by Rev. Mr. Catto, was for a time almost the only house where the cause of the slave could be freely pleaded."

He contrasted Catto with weaker men. Someday, he predicted, black Americans would shake their heads when they learned that "in the year one thousand eight hundred and forty-eight, when the whole world seemed moved on the question of human rights . . . ministers of our own complexion . . . stood side by side with the oppressors."

The trustees of Bethel A.M.E. Church, divided on the issue, could not stomach the noisy hubbub nearby. "They saw the people, eager to hear the truth, blocking up the street in front of Little Wesley, unable to gain admission within its narrow walls," Douglass wrote, "and ourselves begging the use of their house, and they closed it against us."

Against us. The words rang through the Brick Wesley meetings. Who were the cause's true allies?

On Remond's motion, women were allowed to take part in the proceedings. This practice was very new—Catto frowned on it. But in Brick Wesley, neither he nor anyone else objected. They could hardly do otherwise—at least two women in the room, Harriet Purvis and Hetty Reckless, had long since proven their allegiance to the cause, in the well-remembered crucible of Pennsylvania Hall.

As the meeting's various committees (nominations, finances, attendance, drafting) began their work, three men kept the assembly entertained by joining in a song.

> I hear the cry of millions, of millions, of millions,
> I hear the cry of millions,
> "Oh, set the captives free!"

This was becoming an anthem, saluting heroes living and dead. ("I hear the voice of Remond, on prejudice 'gainst color.") The song grew and changed with generations; one stanza saluted the Biases' white friend Charles Torrey, who was arrested in Baltimore in 1844 for smuggling slaves to freedom and died in a Maryland prison. ("I hear the voice of Torrey, crying from the grave.")

Much of the meeting's long agenda concerned churches and clerics who had been silent on slavery or had become its apologists. Speaker after speaker named names, and soon this naming—especially of colored clergy—threatened to swallow up the meeting.

Douglass and Delany spoke, calling on churches to wean themselves of slaveholders' rich tithings, and churchgoers to separate themselves from any church that wouldn't. In the middle of Douglass's "cutting and sarcastic" speech, a man stood up and interrupted.

He was an elder from a church Douglass was attacking. The elder said Garnet, who had not yet arrived, possessed a note from the church's pastor that would prove Douglass a liar. Eyebrows went up. Garnet and Douglass had sparred so fiercely in the past that it was easy to imagine that the elder was right. Then, dramatically, Garnet stomped in.

The minutes, prepared and signed by Catto as the meeting's secretary, described what happened next: "Mr. Garnet having arrived, the note was called for and read, when the house decided that the remarks of Mr. F. Douglass were strictly true."

So Douglass was not a liar. And Garnet did not throttle him. Casting about for unity, someone offered a simple slogan. In a political era fueled by four-hour speeches and forty-stanza poems, the colored meeting contemplated five words of the Irishman who, with a mighty paw and a mischievous quip, had pulled Douglass onto a Dublin stage in 1845.

"Resolved, that slavery exists in this country because the people will its existence. . . . Resolved, that by adopting the language of the illustrious O'Connell—'We will Agitate, Agitate, Agitate'—until the people will be changed." This resolution was unanimously adopted.

Now Garnet, Catto, and the rest of the five-man drafting committee huddled in the next room to hammer out a plea to all "Colored Citizens of the City and County of Philadelphia." The statement began, "Equality, Brotherly Love and Liberty to all men. This is our theme." Then it aimed a new blast at mealy mouthed ministers, quoting a white abolitionist who called churches "the bulwark of American slavery."

The call for churches to take an antislavery stand posed a fearful dilemma for many colored clergymen. Even the A.M.E. Church, while opposing mistreatment of slaves, had not flatly condemned slavery yet. Ministers had good reason not to speak out: Bethel and other colored churches in Philadelphia had been torched or stoned or cayenned for merely being colored churches, much less declaring themselves outposts of abolition.

But no such dilemma troubled Catto. Indeed, the statement aimed daggers at men and institutions he had personally known. It listed slavery's strongest Christian defenders—leading thinkers of America's Methodist, Baptist, and Episcopal faiths and others who had cited Bible passages that purported to endorse slavery, even to portray Jesus as having forgiven those slaveholders who applied the lash. The list began this way: "In the Presbyterian church, slavery has its advocates in the persons of Charles C. Jones, of South Carolina." It did not mention Catto's old pastor, Thomas Smyth.

The list identified as "pro-slavery" the Presbyterian board that only months earlier had prepared to send the Cattos to Liberia. What had

Catto learned during the interval when his family was in Baltimore and his heart was "set on Africa?" The statement he helped draft called on churches "to exclude slaveholders and the apologists from their pulpits; to withdraw their support from the American Board of Foreign Missions."

Then came a call for abandoning any church that welcomed slave owners and slave traders into her flock.

"Come out from among these men-stealers and men-slayers. They live and reign upon the broken hearts and prostrated liberties of your brothers and sisters, parents, children, husbands and wives. . . . They use the sacred Bible to sustain these enormities, and from their pulpits, and down their aisles the voice of your brothers' blood, louder than that of the murdered Abel, cries, 'Come out of her, and be ye separated!'"

Man-stealers was a phrase that Douglass used in speeches and writings. The "voice of your brothers' blood" had the biblical clatter of bones favored by Garnet. The gentler passages concerned the larger equation— that only a massive, unified effort could ever hope to loosen slavery's grip. The writing came from men who had studied scripture as well as the mechanical properties of a steam-driven mill.

"The rain from the clouds falls in single drops to the earth, and swells the resistless streams that sweep onward to the ocean. The condensation of steam gives velocity to complicated machinery, and a union of kindred hearts, trusting in God, is the power in his hands by which he sways and governs the moral world. . . . By being united ourselves, we can break the union of slaveholders. Their bond of union is slavery and is formed in hell—let ours be composed of peace, love, mercy, and freedom."

The meeting's leaders had not always spoken as one. Garnet had confounded the antislavery movement with an early plea for slave uprisings. And something in Douglass made him lash out at his allies. He went after Garnet and Remond in public meetings, on issues both profound and personal. Did the Constitution address slavery? Did Garnet's back-to-Africa argument help the race or hurt it? Was Purvis's vast inheritance the "blood-stained" money of slaveholding forebears? (As if that mattered now, as if Douglass had forgotten how many mulattoes, likely including Douglass himself, were fathered by white masters.) He managed to hurt a loyal friend by publishing not a word about Delany's landmark book, the who's-who of colored pioneers in every field, including Catto and, of course, Douglass.

Even so, these men signaled their admiration of each other in enduring ways. Douglass named a son Charles Remond Douglass. Delany, who had named his first-born Toussaint, named his second son Charles Remond Delany. Catto had already named one boy Garrison; the next child born to him would get the middle name Garnet.

When the October 2–3 meetings ended, Delany was hoarse from speech making and dizzy with exuberance. He had seen many people head home upon discovering that the only remaining places from which to hear the proceedings were in the middle of Lombard Street. The connection between speaker and listener had been electric: "Remond, Garnet and Douglass poured forth the most thrilling peals of eloquence, which were repeatedly loudly responded to by the mutual aspirations of assembled hundreds."

Additionally, Delany wrote, he and Remond and Garnet and Douglass "all had the pleasure, for the first time in our lives, of meeting and shaking glad hands together! . . . This was a meeting the remembrance of which can never be effaced."

They talked of meeting in Delaware, a slave state—"to beard the lion in his den," as Delany put it. "Thus gloriously goes onward our march to certain victory," he wrote. "With the master-grasp of Garnet, Remond, Douglass, Purvis, and others, who are nobly fighting side by side. . . . [W]ith the host of noble men and women at their backs, with the feeble aid that I shall render, the monster now staggers, and must soon fall."

Perhaps. Transatlantic alliances were surely about to bloom; Daniel Webster and other old sympathizers were holding their own in Congress. The drafting committee had risen to the delicate business of awakening the rest of Philadelphia's twenty thousand Negroes—"to arouse this class of persons to a sense of their manhood," in the words of Douglass.

"Their numerical greatness, and geographical proximity to slavery, gives them a mighty lever of influence," he wrote. "Make the colored people in Philadelphia what they ought to be, and there is no power in the land which can long oppress and degrade us."

Whatever rivalries had split them, the giants of the race were shaking hands and standing together. Having sustained myriad blows and bruises, they were going back for more. What brickbats could fly their way that they had not already encountered?

★ CHAPTER 5 ★

Lessons

WHEN WILLIAM CATTO convened the next meeting at Brick Wesley on December 18, 1848, the announced purpose was to advance the statewide effort to regain the right to vote. Instead, the debate turned as treacherous as the hard-packed ice outside.

Catto's gift for quiet persuasion was not winning the day. Speakers derided each other for weak morals, for membership in "pro-slavery" churches, for wasting energies on the "tomfooleries and extravagances" of the colored Odd Fellows order, which had lately broken away from the white Odd Fellows. So many accusations flew across the pews that Charles Remond had to remind people why they were meeting: to work at overcoming "the great disadvantage of our *dis*franchised condition."

Catto had called the session to hear a much-awaited report. Robert Purvis, Gould Bias, and eight other city men had just returned from a larger meeting in Harrisburg. A campaign was being launched to rally Pennsylvanians of both races around extending the franchise to black men. Returning the franchise, actually—the legislature had taken it away in 1838.

The odds were bleak. Lehigh County, sixty miles away, debated banishing Negroes altogether. The Free Soil Party had sputtered in November, allowing Zachary Taylor, a Whig owner of three hundred slaves, to win the presidency. But the movement's optimists still pondered the what-ifs. Colored men could vote in Maine, Massachusetts, New Hampshire,

Rhode Island, and Vermont; in New York, too, if they owned $250 worth of property. Ohio courts memorably ruled that a man could vote if a judge deemed him "more than half white." What if all fifty thousand Negro men in the North could vote? In Trenton, Hartford, Harrisburg, and Columbus, suffrage petitions rose, fell, and rose anew.

With that in mind, sixty-five Negro delegates from across Pennsylvania, along with Remond from Massachusetts, had sat down in a Harrisburg tavern known as Shakespeare's Saloon and composed an elegant, if wordy, appeal to Pennsylvania voters.

"When the last scroll of time shall be wound up on the great windlass of eternity it will present the indestructible names of your Penns, Franklins, Rushes . . . and a host of others whose highest aim was justice to mankind," the appeal said. "Shall these transcendent spirits look down from their peaceful abode on your amended Constitution, and there behold a *barrier* against the exercise of civil rights?"

Purvis and the other men used eight syllables to define the foe— "complexional intolerance" accounted for their disfranchisement. Not ignorance, impiety, or degradation: If such things barred voting, white men aplenty would be barred as well.

This explanation reflected a shift by one of the group's most admired men. The coal dealer William Whipper had long argued that his fellow Negroes' degradation and depravity *caused* prejudice. But experience convinced Whipper that white hate was immutably ingrained and that his old argument was "fit only to be used by our oppressors."

The Harrisburg convention pledged to raise a princely five thousand dollars to underwrite lecture tours and print ten thousand pamphlets. The Philadelphia men promised two thousand dollars of this. The figures seemed outlandish. With few exceptions—Purvis's inheritance, Whipper's coal business, the Fortens' sailmaking firm—no one at the Brick Wesley A.M.E. Church meeting had access to such sums. Some had not seen that much in a lifetime.

A young sign-painter, David Bowser, got up and dared people in the church to open their purses. Dr. Bias called on "young and old, male and female, to lend their assistance, both physical, moral and pecuniary, to obtain our God-given rights."

Catto, reporting the meeting to the *North Star*, omitted the disagreements. But the zeal of the October meetings had ebbed with Taylor's presidential victory and the arrival of winter. Many seats in the church were empty. The organizers shook their heads.

* * *

OCTAVIUS WAS TURNING TEN. He was not the eldest of the ever-increasing Catto brood that now included a new brother and sister. But from an early age he showed promise. He took well to all his lessons at the Lombard Street Colored School, and he had his father's physical strength and grace.

Persuasive soon turned up in people's impressions of the son as well.

He had dark brooding eyes set against caramel-colored skin—"very light and very bright," an acquaintance wrote. In his high cheekbones one could imagine traces of the Indian bloodline that had spared his mother's family from paying the Negro tax. At the corners of his fulsome lips there played the slightest hint of mirth.

He was said to be a star pupil: "outstanding scholarly work, great energy, and perseverance in school matters." Adults may have made the air around him thick with praise, for he fairly shimmered with confidence. Before long, he was writing gaudy notes to girls about "true poetic fervor."

His full name was a wicked mouthful for a child. Some of his brothers and sisters had the same names as a parent, a grandparent, an aunt—William, Mary, and Frances. Others got names that, as was the fashion, saluted heroes and served as little primers of history.

There was Garrison Catto. The next boy, Beman, arrived after his father had come to know Rev. Amos Gerry Beman, a colored abolition leader whose pulpit was in New Haven but who traveled to meetings in New York and Philadelphia. (Rev. Beman named his own son for Charles Torrey, who died for the cause in a Maryland jail.)

For Beman's middle name, William Catto turned to the movement's eloquent amputee. Thus, one Catto son went through life with *three* names of men in the struggle against "complexional intolerance": Beman Garnet Catto.

But Beman had it easy compared with his big brother, the only Catto child burdened with a Latin lesson for a name: Octavius Valentine. Why the middle name? The baby arrived six days after Saint Valentine's Day.

People soon took to calling him O.V.

★ ★ ★

THE LOMBARD STREET SCHOOL, shabby and crowded with 446
pupils, was the city's only public grammar school for Negroes. A principal
and two assistants taught 226 boys; the girls' ratio was similar. This was
progress—two decades earlier, when the school board began sending colored children there, the principal alone had taught 199 pupils.

No South Carolina–style law barred Negroes from teaching Negroes
in Pennsylvania, and by the 1850s the homes of the Purvises, Fortens,
and other better-off families were like plump seed pods bursting with
aspiring teachers. A Forten daughter, Margaretta, followed Sarah Douglass's example and opened a tiny school. The cabinetmaker James Le
Count's children all clamored to teach. But the school board customarily turned colored applicants away, so William Catto and other black parents entrusted their children to the white principal of the Lombard Street
School, James Bird.

And they adored him. Parents had come to realize that most white
teachers instructing their children were the bottom of the barrel, ne'er-
do-wells who couldn't hold more coveted jobs at white schools, and who
often as not neglected or despised their black charges. Mr. Bird was the
exception.

When the school board decided to transfer Bird, old James Forten himself had goaded the state Abolition Society into helping him get the decision reversed. Eventually the board renamed the Lombard Street School
in Forten's memory, making it the first Philadelphia school named for a
Negro. Notwithstanding that gesture, generations of students and alumni
knew it by its nickname, the Bird school.

Most pupils walked to school. The only Negroes who could ride the
bulky horse-drawn omnibuses were white passengers' servants. For Catto
and son, this meant mile-and-half walks south to school and church. The
Cattos rented rooms on Kessler Alley, along the northern reach of the city
proper. Cheap row houses were bunched beside train yards and factories
in a district nostalgically known as Spring Garden. Men carried pistols,
women avoided walking unescorted, and a name appeared in charcoal and
chalk on every available wall, written in the scrawl of a gang of white boys
and men: *Flayers.*

Among the seven families who rented on Kessler Alley were fourteen
children under age twelve, including four young Cattos. The neighboring

men were a box maker, a tinsmith, a carter and a weaver, a lamb's-wool spinner from England, and a laborer from Germany. One man earned his living as an astrologer. The second oldest was thirty-eight, an Irish cordwainer—shoemaker, that is. The oldest was William Catto, turning forty that year. Did younger families look up to the only minister on the block?

The Cattos were also the only Negroes on the row. Many colored families lived closer to South or Lombard Street, or in the myriad alleys south and east where cheaper housing stood—St. Mary, Bedford, and Emeline streets, McClaskey's Court, Hog Alley. In the close-packed neighborhoods of the poor and almost poor, the races mingled.

A child could witness a revolution a-borning at Broad below Spring Garden, but not the one envisioned by the Douglasses and O'Connells. The smoldering smokestacks of the Baldwin Locomotive Works loomed on the city's brow. The factory rose three stories over Broad Street; the yards extended nearly a mile. Tradesmen and apprentices stoked furnaces and maneuvered buckets of molten steel or molded iron tires and tested the intricate valves of Locomotive Engine Model 4-4-0. The works employed four hundred men and boys, placing it on the front rank of American manufacturers. Thirty-seven locomotives were on order for 1850 alone. Matthias Baldwin opposed slavery but did not mind that Southern railroads bought his 4-4-0.

* * *

A WALK FROM Kessler Alley south down Fourth or Fifth Street took father and son past the doors of black men William Catto had come to know in the meetings.

David Bustill Bowser worked in his home at 841 North Fourth. He was Sarah Douglass's cousin and had learned painting from her brother. Midway in age between the older and younger Catto, Bowser wanted to paint portraits. He favored a lush romantic style that wrapped his subjects in a gauzy, golden light. For the moment, his livelihood was finding shop owners willing to hire a Negro to paint their signs.

Customers or no, Bowser could be counted on. In the December suffrage meeting, Bias and Remond had made fine exhortatory speeches but Catto's report noted a "hearty response from the audience" when young Bowser rose and told the assembled bickerers to put up or shut up.

Catto's contact on Fifth Street was the clerk in the Anti-Slavery Society's office—an address already hallowed or cursed, depending on one's views. William Still, in his late twenties, was a clerk in title only, and on two spring days in particular, visitors to 107 North Fifth would have found him shaking with excitement.

Still's main duty was to interview newly arrived fugitive slaves to determine needs and sniff out infiltrators. This was the office where, in 1849, Still and the white abolitionist J. Miller McKim opened a two-by-three-foot box marked "This Side Up"—and up popped the pungent, ecstatic form of Henry Brown, alive after a twenty-seven-hour journey. Aided by allies at both ends, "Box" Brown had shipped himself north from Richmond to freedom and fame.

Here, too, Still had questioned an older fugitive named Peter, and each answer made his heart pound harder. What made Peter's story familiar? It mirrored what the free-born Still had heard all his life. Finally, he asked Peter: What if I told you I am your *brother*? Still's mother had abandoned Peter decades before when she had made her own escape from slavery, settling in New Jersey. Still, who was born in New Jersey, had never met Peter; now he hugged him and reunited him with ten siblings and their aging mother.

Other doors opened onto sadder stories, as witnessed by Society of Friends volunteers in the late 1840s who walked the same streets as the Cattos to compile a census of the Negro community.

Leah Hubbard lived alone at 113 North Tenth. She was like O.V.'s grandmother in that she had been kidnapped into slavery a half century ago. But no white guardian had filed "ravishment of ward" papers for her, and she had remained a slave for years. The Friend who interviewed Hubbard wrote: "Free born but reduced to slavery when a child."

No Underground Railroad drama ensued. Hubbard had regained her freedom by the much more common, slower route—saving money, year by year, until she had the seventy dollars it cost to purchase herself from her master. By then she was nineteen.

Now she did whatever day work she could get and paid seventy-five cents weekly rent. The Friends' volunteer wrote of her room, "Poverty and dirt."

Perry Morris, a stevedore in Lombard Row: "free born but wrongfully sold at 12 and served till 24." Wignette Robinson, a laborer, and his wife, a washerwoman, had five children but two of these were "in slavery in Delaware." Silva Copeland and her two little children lived in a garret; "Husband is a Slave in Richmond Virginia."

This breaking of families was slavery's relentless scythe, marking the lives of Negroes North and South. Nearly every "free" household contained a broken heart. Henry Bibb escaped to Canada and started a newspaper but ran south again and again in attempts to retrieve his wife—only to learn that she had been made her master's "concubine." William Still's newfound brother, Peter, likewise ran south, trying and failing to rescue his wife and children from an Alabama master. Box Brown's Virginia owner announced one morning at breakfast that he needed cash—and proceeded to sell off Brown's wife and children.

Brown wrote of clutching his wife's hands and vowing to reunite "in heaven," and of seeing his eldest child looking at him from a wagonload of children "and pitifully calling, 'Father! Father!'"

The scythe cut hardest among the lowly and the recent arrivals but did not spare Negroes of any origin or class. Ann Jones, of 239 Lombard, was born free but "when quite small" was made the ward of a Philadelphia man—who sold her to a Virginian. Then she was sold and resold. Eventually she saved $250, sued for her freedom, and won. "She is now old and quite infirm."

Another word that cropped up in the Friends report was *mob*.

Hester Dill, living alone on Lombard Street, was born in slavery and freed by manumission—only to see her possessions destroyed by whites in the North. "Broken up and lost all . . . by a mob," the report said. Thomas Trotter of Bedford Street lived "weakly, having suffered from beating by the Mob." Penina Moore and her kin in McClaskey's Court were "broken up in the red row mob and lost good furniture besides $100 in money." That 1835 mob, formed after a deranged black servant attacked his employer, ransacked and set fire to a Negro shantytown known as Red Row. White families put candles in windows, as if to say, not us, not this house. On other streets, Negroes nailed their doors shut in futile efforts to fend off the rioters.

Like Catto, Abner Rilley of North Fifth Street had a child in the Bird school. The Rilley adults were a waiter, a barber, and a dressmaker and so could afford to take in an orphan boy. That child, the Friends' report explained, had lost his mother to an illness begun "at the time of the 1st of August riot."

On August 1, 1842, Bias and others had led twelve hundred Negro temperance marchers up Fourth Street, beneath a banner depicting a man who had broken the chains of enslavement. Before they reached their destination—the State House—they were met by a white crowd twice their number. The whites broke up the parade, chasing down marchers and hurling "missiles of every description . . . with frightful force." At six o'clock the next morning, the mob reassembled with bludgeons in hand and started entering homes. At the same hour, Irish workers set upon their black counterparts in the riverfront coal yards.

The mob controlled part of the city for three days. Bed linens and silver were ransacked, windows smashed, furniture broken, residents driven out. A church burned, as did the meeting hall that Stephen Smith, the coal merchant and clergyman, had financed out of his pocket. Some Negro families fled to New Jersey woods and marshes. Purvis, up all night with his rifle on his knees, wrote of "our utter and complete nothingness in public estimation."

The banner that triggered all this destruction was rumored to portray a slave who had broken his chains and set a town afire. To be sure, Bias and the others had chosen a portentous date for the parade—August 1, the anniversary of abolition in the British West Indies—but all the temperance banner's man was doing was breaking his chains of drink. A few days after the riot, a reporter inspected the banner and wrote: "The banner contains nothing more than the figure of an emancipated slave, pointing with one hand to the broken chains at his feet, and with the other to the word 'Liberty' in gold letters over his head. The burning town turns out to be a representation of the rising sun, and a sinking ship, emblematic of the dawn of freedom and the wreck of tyranny."

The question Angelina Grimké had asked in 1838 lingered. What was a mob? What drove it? A witness to the temperance mob said he heard countless expressions of a jealous rage, whites angry that Negroes were "living just like white folks." This witness wrote that contempt has turned to "envy, and the most ferocious hatred."

The spark for a riot was usually a rumor. A mixed-race abolition meeting gave rise to a talk of black men promenading with white women. The rumor sluiced across a city and soon battalions of men and boys were forming in public squares, stockpiling brickbats, brass knuckles, pistols, clubs, firemen's spanners, and flaming barrels of tar.

Some weaponry was more exotic—the hornet's nest tossed through a West Chester window, the Harrisburg bombardment of Frederick Douglass with rotten eggs and cayenne, finely milled to induce blinding; the bottles of vitriol heaved into a Boston crowd outside a slave's trial. Mere drops of sulfuric acid—vitriol—caused agony and disfigured the flesh. (Box Brown had sprinkled it on his finger to get excused from work in order to start his escape, but the acid had "very soon eaten in to the bone.")

People used the words *riot* and *mob* as shorthand. Did you escape to the fields in New Jersey during the Flying Horses riot? Being shorthand, the words did not convey that some rioters were "gentlemen of property and standing" or that city leaders tended to blame Negroes' parading or promenading.

The shortest route from the Catto home on Kessler Alley to the Bird school was Sixth Street, past the new Odd Fellows Hall, erected recently on a lot that had been in ruins. A father might pause here to tell his ten-year-old a matter of local fact: This is where men burned the abolition hall.

★   ★   ★

IN THE BUSINESS DISTRICT, the Cattos could hear Arch Street's tailors hawk bombazine blouses and Russian furs, as bankers and lawyers and cotton brokers moved about in top hats; workingmen wore slouch hats and wide-brim Kossuths.

Jobs at the docks as stevedores or caulkers had gone mostly to Irishmen by now. Negroes were domestic servants, waiters, launderers, caterers, dressmakers, coachmen, and bootblacks, pickers of rag, pickers of bone. In summer, when streets grew foul with animal carcasses and horse manure, some men worked as scavengers. In winter, dark-skinned West Indies women stirred soups in iron pots on the street corners and cried out to passersby, "Peppery pot! Smokin' hot!" A bowl cost a few pennies.

The sturdiest commerce for Negroes was curiously safeguarded by the deepest moats of prejudice. With rare exception, a white physician would not draw Negro blood, nor a white dentist peer in a Negro mouth, nor a white undertaker risk offending other customers by embalming a Negro's remains, nor a cemetery lay those remains to rest in a field with white decedents. So colored customers turned to colored proprietors, to men William Catto saw at the meetings: Gould Bias, physician; Thomas Kinnard, dentist; James Le Count, undertaker; Robert Adger, purveyor of used furniture; Jacob C. White, barber, bleeder, and cemetery operator. Their children went to the Bird school. O.V.'s best friends were Jake White Jr., and young Robert Mara Adger. Professional schools were closed to blacks, so men like Bias and Kennard were largely self-taught.

A visiting colored writer in town for an antislavery meeting marveled at red-brick homes, each with "little, low, white, unrailed stoops, placed two and two together, square after square, as far as the eye could reach; and when the stoops recede from view, rows of plain white window shutters, and semi-circular topped doors." The city presented "a kind of holidayish or Sunday appearance, . . . a clean, neat, white-cravated, straight-coated, broad-brimmed double-chinned, portly, sturdy Quaker, attired in his Sunday best."

Farther south, and closer to the Little Wesley Church, the Sunday-best appearance began to drop away. After the narrow brick three-story "trinities" of Spruce and Lombard and Rodman streets came South Street and the township of Moyamensing, where cheaper-built boardinghouses and shanties occupied a lattice of courtyards and alleys, filling up in recent years with refugees from slavery and refugees from the famine.

For pupils of the Bird school, the getting-to-and-from was as memorable as the schooling. John Wesley Cromwell told of white gangs so feared that no black church in the vicinity "felt safe to open its doors." Negro children and adults alike were warned against setting foot south of the "dead line," South Street, after dark. A friend of O.V.'s, William C. Bolivar, recalled running to school on hard-packed snow in hostile territory.

"There was indeed some rare marathon sprinting to escape both the cold and the hoodlum," Bolivar wrote. He said the biggest threat was "the idle volunteer firemen."

★ ★ ★

IT WAS A PECULIAR little island world, this place where the Cattos and other free black Americans resided as the century's midpoint approached—"a nation within a nation," Martin Delany said. For all intents and purposes, Philadelphia was its capital.

Richard Allen and Absalom Jones founded Negro religions there. James Forten's sail loft and William Whipper's and Stephen Smith's coal brokerages made modest fortunes there. Negro intellectuals and agitators from across the North—Remond and Douglass, Delany and Henry Highland Garnet and James McCune Smith—came to lecture and confer. An industry of caterers and cooks rose up there, so skilled that diners wrote odes to them. An all-colored Philadelphia orchestra won such renown that Queen Victoria invited them to play for her. She presented the conductor, Francis Johnson, with a silver bugle.

The city was to some degree a zone of comfort and safety, because of its abolitionist community—and because the Quakers' tiny numbers belied their wealth, connections, and lustrous past. The Pennsylvania Abolition Society never exceeded two thousand members, but one of its early presidents had been a reformed former slaveholder, Benjamin Franklin. Bold men and women, colored and white, made the city a grand junction of the Underground Railroad. Geography, too, favored this port city, a day's ride from the line drawn in a South Street office by the astronomer Charles Mason and the surveyor Jeremiah Dixon.

Negroes had become joiners. They had to if they wanted death payments for their loved ones or money for burial. There were Good Samaritans and Masons, Sons of St. Thomas and Sons of Temperance and the all-Negro Grand and United Order of Odd Fellows. By the time the Cattos lived in Kessler Alley, the Negro fraternal and mutual-aid societies in the city had grown in three decades from 15 to 106.

The A.M.E. Church and the Odd Fellows—by then the nation's two largest Negro organizations, with congregations and lodges across the North—called the city their home. Philadelphia, Frederick Douglass wrote, "holds the destiny of our people."

The city did not have Charleston's laws against Negroes' lighting a pipe; nor did it intercept Negro mail or imprison Negro sailors upon stepping ashore or condone the regular ravaging of female servants by male masters. No one riding in the Pennsylvania countryside saw the sight a young Sarah Grimké had once seen near Charleston: a black man's severed head, mounted on a pike to teach other slaves a lesson.

On its docks and in its drawing rooms, however, Philadelphia had its own barriers. Morris Brown, banished from Charleston over suspicions he had aided Denmark Vesey, became an early leader of the A.M.E. Church and lived to see it flourish. But he also saw its first church, Bethel, become such a target in Philadelphia that congregants took to lining the windowsills with paving stones to fend off the next mob.

Negroes clamoring to see an 1848 exhibit of Renaissance art were told to arrive after white patrons had come and gone. (Remond, Bias, Bowser, and Lucretia Mott boycotted, declaring that any Negro who attended was "consenting in his own degradation.") White Philadelphians could bring black servants aboard the omnibuses, but no other Negro could take such a ride, even if he was a world-renowned writer.

William Wells Brown, along with Douglass and Delany, was among
the few American Negro authors in print by the time he visited Philadelphia in the early 1850s. Born in slavery, Brown had been a "soul driver,"
hauling other slaves to auction and prettying up the older ones for sale
by plucking out gray hairs or darkening them with dye. He had managed
to escape and become a writer; now he was returning from five years in
Europe, where he had hobnobbed with the literary crème de la crème. In
Philadelphia, the Purvises and Motts welcomed him—and warned him of
the city's ties to slavery "in a commercial point of view."

In Chestnut Street, Brown was denied a seat on an omnibus. "I was
told that 'We don't allow niggers to ride in here.'" This incident became
fresh fuel for his speeches against slavery, along with the fact that his
grandfather, a slave, had helped the colonials fight the British. Brown had
dined with the great (Charles Dickens and Alfred, Lord Tennyson) and
less great (Edward Bulwer-Lytton, author of "It was a dark and stormy
night"). He had ridden omnibuses in London and Paris with no questions
asked—"But what mattered that? My face was not white, my hair was not
straight; &, therefore, I must be excluded from a seat in a third-rate American omnibus. Slavery demanded that it should be so."

Such stories became some of the movement's cheapest and best
ammunition. Each outrage, as people said, became another bright thread
in a fabric of such remembrances, another line in the litany of a Remond
speech or a *North Star* editorial, another stanza appended to *I Hear the
Cry of Millions*.

All through the Cattos' world, men and women, black and white,
added bright threads to this cloth.

Amos Beman, the Connecticut preacher, added the stories of two letters he had saved, one from a dozen college boys, the other from a famous
scholar.

Beman had enrolled at Wesleyan University during its brief experiment with admitting Negroes in the 1830s. "Young Beman," the letter
began. The writers said they were white students and admonished Beman
and the several other Negroes to stop attending class—and "if you fail to
comply by this peaceable request, we swear, by the ETERNAL GODS, that we
will resort to forcible means to put a stop to it."

This letter was signed "TWELVE OF US."

Beman left Wesleyan, became a Congregationalist pastor, made his
New Haven church into an Underground Railroad stop, and led the

decades-long campaign to get voting rights for Negroes in Connecticut. He wrote to a world-renowned lexicographer in 1843, asking what books the man might recommend on the history of African people.

"Of the wooly haired Africans . . . there is no history, & there can be none," Noah Webster replied. "That race has remained in barbarism from the first ages of the world."

Many of the movement's staunchest white supporters told of moments that changed the direction of their lives.

It was true, as William Catto said, that written accounts of slavery "fell far short of the realities he had seen with his own eyes." But seeing such realities sometimes transformed white witnesses—such as the Grimké sisters or the Briton who had heard a South Carolina planter brag of deflowering his slave girls or the young Northern reporter, Walt Whitman, who had lived in New Orleans and seen enough to become a Free Soil delegate and a writer of antislavery verse.

The remembrances included excitements, too—such as William Still's reunion with his brother, or Box Brown's delivery, or Frederick Douglass shaking hands with his blind admirers in Britain. Or a game that children played one day in James Le Count's house.

Le Count was a colored carpenter who, like many in his trade, added to his income by doubling as an undertaker. All the same, Le Count's children knew they would disappoint their parents if they grew up to be coffin makers. Visitors to the home on Rodman Street could expect to hear young voices doing multiplication tables or reciting verse.

And like Jacob White Sr.'s house on Old York Road or the Purvises' or the Biases' houses, their home served a second purpose. A little Le Count cousin named Lydia discovered this by slipping into the coffin room during a game of hide-and-seek. As descendants tell it, Lydia climbed into one of the freshly nailed coffins to find that it contained a live man.

James Le Count was hiding fugitive slaves.

The discovery of the coffin man prompted a family meeting. The children were warned not to play in that room again and never to tell anyone what had happened.

Purvis provided many threads—he went through life chalking up racial encounters and telling the tales in the manner of a world traveler showing you his oft-stamped passport: the day the great O'Connell mistook him for a white slaveholder and refused to shake his hand; the trans-Atlantic ticket thrown back in his face, only to have a white planter befriend him on the return voyage; the summer stays in Saratoga and other white resorts where he "mingled without question among the beaux and belles"; and the story of Purvis's favorite possession, the portrait of Cinque.

He had been so inspired by the *Amistad* slave revolt that he had commissioned a portrait of its leader, Cinque, and hung it in his house on Lombard Street. There, one of the many fugitives the Purvises harbored asked about the painting, and Purvis told him about the *Amistad*. The fugitive got to Canada, went south to rescue his wife, was recaptured—and then, claiming inspiration from the painting and the Amistad story, led 135 slaves in a famed mutiny on another ship, the *Creole*.

Then there was the Negro telescope.

Robert Bridges Forten was the same age as William Catto but had grown up in Philadelphia and had the advantage of being James Forten's son. He served with his father and brother-in-law as a delegate to the American Anti-Slavery Society in 1836—you could not be a Forten or a Purvis and sit idly by—and became a manager in his father's sailmaking concern. Robert was also an amateur scientist.

That interest gave him something in common with his friend, the ubiquitous Daniel Payne, whose curiosity about the 1832 solar eclipse had left him half-blinded. Payne was now in Philadelphia, preaching for the A.M.E. and living out his dream of soaring north in his pink teaching robes. Payne was doing what he always did—starting a school—and Robert Forten enthralled the pupils with the nine-foot telescope he had built on his own.

Young Forten had ground and polished the telescope's lenses himself. He had even submitted the telescope for display at the city's science museum, the Franklin Institute, which by the 1840s had been open for two decades. The directors not only displayed the telescope—they awarded it their prestigious Scott Medal, given annually to "useful inventions by men and women."

The museum was then and is now a great emporium of science, medicine, and industry, and a treat especially for children, with its vast planetarium, shiny black Baldwin Locomotive, and two-story model of the human heart. But in the Cattos' early years in Philadelphia, the institute was open only to white visitors.

The Fortens and Purvises and their allies made a point of testing such rules and expecting their offspring to do likewise. Not long after Robert Forten's telescope won its medal, a Purvis boy and a Remond girl tried to do what countless other schoolchildren had done: visit the Franklin Institute. The doorkeeper turned them away. (Purvis rebuked his distraught son: "Why didn't you die, rather than submit to this insult?") The family sued the museum and lost.

There is no record of the directors' having pondered the irony of honoring an inventor while barring the inventor's race. On the long list of Scott Medal winners, alongside Jonas Salk's vaccine, Marie Curie's atomic findings, and Orville Wright's biplanes, an entry from the 1840s says only, "R. B. Forten—Telescope."

★ ★ ★

ANYONE WHO VISITED Moyamensing saw many colored families living far below the station of the Fortens or even the Cattos.

The same December week as the Brick Wesley meeting on voting rights, the coroner of Philadelphia County published his annual report for 1848. He devoted a section to deaths recorded that year among the city's Negroes.

"Many were found dead in cold and exposed rooms and garrets, board shanties five and six feet high, and as many feet square, erected and rented for lodging purposes, mostly without any comforts, save the bare floor, with the cold penetrating between the boards, . . . some in cold, wet and damp cellars, with naked walls, and in many instances without floors; and others found dead, lying in back yards, in alleys."

Douglass, who rarely invoked scripture, reprinted the coroner's words in his newspaper with this quotation from Isaiah: "How long, Lord? How long?"

★ ★ ★

THE PENNSYLVANIA SUFFRAGE drive foundered. Tens of pamphlets were printed rather than the promised ten thousand. The legislature finished its February–March session and went home from Harrisburg without addressing the question.

One of the men who had been at the Brick Wesley meeting fumed. He said, We have no one to blame but ourselves. Writing in the *North Star* and signing as "Observer," he indicted the city's respectable Negro class for having grown too protective of its respectability, too busy attending fraternal society meetings, too complacent.

"Let the quiet of the church, . . . the accumulation of dollars and cents, the anniversaries of Odd Fellow societies . . . the suppers of Good Samaritans and Fancy Balls and parties, be made subordinate for the time being, to the great and true idea of our moral, social, political and religious recognition," Observer wrote.

Observer—probably Remond, since he gave his address as Salem, Massachusetts—went on to offer a blistering portrait of the nation within a nation.

"Suffer me to live on South-street, and beat and stab me for walking on the next street below, after 10 o'clock in the evening. Tell me I may walk in an Odd Fellow Society, and mob me for walking in a Temperance procession. Permit me to pass in a Free Mason procession, and club and stone me to death for being in an Anti-Slavery procession. Go when, where and with whom we please as servants or slaves—but denied place above or beneath ground—scarcely breathing air, or drinking water as gentlemen.

"As musicians we may play in the centre of fashionable circles, but must not presume to walk or march on grand parade occasions, ride side by side with our white employers or masters, carry the children in our arms, kiss them and be kissed in return as servants or slaves, but must not come within hailing distance as friends or equals. Such then is our true condition; four millions of people living, acting, dying, not as God wills, but as slavery demands and prejudice complies."

Shame on those who "wait for their white friends to do and dare for them," Observer wrote. He predicted all struggles for freedom and equal rights would fail "until we shall grow more uneasy in our chains as slaves, and self-respectful, confident and daring in our demand for our rights as nominal freemen. . . . And I ask if our fate is to be sealed through our own inertion? or whether as a people we are doomed and damned by Slavery's fist?"

He closed by adding that his "colored friends throughout the country know this is no fancy sketch, but every day reality."

★ ★ ★

A WHITE WRITER happened to offer his report on Negro Philadelphia just then. He, too, wrote anonymously and published his account in a leading abolition paper, the *National Anti-Slavery Standard*. He bent over backward to give Negroes their due but used the same words employed by slavery apologists: *depraved, immoral, filthy*.

"The better class of coloured men and women in Philadelphia are as virtuous, as cleanly, as industrious, as intelligent, and in every way as worthy as the corresponding class of whites. In point of sobriety and economy, they are at least equal to their white brethren, and discharge their duties as citizens, fathers, mothers, wives and children, in all respects, like other people of good character and standing. . . .

"But now the other side of the story must be told," he wrote. Among whites, "not more than one-eighth are unmitigatedly vicious and depraved; with the coloured people we fear we must say that not more than one-eighth are otherwise. It will readily suggest itself to every one that there are great excuses for this state of things in the oppressed condition in which the coloured race has so long have lain, and in the fact that great numbers of the worst of our coloured population are runaway slaves. . . .

"The worst and largest collection of them reside in Lombard Street and its vicinity—being like all poor people in cities, crammed into lofts, garrets and cellars, in blind alleys and narrow courts, with no advantage of sewerage, gas or water, and with not a fresh pure breath of air from one week to another. Under these circumstances, they cannot help being horribly immoral and disgustingly filthy."

The same white reporter visited St. Mary's Street, where the Negro-owned dance halls had names such the Astor House and the California House. Within walls darkened by years of smoke from tallow candles, musicians played, bartenders served whiskey in porter bottles and glasses of lemonade, and young Philadelphians danced. Here, the writer tried to maintain a researcher's remove but found himself transfixed.

"The coloured people are naturally strongly addicted to music and dancing. . . . The 'dance houses' of these people are numerous and always well-attended. The 'Astor House' and other similar high-sounding establishments . . . are the earthly paradises upon which are fixed all the waking hopes and midnight dreams of the belles and gallants of the dark hue."

On Saturday nights, he wrote, they "exchange vows and protestations, imbibe soft nonsense and lemonade with a stick in it. . . . They dance as if there never was any more dancing to be gotten on earth."

★　★　★

IN PEACEFUL INTERVALS, hopes stirred that white mobs were creatures of the American past. The touchstone was Pennsylvania Hall—people assured each other that that degree of violence would not come again.

Steps had been taken to expand the police force, and a regiment of soldiers had been assigned to the city. It was said that a black family could expect to be insulted but no longer assailed for celebrating July 4 in Independence Square. The fire companies and gangs, their ranks augmented by famine refugees, seemed content to fight each other—"wounds & bruises the consequences, but no lives lost," the merchant Thomas Cope noted after a street brawl or "broil" between warring fire companies in 1849. People could hope their city and country were, like the boy in the Book of Corinthians, maturing. *When I became a man, I put away childish things.*

This same hopefulness crept into the antislavery debate. Appeals to decency and reason were offered in Washington, Trenton, and Philadelphia.

In 1849, a young congressman drafted a plan for gradual abolition in the District of Columbia. He made concessions to the South—Uncle Sam would compensate owners for each slave freed, Southern officeholders could still bring their own slaves to the city, and fugitives would get no haven: Washington marshals would return "property" to owners. But these concessions did not sway the Southern bloc and angered abolitionists. Boston's Wendell Phillips branded the congressman, Abraham Lincoln, "that slave hound from Illinois." Lincoln withdrew the bill.

Lucretia Mott, turning sixty, still believed in persuasion. The year before she had participated in the first women's rights convention at Seneca Falls, New York. She noticed that some of Philadelphia medical schools' numerous Southern students were dropping by the Anti-Slavery Society office on North Fifth Street, and she had an idea. The students were far from home and young enough to be open-minded. Throw in the novelty of a female speaker—these boys were raised in polite homes and would at least hear her out. So Mott invited the medical students to hear her speak in the Cherry Street Meeting, and on a February evening in 1849, she delivered a widely reprinted address.

"It has been my privilege and pleasure to meet with some of you in the Anti-Slavery rooms . . . though perhaps from mere curiosity, to see what the 'despised abolitionist' was doing," she said, hoping to elicit smiles. "There are many now looking at the subject of Slavery . . . sympathizing with condition of the poor and oppressed in our land. Although many of you may be more immediately connected with this system, yet it is coming to be regarded as not a mere sectional question, but a national and individual one."

Then Mott began to itemize slavery's evils and to suggest ways a student could help hasten its end. As she spoke, some in her audience stood up and walked from the room.

★ ★ ★

NOW THE NEGRO suffrage drive intensified in New Jersey. For two sweltering late-August days in 1849, Zion A.M.E. Church in Trenton hosted meetings. Colored men arrived from towns as small as Swedesboro and as large as Camden and Newark. A dentist, John S. Rock, rode up from Salem County. Catto came from Philadelphia and involved himself in running the meetings and drafting the statement. A Camden teacher, Ishmael Locke, had come to know Catto and joined him in the drafting. This knot of men set out to persuade at least twenty-three of New Jersey's forty-four white legislators to place before the voters a change in the state's constitution.

Catto was becoming a familiar face at A.M.E. pulpits in Trenton and Camden as well as Philadelphia, sometimes bringing his family. Part of this was necessity. The growing church needed preachers willing to "ride the circuit." And pastoral New Jersey towns offered children a respite from depravity and disease. Smallpox, yellow fever, and tuberculosis rolled through the cities in terrible tides, taking the young and the weak. Cholera killed a thousand Philadelphians in 1849; dysentery, the summer scourge, took five hundred.

His travels kept Catto in the realm of the Remonds, Douglasses, and Garnets. He preached once in Camden with Rev. Henry Highland Garnet. When the A.M.E. needed a temporary or "supply" minister in Bordentown, New Jersey, or Buffalo, New York, he raised his hand. At the church's annual conference, Catto along with Stephen Smith and Dr. Bias persuaded a majority to condemn colonization as a slaveholders' ploy. The A.M.E. was still years away from calling for an end to slavery itself.

And when the New Jersey suffrage meetings convened, Catto could bring with him to Trenton the lessons learned in the ill-fated Pennsylvania drive.

Petitions would be printed, circulated, and delivered to the legislature. Signatures of whites and blacks were to be kept separate. Arguments would blend allusions to New Jersey's glorious traditions with a hardheaded logic about manhood, or citizenship: If a Negro was man enough to be on state tax rolls, then surely he was man enough to vote.

Amid paeans to "the wisdom, justice, and truthfulness of your honorable body," the proposal for amending the state constitution had a sweet simplicity: "to leave out the word 'white' in Article 2nd, Right of Suffrage."

The petitioners noted that they were taxpayers who had "never by insurrection, mobs or tumults" endangered public safety. They asked, If a foreigner can vote after five years in America, why can native-born Negroes not win this right in a lifetime?

By autumn 1849, petitions filled with signatures arrived from at least six counties. Newspapers told of a legislature closely divided. The vote would come early in the new year. Catto and Locke and the other men headed home and waited for word.

★   ★   ★

AS THEY WAITED, a familiar image reared its head in Philadelphia streets. A series of anonymous lithographs depicted bug-eyed black men planting thick lips on willing mouths of white women. Black hands reached for white bosoms and waists. Pennsylvania Hall was an amalgamators' brothel, with mixed-race couples strolling arm-in-arm as mulatto urchins scampered about. The picture was titled, *Abolition Hall, The Evening Before the Conflagration . . . drawn by Zip Coon.* He was a character in minstrel shows.

Black man, white woman. Black abolitionists wearied of such talk. Why were whites who decried "amalgamation" silent about slaveholders who impregnated slaves and even sold off their own mulatto progeny? "I charge it back upon them, that *they* are the amalgamators, and not we," the New York editor Samuel Cornish wrote in his newspaper, the *Colored American.* Rattling off names of prominent whites who had fathered mulattoes, Cornish wrote: "I now call to the stand, Thos. Jefferson."

But the image persisted.

On the evening of October 10, 1849, a rumor circulated that the colored proprietor of the California House tavern in St. Mary's Street had just taken a white wife. By 9:00 P.M. this street of colored homes and dance halls was filling up with white men.

A newspaper described the night scene: "It appears that a gang of men and boys amounting, it is said, to several hundreds, and mostly armed, hovered about St. Mary's street, which is chiefly inhabited by colored people. At the same time, there were several knots of colored men hanging about, and two or three collisions occurred. . . ."

"Before 10 an attack was made upon a tavern . . . called the California House. This place was kept by a colored man, who was reported to be married, or at any rate, living with a white woman." Up the street came a wagon with a flaming barrel of tar.

Blacks hurled stones at the wagon, but the white crowd overwhelmed them and swarmed into the tavern, smashing chairs, tearing out gas fixtures, and setting fires. As flames spread, patrons and bartenders were "driven out and fired upon, with many other colored persons, who were seen flying from their houses in extreme terror, chased by gangs, who pelted them with brickbats, and fired after them with guns."

For the first time anyone could remember, black men took out weapons and fired back. Whites returned the fire in volley after volley.

Six squares north, the State House's fire bell rang through the night. Firemen rushed to the tavern and began putting hoses to hydrants. They turned to find their hoses cut, and pistols aimed at the firemen. Police, too, were driven back with guns and knives.

Militiamen arrived in the night to find the tavern gutted and the street calm. So the soldiers marched away—and within hours, shooting began anew. This cat-and-mouse game played out twice. At Sixth and Lombard, where Bethel Church and the Bird school stood, a newspaper said a colored boy running an errand was shot three times in the leg.

All told, the riot left three white men (including two firemen) and one Negro dead. Nine whites and sixteen Negroes went to hospitals with wounds, and many more were hurt. The identity of the instigators was quickly known. Thomas Cope wrote it his diary even as "the alarm bell is still ringing." Impressed that the gang seemed to anticipate the militia's every move, Cope wrote, "The Killers, no doubt, have spies."

They were mostly Irish and from the city's most feared gang. A fireman later testified that he heard the name shouted that night, as "the mob sang out, 'Go it, Killers.'"

CHAPTER 6

The Irish, the Killers, and
Squire McMullen

THE KILLERS' TALE starts with America's Irish Catholics. In Philadelphia, that story turns on an event in 1844 that Protestants came to know as the Bible fight. Catholics, on the other hand, would refer to it for decades to come as the nativist American riots.

From the most pompous Whigs to its poorest Negroes, contempt for Irish Catholics was as much a part of Philadelphia as streets of cobblestone. It had been far worse in Ireland, where, since the late 1600s, Catholics had been an oppressed race, and *race* was the correct word. They were considered *that* different from Protestants. Catholics could not educate their children, manufacture books, carry weapons, or live in a city. They could not buy or inherit land from Protestants. No priest could enter Ireland. Catholic orphans were raised Protestant. Catholics' taxes supported the Protestant Church.

The Irish-born Protestant Edmund Burke, a member of Parliament, described the laws against Irish Catholics as "well fitted for the oppression, impoverishment and degradation of a people." The laws, he said, made them feel less human.

That sentiment accompanied Irish immigrants to the colonies. The British philosopher George Berkeley wrote in 1736 after visiting Rhode Island and seeing slavery on its plantations: "The Negroes have a saying, 'If Negro was not a Negro, Irishman would be Negro.'" Berkeley thought that Indians in America were dressed and housed better than the Catholic cottage dwellers in Ireland.

In 1797, the year John Adams came to Philadelphia to be sworn in as president, Benjamin Morgan lost a close race for state senate. Many of his wealthier supporters had fled the city because of a yellow fever epidemic. Morgan blamed his defeat on the "deluded masses . . . of Irishtown." Irishtown? Another name for Southwark.

From 1790 to 1840, 70 percent of arriving immigrants were Irish—and after 1820, 80 percent of them were Catholic.

In the 1790s, the Congress declared that only "white" persons could become citizens, but it was not clear who was white and who was not. And that indecision about race was not limited to skin color. At that time, the Irish were sometimes referred to as "niggers turned inside out," and Negroes were sometimes called the "smoked Irish."

In fact, years later in Philadelphia, a white comedian in blackface portraying a slave told this joke at burlesque houses: "My master is a great tyrant. He treats me badly, as if I was a common Irishman."

★ ★ ★

SO THE IRISH went from a people stepped on by a caste system to a new land where in one generation they became the people with the big feet. This is not to say that Irish Catholics were not mistreated by the rest of white America in the 1800s. There really were signs in front of businesses that said "Irish need not apply," and they were scorned, laughed at, and taken advantage of by nearly everyone. But their *whiteness* distinguished them from blacks and gave them a new way of looking at themselves. Exactly how that inner illumination to *become* white occurred is unclear, for it was surely something new for them. And it must have been hard—thinking less about their homeland, their religion, and any animosities they felt, and less, too, about "any natural sympathies they may have felt for their fellow creatures, to a new solidarity based on color."

Their whiteness had done no good for them in Ireland, but they had to hope that things would be better in the white United States. Here, they saw that white equaled freedom and black meant slavery—or, at a minimum, much less than white. Here, being white meant being a citizen, being part of something good. Here, white would pay off.

While the Irish immigrants were transforming, so was the laboring world around them. The apprentice and indenture system, so common in the 1700s, was giving way to wage labor. Loyalty, training, and education were all parts of the master-apprentice relationship, but a wage laborer could expect only wages from his employer. For many Irishmen living in the south-of-Philadelphia districts of Southwark and Moyamensing, that employer was the Navy Yard, opened in 1801 on the Delaware River at Federal Street. Their work was often called "donkey labor," and it was common to hear Gaelic on those docks as Irishmen loaded cargo from wagons onto ships and from ships onto wagons. But with a growing number of escaped slaves and free black men coming north to compete for jobs, Irish Catholics feared for their livelihoods.

By 1811, Negroes lived among the Irish south of the city line on South Street. Negroes were sharing the same narrow, shabby three-story rental housing but not sharing a community. Racial ghettos did not exist then, and the poor areas of cities were racially diverse. Looking back two hundred years, it is easy to say there could have been an alliance between the Irish, persecuted for their religion, and the Negroes, persecuted for their color. But one persecuted the other instead. Negroes in Philadelphia County endured waves of violence from Irishmen in the 1830s and 1840s, from the Flying Horses riot in 1834 to the California House fifteen years later. The attacks often occurred in the outlying districts of Moyamensing and Southwark, where the groups intermingled most.

Life in the city's poorest areas must have been like this, the historian Noel Ignatiev notes: The Irish and Negro families lived next door to one another in alley blocks near Seventh Street. The women hung laundry out together, gossiped and took care of each other's children in emergencies. The Irish husband worked on the docks, while the Negro husband sharpened knives and scissors on the streets with a sandstone wheel. Each of their teenage daughters brought in needed extra money by cleaning houses for a local saloonkeeper. They both have 17-year-old sons, and the boys don't go to church. Their small children play with paper boats in garbage-filled gutters. Each mother has lived through the worst, watching a small child die of croup in the drafty, ill-heated rooms. In the Flying Horses riot, the Irish woman puts a burning candle in her window so that her home would be spared by the looters. The Negro family's house was trashed. What do they say to one another now?

Negroes trying to take jobs away was only one worry for the Irish. They also had to contend with the nativists—an anti-immigrant, American-born mix of English-blooded Protestants and men who identified themselves as Whigs or Republicans. Some saw Irish Catholics as inferior;

others insisted the Pope's followers should have their numbers and freedoms controlled. Then came temperance advocates, who railed at Irish drinking. And native-born workingmen, who blamed the low wages paid to the Irish for hurting the labor market amid the wage cuts and depression of the late 1830s. These groups had one thing in common: They zealously spoke out against the Irish.

This anti-immigrant, anti-Catholic zeal took on the trappings of a political movement throughout the North as nativists campaigned for local and state office. They proposed to erode immigrants' rights, denying men the vote until they had lived in the United States for twenty-one years, and barring them from public office.

But Irish Catholics in Philadelphia and New York and Boston did have an ally.

While Quakers, few in number, looked out for the Negroes, the Irish workers had in their corner the large and growing Democratic Party. Founded in the 1830s, the party stretched one arm to Southern slaveholders and the other to Northern workers, a surprisingly good fit in the same coat of white supremacy. Martin Van Buren, an architect of the newly formed party, said it combined "the plain Republicans of the North" with "the planters of the South." The bread and butter of those "plain Republicans" were Irish immigrants. And the Democratic Party in Philadelphia won their support by defending them against the accusations and fearmongering of the nativists and Whigs.

The Democratic Party knew Irish immigrants' hearts well—knew them better, in the end, than the old friend trying to win them from across the sea, the Liberator.

Ireland, since the twelfth century, had been stridently against slavery, having liberated its British slaves in 1177. As early as the 1820s, Daniel O'Connell publicly repudiated the enslavement of Negroes anywhere. West Indian slave traders offered to underwrite his campaign to create an Irish parliament. All he had to do was focus his liberation speeches on the Irish, not the Negro.

In response, he said, "Gentlemen, God knows I speak for the saddest people the sun sees; but may my right hand forget its cunning and my tongue cleave to the roof of my mouth if to save Ireland, even Ireland, I forget about the Negro one single hour."

Over the next two decades, it would take all his courage and cunning to keep that vow.

O'Connell was a political and organizing genius. He launched the "Catholic Association," fueling it with dues collected weekly in churches, shaping it into the world's first mass political party. He led a Catholic emancipation campaign at a time when Catholics could not hold public office.

By the 1840s, O'Connell saw Irish Americans, by and large, standing solidly against abolitionists and free blacks. Racial tensions in cities such as Philadelphia rose as fugitive slaves and Irish immigrants arrived at the same time. Both groups were poor, uneducated, ill-suited to living in cities, and confronted with a heavy load of hatred and contempt.

O'Connell, who had ardently supported Britain's freeing of its West Indies slaves in 1833, was at the peak of his power as an orator and organizer of a free Ireland movement, a movement financed by thousands of supporters in the United States. Back home, a change in British law let Catholics sit in Parliament and O'Connell was the first, elected to the House of Commons. But what he really wanted was an Irish parliament.

This red-headed lawyer from County Kerry now sought to influence the hearts and minds of the Irish across the ocean. He needed these new Americans' donations to the cause, but he also called on them to support Negro freedom in the United States. It was a balancing act: Raise money for freedom in Ireland and appeal to Irish Americans to act more like their antislavery ancestors and less like white Americans. O'Connell jumped on that tightrope and spent the rest of his life keeping his balance.

Thus did O'Connell, at the 1840 World Anti-Slavery Convention in London, sign the famous "Address from the People of Ireland to their Countrymen and Countrywomen in America," written by Irish and American abolitionists and carried to the United States by Charles Remond in 1841. O'Connell, then campaigning to be lord mayor of Dublin, had no part in writing the address, but his signature carried weight.

The address appealed to the birthright, the Irishness of Irish Americans: "Treat the colored people as your equals, as brethren. By all your memories of Ireland, continue to love liberty—hate slavery—CLING BY THE ABOLITIONISTS—and in America, you will do honor to the name of Ireland."

But Irish immigrants were fast becoming Americans and they spit out the address like bad meat. The broadside that Remond unfurled in hall after hall—it stretched from dais to doorway—caught their eye but did not change their minds.

The nation's most influential Irish leader, Bishop John J. Hughes of New York, questioned the address's authenticity and said it was "the duty of every naturalized Irishman to resist and repudiate the address with indignation." He continued, "I am no friend to slavery, but I am less friendly to any attempt of foreign origin to abolish it." Irish miners in Pottsville, Pennsylvania, too, denounced the call to consider Negroes their brothers. America's leading Catholic newspaper, the *Boston Pilot*, labeled abolition "a British plot to weaken the United States." The paper questioned how O'Connell could "reconcile his advocacy of moral force with support for the abolitionists, whose doctrines 'would bathe the South in blood.'"

On the scale of injustices as measured by slavery on one hand and foreign involvement in internal American disputes on the other, the miners, the Church, and the Catholic press agreed: Poking your nose in someone else's business was the weightier problem.

William Lloyd Garrison despaired. "Not a single Irishman has come forward, either publicly or privately, to express his approval of the Address, or to avow his determination to abide by its sentiments." He sent sad reports to friends in Ireland, saying the anti-abolitionists were succeeding in drowning out the address. "I fear they will keep the great mass of your countrymen here from uniting with us." He asked for help. Abolitionists in Ireland vouched for the authenticity of the address and gathered ten thousand more signatures.

But it was too late. Irish immigrants were Americans and Democrats now. And they were whiter than ever. "Abolitionist" was an epithet to hurl at those who didn't know the facts. All the arguments by O'Connell were foolish "niggerology."

In 1842, a month after Garrison's lament about Irish American sentiments, a largely Irish mob in Philadelphia attacked a Negro temperance parade and burned a Negro church. O'Connell—his donations from America dwindling after he likened Ireland's workingmen to Negro slaves— nevertheless spoke out: "Philadelphia has disgraced itself. . . . [W]here were the Catholic priests? Why did they not raise their voice against the iniquitous proceeding?"

★ ★ ★

THREE WEEKS after the August temperance parade riot, a Philadelphia Irishman wrote home to Ireland: "We have had a serious time lately with the colored people and the whites, the *catholicks* being the worst of the two. . . . Nearly every man who was guilty of cruelty and violence to the colored man was an Irishman."

He went on to say that most of the Irish, immigrant or not, could not find work and were convinced that Negroes "have no right to stay in the city, and that if they can drive them out . . . they will have their places and enough work to do."

During the riot, an Irish woman on Gaskill Street, a sliver of a thoroughfare thirty feet from South Street, told the crowd: "There's a house that I want to have mobbed. There's some Negroes living in there, living just like white folks."

By now, Philadelphia was more than a busy seaport—it was home to textile mills and iron works, makers of steamships and steam locomotives. The city and county population was hurrying past 250,000, swelled by Germans, Irish, runaway slaves, and rural Pennsylvanians looking for work. The growth made jobs and housing scarce and poverty more common. The area closest to South Street and west of Sixth was the saddest part of Philadelphia, where the poorest people—Negroes and Irish—lived.

The friction was apparent to visitors. An Englishman, John Finch, wrote: "Competition among white working men here is even now reducing . . . wages daily; but if the blacks were to be emancipated, probably hundreds of thousands of them would migrate into these Northern states, and the competition for employment would consequently be much increased that wages would speedily be . . . lower." Finch called for them to "remain slaves as they are. Hence we see why the abolitionists . . . are more unpopular in America than Socialists are among the priests . . . in England."

One occupation that did not suffer from unemployment or racism was the tavern owner in Moyamensing. In 1842, the district boasted 450 liquor dealers, most of them Irish. The Moyamensing Temperance Society had a lot of work to do, but it apparently made a dent in liquor profits—arsonists tried twice to burn the Temperance Hall. Following the parade riot, civil authorities declared the hall a nuisance. Their reasoning: If it burned, the flames would threaten nearby houses. A grand jury agreed, and the building—a new brick one—was torn down instead.

O'Connell kept tugging at the moral fiber of Irishmen in America. He wrote to the Pennsylvania Anti-Slavery Society in 1843, "Over the broad Atlantic, I pour forth my voice, saying, Come out of such a land, you Irishmen; or, if you remain, and dare countenance this system of slavery . . . we will recognize you as Irishmen no longer."

He knew that his words might forever close his donors' pocketbooks, though he did receive money from one non-Irishman—Robert Purvis. "If they make it the condition of our sympathy, or if there be implied a submission to the doctrine of slavery on our part in receiving their remittance, let them cease sending it at once."

And that's what happened in the South as Irish freedom organizations disbanded. In the North, his abolitionist rhetoric was ignored. But O'Connell continued to speak: "America, the black spot of slavery rests upon your star-spangled banner."

Years later, Frederick Douglass pondered "the terrible outrages committed from time to time by Irishmen upon Negroes." He said the mobs in cities such as Detroit, Chicago, Cincinnati, and New York proved to him that "the Irish people are among our bitterest persecutors. In one sense it is strange . . . that they should be such, but in another sense it is quiet easily accounted for. It is said that a Negro always makes the most cruel Negro driver, a northern slaveholder the most rigorous master, and the poor man suddenly made rich becomes the most haughty insufferable of all purse-proud fools. . . .

"But there is something quite revolting in the idea . . . that the persecuted can so suddenly become the persecutors."

The Irishman Douglass admired most was gone by then. An ailing, trembling Daniel O'Connell had used his final speech in Parliament to seek aid for his countrymen "starving in shoals, in hundreds—aye, in thousands and millions." O'Connell's doctors sent him to Europe in hopes of a cure, but he died there. A steamship bearing his coffin home passed a vessel of refugees from the famine, leaving Ireland for America.

Upon learning the funeral ship was O'Connell's, the emigrants raised their voices in the Gaelic *caoin* of loss, a high and mournful keen.

★ ★ ★

MORE THAN A MILLION Irish died—many from starvation—and more than a million fled the manacling public policy, poverty, and starvation of the famine. From 1845 to 1855, nearly a quarter of Ireland's people emigrated, most of them Catholic. The catastrophic failure of the nation's staple, the potato crop, did not affect other food sources; the fungus *Phytophthora infestans* spared other crops. Yet people still starved. In "Black

'47," as the Irish called it, Queen Victoria's military loaded Ireland produce onto ships bound for the rest of the British Empire. These exports included 9,992 calves.

In April 1847, Hannah Curtis wrote to her brother, John, in Philadelphia: "People are in a starving state. The poorhouse is crowded with people and they are dying . . . from 10 to 20 a day." She asked him to send money so that her family could leave Ireland. They arrived in Philadelphia in 1848, the same year as the Catto family.

The famine pushed the Irish out of Ireland, but hundreds of thousands had already left for America's big Northern cities. About twenty thousand immigrants arrived in the United States annually in the 1830s, twice the previous decade's rate. They settled in large numbers in New York, Boston, and Philadelphia. In 1842 alone, nearly fifty thousand came.

Philadelphia by 1844 was about 10 percent Irish, and in the districts of Southwark, Kensington, and Moyamensing, the figure was higher. Employment was sporadic for these rural people who had crossed an ocean to become city people. Moyamensing's street corners were crowded with men, young and old, out of work. Those who found unskilled labor earned 63 to 80 cents a day. Women worked in match factories for $2.50 to $3.00 a week. (A dollar then would be about $25 today.) Irish girls earned $1.00 to $1.50 a week plus board as household servants, taking some of these jobs from Negroes. Nearly all the twenty-five thousand immigrant Irish living in and around Philadelphia bore the stain of poverty.

In the winter, the streets of Moyamensing were filled with horse-drawn sleighs. Cholera, yellow fever, and the other epidemics that struck the city with regularity struck the poor in Moyamensing the hardest.

It was no comfort to the ill and dying that Philadelphia was the nation's capital of medical education. About a thousand students attended medical schools in the 1840s. Newspapers and magazines rippled with "Cures" sold by local patent medicine makers. "Panacea" claimed to cure everything, including cancer. "Expectorant" promised to "arrest with certainty the various pulmonary affections under which thousands sink into the grave."

While the "cures" did not help, touring Protestant revivalists promised Philadelphians that religion would help them. Beginning in the late 1830s, evangelists found willing listeners among rich and poor, literate and illiterate. This movement embracing that old-time religion affected even the volunteer fire companies, some of whom organized their own lecture series on the values of fundamentalism.

This was also a time when city services barely addressed the public's needs—just water, sewage, the occasional quarantine, and a bit of justice. Constables served summonses, part-time night watchmen lit the lamps, and neither labored long to prevent crime or capture criminals. A real city police force was a decade away. The lack of one made it easier for mobs to burn Pennsylvania Hall, assail a temperance parade, and destroy California House. The militia served a state unwilling to pay for guns or uniforms. Criminals were most often caught by citizens who brought them to the man on the courts' lowest rung—the local alderman, who had the authority to put people in jail.

White men's attacks on Negroes were common enough to be talked about in a sporting fashion—"Hunting the Nig." The economic depression that stretched into the 1840s inflated the ranks of the poor. Hopelessness and fear grew, along with violence on the streets within racial lines and across them. The worst of that violence, in 1844, became a sort of coming-out party for a tough, charismatic young Irishman from Moyamensing.

★ ★ ★

TO UNDERSTAND WHAT HAPPENED in 1844, it is necessary to understand the mistrust and clenched fists that marked the uneasy relationship between Protestants and Catholics.

The Pennsylvania legislature created public schools in 1834. They were to be coordinated by local school districts, organized by ward, and overseen by boards of controllers. The legislation said nothing about race, but Negro children could not enroll. The Catholic bishop Francis Kenrick of Philadelphia complained immediately—not about the exclusion of Negroes but the exclusion of the Roman Catholic Douay Bible.

The King James Bible was read daily. A teacher would read aloud—typically, ten verses—without explanatory comment. For Bishop Kenrick and Catholics, whose theology depended on explaining the scriptures, such reading was a slap in the face.

The bishop tried to persuade school controllers to include the Douay Bible for Catholic students and to remove the antipapal pamphlets that were turning up in schools. And he asked his parishioners to mind what happened in the classroom. The controllers ignored his Bible request but did order antipapal writings removed—a directive that was ignored. Protestants and Catholics agreed wholeheartedly that God should be in the schools but disagreed on how his story should be told.

In 1838, the year Protestants and Irish joined together to burn Pennsylvania Hall, the legislature stuck its thumb in the eye of Catholics by decreeing the Bible—the King James Version—a textbook. Schools across the state were already using this version. But now it was clear that the Protestants were going use whatever book they wanted.

This same schism opened up in the schools of New York City, with its larger share of Catholics. In 1841, church leaders there fought back. Bishop Hughes demanded school controllers give the diocese all taxes levied on Catholic residents, funds that would be used to open parochial schools. The city refused, so the bishop dipped his chalice deeper into political waters by fielding candidates for City Council. His give-back-the-tax slate lost but garnered enough votes to snatch victory from the Tammany Democrats. He also won national headlines and the enmity of nativists for influencing an election.

A Philadelphia school fired a Catholic teacher in Southwark in 1842 for refusing to start the day by reading the King James Bible. Protestant nativist fervor was peaking, with ministers across the nation imploring congregants to put the sacred back in Sunday by suspending train travel and mail delivery. City clergy launched a drive to halt Sunday liquor sales, not a popular notion among Irish tavern owners or their customers.

Catholics in Philadelphia found themselves hemmed in by Protestant-crafted restrictions. Priests could not administer last rites in public hospitals. Catholic sailors were made to attend Protestant services. As for five thousand Catholic students in public schools being exposed to the King James Bible, Bishop Kenrick kept agitating. But each time he wrote a letter or made a statement, Protestants saw it as a papal attack on their Bible.

Finally, schools agreed to let Catholic students skip Bible reading if their "parents are conscientiously opposed." Pupils could leave the room before morning hymns were sung.

But Protestants saw the decision as the start of a "Vatican plot" to take religion out of schools. An editorial said Protestants had run the schools properly for years "and now come the 'Bishop of New York' and the 'Bishop of Philadelphia' to interfere, . . . creating confusion within their walls and excitement without."

Old hates rooted in Ireland were rubbed raw by the Bible clash. American Republicans—a nativist party—announced on April 27, 1844, that they would open an office in the Third Ward of Kensington, the belly of Irish life along the Delaware River northeast of the city. The residents, many of them weavers who worked on hand looms in their homes, threatened to destroy the building if it opened.

The opening was delayed, but something else gnawed at the Protestants. In February, a teacher had complained to Alderman Hugh Clark, a Catholic and a school director in Kensington, that the exodus of Catholic students before morning devotionals was disruptive. At Clark's suggestion, the teacher suspended the daily religious exercises until a quieter plan could be determined.

Word of this became a game of whisper down the lane—Clark had ordered an end to Bible reading in the classroom. Protestants were angry about the Catholic bullies who had stopped their nativist office opening. That event was rescheduled for May 3, and nativists from across the city were invited this time.

The American Republicans built a platform against the schoolyard fence at Second and Master streets, about a block across cobblestone streets from the Nanny Goat Market, a wooden, open-sided shed with stalls for merchants. Neighborhood women, who lived in brick or wooden frame houses or courtyard shanties, shopped here every day. The streets were narrow, dark sleeves that buttoned up each night. Many single Irish men lived here.

Just a few hundred nativists came, outnumbered by an Irish crowd not there to applaud a speech on the need for stringent immigrant residency rules. The audience tore down the speaker's platform. The speakers fled. As riots go, this Friday incident was barely a melee. Embarrassed and incensed, American Republicans blanketed the city with notices of still another rally in the same spot in three days.

This time, three thousand nativists came to Kensington on a Monday. Catholics came as well, including William McMullen, who likely walked more than three miles with his friends from the Moyamensing Hose Company, a volunteer fire corps of Irish Catholics. McMullen was the kind of young man who walked to—not away from—a fight.

The May 6 afternoon started much like the previous rally, with nativist speakers harangued by Irishmen in the audience. About three o'clock, John O'Neill, an Irish hauler of goods, drove his horse and wagon through the crowd. Within ten feet of the platform he "dumped a load of dirt or manure"—which one was unclear, but the insult was not. Soon it began to rain and everyone sought shelter in the Nanny Goat Market.

Nativists entering the market—the Irish market—was the tinderbox. "Keep the damn natives out of the market house," an Irishman hollered. Shouts became shoves and shoves became fights. Bricks, clubs, and pistols were now in the hands of men.

An Irishman trying to calm people was shot in the face. Outnumbered, the Irish fled the market and were chased down Master Street by nativists throwing bricks and paving stones. But the Irish were fighting on their own ground, and soon musket fire from windows peppered the nativists, who had little shelter in the market. Many shots came from the Hibernia Hose House, a volunteer fire company across from the market. The first Protestant shot and killed was George Shiffler, an apprentice leather worker who was eighteen years old. Catholics came out of homes on Cadwalader Street to battle the intruders. Another Protestant was shot and killed in the market, and two more wounded. People said one of the men who shot young Shiffler was William McMullen.

Protestants gathered reinforcements in nearby Northern Liberties and began marching down Cadwalader Street with muskets, pistols, sticks, and bricks, breaking doors and windows. Any home where a gun had been seen was fired upon. It was four thirty.

The riot had raged for an hour when the county sheriff and deputies arrived. The sheriff was an Irish Protestant, Morton McMichael, who as a volunteer fire chief had helped save the colored orphanage from a mob in the aftermath of the 1838 Pennsylvania Hall fire. The violence stopped. Children lit bonfires as night fell.

The sheriff asked his friend, General George Cadwalader, commander of the city division of the state militia, to "muster his volunteers" in Kensington that evening to maintain order. But Pennsylvania law had no riot statutes and was vague about whether local authorities could summon the militia. Victims could sue if troops hurt anyone. One street that the general was asked to protect, Cadwalader Street, was named for his grandfather, a brigadier general in the Revolutionary War, and his grandfather's brother, a physician. Nevertheless, the general said no to the sheriff.

At ten that evening, the nativists returned in force and began breaking into homes across from the market. Bonfires illuminated figures in the night destroying furniture and shattering windows. By then some residents had retreated to the woods.

The Irish and their homes had been targets. Now, nativists surrounded a seminary. The Sisters of Charity were away on a mission in Iowa, and only Mrs. Baker, a caretaker, was inside. When she came out pleading to leave the seminary alone, people stoned her and set the building ablaze. A limb of the Roman Catholic Church was under attack.

Irishmen who had been protecting nearby St. Michael's Catholic Church came running and "fired a volley of buckshot into the crowd." Shot dead was John Wright, the son of a city salt merchant and believed to be an innocent bystander. Another man, Nathan Ramsey, from Northern Liberties, died later in May from a chest wound inflicted that night. The mob dispersed, and the violence of May 6 was over. The body count: three Protestants and one bystander killed, and three Protestants wounded. No Irish deaths were recorded, but there were injuries, most from "faulty weapons exploding in the users' own hands."

That was Monday. By nightfall, the American Republicans were offering a one-thousand-dollar reward for Shiffler's killers and announced with signs across the city a meeting in the yard behind the State House— Independence Hall—on Tuesday afternoon. A clergyman added these words to the signs: "Let Every Man Come Prepared to Defend Himself."

The Native American newspaper wrote that Tuesday morning: "The bloody hand of the Pope has stretched forth to our destruction. Now we call on our fellow citizens, who regard free institutions, whether they be native, or adopted, to arm."

Several thousand came to the State House yard for the rally. Angry speeches prompted shouts of, "Let's go up to Kensington!" The cry became a chant. The crowd ignored one speaker's call for peaceful action and several hundred men and boys began marching north. Some had guns. One marcher carried a ripped, dirty American flag with a sign that said: "This is the FLAG that was trampled UNDERFOOT by the IRISH PAPISTS."

Kensington was expecting trouble. More people fled north to the woods, taking their belongings. Muskets were delivered that morning, and residents were ready to use them. When the nativist army reached Kensington, it ignored the Nanny Goat Market and went to the Hibernia Hose House. The nativists opened a side door and dragged out the hose carriage. But the Irish upstairs opened fire. Muzzles flashed in windows and doorways on the alleys in a ferocious crossfire, thudding like hailstones and killing four nativist men: a Southwark marble mason, a Kensington ship carpenter, a Southwark rope maker, and an apprentice shoemaker who died near where Shiffler had fallen. Eleven nativists were wounded, including a dentist whose arm had to be amputated.

Nativists fought back by lighting fires. Wood-frame structures on Cadwalader burned quickly, the flames spreading to alley houses and then to the Hibernia Hose. A burnt body was found in the ruins of one house. Joseph Rice, an Irishman standing in his yard watching the fighting, was shot to death. His killer was seventeen.

The militia's arrival brought fighting to a halt. Whatever legal dilemmas General Cadwalader had were dilemmas no more. He posted men at St. Michael's, whose pastor had called for Douay Bibles in schools. The pastor gave soldiers the church keys and left. In the morning, firemen wetted down smoldering embers. Arson aimed at homes of whites was new to Philadelphia, and visitors came to stare. By mid-morning, nativists began arriving, searching empty Irish houses for weapons. New fires began in some of those homes, drawing away the militiamen guarding the church. More fires were set at the church, and then at the seminary and then at school director Hugh Clark's house.

Not much was left standing near the Nanny Goat, so the men with torches headed south toward another Catholic church, St. Augustine's at Fourth and Vine. They spared a German Catholic church on the way. St. Augustine's was inside the city, and Mayor John M. Scott was not going to let the violence of Kensington into Philadelphia. He asked residents to patrol the streets. He climbed St. Augustine's steps that night and implored several thousand nativists to go home. Instead, someone hit Scott in the chest with a rock.

Minutes later, orange fire and black smoke colored the church vestibule. The crowd stopped firemen from battling the fire and cheered when the steeple fell. In the hubbub over the mayor's injury, a fourteen-year-old was said to have slipped in and kindled the blaze.

So the three-day battle in Kensington ended in Philadelphia. The city found money to pay for troops to guard every Catholic church. Protestant and Catholic leaders met at the State House and called for peace, and for authorities to use "whatever force is necessary" to save lives and property. General Robert Patterson, head of the state militia, imposed martial law and cancelled public meetings. The bishop cancelled Sunday mass. At least ten had been killed and twenty hurt. The riots of 1844 had stopped, but they had not ended.

★ ★ ★

SOMEONE HAD TO BE BLAMED for the riots, for the city's shame. The *Pennsylvania Freeman*, the abolitionist weekly, blamed the city itself, and compared the fires in Kensington to the burning of Pennsylvania Hall: "Philadelphia is ruled by the mob, and it is farcical to pretend that civil law protects . . . the property or persons of our citizens."

Catholics anointed themselves the victim, pointing to their neighborhood in ashes and two churches and a seminary destroyed. They doused the American Republicans in names and epithets, drenching them as "church burners."

In June, a sixteen-man grand jury—including two American Republicans and the father of a wounded nativist—blamed the Catholics. The jurors said trying to banish bibles from schools had caused the riots, as had the disruption of American Republican meetings "by bands of irresponsible men, some of whom resided in this country only a short period."

People blamed the sheriff and the militia for not doing enough. Legislators authorized the militia to fire on riotous mobs after "sufficient warning." Authorities examined but fell short of proving William McMullen's suspected role in the killing of Shiffler.

By July, nativists had the upper hand in the debate over blame, and their political sway was increasing. At the same time, the governor quietly approved a Catholic's request to form a private militia to guard St. Philip de Neri, Southwark's first Catholic church. He allowed the volunteers to arm themselves with twenty muskets from the Frankford Armory.

Almost five thousand marched in the city's July 4 parade and as many as a hundred thousand watched. The grand assemblage began in Southwark, with farmers and butchers marching first to honor the city's breadwinners. Seven model ships, including a seaworthy twenty-eight-foot craft, saluted seafarers and shipbuilders. Black carriages bore the saddened families of Kensington riot victims. The nativist American Republicans sent marchers from every ward.

Sheriff McMichael had worked to keep the day calm. He seized a suspect shipment of muskets in Kensington and made sure soldiers were in Southwark to keep the Irish Democrats of the Weccacoe Hose Company from attacking the nativist Weccacoe Engine. The Weccacoes had tangled before. The militia was put on alert.

The Irish were on alert as well. A nativist raid on St. Philip's was rumored. A hundred volunteers drilled with broomsticks in the aisles of the church; the guns from the armory were broken or had parts missing.

On July 5, the repaired firearms arrived in a wagon. People saw the muskets arriving. The word spread. The Irish were arming the church for . . . *something.*

Nativists gathered outside on Queen Street, named in the 1700s by Swedish settlers to honor their queen. The sheriff and two aldermen searched the church, found the muskets, displayed them, assured the crowd that the guns were not loaded, and told everyone to go home. That night, a second search uncovered more guns—hidden guns.

The next day, Saturday, word of the church's secret cache caused crowds to form anew, defying Cadwalader's orders. As had happened in Kensington, fearful residents fled their homes. Others put American flags in windows to signal solidarity with the mob. That evening, the sheriff and militia arrived with three cannons to protect the church.

Cadwalader had his men begin clearing the streets. People stoned the soldiers. The general had had enough. He gave orders to fire. The crowd mocked him. A former Whig congressman, Charles Naylor, jumped in front of the guns, shouting, "My God, don't shoot!" He was arrested and put under guard in St. Philip's. The crowd finally dispersed.

On Sunday, three militia companies remained, but nativists rolled their own cannon up from the waterfront and demanded freedom for Naylor, popular with the masses despite being a Whig. The crowd grew larger and uglier. The senior militia officer on hand, an Irishman, let Naylor go. Naylor urged the crowd to go home, but many stayed.

Young men loaded the cannon with scrap iron and bolts, wheeled it to the church's rear, fired, and missed. They rolled the cannon back to the docks, reloaded it with bolts and nuts, returned and fired again, still doing little damage. But everyone heard the blast and no one wanted another Kensington. So the American Republicans made a pact with the Hibernia Greens, the Irish militia guarding St. Philip's. The nativists would guarantee the safety of church and militiamen if the Greens left the church.

Stones pelted the Greens as they marched away two-by-two. The Protestant mob, ignoring entreaties of nativist leaders, punched a hole in a wall with a battering ram and poured into the church. But no Greens were seriously hurt and the church still stood.

Which is exactly when the militia and the sheriff's deputies arrived, perhaps two hundred in all, marching down Second Street and onto Queen. Cadwalader ordered the American Republicans to cede the church to him. As before, he had his men clear the streets, the crowd replied with stones, and the general gave orders to shoot. But this time the soldiers did shoot, killing two men from Southwark and wounding four. For the first time, authorities had fired on a gathering of citizens to uphold order in Philadelphia.

Nativists commandeered two more cannons from a ship that night and rolled them to Queen Street, muffling the wheels to fool the soldiers. The cannons' first blast killed two and wounded three. Militia artillery fired back at the cannon flash, wounding three Protestants. The fight lasted two hours, until the militia captured a cannon. What began as Protestants against Catholics had become a battle between militia and populace. The toll climbed to fourteen dead and forty wounded.

The governor sent militiamen from across the state. As many as two thousand marched into Southwark and Moyamensing and stayed two weeks. Former sheriff John Watmough was arrested for cursing at the soldiers who had fired on residents, and for remarking that the soldiers should have been shot. He was admonished to act like a gentleman. McMullen stood guard in front of Moyamensing's Catholic churches for two days.

The riots of 1844 were the bloodiest the Catholic community in America had ever seen. They spurred calls for a citywide professional police force—a move New York and Boston had already made—and for annexing Southwark, Moyamensing, Kensington, and other outlying districts to the city so that order could be more easily maintained.

Nativists' political power peaked that year. Their candidates won local office. The new county auditor was the American Republican dentist who lost an arm in the riots.

As for the city's Negroes, one fact regarding the 1844 riots was clear: They had nothing to do with it. An anonymous poem reminded everyone of that.

> Oh, in Philadelphia folks say how
> Dat Darkies kick up all de rows,
> But de riot in Skensin'ton,
> Beats all darkies twelve to one.

And I guess it wasn't the niggas dis time.
I guess it wasn't de niggas dis time.
I guess it wasn't de niggas dis time, Mr. Mayor,
I guess it wasn't de niggas this time.

★ ★ ★

WHEN THE RIOTS ended, young Irish men like McMullen had come of age. They had risked their lives in combat against the marauding nativists, and their names were known in taverns and churches from Kensington to Southwark. They were heroic figures in communities lacking heroes. McMullen was only nineteen.

He began rising through the ranks of two organizations that were themselves on the rise. Both tapped the energies and resentments of being called "niggers turned inside out." One was the Moyamensing Hose Company. The other was the Killers.

The Killers were one of more than fifty gangs prowling Philadelphia streets by the end of the 1840s. Their names were chalked on walls and fences, graffiti of another century: Whelps, Bouncers, Flayers, Shifflers, Hyenas, Schuylkill Rangers, Buffers, Forty Thieves, Snakers, Stingers, Smashers, Gumballs, Rats, and Bloodtubs.

With guns and knives, the gangs were better armed than the night watchmen and constables. Some fought for their territory, others just declared it. The Flayers ruled Spring Garden's streets. The Schuylkill Rangers operated without rival west of Broad Street and south of the city, pummeling passersby and blackmailing barge and ship owners on the Schuylkill. But the districts most infested with gangs were Moyamensing and Southwark. The Shifflers were named for the Protestant martyr of Kensington. They operated in Southwark, as did the largest and most violent gang, the Killers.

The gang became the basis for a novel: "They were divided into three classes: beardless apprentice boys who after a hard day's work were turned loose upon the street at night, by their masters or their bosses. Young men of nineteen or twenty, who fond of excitement, had assumed the name and joined the gang for the mere fun of the thing, and who would either fight for a man or knock him down, just to keep their hand in; and fellows with countenances that reminded of the brute and devil well intermingled. These last were the smallest in number, but the most ferocious of the three."

A pamphleteer romanticized the Killers as successors to "the Jaco-bins of revolutionary France." But that was so much folderol. They were young, white toughs who liked to knock a man down, especially a colored man. Newspaper headlines and stories, like mirrors, reflected the violence caused by the Killers and other gangs:

April 29, 1847: Murder of a black man by three bouncers

July 5: Fight between locals and "Killers" at Gloucester Point, New Jersey

July 8: "The complaint that the citizens of Southwark are con-stantly kept in dread of the frequent street fights of the rowdies. Gangs attack each other in open day."

July 12: "Another of those disgraceful fire riots. . . . The mob city is the familiar term for our beautiful town. . . . There are perhaps, in the city and suburbs . . . 5,000 riotous and disorderly persons, principally boys and young men between the ages of 15 and 26."

July 28: "Four Killers arrested for an attack on a constable"

In warm weather, the Killers relaxed by renting a boat, sailing the Del-aware, and compelling "contributions" from waterfront residents of "hams, fowl and eggs." On the way back, they might attack or threaten incoming ships and bring fruit, vegetables, and whatever other cargo they could steal back to Moyamensing. Neighbors lauded their generosity, yet feared what they might do.

One Sunday afternoon on Spafford Street in Moyamensing, men and boys of the Killers were playing ball and drinking bad whiskey when a bystander walked under a tossed ball. The audacity. The Killers struck him so hard that he spent his afternoon in the hospital. The Killers spent their afternoon doing more of the same, drinking, playing, and mobbing strangers. Police were nearby but did nothing.

The Killers had connections—"spies," as a diarist wrote after the attack on the California House. A nod and a wink from authorities was part of the Killers' mystique.

As the violence of the gangs grew, so did violence from a less likely source—firemen. Fire companies manned by volunteers had been around since the 1700s, but the 1840s saw a flood of two dozen new ones. In poor neighborhoods, the companies gave pride and influence to people who had none. As a boy, McMullen was said to have held candles for carpenters and bricklayers who were building the Moyamensing Hose House on Eighth Street below South.

Engine companies had between forty and seventy men; hose companies were usually half that size. The engine companies carried the pumps and the hose companies connected those pumps to fireplugs. They carried spanners to wrench open the plugs.

Fire companies usually had a religious or political affiliation, like the two Weccacoes or the Shiffler Hose. And the companies were entirely white. Years before, an effort by Negroes to form their own led twenty-five engine and hose companies to warn: "The formation of fire-engine and hose companies by persons of color will be productive of serious injury to the peace and safety of citizens in time of fire, and it is earnestly recommended . . . to give them no support." The African Fire Association dissolved ten days later.

The companies had genteel roots in colonial days. By the 1840s, they evolved into clubhouses of the workingman. Many engine and hose houses had sleeping quarters for volunteers. The firehouse joined the tavern, church, and outdoor market as meeting places for the Irish in the United States.

Success was measured in getting to a fire first. Firemen would not leave without their muskets and pistols, because in addition to fighting fires, they battled rival companies. Some of them lit fires, then lay in wait for their rivals. And while they were volunteers, their protection was not free. Residents often had to pay for protection, lest they be defenseless when their home mysteriously caught fire.

"A dangerous body of men," Sidney Fisher wrote in his diary of city life. Fire companies "are influenced by an esprit de corps, act together &, being composed of the young & . . . the lower classes, have the power to do a great deal of mischief. They defy the law, terrify the magistrates & newspaper, have constantly violent affrays & consider themselves an important body with peculiar rights & privileges."

A City Hall investigating committee concluded what neighborhood people already knew: that nearly every "case of riot brought before the courts . . . had its origin in the fire companies, their members, or adherents. Each fire company was allied with (and in some cases, indistinguishable from) street gangs, which had infiltrated it and taken it over."

Matthias Baldwin knew it, too. The locomotive baron's apprentice system for boys had this among its many rules: A Baldwin apprentice could not join a volunteer fire company.

The company that attracted the most notoriety in Philadelphia was the Moyamensing Hose, headed by McMullen. People called them the "rowdy boys of Moyamensing." Each had a 27 tattooed on his hand, because Moya Hose was the twenty-seventh volunteer company begun in the city. Its biggest rival was Shiffler Hose. One summer, the Moyas set four fires and four ambushes to capture the Shiffler's carriage. They succeeded in September.

Firemen were seen by their neighbors, especially younger ones, as tough, well-known, and great-looking in those colored shirts—the Moyas wore red. McMullen and the Moyas helped themselves win battles with Hibernia, Hope, Franklin, and other fire companies by joining hands and spanners with the Killers. As the City Hall investigation found, some gangs unofficially joined fire companies and were seen on a company's run. The Shiffler gang aligned with Shiffler Hose and the Bouncers were tied to Weccacoe Hose. The gangs helped companies exercise control in their neighborhoods and keep rival companies out. Sometimes the alliances shifted, but the ties between Killers and Moyamensing Hose lasted. This joining brought together the two most feared Irish Catholic street organizations, with McMullen as the leader.

McMullen. His name was a synonym for power. As a young man, he was "Bull," pugnacious, a fighter, a figure worthy of fear and respect. People followed him, because he was the personification of Irish Catholic success. He would become the "Squire," whose whisper could get a man a job, free him from prison, or run him for office. Moyamensing was his feudal land and he was there to protect it any way he could. His whisper could have a man shot.

He was born in 1824. His father was Archibald McMullen, an Ireland native who hauled cargo away from the docks on "a low, sturdy cart" until he had saved enough to open a little grocery store in Moyamensing. His son was born in the family home on the southeast corner of Seventh and Shippen and would die just two blocks away.

McMullen's Moyamensing was full of young men without families at home and an Irish minority culture that taught one lesson: Fend for yourself. Poverty exhausted Moyamensing, with its narrow alley houses kneeling behind bigger ones on South and Shippen streets. Archie's boy was a smart lad who passed the test to enter the prestigious Central High School but left after a few months. His father placed him with a printer and a carpenter, but neither trade suited him. In the riot year of 1844, McMullen's reputation as a tough guy won him his first political job at age twenty. He worked the polls as a bookman for Democrats supporting James K. Polk for president, handing out printed ballots on which votes were cast, and checking the books for voters' residency. But his foremost task was keeping opposition voters from the polls. A Jacksonian Democrat, he helped Polk capture Pennsylvania. The Irish voted as a bloc for Polk, helping defeat Henry Clay. A fellow Whig told Clay: "Ireland has re-conquered the country England lost."

McMullen joined the navy, but the strong man never felt at ease on a rolling deck or taking an officer's orders. He came home to work in his father's store and into the waiting arms of his friends at Moyamensing Hose. The "rowdy boys" not only fought nearby fire companies; they ventured out of the district to fight with "torches, knives, iron spanners, sling shots and pistols." In the city, there was a "general fear of the fireman, a most degrading and contemptible subservience to them by politicians of all kinds."

In late 1845, McMullen was served with a warrant for wielding a knife on an alderman trying to arrest him. Two months later he was arrested in Southwark for stabbing a policeman and hurting another who tried to intervene. He stopped punching when a gun was put to his head. Only then did he tell his Moya mates to stop fighting.

An alderman jailed McMullen. To avoid a trial, he and members of the Moya Hose and the Killers—indistinguishable at this point—enlisted to fight in the Mexican War. They joined Company D of the First Pennsylvania Infantry under Captain Joseph Hill. The Moya boys forced out Hill, a supposed nativist sympathizer in 1844, and McMullen took over. They fought with police in New Orleans but McMullen got them out of that jam. Company D fought under General Zachary Taylor and was cited for "the extremest of bravery" at the battle of Mexico City.

McMullen returned home a hero in 1847 and was elected president of the Keystone Club, an organization of Democratic Party workers in Moyamensing. He was twenty-three and beginning to assume control of the Fourth Ward. He was still the Bull, not yet the Squire.

CHAPTER 7

"Arise, Young North"

THE REPORT FROM TRENTON was as bracing to Catto and the other colored petitioners as the February air. A white committee chairman had found merit in their petitions.

The chairman's analysis filled several pages. The colored proposal, he pointed out, would trigger the complicated mechanism for amending the state constitution, albeit by deleting only one word. If majorities in both houses voted yea, a referendum would go on ballots across the state. White men in lines at polls could contemplate Negroes lining up with them. Such a vision had vast practical, political, and social implications.

This 1850 proposal was not New Jersey legislators' first pass at colored suffrage—it was merely the first measure not "laid on the table" to die. It came up for consideration as powerful tides churned for and against Negroes' rights in capitals across the nation.

Frederick Douglass, to whom people in the Cattos' world increasingly looked for cues, had begun to retreat from the Garrisonian belief that "moral suasion" could bring about slavery's end, and he was taking others with him. He disparaged his mentor's philosophy as having freed few slaves and as offering no clear "principle of action, . . . no light on the pathway to duty." Along that pathway, he and others believed, was the ballot box. Voting-age black men were few in number compared with whites, but their votes could tip the scales in close elections. Therein, the reasoning went, lay a route to political power. Douglass's newspaper carried progress reports from suffrage drives in Harrisburg, Trenton, Albany, and Columbus.

In truth there was not much progress to report. Amos Beman had argued unsuccessfully for voting rights in Connecticut since the early 1840s; Henry Highland Garnet and James McCune Smith directed pamphleteers in New York State, fueled by Negro suffrage clubs that had sprung up in Brooklyn and Manhattan. The Langston brothers, Charles and John Mercer, led a drive in Ohio, where the "more than half white" rule meant Charles Langston, who had faced the tar-barrel mob with Martin Delany, was light enough to vote but the darker Delany was not. Other campaigns had risen and fallen in Michigan, Indiana, Illinois, and Iowa. The petition drafted in Shakespeare's Saloon joined fifty others submitted to Pennsylvania legislators since the state took Negroes' votes away in 1838.

Rhode Island and Wisconsin had recently given the ballot to black men, but a commission in Wisconsin took it back. New York let black men vote only if they owned at least $250 in property. (Two Smiths saw a way around this: The wealthy white abolitionist Gerrit Smith offered Negroes slices of his upstate lands. Buy the slices! the black physician James McCune Smith exhorted; buy just enough to attain the vote.)

Against these game but failing efforts, there rose another tide. The twentieth century would have a term for it—*white backlash*.

If anyone needed a reminder of the Nat Turner uprising, Charleston provided one. On a brutally hot July night in 1849, three dozen black men broke out of the workhouse, where slaves were disciplined. (Rev. Thomas Smyth's wife reported to a relative that her cousins in the militia helped suppress "the insurrection.")

Northern legislators calculated that any weakening of slavery might hasten the influx of freedmen—more owners were freeing their slaves through bequests and manumissions. Illinois, Indiana, and Iowa banned new Negro arrivals. The District of Columbia strengthened its Black Code to make the city's ten thousand free Negroes register. Maryland considered enslaving any Negro convicted of a crime. The Oregon Territory banned Negroes from the stream of settlers trundling out to stake claims, thus adding a whites-only clause to the "Go west, young man" formulation.

A religious journal, the *Watchman and Observer* of Richmond, Virginia, published a front-page essay in seven installments over the pseudonym Laocöon—the name of the Trojan priest who warned against accepting the gift of a wooden horse. The new Laocöon warned of a Trojan horse teeming with free Negroes.

He said they were becoming a burden on Virginia and called on the legislature to send them to a colony he would dub Virginia In Africa. He predicted the Virginia of "our grandchildren" would have a million free Negroes by 1950. After France's revolution, slaves in the French colony later known as Haiti had slaughtered their masters. Laocöon asked: Did Virginians wish to be next?

Some of his arguments weirdly echoed what colored petitioners were already saying and doing in the North. Laocöon predicted Negroes would soon "come to the doors of your legislative halls and ask: 'Are we not men—men of property, men of intelligence, and of numbers sufficient to be known, recognized, heard among you?'" That was precisely what was under way in Trenton.

Laocöon's Southern views had support in the North. Citizens of Mercer County, outside Cleveland, endorsed the same idea that had so intrigued Colonel Augustus Pleasonton after Pennsylvania Hall burned: Expel them. The Pennsylvania legislature, having turned aside fifty-one colored suffrage petitions, considered subsidizing passage to Liberia for free Negroes who went willingly—and for those who did not, the bill would "exile undesirable free Negroes to Africa." Robert Purvis, William Catto, and forty-two other colored leaders dispatched Delany to Harrisburg with their "remonstrance" against this measure.

The exile bill failed, but less because of colored remonstrances than for practical reasons—the difficulties foreseen in "the removal & transportation of many thousands of unwilling people," as one Pennsylvania commentator put it. In Illinois, a U.S. Senate candidate voiced similar concerns. "My first impulse would be to free all the slaves, and send them to Liberia—to their own native land," Abraham Lincoln said. "But a moment's reflection would convince me that whatever of high hope (as I think there is) there may be in this in the long run, its sudden execution is impossible. If they were all landed there in a day, they would all perish in the next 10 days; and there are not surplus shipping and surplus money enough in the world to carry them there in many times 10 days."

In Philadelphia, a typographers union leader, purporting to speak for the fledgling industrial-labor movement, said Negro aspirations not only imperiled white men's wages but flouted science and scripture. Would whites ever let blacks "stand beside us on election day, upon the rostrum,

in the ranks of the army, in our places of amusement, in places of public worship, ride in the same coaches, railway cars, or steamships?" John
Campbell wrote. "Never! never! . . . God never intended it." His book,
Negro-Mania, sold widely. The Utah Territory's governor, Brigham Young,
kept a copy in his office.

In this charged atmosphere, the chairman of the New Jersey Assembly's judiciary committee announced his belief that William Catto and the
rest of the colored suffrage petitioners were right.

The chairman asked fellow legislators to ponder how foreigners gained
citizenship and ballots after five years in the United States while native-
born, tax-paying Negroes suffered "taxation without representation," much
like "our venerated forefathers." He observed that the petitions were well-
crafted and had been submitted in excellent order.

Debate was joined. Supporters said men who could not vote should not
be taxed. Opponents said vote or no, property owners should be taxed for
services received from the state. The white assemblymen cast their votes.
The yeas were twenty-one, the nays twenty-three.

Two votes! The frustrations of campaigns in other states nagged the
colored men anew. What if they had printed more broadsides, spoken at
more meetings? There had been distractions. The organizers had duties
as ministers, teachers, and parents. Another Catto baby, Erskine, had just
arrived, and Ishmael Locke's wife was about to deliver a son (ardent scholars, the Lockes named him Pliny). And Locke had new duties in the eve-
nings, when most political meetings were held. Quakers had hired him to
run a modest experiment in Philadelphia—a night school for colored boys,
taught by colored teachers.

To be sure, getting within two votes of a Negro rights victory was a rarity in any American legislature in 1850. Even as the Trenton petitions were
being voted down, however, reports of a more dramatic vote arrived from
the West. Californians, their ranks swelled by transplanted northeastern-
ers afflicted with "the gold fever," ratified by twelve thousand to eight hundred a proposed state constitution banning slavery. New constitution in
hand, California applied for statehood.

The Mexican War had barely ended. If Californians got what they
wanted, the biggest territorial prize of the war would enter the Union in
the "free" column. That would tip the balance of "slave" and "free" states
maintained since the Missouri Compromise of 1820, the uneasy truce
governing the slavery question in the western territories. The South's advo-

cates turned livid. John Calhoun and others spoke of Northern betrayal, and of Southerners who, unless the West was opened to slavery, were ready to secede.

By relying on the Missouri Compromise, the "gag rule" in Congress, and the noncommittal language of the Constitution itself, the government had for seventy-five years sidestepped the subject of slavery. Now the subject became unavoidable. If California went "free," the South would need something in return.

★ ★ ★

A NEGOTIATION BEGAN in Congress in February 1850 and stretched through August. The goal was to avoid a showdown, to ease the "agitation" over whether to extend slavery into the territories. This mission fell to Henry Clay of Kentucky, Daniel Webster of Massachusetts, and John Calhoun of South Carolina. One writer called them the trusted centurions, "men who had grown grey in watching the Constitution, . . . who had received it in their childhood from its framers, and who had guarded its safety for nearly half a century with almost superstitious love."

Clay favored slavery but had negotiated the previous Union-saving compromise thirty years earlier. Webster was a lukewarm but reliable abolitionist who had once stood on Plymouth Rock to decry the "odious and abominable" slave trade. Calhoun had told the Senate that slavery was "a positive good" and tried to prove it with the census. He had famously muttered, "If a Negro could be found who could parse Greek or explain Euclid, I should be constrained to think that he has human possibilities."

On February 5, Henry Clay, now seventy-three, laid out what became the main elements of the Compromise of 1850: California would enter the Union as a "free" state. Trafficking of slaves, not slavery itself, would be banned in the District of Columbia, closing down slave markets that had long flourished in the nation's diplomatic front-window. (Anticipation of the ban set off a flurry of last-minute slave sales there.) Voters in New Mexico, Utah, Arizona, and Nevada would decide whether their territories were slave or free. Texas would drop its claim on some of these Mexican War–won lands in return for Washington's assuming the Lone Star State's ten-million-dollar war debt. And a new statute would shore up the nation's ill-enforced 1793 law returning fugitive slaves to owners.

"Stipulations" Calhoun called this last element. By March he was so riven with tuberculosis that another senator had to read his last speech to the Senate as Calhoun sat and stared. Let western settlers chose between "slave" and "free," the speech said, and let the trade end in Washington. If the North would "do her duty by causing the stipulations relative to fugitive slaves to be faithfully fulfilled," then the nation would see a peaceful end to "agitation of the slave question." Calhoun died four weeks later.

Webster, too, defended the Compromise, and stunned his abolition friends by denouncing *them* on the Senate floor, saying two decades of antislavery society activities had yielded "nothing good or valuable." He said Northern officials needed to enforce the fugitive slave law without making excuses.

A protest was swiftly organized in Boston's Faneuil Hall. People called Webster a "doughface," a Northerner who sided with slaveholders. The *Liberator* said Webster had "betrayed the cause of liberty, bent his supple knees anew to the Slave Power."

The fugitive bill's term of art was "person held to service or labor." Illinois' Stephen A. Douglas, championing the bill on the Senate floor, said the measure merely equated fugitives "from labor" with people wanted in criminal cases. Besides, he said, the bill established due process for Negro detainees—the right to a hearing and a lawyer.

In fact, the bill was laden with carrots and sticks. Defendants could not testify and were not afforded juries. Specially appointed federal commissioners would issue writs for wanted persons, hear the cases, and make the decisions. A sworn complaint from a slaveholder sufficed to trigger issuance of such a writ—and a commissioner who failed to do so would be fined a staggering one thousand dollars. A commissioner's pay depended on his rulings: a five-dollar fee for each defendant freed, ten dollars for each one sent to bondage. The official explanation was the added cost of paperwork.

Finally, the bill empowered commissioners and marshals to draft "bystanders" to help capture an accused fugitive; bystanders could be arrested for refusing. This was the "posse comitatus" clause: "[A]ll good citizens are hereby commanded to aid and assist in the prompt and efficient execution of this law, whenever their services may be required."

In September 1850, the Fugitive Slave Act and the Compromise's other elements were voted into law. Clay said "the dove of peace" was winging its way from the Capitol dome with tidings of "harmony to all the remotest extremities of this distracted land." A Philadelphia newspaper predicted the Compromise would "satisfy all reasonable men of every section, and give peace and quiet" to this volatile issue. Cannonades sounded and fireworks lit the Washington night. Rightly so: Politicians had laid aside partisanship in the name of the national interest. A crowd of two thousand marched to the homes of Webster and Clay and serenaded the old men with "Hail, Columbia!" and "The Star Spangled Banner."

Calhoun was gone now, but on his way out he had, in effect, taken the peculiar ordinances of Charleston Neck and made them the law of the nation.

The first arrest came eight days later in New York City, where a black man, James Hamlet, was pulled off the streets. At a mass meeting, James McCune Smith reported that Hamlet's wife had gone into shock and died. Women's cries filled the hall; Smith said President Millard Fillmore and Daniel Webster should be called to account for her death, and her tomb should be inscribed "First Victim" of the Fugitive Slave Act. "My colored brethren, if you have not swords, I say to you, sell your garments and buy one," another speaker, John S. Jacobs, identifying himself as a fugitive from South Carolina, said. "Let them only take your dead bodies." People cheered.

Hired slave catchers and freelance kidnap gangs were reported crossing from Maryland into Pennsylvania. Elizabeth Parker and her sister Rachel, free-born Chester County girls, vanished; a gargantuan effort of neighbors, lawyers and legislators tracked them down and months later brought them back—Rachel from a Baltimore jail, Elizabeth from New Orleans, where kidnappers had sold her under a fake name.

A Baltimore slave catcher went unpunished for shooting a fleeing Negro to death in Columbia, Pennsylvania. Philadelphia's most notorious slave catcher, the former constable George Alberti, went briefly to jail for kidnapping a free-born infant, along with the baby's fugitive mother—but the governor pardoned Alberti. A colored church in Rochester was said to lose all but 2 of 114 congregants as families fled north across the border. More than two thousand Negroes moved to Canada in the first three months of the law.

The act touched a distinctly American nerve. Armed marshals entering a home and swiping a man from his family at the whim of some far-off plantation prince brought images of redcoats to mind. A generation of colored families was about to be scissored up like wrapping paper, and bystanders were no longer innocent. The historic attempt to quiet the "agitation" over slavery had instead entangled every citizen in it. A newspaper in Columbus, Ohio, remarked, "Now we are all slave catchers."

Angry prose and poetry issued from abolition presses. Poems called "Blood Money" and "The House of Friends" portrayed the compromisers as "terrific screamers of freedom" who in the end had behaved like Judas. Much was made of the ten dollars the special commissioners would earn for each defendant sent into slavery.

> "What will ye give me and I will deliver this man unto you?"
> . . . They make the covenant, and pay the pieces of silver . . .
> And still Iscariot plies his trade.

The poet was a Northern reporter who had been to New Orleans and had witnessed a slave auction. Young and unknown, he signed himself Walter Whitman. "Arise, young North," he wrote. "Our elder blood flows in the veins of cowards."

The law instantly imperiled free people as well as fugitives. Whether a free-born Purvis or Catto, or a former slave like Leah Hubbard or Box Brown, a person accused in a fugitive writ would be handcuffed and detained.

Declarations of defiance came from colored leaders from across the North. Catto and William Still convened a meeting in Philadelphia in October 1850 in Brick Wesley A.M.E. Church. Older antislavery men came— Purvis, Gould Bias, John Burr, John Bowers. Younger people crowded the benches this time as well.

The drafting committee broadened from the usual preachers and teachers to include barbers, launderers, a peddler of cakes, a clothier, a laborer, and a waiter; free-born and former slave alike. Catto, who had earned livings by hand and head, was chairman. They drafted ten resolutions that the meeting endorsed "with great enthusiasm." Quoting from the Bible and Patrick Henry, they denounced the fugitive law as a "clear palpable violation" of the Constitution.

As they had in the Harrisburg and Trenton suffrage petitions, Catto and the other drafters emphasized that they paid taxes and lived peaceful lives. They tried to describe the effect on families when slave catchers went into homes and took parents from children, or sent them fleeing for Canada or Britain.

"Having already witnessed . . . the cruel operations of this law; having felt such anguish as no language can describe in seeing the wife flying from the home and the embraces of her husband, and the husband compelled to fly from his wife and helpless children, . . . we ask, calmly and solemnly ask the American people, what have we done to suffer such treatment at your hands?"

They pledged to defy the act "to the death."

News of their pledge went nationwide in the *Liberator*, which now boasted subscribers in California. Reports of resistance by blacks and whites alike rocketed across the North. An antislavery mob in Chicago boarded a slaveholders' canal boat, wrested six fugitives away, and got them aboard a Canada-bound steamer on Lake Erie before their owners could catch up. At Chardon, Ohio, east of Cleveland, fifty "respectable, influential and wealthy citizens" announced they were forming their own militia to resist the Fugitive Slave Act "by force of arms."

At a Boston rally, the former slave Samuel Ringgold Ward boiled the question down to "whether a man has a right to himself."

Ward, known for eschewing Victorian rhetorical flourishes and cutting knifelike to his point, was a minister, teacher, and editor. The new law imperiled him directly: He was still a fugitive. He was three when his mother bundled him out of slavery in Maryland. He attended the New York City Manumission Society's respected African Free School with Garnet and James McCune Smith, was mobbed and jailed for his antislavery pronouncements, became a pastor in Cortland, New York, and helped start the Free Soil Party in 1848. Now Ward rose in Faneuil Hall to denounce Webster and the other "Northern doughfaces who are willing to pledge themselves if you will pardon the uncouth language of a back-woodsman, to lick up the spittle of the slavocrats, and swear it is delicious."

He said the law would even require village postmasters to carry handcuffs and serve fugitive writs on free Negroes, "though I pledge you there is one, whose name is Sam Ward, who will never be taken alive."

Martin Delany picked up this cry in Pittsburgh. With an unlikely ally, the mayor, at his side, he told a vast audience that the founding fathers had it right, a man's home is his castle. Delany said no marshals would enter his castle. Even if President Fillmore himself served the writ, with "the Declaration of Independence waving above his head as his banner. . . . O, no! He cannot enter that house and we both live."

Kidnappers and slave catchers had not been absent long from the Cattos' world. Robert and Harriet Purvis were in their teens when a kidnap ring worked Philadelphia's southern tier, bundling Negro children as young as nine onto Delaware River sloops to see what prices they would fetch in Baltimore or New Orleans. Two Forten relatives, a man and a boy, were stolen and sold and later turned up in Louisiana and Mississippi. Octavius Catto had something in common with his young friend Robert M. Adger: Both boys' grandmothers had had their freedom curtailed by kidnappers, slaveholders, or "force & arms" on the palmetto-lined streets of Charleston.

Kidnapping had faded in the North by the late 1840s. The Fugitive Slave Act, however, made this crime more profitable and less constrained by law. What would stop kidnappers from faking a slaveholder's claim for a freeborn Negro? A commissioner would have to issue a writ, and the Negro could not testify. Once the victim was taken south, his captors could try to sell him before anyone was the wiser.

In the Lancaster County village of Christiana, just above the Mason-Dixon Line, local people—men and women, colored and white—fought off armed slave catchers who, along with a U.S. marshal from Philadelphia, had come to seize four fugitives.

The four escaped, and their Maryland owner, Edward Gorsuch, was killed in the showdown. President Fillmore mourned the "estimable" Gorsuch but assured Americans that the number of agitators trying to undermine "the law for the return of fugitives from labor" was believed to be "daily diminishing."

In the Cattos' world, the Christiana resisters were celebrated. Much was made of the fact that they included black and white. Underground Railroad operatives helped the fugitives hopscotch their way from Lancaster County to Philadelphia, then to Rochester and Canada. One of them probably got the free medical checkup—he stayed in the Philadelphia home of Gould and Eliza Bias.

At Rochester, Douglass took three Christiana men into his house, using his old "D.F." reversed-initials trick to send word of their arrival. "I could not look upon them as murderers. To me, they were heroic defenders of the just rights of man," he wrote. "So I fed them, and sheltered them." (His daughter Rosetta remembered who really fed them: "It was no unusual occurrence for Mother to be called up at all hours of the night to prepare supper for a hungry lot of fleeing humanity.")

When the leader of the resisters reached Canada, a fugitive named Henry Bibb took him in and wrote of his derring-do in Bibb's newspaper, *Voice of the Fugitive*. Bibb, too, had lived a life of agonies and escapes. He had been chased, captured, spread-eagled, whipped, sold, and resold. By the time he set the Christiana story in type, he had earned the right to a moment's glee.

"The Christiana Hero Is in Canada," the headline said.

Not everyone escaped. Twenty-nine blacks and three whites were arrested. The Christiana trials began in Philadelphia in November 1851. A courtroom was readied for evening sessions, with lamps "of the chastest design" and ceiling ventilators controlled from the judge's bench. The room was on the second floor of Independence Hall.

The building had become a municipal catch-all by 1851—police station, mayor's office; dog pound in the basement; unruly lines of voters at ground-floor windows on election days. The trial upstairs drew national attention. Pro- and antislavery crowds (including Lucretia Mott) swirled outside. A colored committee led by Bias, Burr, and William Forten raised defense monies, with James McCune Smith helping in New York. Donations arrived from as far away as San Francisco and Detroit, where black women pooled thirty dollars for the families of "our noble-hearted liberty-loving patriots of Christiana."

In court, seven prosecutors, including Maryland's attorney general, faced five defense lawyers, led by Thaddeus Stevens, the abolitionist legislator from Lancaster, Pennsylvania. To prosecutors' annoyance, defendants wore red, white, and blue scarves. Stevens presented evidence that "a gang of professional kidnappers" was snatching Christiana Negroes—"they have never afterwards been seen or known of." A witness said the pardoned slave catcher, George Alberti, had turned up in Christiana. Stevens had a Philadelphia judge, William D. Kelley, testify that one prosecution witness was a known liar.

Kelley was more politician than abolitionist, but one thing set him apart: He had grown up with children of both races. His childhood friend was Robert Bridges Forten.

The defendants were acquitted. Abolitionists rejoiced—though some said the trials merely proved how far the government would go to enforce the new law. Samuel Ringgold Ward and his wife were on an antislavery lecture tour in Ohio when they read the news. They talked and concluded that neither resistance nor persuasion could cure a country "hopelessly given to the execution of this barbarous enactment." They decided to gather up their children, "wind up" their affairs and "go to Canada."

★ ★ ★

THE FUGITIVE SLAVE ACT became a wondrous recruiting tool for antislavery meetings. Austin Bearse, a retired sea captain from Cape Cod, offered his recollections to a writer who, at abolitionists' urging, was researching a novel on slavery.

Bearse said that in the winters of the 1820s, he and other New England sailors left their snowbound ports to pick up extra work along the Southern coast. As first mate on the brig *Milton*, he had moved slaves upriver from Charleston for the rice harvests, first stopping overnight at a landfall known as Poor Man's Hole.

During these stops, the crew allowed slaves' loved ones aboard for a night's visit. "In the morning it used to be my business to pull off the hatches and warn them that it was time to separate," Bearse remembered, "and the shrieks and cries at these times were enough to make anybody's heart ache." He told of a scene in Charleston Harbor in 1828.

Slave traders brought aboard four handcuffed men who were being shipped to a buyer's agent in New Orleans. But as the *Milton* eased away from the docks, an old Negro woman "came screaming after them, 'My son, O, my son, my son!'" "When we had got more than a mile out in the harbor," Bearse wrote, "we heard her screaming yet."

The four slaves included a carpenter and a blacksmith and impressed Bearse as "resolute fellows." When the *Milton* reached the Gulf Stream, he removed their handcuffs. Mark our words, the men told Bearse—we will never live to be slaves in New Orleans. The *Milton* transferred them to the agent and proceeded on its way.

Sometime later, Bearse's captain saw the same agent, who said that within forty-eight hours after the transfer, each of the four slaves had taken his own life.

The author who interviewed Bearse also read the Weld-Grimké book *American Slavery as It Is* and kept it under her pillow for inspiration. One publisher turned her novel down, calculating that an antislavery woman writing on slavery would offend Southern customers. When her novel finally came out, Southern legislatures banned it and the author was showered with hate mail. A package sent to her from the South had a note about the "damned niggers," pinned to a Negro's severed ear.

Harriet Beecher Stowe never saw the ear—her husband opened the package and kept it from her sight. Not that it would have mattered—by then, four presses were running day and night to keep up with the demand for copies of *Uncle Tom's Cabin*.

★ ★ ★

THE FUGITIVE SLAVE ACT also drove Martin Delany to write. His 1852 *Condition, Elevation, Emigration and Destiny of the Colored People of the United States* offered a who's-who of 161 accomplished colored Americans—from Richard Allen to William Whipper—and the text of the Fugitive Slave Act. The act convinced Delany that American Negroes should found a nation in Africa, if only for their children's sake: "To use the language of the talented Mr. Whipper, 'they cannot be raised in this country, without being stoop-shouldered.'"

Delany laid out a scheme for raising funds, buying African land, and structuring a government. He offered past examples of "necessary emigrations"—the Puritans sailing from England, the Jews escaping Egypt. American Negroes were captives, he said, like the Poles in Russia or the Irish in Great Britain—"We are a nation within a nation."

No presses ran at night to meet demands for Delany's book. But it had a mad charm—the foreword said he had written it in less than a month while "in the city of New York on business." Amid his list of colored newspapers, from the *Anglo-African* and the *Elevator* to the *Ram's Horn* and the *Struggler*, Delany plopped in such sentences as, "Another issued in New York city, the name of which we cannot now remember." The book offered a wondrous guide to the achievements of Negroes. William Catto was touted twice—for "improving" the rice mill to five hundred bushels daily, and for forsaking his Liberia plans to "make himself more useful" as a preacher in the North.

Those words may have buoyed Catto in a difficult time. The A.M.E. Church had made him steward of its Book Concern that year, a weighty honor in a church that relied on its publications for revenue. But Daniel Payne wrote that Catto, selected for his "superior natural endowments and . . . pulpit oratory," proved "destitute of the tact and pluck which come from business training." He quit the post within a matter of months.

Some of Catto's choices in life sat badly with other colored men and now, with his name turning up in books and newspapers, one of them let him know it. A minister who had signed on with the Colonization Society berated Catto and Payne. Men that clever could have done well in Africa, the minister wrote. *Very* well.

William Catto left Charleston "with the intention of going to Liberia, but the people of the Northern States advised [him] not to go," Rev. Daniel H. Peterson wrote in his 1854 book on Liberia. "That was a great error. . . . [T]hey would have been doubly useful in the Church, and would, by this time, have been men of wealth and eminence. But they are just as they were, and no better, like many others who would rather remain half-free and half-slave, in a country that they cannot travel without being stopped and examined as though they were thieves and robbers."

Liberia's coastal cities had no newspaper. Why not send the *North Star*'s editor? Frederick Douglass would accomplish more good there and "would make five times as much money." Besides, Peterson wrote, "many things which we are endeavoring to do in the United States, are like pouring water upon a goose's back."

★　★　★

LEAVING THE COUNTRY was not a new idea; Delany and Garnet endorsed various back-to-Africa proposals over the years. But now the Wards' conversation about Canada was repeated in a thousand colored homes. The Purvises considered London. "For ourselves we might endure to the end—as we have suffered so long," Harriet Purvis wrote to a friend, "but for our children it is a question of whether we ought to seek another home."

Her brother, Robert Forten—the telescope maker—sent his shy, serious daughter Charlotte to Massachusetts to stay with the Remonds and attend school in Salem. Charlotte, just three when her mother died, hoped her father would come and join her. Instead he chose Canada and eventually, Britain, leaving a heartbroken Charlotte behind.

Thanks to the Underground Railroad, thousands of fugitives had settled in Canada by 1850, and after the Fugitive Slave Act, many more followed—by various estimates, as many as thirty thousand. A song was sung to a tune popularized in Gold Rush days, "O! Susannah." Versions abounded, with refrains like the one in Henry Bibb's newspaper:

> Farewell old master,
> Don't come after me!
> For I'm on my way to Canada
> Where colored men are free.

The race's most visible men and women felt the ground beneath them crumble. They lost the writers William Wells Brown to Britain and Mary Ann Shadd to Canada; Rev. Alexander Crummell, who at sixteen had carried his friend Henry Garnet away from the New Hampshire mob, headed for Liberia. They might lose Purvis, Ward, and Garnet. Churches and colonization societies offered passage to Africa or the West Indies. Douglass wrote of feeling "like a besieged city, at news that its defenders had fallen at its gates."

Garnet sailed to Britain—and after putting up with Jim Crow quarters on the way over, basked in London's tolerance as other black leaders had. Britons at an antislavery convention applauded his call for a boycott of slave cotton; he told them the motto of colored Americans was, "Onward! Upward!" Then came word from his wife, Julia, that their two boys were desperately ill. He sent money for doctors, but Julia never received it. One boy recovered somewhat; the other died in early 1851.

Devastated, Garnet accepted a church's offer of a Jamaica mission post. Bringing along a fugitive girl they had adopted, the Garnets sailed from Britain in December 1852. He and Julia looked forward to a respite from tragedies and politics—but on this voyage their other boy took ill again, and on arrival in Kingston they laid him to rest.

Garnet wrote to the abolition leader Gerrit Smith, "Unless Providence bids me otherwise, I never mean to reside in [the United States] again."

★   ★   ★

DANIEL PAYNE WENT up to Rochester to see Douglass. They needed to speak about "whether it was best to stand our ground or flee to Canada." The tiny, bespectacled Payne and the hulking Douglass, his shock of hair now starting to go gray, took inventory.

Payne had built the A.M.E. Church into a national network with a popular weekly paper and a "book concern." He probably wanted to push Douglass off platforms for saying A.M.E. leaders lacked the boldness of such upstarts as William Catto. But Douglass was too large for Payne to push, and both men were running out of options. Dreams of a European-style worker movement or an Irish-black alliance had faded. The Fugitive Slave Act not only constricted the freedoms that had drawn men like them to the North; it placed them and their families in peril.

Douglass could go into exile with admirers in London or Edinburgh. Payne, too, had enough church contacts to secure a post abroad. But how would this look to the world? If two of the race's top men fled in this "trial-hour?"

The *North Star*'s editor had intended to stay in the United States at least as long as Garnet remained. But Garnet, faced with family tragedies, was wavering. And Samuel Ringgold Ward? "Why, Ward, Ward, he is already gone," Payne said. "I saw him crossing from Detroit to Windsor."

Douglass's eyes widened. Losing Ward was "a stunning blow," he wrote later, "for no other could bring such brain power to bear." From Canada, Ward, too, was headed for Jamaica, another place where British abolition law meant colored men were free.

What about you, Douglass asked Payne. Will you stick around?

Payne said he would. "We are whipped, we are whipped," he said, but the fight was not over, "and we might as well retreat in order."

★ ★ ★

IN PHILADELPHIA, WILLIAM CATTO undertook his own orderly retreat.

The new law meant he, too, had to proceed warily. For all he knew, the 1848 warrant for a William Catto of Charleston languished in a bailiff's desk in Maryland—the state where the Biases' white friend Charles Torrey had died in jail, and where legislators now proposed to enslave free Negroes convicted of crimes. What if marshals came for him on the old warrant?

The next time federal census takers came to his door, he did not say his birthplace was Charleston. For the time being, at least, he became William T. Catto, mulatto minister, free-born; birthplace, Nova Scotia.

He prepared his family to move north into central New Jersey. The A.M.E. needed someone to cover five pulpits on a forty-mile "circuit" from Bordentown on the Delaware to Freehold and Cooks Mills, near the ocean at Long Branch—someone willing to travel.

He knew the state a bit, having preached in Trenton in 1849. He knew Ishmael Locke from Camden, and John S. Rock from Salem County, who aspired to practice law and who had helped the suffrage effort. In June 1850, Catto shared speaking duties in Camden with the great Garnet himself, at the laying of a cornerstone for the rebuilt Macedonia Church, Camden's oldest A.M.E. congregation.

Camden was a leisure-time haven for those unafraid of mixing races. You could leave your temperance vows in Philadelphia, ride the ferry over, buy a hot corn and a pint of German lager and bet on interracial prizefight-ing or a cricket match, or stroll the boardwalk with your sweetheart on a summer's evening as paddleboats plied the Delaware and the sun dipped into the silhouette of Philadelphia's smokestacks and spires.

One of the A.M.E. pulpits on Catto's new circuit was in Allentown, a village midway across New Jersey. Allentown also had a boys' academy with a good reputation. Catto's soft-spoken Sunday orations tended to draw interest wherever he worked, and one of Allentown's leading white citizens came to know him. Former Congressman William A. Newell lived just down the hill from the boys' school.

In Congress, Newell had been no abolition dynamo—he thought the 1850 compromise had merit. But behind his enormous mutton-chop whis-kers was a studious Presbyterian with previous careers as a physician and a maritime lifesaving expert. He had helped pioneer the "life-car," an egg-shaped steel capsule that rode rocket-fired "life-line" cables to stranded ships and whisked passengers ashore, five or six at a time. Now, Newell fired a life line to Catto and whisked his most-favored son into the acad-emy. In all likelihood, Octavius was its first colored pupil.

William Catto had been through something akin to this at the Pres-byterian seminary in Columbia, South Carolina, not so long ago; surely his son would have it easier in Allentown. But William was thirty-seven when he went to the seminary. Octavius was fourteen. The experiment of placing a light-skinned Negro in a school of white boys lasted one aca-demic year.

Then came word from Philadelphia of a new possibility.

★ ★ ★

ISHMAEL LOCKE'S NIGHT CLASSES were a modest success. Enlist-ing the help of colored craftsmen, Locke started a kind of trade school and within a year or so, sixty colored boys were apprenticing as cabinetmak-ers, boot makers, tailors, barbers, plasterers, undertakers, and musicians. This effort had its ups and downs—"graduates" struggled mightily to find work—but Locke was proving that Negroes could teach Negroes. In 1851, the Quaker managers acceded to the plea of colored ministers on the aux-iliary board and made plans to open a full-fledged school. One of the min-isters was William Catto.

The project known as the Institute for Colored Youth (I.C.Y.) limped along for years with no "institute" and few youths. A Quaker slaveholder's bequest had set the experiment in motion two decades earlier—Richard Humphreys, a goldsmith, had "seen the realities of slavery," as Catto once put it, and willed ten thousand dollars to "instructing the descendants of the African race in school learning in the various branches of the mechanical arts and trades and in Agriculture . . . in order to prepare . . . them to act as teachers."

The managers initially purchased 136 acres outside the city and sent some fifteen Negro boys to learn gardening, the Bible, and the making of brooms. Neither teachers nor pupils had their hearts in it. The ministers on the auxiliary board wanted a real school in the city, with "literary subjects" as well as trades—Negroes such as William Catto had not braved mobs and marshals to see their children taught broom-making.

Funds from the Humphreys bequest went to purchasing a lot and putting up a schoolhouse. The door of the new school at 716–18 Lombard Street would be ready to open for daytime classes in the fall of 1852. All that was needed was a faculty.

Except at tiny private schools such as Sarah Douglass's and Margaretta Forten's, no one hired black teachers. The Quakers relied on white women to teach Negroes. But the I.C.Y. managers—Quaker merchants—were impressed enough with what Locke accomplished that they took another chance. In 1852 they published this notice:

TEACHER WANTED

THE Managers of the "Institute for Colored Youth," desire to engage a competent Teacher for their new High School in Philadelphia, for the instruction of colored youth in the higher branches of an English education and the Classics.

Satisfactory references as to moral character, literary acquirements, and ability for the government of such a school, will be required.

A colored man would be preferred, qualifications being equal.

That colored man was Charles L. Reason. He was thirty-four years old when the managers entrusted him with the future of their experiment.

A New York child of Haitian immigrants, Reason had aspired to the ministry but an Episcopal seminary rejected him for his color. He attended New York Central College, one of three in the nation accepting Negroes, and before that was a classmate of Garnet, Ward, William Wells Brown, and James McCune Smith at the African Free School. Like the Bird school's pupils, Free School students learned to sprint—white boys of lower Manhattan routinely pelted them with stones and epithets.

Thus did Reason arrive in Philadelphia well prepared.

His plan for the I.C.Y. was daunting and elaborate. Families would submit applications and pay ten dollars for tuition, books, and stationery; the poorest pupils could attend free. Boys and girls alike would study algebra, trigonometry, poetry, the classics, and the sciences. In keeping with Richard Humphreys's will, students would learn to teach.

Reason set the standards high—applicants had to pass exams in "Reading, Writing, Spelling, Arithmetic as far as Fractions, and in the Geography of the United States." He insisted on a library respectable enough to open to the public. He used his contacts in the black intelligentsia to arrange guest lectures; these, too, were open to all. The little faculty began to attract stars. Sarah Mapps Douglass signed on, and the I.C.Y. annexed her school for girls. A veteran of Pennsylvania Hall, she already had a following, and she too, was inclined to innovate: She began teaching human physiology to girls.

A mathematician by training, Reason favored math and the sciences. He announced the areas of study: "Composition, History, Algebra, Geometry, . . . Plane and Spherical Trigonometry, Surveying, and Navigation, Natural Philosophy, Chemistry, Mechanical Drawing, and Drafting, Anatomy, and Physiology." In the future, he said, he expected to add "other advanced studies" and some languages to the mix.

The I.C.Y. boys department opened in the fall of 1852 with six pupils.

Enrollment grew pyramid-style, with a goal of graduating more students each year. Seniors knew that when spring classes ended, grade averages, good or bad, would appear in the best-read paper in black America, the A.M.E.'s *Christian Recorder*. Final examination questions included: "Inscribe a regular decagon, and a regular polygon of twenty-four sides in a circle, and prove the work." And "Parse every word in the following stanzas," including:

> O matre pulchra filia pulchrior,
> Quem crimmosis cunque voles modun

Debellate, monet Sithoniis non levis Evins,
Cum fas atque nefas exiguo fine libidinum.

And: "Standing due west of a house which faces North West, I hold
a foot-rule 8 inches from my eye, and observe that the rays from the two
extremities of the house, intercept 1.3 inches on the rule. Knowing that
the house is 60 feet long, what is the distance of its nearest corner from
the place where I stand?"

Commencement programs tested the audience's skills, with sections
printed in Spanish, Latin, and Greek.

Each year, as many as half the seniors did not graduate and were
held back for more studies; even that unpleasantness was announced in
the papers. Professors from Haverford and other Quaker colleges (which
had no intention of actually admitting Negroes as students) proctored
the examinations. Suspensions and expulsions were commonplace. Insolence was not tolerated—a boy's diary told of a teacher clubbing him with
a textbook. Where had the teacher learned that? He was a graduate of
the I.C.Y.

Instruction was strict, exams rigorous—and parents clamored to enroll
their children. Families in far-flung cities applied. Waiting lists grew.
"There were always more pegs than holes," William Bolivar, an alumnus,
wrote. Nearly half the pupils were out-of-towners, boarding with local
families or relatives. In three years, enrollment grew from 6 to 112.

William Catto moved back to Philadelphia in 1854 and enrolled Octavius. The minister's friend, Jacob White Sr., put Jake Jr. in the I.C.Y.,
too. Jake had been Octavius's tall, skinny playmate since Bird school
days, when the Cattos' Kessler Alley address was close to the Whites'
on Old York Road. The two boys learned from the same teachers, heard
their fathers espouse the same views, and walked—or sprinted—the
same streets.

Another classmate from the Bird school, Robert M. Adger, was accepted, too. Younger friends of the Cattos followed—Bolivar, William
Minton, J. W. Cromwell, the three daughters and son of James Le Count,
and eventually Ishmael and Mary Locke's little boy, Pliny.

The ratio of students to teachers was roughly 20 to 1. That put
the institute ahead of the public high schools in Philadelphia—then
and now.

★ *Firemen aiming a hose at nearby buildings as the abolitionists' Pennsylvania Hall burned in 1838. (Courtesy of The Library Company of Philadelphia.)*

★ *Photograph of the Pennsylvania Anti-Slavery Society, circa 1850–1851.* BACK ROW, FAR LEFT: *Mary Grew.* FAR RIGHT: *J. Miller McKim.* FRONT ROW, BEGINNING FOURTH FROM LEFT: *Robert Purvis, Lucretia Mott, James Mott (Lucretia's husband). (Courtesy of the Friends Historical Library of Swarthmore College.)*

★ Frederick Douglass in 1848. He later gave this daguerreotype to Susan B. Anthony. (Courtesy of Chester County Historical Society, West Chester, PA.)

★ Rev. Henry Highland Garnet, the eloquent one-legged New York clergyman who was the first black man to address the U.S. House of Representatives. (Courtesy of The Library Company of Philadelphia.)

★ Martin R. Delany, civil rights leader, author, explorer, physician, and the highest-ranking black military officer in the Civil War. (Courtesy of The Library Company of Philadelphia.)

★ William Lloyd Garrison, one of
the early and most important white
abolitionists of the 1800s. (Courtesy of
The Library Company of Philadelphia.)

★ Charlotte Forten, a product of the
Forten-Purvis "dynasty of social activists."
She joined antislavery efforts in Boston
and Philadelphia at an early age. (Courtesy
of The New York Public Library.)

★ William Still, who managed the Underground
Railroad in Philadelphia and helped hundreds of
fugitive slaves make their way to freedom. (Courtesy
of The Library Company of Philadelphia.)

★ Octavius V. Catto, circa 1870.

ROBERT SMALL,
Pilot of the Steamer Planter, Charleston, S. C.
Entered according to Act of Congress, in the year 1862, in the
Clerk's Office of the District Court of the United States for the Eastern
District of Pennsylvania, by
McALLISTER & BROTHER, 728 Chestnut St.
PHILADELPHIA.

★ *Robert Smalls, the slave who piloted the* Planter *out of Charleston Harbor and into Northern hands. Smalls became a war hero and went on to run for Congress. (Courtesy of The Library Company of Philadelphia.)*

★ Fanny Jackson Coppin, the former slave who educated herself and then devoted her life to educating black children. (Courtesy of The Library Company of Philadelphia.)

★ RIGHT: Jacob White Jr., who was involved in more than a dozen civil rights and civic associations. He was also Octavius Catto's best friend and Philadelphia's first black public school principal. (Courtesy of The Library Company of Philadelphia.)

★ LEFT: Ebenezer D. Bassett, the principal of the Institute for Colored Youth from 1855 to 1869. He resigned after being named the nation's first black diplomat—minister to Haiti. (Courtesy of The Library Company of Philadelphia.)

★ RIGHT: Daniel A. Payne, a Charleston-born cleric who went north so that he could teach black children. He opened a college and became a bishop in the A.M.E. Church. (Courtesy of The Library Company of Philadelphia.)

★ Captain William McMullen, 1861, leader
of the Independent Rangers in the Civil
War. (Courtesy of The Library Company
of Philadelphia.)

★ William McMullen, the Squire,
who ruled South Philadelphia
for half a century.

★ Frank Kelly, the young
Moyamensing Hose man and
Democratic operative.

★ *Octavius V. Catto, 1871.*
(Courtesy of The Library Company of Philadelphia.)

ON MARCH 4, 1853, two grand inaugurations occurred. In blizzard-bound Washington, President Franklin Pierce asked twenty thousand listeners to respect "the rights of the South" and obey the laws of the Compromise of 1850 "cheerfully." In Philadelphia, Charles Reason inaugurated the Library and Reading Room of the Institute for Colored Youth.

The library began with thirteen hundred volumes, from *Rural Chemistry* and *Civil Engineering* to biographies of Julius Caesar, Marie Antoinette, Hannibal, Isaac Newton, William Penn, Cortez, and Patrick Henry. Also, lives of religious greats: Martin Luther, Mohammed, the Quakers' George Fox; histories of Egypt, Rome, Macedonia, Persia, New York City, and—notwithstanding Noah Webster's views—Africa.

"Education ought to be and must be a family ambition, an inbred pride, a universal emulation," Reason told his audience that night. "It must become a habit."

Two springs later, the I.C.Y. librarian, James Bustill, reported 233 male and 217 female visitors in a year. Books were loaned 4,088 times and read in the Reading Room 1,554 times—rivaling rates in the city's older libraries. The colored librarian saw parents heeding the principal's call. "Widowed mothers, though pressed with many cares, and conversant with many sorrows, have come, leading their youthful sons and daughters to slake their thirst at this foundation of knowledge. Fathers, long lukewarm on this subject, have been roused to enthusiasm by the zeal of their children."

Bustill exulted, "Oh! This is a glorious spectacle to gaze upon children bringing parents who have long dealt in mental darkness, to behold this marvelous light illuminating the mists of prejudice and realizing the dawn of a promising day."

FOR YOUNGSTERS STRAGGLING into classrooms on a Monday in January, what could be better than gossip and distraction involving the principal? The news was that on Saturday night, he had managed to get booted out of a Philadelphia lecture hall because of his race.

A photograph of Reason conveys a formal bearing, ample mustache, and thoughtful gaze; he could have passed for a librarian himself. But he began a tradition for I.C.Y. principals: Be a subversive; keep one hand in the equal-rights fight at all times.

Reason joined the revived local Vigilance Committee to aid fugitive slaves. Within days of the library's opening, he was in William Still's office processing a fugitive from Baltimore. He spoke against colonization. He brought his friends Remond and Garnet to the I.C.Y. for lectures. Parents reading the weekly *Freeman* saw the principal's advice to fugitives— advice one I.C.Y. parent, William Catto, would certainly have supported. Use caution in letters to friends and family in the South, Reason warned. Authorities were opening more Negro mail than ever.

In January 1854, a visiting Massachusetts abolitionist, Lucy Stone, invited Reason and a few other colored Philadelphians to her Saturday night lecture titled "Women's Rights." The managers of the Musical Fund Hall refused to seat the Negroes. Stone protested but said she had learned of this refusal too late to cancel her speech.

Word of the episode spread quickly—a testament to the telegraph and the honing of colored political reflexes. "We who have to endure the cuffs of proslavery can ill bear to be deserted by our friends," Frederick Douglass editorialized in Rochester. A letter from Reason, along with his I.C.Y. title, appeared in Philadelphia papers. He said Stone not only had "failed to exonerate" herself from the hall's whites-only policy but had learned of the policy in plenty of time to cancel. He noted that a similar incident in New England had triggered boycotts by such white luminaries as Charles Sumner and Ralph Waldo Emerson. Reason asked readers: "Is Lucy Stone or any Garrison Abolitionist of Philadelphia less true to us than these?"

Reason's words about Garrisonians also rubbed salt in a widening wound. Garrison's "moral suasion" doctrine felt increasingly obsolete to black abolitionists. The daily terrors of the Fugitive Slave Act convinced them of the need for something more concrete—a "principle of action," as Douglass said. Garrisonians did not dirty their hands in party politics; black abolitionists said it was high time to dirty their hands and run antislavery candidates. At one meeting, Douglass traded angry barbs with his old mentor, William Lloyd Garrison.

Like lovers in a breakup, Douglass and Garrison confided in mutual friends. "I stand in relation to him something like that of a child to a parent," Douglass wrote of the owlish man who had stood with him through mobbings and eggings. Garrison told an ally, "With Douglass, the die seems to be cast. I lament the schism, but it is unavoidable."

* * *

THE GOVERNOR OF PENNSYLVANIA was making a rare appearance before a colored audience when a tall, thin Negro stood up like an exclamation mark.

When would the state confer political rights on its forty thousand disfranchised colored men, the black questioner wanted to know. When would Pennsylvania "acknowledge the common brotherhood of her children?"

Governor James Pollock was a guest of the I.C.Y. that spring day in 1855. His questioner, Jacob Clement White Jr., peppered Pollock with words such as *citizenship* and its nineteenth-century synonym *manhood*, in a calm and practiced voice. White sketched a vision of equality, and his earnest gaze suggested he believed it.

"You see us, sir, a little family by ourselves, set off from the other youth of this great Commonwealth. . . . We are glad, therefore, that in the midst of your numerous engagements, your Excellency has given us an opportunity to present ourselves before you, that you may see that though not recognized in the political arrangements of the Commonwealth, we are nevertheless preparing ourselves usefully for a future day, when citizenship in our country will be based on manhood and not on color."

Jake White was eighteen. A young black man confronting a white governor would have made news in 1955, much less 1855. Negro newspapers as far off as Canada reported the scene. Pollock "continued to address the scholars at some length, counseling them to get knowledge; to cultivate the love of morality, Christianity, & etc., which was all very good," a writer said. "But of our rights, of which we have been so long robbed, and have suffered so severely in consequence thereof, he said nothing. Of course he could not have forgotten the fact, as the address of the pupil so justly made allusion to it."

Pollock cared about schools. He was the first governor to make such a visit. For his troubles, he had been pelted with words by a gangly pupil. Reason and the school's other Negro teachers had not lifted a finger to halt the pelting. Had Pollock detected in the principal's broad brow an effort to smother a smile? What sort of school *was* this?

All the same, the gangly boy had spoken well.

"How Much I Yearn
to Be a *Man*"

I N JAKE WHITE JR.'S unquavering voice, something new could be heard. A phenomenon stirred in black America by the middle of the 1850s. Emboldened Negroes, some quite young, stood up and drew attention to themselves in unlikely settings. Sometimes white allies stood with them, sometimes not.

A young Negro schoolteacher sued a New York streetcar line for ejecting her, screaming, from a whites-only car in the Lower East Side; within weeks her suit received donations and letters of support from Negroes as far away as California. In Boston, black advocates asked the Massachusetts legislature to desegregate the public schools, anticipating *Brown vs. Board of Education of Topeka* by ninety-nine years. In Ohio, Martin Delany's friend Charles Langston went to jail for helping Oberlin College students and teachers swarm a slave catcher and free a fugitive.

At his sentencing, Langston turned to the judge and prosecutor and dared them to join the rescues—"Your children to all generations would honor you for doing it, and every good and honest man would say you had done *right!*" (A stenographer noted "prolonged applause, in spite of the efforts of the Court.") New verses were appended to "I Hear the Cry of Millions," an anthem of an ever-changing struggle.

> I hear the voice of Langston, of Langston,
> I hear the voice of Langston, from Cleveland City Jail,
> "Oh, set the captives free."

A Syracuse band composed the "Underground Railroad Quickstep" to raise funds for the network and salute its local agent, former slave Jermain Loguen. Charlotte Forten wrote a parody of "Columbia, the Gem of the Ocean." Her lyrics asked when children of every "hue" would find protection "'neath the folds of the red, white and blue." The eternal self-doubter, she rated her lyrics "miserable." Before the decade ended, young colored men were singing them at protests in Boston and Philadelphia.

A younger generation was coming up and keeping the music playing.

Old laws were being challenged. So were old admonitions about public speeches, writings, parades in the public square. A handful of writers, poets, and biographers got works into print. Frederick Douglass completed a second autobiography. William Catto began a book on Philadelphia's colored churches. Martin Delany, irked at the meekness of Stowe's *Uncle Tom*, began writing a novel about a defiant slave.

Garrison's *Liberator* published two of Charlotte Forten's poems; a third appeared in the *Christian Recorder*, thanks to Daniel Payne. The A.M.E. bishop paid her a dollar. He also helped a former slave named Frances Jackson, who was known as Fanny, afford Oberlin's tuition. That was Payne: Johnny Appleseed to the next generation, planting seeds that grew into scholars and schoolhouses everywhere he went.

Not that these two girls needed much help. Though born far apart— Fanny Jackson in slavery, Charlotte Forten in comfort—they were the same age and color, and by their late teens were gripped with a nearly identical sense of mission and a fiery resolve.

Forten wrote in her diary of reading a Charles Dickens story one Sunday, and Frederick Douglass's collected speeches the next. At age eighteen, she seethed at how her white classmates, otherwise "kind and cordial . . . feared to recognize me" in the street.

But then she wrote: "It is ignoble to despair; let us labor earnestly and faithfully to acquire knowledge, to break down the barriers of prejudice and oppression, . . . hoping and believing that if not for us, for another generation there is a better, brighter day in store, when slavery and prejudice shall vanish before the glorious light of Liberty and Truth."

Jackson became one of "the talented thousandth," as modern authors have dubbed the few Negroes in Oberlin College before 1861. Even at Oberlin, female Negro students were a curiosity that white visitors came to observe. Jackson felt their stares.

"I never rose to recite in my classes at Oberlin but I felt that I had the honor of the whole African race upon my shoulders," she wrote. "I felt that, should I fail, it would be ascribed to the fact that I was colored."

★ ★ ★

THEY GREW UP amid powerful expectations of joining their parents' quest for abolition, education, and equal rights, a quest that kept intensifying all through the 1850s. Emma Lapsansky-Werner writes that Forten, White, Jackson, and Catto were stepping into adulthood "preparing to lead the struggle for equality."

The rise of black schools and scholars was a revolution in itself. South Carolina legislators closed Payne's first school and Wesleyan collegians threatened the "forcible" ouster of Amos Beman. Armed New Hampshire farmers cut short Henry Garnet's freshman year and New Yorkers stoned Charles Reason's Free African School classmates in the street. Virginians banished Martin Delany's family for "playing school"—all examples of how William Catto's generation had bled to reach the schoolhouse door. Octavius Catto and his friends grew up believing education was their birthright.

The vast majority of black children in every region were still shut out; in the North, schools such as James Bird's and the I.C.Y. were the exception, and in most of the South, anything beyond rudimentary teaching of slave children was unlawful or out of the question. Even the luckiest were not so lucky. Rochester's school board closeted Rosetta Douglass and Philadelphia's white gangs motivated Billy Bolivar's "marathon sprints" to school. But these children came from families practiced at sifting the ashes of defeat for fresh ammunition. Rosetta's father moved her to a new school and bedeviled her old one until it integrated in 1857.

Learning was becoming the "dangerous instrument" after all. Education and equal rights were goals as closely interwoven as the reeds of a low-country basket or the gears of a Baldwin locomotive. Students aspired to teach the oppressed and to train the heart in "hatred of oppression," as Charlotte Forten wrote in a school hymn in 1855. Fanny Jackson grew fond of the expression, "Knowledge is power."

Colored classrooms sprang up in front parlors and church basements in North and South alike—the Southern efforts were more covert. ("For God's sake, don't let a slave be cotch with pencil and paper," Elijah Green of Charleston recalled. "You might as well had killed your master or missus.") A slave boy in Richmond named Anthony Burns borrowed a primer from a plantation owner's sister and once he had learned the rudiments of reading, he began teaching other slave children. A Philadelphia girl named Cordelia Jennings started a school in her mother's house as soon as she completed her senior year at the I.C.Y. and drew fifty paying pupils. A slave mother in Winchester, Virginia, entrusted her children to the Underground Railroad—and when they reached Pittsburgh safely, one of them, Sarah Miller, the same age as Octavius Catto, started a school in her room. Then she married a freeborn A.M.E. minister, Benjamin Tucker Tanner, and the couple paid a muted homage to the Ossawatomie, Kansas, raid on pro-slavery forces by naming their son Henry Ossawa, who would grow to be an artist to whom homage was paid.

Charlotte Forten and Jake White won their first teaching posts at the high schools they had attended—she in Salem, he at the I.C.Y. Octavius, two years younger, was close behind. All four of James Le Count's children, too, were preparing to teach.

Education fueled the struggle for civil rights, and the strugglers returned the favor. Colored writers from two generations touched on this in a statement prepared for Connecticut's Negro suffrage campaign in 1855. Rev. Amos Beman and the teacher Ebenezer Bassett, forty-three and twenty-one, respectively, wrote, "All people should aspire to the full attainment of their political rights whenever or wherever they are deprived of them, as the only manly course for them to pursue . . . and as the only noble example for them to set for their children."

J. W. Cromwell, an I.C.Y. pupil, grew up so infused with the dual missions that his daughter remembered learning to read from two books that, she said, "typify the things for which my father stood: sound education and the championship of right and justice." The books were a history of the Underground Railroad and an Oberlin College catalogue.

★ ★ ★

THE CONNECTICUT SUFFRAGE DRIVE that Beman and Bassett led was, like those of other states, in another Sisyphean round of not quite persuading legislators to make the franchise color-blind. At the same time, organizers in states with limited black suffrage were trying a novel tactic—candidacy.

New York state's first black candidate was John B. Vashon, a lawyer who had grown up in Pittsburgh. An impressive family, the Vashons were of the stature of the Whites or Fortens—"a dynasty of social activists," as Lapsansky-Werner describes those families. Vashon's father had founded Pittsburgh's antislavery society, headed a temperance league, and owned a bathhouse that served whites by day and sheltered fugitive slaves by night. A lawyer tutored young Vashon until he passed the New York bar examination, and the antislavery Liberty Party ran him for state attorney general in 1855. He lost.

In Ohio that year, a splinter group of antislavery Democrats nominated Langston's brother for clerk of Brownhelm Township, near Oberlin, daring voters to elect a Negro for the first time in the nation's history. John Mercer Langston was an Oberlin graduate. Though snubbed by law schools, he, too, found a tutor and passed the bar. He won.

Even the temperance drives of older men such as William Whipper and Jacob White Sr. were turning political. An essayist in 1854 envisioned sobriety less as the moral high ground and more as a way to equip his race with an army of clear-eyed men—"men to fight their battles, and contend with our enemies for our rights." The essayist was Jake White Jr., writing at age seventeen.

Jake's parents traveled the same circles as the Biases, Fortens, Cattos, Vashons, and Purvises—preachers, physicians, and merchants who led double lives as organizers and agitators. Jacob Sr., and his wife, Elizabeth, had been welcoming Underground Railroad passengers into their home for a quarter century by the time their son confronted Governor Pollock in 1855. Elizabeth was a seamstress; Jake Sr., by turns a barber, a dentist, a "bleeder" who applied the leeches and the heated glass cups used to drain infections from the bodies of the ailing. This work lent itself to Negroes treating Negroes—white physicians generally did not minister to colored patients lest their white customers revolt.

If the "cupping and leeching" failed, White Sr. offered one more service—he operated Lebanon Cemetery on Passyunk Road, one of two colored cemeteries in the region. His friend, Rev. William Catto, was on the board of directors.

The Cattos and the Whites had known each other since the late 1840s when both lived in Spring Garden, and by the middle of the 1850s, the two fathers and two sons were all but inseparable. When Catto left the A.M.E. Church in 1854, his next leap to a new pulpit brought him to First African Presbyterian, at Seventh and Shippen streets, where White Sr. was an elder. The 182 congregants voted Catto their pastor.

Elder sounded sedentary. White Sr. was more like a militating manager. When the church interior needed an overhaul to keep up with nicer-looking houses of worship, he dragooned the faithful until the funds were raised—$1,436.20, by his calculations. Frederick Douglass's blasts at cowardly clergy sounded fresh in 1848, but White Sr. had decried the churches' "deathly silence" on slavery as early as 1836. Jake Jr.'s first published essay asked Negro customers to boycott "slave-grown goods"—an admirable cause for a fifteen-year-old, but one his father had pushed since the year Jake was born.

Jake Jr. was an early writer, note-taker, and joiner. He started joining social and fraternal societies in his teens and joined fourteen in all. He usually was elected secretary, recording secretary, or corresponding secretary. He was a boy who was no great athlete but filled out the scorecards, who wrote about the race's future while saving every invitation and ticket stub as if to make a record of the past.

He was said to be "quiet, soft spoken, active and very dignified." When his beard came in, he trimmed its corners to ninety-degree angles—"square cut along the distal edge," an acquaintance wrote. This gave him an older, "almost patriarchal appearance," and along with his zeal for record keeping, set him off nicely from his shorter, younger friend, the outspoken, argumentative, charming Octavius Catto.

★ ★ ★

POLITICAL AND PRECOCIOUS as Jake was, another young person of the "better classes" was surpassing him. A *girl*. Women at political events were considered bold and brazen; Rev. William Catto tried to bar them from an 1857 meeting. Barely a generation had passed since Angelina Grimké had balanced her notes on two men's hats to address a state legislature—and she was white. Charlotte Forten was colored.

But she was a Forten, and by the time Jake White had confronted Governor Pollock, she had already walked with thousands in a protest parade. She suffered recurrent bouts of "lung fever," sadness, and self-reproach. Her widower father, Robert Bridges Forten, regularly sent her away—to the pastoral safety of her country cousins, the Robert Purvises, and then, for the sake of a superior education, to the Remonds of Salem, Massachusetts.

She took the measure of the offstage Charles Remond: His "gloomy countenance gives me fits of the blues regularly every morning. And the blues are not the pleasantest companions in the world," she wrote. But Remond's little sister, Sarah, made up for that.

Sarah Remond, turning thirty, had become a sensation on the lecture trail, upending notions of colored women's limitations and all but eclipsing her brother. She went to Britain, believing she "might for a time enjoy freedom," and there spoke of the unspeakable—male slaveholders' crimes against female slaves. In her slow, stately cadences, she likened the slaves to British needle workers, "made to 'stitch, stitch, stitch' till weariness and exhaustion overtook them." But those destitute women at least kept their babies, she said—"while the slave-woman was victim of the heartless lust of her master, and the children whom she bore were his property."

She already had a lifetime of stories to tell—of being shunned by the Salem school, barred by the Franklin Institute, and thrown down a stairs in a Boston opera house for refusing to leave the all-white "Family Circle." (The fall injured her shoulder and tore her dress; she sued and won five hundred dollars.) A typical entry in Charlotte's diary when Sarah visited: "As usual we lay awake till morning, talking about her lecturing experiences."

Not that all this was foreign to Charlotte—she had grown up amid aunts, uncles, and grandparents who had led or joined every Philadelphia antislavery and equal-rights initiative in the previous quarter century. By age seventeen she was corresponding with John Greenleaf Whittier and dining with William Lloyd Garrison, who took the occasion to explain his strategy of "nonresistant" moral suasion. She wrote that Garrison had spoken "beautifully" but had not swayed her, for, she said, "I believe in 'resistance to tyrants' . . . and would fight for liberty until death." She nearly had her chance a few days later.

Anthony Burns had been arrested in Boston in May 1854 under the Fugitive Slave Act. New England's legion of abolitionists—Garrison, Wendell Phillips, Theodore Parker, the Remonds, Ralph Waldo Emerson, Henry David Thoreau—rushed to his defense. But a commissioner ordered him sent back to Virginia. Burns, nineteen, was the slave who in boyhood had borrowed a primer, learned to read, and then taught other children. He had a scar across his face, and a broken hand with a bone poking out an inch or more.

Abolitionists of both races stormed the courthouse but failed to free him. In the melee they stabbed to death a marshal, James Batchelder. On June 2, tens of thousands of people filled Boston streets as militiamen with cannon and bayonets led a manacled Burns to a ship. His supporters decried using soldiers on a slave owner's errand, but the commanding officer, Lieutenant Darius Couch, had little patience for abolitionists. The crowd was divided—some pointed at Phillips and Parker and shouted, "Murderers of Batchelder!" Others jeered the soldiers— "Kidnapper!" Charlotte Forten and Sarah Remond stood with Anthony Burns's supporters.

A man flung cayenne pepper into the crowd; another, a bottle of vitriol. People gasped and ducked but the soldiers kept moving, their prisoner "hemmed in by a thick-set hedge of gleaming blades." A white abolitionist in the crowd, Samuel Gridley Howe, noticed "a comely coloured girl" with clenched fists and "tears streaming down her cheeks." He pushed through to reach her side and tried to console her.

It is not known whether that girl was Charlotte Forten. But she stiffened in a Forten-Purvis way when Howe tried to assure her that Virginians would not hurt Burns. *"Hurt!?"* the girl said. "I cry for shame that he will not *kill* himself! Oh! why is he not man enough?"

Of course, Burns was hurt—shackled in a Virginia cell for months and nearly starved before Northern abolitionists bought his freedom. He eventually became a minister to colored expatriates in Canada. He could have made more money—a New York promoter offered him a hundred dollars a week to tell his story to freak-show audiences. Burns said, "He wants to show me like a monkey!" and turned down the offer from P. T. Barnum.

★ ★ ★

CHARLOTTE'S HOME LIFE was contained in an elegant bubble, provisioned with novels, newspapers, and sheet music. Each Sabbath, she strolled in Salem's woods, "in perfect silence . . . [to] commune with Nature and with Nature's God." She divided her time between Salem and Philadelphia, where she stayed at her Uncle Robert's Byberry estate, with its "fine series of barns" and "magnificent orchards."

White abolitionists embraced Charlotte and her peers. Mott cousins tutored Rosetta Douglass. Ellen Wright, a Mott niece, befriended Robert Purvis's daughter Hattie at a school in New Jersey—a mixed-race boarding school, run by Theodore Weld and the Grimké sisters. "I am getting old," Hattie wrote to Ellen on the day after her seventeenth birthday. She told of tutoring her brother and sister in the house at Byberry, because in public school "they are made to sit by themselves because their faces are not as white as the rest of the scholars. Oh! Ellie how it makes my blood boil."

Charlotte's diaries, rare mementoes of black life in the nineteenth century, are shot through with the word *refused*. In the summer of 1857, she and a colored friend from Salem were denied service at a Philadelphia "ice cream saloon." They tried two other ice cream shops and were twice "refused." Her friend bought a train ticket, but a conductor pointed her to the Jim Crow car—"which she of course indignantly refused" and instead climbed off the train. "Oh, how terribly I felt," Charlotte wrote. "Could say but few words."

She craved Dickens and persevered with Tennyson ("requires study, but richly does he repay it"). And though the history books did not mention such events as the Flying Horses riot or Pennsylvania Hall, Charlotte had that history at her disposal, too, from graying aunts and uncles who had lived through those attacks.

She was still in her teens when she joined the women's antislavery society in Salem in 1855. The women knew the Forten name—her mother and her aunts had helped found the group's Philadelphia counterpart two decades earlier. In Massachusetts, Wendell Phillips thanked her personally for staying in America when other Negro allies were leaving—he said Charlotte owed that much to her grandfather James.

Violence shaped her generation. Charlotte Forten, Jake White, Octavius Catto, and their friends had been children in 1849 when the gunfire of the California House riot was heard outside the Bird school. Some were old enough to recall the temperance riot seven years earlier, or the other assaults on colored Philadelphia of the 1830s and 1840s.

At the same time, an important difference between William Catto's generation and his son's lay in their perceptions of physical danger.

Most of the older people had fled one mob or another. The leaders—Douglass, Delany, Garnet, Remond, Beman, and the Langstons, Purvises, and Fortens—had been chased and beaten and had had their mail opened, their homes surrounded, their friends imprisoned, their lives threatened, their bones broken. That had been the accepted price of black political activity; at times, even of black residential life. Their sons and daughters came to adulthood in the 1850s hearing the stories but less frequently bearing the blows.

Octavius, Charlotte, and others pointed back to a touchstone event, a blazing night, as if they were old enough to remember it. Catto and other young men once assured a fearful landlord that the days of "burning down halls in Philadelphia" were gone. That was easier said by those who had not been there.

They were becoming distanced from slavery as well. The Fortens had been free since the eighteenth century, the Whites nearly as long. The Cattos and Adgers had made their way north more recently and their memories of Charleston were just a decade old. Slavery was in the stories about their grandmothers.

The distance was great enough that Rosetta Douglass, the same age as Octavius, could write to her father complaining that her Philadelphia landlady was so strict, "I feel in bondage." Her father, whose new autobiography was titled *My Bondage and My Freedom*, must have laughed.

Rosetta wrote that all she had hoped for was "innocent fun." She said one of her recent gentleman callers was Octavius Catto—"Mr. Cato," she called him. She assured her father: "Respectable, too."

The distance was shorter for Fanny Jackson. Born in slavery, she remembered the aunt who worked for $6 a month until she could purchase her niece's freedom for $125. Jackson was born the same year as Jake and Charlotte, 1837, in a place where Negroes had come under an almost incomprehensible assault—the District of Columbia.

In 1835, a colored man named Snow had flirted with white mechanics' wives, setting off a riot that raged for days and came to be known as the Snow Storm. White men drove people out of their homes and destroyed black schools. Negroes lived in fear for months.

That was the Washington in which Fanny's life began. Her grandfather, freed by his master, had worked his way up to caterer by waiting on Washington tables, even those of Cabinet members; a customer dubbed him the city's "most experienced & fashionable waiter." He saved enough to buy his six children out of slavery. But he decided one daughter did not deserve freedom. That was Fanny's mother.

Why did he leave her in slavery? "On account of my birth," Fanny wrote in a memoir. She did not say who her father was.

Fanny was about twelve when her aunt purchased her freedom. That was in 1850, when the Fugitive Slave Act's new residency restrictions caused colored Washingtonians to move north if they could. Fanny's family sent her to relatives in New England, and she went to work in Newport, Rhode Island, for a white couple named Calvert. She stayed six years.

The Calverts were aristocrats, descended from Lord Baltimore and Mary Queen of Scots. They taught their maid little beyond the domestic arts. So Fanny used her seven-dollar monthly salary to hire a tutor, an hour a day, three days a week. She learned to play the organ at the local colored church. She rented a piano and kept it at her aunt's.

When Fanny announced she was leaving to seek formal schooling, Mrs. Calvert offered her money to stay. Fanny said no. "My life there was most happy," she wrote later, "but it was in me to get an education and to teach my people. This idea was deep in my soul. Where it came from I cannot tell, for I had never had any exhortations, nor any lectures which influenced me to take this course. It must have been born in me."

Someone told Daniel Payne of this former slave who said she yearned "to teach my people." Payne, working at his old dream of launching a Negro college, had set his thick-lensed sights on a spot in Ohio, not far from Oberlin and its dizzying abolitionism—the college celebrated West Indies Emancipation Day, August 1. (On July 4, students raised money for antislavery societies.) The school had a few Negroes among its twelve hundred students. Fanny could not afford Oberlin—so Payne helped pay her tuition.

She arrived at the Ohio campus in the summer of 1860. Oberlin, founded by Congregationalists, espoused racial tolerance. The Langston brothers taught there. Charles Langston and a white professor, Henry Peck, had led students in the 1858 rescue of a man from slave catchers, inspiring new verses in "The Cry of Millions"—"I hear the voice of Professor Peck." Still, college dons warned Fanny: If her presence in class discomfited white students, she would be asked to leave. She boarded with the Pecks.

Fanny never spoke of her father (he was said to be a white politician in Washington, a Southerner) and rarely of her childhood. One day, "at Mrs. Peck's, when we girls were sitting on the floor getting out our Greek," a white girl from Maine "looked up from her textbook and all at once blurted out, 'Fanny Jackson, were you ever a slave?'"

Fanny said yes. The Maine girl burst into tears. They did not talk about it again, Fanny wrote, "but those tears seemed to wipe out a little of what was wrong."

★ ★ ★

IN COLORED COMMUNITIES as old as Philadelphia's and as new
as San Francisco's, young men joined their fathers in literary societies
with such estimable goals as "diffusion of knowledge, mental assistance,
moral and intellectual improvement" and rules against drink and "profane
swearing." In this, they differed little from the Bonneau Society's call for
"Improvement of Our Mental Faculties" in Charleston a quarter century
earlier. But the Bonneau society could not have chanced a debate such as
the one staged in Philadelphia on August 2, 1854: Would the downfall of
the republic "be beneficial to the interest of the Colored People?" Or this
lecture, from a minister with Underground Railroad connections: "Does
the Bible Sanction Slavery?"

The sponsor of both events was the Alexandrian Literary Institute.
The group was casting about for a new name—Negroes were naming
everything from sons to sewing clubs for the race's heroes (one I.C.Y. pupil
was Toussaint L'Ouverture Martin). Underlining a belief in marrying aca-
deme to advocacy, the Alexandrians renamed themselves for Benjamin
Banneker. The late Negro astronomer, mathematician, and surveyor who
had helped draw the District of Columbia's lines won Thomas Jefferson's
friendship and nonetheless accused Jefferson of contravening his most
famous words ("created equal") by owning slaves. Fifty-eight Philadelphia
colored men were dues-paying members of the Banneker Literary Institute
by 1856.

The organization spent eighty-seven cents to frame its disciplinary
rules and post them on the wall of the rented meeting room. "Indecorous
language" was banned, as was standing up or exiting without prior approval
of the chairman. The rules were often enforced with evangelistic zeal.
Banneker minutes for 1856 list twenty members expelled for infractions.

There were Banneker committees on discipline and debates, the
library and the open-to-the-public evening lectures. Attendance was
totaled and averaged. Sometimes the averages sagged—the annual report
for 1857 says that an average of 10 members came to the weekly meetings; 10.5 attended evening lectures; the debates, a lonely 2.8. But a lecture on the antislavery movement drew a crowd. When the minister spoke
on whether the Bible sanctioned slavery, the house was full.

Nothing was simple in the Bannekers' universe. When a black me-
chanic sent word that he had invented a new fire extinguisher ("a credit to

our race," he predicted), the Bannekers appointed a committee, which in turn proposed a concert to raise money for the inventor's efforts and suggested advancing this idea by creating another committee. There was a committee on zoology.

One of the society's founders was William Catto, now in his mid-forties. That placed him in the Bannekers' old guard. The younger ranks included Jake White Jr. He ascended to the post of secretary and soon was churning out handwritten minutes, memoranda of code-of-conduct infractions, and annual reports.

"To those who have been with us in all our trials and difficulties I would say, persevere," White wrote in 1857. "A bright day shall yet dawn upon us and . . . the Banneker Institute will be looked up to as the source from which emanates light and knowledge, and the names of those who have labored to place her in that high position will be handed down with grateful recollections to an enlightened posterity." He was nineteen.

Younger still was the boy whose Banneker application was rejected despite ties of family and friendship. Too young, the membership committee told an impatient Octavius Catto. The committee suggested he reapply when he finished high school.

His efforts to join the Bannekers became a kind of template for him. Ask, argue, be denied, ask again, argue again, eventually win the day. Or, in defeat, win admirers. Banneker members had voted him down but had also invited him to try again.

Persistence, persuasion—they knew where he had acquired those talents. They had seen that "quieter and more persuasive way" his father delivered a sermon, a suffrage speech, a tirade against colonization.

Sometimes Octavius turned impatient at a rebuff and walked away on "pedestals," as he once said of a younger boy's haughty airs. More often, he kept asking and arguing until people rolled their eyes and said yes.

★ ★ ★

BY OCTAVIUS'S JUNIOR YEAR, the I.C.Y.'s reliance on colored teachers for colored pupils had drawn so much notice that visitors from other states came to gaze and gawk. The scenes resembled Fanny Jackson's Oberlin classes—except the only whites were visitors.

A white Maryland minister used the I.C.Y. to rebut the better-off-as-slaves theory. Writing in 1857, Rev. John Dixon Long dared Southerners to observe Philadelphia Negroes—"their 18 to 20 churches [and] . . .

their classical high school, with its colored professors from New England and Jamaica—a school such as I have never seen on the Eastern Shore of Maryland."

A new principal in 1855 replaced Charles Reason, who had married a woman from New York and moved there to run a school. The I.C.Y. managers published another notice asking colored teachers to apply, and Ebenezer Bassett, one of the young leaders of suffrage drives in Connecticut, raised his hand.

Ebenezer Don Carlos Bassett was the son of a Pequot Indian and a mulatto slave. He had bronze skin, wavy hair, and a well-twirled mustache, causing one writer to say he looked more like a Spanish dance instructor than a school principal. He knew the classics and had charmed his way into two years of Yale classes before the college officially integrated. He seemed an altogether fitting successor to Reason: Already he had headed up a small grammar school in New Haven and helped Rev. Amos Beman agitate for the vote.

In 1854, Bassett wrote his U.S. senator a query. Senator Francis Gillette of Connecticut replied, "I am under the sad necessity of saying, that free persons of color coming into [Washington] . . . are presumed by the laws to be absconding slaves, and are liable to be arrested, and if unable to prove their freedom, to be sold into slavery for life to pay their jail fees." Gillette's letter—which Bassett forwarded to Frederick Douglass's newspaper—warned that any Negro visiting Washington needed letters of reference from whites. Bassett's torpedo had hit its mark, exposing the perils free Negroes faced, not in Charleston or New Orleans but in the nation's capital.

The I.C.Y.'s new principal was barely older than his pupils. The notice of his hiring in November 1855 did not mention that he had just turned twenty-two.

Bassett added trigonometry, higher algebra, Latin, and Greek to the curriculum; he did not share Reason's passion for the sciences. He left that to the new head of the I.C.Y. sciences department—who was a man of the hemisphere. A printer's son, born in Jamaica, Robert Campbell was a free spirit who had run a school in Kingston and taught in Central America before he came north.

I.C.Y. teachers, like most schoolteachers, might specialize in one subject but teach three or four. Bassett taught mathematics, natural sciences, and the classics, and about once a year gave an evening lecture titled

"The Atmosphere (Illustrated with Experiments)." Campbell, desiring to sharpen his science background, bought tickets to a series of seminars at the Franklin Institute in 1856. The tickets were slow to arrive. Campbell asked once, twice, thrice—and finally was told Negroes were not welcome. He asked whether the museum's directors supported this policy. The directors gave an indirect answer. They offered Campbell a free pass as a science teacher, "under the circumstances."

Campbell seized on this. Did the museum always offer passes to science teachers? No. In that case, Campbell replied, "under the circumstances" he would not accept free admission. "I could not without making a sacrifice of principle," he wrote to the I.C.Y. board. The board mollified him by getting the University of Pennsylvania to let him audit science courses—thus integrating that all-white college, if only briefly.

Other countries and cultures fascinated Campbell. He was an unlikely nineteenth-century man, having already lived and worked on two continents, and his travels were not over. In old I.C.Y. faculty portraits, he is the man in the turban.

★ ★ ★

BASSETT BUILT ON Reason's intermingling of academia and advocacy. He went to abolition meetings and wrote letters to editors. He likened an antislavery oration by Senator Charles Sumner of Massachusetts to a speech by Demosthenes twenty centuries earlier. He kept the I.C.Y. lecture invitations going out to the likes of Remond, Garnet, and Douglass.

Generally, the I.C.Y. managers gave Bassett leeway, even lending him money as his young family grew. When Douglass agreed to speak at the school, however, the board asked Bassett to limit the lecturer's topic to the "peaceable principles of Friends."

Limit *Frederick Douglass*? I think not, the principal replied. Speakers such as Douglass and Garnet were "a continued and unanswerable argument in behalf of the ability, energy and worth of the colored race," Bassett wrote to the managers, "and their presence in the community cannot but be beneficial to their own people, as well as to others." The I.C.Y. was becoming a hub of the black intelligentsia.

The principal assigned extra work if he thought his pupils too sluggish. ("Mr. Bassett is mad as a bug," J. W. Cromwell wrote after a class.) Rote answers were not good enough for Bassett—colored pupils had to learn to think on their feet.

His efforts bore fruit. A visiting educator marveled at the poise and preparation of I.C.Y. students in the public examinations before commencement. Bassett heard from families, too. "You cannot think how proud I am of that Institute, and how grateful I am to the managers for its library, its schools, its lectures, and its colored teachers," a parent wrote. "Oh, it is a great thing for our people."

Even the managers boasted that their experiment was drawing "the attention of intelligent persons in various parts of the country." Visits by Southerners presented Bassett with a wry opportunity. He took to showcasing his darkest charges, his blackest blacks. A colleague remembered Bassett's telling and retelling the story of one visit.

The guest had written a book offering scientific proof of Negro inferiority. He had heard "of the wonderful achievements of this Negro school" and brought a mathematician along to challenge Bassett's top pupils.

Jesse Ewing Glasgow Jr. was a whitewasher's son, an eager student, a future Banneker member, and Octavius's and Jake's beloved friend. He also was described as a "very black boy." Bassett called him to the blackboard.

"Just as fast as they gave him the problems," Jesse solved them on the blackboard "with the greatest ease. . . . This decided the fate of the book, then in manuscript form, which, as far as we know, was never published."

* * *

JESSE GLASGOW WENT on to college. Most American colleges turned Negroes away, but the University of Edinburgh offered a scholarship and by decade's end the "very black boy" was studying in Scotland, besting white classmates to win prize after prize.

His journey embodied one of the sweeter ironies of the 1850s. For Negroes who found the means to leave, exotic avenues beckoned, each promising a version of freedom somewhere else.

Martin Delany, ever more certain Africa was the answer, published a notice seeking volunteers for a trek up the twenty-six-thousand-mile Niger River, with the aim of securing enough arable, cotton-friendly land to support a nation of former American Negroes. Not a colony—a nation. Delany was clear on that. Douglass and Payne thought he had gone soft-headed; the I.C.Y.'s Robert Campbell saw the notice and volunteered. Entire towns in Canada West, as Ontario was called, became havens for colored expatriates. So many were farmers, merchants and hotel keepers in Amherst-burg, near Detroit, that people said "$400,000 worth of Southern slaves were walking the streets."

Two of Robert Adger Sr.'s fourteen children ventured from the family's South Street used-goods emporium to the far side of the world. An 1850s gold rush had attracted a handful of colored Americans to Australia, where British law made slavery illegal. James Adger opened "a first-class hair-dressing saloon, being favoured by the Governor and gentry of Sydney." Daniel Adger visited, basking in the novelty of freewheeling chats with passengers and crew on the voyage across two oceans. A British traveler predicted young Adger would enjoy Australia and asked him: "Why don't more of the colored people leave for parts where they can have better rights?"

Foreign places promised more than legal freedoms and paid employment. They promised *manhood*. In that word, David Blight writes, "the combined anguish and hope of generations met and found meaning."

Most states, North and South, denied Negroes the basic stones of the civil mosaic: the right to testify, to serve on juries, ride public conveyances, and vote. Even the Quakers "aid in giving us a partial education—but never in a Quaker school, beside their own children," Samuel Ringgold Ward said. "Whatever they do for us savors of pity, and is done at arm's length." Denial of a museum ticket or a seat on a train hurt Charlotte Forten less than the averted glances of white schoolmates when they saw her on Salem streets. "These are but trifles, certainly to the great, public wrongs which we as a people are obliged to endure," she wrote in her diary. "But to those who experience them, these apparent trifles are most wearing and discouraging."

Finally, there was the violence that white Northern men periodically visited on their colored neighbors. Like a disease in remission, the attacks had ebbed in the 1850s but had never gone away. A white Cincinnati gang's assault on a black home compelled a young colored man, William Parham, to write this to his friend Jake White Jr.: "I have almost concluded to go to Jamaica. What think you of it? . . . I shall [likely] make an effort to get out of this slavery-cursed and Negro-hating country as soon as I can. . . . My dear friend, you do not know how much I yearn to be a *man*, & having found that I can only be so by leaving the country, I am willing to accept the conditions."

★ ★ ★

MOST BUSINESS at the monthly meetings of the Philadelphia Presbytery was routine. Ministers and lay elders considered whether to grant a
preacher permission to transfer to a pulpit elsewhere, or to nominate a
man for mission work among the Indians, the Africans, even the Italians.
But on this occasion, the chairman announced that the only colored minister in the room had started writing a book.

This was the exotic avenue William Catto chose in 1857. Not leaving the country—he had flirted with that Africa business before—but
embarking on a trek around the city that would put him in rarified air with
the Delanys and Douglasses and some two dozen other American Negro
writers who had gotten books into print.

He was writing a history of First African Presbyterian Church, "and
the Presbytery cordially recommend the volume to the patronage of all
who feel an interest in the welfare of the African race." First African was
marking a milestone—fifty years' existence in a city not altogether accepting of Negro churches. The book would include "sketches" of each of Philadelphia's seventeen other colored houses of worship.

Catto, in his late forties, professed to be comfortable with the Presbyterians. He said their interpretations of scripture "are addressed more to
the conviction of the conscience and understanding of the people, than to
the prejudices and passions; . . . they are, however, good cultivators, and
though their growth may be slow, yet they are sure and steady." The son on
whom he had pinned his hopes was in a well-regarded school with colored
teachers and had the prospect of future admission to the city's best colored literary society—both enterprises in which William Catto had played
a part. With Octavius thus ensconced, he could embark on a project of
his own.

He trudged around Philadelphia, gathering data on all eighteen Negro
churches, identifying founders, totaling the number of Sabbath schools,
teachers, lecture rooms, communicants. He listed seating capacities, building materials, property values. By August 1857, he was sending out a letter
offering the slender 111-page book for twenty-five cents, or five for a dollar.

A Semi-Centenary Discourse, neither riveting nor polemic, received
favorable if brief notice in religious journals. Catto's prose relied heavily on
the words *neat*, *brick*, and *edifice* and provided facts to chroniclers of black
life for decades to come.

He sketched Bethel A.M.E., the biggest of the eighteen churches, as "a large brick edifice substantially built, plain, but neat; it is 62 feet wide, 70 feet long, with a basement story divided into a lecture room, class rooms, and minister's study with a library attached. Church & lot where it sits worth $60,000, a low estimate. Audience room can seat 2,500. Church has 1,100 communicant members . . . Sabbath school containing 350 children, 2 superintendents, and 25 teachers (11 males and 14 females)."

Catto listed the A.M.E. bishops, among them two Charleston men who had come North before him: Morris Brown, whose Charleston church had been demolished in the wake of the Vesey terror; and Daniel Payne, who had been so disappointed with Catto's brief tenure at the A.M.E. Book Concern.

Catto's tour from church to church was like his ministerial career in miniature. By the time his book was published, he had switched faiths three times and had preached in at least eight towns and cities in four states. He had moved his family in an age when intercity travel was tedious and trying—rocky by sea, bumpy by stage, sooty by rail—and more so for those confined to cargo rooms and "pauper cars." Negroes moving from city to city became well acquainted with Jim Crow.

The book began with the sermon Catto delivered on the church's fiftieth anniversary. He offered the history of its twists and turns, the names of the founders, and—tipping his hat to the efforts of the elder Jacob White—the cost of the improvements. He made little reference to slavery or politics, except to invite his audience to identify with an earlier people striving for liberation. All knew the story of the Hebrews, "their final departure from Egypt to a land of freedom, the land of Canaan, where they could worship God under their own vine and fig-tree, none to molest or make them afraid."

Then he eased into present tense. "We can well imagine what their hopes and anticipations were when they found their journey toward the promised land really begun, as in their tribes and families they take up the line of march."

The *Discourse* became Catto's legacy, his contribution to the cloth of common remembrance—his neat, brick edifice.

★ ★ ★

HALF A BLOCK west of Catto's pulpit, the neighborhood's newly elected alderman was setting up his court. Passersby on Eighth Street hallooed congratulations. The alderman waved a thick arm, though in his nickedup fighter's visage a smile was not always easy to detect. It was also hard to tell whether Bull McMullen was carrying his dagger.

His "court" consisted of a wooden desk in the front room of his rented house at 730 South Eighth. A desk, a door, a name respected in the neighborhood was all an alderman needed. As for the dagger: he'd carried one now and then since the nativist mobs of 1844.

His house was well placed—a few feet from the local police station, a few more from the tavern he had opened at Eighth and Emeline streets in 1854 (amid the "Temperance Fever"—*that* showed the reformers) and five doors from the Moyamensing Hose House. This spot was an easy walk for his Irish constituents, and was within a block of the Adgers' store, the Quakers' colored high school, and other Negro meeting places. Not that the alderman cared so much, since those people could not vote.

The territory had changed under William McMullen's boots. The police department had been stocked with nativists by a nativist mayor, then expanded to an army of a thousand officers, modernized by telegraph wires and freed to enter the old townships. The townships were no more, tucked under the city's expanded municipal awning by the Consolidation Act of 1854. Moyamensing and Southwark became the Fourth Ward.

The Negroes had grown in number and insolence to where the new alderman could barely look out his front window without seeing a colored waiter, preacher, or teacher roll by, or a scrubbed-up child running home from school. The famine had sent more indigent Irish his way than even McMullen could place in jobs or houses or twelve-and-a-half-cent rooms that slept six men, side by side, renting their sliver of floor for two cents a night. But they were his people; they relied on him for the odd favor, and he on them for votes.

He had been accused in 1852 of faking Irishmen's naturalization papers by the hundreds, in order to have them vote. The nativist police had stormed his Keystone Club over that one, arresting him but only after he had backed them down with the sharp point of his dirk.

The old time fire companies, too, now found themselves contending with endless deprecations from grand juries, editorialists, and "municipal reformers"—the one species McMullen might despise more than nativists and Negroes.

McMullen, in his thirties, was already a survivor of mythic proportion. He had endured riots, arrests, firemen's wars, the Mexican War, and murder attempts by the Protestants of Shiffler Hose, who never doubted that he had killed George Shiffler in 1844. A Shiffler Hose man—the lucky fellow who had drawn lots for the glory of murdering McMullen—twice fired on him from close range in 1852. Twice, the carefully tested pistol misfired, leading the shooter to declare that McMullen was "protected by the Evil One. "

In the mayoral election of 1856, a Democrat named Richard Vaux calculated that the way to overcome his patrician Quaker roots was to throw in with McMullen and his "roughs" from Company No. 27, the Moyamensing Hose.

Up and down the ballot, Democrats in Pennsylvania were having a good year. The state party's newspaper, the *Pennsylvanian*, said the fledgling Republican Party was too busy helping the Negroes to lift a finger for the white workingman. Slavery was a necessary "form of race control," the paper argued. Freeing the slaves, now thought to number more than three million, would "jeopardize the peace, safety, & prosperity of Southern whites; a war of race would inevitably break out." The *Pennsylvanian* asked readers which fate would be better for the Negroes: "freedom, followed by speedy extermination—or mild slavery, accompanied with health & happiness?"

This "mild slavery" argument was important, because the newspaper reflected the views of the state's top Democrat, James Buchanan, who was running for president.

Buchanan's opponents, the Republicans, were a party born in reaction to a single act of Congress. The measure sounded harmless enough—the Kansas Nebraska Act—but its effect was to destroy the Missouri Compromise.

The growth of the territories west of Missouri and the national push for a railroad connecting California to the East led to a sectional battle over where the eastern terminus of that railroad should be—in the South or in the North. The Democratic senator from Illinois, Stephen A. Douglas, lobbied for Chicago as the eastern end. And he offered a carrot to Southern colleagues in 1854—throw out the Missouri Compromise and its ban on slavery north of Missouri, and permit residents of Kansas and Nebraska to choose whether they wanted slavery or not. This "popular sovereignty," as Douglas called it, sparked the violent clashes over slavery that others called "Bleeding Kansas."

The Republicans shied away from campaigning as abolitionists, but Buchanan did his best to affix that label. Democrats had to remind voters that "the Union is in danger," he told an ally. He said all Republicans were "Black Republicans" and "disunionists" and said that charge "must be reiterated again and again."

For their part, Republicans tried to persuade workingmen that slave labor undercut free man's wages. Don't be fooled when a Southerner says "niggerism is the only element in the contest," Judge William Kelley of Philadelphia exhorted. What if your boss owned *you*? "Think of it, my fellow citizens, you who earn your bread by the sweat of your brow. Think of it, sons of mechanics, laboring men."

Some Republicans tried to appeal to white Southern workers. Simon Cameron, running for Senate in Pennsylvania, wrote: "These poor white men . . . who are our brothers, and our natural allies, must be taught . . . that we are battling for their rights. They will learn in time, that by acting with us, they will cease to be the 'mudsills of society.'"

But in North and South alike, laboring men favored the Democrats in 1856. By year's end James Buchanan was crafting his inaugural message, and his fellow Democrat, Vaux, was being sworn in as mayor of Philadelphia. (Too bad only white men could vote, the colored janitor and messenger Amos Webber wrote in his diary; he'd gladly have voted against Vaux and the other Democrats. *"Demagoges,"* he called them.)

Vaux and Buchanan owed their victory margins in the city to Bull McMullen. As mayor, Vaux thanked him by hiring Moyamensing Hose men into jobs where their know-how in street fights served them well. He made them police officers.

He had even offered to make McMullen a lieutenant—but McMullen declined, instead joining the Board of Prison Inspectors, who toured the jails Wednesdays and Saturdays and had the power to free a prisoner early, or keep another late. (Vaux understood—he'd been an inspector himself.) And McMullen had made his triumphal run for alderman, defeating a rich incumbent.

An alderman was something like a justice of the peace—a neighborhood judge, mediator, and sheriff rolled into one. The position was coveted. If on a Tuesday you freed a man you had sentenced on Monday to thirty days' jail for public drunkenness, you were likely to have certain generosities offered to you. All manner of litigants crowded in; spectators came to hoot at the burglars, leer at the prostitutes, mimic the immigrants, and giggle at the drunks. In alderman's court, the theater was lively and the price was right.

A desk, a door, a respected name. Neighbors would soon crowd into McMullen's front room with their claims. A Negro bootblack from Emeline Street, an Irish stevedore out of work in the bank panic and staving off eviction. A landlord with a billy in his sleeve, ready to do the evicting; drinkers and temperancers, policemen and probationers, neighbors of every color and class—they would all be coming to his court.

After a while, he decorated the wall with a portrait of James Buchanan.

★ ★ ★

ON MARCH 4, 1857, Buchanan assured the thousands at his inauguration that American slavery's future in the West was neither a presidential nor a congressional matter but "a judicial question, which legitimately belongs to the Supreme Court." This was a curious view to air in the building where Congress had crafted the Missouri Compromise, the 1850 Compromise, the Fugitive Slave Act, and the Kansas Nebraska Act. What was the new president thinking?

That became clear two days later. Amid the blooming of colored schools, colored politics, and hopes for colored rights, the Supreme Court ruled 7 to 2 that colored Americans had no rights.

In the majority opinion in *Dred Scott*, Chief Justice Roger Taney, a seventy-nine-year-old pro-slavery man from Maryland, decreed that Negroes "are not included, and were not intended to be included, under the word 'citizens' in the Constitution." Nor did the Declaration of Independence apply to them, for they were "so far inferior that they had no rights which the white man was bound to respect."

The decision incinerated with one match every pending suffrage petition and discrimination suit in the land, and extended the Constitution's protective armor to every black law and Jim Crow exclusion.

Another justice, reflecting later, said Taney's thinking resembled that of Washington's past architects of slavery solutions, from John C. Calhoun back to the founding fathers: a desire not to address the volatile question of the rightness or wrongness of slavery but to calm the nation down. Taney believed the court could "quiet all agitation on the question of slavery in the territories" by ruling that Congress had no say in it.

William H. Seward rose on the Senate floor to allege that the decision was the fruit of a conspiracy to protect and expand slavery. He claimed

Taney had found a kindred pro-slavery spirit in Buchanan. The president's inaugural audience had been "unaware of the import of the whisperings carried on between the President and the Chief Justice," Seward said. He pointed out that the ruling was announced just two days later.

Buchanan furiously denied Seward's claims, though clues suggested the new president had advance word of the ruling. Conspiracy or no, Roger Taney's court had issued as law the same message J. J. Gurney had heard as lore, in Philadelphia streets a generation earlier, in the tale of the white boy who took the black boy's marbles and said, "You have no rights now." The court had even used the same words. *No rights.*

The difference was that the black child in Gurney's story "submitted in silence."

★ ★ ★

BLACK AND WHITE abolitionists climbed rostrums again. Their words had razor edges. "The time has gone by for colored people to talk of patriotism," Charles Remond said in New York. "We owe no allegiance to a country which grinds us under its iron heel and treats us like dogs." At another meeting, in New Bedford, Massachusetts, he called for a simple declaration "that we defy the *Dred Scott* decision." He nearly persuaded a majority to support the idea Garnet had been derided for in 1843: a call for the slaves to revolt.

In Pittsburgh, Rev. Benjamin Tanner, who had succeeded William Catto as A.M.E. book steward, announced he would "remove to Canada in the name of God"; another speaker urged all Pittsburgh Negroes to do likewise. A New Haven speaker advocated an exodus to "a black man's country," Haiti. A colored Cleveland businessman incorporated a land company with intentions of founding a colony in Central America. A Missouri congressman requested federal grants for the same purpose. Robert Purvis said in Philadelphia that *Dred Scott* confirmed "the already well-known fact that under the Constitution and Government of the United States, the colored people are nothing."

In Boston, organizers responded by creating Crispus Attucks Day on the anniversary of the 1770 Boston Massacre, in which Attucks, a black man, was first to fall. The event included speakers of both races, and a new colored choir, the Attucks Glee Club. Charlotte Forten traveled from Salem to hear the club sing her parody of "Columbia the Gem of the Ocean," a song known in those days as "The Red, White and Blue."

Oh! When shall every child of our Father,
Whatever his nation or hue
Be protected in all thy dominions
'Neath the folds of the Red, White and Blue?

Frederick Douglass declared *Dred Scott* a triumph for the Supreme Court's "slaveholding wing." The *Provincial Freeman's* editor, Mary Ann Shadd Cary, saw a vindication of her decision to leave Pennsylvania for Canada. "Your national ship is rotten and sinking," she wrote, addressing fellow Negroes back in the states. "Why not leave it?"

Wait and sift the ashes, William Still counseled. "Great evils must be consummated, that good might come."

★ ★ ★

IN PHILADELPHIA, a national conference of colored Presbyterian and Congregationalist ministers resolved that *Dred Scott* was meant "to degrade and rob the free people of color of civil and political rights, to perpetuate Slavery" and was "a sin against God, and a crime against humanity." The ministers saluted the two dissenting justices by name.

That October 1857 conference amounted to a three-day, five-state civil rights convention, a reunion of such preachers as Garnet, Beman, and Catto. Garnet, who had finally given up on Jamaica, came down from his Shiloh Church pulpit in New York City. Beman came from New Haven, Bias and Catto from the city.

After the *Dred Scott* resolutions were voted, Catto moved to have churches recruit students for Oberlin and "all other institutions of learning which open their doors" to all races. That meant three colleges in all. No one dissented. He also heard his book on the churches praised by the most famous man in the room: "Rev. Mr. Garnet moved that the Convention take great pleasure in recommending to the churches, the Rev. William T. Catto's *Semi-Centenary Discourse*."

Catto let the group know that he had "had the pleasure of presenting a copy of his book to the President of the United States," and that Buchanan himself "recommended it." Strange—to hear a colored abolitionist tout the same president who had applauded *Dred Scott*. But he was the president, after all.

That same week, the chairman of the Philadelphia Presbytery announced that Catto had "received a call" from another colored congregation to serve as its pastor. The church was Fifteenth Street Presbyterian—in Washington, D.C. The chairman asked Catto: What think you of this?

Catto said he "felt it to be his duty, when the way was prepared, to accept the call." The way was prepared. The Presbytery commended him to its Washington counterpart "as a member in good standing with us." This routine step also equipped Catto with the pass every Negro needed in the nation's capital, a letter of reference from whites.

With his book in print, his son in school, and his pass in his pocket, William T. Catto was on the move again.

★ ★ ★

A FEW MONTHS after the colored ministers' 1857 conference, a smaller meeting convened in Philadelphia. Douglass came from Rochester, Garnet from New York. They met with William Still and a white abolitionist at the home of the colored coal broker, Stephen Smith, on Lombard Street. Another rendezvous of giants—the richest Negro in the city, the race's two greatest orators and a leader of the Underground Railroad.

Such a meeting usually drew notice in the colored press. But years passed before the colored participants told of this rendezvous with a white abolitionist. Douglass observed that when his allies mentioned this man, "their voices would drop to a whisper."

★ ★ ★

THE CONDEMNATION OF SLAVERY and *Dred Scott* that the colored Presbyterians had issued was a rarity for clergy of either race in the late 1850s. Preachers had to think twice about triggering the wrath of mobs outside—and higher-ups inside. In Philadelphia they thought about Rev. Dudley A. Tyng.

The Episcopalians had moved young Tyng from his Cincinnati posting in 1855 to run the Church of the Epiphany at Fifteenth and Chestnut streets, where his father had once been pastor. Against warnings from the church's board of vestry, Tyng preached antislavery sermons. Word of this internal dispute got out, and on a Sunday night when the popular young minister rose to address this matter, the pews were full.

Tyng went down a list of the nation's ills until he came to slavery. This evil implicated "all who are party to it, great and small, North and South," he said. Then he revealed that well-heeled worshippers had privately implored him to drop this subject. Now everyone leaned forward to hear. Tyng was telling church secrets.

He said the message had come from Philadelphians "of the highest standing." He said their entreaties gave him a glimpse of "how all-pervading was the power of slavery." A prominent physician on the vestry board stood up and interrupted. Some matters were "inappropriate" for sermons, the vestryman said. But Tyng kept speaking.

One worshipper of some renown, Pierce Butler, quit Epiphany rather than hear Tyng preach abolition. And two weeks after the sermon on the nation's ills, Tyng was replaced—by an Episcopal minister from South Carolina. Almost immediately, word spread that the new pastor had slaves of his own.

Many in Tyng's flock marched out with him and helped him start a splinter church. A Boston publisher reprinted his antislavery sermons. Sarah Remond told his story on her British lecture tour. She and others Tyng supporters said the real culprit in his ouster was a city that winked at slavery.

Tyng "is a young man, and his courage in advocating the cause of antislavery in the city of his residence cannot be duly appreciated by those at a distance," the *Cincinnati Christian Leader* said. Philadelphia "is a city of merchants who trade with the South, and the love of gain has eaten all sympathy with the wretched slave."

The leader of the effort against Tyng was actually more than a merchant with southern customers. Pierce Butler had inherited his family's rice and cotton plantations in the Georgia low country, and with them, nine hundred slaves.

Butler had cut a dashing figure in Philadelphia, marrying the British Shakespearean actress Fanny Kemble. But she had divorced him, having grown fed up with his profligate ways and his owning of slaves.

His financial advisers sat Butler down at the end of 1858 and told him he would have to liquidate some assets to cover his debts.

★ ★ ★

FOR BLACK ABOLITIONISTS, "there were many signs of hope in the political storm over slavery in the 1850s," David Blight has written. "But in neither North nor South could black leaders escape the daunting realities of racism." The same was true for the aspiring young leaders in Octavius

Catto's generation. This paradox of hopeful signs and brutal reminders intensified as the decade rolled to a close.

For Banneker Institute men, the reminders began in January 1858, when a letter for Jake White Jr. arrived with a New Orleans postmark.

The sender was George E. Stephens, a Banneker member and a close friend of White's. He had taken temporary work on a government ship and wrote as the voyage to southern ports was nearing its completion.

Stephens was the son of free Negroes who had come to Philadelphia in 1832, the year before he was born. He would have been born in eastern Virginia, but his parents and hundreds of other black families had rushed from there, fleeing the waves of repression that followed Nat Turner's murderous uprising.

In Philadelphia, Stephens lived with his parents in a brick house on Currant Alley. He learned cabinetmaking from his father, but when he cast about for apprenticeships with carpenters in the city, none would hire him. That was a common fate for would-be colored tradesmen. The Abolition Society, surveying the city's able-bodied Negroes in 1856, found more than a third "compelled to abandon their trades on account of the unrelenting prejudice against their color." An employer who hired them often found his white workers throwing down tools in protest. And that was in good times. Stephens happened to be job-hunting in the Panic of 1857–1858.

He took a short-term job as a ship's carpenter for the U.S. Coastal Survey. The iron-hulled *Walker* steamed down the Delaware in November 1857 and followed the turns of the Atlantic coast, its crew sounding the depths and charting the Gulf Stream's currents.

This made Stephens a temporary citizen of that bracing, equalizing world of sailors at sea, where the pay was steady, the food bearable, and "no distinction as to color," as another friend of Jake White's wrote from a Pacific whaling ship.

On December 2, 1857, the *Walker* made landfall for two weeks in the port of Charleston. Stephens was sent ashore to purchase fresh supplies.

He walked about the city for several days. In King Street, he passed slave markets; he could hear the auctioneers. His heartbeat quickened and he tried to avert his eyes. He saw a scene at dockside quite like what the Cape Cod sailor Austin Bears, had seen in the 1820s—two hundred Negroes, "half-clad filthy looking men and women" standing in silence, about to be marched onto barges and carried upriver. Stephens wrote that

Charleston was the "half-way house on the pathway of wrong to the region of the damned."

He ran into a colored man he knew—a free, well-off man named William McKinlay, who had gone to school in Philadelphia. Relieved to see a familiar face, Stephens took out cigars and proposed to celebrate their chance reunion in Charleston with a smoke.

McKinlay drew back as if the cigars were diseased.

He explained to Stephens: Local law imposed twenty lashes for Negroes who lit pipes or cigars, carried a cane, or spoke or sang too loudly in the street. For accidentally bumping a white passerby, Stephens wrote to Jake White, "they would have had me flogged."

★　★　★

ANOTHER MEMBER of the rising black generation was in Charleston in those days. Robert Smalls had been born a few weeks after Octavius Catto and forty miles south, in Beaufort. Smalls, too, had shown his intelligence at an early age and was learning all he could. The difference was that Smalls was a slave.

He and his mother and sisters were owned by Beaufort planters named McKee. Smalls suspected patriarch John McKee might be his father. His mother worked as a domestic in the McKee home, a rambling house shaded by live oaks and overlooking Beaufort's harbor.

As rice planters went, the McKees—like the Butlers in nearby Georgia—were considered humane. They had a woman teach the slaves rudiments of reading and writing—discreetly, in the light of the black laws. They had Robert Smalls work on their boats. He learned to navigate the shoal-laden harbors, and the rivers that were thoroughfares for commerce, moving slaves inland for harvests and rice downriver to the mills.

Smalls was a boy when his owner began letting him hire out to Charleston tradesmen, dividing his pay with his master. By 1856 he walked the streets unguarded; he told of slipping into meetings of Negro "secret societies," as he called them. Those groups, such as the Bonneaus and Brown Fellows, had their tiny libraries for "literary improvement," but for all intents and purposes Smalls had no access to books. Close as he was in age to freeborn children, such as Octavius Catto, he was light years behind them in formal education.

But he knew how to steer a boat through Charleston harbor.

★ ★ ★

ON THE THIRTEENTH DAY of the *Walker*'s fourteen-day visit, Charleston authorities learned that a free black sailor was walking the streets. George Stephens was arrested.

Notwithstanding the past efforts of lawyers from Boston and London and the edicts of federal courts, the Negro Seamen's Act of 1822 was still the law of South Carolina. Visiting black sailors could still be incarcerated, even enslaved.

A *Walker* lieutenant with Charleston relatives learned of the arrest and prevailed upon city officials to let the prisoner go.

Stephens wrote to Jake White Jr. three weeks later. "You, sir, have not perhaps been south of Masons and Dixons line, and Judge slavery therefore by the testimony you receive," his letter said. "You must witness it in all its loathsomeness. You must become a witness yourself. . . . The finger of God is laid upon Charleston."

★ ★ ★

BY THE TIME Stephens returned from the South, his fellow Bannekers were full of anticipation. They had applied to join Philadelphia's citywide league of literary societies. Belonging was a stamp of approval from learned men; integrating the all-white league would be a victory for the Bannekers and for colored intellectuals everywhere. In April, the league sent a delegation to observe their activities and look over their books.

Jake White Jr., monitoring the application's progress, invited the league's men to sit in on a Banneker Institute evening debate. The subject was the Kansas-Nebraska Act of 1854. George Stephens was arguing against the act.

He had plenty of ground to cover. By reintroducing slavery in territory stamped "free" in the 1820 and 1850 compromises, the act had rocked the national boat almost to capsizing. The prime sponsor, Senator Douglas of Illinois, observed that he could ride from Boston to Chicago "by the light of my own effigy." The effigy-burners were not all abolitionists, but they were sure Douglas, with one eye on a presidential run, had broken the national truce over slavery for the sake of Southern votes. His deed would "rouse up every sleeping energy of abolition fanaticism in the land," an Illinois newspaper warned. Armed pro- and antislavery men were already warring in "Bleeding Kansas."

George Stephens had lectured for the Bannekers on subjects ranging from love and morality—always a crowd-pleaser—to religion and colonization. The *Weekly Anglo-African* judged him "a promising young man, a ready and fluent writer . . . [who] possesses a vigorous intellect and an easy flow of ideas." In the Bannekers' debate of April 22, 1858, he condemned the new law and reviled its sponsor, Douglas. Everyone agreed that Stephens won the debate and comported himself properly.

Everyone, that is, except one of the visitors from the literary league, who protested Stephens's remarks. Within a few days the visitors made their recommendation. No mention was made of Stephens. The Bannekers' rules and minutes were in order, they said. But the Banneker application was rejected.

In his written report, a bitter Jake White Jr. said the sole reason the league cited was color. "Acting upon this," he wrote, "we were excluded by them."

★ ★ ★

UPON COMPLETING HIS senior year at the I.C.Y., Octavius graduated—no small feat, considering the school's stingy approach to awarding diplomas. To graduate was to join what Roger Lane called "a surviving elite within an elite." On top of that, Octavius was named valedictorian. If the tiny number of competitors made this title lose its luster, he could at least share bragging rights with his friends from the previous two graduating classes, Jake White Jr. and Jesse Glasgow: valedictorians all.

And lest the school's rigors had not been enough, Octavius signed up for tutoring in the classics, Latin and Greek. All sorts of advantages could derive from such studies—particularly for those who aspired to be educators, orators, lawyers, leaders. His tutor was a professor in Washington, D.C. This additional learning brought him back, if only briefly, to his father, who had moved down to Fifteenth Street Presbyterian Church in Washington.

Diploma in hand, Octavius reapplied to the Banneker Institute, and this time he won the two-thirds vote required for admission. *Finally!* By then he knew most of the men in the room. Within months he was succeeding Jake Jr. as Banneker secretary and preparing to deliver evening lectures on subjects ranging from ancient Egypt to modern language.

The Bannekers still had lofty notions—that a well-run colored literary society would show "those in authority in our government that we are susceptible of the highest degree of mental culture and worthy of the rights which have been so long withheld from us."

They were not unique—the Industrial Revolution had seeded countless fraternal societies seeking "definition-by-association," as one historian puts it. The city had two Library Companies, one white and one colored. An entire store sold Odd Fellows' and Masons regalia. Gould Bias was an Odd Fellow; David Bowser, a Banneker member and an Odd Fellow "grand master." Banneker meetings were a haven in which young black men could light cigars, speak their minds, and debate ideas at a safe remove from the street. The Thursday evening meetings were private—colored public meetings ran the risk, as Bolivar wrote, of whites intruding for the sake of curiosity "or to combat."

Members donated a book a year to the Banneker shelves and paid annual two dollars' dues—beyond the means of most of the waiters, washers, coachmen, and maids of colored Philadelphia in the late 1850s. Bannekers could be contradictory: They celebrated West Indies emancipation day, August 1, but once debated whether slavery had saved Africans from "heathenism." Jake White argued "for." (Did he argue from the heart? The records do not say; his other writings and speeches were pure abolitionist.) Lectures lamented the plight of the destitute, but the five-to-twenty-five-cent admission kept the destitute away.

Parker T. Smith resigned as Banneker president in 1855, saying the meetings had gone to the Devil—"strict order and parliamentary etiquette," he wrote, had yielded to "strife and contention." But Smith came back. So did others. A quality that beams from the old Banneker papers is the affection members had for one another.

In a largely hostile 1850s world, a few dozen young men and their fathers read, argued, and debated. They met weekly from September to June, convening at eight and unfailingly adjourning at ten, sometimes borrowing the I.C.Y. lecture room as membership grew. A cancelled meeting often meant something bigger had come up. They made way for the I.C.Y.'s annual examinations—and once they canceled because Frederick Douglass was in town to speak that night.

Bannekers mourned losses together and pined for each other's company when they were apart. Parker Smith briefly joined the Canada exodus—but wrote to Jake White that he was "home sick" and would return to Philadelphia as soon as he could. "Give my love to every body," Smith wrote, "and consider yourself entitled to the largest share."

The death of a beloved young friend prompted members to draft a message of "inexpressible grief." When a loyal white ally in the equal-rights struggle died, the Bannekers signed their mourning note "as a band of brothers."

Octavius's friend Robert Adger was expelled from the Bannekers for a rules infraction, then readmitted, then expelled once again. He remained in the band of brothers all the same.

Adger, too, had grown up in a household steeped in abolitionism—and in second-hand goods. Furniture, china, silverware, and featherbeds were bought and sold in the Adger store at 825 South Street. Portraits of Douglass and Garrison lined the walls. Shelves creaked with writings about the race—the tale of Peter Still's escape from bondage and his reunion with his brother; the Weld and Grimké antislavery tracts and the novel they fueled, *Uncle Tom's Cabin*; John Campbell's *Negro-Mania*; pamphlets and petitions from a quarter century of Negro conventions; writings against colonization, the Fugitive Slave Act, and *Dred Scott*; arguments for temperance and the right to vote.

The store was, roughly, the geographic center of colored Philadelphia and was such a landmark that some called the spot Adger's Corner. The sixteen Adgers—Robert Sr., Mary Ann, and fourteen sons and daughters—lived next door. (That was before James sailed for Australia.) Living on South Street, the Adgers were on the northern boundary of old Moyamensing Township, the new Fourth Ward, with its white gangs and fire companies. But Adger Sr. saw to it that his premises were secure—customers were greeted by a snarling, chained cur of indeterminate breed.

The Adgers were also, along with Jake White Jr. and their mutual friend, William Dorsey, unofficial curators of the colored city. They saved not only books and broadsides but invitations, menus, and bills of sale—Robert M. Adger once said future generations needed "to tell their children what our past condition was." So the dog guarded both the present and the past.

Exactly what the Adgers' collection included was hard to know. They did not organize an archive of handmade scrapbooks, as young William Dorsey did. When a reporter from the *Philadelphia Press* asked in 1860 whether there was a written inventory, Adger Sr. just smiled and said he knew where everything was.

People spoke of one item in the collection. They remembered the ill-fated temperance parade of 1842, the banner that sparked a bloody siege, and the rumor that the banner depicted a Nat Turner or Denmark Vesey breaking free and setting a town ablaze.

People said Robert Adger Sr. saved the banner.

★ ★ ★

BY AUGUST 1858, the fury over Kansas had Republicans hopeful of gains in Congress. A crowd estimated at twelve thousand watched the first debate between Senator Stephen A. Douglas and his Republican challenger, in the town square of Ottawa, Illinois.

Douglas likened his rival to "the little abolition orators who go around and lecture in the basements of schools and churches." He said the man deserved a medal from the infamous "Fred Douglass." Did Illinoisans want Negroes in their meetings and voting lines? Marrying their daughters? Because that would happen if his opponent won.

Abraham Lincoln got up to reply. Clean-shaven and towering over Douglas, he said the senator had concocted from whole cloth "this tendency of mine to . . . set the niggers and white people to marrying together." He denied favoring political or social equality for Negroes and said Douglas had so twisted up his words that they could "prove a horse chestnut to be a chestnut horse."

All the same, he said, a black workingman deserved a fair wage, like any other man.

Douglas labeled Lincoln the candidate of "Black Republicanism" and lest any voter in the crowd miss this phrase he repeated it eleven times in the three-hour debate.

★ ★ ★

AT THE END of 1858, the I.C.Y.'s Robert Campbell chose Africa. He was joining Martin Delany's Niger Valley trek. Campbell's students presented him with farewell gifts—a gold watch and a copy of *Cosmos*, Alexander von Humboldt's five-volume book on the physical properties of the earth and the universe.

Campbell's plans appealed to the colonizationists on the I.C.Y. board, and the minutes exuded a certain Ferdinand-and-Isabella pride. The school's colored Columbus was sailing off to found a cotton-growing nation, "with the view of interesting the colored people of this country in emigrating thither to form settlements . . . and to open commercial relations with other countries."

The managers decided hiring a full replacement in mid-winter was "inexpedient." Instead, Bassett would handle some of Campbell's classes, and a young assistant would be hired to lighten the principal's load. An assistant would cost less and could come from the ranks of recent graduates, in keeping with the era's so-called Lancasterian schooling theory. Youth was a plus, not a minus. Charles Reason was said to have taken his first New York teaching post at age fourteen.

A committee proposed hiring the most recent I.C.Y. valedictorian at an annual salary of $150. The managers nodded approvingly at the name, and by the close of business on January 17, 1859, Octavius Catto had a job. He was one month short of his twentieth birthday.

The *Weekly Anglo-African*, published in New York, ran an item about the I.C.Y.'s hiring of both Catto and White Jr. The paper observed "that the teachers of the Institute are all colored: that is, we have black men teaching black boys spherical trigonometry."

As Bassett's new assistant, Catto taught English and mathematics. He was an athlete, said to excel at cricket and its fast-growing American cousin, "town ball." (In New York City, they were calling it "base ball.") He could be impatient to the point of pettiness. Twice he canceled his Banneker lectures, complaining in one instance that he hadn't been given enough notice; in the other, that his audience was too small.

He believed in corporal punishment—he was the I.C.Y. teacher who had disciplined J. W. Cromwell. "Mr Catto gives me a slap on my face with a book for giving impudence as he calls it," the Virginia native wrote in his diary. Catto also warned him against "walking about with my Virginia pedestals."

★ ★ ★

AS CATTO MOVED into his role as a Banneker officer, a restlessness began to infect the group's thinking. With the white literary league's rejection, no one needed to fool himself that "respectable" behavior and well-kept minutes would change the minds of men. And George Stephens was a walking reminder of how slavery, seemingly far away, could slip a tentacle around one of their closest friends and dispatch him straight to hell.

Top antislavery men were joining the Bannekers—Bassett of the I.C.Y. accepted an honorary membership, as did William Still. (Of all the literary societies, Still wrote, only the Bannekers stood a chance of being "of service and credit to the colored people of Philadelphia.") So did another Underground Railroad man, William Henry Johnson.

A Banneker committee preparing the annual August 1 antislavery picnic wrote that the occasion "gives abolitionists a fine opportunity to expose the hollow-heartedness of American liberty and Christianity." At the same time, Catto, White, and others began planning a new event in the city, to be held on the Fourth of July. There was reason to think the police would not be the enemy this time. The new mayor, Alexander Henry, gave officers new badges and curbed the spoils system that his predecessor, Vaux, had used to hand out police badges to Moyamensing Hose men.

The July 4 Banneker event was to be an incursion into the public square, where Negroes had been unwelcome. Or unwilling: When slave catchers snatched a Negro off Philadelphia streets in 1857, a commissioner sent him south before abolitionists of both races could mount a protest. A letter in the *National Anti-Slavery Standard* said the real culprit was "the mute indifference of the four hundred thousand people . . . in this great and loud-professing metropolis." So a point needed proving. If Boston could turn out thousands, black and white, against a rendition, could Philadelphia?

CHAPTER 9

A Chance on the Pavement

OCTAVIUS BEGAN his teaching career in a season of revelations.

As the ice melted on the Schuylkill, he and five other colored teachers labored to keep their I.C.Y. pupils focused on Virgil and trigonometry in a semester bursting with livelier facts. Reports of "outrages" and "usages" of Negroes filled the columns of the *National Anti-Slavery Standard*, Frederick Douglass's monthly, even the daily papers. There was talk of reviving the transatlantic slave trade, and defenses of "mild slavery" by a president whose line of loyalists ran from Alderman McMullen's office to the brick-and-marble mansions of the city's favorite spendthrift, Pierce Butler. The season was the spring of 1859.

President James Buchanan had named a new commissioner, a Quaker, to hear fugitive cases in Philadelphia. Previous appointees had sent defendants south with brisk efficiency. The abolition community wondered what sort of Quaker would take such a post.

In the city of the Institute for Colored Youth, the ranks of colored youth were increasing, their voices sharpening. The next year's census would find that most of Philadelphia's 22,630 Negroes were under age thirty. And the same I.C.Y. managers who winced at hosting Frederick Douglass became concerned that the students' orations were taking on overtones of "war, hatred and revenge."

Principal Bassett and his new assistant did little to tamp down the orations. The principal—having reached the wizened age of twenty-five—
delighted in holding up modern politics to ancient lamps; in comparing,
say, Charles Sumner to Demosthenes. Catto had his recent classics tutoring to draw on. He was not only teaching; he was starting to fuel his own
orations with allusions to thinkers as modern as Douglass and as ancient
as Aristotle. The latter's warning, that a free people "unable to face danger bravely are the slaves of their assailants," applied well to free Negroes
reaching adulthood in 1859.

One assailant all but tipped his hat to them from the pages of a weekly
newspaper.

The *National Anti-Slavery Standard's* writer had knocked on the door
of George Alberti, the most notorious of Philadelphia slave catchers, to
seek an interview. To the astonishment of the visitor—the redoubtable
Miller McKim—Alberti showed him in, sat him down, and began a spirited defense of forty years of snatching Negroes off the streets.

The former constable had first been linked to such kidnappings
in 1815; the abolition society in 1839 termed him a "well known slave
catcher." He had been jailed and pardoned in 1851 for taking a freeborn
infant. Now nearly seventy, he assured McKim, who was forty-eight, that
he was neither retired nor repentant.

"No sir, slavery is according to the law of God! The slaveholder has
as good a right to his niggers as he has to his horses; if they run away, as
a good citizen I have a right to catch them. . . . I would catch a nigger on
Monday, if I had the chance."

McKim asked: "On Monday? Why not tomorrow?" Alberti replied, "I
believe it would be a sin for me to do it on Sunday."

Alberti had been implicated in seizing Negroes who were not fugitives, as well as those who were. Either way, there was money to be made,
especially after the 1850 fugitive law and the rising demand for slaves in
far-flung Texas. McKim had heard his name for years; he had once intercepted a letter to Alberti and used it to help a fugitive escape. He asked
one last question: How many had Alberti taken in all?

"Easy a hundred," Alberti said.

By coincidence, the Alberti article was circulating as men from Virginia came into the city to hire a lawyer.

Several attorneys turned them down. Then the Virginians approached
a rising talent of the local bar and the Democratic Party, a lawyer who,

after a discussion of fees, agreed to take their case. Benjamin H. Brewster would serve as counsel to their employer, a Virginia planter, in a claim about to be brought under the Fugitive Slave Act.

★ ★ ★

DEBATES IN THE city's antislavery meetings were intensifying just then. Buchanan's Democrats had stumbled in the 1858 elections, thanks to the Panic of 1857–1858 and the violence in "Bleeding Kansas." The rise of a Republican Party, timid though its leaders were about abolition talk, brought hopes of stopping slavery before the earth was "swept into eternity," as Garrison had quipped of the gradualists. In March, William Still reported an intriguing idea: A speaker at a meeting proposed attacking discrimination in the North even while pressing to end slavery in the South.

The speaker mentioned various "usages" and injustices—Negroes not allowed in the city's museums, "except at certain hours," or into the Academy of Music, "except in the fourth story, in a little place set apart for them," or in the new passenger railway cars. Fare-paying Negroes had to ride outside on the muddy platform, behind the horse. Those who tried to keep their seats, such as the poet Frances Watkins, were insulted or ejected or both. The speaker called for circulating "petitions or remonstrances, through the community, with a view of remedying the evils complained of," Still wrote in the *National Anti-Slavery Standard*'s March 19 edition. "The suggestion, thought I, was a capital one."

He did not report the speaker's name or that of another speaker who warned that petitioning would kindle more prejudice. Better to hew to "the great principle," abolition, and let Northern prejudice run its course, like a fever. Someone else countered: The fever can be attacked! Colored Bostonians had won changes "due to petitions and remonstrances," this speaker said—"it was the sort of work they should all do." Colored New Yorkers had successfully sued railways to integrate; the Massachusetts legislature had agreed to let Negroes into the schools. Still his readers asked: Why not petition to open up the streetcars in Philadelphia?

"I can scarcely understand why this matter of prejudice should be allowed 'to take care of itself;' why the colored man should be expected to mutely submit to such outrages in the North," he wrote. "Indeed, I am fully of the opinion that as efforts are put forth to overthrow slavery in the South, corresponding efforts should be made to destroy the bulwark of prejudice in the North."

Still had lately become landlord of a South Street rooming house. He could be sneering and self-important, and he had a puritanical streak. He claimed that a woman who had raised money to buy her children out of slavery in Kentucky was a swindler and a whore; she sued him and won a hundred dollars. But his words carried weight for colored readers of the *Standard*. The number of fugitives he had helped was second only to Harriet Tubman's and could be multiplied by those who had heard the stories or read about Box Brown or been reunited with a loved one, thanks to Still. Jake White Jr., augmenting his I.C.Y. salary by hawking out-of-town papers, told the *Weekly Anglo-African*'s editors he could sell fifty extra copies a week if the edition included a letter from William Still.

Any effort to open up the streetcars would draw wide attention, Still knew. Negroes would have to choose the right moment to "remonstrate" for equal treatment on this popular new conveyance. The cars were the talk of the city. "No public improvement," Mayor Henry said, "has ever promised more benefit to the community." Doctors on house calls were giving up their carriages and requesting discount fares. The ride over rails was swifter than the bump-and-clump of the old omnibuses on paving stones. "So gentle is the motion that the passenger can read his journal without difficulty," a report prepared for inquiring British engineers said. "In case of necessity, troops can be transported from one part of the city to the other at ten miles an hour."

That suited the mayor. Alexander Henry's predecessors had been former soldiers or firemen; he had a degree from Princeton. His thousand policemen, with new pistols and star-shaped badges, patrolled a city that the consolidation had expanded from 2 square miles to 129. The cars could speed his great wish: to shake off like an old coat the city's pattern of brawling gangs and bloody assaults on Irish, abolitionists, and Negroes. Charlotte Forten's grandfather James had called Philadelphia "the Mob City"; Mayor Henry wanted visitors to think of it as the Modern City.

Less clear was whether he and his police would make the streets and meeting halls safer ground for colored citizens, or, as previous police and mayors had, more perilous.

Not everyone favored the passenger cars. Pastors and proprietors were incensed to find their streets laid open by rail crews. Sidney Fisher, the diarist who had once described the "mob of well dressed persons" storming Pennsylvania Hall, suspected railway owners were corrupting city officials even as their rails corrupted the street-bed, causing much lagging and lurching for citizens who, like Fisher, could afford a carriage and a driver.

"It spoils the road for driving," he wrote, "but all the people in Germantown can by it go to town for 10 cents every 10 minutes." He also noted the rise in the value of property near the railways. "All the families who own much land here have been enriched"—he mentioned the Logans, Wisters, and Norrises, each with hundreds of acres. Fisher said his friend Pierce Butler's two hundred country acres had soared in value.

And as Fisher was well aware, Butler needed cash just then.

★ ★ ★

THE BUTLER FAMILY'S roots were intertwined with America's. Pierce Butler's grandfather represented South Carolina in the Constitutional Convention and in 1804 had made the family's Georgia land a haven for a friend on the run, Aaron Burr. As other people had city homes and country retreats, the Butlers had empires of cotton and rice on the Georgia coast and villas in Philadelphia. Before his divorce, Pierce Butler and his actress wife had toured Europe with Franz Liszt and met Queen Victoria and Prince Albert. Back home in Philadelphia, the Democrats sent Butler to the Electoral College in 1856 to help elect his candidate, Buchanan.

Then the Panic of 1857–1858 and poker had depleted the family's wealth, and by early 1859 Butler's financial advisers—who included Sidney Fisher's brother and their friend George Cadwalader—calculated his debts at three hundred thousand dollars. People said twenty-six thousand dollars of this derived from one hand of poker: Butler had bet on four deuces and lost to four kings.

"Pierce Butler has gone to Georgia to be present at the sale of his Negroes," Fisher's diary entry for February 17, 1859, begins.

"It is a dreadful affair. . . . There are 900 of them belonging to the estate, a little community who have lived for generations on the plantation. . . . Butler's half, 450, to be sold at public auction & scattered over the South. Families will not be separated, that is to say, husbands & wives, parents & young children. But brothers & sisters of mature age, parents & children of mature age, all other relations . . . will be violently severed. It will be a hard thing for Butler to witness and it is a monstrous thing to do. Yet it is done every day in the South. It is one among the many frightful consequences of slavery and contradicts our civilization, our Christianity; . . . what can be done?"

People said Butler was a "kind master" who kept families intact; his oldest Negroes remembered his grandfather. He could have taken gentler measures than an auction—sell some land, or, as many slaveholders did, allow slaves to purchase themselves. Even as he was preparing for the auction, the *National Anti-Slavery Standard* published a Maryland slave's letter asking Philadelphia readers to buy freedom for his two sons, his wife, and himself.

But letting four hundred slaves buy freedom piecemeal would not get him three hundred thousand dollars quickly; it would also smack of abolitionism, and Butler was no abolitionist. He headed for Georgia, unaware that a New York reporter was headed there as well.

★ ★ ★

PHILANDER DOESTICKS had the scoop of his career.

His real name was Mortimer Thomson, but in the style of the day he used the "Doesticks" pen name, which apparently amused readers of the *New York Tribune*. His story ran down column after column, nine thousand words in all, and caused the March 9, 1859, edition to sell out; the editor, Horace Greeley, ordered extras printed.

Butler and his broker had staged a two-day auction at a Georgia racetrack, convenient to the train depot. The slaves were put in horse stalls for inspection; 436 adults and children, including some 30 infants, were sold. Doesticks went incognito, masquerading as a customer. He knew he had a story when he discovered the hotels of Savannah were full of prospective buyers.

At the racetrack, he saw a slave couple beg to be purchased together, only to be pulled apart amid sobbed farewells. He saw women disrobed, peered at, and picked over by customers in "indecent" ways. He reprinted the sales list Butler's broker provided: "107—Linda, 19; cotton, prime young woman. 108—Joe, 13; rice, prime boy. Sold for $600 each." He reveled in the absurdities: "Here and there, scattered among them were strange men with banjos, hired by the management to stimulate cheerfulness and gayety that was not, however, realized."

He saw Pierce Butler walking about with sacks of newly minted quarters, handing each of his favorite servants a dollar in coins as a parting gift. As the auction ended, Doesticks watched the separating "of parents and children, of brother from brother, . . . the tearing asunder of loving hearts." Butler's broker served champagne to the buyers.

Within weeks, newspapers in Washington, Philadelphia, Chicago, and London reprinted Doesticks's story. He called it the biggest slave sale in years; historians say it was the biggest in U.S. history. Sarah Remond cited it in lectures, reminding British audiences that the seller was a Northerner, former husband of "your own Fanny Kemble." Worse, she said, "Mr. Butler has in no wise lost caste amongst his friends; he still moves in the most respectable society." She mentioned that Butler "brought about the removal" of his church's antislavery pastor, Dudley Tyng.

Southern editors railed at Doesticks's sneery depiction of the buyers as "a rough breed, slangy, profane and bearish, being for the most part from the back river." Fisher wrote in his diary that Doesticks's story "tho doubtless exaggerated is in the main true."

Fisher personified the ambivalence of influential, educated whites in what Roger Lane has called "the northernmost city of the South."

Slavery, Fisher had written, "contradicts our civilization"—had anyone said it more clearly? His villa in Maryland and his ties to the South through family and friends made him privy to the "outrages." His friend George Cadwalader told of dining at a planter's home where mulatto servant boys bore a striking resemblance to the host—and then, of seeing the same boys the next day, being taken away to be sold. On a rainy ride through Maryland in late 1858, a constable told Fisher of earning eight dollars a year for "whipping Negroes," ten lashes each, for singing too loud or dancing too late. The constable showed Fisher a plaited-leather whip and a post and said the twenty free men and women he had whipped there took it with grace. An incredulous Fisher asked, "They did not mind it?" Well, the constable said, "they made an almighty howling."

Fisher's essays on politics and law were widely read; he had criticized *Dred Scott* and said the West should remain "free." He dined with mayors and governors. Though his circle included such slave owners as the Middletons and Butlers, he also knew the Republican judge William Kelley and the antislavery society's Miller McKim. An antislavery soapbox would have been his for the asking. But he confined his harshest judgments to his diary. When it came to the brutalities, he was silent Sid.

"For the sake of preserving . . . peace and order, which in reality means his own property and enjoyments . . . he is willing to sacrifice the right and the truth, to yield to all the demands of the South, and to maintain slavery without so much as asking whether it be not in itself a wrong and a crime." Fisher wrote that of a cousin who had married into a slaveholding family. But the words could have applied to his city, his country, himself.

★ ★ ★

FOR THE OTHER PHILADELPHIA, Catto's Philadelphia, the news of the Butler auction capped off an unusual sequence. The Alberti interview was published February 19; a month later, Still's call for "petitions and remonstrances" and Doesticks's bombshell appeared. The papers had shown that the city had in its midst a leading slave catcher and a leading slave seller. Also a slaveholder's attorney—but that news had not surfaced yet.

The auction story was still in the papers when a message reached the Vigilance Committee from a Chestnut Street boardinghouse where Southern tourists stayed. A slave in her fifties was hoping to escape. The vigilance men arranged a secret meeting.

Three days later, a telegram arrived. Harrisburg's Vigilance Committee was sending an urgent plea. At dawn, three federal marshals with Colt revolvers had slipped into a crowded market and encircled a colored man in a red flannel shirt and a battered hat as he was buying fish for his wife's breakfast.

The Negro cried out for help, but the marshals waved their pistols to back the crowd off. By breakfast time, the prisoner was in manacles and on an eastbound train. His case would be heard by President Buchanan's new appointee.

The marshals had told people in the market that the man was wanted for burglary. That was a familiar line. After nine years of tumultuous enforcement, marshals knew better than to tell a crowd that they were taking a prisoner on a Fugitive Slave Act writ.

The burglary story did not last long. People in the market, black and white, knew the arrested man not as a thief, or a fugitive named Daniel Dangerfield, but as Daniel Webster, a local fence maker in his twenties whose family had lately been decimated by disease. He was well liked.

Herein lay the Fugitive Slave Act's hidden flaw, a consequence its authors had not foreseen. White Northerners who had never cared a whit about abolition looked up to discover pistol-wielding marshals dragging away a bootblack, a fence maker, a washerwoman, a neighbor. A man such as Webster.

His odds were terrible. Previous commissioners had so routinely ruled against defendants that they had sent one man south only to be returned by a slave owner who said, this is not my missing Negro. "The most we expected to do was to make a good fight," Miller McKim wrote, "and build up public opinion." Amid pledges to "dispute every inch of ground," he and Robert Purvis began lining up lawyers. Then came word that the slave-holders had hired the ambitious Democrat Brewster as their lawyer; and that Brewster had already met with the commissioner—twice.

McKim and the Vigilance Committee lawyers rushed to the court-house. They found Webster, handcuffed, seated alongside a marshal. McKim demanded, "Who put those manacles on you?" The marshal, a man named John Jenkins, said, "I did."

Court employees and "hangers-on" watched as the two men argued.

McKim was part manager and part fire-breather; someone called him "that prudent, rash man." His hair sprang up in tufts that defied a comb. Born in Carlisle, Pennsylvania, he had gone to Andover and Princeton and had embarked on a career as a Presbyterian minister when one day's read-ing—a Garrison antislavery tract—caused him to give up his pulpit and join the abolition movement. He was officially a "publications agent"; in truth he worked full-time for the Underground Railroad. He was married and had befriended an older woman, Lucretia Mott—their letters are so affectionate that one has to wonder—and he had helped Still liberate Box Brown. His wits having lately been sharpened by interviewing Alberti, he began firing questions at the marshal.

McKim demanded that Webster's manacles be removed. "It is an outrage!"

Jenkins said he'd remove the handcuffs "directly." But he wanted McKim to know: In the Harrisburg market, the Negro's cries for help had "brought about a hundred niggers around us." He said Webster had tried to grab a butcher's knife.

"Wishing you no harm," McKim replied, "I am sorry he didn't succeed."

"I have no doubt it would have pleased you if he had plunged the knife into my heart," Jenkins, who had been a marshal in fugitive-slave cases for a half-dozen years or more, said. "It's not the first time I have been insulted by people of your kind."

The former preacher reached back to his training for a "Do unto oth-ers" argument. What would any man do if put in irons and marched toward enslavement, he asked. What if it were *you*? "Would you not want to get hold of a butcher knife?"

"Perhaps I would. But in this case I am only doing my duty," Jenkins said. Hangers-on nodded approvingly. "I have no feeling in the matter."

McKim retorted, "That is my objection to you."

The marshal said he'd removed the handcuffs during the train ride. Webster agreed that Jenkins "was very kind to me in the cars." Then he began to cry. "My poor wife! Little did I think this morning that I was to be jerked away from her all of a sudden!"

McKim asked whether he had children. "I had two, but they are dead," the Negro said. "I buried the second one last week." The room went silent.

Jenkins reached into his pocket, took out a key, and unlocked Webster's handcuffs.

The commissioner, John Cooke Longstreth, arrived. He defended as proper his having met with Brewster to smooth out legal flaws in the slave-holder's writ; in this step by the new appointee, Webster's lawyers saw a bad sign. A better sign: Over Brewster's protests, Longstreth granted two days' delay. The trial would begin at ten o'clock Monday. The defense had pleaded for time to prepare its case and muster its witnesses.

And its army. McKim devoted the next two days to spreading the word. One woman wrote, "Miller feared there was no hope for the slave, but he was anxious that as many as could, should go to the Commissioner's office on Monday."

A quarter century of "remonstrating" had sharpened McKim's sense of how much the press could help or hurt the cause. "The Saturday afternoon and Sunday morning papers gave publicity to the facts. The community was deeply moved," he wrote. One newspaper mentioned the tears welling in Webster's eyes when the Negro spoke of his children.

★ ★ ★

AS PUBLIC ATTENTION was drawn to Webster's impending trial, a less visible drama began to unfold a few hundred feet away, in the boarding-house on Chestnut Street.

The message to the Vigilance Committee had come from Cordelia Loney, a house servant to one of the guests. Her owner was a wealthy Virginia widow who had friends in Philadelphia. Having accepted "invitations from some of the *elite* of the city," the widow had booked into the boardinghouse and brought her Negro servant for a month-long stay.

Entourages from the South were a staple of the city's tourist trade. The heat of Southern summers inspired excursions by those who could afford it; many came to see sons graduate from Philadelphia's medical schools, where more than half the students were from the South. One daughter of North Carolina slaveholders, in town for her fiancée's graduation, was startled to meet a lady abolitionist. Thankfully, she noted, "all the other persons that I have seen here are warm friends of the South." Regional differences were noted—Philadelphians swore more and drank more; and the easy source of pleasure for slave-owning Southern men was not available. "Since you have been in Philadelphia," a Virginia college boy wrote to a friend, "how do you like [seducing] white gals?"

Many tourists brought household slaves to Philadelphia but warned them against speaking with colored maids and waiters. The warning was well-founded. A cook helped smuggle Miles Robinson to freedom by hiding him in a closet of pots and pans on a steamship bound for Philadelphia. A maid at Bloodgood's Hotel on Walnut Street started a famous rescue by alerting William Still to Jane Johnson's whispered entreaty, "I am not free but I want to be." Five black porters went to jail for grabbing Johnson's owner while Still and Passmore Williamson rushed her away. The porters had the good fortune to be sentenced by Judge Kelley, who jailed them for just a few days.

This anonymous network of Philadelphia maids, waiters, porters, and cooks turned up in 1857 in *The Garies and Their Friends*, one of the first novels published by a colored American. The author, Frank Webb, depicted life in his home city—a white mob storming colored homes, a fancy-dressed mulatto who tried to pass as white. Webb portrayed one hotel as "the great resort of Southerners, who occasionally brought with them their slippery property; and it frequently happened that these disappeared from the premises to parts unknown, aided in their flight by the very waiters who would afterwards exhibit the most profound ignorance as to their whereabouts." The novel's waiters sweet-talked Southern customers, refilling their drinks and pining for days of "Ol' Massa" till tips were secured—and promptly delivered to the Vigilance Committee.

Cordelia Loney sent her entreaty to the real Vigilance Committee through colored workers at the boardinghouse. A vigilance man quickly set up a secret meeting. Loney impressed him as "very neat, respectful and pre-possessing," about fifty-seven years old. She had long been a servant to the wife of a Virginia planter, a man with many slaves.

Loney said she dressed her mistress each day, drew her bath, combed her hair, and laced her shoes. She had tended the master's sickbed during his long decline. The widow had lately pulled her closer, inviting Loney to say nightly devotions with her at bedside.

The Vigilance Committee's man asked: Did Loney have any family with her who'd need to be part of an escape? She said no.

He laid out her options. She could sue under the state's 1847 Personal Liberty Law, which, in essence, conferred freedom on anyone setting foot on Pennsylvania soil. But *Dred Scott* had played havoc with such laws and she could only hope for a sympathetic city judge such as Kelley or Joseph Allison. The committee would provide lawyers.

Or, she could bundle up her belongings, and at a designated hour of night, slip out to Chestnut Street and be whisked away by the sure hands of the Underground Railroad. They'd hide her for a few days and start her off for Canada. Loney chose that option.

Then the vigilance man hesitated. Loney had described an almost comfortable life. Her mistress prayed with her. Was Loney certain of wanting to flee that pious owner?

Oh, yes, she said. That pious owner sold away my two daughters and two sons.

★ ★ ★

BY THE TIME Commissioner Longstreth's office opened on Monday morning, McKim could report that "the city was in a hopeful state of excitement." The street outside the office was filled with what a Brewster confidant called "an immence throng of negroes and Abolitionists who surrounded the building."

McKim was impressed at how many young men of both races turned out, itching for confrontation. Some arrived with weapons in their pockets and had to be persuaded that they'd only hurt the cause in the public's perception.

The crowd was white and colored, male and female, young and old. There were members of the Vigilance Committee, the various antislavery societies, the Banneker Institute. They ranged in age from James Mott, age seventy, to his grandson, age nineteen. Lucretia Mott and Mary Grew led a contingent of two dozen women; there was Passmore Williamson, the white hero of Jane Johnson's 1855 rescue, and the men and women of the Purvis-Forten "dynasty of social activists," including Charlotte Forten.

Another illness had forced Charlotte to convalesce at the Purvises' country home. She had come down from Salem in March, weak but well prepared, having stood with Sarah Remond in the bayonets-and-vitriol maelstrom over Anthony Burns's rendition in Boston. This time she would have a story to tell Sarah.

When the court opened, people filled every seat. In the momentary hubbub, a bent figure in a pale bonnet scooted across the room and sat by the Negro defendant before anyone could stop her. Thus ensconced, Lucretia Mott fixed her gaze on Benjamin Brewster. By Tuesday, he was asking to have her moved, and years later he was said to remark that "having dared to face Lucretia Mott, he could dare to face anything."

Brewster had already served as federal commissioner for land disputes arising from the transcontinental relocation of the Cherokees. He had been talked about as a candidate for district attorney in the forties. He made no secret of his political aspirations or his aristocratic roots. To Webster's supporters he became the Slave Power's symbolic face.

Brewster's was also an unforgettable face. A fire in boyhood had so permanently maimed and blackened the side of his head that he often wore a white silk hat and ruffles to conceal his disfigurement. Enemies mocked this affectation, but "his stormy eloquence & ugliness please the masses," an admirer wrote. As Webster's case ground forward, even McKim marveled at how Brewster had shed "his vaunted gentlemanly bearing" to argue with passion that the Fugitive Slave Act, however disputed or despised, must be upheld: "I came here not to indulge in camp-meeting oratory," he said, "but to speak of what is law."

His opponents knew the law made their case almost impossible. In lowered voices, they warned their client. Webster said he asked only one thing: "a chance on the pavement."

One of the men quickly replied, "He shall have a chance" and began discreetly enlisting young volunteers, white and black, in a plan.

The opportunity would come the next morning as police escorted Webster through a courthouse door. The ever-growing crowds of supporters and opponents milling in Chestnut Street and jeering at each other would provide cover.

The volunteers would group themselves in squads as the officers prepared to move Webster. A carriage would pull up. On a signal, groups would set upon each policeman. They would mob him. They would try to pin each officer's arms, if only for seconds, while Webster sprinted to the carriage. The men would be arrested, perhaps bludgeoned by the police, and undoubtedly set upon by the crowd. And Webster would get his chance.

In the morning, the pieces were moved into place. Young men eased through the crowd outside the courthouse door. A carriage pulled up.

Then came word that Longstreth had moved the case to a larger room to accommodate more spectators. The marshals were already bringing the prisoner through a different door. The opportunity evaporated.

The throng grew, filling stairwells and corridors. Webster was escorted by "a strong guard of Deputy Marshals [and] a dense and excited crowd." White men hissed at Webster's supporters. Police cleared corridors several times, ejecting more Negroes than whites. Mott's sister told of elbowing her way in "amid the roars of the crowd."

Defense lawyers spent a morning in court tweezering at flaws in the slaveholders' documents. That served McKim's purpose—"a good record made up for publication in the evening papers."

William Furness stopped by. The Unitarian minister had been a lonely antislavery voice among the city's white clergy since Dudley Tyng's removal. "I looked the other day into that low, dark and crowded room, in which one of the most wicked laws that man ever enacted was in process of execution," he told his congregation. "The . . . heated atmosphere of the place well became the devilish work that was going on."

He told of glimpsing Webster "in his old hat and red flannel shirt and ragged coat"—and at his side, "cheering her poor hunted brother with the sisterly sympathy of her silent presence," was Mott. Furness wondered: How did she do it? She had regained that spot even after Brewster protested and bailiffs rearranged chairs. She sat as if in "celestial light"; to Furness's eye, a halo over Mott's bonnet would not have seemed out of place.

Celestial—and crafty. During a recess, Mott found Commissioner Longstreth alone, writing at a table in the courthouse basement. "I ventured to step forward, and, in an undertone, expressed to him the earnest hope that his conscience would not allow him to send this poor man into slavery. He . . . replied that he must be bound by his oath of office." Mott left him with a line of verse by James Russell Lowell: "The traitor to humanity is the traitor most accurst."

In court, the slaveholder's witnesses testified that they'd heard the fugitive Dangerfield was living in Harrisburg. They had gone there and spotted him. William Bogue testified with a "saucy" air that his main purpose in coming north was business. In the hotel trade, he was here as a "buyer." He said he was not a slave buyer but did, on occasion, "deal in that article." That *article*! Spectators shook their heads.

Webster's lawyers argued that the defendant was not someone's chattel but a man; at the same time they hoped to prove he was not *the* man, the runaway named in the writ.

By Tuesday, the case was boiling down to two knotty discrepancies.

One was time: The slaveholder's Virginia witnesses said Dangerfield had run away in 1854. Webster's witnesses swore they'd known him in Harrisburg in 1853; one man claimed to have met him in Philadelphia in 1849. But U.S. marshal Jenkins testified that on the train—after he'd removed the manacles—his prisoner marveled at Philadelphia's size and blurted out that he'd never seen the city before.

The other was height. The slaveholder's witnesses said the missing slave was about five-feet-six. Defense lawyers claimed Webster was taller, but the fugitive law barred him from testifying. So Webster stood in the middle of the room while Longstreth measured him. Brewster shouted objections at the young commissioner—*Have him get his boots off, your honor.*

Webster removed his boots. The commissioner measured and made a note: boots on, five-feet-ten, boots off, nearly five-nine.

So Webster was slightly taller than the man Virginians remembered. A simple explanation existed, but Brewster was in no position to offer it. As lawyer for the side which, generally speaking, believed Negroes were better off as slaves, he could hardly argue that after five years' freedom, a man might stand taller.

★　★　★

LONGSTRETH ANNOUNCED THAT he would hold court on Tuesday until the trial was complete. The final arguments began in the evening and lasted through the night.

The chief marshal dozed off, as did Webster. "The officers rested their heads on the ends of their maces," McKim wrote, "and the doorkeepers slept at their posts." Mott's ailing sister, Martha Wright, left after eight hours over Mary Grew's entreaties to stay. Mott and the other women continued to sit upright.

The arguments ended at 5:50 A.M. Longstreth called an adjournment until 4:00 P.M. and said he would announce his ruling then.

By noon, public interest in the case "reached a point of intensity that was painful," McKim wrote. He said revivalists who ran a Sansom Street prayer meeting waived their ban on controversial subjects in order to pray "for the deliverance of Daniel."

When Longstreth returned to the bench, the room was full again, peopled with those, the judge noted, who "had seen the sun set and rise in the court room." The crowd in the street was enormous. He began to read his decision slowly, in a "hard voice" that seemed to signal the usual outcome.

Then Longstreth said one encouraging thing: that in addition to property, the case "involved the liberty or bondage of a human being."

He said he was satisfied that the writ was in order and that the slave owner had a legitimate claim on a slave named Daniel Dangerfield. Then he moved to the questions of time and height. He said testimony showed Webster was in Harrisburg by 1853; Dangerfield had not fled Virginia until 1854.

McKim heard a voice somewhere in the courtroom say *Thank God*.

Then another voice, and another, until the words "were leaping from every mouth . . . beamed from every glistening eye." Now Longstreth was explaining that Webster measured five-feet-ten, slightly less with his boots removed, thus two to three inches taller than the fugitive Daniel Dangerfield—and the sound of tears and "hurrahs" began to fill the room even as the commissioner ordered "the prisoner to be discharged."

A man in the audience threw open a window and waved his handkerchief to signal the outcome—and the street answered with a roar.

They did not all shout as one; some white citizens screamed epithets. Webster came to the courthouse door in a rain of hurrahs and hisses. Young white men pressed forward.

By one account, Mott employed an old tactic. She hooked her arm through Webster's and began walking. Slowly, the little white grandmother and the tall Negro in the red shirt made their way through the roiling, screaming crowds.

People parted enough to let them through.

Colored men hoisted Webster to their shoulders and put him on a carriage. They unhitched the horses and pulled the carriage through the streets. "You never saw such an excited & happy crowd," Mott's sister wrote. She told of hearing an old colored man declare that "if Mrs. Mott didn't have a high place in Heaven he didn't want to go there."

A victory meeting was planned for two days later in Sansom Street Hall, with its frescoed interiors and room for a thousand people. Webster and his wife stayed at the Purvises' country house and prepared for a journey north. Whites were overheard vowing to abduct Webster to Virginia. Neither side's young men were ready to end this drama.

★ ★ ★

THOUGH LONGSTRETH HAD SAID he'd ruled on facts, "Others are inclined to believe that the pressure of public sentiment—which was, strange to say, almost universally on the right side—was too overwhelming for the commissioner," Charlotte Forten wrote. She said Longstreth's family, "even his wife, it is said, declared that they could discard him if he sent the man into slavery. . . . It gives one some hope, even for Philadelphia."

Mary Grew, who had been preparing the antislavery society's reports for a quarter century, wrote that the Webster case was "proof of a great change wrought in popular feeling; in which change we saw the result of twenty-five years of earnest effort to impress upon the heart of this community anti-slavery doctrines and sentiments."

Webster's young supporters could not wait for the victory meeting. Blacks and whites marched to the Motts' and gave three cheers. As the hour grew late, some headed for Benjamin Brewster's address and hooted for him to come out.

In the courtroom he had wrapped himself in the law. Now Brewster wrapped himself in the flag, and with a Stars and Stripes draped capelike on his shoulders, he stepped to his doorway and dared the crowd to shoot. People hooted a while longer and dispersed.

★ ★ ★

AT THE VICTORY MEETING, people were resolving to never let another Negro be sent south from Philadelphia when noises erupted at the back of Sansom Street Hall. Charlotte Forten turned to see men running up the aisles. "We thought we should be crushed but I did not feel at all frightened," she wrote. "I was too excited to think of fear. The veterans in the cause said that it reminded them of the time when the new & beautiful Pa. Hall, which afterward was burned to the ground—was mobbed."

Martha Wright, sitting with Harriet Purvis, described "a disorderly multitude of sympathisers with the South [who] by constant cheers and groans drowned the voice of speakers. . . . The mob voted themselves the citizens of Philada. & . . . resolved that they wd. not associate with niggers, and there were many present, so designated, from Robt. Purvis & family, to the deepest shades, & some were much terrified."

Passmore Williamson sent word to the police. Miller McKim saw young antislavery men with knives and guns; these children of Underground Railroad families wanted to drive the train *above* ground. But "the veteran Abolitionists, men and women, were quiet and composed. They kept their seats, ready, if the appointed guardians of the peace should fail of their duty, to weary out their enemies, as they had often done."

"Their enemies" were surging toward the speakers when the doors swung open, and in rolled a wave of men with badges. "It was grand to see the police with their stars, step in & confront the mob just as they reached the platform," Martha Wright wrote. Her young nephew pointed to the mob's ringleaders. "He was pale as death, as were most of the men, but full of fire."

McKim wrote: "Happily, and for the first time in the history of our movement, the police did their duty."

★ ★ ★

AS THE WEBSTER TRIAL was concluding, Cordelia Loney packed her things. She waited for the designated hour of the designated night, slipped out to meet her Vigilance Committee contact and was gone.

The discovery of her absence provoked uproar in the Chestnut Street boardinghouse.

Colored employees did what their fictional counterparts had done in *The Garies*. They professed ignorance of Loney's escape, even as they relayed information to the Vigilance Committee. They reported that Loney's owner felt betrayed and helpless—she was unaccustomed to traveling alone, lacing her own shoes, and combing her hair. Other Southern guests rallied to her side and began quizzing their own servants.

The servants, too, volunteered nothing. Some guests offered them rewards for information on Loney's whereabouts. When that did not work, William Still noted, "Some charged the servants with having a hand in her leaving."

A local Episcopal minister who was friends with the widow promised to use his contacts among the better-off Negroes. In the street he spied a Negro caterer, Thomas Dorsey, "who he thought knew nearly all the colored people about town." The white pastor told Dorsey about Cordelia Loney—how she had fled a kind mistress, broken the law, and was sure to land in degradation among the "miserable blacks down town." Could the caterer help find her? For good measure, the minister quoted scripture justifying slavery.

Dorsey was the same generation as William Catto and had a son close in age to Octavius. The older Dorsey had escaped slavery many years before, and in Philadelphia had slowly built up a successful catering business. The Dorseys owned their house on Locust Street and counted the Adgers, Whites, and Cattos among their friends. Dorsey's wife, Louise, was the protective landlady who shooed suitors away from her boarder Rosetta Douglass. The Dorseys worshipped at St. Thomas, so technically at least, they were of the same faith as the minister now asking him to help track down a runaway slave.

Dorsey answered the white churchman "in not very respectful phrases," as Still put it. First of all, Dorsey said, he would hear no more of Servant obey thy master. Scripture did not say that. The Lord never meant one man to own another.

Second, "it was all false about the slaves being better off than the free colored people." Third, the minister would find just as many degraded whites as Negroes if he would trouble himself to walk "down town."

Finally, Dorsey said he was not going to help retrieve the missing woman. He said that if he knew where Cordelia Loney was, he would sooner "give her a hundred dollars to help her off, than to do aught to make known her whereabouts."

A few weeks later, a message came from Daniel Webster. "We hear with joy that he is safe in Canada," Charlotte Forten wrote. "Oh, stars and stripes, that wave so proudly over our mockery of freedom, what is your protection."

William Still reported that Cordelia Loney, too, arrived safely in Canada.

★ ★ ★

LIFE INSIDE the Chestnut Street boardinghouse quieted down by the end of April. Southern parents arrived for the medical school commencements; waiters worked the guests for tips. Five blocks south, pupils and teachers prepared for the rigors of final examinations and the awarding of diplomas at the I.C.Y.

The end of each spring semester at the I.C.Y. was momentous. Teachers determined who would graduate and who would not. Managers went over salaries; this year, they determined that young Catto had done well enough in his first semester's teaching to merit a raise, from $150 a year to $200. Commencement was becoming a grand rite. Several thousand colored Philadelphians and invited white guests—the mayor, the district attorney, judges—watched a half dozen boys and girls figure, translate, and orate, and if they did well enough, walk across a wooden stage and collect a diploma (and maybe a ten-dollar prize for best in mathematics or languages) from Mr. Bassett or Miss Douglass to the sound of deafening cheers.

Commencement also marked the beginning of the season when Ebenezer Bassett and his young teachers had more time for other matters.

Catto and Jake White Jr. focused their attention on July 4—on reclaiming a holiday once so fraught with danger for Negro celebrants that they marked July 5 instead, or celebrated August 1, West Indies Independence Day, at pastoral "pic-nic" spots outside the city. The Fourth was shunned in protest, too. As the poet John Greenleaf Whittier and his friend Theodore Weld had vowed to stay unwed until slavery ended, Henry Highland Garnet, James McCune Smith, and other Negro intellectuals had a July 4 pledge: No celebration until emancipation. Of course, Garnet and Smith were getting up in years. The young Banneker members had made no such pledge.

★ ★ ★

ON JULY 4 at Independence Square, boys hawked peanuts, cakes, and candies from tattered baskets, and girls presided at lemonade stands. Workingmen tested their strength by climbing poles or hefting sledges. Top-hatted judges with knotted cravats made the customary speeches about the founding fathers, and a prominent lawyer read the Declaration of Independence aloud. Brass bands and firecrackers tickled every ear. Pennsylvania Hospital reported the customary injuries: "Thumb shot off, pistol." "Finger blown off, pistol." Down at the Navy Yard, bigger guns thundered salute after salute, and a hundred pennants flapped and fluttered on the stays of a hundred ships.

The difference on this July 4 was the Negroes.

Dressed to the nines despite the afternoon heat, and flanked by marching musicians, Catto, White, and a phalanx of Banneker Literary Institute members strode into Franklin Hall at three thirty. Hundreds more colored people followed. The Bannekers had persuaded some sap—a Quaker, no doubt—to rent the hall at Sixth and Arch, two squares from the white July 4 celebration, and even closer to where Pennsylvania Hall had stood.

The colored conductor raised his baton and the trombones began to boom. "O, Co-*lum*-bia, the gem *of* the Ocean." But someone had negrified the lyrics, and young colored men sang at the top of their lungs about a future time when the flag would protect every child of every "hue." They were singing Charlotte Forten's lyrics.

Speakers decried the holiday's empty meaning for "disfranchised" Americans. Jake White Jr. asked: Why celebrate a history marked by "multiplied instances of bad faith?" He described the burden borne by every colored American. "If we sit at home, we feel it—if we walk the streets, the influence of prejudice surrounds us at every step—if we sleep, our dreams are of the weight of oppression we are obliged to sustain."

From his first youthful essay on "free" produce to his evocations of the Bannekers' goals, White constantly envisioned a day "in futurity" when every child's teacher would rival the I.C.Y.'s, slavery and prejudice would fade into history lessons, and a column of clean-living Banneker men would march to Harrisburg and Washington and pry the race's citizenship papers from the closets of the capitals as surely as William Still and Miller McKim had pried a man from a box.

Getting there would require a greater battle than "the conquests of a Napoleon, . . . the victories of an Alexander." But someday, "not very far in futurity, our grievances will be redressed," White said, and Negroes would celebrate July 4 "with our once-cruel opponents and oppressors."

Then he sat down, and another young Banneker, Henry Minton, stood up and made history. He was probably the first Negro to read the Declaration in public on July 4 within sight of the spot where it was written.

William Henry Johnson, a Banneker man who had worked for the Underground Railroad in New York State as well as Pennsylvania, said the Declaration's signers "were, to all intents and purposes, anti-slavery men." He said the problem was their heirs who'd authored *Dred Scott* and the Fugitive Slave Act. "And by the way, there are *tories* today," Johnson said, "and their business is to hunt down the poor fugitive negro, and to handcuff and drag him hundreds of miles from his home to be tried as a slave, and to be remanded . . . within sight of the hall where independence was declared."

As much as the speeches themselves, who was delivering them—and where—was the point. The Bannekers had stepped from the safety of their Thursday night meetings to claim a corner of the public square, leading an all-black "disfranchised Americans" rally on July 4 within sight of the national birthplace, and without igniting a white mob. Precedent was broken, the *Weekly Anglo-African* said. Catto and two other men engaged a printer to commit the day's speeches and resolutions to a thirty-one-page pamphlet.

They wrote that the pamphlet reflected "a desire . . . to make known to all men . . . why we, as proscribed Americans, should not let the day pass unnoticed by."

★　★　★

THE *WEEKLY ANGLO-AFRICAN* reported another first that day—the first baseball game played "between players of African descent." The Monitor and the visiting Unknown club went nine innings on a field in New York City. "Quite a large assemblage encircled the contestants, every one as black as the ace of spades." The only white player mentioned was "the venerable Joshua R. Giddings," an Ohio congressman who had stood strong for abolition—much stronger than, say, his close friend Abe Lincoln.

Giddings was cheered when he batted. His left-handed pitching motion baffled hitters. He was known for playing "with perfect abandon" in games with colored men. By mid-game the visiting Unknown club was well-known, having scored fourteen runs in the top of the fifth. The final score was Unknown 41, Monitor 15.

Thomas Hamilton's black publications in New York, the *Weekly Anglo-African* and the *Monthly Anglo-African Magazine*, were a window on the changing landscape of Negro life in 1859—the baseball game, the July 4 Banneker event, even the first thirty chapters of Martin Delany's novel.

His mother's home teaching had paid off. Delany had already published his short-lived but marvelously named Pittsburgh newspaper, the *Mystery*; his essays and field reports for the *North Star* before he and Douglass drifted apart, and his guide to Negro accomplishment, *The Condition and Elevation*. Now came his rejoinder to the God-praising colonizationist Negroes in *Uncle Tom's Cabin*. Amid purchasing provisions and consulting Niger River charts, he found time to start *Blake; or, The Huts of America*.

The hero of the novel is Jamaican-born Henry Blake, who at an early age is tricked into bondage in Mississippi. Blake is "a black—a pure

Negro—handsome, manly and intelligent." He marries Maggie, a slave, and they have a son. Their owner, who also owns Maggie's mother, makes the familiar promise of the Christian master: He'll not sell Maggie and Henry apart. The turning point in the novel comes when the master, needing a quick profit, breaks his word and sells Maggie.

Henry vows to rebel. Maggie's mother cries words from Isaiah—"How long! O Laud how long!"—but she begs Henry to peaceably accept whatever fate God bestows on Maggie. The story continues: "Religion!' replied Henry rebukingly. 'That's always the cry with black people. Tell me nothing about religion when the very man who hands you the bread at communion has sold your daughter away from you!'"

Henry risks all, battling slave catchers and brandishing a butcher's knife, like the knife Delany had clutched in 1848 as he and Charles Langston waited out a mob. Blake was still fighting for his life in chapter 30 when the financially ailing *Weekly Anglo-African* ceased publication. Readers would have to wait to learn Blake's fate.

Delany hoped sales of *Blake* would help finance his Niger Valley trek; he imagined he "could make a penny by it," as he wrote to William Lloyd Garrison, asking about publishers. That would be better than accepting funds from the cotton and colonization forces eager to underwrite the colored men's trip.

Delany softened his message for no one; his stentorian voice was accompanied by what William Wells Brown called "a violence of gestures." His *Condition* book, amid its who's-who of Negro scholars, scientists, mechanics, and millwrights, went out of its way to condemn the prejudices of white abolitionists. Many of them distanced themselves from him after that.

He was in some ways like a traveler from another time. He celebrated his African origins at a time when others in both races were debating how to save that continent's "heathens." Even Garnet was tilling this swampy plain, assuring British donors that *his* new emigration project, the African Civilization Society, would speed "the triumph of the Gospel in Africa." No doubt, Garnet was hustling the Britons much as Philadelphia waiters hustled Southerners for tips; but Delany would sooner go penniless than pander to rich whites. Fredrick Douglass observed of Delany: "He stands up so straight that he leans back a little."

Daniel Payne, who had famously objected to the "cornfield ditties" former slaves sang in church as too primitive, said Delany was too African.

Delany had "fine talents, and more than ordinary attainments [and] . . . he knew much of men & things in Africa, England, Scotland. . . . His oratory was powerful, at times magnetic," the church leader wrote. "But he was too intensely African to be popular, and therefore multiplied enemies where he could have multiplied friends by the thousands."

Delany, perhaps more than Douglass and others, was open to experiments. While he was writing *Blake* and preparing for the Niger, he also sent a cryptic letter to a young white antislavery man in Chambersburg, Pennsylvania, named John Henrie Kagi. Delany asked for news of "uncle's movements."

Kagi, in his twenties, had become a kind of military aide to the white abolitionist that Douglass, Garnet, and the others had secretly met with in Philadelphia in 1858. "Uncle" was John Brown.

★ ★ ★

FREDERICK DOUGLASS NEVER forgot his first visit with Brown a dozen years earlier. Garnet and others—always lowering their voices—had urged him to introduce himself. So he had made his way to a cabin in Springfield, Massachusetts.

"Its furniture would have satisfied a Spartan," Douglass wrote. The table of pine planks was "innocent of paint, veneering, varnish, or tablecloth." There, "under the misnomer of tea," Brown served Douglass steaming portions of beef soup, cabbage, and potatoes, "such as a man might relish after following the plow all day or performing a forced march of a dozen miles over a rough road in frosty weather."

Douglass studied Brown: nearly six feet tall, lighter than 150 pounds; hair coarse and graying and low on the brow, woolen clothing and a cravat of cowhide. "His eyes were bluish gray, . . . full of light and fire. When on the street, he moved with a long, springing race-horse step, absorbed by his own reflections."

Brown said he had followed the career of Douglass and other abolitionists and had decided "moral suasion" would not end slavery. Douglass knew of the Grimké sisters and argued that other slaveholders could be converted. Yes, Brown said—if "they felt a big stick about their heads." Then he commenced to explain that God had molded the Appalachian Mountains to accommodate a guerilla-style war against slavery. He said the key was to ignite a revolt that would grow to encompass several million slaves.

Douglass did not take him seriously.

In the 1850s, however, Brown had proven in Kansas his willingness to murder in the name of abolition. Following an attack in Lawrence by pillaging pro-slavers, Brown wreaked vengeance by having his raiders pull five men from their homes, split their skulls with swords, cut off their hands, and leave their bodies outside.

He had recruited a band of would-be soldiers and suppliers. He had staged a secret "convention" of forty men, including Martin Delany, in Canada, where Brown had unfurled his "constitution" for a post-slavery America. He had invited Douglass and a few other colored American leaders; only Delany attended. Brown began dispensing titles and instructions; he made young John Kagi "Secretary of War."

By late summer 1859, Brown's footprints were all over the Cattos' Philadelphia. He had dined at the generous table of the Dorseys, in Locust Street, had gabbed and argued into the night with Thomas Dorsey and the other older Underground Railroad hands. He boarded in two Banneker members' homes—the Mintons, on Lombard Street, and David Bowser's shabby studio rooms up on North Fourth.

Robert Adger, close friends with the Dorseys' son William, remembered seeing Brown at their house. He said one other Negro "knew John Brown and was with him in this city often [and] . . . was nearer to him than I, that is he knew of his plans etc." He said that was Ebenezer Bassett of the I.C.Y.

In September a group of colored Philadelphia leaders wrote to Douglass, imploring him to rush to Chambersburg for "a convention to come off right away." They urged him to contact Kagi. Their letter made no mention of Brown or of a plot or any suggestion of danger—except an ominous pledge: If Douglass went, they would guarantee the safety and care of his family—"during your absence, or until your safe return to them."

Douglass declined. He had already attended one urgent "convention" near Chambersburg. Kagi had led him from the town to a quarry where a huddle of two dozen grimy unshaven men with pistols, rifles, and ammunition sat about on seats of rock as John Brown did the talking.

Brown laid it out: the topography of Harper's Ferry, Virginia, the merits of taking prominent local citizens hostage, the uprising that was sure to ignite among the enslaved peoples of western Virginia and crackle across the South and West until all four million slaves were raising arms against their masters.

Brown explained the intricacies of his "constitution" and kept explaining until some of the men nodded off. ("It was the first thing in the morning and the last thing at night [and] . . . it began to be something of a bore," Douglass wrote.)

Then he asked Douglass to join him. Douglass's name would bring towering legitimacy in the eyes of Negroes, Brown said. As the morning sun warmed the quarry, Brown wrapped his arms around him and beseeched him once more. "When I strike, the bees will begin to swarm," Brown said, "and I shall want you to help hive them."

Douglass, who had borne his share of bee swarms, declined.

He wondered later whether he had demurred out of cowardice or common sense or both. Other colored leaders faced the same dilemma. "All make such excuses, until I am disgusted with myself and the whole negro set," a Brown recruiter wrote. *"God dam em."*

Douglass was speaking in Philadelphia on an October night when the news from Harper's Ferry flashed through the hall. John Brown and twenty-one other armed men, sixteen white and five black, had seized an arsenal containing thousands of rifles and a mountain of ammunition. Two townspeople were killed, ten slaves freed. Sixty miles from Washington, white and colored "insurrectionists" prepared to arm slaves for a war against their masters. The raiders cut telegraph lines and a captured a railroad station, stopping a Baltimore-bound train. Never had the nation seen such an attack. "It was something to make the boldest hold his breath," Douglass wrote.

"All of our men became hopeful, men like Stephen Smith, Robert Purvis," Billy Bolivar wrote. These were men who "had so long, intelligently and faithfully, tried by reason to make the people of this country convert to abolition." Now they waited to learn if another way would work.

★ ★ ★

THE SLAVES DID NOT revolt. Within thirty-six hours Brown's raiders were all captured, killed, or on the run. Kagi was shot to death. Days later, one of the few to escape, a Negro named Osborne Anderson, reached an address on North Fifth Street in Philadelphia. William Still answered his door to find Anderson, "footsore and powder begrimed" and sent him north to Canada. Brown and others were tried, convicted, and sentenced to hang.

Anyone in on the plot could face prison or the gallows. Brown's captors found letters in his carpetbag implicating abolitionists of both races: Gerrit Smith in New York, Samuel Gridley Howe in Boston, the ball-playing Ohio congressman Giddings—and Frederick Douglass.

He was staying with the Dorseys on Locust Street. A telegram arrived in Philadelphia, instructing the sheriff to arrest Douglass. The telegraph operator on duty that night was a white man in his twenties who happened to be "an ardent admirer of the great ex-slave." He stuck the message in his pocket, alerted Miller McKim—and three hours later, delivered the message to the sheriff.

By then, Douglass's friends had put him on a ferry, the first leg of a hasty trip home to Rochester, then to Canada, and finally to Britain.

The extent of his involvement was disputed almost from the moment of Brown's capture. Douglass admitted delivering one recruit and one supporter's ten-dollar donation to Brown at Chambersburg but insisted he'd argued against the plot. Brown's daughter said later that her father and Kagi had come back from the quarry meeting with a pledge from Douglass to follow Brown "even unto death." Douglass's son said Southerners had concocted this story to discredit his father.

Even so, when Douglass booked passage on a steamship from Quebec to England in November 1859, he knew he "was going into exile, perhaps for life."

For months, repercussions of Harper's Ferry shook the nation. Legislators drafted bills deporting free Negroes or requiring them to register. In Newport, Kentucky, a crowd described as "gentlemen," believing they had unmasked the next John Brown, tore apart a white abolitionist editor's presses and hurled his type into the Ohio River amid shouts of "shoot him" and "cut his throat."

"I do not exaggerate in designating the present state of affairs in the Southern country as a reign of terror," the British consul in Charleston reported. "Persons are torn away from their residence and pursuits [and] . . . letters are opened at the Post Offices; discussion upon slavery is entirely prohibited under penalty of expulsion."

Some colored leaders chided Douglass for doing what he and Payne had once vowed never to do. Rev. Sella Martin, writing in the *Weekly Anglo-African*, imagined Douglass safely penning "letters from the broad latitude of Canada West" while others stood in the fierce winds below the border. All the same, Douglass was on the run. The governor of Virginia said he would like to hang him, asked a prosecutor to indict him, and commissioned a private detective to track him down. Slaveholders took the manhunt to heart—"If you manage to get holt of that Boy," a Mississippian volunteered, he would have one of his Negroes whip him "until he says thank you Sir, or Please Master." Douglass had become a symbol of the plot he had hesitated to join.

The failed raid energized the Negro political world. Brown had stirred up Garnet's old "Arise, arise" call for slave revolts. In a sermon the *New York Herald* termed "not distinguished by a tone of moderation," Garnet now predicted sleepless nights for slaveholders, adding, "All that was needed was a box of matches in the pocket of every slave." In Hartford, men scaled the dome of Connecticut's state capitol to drape a shroud over its Liberty statue. In Detroit, Negroes filled Second Baptist Church to hear speeches of abolition and resistance. "On to battle, we fear no foe," black men shouted. As the meeting was ending, they sang the Marseillaise.

A new verse was appended to the anthem. "I hear the voice of John Brown, from Harper's Ferry, too . . ."

Antislavery societies and colored organizations planned vigils for the hour of Brown's December 1859 execution—even as a counter-chorus of white lawyers, manufacturers, merchants, and mechanics painted banners and printed song sheets for a rally supporting the South. The Banneker Institute planned a mass meeting as well; Catto and four other members arranged to rent a hall. Anticipating clashes, Mayor Alexander Henry flooded the streets with his "star police," under orders to carry their pistols.

By late November, the forlorn figure of a large woman in shabby clothes trudged among the homes of the Stills, Motts, McKims, and Dorseys. Not everyone in these families had supported John Brown's tactics; all the same, they took in his wife. Mary Brown had lost two sons at Harpers Ferry, and Virginia was about to hang her husband.

The wait for the execution grew unbearable. A white woman, Susan Lesley, was coming out of one of Furness's antislavery sermons with her young daughter when she spotted Mary Brown standing alone outside the church. "Immensely large, strong-looking," Lesley thought, and "wearing the dress of a *very* poor woman."

Lesley went over to speak with her. Mrs. Brown perked up a little. Then she hoisted Lesley's little daughter, gave her a kiss, and began crying.

Wendell Phillips came down from Boston to deliver one of his more popular lectures—a narration on Toussaint L'Ouverture. Phillips let it be known in advance that he'd draw comparisons between the hero of Haiti and John Brown. The event's organizers received a warning: If Phillips spoke as planned, the lecture would be halted by "roughs" from Moyamensing led by Alderman McMullen—or as Phillips put it, "a highly distinguished leader of riots."

When the doors opened on November 28 at 8:00 P.M., McMullen and his men filled the back of the hall. As Phillips began speaking, they shouted "kick him out" and "hang him." Then they began to quiet down in the presence of 120 police. People credited Phillips's storytelling as well. Moyamensing Hose men who had been likened to Jacobins heard him tell of Haitian slaves' triumphs over well-armed French soldiers. The men who had come to silence the speaker became silent themselves and "sat spellbound until the end."

On December 2, the day of the execution, abolitionists wore black and draped their doors in mourning. The city's Southern medical students countered with red ribbons and strutted about the city, Susan Lesley wrote, "telling how many 'niggers' they owned."

Even as the students promenaded, six hundred Negroes and sixteen white sympathizers crowded into Shiloh Baptist on South Street to sit in vigil. A visiting black minister took pains to explain why his church, Mother Bethel A.M.E., was not hosting this meeting. Another minister denounced the "truckling" of some local blacks to whites in this crisis time. When Shiloh's pastor, Jeremiah Asher, said members of his own family were still trapped in slavery, shouts went up from every pew: "So is mine!" "So is mine!"

Speakers in two cities likened Brown to Christ. A Concord, Massachusetts, audience clapped when Henry David Thoreau called the Crucifixion and Brown's hanging "two ends of a chain. . . . He is not Old Brown any longer; he is an angel of light." Robert Purvis, addressing a rally in Philadelphia's National Hall, was not as well received.

One historian calls the moment when Purvis stood and spoke "so extraordinary"—a Negro abolitionist addressing an audience dense with pro-slavery men. Listeners "burst into hissing and applause, with wild interruptions at every phrase."

Purvis, as ever, minced no words. "Coward fiends of Virginia," he called the executioners. "John Brown dying on the scaffold was the Jesus of the 19th century!" Some men shouted back, "Hang the nigger!" "Throw him out the window!"

A thicket of policemen separated speaker from audience. The mayor and his police chief, Samuel Ruggles, had gone to unusual lengths to protect an abolition meeting and it had ended without further incident. They went to even greater length to protect John Brown's body as the train bearing his casket arrived in Philadelphia, en route to a family burial ground in upstate New York.

Anticipating trouble, the mayor contacted Miller McKim and arranged to have a decoy casket move through the streets. Sure enough—white crowds massed around the counterfeit cortege. In the meantime, a cart disguised as building supplies delivered the remains of John Brown to a ferry, departing on schedule from the Walnut Street wharf of the Almost Modern City.

★ ★ ★

THE GREAT UNION MEETING of December 7, 1859, was a model of promotion. For days, a person could not walk the streets without seeing reminders draped from streetcars' flanks. Cannonades from ships in the Navy Yard announced the meeting was starting.

Jayne's Hall, built to hold six thousand, became "tightly packed long before the hour . . . and the street in front of the building presented a dense mass of persons who had no hope of gaining admission. . . . The business men were strongly represented. . . . Workingmen were there, also." So were men from prominent families: Ingersoll, Randall, Cadwalader; a young financier named Anthony J. Drexel. The lawyers included Benjamin Brewster. Speakers pledged to honor the South's "rights" and found in Harper's Ferry new proofs of the happiness of the slaves. They also scolded the mayor.

"We have more convicts in the Eastern Penitentiary" than abolitionists in the city, the attorney Josiah Randall, a Democratic leader and a confidant of President Buchanan's, said. "These Abolitionists, though small in number, are active and untiring in their treasonable efforts, and they have recently, under the protection of the armed municipal police, met together and promulgated the most abominable opinions and sentiments. It is much to be regretted that the chief magistrate of our city did not follow the example of his predecessor and take efficient measures to suppress such meetings."

That the thousands of slaves living near Harper's Ferry had not joined the raiders proved "the slaves are happy and contented," Randall said. "They desire no change."

The audience greeted Brewster with three cheers "and a tiger," a manly roar. He said slavery was not only lawful but made the nation strong—"for how, without such help, could the early settlers have subdued this savage wilderness, and cleared the way for the free white man? . . . [B]y [slave] labor do we produce our great staple cotton, with which we command the markets of the world, and by which alone we have maintained peace with other nations, and hindered their rulers from inflicting upon us those injuries that would have retarded our growth and suppressed our national greatness."

People stood and clapped and shouted and stomped. Thousands more pressed in from Chestnut Street. Those inside Jayne's Hall felt the floor begin to move.

So many had massed in one area that the structure became a "dense and swaying concourse, [which] threatened the very stability of the floors," until some people went quickly outside, staggering gratefully onto the pavement's permanence.

The outside crowd called itself to order, chose a chairman, heard nominations, and elected two dozen vice presidents and secretaries of its own. All sang a song of many stanzas that had been printed and handed out at the rally.

> The South shall have her rights—o'er her
> Our eagle spreads its wing—
> The treason plotters, brown or white,
> Shall from the gallows swing.

One week after the Jayne's Hall rally, the other side met again. This event was the antislavery societies' annual fair, with speeches by Purvis, Mott, Furness, Miller McKim, Mary Grew, and a Boston luminary, the abolitionist George William Curtis. He would speak in the evening at National Hall.

Unsigned advertisements in the newspapers called on Philadelphians to gather in front of the hall that night and prevent Curtis's lecture. Older people remembered the anonymous placards that turned up in streets before Pennsylvania Hall was attacked—except this was more brazen. Someone had paid plenty of money for the ads.

Mayor Henry asked organizers to cancel the lecture and stave off a riot; they refused. He asked again, visiting with the group at Furness's home before the event. Pressure was being brought to bear on him by "the wealthiest houses" of commerce, according to Wendell Phillips. But the abolitionists were unyielding. One of them, Isaac Clothier, wrote that everyone in the room feared injury or death. They started walking the few blocks to National Hall on Market Street.

Halfway there, they heard "a terrible noise in Market Street & a great crowd."

★   ★   ★

JUDGE WILLIAM KELLEY was assigned to introduce Curtis that night. Kelley was a new father, his wife having three months earlier given birth to a baby girl, Florence. Little Florrie was in for a lively childhood—pro-slavery men took her father's name in vain and by her eleventh birthday would aim rotten eggs at his portrait in a parade. Inside National Hall, he took aside Clothier and pulled up his sleeve to reveal a slender wooden "billy." Then he took Clothier down a staircase to the street. Have a look, the judge said.

Outside were amassed four hundred policemen, checking their pistols and pulling up their collars against the December air. The officers were outnumbered 10 to 1 by the angry throng that had gathered. Clothier decided this was the most exciting night of his life.

Chief Ruggles had also positioned fifty officers in front of the speaker's rostrum and scattered fifty more in the hall. The mayor had said all week that he might not agree with Curtis and the other antislavery people but would defend their free-speech rights. As the hisses and catcalls increased, Henry sat down by Curtis on the speakers' platform. This brave gesture almost backfired when someone mistook Henry for a troublemaker and was about to heave him bodily from the platform when others shouted that he was the mayor.

Hecklers inside and outside the hall were in a frenzy when Curtis rose to speak. Many were Southern medical students. A leader of the crowd was Joseph Allen, a former policeman with an endearing nickname, Rat. Another was said to be from the Killers gang. And Josiah Randall's son,

Robert, was so obviously whipping up the crowd's taunts that Ruggles's officers began to tail him.

Amid this hubbub came a sound of windows breaking and the gasp of a hundred breaths sucked in at once. People who saw the high glinting arcs realized too late that the objects were dark glass bottles. Vitriol. The bottles shattered and a woman screamed.

Stories spread about who had been hit by the acid and how badly. One account said a young man's face was disfigured. Another said vitriol struck Lucretia Mott herself. In fact, the worst injury was to a young white woman from Chester County, a Quaker named Emma Fussell. Some of the vitriol landed on her bonnet; some struck her face.

She crumpled to the floor as police officers rushed in. They arrested fifteen men.

Chief Ruggles saw people running for cover and sensed order slipping away. He had officers load their fifteen prisoners into a freight car, conveniently moored on a railroad siding in the grain-and-flour store that occupied the ground floor of National Hall. Then he let it be known that if the hall burned, police would safely evacuate everyone else before turning their attention to the prisoners.

Things began to quiet down.

The vitriol burned Emma Fussell's face and she was in bandages for weeks. The scars healed, but she kept a memento—"her bonnet riddled with holes."

The arrested men included Rat Allen and two other former policemen, a constable, and medical students from Georgia and Kentucky. From these future physicians, police confiscated a billy club, a "murderous looking dirk knife," and a fully loaded Colt.

Then there was Robert Randall, the legislator, charged as a ringleader; and John Scott, the purported Killer, charged with creating disorder in the hall.

★ ★ ★

HUNDREDS OF COLORED PEOPLE were already waiting at Eleventh and Pine streets the next night when Catto, William Minton, and four other Banneker men arrived to open the hall. Whites had made predictable threats against the meeting. The Bannekers asked Negro merchants to close early so everyone could attend, threats notwithstanding, and the early crowd was a thrilling sight. The reporter on hand from the *Weekly Anglo-African* would have a story to tell.

The Bannekers had put down a one-dollar deposit on the New Masonic Hall, one of the few willing to rent them space. The Bannekers had rented from the Masons before, for an anniversary gala. They had been good customers.

But tonight Catto and the others found the hall's doors locked.

Murmurs went through the crowd as the young men began pounding at the door. The rental agent for the Masons came out and Catto and the others gathered around him. He said his board had decided a Negro meeting was too dangerous. The vitriol episode had scared them. The agent had his instructions: Return the deposit and keep the hall closed.

But hundreds were waiting! A negotiation began. The board might open the hall in return for a promise of no publicity. No, the Bannekers wanted publicity and a reporter was already there. By now it was after dark and murmurs were turning to shouts. Catto and the others tried to assure the rental agent that "the time for burning down halls in Philadelphia had long since passed."

The time for closing halls had not passed. The Masons would not relent. A thousand colored citizens went home cold and angry, stamping their boots.

★ ★ ★

THE DIARIST SIDNEY FISHER perceived quickly that however suicidal the raid, however bloodthirsty the reaction, John Brown had actually achieved his purpose; that is, he had shown that some men were willing to die to force the great question into the open. Fisher even found himself agreeing. Something had to happen.

"Slavery occupies all conversation now," he wrote. "Slavery is a wrong, an injustice. It must either destroy the moral sentiment of the country or be destroyed by it."

The opposite view was being articulated just then in the closing days of the 1850s, by a political leader from Pennsylvania, a Democrat.

"Notwithstanding our demerits, we have much reason to believe, from the past events in our history, that we have enjoyed the special protection of Divine Providence ever since our origin as a nation," the Democrat wrote. He predicted Harpers Ferry's bloodshed would unite Americans in defense of such cherished institutions as freedom—and slavery. He lauded the latter as if it were a charity and a wonderful one at that.

The American slave "is well-fed, well-clothed, and not overworked. . . . Both the philanthropy and the self-interest of the master have combined to produce this humane result." The writer did condemn recent talk of renewing the trans-Atlantic slave trade. He said reopening a competitive market for slaves would jeopardize "the present useful character of the domestic institution, wherein those too old and too young to work are provided for with care and humanity, and those capable of labor are not overtasked."

By then, many Americans had read accounts to the contrary, from the Weld-Grimké *Slavery as It Is* book to the Doesticks article. Many more had read *Uncle Tom's Cabin* or packed theatres to see it staged. Yet a major Northern politician was offering a serious and rosy vision of slavery in 1859. He was the man Pierce Butler and the Randalls helped put in office, whose portrait gazed down over Alderman McMullen's desk in Moyamensing. The text was President Buchanan's annual message to Congress.

★   ★   ★

DAVID BOWSER BEGAN painting a posthumous portrait of his late boarder, John Brown. He softened the eyes and hair until the man who had ordered five Kansans hacked to death looked docile, even angelic. On the shoulder of his subject's blue cloak, Bowser painted an epaulette of gold, as if to signal that Brown had died in the service of his country.

Which, as far as people in the Cattos' world were concerned, was exactly what happened.

In Edinburgh, the farthest-flung Banneker member, the "very black boy" Jesse Glasgow Jr., interrupted his studies to write a history of the raid for a Scottish publisher. The title made Glasgow's feelings clear: *The Harper's Ferry Insurrection . . . the Trial and Execution of Captain John Brown, Its Hero.* The forty-seven-page pamphlet sold for a shilling and included Glasgow's plea for readers to donate to the Underground Railroad or others working toward "the colored man's freedom and manhood in America."

A letter in Brown's possession at his arrest was said to be from Ebenezer Bassett. Brown's diary revealed a list of seven "Men to Call for Assistance." Dated a week before Harpers Ferry, the list included: "E D Bassett, 718 Lombard Street, Philadelphia."

Bassett had widened the trail blazed by Charles Reason at the I.C.Y., the proud project of well-heeled Quakers who shunned violence. Now everyone could see that he was something else as well—connected, as if by telegraphic cable, to America's number-one fanaticist. John Brown had even written down 718 Lombard as a place to go for help.

The schoolhouse!

Yet it was all in past tense now. Brown's raid had come and gone and no perceptible harm had come to the two-story brick schoolhouse. The I.C.Y. managers had come to accept the mysteries of Bassett's life as a political leader of other young colored men and did not demand explanations. At least, not officially.

"I remember the distressing position Bassett was in," his student Robert Adger wrote later. "But we had at that time a lot of young fellows who stood together and . . . gave good account in many broils . . . fugitive slaves cases, etc."

★ ★ ★

ONE "BROIL" INVOLVED a turncoat.

Catto and friends often met at a cigar store. One of the group was a fugitive slave. George Steel, a waiter, lived with his mother. Two bad things happened to Steel—his former master came with other men looking for him and his mother. And a Negro named John Francis told the master where he could find them.

A slaveholder himself in Charleston, Francis was staying in William Still's boardinghouse—across the street from the cigar store. Steel and his mother left the city as word of his treachery spread. A meeting was held in the street that night. "The indignation of the colored people knew no bounds," William Henry Johnson, who was there, wrote. Three men marched to the boardinghouse, the crowd surging behind. Still opened the door. He said he would defend his boarder "to the bitter end."

Johnson observed, "This did not amount to much." They pushed Still aside and went to Francis's room. Confronting the "base informer," they ordered him to leave the city. Francis looked out the window and saw the crowd. He asked for "safe passage across the Gray's Ferry Bridge." He got it and left town, never to be seen again.

* * *

IN 1860, MARSHAL JENKINS and his men seized another Negro.

The arrest of Moses Horner bore curious parallels to Daniel Webster's arrest almost exactly a year before. The slaveholder's counsel was Brewster. The accused was grabbed near Harrisburg. This time, the writ was vague about the fugitive's height.

A Virginia slaveholder had sworn out the writ for Horner, "a slave . . . in absolute right and for life." He was twenty-seven, "neither very bright nor very dark, . . . somewhere between 5 feet 9 inches and 6 feet, appearing different as he sometimes carries himself erect and sometimes a little stooping about the neck and shoulders."

The marshals made their move at night, rousting Horner from his bed. They hurried him down unlit lanes to a railroad depot and placed him under guard in a smoking car.

Legal twists and turns landed the case in the courtroom of a federal judge, John Cadwalader. Where Longstreth had given the defense two days, Cadwalader gave them three hours. Where Longstreth had moved the boiling-over cauldron of the Webster case twice to seat more spectators, Cadwalader let marshals remove some spectators from his courtroom at Fifth and Chestnut. Specifically, the Negroes.

Rather than a judge whose parents were Quakers, Horner had a judge whose brother owned slaves. That was George Cadwalader, the general who had put down the Bible riots, the adviser who told Pierce Butler to auction four hundred slaves.

Given three hours to prepare a defense, Horner's lawyers found one witness who swore he had known Horner as a free man in the North since before the date of his putative escape from the South. Brewster presented several Virginia men who said the opposite.

Cadwalader quickly ruled against Horner, setting off "demonstrations of joy" by pro-slavery spectators. (A Harrisburg paper said Philadelphians were taking up their shameful habit of bowing to "King Cotton.")

Horner's lawyers, desperate to prevent his being sent South, rushed to a city judge, a Republican, Joseph Allison—who ordered the marshals to come to his courtroom the next morning and show cause for holding Horner prisoner. Cadwalader was a federal judge, so this local writ of habeas corpus had little force and the marshals knew it. They ignored

Allison's order and prepared to walk Horner to a heavily guarded carriage that would take him to a Baltimore-bound train.

The walk was a distance of about sixty yards, across an intersection clotting up with more than fifty white policemen and perhaps five hundred young Negroes.

One of the young men was Alfred M. Green, a Banneker member. He held a cane in his hand.

Green was twenty-seven. His father was an A.M.E. minister who had moved from Pittsburgh to Canada after the Fugitive Slave Act and had urged his flock to follow. Rev. Augustus Green had written *A Discourse for our Time*, a pamphlet praising the safer, calmer life of Canada. Green's son had other ideas. He sought out arguments and excelled at the give-and-take of Banneker debates. Having already lived in two countries, he adapted quickly to new situations.

The courthouse doors swung open and a platoon consisting of Jenkins and four other marshals began walking Moses Horner toward the carriage, its driver seated high and swiveling his head left and right at the milling, shouting crowd. The marshals had gotten the manacled Horner seated when two colored men shouted, "Rescue! Rescue!"

Police ran to the carriage, but Alfred Green and two other colored men outran them. Green grabbed the horses' traces "and with an uplifted cane was striking at the driver." The other two colored men each grabbed a bridle and wrenched the horses toward the curb as hard as they could.

Other colored men lunged at the coach and were driven back, once, twice, three times. Police grabbed and grabbed until ten Negroes were arrested and the carriage's path was clear. The marshals got Horner to the train.

Charges were dismissed against five of the arrested men. That left Alfred Green and four others facing trial. Purvis went to the courtroom, inspired by what he called "the noble little band, . . . the men who generously, heroically risked their lives to rescue the man who was about being carried back to slavery." When Purvis tried to post bail, John Jenkins barred his way. The marshal said, "I have my orders." What orders? "To keep out all colored people."

A chief marshal reversed this order and made an apology to Purvis that nonetheless left him "burning with indignation." Cadwalader ruled that the marshals had barred Negroes not for their color but for being dis-

ruptive. Marshals needed discretion to maintain order, the judge wrote—
especially with rumors of a "rescue" afoot.

"The testimony shows that colored persons of good character, whose
usual deportment was quiet and orderly, were not able to command their
feelings on the day . . . so as to abstain from acts of lawless violence," Cadwalader wrote.

Catto and the Bannekers went to work. The arrests were on a Wednesday. By Friday they were launching a defense fund for the five Horner rescuers. Graying men such as Stephen Smith attended the meeting, but men
under thirty led it—Catto, White, Thomas Charnock, William Minton,
all friends of the arrested men.

The committee put a plea for donations in the colored and abolition
press. They praised the lawyers who had defended Horner and Webster.
As for the other side's lawyer, by helping to consign "his brother man to
the chains of interminable slavery," Benjamin Brewster had earned "the
supreme contempt and execration of every lover of freedom."

The poet Frances Watkins was moved by their advertisement. The
"rescuers" had rushed the carriage knowing they would go to prison. Watkins called on readers to open their purses. "Shall these men throw themselves across the track of the general government & be crushed by that
monstrous Juggernaut of organized villainy, the Fugitive Slave Law, & we
sit silent, with our hands folded, in selfish inactivity?"

Alfred Green's term in the city's Eastern State Penitentiary began in
late spring 1860 as the weather warmed up. He used the jail's nickname
for his return address when he wrote to a Banneker friend: "Cherry Hill
Prison, Summer Retreat."

The prison operated under a Quaker reformer's theory that solitary
confinement in darkness made a man see the light and change his ways.
Jail affected Green as it did most political prisoners: It steeled his resolve.
He wrote of decent treatment by his jailer, the only face he saw each day,
and said he was sustained by a growing belief that a just God's wrath
would "be meted out on this guilty, hypocritical and ungodly nation."

Some months later, Mary Grew wrote her annual report for the anti-
slavery society. The year's only fugitive trial in the city had been Moses
Horner's. "On the whole, though the Slave has been taken back. . . . We
have made a good fight, & the enemy has gained a damaging victory. The
feeling of the community is in our favor, and our opponents are tired of
the contest. The marshal & several of his officers have expressed to our

friends their 'hope in God that they might never have another case.' . . . My impression is, that the business of Slave-catching, in Pennsylvania has about come to an end."

★ ★ ★

THE FRENZY TO UNMASK John Brown's abettors ebbed in 1860 as pro- and antislavery forces became engrossed in choosing Buchanan's successor. The city's Democrats met to hammer out their ticket, with Stephen A. Douglas for president at the top and Samuel J. Randall for state Senate, at the bottom, along with his brother, Robert, for state representative.

Sam Randall, Josiah's older son, had learned what Buchanan and former mayor Vaux already knew—that McMullen's reach extended into many polling places in the new, 129-square-mile city. Some Democrats, gagging on the Buchanan feast of pro-South, pro-slavery talk, had bolted the party. But those Democrats were in the minority on the warm day in 1860, when in a dark, overcrowded hall at Ninth and Shippen streets, the Randall-McMullen alliance controlled the nominations meeting.

As the hour grew late, someone rose to accuse that alliance of securing the state Senate nomination for Sam Randall by employing "corrupt means."

Such words were not new to the ears of McMullen's Fourth Ward men, some of whom—including McMullen—had been in and out of court on charges of doctoring ballot boxes and faking Irish voters' naturalization papers. The usual roughs were converging on the dissenter when the night's big winner, Sam Randall, took the floor.

Full-faced and dark-haired, Randall was known less for soaring oratory than studied backstage skills. He had served on the Common Council and was cultivating a legislator's knack for hoarding and dispensing political capital to ease the disputes of his district's warring tribes—except when it came to the Negroes. Since Harper's Ferry, they and their abolition friends had all but become the Democrats' official national whipping-boy, and conveniently, Negroes could not vote.

Randall held his hands out to calm the noisy hall. The point, he reminded them, was not just to elect Stephen Douglas. "Let us go out peacefully and use our best endeavors to beat Abraham Lincoln," he said. "Anything to defeat *Black Republicanism!*" The assembled white Democrats cheered.

★ ★ ★

AS FOR THE other Douglass, he joined Sarah Remond in Britain, toward the end of a tour that surpassed fifty lectures. She hardly needed the booming Douglass at her side; in her stately voice she decried the "unspeakable" use of slave women by their masters. "You may infer something of the state of society in the South," she said, from the presence of eight hundred thousand mulattoes, many of them sold away by their own white fathers.

She repeated the stories of the Tyng ouster, the Butler auction, the jailing of a Maryland Negro for possessing *Uncle Tom's Cabin.* Though once a nonviolent Garrisonian, she had no quarrel with John Brown's attempt "to carry out his great idea." This drew approving shouts of "Hear, hear!" Douglass said the Harpers Ferry raiders were no more criminals than men who boarded a pirate ship, cudgeled the captain, and seized the vessel. He did not mention that he'd aided the boarding party.

In spring, Douglass received an awful letter. His daughter Annie had sickened and died while he was safe in Europe. "My darling sister is now an angel," Rosetta Douglass wrote, ". . . gone to Him whose love is the same for the black as the white."

Douglass slipped back into a divided country and quietly hurried to Rochester. He heard this news: A tall black man in Knoxville, Tennessee, had been set upon by "a furious crowd with knives and bludgeons." Someone had mistaken the man for Douglass.

Sarah Remond stayed in Europe. Britons inscribed a watch for her: "Presented to S. P. Remond, by Englishwomen, her sisters . . . Feb 2d 1860." Thanking them, she said she had been "received here as a sister by white women for the first time in my life."

★ ★ ★

AMID THE RAISING of funds for the Moses Horner defendants and the annual intensity of I.C.Y. examinations and commencement, Catto and his friends took up other business. They prepared and signed an invitation to Mary Brown. Could the white widow attend a special colored concert in her honor?

The invitation came from older men such as the coal-broker Smith, the caterer Dorsey, White Sr., the cemetery operator; Adger, the used-furniture seller; Catto, the eternal circuit-rider; and their children, Jake,

William, Robert, Octavius. A public alliance of two generations—the Underground Railroad men and their sons.

They affected a gallant tone, promising excellent music from colored orchestras, choirs, and soloists, hoping to offer cheer in the hour of "your late sudden bereavement." Fifty-nine colored men affixed their names and published the invitation. No small thing, this, in early 1860, to associate oneself with John Brown's widow in the northernmost Southern city. And to announce it—that was certainly going *above* ground.

Mary Brown accepted.

CHAPTER 10

The Wolf Killers

O N A WINTER night in 1860, a northbound train pulled into Cincinnati and disgorged forty bedraggled colored women and children.

They were ending a journey of five hundred miles. They were refugees—not from slavery but from Arkansas. In 1859, the Arkansas legislature passed a law declaring that the state's free Negroes—six hundred or so, compared with its forty-seven thousand slaves—were potentially trouble and must leave.

Slave owners loathed abolitionists but saved a special emotion—call it dread—for their free Negroes. Arkansas was emptying its state attic of the dangerous debris that had collected there. If the free Negroes remained in the state, they would be enslaved. Their deadline was January 1860.

So hundreds of men, women, and children, by foot, train, wagon, and boat, left the state in a sudden cold-weather trek, all headed in the same direction, all going North, an exodus caused not by famine or flood but by the hand of man.

Other states already had passed laws closing their borders to colored immigrants. Illinois said no, as did Indiana and Oregon. Minnesota's legislature was considering the exclusion. New England was too far, and even Pennsylvania, the state just on the other side of the Mason-Dixon Line, was too great distance in the plunging temperatures of January. Who would let them in?

Finally, Ohio beckoned. "We learn that the upward-bound boats are crowded with them," a Cincinnati paper reported. They were fortunate enough to be greeted by the colored leaders of the city in a formal reception at a colored-owned boardinghouse where Frederick Douglass once spoke from the balcony.

The poet Frances Ellen Watkins's "Appeal to Christians Throughout the World," was a thank-you to Ohio and vitriol to Arkansas. She asked ministers and editors and mayors to be "united in protest again this forced winter exodus." "We turn to the free North," she said, "but even here, oppression tracks our steps," detailing the states that would not provide rest "for the souls of our weary feet. . . . In Ohio, we found hearts."

At the same time, another racially motivated exodus was beginning in Philadelphia, but this one was voluntary. Many Southern medical students studying in the city chose to secede. Some left after being caught with dirks and revolvers at the George William Curtis lecture. Some may have just not wanted to listen to any more drivel about abolition. But 244 of them headed South to attend schools closer to home.

Not only did Philadelphia have about twenty-two thousand colored residents in 1860, far more than any other Northern city, but the city also had more Negroes in relation to the white population. Boston had one Negro for every seventy-seven whites; New York City had one in sixty-three. Philadelphia one in twenty-four. (That twenty-two thousand count was likely low; white federal census takers were not smitten with the idea of venturing into colored neighborhoods; and Negroes, aware that state officials were in favor of colonization, were not eager to cooperate with a white man knocking on the door and asking to count them.)

Though Negroes lived citywide, their world was, by and large, not seen by whites. Whites saw the colored shuckers of oysters but did not see the lack of colored lawyers or bankers. The *Press*, a Republican newspaper and the most abolition-friendly of the city's dailies, sent a white reporter out in 1860 to remove the shutters from the colored city.

The reporter visited three homes with pianos and saw portraits of John Brown, Frederick Douglass, and Harriet Beecher Stowe. He found a better class of Negroes living on Rodman Street west of Ninth with "its rows of tall, beautiful houses, and . . . the clean pavements and street. . . . [I]n the doorways the families of colored men were seated. . . . There was no loud laughing or talking."

He wrote that he had not seen "such decorum" on "any street in the city" and was chastised by one colored man because "streets like this you never visit . . . [and] never [go] . . . into these cheerful homes or speak with these families of our better classes. . . ."

And the reporter went to the area near Mother Bethel Church where "upon Sunday mornings . . . [f]olks of all shades of color saunter down the streets; beautiful quadroon girls, perfumed, fashionably dressed, dandy beaux, staid colored gentlemen, etc."

He detailed some of the problems and prejudices facing the Negroes. "They seldom inherit money. . . . At theatres, and concerts, lectures and churches, the negro is restricted to a remote gallery. In mechanical pursuits, if a colored apprentice or journeyman be employed, there is an immediate rebellion upon the part of the white laborers."

And because they were poor and were not permitted on streetcars, many were forced to live in the worst housing in the city's worst areas on streets such as St. Mary's, Baker, and Bedford. The reporter wrote he could not "speak at length" about the wretchedness he had witnessed, and then he did just that.

"There were Negroes in all conditions of bodily mutilation. We saw one afflicted with a tumor nearly a foot in diameter; one with a ghastly scar across his jaw made by an axe in the hands of an enemy; one whose leg was almost fleshless from a scalding received when stupefied with rum; many one-eyed, some deaf, some entirely blind."

In this squalid area, perhaps one in five who listened to prayers and hymns in the warm Christian confines of the Bedford Street Mission was Negro. New York had its Five Points; Philadelphia had its "infected region," as city officials called it, unless those officials were a welcoming committee describing it to out-of-town visitors. Residents knew to watch where they stepped because the narrow streets were often used as a public sewer, and pigs, goats, and chickens made their homes on those streets, too.

A school teacher curious to see the seamier side of life turned up a dirty alley near Bedford and found herself in a "still dirtier yard, built up on each side with what I supposed to be cow stables, but . . . no poor cows were lodged in these sheds, which are about 10 feet square and 6 in height. A little round hole cut in front of each was the only admittance for air and light, except the doors, which, although fastened by a padlock, swung two or three inches from the post. They were really not good enough for animals, and yet they were used as boardinghouses for those poor human beings." Rent was ten cents a night, in advance. And those who did not pay could land in the alderman's office.

Poverty and disease and alcoholism were the lynchpins of the squalor in "the infected region," but for the men and women trying to bring God's word to its tarnished souls, racism was there as well. Rev. Benjamin T. Sewell ran the Bedford Street Mission, and he explained the degradation he witnessed every day: "Many a husband . . . is weeping with his offspring while the mother of his little ones is drunk on the streets, or locked up as a vagrant in Moyamensing Prison or living with some dirty negro."

While Negroes were being castigated on Bedford Street, a Negro was being celebrated in Boston. A dead Negro. The question John S. Rock, a speaker in March 1860 on the ninetieth anniversary of the Boston Massacre and the death of Crispus Attucks, asked was whether the right dead Negro was being honored. No one had ever asked questions quite like this, at least not in public. But Rock, surely the only colored dentist-doctor-lawyer in the nation, did just that.

"I am not yet ready to idolize the actions of Crispus Attucks, who was a leader of . . . those who resorted to forcible measures to create a new government which has used every means in its power to outrage & degrade his race & posterity," he thundered. Rock said that the nation's only events deserving commemoration were the founding of the Anti-Slavery Society in 1833 and the insurrections of Nat Turner and John Brown.

"I believe in insurrections—and especially those of the pen and of the sword. William Lloyd Garrison is, I think, a perfect embodiment of the moral insurrection of thought; . . . John Brown was, and is, the representative of the potent power, the sword, which proposes to settle at once the relation between master & slave—peaceably if it can, forcibly if it must. This is, no doubt, the method by which the freedom of the blacks will be brought about in the country. It is a severe method; but to severe ills it is necessary to apply severe remedies. Slavery has taken up the sword, and it is but just that it should perish by it."

The young orator from South Jersey, now living in Massachusetts, was not finished. He said money was the key to the Negro's future. He predicted a day Negroes would gain economic power and have spending money in their pockets. When that day came, he said, "Black will be a very pretty color."

About a week before in New York City, slavery was also the topic, but this time the speaker was a white man, a midwesterner, and he was talking not about destroying slavery with a sword but about containing it with the law.

Abraham Lincoln, who already had acquired a reputation as an eloquent public speaker in his debates two years earlier with Senator Stephen A. Douglas, was making his first major speech in New York, and he did well. "No man has ever made such an impression on his first appeal to a New York audience," the *Tribune* trumpeted. The newspaper wrote that it was "one of the happiest and most convincing political arguments ever made in this city."

What Lincoln posited was that the federal government had the power to stop the spread of slavery outside the South. Neither the words nor the sentences, in and of themselves, lift off the page with their cadence or power—"Does the proper division of local from federal authority, or anything in the Constitution, forbid our federal government to control as to slavery in our federal territories?"

Nonetheless, Lincoln's performance that night caused his name to be on the lips of Republicans the next day. The stage was set for his presidential candidacy.

Not as impressed were Negro leaders. Lincoln was talking about limiting slavery, not ending it. He favored colonization, the fancy five-syllable word that had all but become a curse word to most Negroes. He supported enforcement of the Fugitive Slave Act and was not talking about equal rights. No, it was clear. Lincoln was no friend to the Negroes.

★ ★ ★

THE ENORMOUS ISSUES and events of the day were often accompanied by smaller ones, by baseball games, by parades of fraternal groups, by romance after the long I.C.Y. school year, and by a scientific lecture by a proud Negro.

Robert and Joseph Henson held a "grand festival" with music and dancing in Jamaica, Long Island, New York, to celebrate the Henson Base Ball Club win over the Unknowns, the colored baseball club from Long Island.

Amos Webber donned a different sort of uniform on an 1860 Sunday in May in Philadelphia. The janitor wore an apron and collar, jewelry, badges, and an insignia for his attendance at a meeting of the Grand and

United Order of Odd Fellows, Carthaginian Lodge 901. White Philadelphia—for that matter, the white North—was not enamored of the sight of
Negroes in uniform. Uniforms suggested authority and power, and whites
were not going to allow Negroes to wear the uniform of a police officer
or the hat of a streetcar conductor or, heaven forbid, the blue of the U.S.
Army. But Webber and the other members of the Odd Fellows Lodge, outfitted in regalia, paraded through the streets to a black church. They were,
in the same way as the Bannekers were, showing themselves to the city
around them for the first time. The Odd Fellows knew that their public
showing of colors was dangerous, but they did it anyway. On occasion, the
police under Mayor Henry gave them an escort through the streets.

Octavius Catto, now twenty-one, chose that same month of May to
show his manhood, moral vision, and colors by writing a flirtatious letter
to Cordelia Sanders, two years his junior.

It was addressed "Highly Esteemed Miss" in clear handwriting that
lacked his father's flourish but held the margins in straight lines and concluded with his signature, underlined twice. Before that signature was a
poem. (The word "lay" in the third line hearkens back to an old meaning—a poem that is sung.)

> And if, perchance, one pleasing ray
> Of true poetic fervor beams
> Along my unambitious lay
> Thyself hath been th' inspiring theme
>
> Accept it then and believe me
> Yours always and always yours,
>
> Octavius V. Catto

Cordelia, like Octavius, had her roots in Charleston, but her background was different. And different from most other offspring of a slave
mother and a slave-owner father.

Richard Cogdell, a third-generation Charlestonian, bought a fifteen-
year-old slave named Sarah Martha Sanders in 1830. He had been married many years, but over the next two decades, Sarah Sanders bore ten
children by him, including Cordelia, born in 1841.

Unlike so many other white slave-owners who fathered children with
their slaves, Cogdell cared for Sarah and their children, bought them a

house in Philadelphia, and moved them there so that the children could be educated. Upon his death, he left all of his household property in Philadelphia to Cordelia and one of her sisters.

Catto's life as a young romancer was no secret. An 1860 letter from his friend in Washington, William Wormley, mentioned four young ladies that they both knew. Wormley was the scion of one of the best-known colored families in the District of Columbia. His father ran a restaurant, his uncle a big livery stable. His aunt had trained with Sarah Douglass in Philadelphia and had started a colored school.

Wormley was replying to a long, newsy letter from his Philadelphia friend.

> Yea! It filled my heart with joy unspeakable: when I saw that some fair young lady had won the gallant heart of our most noble "Catto." I tell you old boy, you may say what you will about that young lady, but old "Wormley" is in the field yet. . . .
>
> . . . [T]he George Town ladies are all well, and send their best love to you. . . .
>
> Miss Pet Jones has come home from Oberlin. . . . Miss Laurie Browne asked me to give her best "love" to you. Miss Johnson-alias-Dougans sends her very best love to you and says she would very much like to see you so will you come, won't you come, and bring "Blue Dress" with you?" ["Blue Dress" was formal wear.]

Wormley mentioned breezily that he, too, was Oberlin-bound—and thus marked a family milestone. The Snow Storm mobs of 1835 had burned the school his aunt founded and his father attended. Now, a Wormley son was heading off to college.

He added a P.S.: He had gone to hear Octavius's father lecture the night before at Fifteenth Street Presbyterian. The topic was "The 'Condition of Our Race' in the United States," he wrote. "It was excellent. Three cheers for Mr. Catto—hip-hip-hip."

In June, another sort of lecture by a colored man occurred, but this time the speaker was Martin Delany and the scene was London.

Delany, back from his twenty-six-hundred-mile exploration of the Niger Valley, was being honored by the Royal Geographic Society. So was Robert Campbell, the former I.C.Y. teacher who had also made the trek. They were the first Negroes the society had so praised.

★ ★ ★

THE SUMMER AND FALL of 1860 were highlighted by two events in Philadelphia: the election campaigns for mayor, governor, Congress, and the presidency and the beginning of the city's first season of baseball. Negroes could participate in neither.

Taking the latter first, most of the city's young white men had stopped playing town ball and had adopted the New York rules for baseball, with its four bases around a diamond-shaped infield. The Winona, Equity, Mercantile, Keystone, Continental, and Minerva clubs played that year in fields across the city. The Mercantile Club was so popular that a song was written about them—"The Home Run Quick Step."

While one should never minimize the importance of baseball, written as one word or two, the presidential election in 1860 would turn out to be the more important event.

By summer, the possibility that antislavery Republicans might win was palpable. Southern states were talking about secession. Philadelphia big business depended on the South so there was no glee in its count- ing houses at the thought of a Republican takeover. Philadelphia may have been the first stop in the North for Southerners, but it was also the North's most Southern city. The abolitionists had turned out big crowds of late, but none as mammoth as the pro-South rally that nearly toppled Jayne's Hall.

Lincoln understood the aversion that so many had to Republicans and abolition. He ran not as a Republican in Philadelphia but on the Peo- ple's Party ticket. There was more in his campaign literature and speeches about tariffs than about stopping the spread of involuntary servitude. Mayor Henry, who ran for reelection on the People's Party slate, did not support Lincoln and kept as far away as he could from his coattails. None- theless, Henry's opponents painted him as an abolitionist.

And Lincoln opponents painted him even more harshly. Cartoons were published. A print by the celebrated Currier and Ives portrayed Young America as a young man in a slouch hat pondering his vote: Lincoln ally Horace Greeley assures him that the candidate had "no connection with the Abolition party." A clean-shaven Lincoln sits atop a "Republican Platform" of rails he has split. Inside those rails is a caged black man, his big lips and wide eyes in an idiot's grin.

"You can't pull that wool over my eyes," Young America says, pointing at the black man. Below is the cartoon's title, "The Nigger in the Woodpile."

Fortunately for Mayor Henry, during the last week of campaigning, one of the city's more influential Democrats, Alderman William McMullen, was attending the Democratic national convention in Charleston, South Carolina. The convention began April 23 and ran late, until May 3. So McMullen was out of town on May 1, election day for city offices. Henry won by 882 votes in a surprise.

When Lincoln won in November, so did People Party candidate Andrew Curtin for governor. Philadelphians split their ticket, electing some Democrats as well. They chose Samuel J. Randall as their state senator from McMullen's southern end of town, and sent his brother, Robert Randall, to the state legislature in Harrisburg.

Soon after his reelection, Mayor Henry bought uniforms of blue for the city's police.

★ ★ ★

ELATION **IS SELDOM** used to describe the national reaction to the election of Lincoln.

South Carolina passed a resolution to secede but changed its mind the next day. A Lincoln effigy was burned in Florida. Georgia legislators asked for a 25 percent tax on goods from Northern states not abiding by the Fugitive Slave Act. The busy South Carolina legislature called for "police surveillance" on visitors from the North. The reaction in Philadelphia was calmer and more befitting a mercantile city—a newspaper advertisement announced that if the president-elect was bald, then he must be wearing a toupee made by George Thurgland, with offices at 29 South Sixth Street.

The Banneker Institute celebrated Benjamin Banneker's 128th birthday with food, music, and a speech by Catto. Frederick Douglass in Boston and Rev. Henry Highland Garnet in New York prepared speeches for the anniversary of John Brown's death. A crowd broke up a similar Boston meeting before anyone could speak. At Shiloh Church in New York, Garnet said any Southern secessions would advance freedom's cause. "Let the enslavers secede," he said—yank them out of the nation's body like sore teeth.

In Philadelphia, skaters dotted the frozen Schuylkill on ice eight inches deep. As the ice hardened, so did attitudes.

Democrats and businessmen met amid fears of losing Southern trade and blamed the abolitionists. Brewster, the slaveholder's lawyer, said Pennsylvania must decide whether she "would go with the North or with the South or stand by herself." Speakers called for the state's secession from the Union if war with the South began.

To the consternation of Robert Purvis, Lucretia Mott, and Miller McKim, the mayor who had protected the abolitionists now denied them a hall. This time, Mayor Henry said, "The threats of riot were so loud." Then he took part in a pro-South meeting on Independence Square.

The event was described as a "monster citizen's meeting" held "for the purpose of extending the olive branch to the South through promises of concessions." The rally resolved to uphold the Fugitive Slave Act and not to interfere with slavery. Mayor Henry spoke as did one business leader after another. Judges spoke. Their words made an impression on one young out-of-town visitor. He even adopted some of the words in a speech that he wrote. He was a twenty-two-year-old actor. Already well-known in the South, he was just beginning to perform in the North. His name was John Wilkes Booth.

On December 20, South Carolina seceded again and did not change its mind the next day.

South Carolina was overreacting. Nothing was really going to change in 1861, Banneker member George Stephens predicted. The coming Lincoln presidency was just "the fag end of a series of pro-slavery administrations."

★ ★ ★

JANUARY 1861 WAS NOT freedom's proudest month.

Secession gained momentum. Sidney Fisher wrote in his diary: "States are going one after another out of the Union and nothing is done to prevent them. The plan of the government seems now to avoid anything that will irritate the South and bring on civil war."

State representative Randall introduced legislation to repeal Pennsylvania's personal liberty laws—that is, the state would no longer protect a fugitive slave who had believed the state to be a safe haven. Randall, armed with a petition signed by eleven thousand citizens, argued that the founding fathers had not meant to give jury trials to runaway slaves. Later in the month, a judge said the owners of Philadelphia horse-drawn streetcars could legally bar Negroes from inside their conveyances. Among the judge's remarks were these seven words explaining his decision: "views and feelings of the superior race."

In the South, many free people of color went North to escape the possibility of being enslaved. But some stayed back. The governor and other officeholders of the state of South Carolina received letters from mulatto residents who had once called William Catto their friend: "In our veins flows the blood of the white race[,] in some half[,] in others much more than half white blood. . . . Our attachments are with you, our hopes of safety and protection from you. Our allegiance is due to South Carolina and in her defence, we are willing to offer up our lives, and all that is dear to us." Among the twenty-three signers were Richard E. Dereef, Joseph Dereef, Robert Howard, Richard Holloway and sons, and the millwright Anthony Weston. Most of them owned slaves.

The wind off the Delaware River made the January cold unbearable, and 270 homeless people spent January 19 in city police stations. A week later, five thousand workingmen braved the wintry gusts of a Saturday night snowstorm to come to Independence Hall for a peace rally. They rallied for, of all things, compromise and raised their voice against any sort of war with the South.

The Bannekers held a meeting at St. Thomas Church on a Tuesday evening to grapple with what "duty" colored people had in the midst of this national political crisis. The meeting also resolved to petition the state legislature to foil Randall's efforts. That petition said, in part, "It is not part of our business to review . . . the pretended causes of the present national disorder of the country; certainly no one will pretend that the free colored people of the State have anything to do with these great National questions. . . . To sacrifice our freedom, our peace, and our blood to purchase a conciliation with the South . . . would be as blind and impolitic as it is unjust and sacrilegious."

The Banneker member who had spent a night in a Charleston jail scolded the older generation for talking too much and doing too little. He wrote to the *Weekly Anglo-African*: "The bulls of our people seem to be resting in the most profound indifference; not a ripple disturbs the quiet calm of the wide sea of their contentment," George Stephens said. "If I could make my voice heard throughout the length and breadth of this broad land, I would cry from the depths of my soul, 'Arouse, free black men! arouse! Act—act in the living present!'"

* ★ *

THE MAIN ACTOR in the living present had been a Mexican War hero, secretary of war, and U.S. senator. Jefferson Davis announced the formation of the Confederate States of America. At the same time, the president-elect of the United States of America stopped in Philadelphia to mark Washington's birthday. He was on his way to his inauguration.

Sitting in a barouche pulled by four white horses and accompanied by elected officials and luminaries (including Mayor Henry, who stayed close to his coattails this time), Lincoln waved to the flag-waving crowds as he arrived at the State House shortly before six on a clear February 1861 morning and raised the nation's newest flag of thirty-four stars—the latest star for Kansas.

The night before, the mayor had asked him to stay long enough to "consult" with the spirits at the site where the Constitution was written—"as it were, to listen to those breathings rising within the consecrated walls."

The crowd at Independence Hall applauded when Lincoln said there was "no need for bloodshed and war. . . . The Government will not use force unless force is used against us." Perhaps he had listened to the whispers of the walls. He said he had pondered "what great principle or idea" had held the nation together this long—"not the mere matter of the separation of the colonies from the mother land; but something in that Declaration giving liberty, not alone to the people of this country, but hope to the world for all future time. It was that which gave promise that in due time the weights should be lifted from the shoulders of all men, and that all men should have an equal chance."

Lincoln said he would sooner "be assassinated on this spot" than cede that principle. He had just received word of men plotting to kill him when his train reached Baltimore.

A photograph of Lincoln giving his speech that day shows a bramble of hatted heads, too fuzzy to discern whether any of the faces is Negro. Would young Negroes want to see the president-elect? Or were Negroes like Octavius Catto, Jake White, and Charlotte Forten as pessimistic as the abolitionist leaders of their fathers' generation?

Lincoln's stance against war and bloodshed pleased most everyone in the North, but not men like William Lloyd Garrison.

"How is it possible?" the abolitionist and one-time nonviolence leader asked, "that the President can be deluded into the belief that 'there need be no bloodshed or violence' in enforcing the laws. . . . The breach is natural, inevitable and not to be repaired—it is the result of the 'irrepressible conflict' between justice and oppression, right and wrong, which admits to no conciliation or compromise. . . . Let there be no civil war, but a separation between the Free and Slave states in the spirit of Abraham and Lot."

★ ★ ★

AND SO THERE was a Civil War.

After the April attack by five hundred members of a new Confederate army and surrender of the eighty Union soldiers at Fort Sumter in Charleston harbor, men and women in the North were flying flags and raging with war fever.

Tents held busy recruiting stations in Philadelphia's four main squares. Women sewed uniforms inside hotels. Soldiers paraded and drilled. Fife-and-drum teams drilled as well. Storefronts and rooftops were colored red, white, and blue. The shopping thoroughfare of Chestnut Street flaunted flags, ribbons, streamers, and dry goods of the patriotic colors and booksellers did the same, arranging book bindings in the windows to show the colors. Crowds thronged telegraph offices waiting for war news. Black abolitionists, led by Underground Railroad titan William Still, opened an office to help fugitive slaves find employment. He was overwhelmed by the number of men and women seeking work.

His replacement was a forty-year-old Boston carpenter and school teacher born free in Virginia who had already gone back down south to teach former slaves to read and write. John Oliver wrote a letter to the American Missionary Association explaining his zeal: "I have felt a desire to . . . help teach them. . . . with my knowledge of both Slavery and the Slave and the condition in which the former has left the latter, I Believe that I would be of great service to that people. The work of Anti-Slavery men is not yet compleat. . . . [The freedmen] must also at this . . . beginning prepare their minds for this new berth."

In Philadelphia, the kind of violence that once targeted abolitionists now visited secessionists. A mob ran one afternoon to a newspaper office rumored to be flying the Palmetto flag of South Carolina. There was no flag, but the mob stormed the office of the *Palmetto Flag* newspaper, which closed days later. Josiah Randall, the Democratic patriarch whose pro-South speech had drawn cheers at Jayne's Hall in 1859, found his home ringed by patriotic and unhappy young men. Police moved them away.

And Sidney Fisher's diary dutifully noted the latest gossip about Pierce Butler.

"The only news of interest this morning is that yesterday Pierce Butler was arrested on a charge of treason," he wrote. He noted that his friend had returned from a Charleston trip expressing "the strongest opinions in favor of the southern cause." One report said that on the trip, Butler had transported "a number of secession cockades, pistols etc." and was in touch with Confederate officials. His face was said to be "white & slightly quivering lips & nostrils" as soldiers escorted him to a cell in a New York fort, but he'd otherwise kept his composure. Butler's daughter wrote in protest to Lincoln.

Fisher reflected that jail "will keep him quiet and out of harm's way." Briefly, at least. Butler at first refused but finally signed a pledge not to undermine the Union and to get federal permission before he traveled south again. He was out of jail in a month.

It was unclear where the soul of the city really rested. From the firemen to the money men, Philadelphia was awash in Southern sympathies and dependent on Southern commerce. Yet it also had the historic underpinnings of abolition and a free, vigorous Negro community. The city had the trappings of patriotism, but there was little evidence that it had the language. What are we fighting for? When the war ends, what do we win? Answers were not forthcoming. And ending slavery was not on anyone's lips, except for those of abolitionists and colored people.

Actually, the whole issue of slaves and slavery was interfering with the war. Fugitive slaves were fleeing to Union lines and the military commanders were not quite sure what to do with them. Top military figures, such as Generals George McClellan and William T. Sherman, thought they should be returned to their masters, assuming their masters were loyal to the Union.

Lincoln wanted them returned as well, thinking that he could keep the Southern border states, such as Kentucky, out of the Confederacy if he did not interfere with slavery.

The fugitive slaves made the decision for Lincoln. The occasional appearance of a runaway slave at Union lines grew to a trickle and then a stream of as many as 150 a day. Soon, slave owners were also arriving at Union lines seeking their property.

Congress declared that returning fugitive slaves was not a soldier's job. Exactly what would be done with them was not clear—Lincoln wanted

funds appropriated to colonize them in a far-off land. One of those lands was Chiriqui in Panama. Investors presented the president with a plan to move Negroes there. Chiriqui, they said, offered a good harbor, verdant valleys, plentiful coal, and a chance to establish a U.S. military post that would dominate the western Caribbean.

Lincoln was so enamored of the idea that he invited five Negro leaders in Washington to the White House, where he told them, "Your race are suffering, in my judgment, the greatest wrong afflicted on any people." Even if emancipation occurred, he said, they would not be considered equal. The answer was "for us both, therefore, to be separated."

He cited the perils George Washington had braved. He asked the Negro leaders to brave perils, too, and lead their people out of the country. He said the power of his office was not enough to win fairness for Negroes in this country, but he would do all he could to achieve that in Panama: "I would endeavor to have you made equals."

Lincoln's argument was that if they agreed to leave the country, he would have an easier time emancipating them. He assured them they would not be sent to far-off Africa but rather to Central America. "The place I am thinking about [offers] . . . harbors among the finest in the world [and] . . . very rich coal mines. . . . Could I get a hundred tolerably intelligent men, with their wives and children . . . ? Can I have 50? If I can find 25 able-bodied men . . . I think I could make a successful commencement."

The president touted this idea like an auctioneer, pounded it like a revivalist, hawked it like a circus barker. He invoked the name of Washington. He sympathized. He empathized. The Negro men looked at him silently and said they would get back to him.

★ ★ ★

IT COULDN'T BE a very long war. The North had five times more industrial production, twice the railroad mileage, and seven million more people—and that included the South's four million slaves. The war would be over before the baseball season ended.

But with each passing month, more young colored men wanted to be a part of the war. Thousands in Boston, New York, and Philadelphia succumbed to the war fever, rallying to the North's side. But many in the black community still thought they should not fight. Did it make sense to go to war for a Union not making the end of slavery its battle cry?

The *Weekly Anglo-African* called on readers to organize, drill, and be ready but go to war only "when the slave calls." That became the stance for many—fight when the war's aim was to end slavery. The *Christian Recorder* said "to offer ourselves for military service now is to abandon self respect and invite insult."

That did not please the Bannekers' Alfred Green, a man uncomfortable with action delayed. "No nation ever has or ever will be emancipated from slavry . . . but by the sword, wielded too by their own strong arms," he wrote. "The prejudiced white men, North or South, never will respect us until they are forced to . . . by deeds of our own."

Colored volunteers organized their own militia and began to drill. More than eighty-five hundred joined military units and were ready to fight. But the A.M.E. Church said Negroes should not do battle for a nation that "oppressed them." Others were convinced that fighting might ease racial tension and lead to emancipation. And the question arose: If they fought, would they come home to a nation that gave them full rights?

The Lincoln administration said no to the colored volunteers, invoking the law passed just before the Mexican War—no Negroes allowed in the army. (But the navy did permit enlistment by Negroes.) When the colored abolitionist leader John Mercer Langston asked the governor of Ohio, David Tod, to permit Negroes to enlist and to let Langston lead their recruiting and training at no cost to the state, he replied, "Do you not know, Mr. Langston, that this is a white man's government; that white men are able to defend and protect it, and that to enlist a negro soldier would be to drive every white man out of the service? When we want you colored men, we will notify you."

In the war's first months, federal authorities did permit commanders to use former slaves as workers with the military. But those commanders did not want fugitive slaves to be soldiers. Northern legislators felt it would be "degrading" to the nation for colored soldiers to fight and that "insurrections" would result. Some thought the argument meaningless and that the law need not be changed. Negroes would never fight.

Frederick Douglass was not satisfied. He wanted slaves freed immediately and given guns, insisting, "The Negro is the key of the situation—the pivot upon which the whole rebellion turns."

So the war had begun and there was no agreement about why it was being fought. Both the North and South were fighting for preservation, the South to preserve its way of life, and the North to preserve its Union. But for Negroes and white abolitionists, the war was about changing everything.

★ ★ ★

IN APRIL, McMULLEN volunteered and was given a commission as captain, as befitting a veteran of the Mexican War. He formed the Independent Rangers, his own one-hundred-man unit.

McMullen was a supporter of his country, not Lincoln. The war, small, newborn and inviting curiosity, drew the attention of eighty-four men from Moyamensing Hose and the Killers, who signed up for a three-month stint with the Rangers.

Also volunteering to fight for other units were men from the Classics Department at the University of Pennsylvania and the Maennercher Vocal Society. Differences of breeding, education, and wealth were overlooked as every man on the street seemed to be in uniform, or working on behalf of those in uniform. But the Moyas and Maennerchers were never mixed into the same unit. Philadelphia was still a Southern city by many accounts, but it dressed itself in blue. In early June, just before the Rangers went south, McMullen was given a gift, a collection of little cards with photos of Southern rebel leaders, a nineteenth-century version of baseball cards of the enemy. And before his men had captured any of those rebel leaders or attacked a Confederate flank, a song ballyhooing the pluck of "McMullin" and the Rangers was written and sold on the streets.

> Our Country is now in great danger,
> And calls aloud for freeman all,
> To rally around our noble standard,
> And answer bravely to the call.
> So buckle in on freedom's cause,
> The majesty of all our laws,
> The majesty to us given,
> In '76, bestowed by heaven.
> The President, though not our choice,
> Now holds his seat in hallowed land,
> And we'll protect him, though we perish,
> By a brother, hand to hand.

Disunion in our midst is raging,
In social circles, and midst Firemen all,
And McMullin's Band's, the first responded,
To our President's appeal to all.

★ ★ ★

A SPECIAL SUMMER SESSION of Congress in 1861 made it clear that not emancipating the slaves was the policy of the nation. The Crittenden Resolution declared that the war was not "for any purpose of conquest or subjugation, nor for purpose of overthrowing or interfering with the rights of established institutions of those States."

McMullen and his men came home at summer's end to cheers and a parade. The Independent Rangers were at the periphery of the war's first major land battle in Manassas, Virginia, but saw little action in their three months. The crowds didn't seem to care. The Moyamensing Hose building was decorated with flags and a "Welcome Rangers" banner. Ladies waved handkerchiefs from windows on Eighth Street. The hose company carriage was run out, its bells ringing, as were bells of nearby companies.

Just three blocks north, Catto had taken a room in a boardinghouse. Cordelia Sanders, the object of his recent affection, had decided to marry another. If her marriage tore at the heart of the schoolteacher, history neglected to record it. Henry Minton ran his restaurant while Thomas Dorsey catered birthdays and anniversaries—mostly for white clients, who could afford caterers. James Le Count was making cabinets and coffins and sending four children to the I.C.Y. Jake's father, Jacob C. White—carrying an umbrella rain or shine—owned Lebanon Cemetery, where those coffins ended up.

Newspaper advertisements showed that men sought work: "Wanted— A Good, Colored Cook wants a situation"; "A single colored man wishes a situation as Waiter." Though most colored men and women had poor-paying, back-breaking jobs, the community also had its custom boot makers, portrait painters, barbers, undertakers, band leaders, teachers of shorthand, and lumberyard owners.

In September, graduates of the Institute for Colored Youth formed an alumni association and elected Catto as its president.

One of the institute's favorite guest lecturers was at sea just then. Garnet was on his way to England to raise money for his latest African settlement venture. He wrote his wife after he arrived in Liverpool, marveling at how much better this voyage was than his trip twelve years before. "I was caged up in the steward's room and not allowed to go into the saloon, or to eat at the table with white humanity. How changed now." He had "an elegant stateroom" and dined with white humanity. One day, passengers were excited to see two black whales. A white woman said, "Oh! why do they make such a noise and commotion? They are the biggest fishes in the sea—and they are black."

Garnet replied, "Madam, you have accounted for the noise they make."

Lincoln proclaimed September 26 National Fast Day. A young Negro minister in New York quoted Isaiah 58 to mark the occasion. "Is this not the fast that I have chosen to loose the bands of wickedness . . . and to let the oppressed go free?" Preaching was Rev. William J. Alston, a free-born North Carolinian who was one of the "talented thousandth" at Oberlin. He said that slavery had left the nation "basely corrupted" and lamented that before the war, "our wealthy and influential citizens, in both sections of the country, with some honorable exceptions" coexisted too easily with slavery. He called on the president to free all of the slaves.

A month later, the Pennsylvania Anti-Slavery Society held its annual two-day meeting. Garrison, the Motts, Purvis, Mary Grew, Miller McKim, they all were there. McKim said that with two armies now fighting, the slavery question was no longer a moral question but a military one. Perhaps the most notable words came from Theodore Tilton, a white New York City journalist who had spoken in Philadelphia at the December 2 John Brown rally and, in one unforgettable scene that day, stood on the stage with his arms folded, stepped forward, and silently stared down the hissing crowd.

"There is a war because there was a Republican Party; there was a Republican Party because there was an anti-slavery party; there was an anti-slavery party because there was slavery. To charge the war upon Republicanism is merely to blame the lamb that stood in the brook; to charge it upon Abolitionism is to blame the sheep for being the lamb's mother; but to charge it upon slavery is to lay the crime straight at the door of the wolf. So, to end the trouble, kill the wolf. I belong to the party of the wolf killers."

In an effort to show that not all of the city's moneyed class was beholden to King Cotton, men such as Horace Binney Jr., Morton McMichael, and George H. Boker formed a new association, a Republican "refuge for loyalty." They called it the Union League.

Along the Schuylkill's east bank, 609 shoemakers were making shoes and knapsacks at the Gray's Ferry Arsenal, and hundreds of seamstresses were sewing uniforms. Three thousand men were building eleven warships at the Navy Yard while breech-loading rifles were noisily put together at a factory on the west bank of the Schuylkill. Ammunition for those rifles was being made at the Frankford Arsenal. Baldwin Locomotive tripled its production of locomotives to a hundred a year. The city's twenty-four military hospitals and twenty-two other hospitals treated more than 157,000 men by war's end.

Shortly before Thanksgiving, Catto received news from his Washington friend Billy Wormley. Scrawled on the envelope was "ship's letter, U.S.S. Wabash."

Wormley had not gone off to Oberlin after all. He had enlisted in the navy and found himself in the middle of a deafening battle. On November 7, a flotilla of Union ships off South Carolina approached Port Royal and Beaufort. On Lincoln's orders, the navy was endeavoring to blockade harbors and curtail the South's access to trade. The bombarding of Port Royal, led by the Wabash's sixty guns, could be heard as far south as Florida.

The battle was brief and one-sided. Wormley was giddy. "Capt.," he wrote to Catto, "we have taken Beauford and with it 38 guns, 18 or 20 prisoners, 6 or 8 horses . . . plenty of wines, and cigars. . . . Give my love to Minton and all of our friends; . . . the 'Stars and Stripes' now hang over 'Fort Wormley' in place of a secession *rag* which we tore down in fury." He closed with a swagger: "Still the great lover of ladies. Billy."

By the time Catto received the letter, the harbors were blockaded and a swath of South Carolina and Georgia coast was in Union hands. White families fled plantations, leaving supplies and slaves. Almost overnight, Port Royal went from a Confederate post to a haven for freedmen—thousands of them—protected by Union soldiers.

Wormley was not the only man for whom the battle was unforgettable. More than seventy years later, the former slave Sam Mitchell remembered the sounds of the bombardment. WPA Federal Writers Project interviewers talked to him about what happened in November 1861.

He thought the noise was thunder, but the sky was clear. It didn't make sense. His mother, a slave, knew exactly what the sound was and what it meant to her family: "Son, dat aint no t'under. Dat Yankee comin to gib you freedom."

On a Tuesday evening six days before Christmas, Philadelphia's annual antislavery fair opened. Abolition was still a dream, but suddenly it had taken a form—newly escaped slaves who needed clothes, food, and shelter, from the arrivals in Philadelphia to those who had fled to freedom in Port Royal.

The crowds at the fair were larger than usual. One banner flying said, "Anti-Slavery is True Democracy." Another used the words from the Liberty Bell: "Proclaim Liberty throughout all the Land unto All the Inhabitants Thereof."

In 1860, Mayor Henry had not permitted that flag to be flown, fearing it would create a disturbance. In this first year of war, he had no such qualms.

*　*　*

AND THE WAR slid into its second year with optimism slinking away.

Doubts arose about the celebrated military service of McMullen. No one questioned his valor—it was his truthfulness. At a Senate hearing in January 1862, Colonel David B. Birney was pressed to explain what he knew about the Union's embarrassing loss at Manassas. He testified that Captain McMullen had scouted the size of the enemy force. But the colonel had not believed McMullen's report and sent his own men out to scout the enemy.

When a senator asked why he was in doubt, Colonel Birney said, "I had very little confidence in Captain McMullin; that I considered him a very disreputable character. . . . You probably know McMullin's reputation . . . in Philadelphia. He has always been . . . a bully, kind of a character there. He is a fellow of courage, and all that, but he is not a man in whom I would place the most implicit confidence."

*　*　*

NORTHERN TEACHERS and missionaries began arriving at Port Royal. A freedmen's school opened. Some Northerners scoffed at these efforts—Wendell Phillips said the freedmen did not need charity; they simply needed the "yoke" removed. At the same time, the reports from Port Royal stirred interest all through the black and abolition world. On August 23, a fledgling Beaufort newspaper called the *Free South* dubbed Port Royal's new Union overseers the "Department of Experiments."

Miller McKim quit the antislavery society and began something new, something more urgent. He formed an association to provide food, clothing, and funds for the freedmen living in Port Royal and the other sea islands. Charlotte Forten, too, was drawn to events in Port Royal. The freedmen needed teachers.

The freedmen served a need in her as well. Turning twenty-five, Forten wrote in her diary that her youthful dreams of literary accomplishment, travel, and society "can never be mine. If I can go to Port Royal I will try to forget all these desires. I will pray that God in his goodness will make me noble enough to find my highest happiness in doing my duty."

She twice applied to a Boston charity that was sending teachers to Port Royal, and getting no reply, she turned to McKim's committee. By October, she was teaching freedmen's children of all ages in a one-room schoolhouse under the live oaks of nearby St. Helena Island. "I never saw children so eager to learn."

At first the adults were wary of the well-dressed mulatto—they called Forten "dat brown gal," as the white teacher Laura Towne wrote in her diary. Then Forten began teaching her pupils songs. A Union officer, Thomas Wentworth Higginson, observed: "When they heard her play on the piano [they] . . . soon all grew fond of her."

Edward Pierce, a government agent working with the former slaves there, wrote a report in February on the condition of fifteen thousand of them living under Union protection.

> The lash, let us give thanks, is banished at last. No coarse words or profanity are used toward them. There has been less than a case of discipline a week, and the delinquent, if a male, is sometimes made to stand on a barrel, or, if a woman, is put in a dark room, and such discipline has proved successful. . . .
>
> The desire to be free has been strongly expressed, particularly among the more intelligent and adventurous. Every day almost adds a fresh tale of escapes . . . conducted with a courage . . . and a skill worthy of heroes. . . . There is another consideration that must not be omitted. Many of these people [are] . . . anxiously looking to see what is to be our disposition of them. It is a mistake to suppose that . . . they are universally and with entire confidence welcoming us as their deliverers.

While the war droned on, some of its noises were changing. The debate over the role of Negroes in the war was slowly evolving.

The Tammany Hall Young Men's Democratic Club in New York City resolved to oppose freeing the slaves, "unless on some plan of colonization, in order that they may not come in contact with the white man's labor."

Union general William T. Sherman did not want to command Negro soldiers. He thought it "unjust to the brave soldiers and volunteers" if Negroes fought beside them as equals. "I cannot bring myself to trust Negroes with arms in positions of danger and trust."

Not all of his soldiers agreed. Some had no problem trusting Negroes to be in positions of danger. Taking that view was a Union general's aide named Charles Graham Halpine, who wrote "Sambo's Right to Be Kilt" under the name of Private Miles O'Reilly for the *New York Herald*:

> Some tell me 'tis a burnin' shame
> To make the naygers fight,
> And that the trade of bein' kilt
> Belongs but to the white.
> But as for me, upon my soul!
> So lib'ral are we here,
> I'll let Sambo be shot instead of myself
> On ev'ry day in the year.

Negroes were already finding ways to join the war. Runaway slaves were spies, scouts, and mapmakers of roads and streams, troop strength and defenses. A most valuable source of intelligence for the Union was William Jackson, Jefferson Davis's coachman.

As Union losses and casualties mounted, the Lincoln administration inched toward the enlistment of colored soldiers. En route to that precipice, Edwin M. Stanton, who had just replaced Pennsylvania's Simon Cameron as secretary of war, suggested a smaller first step for Negroes—garrison duty in the malarial regions of the South.

In April, General Benjamin F. Butler, who commanded Union forces in much of the South, captured New Orleans and began paying former slaves wages to work as laborers and teamsters for the army.

Treating former slaves as ordinary wage earners had to surprise anyone who followed General Butler's career. He had supported the Southerner John Breckenridge, not Lincoln, in 1860. He had more recently assured the governor of Maryland that he would use his troops to suppress any slave rebellions. But this Massachusetts lawyer was not an easy man to discern, because he also developed the policy that former slaves were assets to the military and should be recognized as "contraband" of war. Rebel armies used them for labor; Butler reasoned that taking them away hurt the enemy. If he recovered Confederate cannons, wouldn't the Union use them? His idea tore apart the Crittenden policy.

On April 16, Lincoln signed a bill ending slavery in Washington, D.C., with the proviso that owners be compensated. The military promptly hired four hundred of these former slaves and kept hiring until this number reached four thousand six months later.

The South, too, pressed Negroes into military duty, relying on skilled and loyal slaves to serve as drivers, cooks, even officers' valets. In Charleston Harbor, Confederate officers entrusted the helm of a steamship, the *Planter*, with its pivot-gun and howitzer, to the most skilled pilot available, the slave Robert Smalls.

Smalls was all of twenty-three years old now, with a wife and three children. His master had let him hire himself out as a waiter, lamplighter, stevedore, and sailor. His ability to navigate the harbor's shallows and shoals was unmatched. He also knew that the channel buoys had been removed and the lights in the harbor darkened to impede any Union attack.

He gathered his family and twelve other slaves and made a secret plan. They would wait till the middle of the night, when the *Planter*'s white officers were ashore. They would make their move at a routine speed, in the hope of attracting no interest. If detected and pursued, they would scuttle the ship and cost the Confederacy a steamer, six artillery pieces, and an entire family of slaves. "They should all take hands, husband and wife, brother and sister, and jump overboard and perish together."

On May 12, 1862, at 4:00 A.M., Smalls started the engines and got under way. He wore the ship captain's floppy straw hat.

Smalls waved to the watchmen on the harbor and, flying the Confederate flag, sounded the all's-well whistle until he was past the range of their guns. Then he quickly hoisted a white flag and headed for a Union ship, the *Onward*, hoping the flag would be spied before navy gunners opened fire on the rebel ship. The *Onward* was about to let loose with its big guns when lookouts began shouting and pointing to the white flag.

The commander of the navy's blockade said many contrabands who reached Union lines were smart, but none smarter than "the very intelligent contraband who was in charge" of the stealing of the *Planter*. The steamer's theft by a slave embarrassed the South and cheered the North, especially when Smalls said that some of its guns had been taken from Fort Sumter.

* * *

EARLY IN THE YEAR, the Smithsonian opened its public lectures to Negroes, and the United States offered diplomatic recognition to Haiti, the last major country to do so.

Rev. William Catto left Washington for a pulpit in New Haven. His son, teaching at the I.C.Y., called on Douglass's twenty-three-year-old daughter, Rosetta, who was staying in Philadelphia with the Dorseys and looking for a teaching job. That was when the protective if imperious Mrs. Dorsey took away her social life. Rosetta wrote to her father about "Cato" and another visitor, William Minton. While she included no details about the meeting—she was just looking for "pleasure in an innocent way"— Rosetta enjoyed the break from her confining routine.

In that letter home, she also wrote, "Mrs. Dorsey told me to night that I was a *street woman* and used some pretty harsh language. She said that my father had told her that she was to keep me from the boys, and said it to me before a room full of folks and it sounded quite badly that you should send me here but that I must be kept from the boys as if that was my particular failing and she was to watch me."

Her father had other concerns. He stridently opposed the president's Chiriqui colonization idea. So did William Catto and Octavius Catto's boss, Ebenezer Bassett. At Shiloh Church in New York, the two men spoke against Lincoln's plan to send freed slaves to Panama, with William Catto accusing the president of "pandering to the mob spirit."

Alston, the minister in New York who had called for Lincoln to end slavery, moved south, taking over the pulpit at St. Thomas in Philadelphia. Moving north from Philadelphia was a "select nine" of baseball players doing something unheard of—going on a road trip. They played in Hoboken, Newark, and New York City before crowds of fifteen thousand, with newspapers calling it the "first invasion" of ball players from Philadelphia. But barely moving at all were the nation's free Negroes, who, despite the wishes of the president, were not emigrating to Haiti or Africa or Panama. The colonization movement was shriveling. There was no room for it. The war was too big.

The war had not changed the racism against Negroes, and in some ways it was worse, especially as Southern victories mounted. Now Republicans as well as Democrats were "cursing the niggers and . . . declaring that the slaves, if possibly emancipated by the war, must be removed from the country."

Negroes had new enemies—Union soldiers. White troops in Harrisburg "are at large in the city and their prejudice against 'the peculiar people' is evidenced by the kicks and cuffs they administer to our poor sable brethren," Jake White wrote. Irish stevedores in Cincinnati burned down homes in a Negro neighborhood after contrabands were hired as strikebreakers. In Brooklyn, Negro women and children working at a tobacco factory were attacked by Irish workers, who then set fire to the first floor. Police rescued the workers from the blaze, but the owner let them go and hired whites to replace them.

The *Weekly Anglo-African* in New York published an editorial after the fire:

Irishmen! The day will come that you will find out that you are making a sad mistake in assisting to crush out our liberties. Learn! O learn, that the protection of the feeblest of your fellow beings is the only guarantee you have for the protection of your own liberty. . . . We call upon the world to bear witness to the dreadful effects which the system of slavery has had upon the Irish people. In their own country they are kind and hospitable to our poor and constantly abused race; but here, so dreadfully corrupted do some of them become that they are prepared for the vilest deed . . . their attempt to roast alive a number of people who never did them the least harm.

Sometimes the pressure and violence were not directed at a factory. Sometimes they landed on a neighbor.

A Philadelphia man "discharged an Irish servant and in his place employed a Negro," Fisher wrote in his diary: "Shortly after, his garden was trespassed on, plants and shrubbery destroyed and a paper stuck on one of his trees, threatening further injury if he did not send away the Negro." And the man did as he was told.

Prejudice did not drape every moment for Negroes, nor did the war's violence and debate touch every life. At the Institute for Colored Youth, students about to graduate studied Latin and Greek for their final exams. The institute was more than ever a civic and political beehive as more Negro adults were walking the streets to Lombard to attend evening lectures on subjects from electricity to the holy scripture. Garnet spoke as did Douglass and Rev. Alexander Crummell, who had come back from Liberia. And young Catto spoke about poetry, in a talk titled "The Genius of Alfred Tennyson."

Walking those streets was a health hazard. They were filled with coal ashes, rotting vegetables, and dead rats cooking in the sun. Mayor Henry proclaimed he would clean them and announced a new policy—getting rid of stray dogs.

The job went to a short, light-skinned mulatto man who wore a cap on his head and a badge on his chest. Jim Francis was the dogcatcher and also the city's official dog killer.

Francis worked under simple rules: Catch unmuzzled dogs and put them in a pound. Wait three days. If no one paid a two-dollar fine and claimed the animal, then Francis or one his colored minions clubbed the dog to death. When the dead dog pile reached a hundred or so, a buyer boiled the dead animals "down into wheel grease." In return for his time, effort, and profusion of dog bites, Francis was paid fifty cents for each dog caught. In a good summer, he would grab two thousand dogs. He also caught stray pigs; in the winter, he swept chimneys.

★ ★ ★

DESPITE THE LAW, three Union military leaders organized Negro fighting units in 1862.

General David Hunter put together the First South Carolina Regiment to mark the one-year anniversary of Fort Sumter. The regiment had no authority from Washington, it was not paid, and officials criticized Hunter for "unfeeling barbarity" in his bullying former slaves to join. The unit disbanded in August, four months after it formed.

The army's first colored regiment was put together by the perplexing General Butler. While he thought well of contrabands working for the army, he thought colored men fighting with guns was a terrible notion. The Negro, he said, had "by long habit and training, a great horror of fire-arms, sometimes ludicrous in the extreme when the weapon is in his own hand."

The abolitionist James W. Phelps, an officer under Butler, disregarded his superior. He began training three hundred Negroes in July for what he thought would be the start of three new regiments. An angry Butler wrote, "Phelps has gone crazy." Phelps resigned.

In August, however, Butler ordered that weapons be provided for fourteen hundred freedmen the state of Louisiana had brought into the militia the year before. These new soldiers were part of the Louisiana Native Guards, First, Second, and Third regiments. Arming slaves was still against the policy of the federal government, so all these men were referred to as freedmen, though it is doubtful that each one was. Butler changed his mind because he had the foresight to realize that the Union needed colored soldiers to win the war. Or he just wanted the plaudits for finishing what Phelps had started.

The first colored unit to go into battle was the First Kansas Colored Volunteers. Ignoring the president and the secretary of war, General James H. Lane formed the unit in September and sent it out on scouting missions and skirmishes with Confederate troops in Missouri. The unit was officially accepted into service in mid-1863.

Colored military units had been organized in Philadelphia, too. They just were not officially in the military, and no one was going to let them fight.

City Negro leaders, including Alfred Green, began forming black regiments in the spring and had six local companies organized, equipped— they had raised money for uniforms and supplies—and ready for battle. An amazed correspondent from the *New York Tribune* wrote, "The blacks here are drilling on their own hook. They could muster 5,000 here easily." One of those companies would have been hard to miss on the field of battle because its troops wore the uniforms of Algerian tribesmen recruited into the French army in the 1830s and 1840s

The uniforms of the Zouaves included a red fez, white leggings, baggy red pants, a blue sash, and a blue vest. The armies of both the Union and the Confederacy had Zoave units in the early months of the war. But the baggy red pants stayed in Philadelphia in 1862. Pennsylvania was still not enlisting colored volunteers.

And when the War Department changed its policy in late August (after one too many Union losses) and permitted Union generals in the South to recruit Negroes, there was no rush in most Northern states for permission to do the same.

* * *

ON SEPTEMBER 22, President Lincoln made a brief announcement, barely more than a handwritten page. He had told his Cabinet in July and now he was telling the world. He had held back, waiting for a Union military success. At great cost, Union soldiers had prevailed at Antietam. The victory was incomplete, but it was what Lincoln needed. He said that in one hundred days—January 1—if the rebellion of the secessionist states had not ended, everyone held as a slave in those states would be free.

It was as if every bell in every tower began pealing the sweet sound of deliverance all at once. Slaves heard the Emancipation Proclamation and knew freedom was coming. Slaveholders heard it and feared rebellions from slaves who couldn't wait for freedom. Ralph Waldo Emerson lifted Lincoln's words to the sky, asking that the laws of nature be ignored for the next one hundred days. "Do not let the dying die; hold them back to this world until you have charged their ear and heart with this message . . . announcing the melioration of our planet."

Colored men began enlisting, a surge of new patriots wanting to fight for a country that was ending slavery. Yet there still was no welcome for colored soldiers in Pennsylvania. But in Massachusetts there was, and Negroes from across the North began heading for the new colored unit there, the Fifty-fourth.

Near Butler, Missouri, the colored unit from Kansas suffered casualties in battle, the first Negroes to die in combat. Robert Smalls, the war's first colored hero, returned to the Union-occupied coast of his native South Carolina to help slaves who had been freed. He met Charlotte Forten and talked to her of enlisting: "How can I expect to keep my freedom if I'm not willing to fight for it?"

She was teaching the story of Toussaint L'Ouverture and the song of John Brown. "I felt to the full the significance of that song being here in South Carolina . . . by those whom he—the glorious old man—died to save."

Even so, a fear of a forced exodus tamped down the joy of Negro leaders. Lincoln was still talking about colonization and Chiriqui, still trying to get Congress to appropriate funds. So Negro leaders across the North met, wrote petitions and letters to the president, and agonized about this cloud hanging over their freedom. At an October meeting in New York's Shiloh Church honoring Smalls, with Garnet, Charles Reason, and hundreds more erupting in cheers when he entered, there was continued applause later in the evening as speakers condemned any effort to force Negroes to leave the country of their birth.

Back in Philadelphia, black leaders were celebrating the December birthday of one of their institutions, the twenty-ninth anniversary of the city's colored Library Company. T. Morris Chester, a Harrisburg native and a frequent traveler to Liberia, delivered a speech titled "Self Respect and Pride of Race." A stenographer recorded his words:

> Remove from the eyes of the rising generation the portraits of Clay, Webster and Seward, and if superior intellects present any attractions, hang in the most conspicuous place the great WARD, the unrivalled DOUGLASS . . . the pathetic PAYNE . . . the gifted GARNET [applause]. . . . If your tastes are of a literary character and you desire to frame professors, there are . . . the polished REASON [loud applause] the talented CRUMMEL [applause] and the culti- vated BASSET [applause] . . . the graceful ROCK . . . artists of the brush by the sanguine BOWSER . . . the close-calculating WHIPPER [applause].

He mentioned Benjamin Banneker, Crispus Attucks, Sarah Douglass, and Nat Turner.

He saluted achievements made "in the face of a violent prejudice." When he shouted the name of Robert Smalls, the applause became a thunderclap. "Let your children look upon such public speakers as the brilliant DELANY, the chaste REMOND . . . and the rising CATTO."

★ ★ ★

THE CHIRIQUI COLONY idea was dying or dead—it had sputtered for lack of treaties with nearby Central American governments, and a test of Chiriqui's vaunted coal had produced dismal results. But fresh hopes for a colored colony materialized in the form of an eager Florida businessman with land in the Caribbean. Using his formidable Washington connec- tions, Bernard Kock had written a detailed proposal and gotten in to see Lincoln on December 31, 1862, the eve of the day when the Emancipation Proclamation awaited the president's signature.

Kock offered a grand solution to the problem of where to send the Negroes once they were freed. He promised to ship, house, and equip five thousand of them for a life of raising cotton on an island he had acquired near Haiti, for a fee of fifty dollars per Negro, payable to Bernard Kock. He had already enlisted political allies from Kansas to Port-au-Prince; he had even named himself governor of Île à Vache—French for Cow Island—and had begun printing one- and two-dollar bills with his name and portrait. Lincoln was wary of this man; historians say he signed the deal but privately told Secretary of State Seward not to countersign or apply the seal of the United States just yet. Nonetheless, the fifty-dollars-per-Negro contract with Lincoln's signature survives to this day.

Nearly five hundred contrabands were readied for the voyage. Food, shelter, and farming tools, courtesy of Governor Kock, awaited them on the balmy shores of Île à Vache.

★ ★ ★

WATCH NIGHT WAS December 31, and never before had America seen such a moment. Negroes, free and slave, waiting for the president to sign a document that would end slavery in the secessionist South.

Emancipation eve, and the collective breath of a nation was held. It was of no matter that the president's motive was to hurt the Confederacy, not benefit the slave. Would he sign? Would pro-slavery pressure be too strong? In Philadelphia, black churches seemed to stretch their walls to make room for the crowds that kept coming. "They sang and shouted and wept and prayed," the white abolitionist B. Rush Plumly wrote to Lincoln. "God knows I cried with them." At St. Thomas, one worshipper asked whether the president would colonize freed Negroes. "God won't let him," someone shouted.

In snow-bound Boston, Douglass and Longfellow and Emerson and Rock and Anna Dickinson waited and shivered with three thousand more for the telegram that would signal Lincoln's signature. They worried that Mary Lincoln, a Southerner, would influence her husband in the way that wives do. "Every moment of waiting chilled our hopes and strengthened our fears," Douglass said.

At a military encampment near Fredericksburg, Virginia, George Stephens of Philadelphia waited as well. He was, on this December 31, a valet and cook to an officer of the Twenty-sixth Pennsylvania Regiment, Sickles's Division, and a correspondent for the *Weekly Anglo-African*, a newspaper Negro workers for the military "read and reread until its folds are worn."

Stephens, the Banneker Institute member who had made a harrowing visit to Charleston, called emancipation eve a "night of atonement," for "the errors and misdeeds of the past year are tearfully and prayerfully remembered, and a new leaf is turned over." He wondered whether "nations have to suffer for misdeeds as well as individuals" and hoped that this "may be the watch night which shall usher in the new era of freedom."

Lost in the joy was the fact that no one was actually freed at the stroke of Lincoln's pen. Three million slaves in secessionist states would be slaves no more, but only after the war ended. A half-million more in border states that stayed with the Union—Delaware, Kentucky, Maryland, and Missouri—were not freed. Nor were slaves in parts of Virginia and Louisiana, occupied by Union troops. But the declaration was wondrous. The government was, for the first time, announcing its intent to free the slaves.

Lincoln, the orator whose words belonged to the ages, stood at a White House window and bowed in silence to the cheering crowds.

In Boston, the crowd cried, cheered, and sang, and did not stop for hours. In New York, Rev. Henry Highland Garnet knelt inside Shiloh and prayed silently from 11:55 P.M. to midnight. Then the choir sang, "Blow Ye Trumpets Blow, the Year of Jubilee Has Come." The next day, Garnet called the Proclamation "one of the greatest acts in all history" and led three cheers for the president. And for "our native land."

At Port Royal, Charlotte Forten, freedmen, white soldiers, freed slaves who had become soldiers, and their white officers, including Thomas Wentworth Higginson, commander of the colored First South Carolina Volunteers, gathered on Emancipation Day.

Forten described "an eager, wondering crowd of the freed people in their holiday attire, with the gayest of head-handkerchiefs, the whitest of aprons, & the happiest of faces." She saw troops parading in red pantaloons, "a fine soldierly-looking set of men; their brilliant dress against the trees invested them with a semi-barbaric splendor. . . . To us, it seemed strange as a miracle, this black regiment . . . doing itself honor in the sight of the officers of other regiments, many of whom, doubtless, came to scoff. The men afterwards had a great feast, ten oxen having been roasted whole for their special benefit."

The same day, from Colonel Higginson's diary:

Prayer by our chaplain . . . proclamation read. . . . There followed an incident so simple, so touching, so utterly unexpected. . . .

Just as I took and waved the flag, which now for the first time meant anything to these poor people, there suddenly arose, close beside the platform, a strong but rather cracked and elderly male voice, into which two women's voices immediately blended, singing as if by an impulse that can no more be quenched than the morning note of the song sparrow—the hymn "My country 'tis of thee, Sweet land of Liberty."

People looked at each other and then at the stage to see whence came this interruption; . . . irrepressibly the quavering voices sang on, verse after verse; others around them joined; some on the platform sung, but I motioned them to silence. I never saw anything so electric; it made all other words cheap, it seemed the choked voice of a race, at last unloosed; nothing could be more wonderfully unconscious; art could not have dreamed of a tribute to the day of jubilee that should be so affecting; history will not believe it; and when I came to speak of it, after it was silent, tears were everywhere."

CHAPTER 11

Manhood

THE EMANCIPATION PROCLAMATION caused no joy or singing among the Democrats. Shudders to be sure, and anger. Freed
slaves were streaming into Northern cities and workplaces. Colonization had slowed dramatically. Democrats were not happy with the
future before them.

On January 8, 1863, Philadelphia Democrats marked the anniversary of the Battle of New Orleans. They elected Charles Ingersoll, whose
grandfather had signed the Constitution, as the Central Democratic Club
president and chose vice presidents from each ward, including William
McMullen from the Fourth. The voice of Ingersoll and the Democrats
could be read six days a week in a newspaper they helped start, the *Age*.

Ingersoll had been arrested briefly the year before for making anti-
Union remarks. He was not cowed by that arrest. "Mr. Lincoln says come
into the Union, but without your property. Give up everything you possess . . . and then return to the Union."

One the few positives Democrats could point to was that disillusionment with the Union losses in the war had given them a one-vote edge in
the combined Pennsylvania legislature. And the legislatures, not the voters, elected U.S. senators. Democratic leaders knew that theirs was not a
tight ship, and that some of their members might jump and vote for the
Republicans.

The Republican nominee for the Senate was Simon Cameron, former secretary of war, and a power broker in the state. Charles Buckalew, former chair of the Democratic State Committee, won the Democratic nod. A state senator and lawyer from rural Columbia County, Buckalew had won a tough intraparty fight against James Campbell. After that win, some of Campbell's supporters were planning to vote for Cameron, not Buckalew.

Party leaders needed a Democrat in Washington. An election victory had to be guaranteed. Some one needed to deliver a message to any wavering legislators, in language unequivocal. Someone gristle tough.

On the morning of the vote, guests taking coffee in Harrisburg hotels were startled by the talk in the lobbies and out along the street. Men coming off the trains from Philadelphia were saying loud enough for strangers to hear that any Democrat voting against Buckalew and for Cameron—Lincoln's candidate—would be shot.

The messenger had arrived. Alderman McMullen was in Harrisburg with a hundred of his toughest cohorts. Cameron immediately went to see Alexander McClure, an assistant U.S. adjutant general in Harrisburg, and implored him to send soldiers into the Capitol building. He said he would win the election if "the members of the Legislature were protected." McClure, preoccupied with running the wartime draft, refused. He wrote later, "I would never permit the gleam of the bayonet in the legislative halls to intimidate or protect legislators in the discharge of their duties."

So in a hall dedicated to open debate, legislators about to cast their votes saw McMullen's armed sentinels standing in every one of the chamber's doorways, "each with a revolver in his right coat-pocket and his hand on his revolver ready for business." Buckalew won by two votes.

Just days before, local Democrats had been frustrated about their lack of power and had pummeled the president with words. Now they had "elected an enemy of your Admn.," as Cameron wrote in haste to Lincoln. A new Senate foe was being sent to Washington, courtesy of the Bull, the king-making Democrat with fists large enough to reach beyond the Fourth Ward. And McMullen had become friends with another powerful Democrat from South Philadelphia, Congressman Samuel Randall.

The tactics of intimidation were not lost on Democrats like Ingersoll, "gentlemen of property and standing," who were gratified by what the roughs of Moyamensing had accomplished. The rich defenders of slavery—Ingersoll had married into a large slave-owning family—and their poorer, streetwise supporters were now a proud, public coalition. Sidney Fisher had rarely seen his brother-in-law, Ingersoll, so energized, "in a state of great exultation at what he considers the triumph of the Democratic Party & said that soon they will resort to mob law & physical force to carry out their views."

Time did not take the edge off Democrat anger toward the president. A month later, another meeting chaired by Ingersoll featured an invitation calling Lincoln "the negro-worshipping tyrant." When two *Philadelphia Press* reporters arrived at the meeting, McMullen told them, "You had better leave or you may regret it" and booted them out.

★ ★ ★

THE EMANCIPATION PROCLAMATION changed everything. The Emancipation Proclamation changed nothing.

Mary Grew, who saw Pennsylvania Hall burn in 1838, looked back on those twenty-five years and said, "What we endeavored to do was *abolitionize* the country. . . . Today, more than three millions are emancipated! The banner of liberty has passed over our South land, and has been a great comfort and joy to a mighty people."

For many, the Proclamation was a call to action. Volunteers in Northern cities raised money to help the freed slaves. For some, raising funds was not enough and they left their homes and went south to help with the sweat of their brow.

Bishop Daniel Payne of the A.M.E. Church, emboldened by the Proclamation and thinking ahead to a time when more and more Negroes would attend college, completed his own remarkable journey—from running a tiny Sabbath school in Charleston to opening Wilberforce College in Ohio, the first college owned and operated by Negroes.

A Pennsylvania legislative committee came out strongly against a State House initiative to control the flow of free Negroes and mulattoes into the state. Their stance killed the bill.

The A.M.E. Church now urged Negroes to fight for the Union. So did the *Weekly Anglo-African* newspaper, asking "Will you vindicate your manhood?"

One Negro soldier in this intra-American war had the foreign name of Meunomennie L. Maimi. Fighting for the Twentieth Connecticut Regiment in Virginia, he wrote home to his Philadelphia-born wife: "Do you know or think what the end of this war is to decide? It is to decide whether we are to have freedom to all or slavery to all. If the . . . Confederacy succeeds, then you may bid farewell to all liberty thereafter. . . . If our government succeeds, then your and our race will be free. . . . When slavery passes, the prejudices that belonged to it must follow."

The governor of Massachusetts had begun the North's first all-Negro military unit, but there were so few Negroes in the state that his call became nationwide. Frederick Douglass, whose son volunteered for the Massachusetts Fifty-fourth, urged an audience of several thousand at Mother Bethel, "Get an eagle on your button and a musket on your shoulder by the speediest means, at any cost, and when you have Uncle Sam's uniform on your back, all the devils in Jeff Davis' dominions cannot keep you out of citizenship. . . . The whole heavens are written over with 'now or never' for the colored people." Then he began to sing.

"John Brown's body lies a-mouldering in the grave . . ."

Douglass had learned to sing in boyhood, when a master made him lead other slaves in hymns; he had later sung antislavery songs for allies in Britain; sung to the rafters of a house of worship he had once derided for its shuddering fear of antislavery meetings; sung to persuade young colored men of Philadelphia not to protest or petition, but to enlist for Uncle Sam. By the second stanza, the whole audience was singing.

Five men volunteered on the spot. "Halloo out your names," Douglass commanded, and one by one, five cheers went up. In the end, so many heeded his call that one company in the Fifty-fourth was all Philadelphian.

As at every important meeting of Negroes, a long list of conspicuous men organized, publicized, and presided. At the Douglass lecture, they offered a long list of resolutions at the meeting's end. Each key man was given a title. Principal Ebenezer Bassett was the event's secretary. But this meeting was different from the hundreds of conclaves before it. The titles may have been the same, but something new was in the air, not buffeted by the winds but somehow leading and directing them: *Fight, and they'll treat you like a man. Be a soldier. Now is the time. We all must fight!*

The opposing wind still roared and rattled. The vestiges of life and attitudes before the Emancipation Proclamation remained. The *Metropolitan Record*, the newspaper of the Archdiocese of New York, wrote: "Since fight we must, may it not be necessary yet to fight for the liberty of the white man rather than the freedom of the Negro?"

The fact that Amelia Howard lived in pro-Union Maryland, one of four border states that had not seceded, did not protect her. A free Negro in her sixties, she was convicted in Annapolis "for enticing slaves to run away." She was ordered sold, and lost her freedom at a public sale in front of the court house to man named Frank Steigleman. He paid twenty-five dollars.

A month later, two Negroes were killed and more than twenty wounded in a riot in Detroit. Whites set more than forty buildings afire and rendered two hundred Negroes homeless. Called the "bloodiest day that ever dawned on Detroit," it all began when soldiers escorted to jail a black man accused of harming a white orphan girl. White crowds jeered and harassed the prisoners and his guards, but the suspect was delivered. Yet the harassment of the soldiers continued, and angry and scared, they fired into the crowd, killing a man and wounding six. Then they returned to their barracks.

The crowd, bloodied but unbowed, was not done. They attacked with bricks and paving stones the first Negro house they saw. Dozens were inside and they shot at the mob but hit no one. Finally, the mob set the house ablaze, lay in wait outside with pistols and clubs, and ambushed the fleeing occupants. When a Negro woman carrying a baby came out pleading for mercy, the mob stoned her back inside. In the end, a merciful member of the crowd got her out safely.

More homes were sacked and burned, and once again Negroes were forced to flee an American city. "The colored population of the city . . . hurried from the mob, scattering in every direction; a large amount going over the river to Canada, while many actually fled to the woods with their wives and little ones," one newspaper reported. Soldiers from neighboring cities arrived to stop the riot.

The same month, Harriet Jacobs wrote to the abolitionist Lydia Maria Child, an old friend. Jacobs, a former slave, had gone south from New York City to help and was running a freedmen's school in Alexandria, Virginia. She was one of many Negro women—among them free-born Charlotte Forten and slave-born Sojourner Truth—who had gone south as teachers, missionaries, and relief workers for contrabands and colored soldiers.

> Since I last wrote . . . the condition of the poor refugees has improved. During the winter months, the smallpox carried them off by the hundreds; but now it has somewhat abated. . . . The Quakers of Philadelphia, who have sent me here, have done nobly for

my people. . . . They have sent . . . tens of thousands of dollars to different sections of the country, wherever these poor sufferers came within our lines. . . . Many have found employment, and are supporting themselves and their families. It would do your heart good to talk with . . . these people. They are quick, intelligent and full of spirit and freedom. Some of them say, . . . "The white men of the North have helped us . . . and we want to help them. We would like to fight for them, if they would only treat us like men."

The colored people could not do enough for the first regiments that came here. . . . The sight of the U.S. uniform took all fear out of their hearts. . . . Many of them freely fed the soldiers at their own tables, and lodged them as comfortably as possible in their humble dwellings. . . . In return for their kindness . . . they often receive insults, and sometimes beatings, and so they have learned to distrust those who wear the uniform of the U.S.

★ ★ ★

THE WAR MADE its appearance in the North in May. Just the Potomac separated Confederate troops from Pennsylvania, and their incursion was imminent. One newspaper called on the state to quickly retrain and reorganize its militia, neither of which was accomplished. Lincoln had approved the use of Negroes to fight, but Pennsylvania had not yet permitted their entry. Nor had New York.

The rolls of the Fifty-fourth were now filled with more than two thousand men. On May 28, an enormous crowd in Boston applauded and hallooed as they headed south to the war. Negro troops had fought the day before in their first official Union offensive, battling with valor in Port Hudson, Louisiana. The attack failed, but before long the battles of Port Hudson, Olustee, and Milliken's Bend yielded shouts of heroism and pride as Negro soldiers proved their mettle.

Their mettle was proven behind the lines as well. By now, thousands worked as laborers and wagon drivers for the Union Army. At the start of what would be known as the "Gettysburg Campaign," Confederate soldiers in Virginia were poised to sweep through Union garrisons in Winchester and Martinsburg and capture a thousand horses on their way to Pennsylvania. But a combination of Negro wagon drivers and laborers, many of them former slaves, rode the horses off "just as Southern forces closed in."

By June, the advancing Southern troops were on everyone's mind. The Philadelphia Athletics' first road trip to play baseball teams in Newark, Brooklyn, and New York was called an "invasion." A bank in Uniontown, Pennsylvania, emptied its safe and took the money to Pittsburgh for safekeeping. Mayor Henry and Governor Curtin pleaded for enlistments to protect the city and state but few answered the call. The governor called for fifty thousand six-month enlistees. Terror moved as quickly as the invading troops. Negroes living in the west and central parts of the state began to flee.

Rachel Cormany of Chambersburg watched the Rebels "hunting up the contrabands and driving them off by droves." "O! How it grated on our hearts to have to sit quietly and look at such brutal deeds. I saw no men among the contrabands, all women and children. Some of the colored people who were raised here were taken along. I sat on the front step as they were driven by just like we would drive cattle."

Her neighbor Tillie Pierce said many of the town's Negroes, free-born and fugitive slave, did get away. "Their flight was invariably . . . toward the woods on and around Culp's Hill. I can see them yet: men and women with bundles as large as old-fashioned feather ticks slung across their backs, almost bearing them to the ground. . . . The greatest consternation was depicted on all their countenances as they hurried along; crowding, and running against each other in their confusion; children stumbling, falling, and crying."

In the nation's capital, too, Negroes were under attack. But the victims were men enlisting to fight, and their attackers were not Confederate soldiers.

The first colored man in the Washington enlistment line was Catto's friend Billy Wormley. Almost at once, whites in the street, including policemen, began shouting threats at the sight of colored men being issued guns and uniforms.

A man in the enlistment line shouted back. George W. Hatton dared police to shoot him if they needed to kill a Negro for enlisting. Wormley said the same. The police glared, but no one fired.

Hatton rose to become an officer in the U.S. Colored Troops and he would see how things had changed since that day on the sidewalks of Washington, D.C.—a colored Union soldier invited by his white superior to punish a captured slave owner. William Clopton was known for his cruelty and colored troops tied him to a tree near Jamestown, Virginia, and bared his back. William Harris of Company E was given a whip.

"Mr. Harris played his part conspicuously," Sergeant Hatton said, "bringing the blood from his loins at every stroke, and not forgetting to remind the gentleman of the days gone by."

★ ★ ★

PHILADELPHIA GREETED WAR with two faces.

Aside from Chestnut Street, busy with people reading the latest war news on boards outside the newspaper offices, the city seemed strangely weary. "Recruiting parties were marching about with drum and flag, followed only by a few ragged boys—recruiting offices empty, taverns and grog shops full. The people looked careless and indifferent. There was no excitement," Sidney Fisher wrote. Just two years before, the city was aflutter with flags, abuzz with the anger and earnestness of a people embracing war.

But the war was no longer new. Union losses were growing. The enemy was already in the state and drawing closer, and, Fisher wrote, "the demagogues have spread abroad the opinion that the administration is corrupt and imbecile, that it is impossible to conquer the South and that we ought to have peace now on any terms."

So whites went about their business, some going to the race tracks at Point Breeze and Suffolk Park—each of which had Negro jockeys—and very few hearkening to the call of the mayor and governor to protect their city and state from the relentless invaders.

The other face was that of colored Philadelphia, proud and eager for tomorrow to arrive.

At the commencement ceremonies for the graduating class at the Institute for Colored Youth, Caroline Le Count won accolades for having the highest grades and had her marks published in the *Christian Recorder.* That day, she joined Rev. Henry Highland Garnet on the dais as they both spoke to the overflowing crowd. The new graduate's topic: "The Cultivation of Taste."

The *Christian Recorder* also printed a poem of praise for the I.C.Y. graduates, especially for Caroline Le Count. It was written by a student at Ashmun Institute, which was soon to become Lincoln University on the outskirts of Philadelphia.

TO CARRIE
By R. B. Jones

The Institute for colored youth
In Philadelphia
Much talent did display, forsooth,
About the first of May.
Five members of the senior class,
Examination stood;
And what do well describe their "pass,"
Are these words, very good.
In Greek and Latin both they read,
And showed themselves well taught;
In mathematics it is said,
That they had fairly wrought.
They climbed the steeps of science well,
That high and towering mount;
But one did all the rest excel,
'Twas Carrie R. Le Count.
Young friends you know these things are true,
Of which I now do speak;
O then I trust that all of you,
Will go and knowledge seek.
Muses, arise and slake your thirst,
At science' purest fount;
Then forth in highest praises burst,
Of Carrie R. Le Count!

The I.C.Y. had become the "heart and hope" of colored Philadelphia, Douglass wrote in his newspaper after twice visiting the school. Its six teachers were *all colored persons,* he exulted. Inch by inch, other doors opened. Soon after the 1863 commencement, two I.C.Y. alumni became the first Negroes ever hired to teach in the city's public schools.

John Quincy Allen bested thirty white applicants for a teaching job in a colored school. Cordelia Jennings won public-school status for the thirty colored students she was already teaching in her home. Principal Bassett, calling Allen and Jennings "pioneers," used their achievements to success-fully advocate for more money from the Quaker managers. Now the I.C.Y. could grow and educate more students to be colored teachers.

Catto was eager for tomorrow to arrive as well. The I.C.Y. teacher was ready to go to war. And other young men rushed to join him. He had no reason to ask his father's permission. They were not living under the same roof anymore. The young men were all breathing in that intoxicating mixture enveloping the land. On a morning in early June, people awoke to see broadsides four feet by eight feet, inked with gumption and four-inch-high letters and signed by fifty-five colored men. The posters were plastered to the walls and fences of Philadelphia.

The headline on the broadsides roared: *Men of Color!*

The Country Demands your Services. The Enemy is Approaching. You Know his Object. It is to Subjugate the North and Enslave us. Already many of our Class in this State have been Captured and Carried South to Slavery, Stripes and Mutilation. For our own sake and for the sake of our Common Country we are called up now to Come Forward!

Let us seize this great opportunity of vindicating our manhood and patriotism through all time. The General Commanding at this post is arranging for the Defence of the City! He will need the aid of everyman who can shoulder a musket or handle a pick. We have assured him of the readiness of our people to do their whole duty in the emergency. . . .

The undersigned have been designated a Committee to have this matter in charge. Members of this committee will sit every day at Bethel Church . . . and at Union Church. . . . Their business will be to receive the names of able-bodied men of color who are willing to share with others the burdens and duties of Entrenching and Defending the City. *Men of Color!*

Never before had there been such an appeal to Philadelphia Negroes by Philadelphia Negroes. The fifty-five signatures belonged to fifty-four Philadelphians and one frequent visitor, Frederick Douglass. The names included fathers and sons—the Whites, the Adgers, and the Cattos. Lit by one generation, the flame of social activism burned bright in the next.

There were more recruiting broadsides in the weeks to follow: *Men of Color, To Arms! Now or Never! This is our Golden Moment.* One broadside offered a challenge: "Are free men less brave than slaves?" Another: "If we are not lower on the scale of humanity than Englishmen, Irishmen, white Americans and other races, we can show it now."

The names at the bottom were almost always the same, considered the "gentlemen of color" in the Negro community: Forten, Adger, Douglass, Catto, Bowser, Whipper, Cassey, Smith, Dorsey, Burr, Minton, White, Green, Alston.

The fifty-four local signers were a distinct part of the colored city—they who could read and write, possessed race consciousness, and controlled their own lives, Emma Lapsansky-Werner writes. They numbered but several hundred. "Race conscious," she explains, meant they believed their own successes or failures influenced opportunities for others. Thirty of the fifty-four owned their homes, and some owned more real estate. But wealth was not the sole measuring stick for status in the colored community. Nearly all these men worked hard for a living, as did most of their wives. The signers were seen as leaders, too, for their involvement in the community—their activity in the Odd Fellows, the Banneker Institute, the churches. Eight-seven percent were thirty-two or older.

Catto was just twenty-four and eager to prove his manhood. The entreaties from the governor and the mayor had made no reference to race. So, with friends and students from the I.C.Y., Catto and Jake White put together a colored company of ninety volunteers. In Washington, D.C., a Negro regiment was already fully mustered in.

On June 16, the night before the Catto unit was to board a train for Harrisburg, Bassett was worried about his teachers, men like Catto and White, and his youthful students, boys like Raymond Burr and Henry Boyer Jr. All so young and about to go to war. He went to see Mayor Henry.

He asked four questions: Did the colored volunteers have to serve after the invaders were repelled from the state? Would the troops be armed, supplied and paid a promised ten dollars from the city's bounty fund? Were they under state command? If disabled or killed, would their families be cared for?

Mayor Henry responded: Catto and his men would serve only for "the present emergency." As soon as practical, their pockets would be filled with ten dollars. The state needed them, but they would be under federal jurisdiction. Aid for families was not guaranteed, but they would get as much attention and care as white soldiers' kin. Overcoats and blankets would be issued, but guns would wait until they arrived in

Harrisburg. Bassett promised that the recruiting committee would raise more troops.

Early the next morning at Independence Square, once a landmark where Negroes could not safely gather, ninety men and teenaged boys were mustered into service by an army captain, William Babe. He marched them to the City Arsenal on Broad Street, where they were outfitted with uniforms and gear. Then to the station for the ride to Harrisburg.

Several mothers intercepted the underage warriors and kept their sons from leaving. The parents of one I.C.Y. student, Joseph G. Anderson Jr., impounded their son at the station, but he ran to rejoin his comrades. A large crowd formed to say good-bye to these first Negro troops representing the city. Parents wept. Sweethearts waved. Faces streaked in tears and stretched with pride. The day was "the most exciting I ever witness," Emilie Davis, an I.C.Y. pupil, wrote in her diary. "We went to see the boyes start for Harrisburg."

"Camp Curtin," on the heights opposite Harrisburg along the Susquehanna River, was already alive with troops arriving for the expected battle. The Catto company would be billeted and trained there.

If the company was allowed to serve.

The military commands in Washington and Harrisburg did not mesh as smoothly as the gears of a Baldwin 4-4-0. The governor and the army commander sent to oversee the troops did not speak with one voice.

Mayor Henry could not have foreseen what happened next. The commander was Major General Darius Couch, who in 1854 had led the troops pulling fugitive slave Anthony Burns through crowds of Boston protesters. Couch knew Governor Curtin had declared martial law and had made a plea for short-term soldiers for the state militia. Couch also knew the federal enlistment rules: Colored volunteers were to be signed up for three years.

Catto and his recruits were signing up for the emergency, to stop the encroaching rebels. Governor Curtin knew they were there for the battle, not the war. Captain Babe knew. But Couch insisted he had no authority to circumvent War Department regulations. Perhaps, in that hour of crisis, he would have been applauded if he had bent the rules to accept ninety new soldiers. Instead, he sent the Catto company back to Philadelphia. The major general was telling them they could not fight for their country.

Emilie Davis heard "that the boyes had bin sent back. I feel glad and sorry."

There is no sure way of knowing how Catto reacted, but this was a young man known to throw his hands up and walk away at lesser slights. Some of the ninety rejected men tried again weeks later—and formed the core of Company A of the Third Regiment of U.S. Colored Infantry, the first black regiment raised in Pennsylvania. But not Catto.

Secretary of War Stanton sent Couch a chastising telegram instructing him to accept volunteers "regardless of race."

★ ★ ★

CATTO'S COMPANY may have been stillborn, but the Fifty-fourth Massachusetts was already in the South, occupying coastal Georgia. Heading the unit was a twenty-six-year-old white son of Boston, Colonel Robert Gould Shaw. During a lull in the war, he visited the plantation of Pierce Butler. Shaw's family had known Butler's famous former wife, Fanny Kemble, years before.

"There are about ten of his slaves left there, all of them sixty or seventy years old," he wrote in a letter home. "He sold about three hundred slaves about three years ago. I talked with some whose children and grandchildren were sold then [and] . . . they maintained that 'Massa Butler was a good massa,' and 'they would give any thing to see him again.' When I told them I had known Miss Fanny, they looked . . . pleased, and one, named John, wanted me to tell her I had seen him. They said all the house-servants had been taken inland by the overseer at the beginning of the war; and they asked if we couldn't get their children back to the island again. These were all born and bred on the place, and even selling away their families could not entirely efface their love for their master."

Even so, Shaw was struck by the old slaves' words for the great auctioning-off at the racetrack in 1859. "They said that was a 'weeping day.'"

When in South Carolina with the Fifty-fourth, he wrote of having tea with "Miss Charlotte Forten," and of her promise to provide him with the words of hymns sung by the Negroes there. And of war, he wrote, "I want to get my men alongside of white troops, and into a good fight, if there is to be one. . . . We don't know with any certainty what is going on in the North, but can't believe Lee will get far into Pennsylvania."

The confidence expressed by Shaw was not seen on the streets of Philadelphia as the war drew closer. Trains to Harrisburg were stopped and their engines taken away. Many businesses closed. The State House bell tolled all day. Colored refugees from Chambersburg and Gettysburg arrived on foot, lugging bundled belongings and telling crowds near Mother Bethel Church of the dangers they had seen.

Negro and white leaders wrote to Secretary of War Stanton urging him to hasten the enlisting of colored troops. Printed in the newspaper June 18, the letter was accompanied by an advertisement for a July 6 Negro recruiting meeting at National Hall. Politicians were closing ranks; the letter's signatories included Benjamin Brewster, once the enemy of abolitionists and the object of Lucretia Mott's unforgiving stare. "I only wish we had two hundred thousand [Negroes] in our army to save the valuable lives of our white men," one white Philadelphian wrote. No matter. A change had come, and now it was irrevocable. Negroes in Pennsylvania would fight for the Union. Catto and his company had just tried days too early.

The day after Catto's return, Stanton gave official permission for the committee that created the "Men of Color" broadside to oversee the immediate recruitment of Negro troops and to form three regiments in the Philadelphia area. He also named Major George L. Stearns, the former recruiter of Negroes for Massachusetts, as the government's Pennsylvania's recruiter. And he laid out rules: no cash bounty from the city, three-year enlistments (or until the war ended), and a salary of ten dollars, less three dollars for uniforms. So they earned seven dollars a month while white soldiers earned thirteen.

The next day was Saturday, June 20. Eight thousand rebel troops were massing near Harrisburg ninety miles away after having dispensed with a state militia force. Also on that day, Miller McKim, the abolition leader who worked so hard to save Daniel Webster, and Congressman William Kelley, the former city judge who hid a billy club in his sleeve at the tense antislavery society meeting in 1859, were named to the recruiting committee for colored troops. They did their work well. Before July, a training camp for troops had opened eight miles north of the city. The camp at Chelten Hills, soon to be called Camp William Penn, was the nation's first and largest for colored troops. Nearly eleven thousand men would be trained there by war's end.

The recruits were greeted by Thomas Webster. He apologized, cajoled, and tried to inspire the region's first Negro troops. His words echoed Douglass, Bassett, and the other signers of the "Men of Color!" broadside. Except that Webster was a white man, the head of an all-white recruiting committee.

"Men of Color . . . the opportunity is offered for which you have waited so long and so patiently. . . . At the very commencement of the struggle, you eagerly offered your services," Webster said. "They were rejected for reasons which, whether well or ill founded, were all powerful at the time. Those reasons exist no longer, and your country now invites you to arms in her defence.

". . . You have been strangers in a land of strangers, and it is now for you to decide whether that land shall be to you and your children more in the future than it has been in the past. . . . Old prejudice declared that you could not fight."

Webster said that contraband soldiers had "gloriously replied to that taunt." He went on, "An opportunity which has no parallel in history is now before you. Shrink from it now, and you justify the taunts and sneers of your enemies and oppressors. Take advantage of it; show yourselves to be men and patriots, and a grateful country watching the flags of your regiments emerging triumphantly from the smoke of battle, cannot refuse the applause which is the due of valor contending for the right."

In a preview of the expected July 6 mass recruitment rally, a smaller meeting was held June 24. And there, a new exultation of Negro valor—the performance of colored troops in the Union victory earlier in the month at the battle of Milliken's Bend, Louisiana—was surely heard. Any indignant feelings Catto had at being turned away in Harrisburg had apparently cooled—his was the first name at the bottom of the meeting's broadside.

★ ★ ★

GEORGE GORDON MEADE, commander of the Army of the Potomac, arrived in the state on Monday, June 29 to do battle with Robert E. Lee's forces. That day, the headline in Philadelphia was: "To Arms, Citizens of Pennsylvania!! The Rebels Are Upon Us." The mayor's appeals for more volunteers had little result, outraging the morning paper: "A precious day was lost yesterday by following the promptings of this do-nothing spirit. There are no Sundays in revolutionary times."

The battle at Gettysburg began July 1 and lasted three days. Despite the paucity of volunteers from Philadelphia, Meade's forces prevailed. One of the victorious generals was Alfred Pleasonton, a small bearded man with a prominent mustache who headed the cavalry. Pleasonton never set foot on the battlefield where ten thousand died, tens of thousands were wounded, and more than three thousand horses were killed. He stayed at headquarters. He was the younger brother of Augustus Pleasonton, the brigadier general of Philadelphia's home guard and a witness to the 1838 destruction of Pennsylvania Hall.

As the news of the success at Gettysburg—and Vicksburg soon after— became the talk of the nation, five hundred colored troops from Camp William Penn paraded through the city. Crowds applauded and cheered. *Cheered.* In Philadelphia, where Negroes faced epithets like *Nigger* as often as they did offal on the streets, crowds cheered. Threats of attack on the city had sparked resentment toward the cause of Jefferson Davis, even among Democrats. Everything that daylight touched was now different.

Catto and his friends Jake White and Ebenezer Bassett were the secretaries for the July 6 recruitment meeting at National Hall, the site four years before of near riots over John Brown's execution. Vice presidents included Rev. William Alston, David Bowser, and Robert Adger. The mood was celebratory as a band played "John Brown's Soul Is Marching On." Frederick Douglass, introduced by Congressman Kelley as a man "who was once a thing," urged those who were turned away the month before to volunteer again. The audience of whites and Negroes cheered lustily at the mention of Gettysburg and Milliken's Bend. They whooped at the name General Benjamin Butler. Bassett read the "Men of Color!" broadside aloud and promised to raise four companies of eighty men each.

Kelley, the first white elected official ever to speak to a primarily Negro audience in Philadelphia, urged colored parents to disown their sons if they did not enlist. To peals of laughter, he said, "You girls, remember the young fellows when they come to spark you. If they are afraid of the smell of gunpowder, you will have to tuck them under the bedclothes when it thunders."

On that same July 6 day, Charlotte Forten, teaching in South Carolina, wrote in her diary about Colonel Shaw, the leader of the Massachusetts Fifty-fourth. If she were ten years younger, her words and emotions would have been described as a *crush.* But at the age of twenty-five, her words were handwritten with admiration and she was clearly *smitten.*

"Tis a splendid looking reg't, an honor to the race." Colored troops were singing "Jubilo." "I am more than ever charmed with the noble little Col. What purity, what nobleness of soul, what exquisite gentleness in that beautiful face! As I look at it I think, 'The bravest are the tenderest. I can imagine what he must be to his mother. May his life be spared to her!'"

He was twenty-five as well, newly married, and talked to her of missing his mother. "Tonight, he helped me on my horse, and after carefully arranging the folds of my riding skirt, said so kindly, 'Goodbye. If I don't see you again down here, I hope to see you at our house,'" in Massachusetts.

★ ★ ★

NEGRO GOOD FEELING about the nation, and the nation's good feeling about Negroes, did not last. Imagine a seesaw, exhilaration about change lifting one end up and unchanged realities keeping the other end down. Whatever pride and confidence Negroes in the North had about their improved stature disappeared in the time it took for a rope to be tossed over a lamp post in New York City. Lynching defiles optimism.

The Civil War was the largest civil insurrection in the nation's history. Second were the July 13–17 draft riots in New York. How many died is uncertain—more than a hundred to be sure, perhaps as many as five hundred. Thousands were injured, thousands lost their homes. Once again colored residents of an American city had to flee. Police had great difficulty stopping the violence because they were, in great numbers, the perpetrators.

A military draft had begun just days before in New York, but any man with three hundred dollars could buy his way out. White working men and policemen were angry about that and the worsening economic conditions and about risking their lives in a war for Negro freedom. Economic conditions and an inequitable draft are difficult to punish, but punishing colored people, that was easy. The punishers hunted in packs and killed by hanging, shooting, beating, burning, and drowning. They destroyed a colored orphans' home and a colored seamen's retirement home. Colored New Yorkers were afraid to step outside.

The Negro abolitionist William P. Powell hid on a roof. "From 2 P.M. to 8 P.M., myself and my family were prisoners in my own house to King Mob. . . . About 4 P.M., I sent a note to [Police] Supt. Kennedy for protection, but received none, from the fact that he had been seriously injured by the mob in another part of the city." White men threw stones, broke windows, and finally entered Powell's home. He took his family, including an invalid daughter, and escaped to the roof of the next house and stayed there for hours. Rain drenched them. "But . . . God . . . came to my relief in the person of a little, deformed, despised Israelite, who, Samari-

tan-like, took my poor helpless daughter . . . in his house. . . . He also supplied me with a long rope." Powell climbed down and hid in a neighbor's
cellar until eleven, when police came. He lost three thousand dollars in
personal property.

A colored man in Brooklyn saw "many men . . . killed and thrown into
the rivers, a great number hung to trees and lamp-posts, numbers shot
down; no black person could show their heads but that they were hunted
like wolves. . . . Hundreds of our people are . . . in the woods. . . . The
mob spirit seems to have run in every direction."

Among the hunted was a notorious one-legged Negro.

Henry Highland Garnet recruited colored troops and also tended to
their spirits as chaplain at the training camp on Rikers Island. He never
stopped talking about abolition. The mob knew his name, knew he lived
on Thirtieth Street, and knew his church was Shiloh.

A visiting British abolitionist, scheduled to speak at Shiloh that night,
arrived to find the church eerily deserted. He raced about until he found
Garnet, seated in "the darkened parlor of his home with four friends. . . .
They braced themselves . . . dreading every falling footstep which seemed
to approach the door." Garnet's daughter Mary had the presence of mind
to cut his nameplate off the door with an ax.

Now the rioters surged down Thirtieth Street, shouting Garnet's name.
They ran past his house.

Shiloh, meanwhile, was "sacked, but not destroyed." Garnet later told
of a scene that would not leave his mind. A colored man was hung on
a tree and then "a demon in human form, taking a sharp knife, cut out
pieces of the quivering flesh, and offered it to the greedy, blood-thirsty
mob, saying, 'Who wants some nigger meat?' and then the reply, 'I!' 'I!' 'I!'
as if they were scrambling for pieces of gold."

The violence ended when the federal government sent troops in.

Garnet thought that the wave of freed slaves coming north had helped
ignite the riots. He and others saw "danger to the white race and their
republican institutions because of the presence of a disenfranchised and
distinct class of laborers in the heart of the Republic" and used those
words in a letter that fall to President Lincoln. The letter revived Martin
Delany's plan of an independent state for Negroes, probably in the 'American tropics,' and requested five thousand dollars in government funds "to
the African Civilization Society for emigration purposes."

Not all Negro abolitionist leaders blamed the riot violence on freed slaves. New York's James Pennington pointed to the "anti-black spirit of colonization" as a cause.

The riots led to Negroes being terrorized throughout the North. Troy, New York, had a riot, as did Boston. Was the violence going to spread further? The military draft in Philadelphia was scheduled for just days after the riots in New York. The *Christian Recorder* tapped the mood of colored Philadelphia: "Our citizens are expecting every day that a mob will break out here, and . . . it is thought, they will not only resist the draft, but will pounce upon the colored people as they did in New York and elsewhere, and if so, we have only to say this to colored citizens . . . : Have plenty of powder & ball in your houses, and use it with effect, if necessary, in the protection of your wives and children."

The local Republican leader John Read wrote to Abraham Lincoln in the midst of the New York riots begging him to send troops to Philadelphia because there were as many as "40,000 blacks, whom the government is bound to protect. In a riot, they will be the first sufferers, and will be savagely murdered."

If there had been a riot, General George Cadwalader, who had tried to keep the peace during the Bible riots in 1844, would have commanded the Union troops in the city. But Mayor Henry and the police were credited with staving off a bloodbath. The same resentments that raged in New York festered in Philadelphia but did not flare into a riot.

While Negroes were the victims of the riots in New York, Troy, and Boston, they were not victims everywhere. In Flushing, New York, they fought back. There, "the colored people went to the Catholic priest and told him that they were peaceable men doing no harm . . . and that the Irish had threatened to mob them, but if they did, they would burn two Irish houses for every one of theirs, and would kill two Irish men for every colored man killed by them. They were not mobbed."

The day after the riots in New York ended, the Massachusetts Fifty-fourth was part of a Union attack on Fort Wagner in Morris Island, South Carolina, which guarded the southern approach to Charleston harbor. Armed with fixed bayonets, colored troops who'd gone two days without rest or rations led the assault across three-quarters of a mile of sand to the Confederate earthen works. One hundred forty-six men were wounded and a hundred were listed as missing or dead. Four officers died.

One of the dead was a corporal named Holloway, a family member of Richard Holloway's, the colored slave owner from Charleston and the old friend of William Catto's. The dead soldier's uncle was Daniel Payne, who had married a Holloway. A.M.E. bishop James Lynch described the slain soldier in a letter: "Bishop Payne's nephew, Corporal Holloway, died fighting. I was told by a soldier who stood by his side that the moment before he fell, he said, 'My gun shall aim for the rebel's heart and my soul for glory.'"

The failed attack on Fort Wagner succeeded in one important way: The colored soldiers leading the assault convinced their white officers of their valor. Charlotte Forten said, "It is too terrible, too terrible to write. . . . Thank Heaven! they fought bravely! And oh, I still must hope that our colonel, ours especially he seems to me, is not killed."

But Shaw was killed that day.

★ ★ ★

IN THE FIRST MONTHS after Emancipation, as freedmen streamed into Union camps by the thousands, information began coursing out of the censored slave world.

Federal interviewers in Union-occupied Beaufort listened wide-eyed to Robert Smalls, the hero of the *Planter*, describe his previous life there as a slave. The transcript revealed as much about the questioners as it did about Smalls.

He had prospered since his dramatic night on Charleston Harbor. He was soon to be made a captain in the Union Navy. In the meantime, he returned to Beaufort and the adjoining islands, where the presence of Northern soldiers, teachers, and abolitionists denoted a world turned upside down. Illiterate, Smalls put his six-year-old daughter, Elizabeth, in the class taught by Charlotte Forten. (According to family lore, Elizabeth assured her father, "Daddy, Miss Forten knows *everything*.")

The American Freedmen's Inquiry Commission men, Northerners acting on congressional authority, asked about farming abilities, capacity for self-government (Smalls said white help would be needed), willingness to take up arms for the Union, and moral proclivities of slave women.

Q. Have not colored women a good deal of sexual passion?
A. Yes, sir. . . .

Q. How is it with the young women?

A. They are very wild and run around a great deal.

He said most girls joined a church by age sixteen, and that made a difference in them "as great as between the sunshine and a hail-storm." Smalls said churches and "secret societies" were Negro nerve centers despite laws against gatherings of more than four colored men. He said Negroes in Charleston knew of the war, were "praying for this day," and given the chance would form ten regiments. But not the slaves on outlying plantations. "They have been kept in ignorance and punished if they attempted to learn."

The commissioners asked about the punishments. Smalls told of men placed in stocks for as long as two days; of an owner who, on a whim, had men whipped, and doused with salty water. "My aunt was whipped so many a time until she has not the same skin she was born with." He described the same device the Grimké sisters and Theodore Weld had reported in their book *Slavery as It Is* in 1839. "In this very place I have seen a man owned by John Verdier wearing an iron collar with two prongs sticking out at the sides like cow's horns," Smalls said. (The Verdiers were respected white gentry in Beaufort; the Verdier house is a tourist attraction today.)

Smalls said one owner devised a series of stocks, built one atop the next, to punish several slaves—after each was made to drink a laxative. A man who misbehaved "was not punished immediately but kept until there were enough [slaves] to be punished to fill the stocks. Then the man to be punished most would be placed in the lowest stocks and the others above him, when they would all be required to take a large dose of medicine and filth down upon each other."

Miller McKim, too, had recently returned from Beaufort when he sat down beside Sidney Fisher in a Philadelphia streetcar. The two men were not close friends, but Fisher saw McKim as "a noted abolitionist, & intelligent & I think an honest & sincere man." As the car carried them across the city, McKim, fresh from weeks of setting up makeshift schools for freedmen's children, told Fisher a story.

Two mulatto slave girls in Beaufort claimed their masters had forced them into "concubinage"—only to be discovered by the masters' wives, who had them whipped again and again. Skeptical, McKim asked women in his traveling party to inspect the girls' "persons"—and the women "found on their lacerated backs full confirmation of their dismal story."

Fisher knew the white families McKim was naming—"some of the best families," he wrote. "I have often heard that concubinage was a source of much domestic unhappiness in the South, but I never before heard that injured wives revenged themselves in this way on the innocent victims of their husbands' crime."

★ ★ ★

IN THE LATE SUMMER, Philadelphians read *A Tale of Two Cities* as the Nevada Territory elected delegates to a state constitutional convention. Colored enlistments dropped. Lower wages than whites and the refusal to appoint Negro officers dimmed patriotism. The *Weekly Anglo-African* called for suffrage, insisting emancipation was not enough. Workmen hammered and sawed new wooden barracks at Camp William Penn.

On September 1, trainloads of spectators came to the camp to hear speeches, watch the troops parade, and see a flag presented. Jacob White Sr. said the colored recruits had penned their names "high upon the scroll of fame." Robert Purvis said, "I thank God that the Government . . . recognized your manhood . . . by calling on you to share in the sacrifices necessary to establish the doctrine of equal rights."

Two days later, passengers on a train to the camp witnessed another sort of sacrifice. A colored soldier stood on the train's outer steps, careful not to step inside where he was not permitted. But a surging group of whites coming onto the crowded car forced him inside. White passengers, angry about this apparent impudence, shouted for the conductor to do something. The conductor did nothing. Suddenly a white man in the center of the car spoke in a strong clear voice: The soldier should not be removed. Passengers said, "Who are you?" He identified himself—"Thomas Smith, president of the Bank of North America." One incredulous passenger said, "I don't believe it." Smith walked over to the disbelieving man and knocked him down. Then the banker gave the soldier his seat and stood by him until his stop.

In the fall, voters in the local elections saw placards on the streets from the Philadelphia Colored Literary Institute urging "our white brethren" to turn up at the polls because "a native born colored man" has more political rights than "a white foreigner."

The signs were a smear, created to rile Democratic voters—Irishmen—
to go to the polls in anger to protect their rights. There was no Philadelphia
Colored Literary Institute.

The men of the city's real colored organizations had to stop what
they were doing and counteract this lie. William Forten, Ebenezer Bas-
set, Octavius Catto and his father, Rev. William Alston, Jacob White Sr.,
Robert Adger Sr., and more signed a letter to the newspaper saying so and
declared that the placards' real purpose was "stirring up vulgar prejudice
against us and fanning the embers of hatred" between Negroes and the
white foreign-born, people like the Irish Catholics. Similar tactics, they
said, had been used in the previous municipal election.

In late November, President Lincoln came to Gettysburg to dedicate
a cemetery to the fallen soldiers. Secretary of State Seward spoke, too, as
did Edward Everett, who had been a U.S. senator, secretary of state, and
president of Harvard University. Here is what Sidney Fisher said of the
addresses: "The orator was Mr. Edward Everett. His speech was long but
commonplace, tho well written and appropriate. Mr. Seward made a good
speech, Mr. Lincoln a very short one, but to the point and marked by his
pithy sense, quaintness & good feeling."

★ ★ ★

ON FEBRUARY 19, 1864, the *Liberator* published a poem urging Negro
enlistment by Robert Bridges Forten, son of James, father of Charlotte
and the creator of his own nine-foot telescope. The poem ended with
the sadness of the Union's pride having been "slain" by the traitors of the
South, but

> The negro's arm shall be the charm
> That gives it life again.

A day later and seven months after Fort Wagner, the Massachusetts
Fifty-fourth joined other units in a battle amid the long-leaf pines of north-
central Florida. Banneker member George Stephens, the former ship's carpenter who was arrested in Charleston for being a walking-around free
Negro, was a soldier in the Fifty-fourth. He told of their march into battle at Olustee, through palmetto bushes and wire grass, singing, "We're
bound for Tallahassee in the morning" and Stephen Foster's "Old Folks
at Home."

As other units' casualties rose, the Fifty-fourth was ordered forward "at double quick," rushing past wounded men who shouted, "We're badly whipped. You'll get killed." The Fifty-fourth put up their own shout: "Three cheers for the 54th and seven dollars a month!" The valorous Fifty-fourth was the last unit to leave the field in a battle the Union lost decisively.

The Eighth U.S. Colored Troops, trained at Camp William Penn, saw its first action at Olustee. Of the 5,000 Union troops on hand, 1,800 were casualties—killed, wounded or missing in the loss, one of the most brutal battles of the war. The Eighth brought 554 men to the battle and had 310 casualties, the most of either side. The killing did not stop when the battle ended. The Union's retreat was so swift that it left wounded colored men alive on the battlefield. Confederates killed many of them.

Despite the continued unequal treatment of Negro soldiers in pay, training, equipment, and advancement, the military, in important ways, treated its Negroes better than the nation did. They could testify in military court, even against whites. And for former slaves from the South, the ultimate authority was the law, not their owner. For the first time in the nation, Negroes and whites were being treated equally in the courts.

Not everyone in government took notice of that development or necessarily thought it was the way it should be. For one important man, the best end of the Civil War was threefold: a victory for the Union, a government for white men, and colonization for black men. Yes, that's the way it should be, said the U.S. senator from Tennessee, Democrat Andrew Johnson.

As Johnson was offering his view of a perfect nation, Rev. Catto had left his Congregationalist pulpit in New Haven and had rejoined the Presbyterians *again*, local newspapers brimmed with advertisements for baseball and cricket equipment, and the most famous Negro singer of the day, Elizabeth Greenfield, the "Black Swan," performed at a fund-raiser at Camp William Penn. In Washington, Senator Charles Sumner denounced the local streetcar system for excluding Negroes and promised new laws to stop the discrimination.

In a time when the names of phony Negro organizations were bandied about on election placards, another real one sprang up to join the likes of the Banneker Institute and the Social, Cultural, and Statistical Association of the Colored People of Pennsylvania. The new Colored Union League formed to press for Negro suffrage. The Banneker's Alfred Green was its secretary and Rev. Stephen Smith its treasurer. Its president, John C. Bowers, said the group would also petition for streetcar equality, for an end to "feeble females, with helpless children . . . compelled to ride on the front platform of the cars often during the coldest and most dis-agreeable days of winter [and] . . . many were prevented from visiting their husbands & brothers at Camp William Penn."

Smith had perhaps the meeting's most poignant comment: He remem-bered what it was like to vote. It had been twenty-six years since any Negro in Pennsylvania had voted.

★ ★ ★

WITH A NAME that sounded more like a mountain of cushions in a child's bedroom than a Union garrison, Fort Pillow stood atop a bluff along the east bank of the Mississippi, about forty miles north of Mem-phis, Tennessee. On April 12, a battle was fought there involving eighteen hundred mounted Southern soldiers and fewer than six hundred Union soldiers, some of them Negro. None of the rebels had fought uniformed Negroes at close quarters before.

General Nathan Bedford Forrest, a Memphis slave trader, commanded the Confederates. Just 14 of his men died in the battle while 248 federal troops were killed. Of the 248, about 170 were black, or two-thirds of the Negro soldiers. Blood reddened the soil and accusations of massacre blackened the air.

A Southern newspaper correspondent tried to explain what had hap-pened. He wrote: "The sight of negro soldiers stirred the bosom of our sol-diers with courageous madness."

Ten days later in Cairo, Illinois, a congressional committee held hear-ings to determine what had happened at Fort Pillow. Survivors testi-fied. Colored private Duncan Harding told the committee that he was wounded, taken prisoner after the surrender, and shot by rebel troops in the thigh as they took him away.

Q. Were any [Confederate] officers about you when you were shot?
A. Yes sir.
Q. Did they say anything against it?
A. No, sir; only, "Kill the God damned nigger."

Several white and black soldiers testified that they saw colored prison-ers, men and boys, shot after the surrender. Two white soldiers said rebel soldiers cursed at them for "fighting with the niggers." Some white prisoners were wounded and killed after the surrender, but the "worst of massacre" were colored prisoners. Many who testified were former slaves.

One was John F. Ray, who said, "I saw a rebel lieutenant take a little negro boy up on the horse behind him; and then I heard General Chalmers—I think it must have been—tell him to 'take that negro down and shoot him,' or 'take him and shoot him,' and he passed him down and shot him."

Q. How large was the boy?

A. He was not more than eight years old. I heard the lieutenant tell the others that the negro was not in the service; that he was nothing but a child. . . . The other one said: "Damn the difference; take him down and shoot him," or he would shoot him. I think it must have been General Chalmers. He was a smallish man; he had on a long gray coat, with a star on his coat.

Union lieutenant William Clary arrived on a gunboat the morning after the battle. After negotiating permission from an aide to General Forrest to take Union wounded onto the boat, he testified, "I rode all around the battle-ground, and saw some of our dead half-buried, and I saw five negroes burning. I asked Col. Chalmers, the general's brother, if that was [what] he allowed his men to do. He concluded that he could not control his men very well, and thought it was justifiable in regard to negroes; that they did not recognize negroes as soldiers." Clary said the men lay on wooden boards and in tents that had been set ablaze. He guessed the fires had already burned for half an hour.

"Their flesh was frying off them, and their clothes were burning."

Q. How many did you see in that condition?

A. I saw five.

★ ★ ★

ROBERT B. FORTEN, father of Charlotte, was now living permanently in England. He had a good job as a clerk. The prejudice against his race there was not as overbearing. But he was unable to ignore the war back home and what might happen if the Union won. He left his new-found country for his old one and joined the army in March 1864. He was put to work immediately recruiting colored troops. He was fifty.

Asked once why he enlisted, a man of education who no longer lived in America and could never be elevated to officer, he said that his "country asked her colored children to rally to her defense, and those of them that had been blessed with education should be foremost in responding to the call."

He said to his concerned mother: "How could I, or any other colored man . . . remain in a foreign land?"

In April, while in Baltimore, he succumbed to typhoid fever.

His death occasioned a rare speech in Congress: a member rising to mourn a colored friend. William Kelley spoke poignantly on the House floor about the death of his childhood playmate and the sacrifices that Negroes were making for the Union. Unequal pay for colored soldiers was "pregnant evidence of the terrible weight of prejudice which has clouded the judgment and conscience of the American people." Among those strongly against raising the pay for colored soldiers was his fellow Philadelphia congressman, Democrat Samuel Randall.

The military funeral provided for the late major was the first ever granted to a Negro in Philadelphia and was attended by sixteen Negro comrades from the U.S. Colored Troops, Lucretia Mott, J. Miller McKim, and numerous colored and white city leaders. They came to the services at Camp William Penn and escorted Robert Forten's hearse on its long trek from the camp to the city and stood by as he was laid to rest within the protective walls of St. Thomas Church. Three musket volleys sounded over his grave.

★　★　★

THE TWELFTH ANNUAL COMMENCEMENT at the Institute for Colored Youth took place over two days in May, beginning with public testing of the graduates and ending on a Thursday evening with the event's keynote speaker walking to the podium at Concert Hall. The first day's examination was held at the school, 716–718 Lombard.

The nine graduates were rigorously tested in Greek, Latin, trigonometry, and English. The audience watched as students parsed Homer and Virgil, quoted verses of the Bible, and solved mathematical problems, such as: What is the area of an equilateral triangle that can be inscribed in a circle of two acres?

Graduates won prizes for their scholarship. J. W. Cromwell, once cuffed on the head by Catto, received fifteen dollars for "excellence in mathematics." Theophilus Minton, whose older brother, William, was a Banneker, accepted ten dollars for "diligence and good conduct." The elder Minton had joined Catto when they visited Rosetta Douglass and when a defense fund was formed for the would-be rescuers of Moses Horner.

Principal Bassett spoke at the commencement for more than an hour. Fourteen-year-old I.C.Y. student Toussaint L'Ouverture Martin recited a poem. Various alumni spoke; Caroline Le Count read an obituary for a schoolmate. Catto watched the poised eighteen-year-old cross the stage and address the hall. Then she watched him do the same.

He was the attraction everyone was waiting for, a graduate who was already a leader in the community, a twenty-five-year-old teacher who had been described as "the rising Catto."

He could see that a third of the audience was white, as many as one thousand. In the gallery above and in the audience below, he could see the fire-ravaged countenance of Benjamin Brewster and the handsome visage of the Rt. Rev. Alonzo Potter, the Episcopal bishop. Some of the whites had heard of this school teacher, this recruiter of colored soldiers, but few had heard him speak. This was the largest audience Catto had ever addressed, and certainly the one with most white people. Behind him sat the school's white managers, teachers, and Negro alumni. In front and above sat students, Banneker members, neighbors, soldiers, all wondering what he would say—say on the spot where Douglass, Sumner, and Garrison had spoken; on the spot where George Christy's Minstrels appeared in blackface as "Gems of Ethiopian Minstrelsy And Characteristics of Negro Eccentricity" and charged white audiences twenty-five cents a ticket to laugh the night away. His father, who had spoken on pulpits and platforms across the North, had never spoken on this stage. Now William Catto's second-born son began a most important oration.

He began with the importance of education and of the institute. He spoke about the need "to pause and remember, that the principles of right, equity, and justice; the very ideas of an improved civilization, . . . the very moral conception of individual and mutual rights of property, contract and government, upon which the people of the North justify their attitude in the present have never been more successfully and generally promulgated than through the teachings of the School.

"And we venture the belief, that had there been, through the Southern part of this country, a system of education for the masses, irrespective of class or color, exhibiting in its energy one half of the zeal which has, within those States, been exerted to keep the conscience unenlightened and the understanding uninstructed, we tonight would not be found at the crisis of a civil war."

He buttressed his argument with words from Aristotle and Martin Luther on the importance of teaching. He offered examples about church and government-run education in the capitals of Europe and then declared that the locally controlled school system in the United States, while flawed, was the best devised.

That took him to the history of the institute and a call for a new, larger, more modern building to house the one hundred students, six teachers, and more than two thousand books. The Lombard Street building was thirteen years old and in a neighborhood that was seeing more and more groggeries and brothels.

He announced that the Society of Friends and the managers had raised thirty-six thousand dollars, ten thousand dollars of which had purchased a 77-by-140-foot "fine lot" on Shippen Street above Ninth, opposite a cemetery (guaranteeing quiet) four blocks from the current site "in a location less noisy and surrounded by influences of a more moral tendency." "We may readily perceive the intention of the Board," he added, "to make this a first class Institute, . . . every man who admires the spirit of disinterested benevolence . . . should . . . feel encouraged."

The institute was small, but growing; some years its graduating class numbered two or three. Catto said the best way to judge its worth was to look at what had happened to the graduates before tonight. Two were taking courses in medicine, sixteen were teaching, including three in city public schools. He said three more were office clerks. He recalled an 1856 graduate, his friend Jesse Glasgow—the "very black boy" who had once stepped to the blackboard to help Ebenezer Bassett demolish a visitor's theory of racial inferiority, and who had gone on to win prizes at the University of Edinburgh, only to sicken and die before he could graduate. He added that one graduate, Sallie Daffin, class of 1860, "the pioneer in our ranks," was teaching freed colored children in Virginia.

Then Catto moved his words onto broader issues and a wider world. He brought up one his favorite causes—colored teachers for colored students. It was a topic that showed both his passion and his propensity, as was typical of his time, to speak at length and then continue. He charged that the schools sent their worst white teachers to instruct colored children.

"It is at least unjust to allow a blind and ignorant prejudice to so far disregard the choice of parents and the will of the colored tax-payers, as to appoint over colored children white teachers, whose intelligence and success, measured by the fruits of their labors, could neither obtain nor secure for them positions which we know would be more congenial to their tastes."

He then praised the nation's president but criticized the nation.

The five hundred former slaves who had sailed for a new life on Île à Vache had met hunger and death instead. None of the promises made by Bernard Kock and his partners had been met. Ten months after they had arrived, Lincoln sent a ship to bring the survivors home. Three hundred and fifty arrived a few weeks before the institute's graduation ceremonies. Catto's audience had heard and read about the rescue.

"Let it be recorded," Catto said, "to the credit of Mr. Lincoln as the purest act which his administration has thus far performed in justice to the colored American. Let the statesman regard it as the jeweled hand of the Present lifting the dark veil of the golden Future."

The I.C.Y.'s white managers shifted in their seats. The speaker was supposed to sketch the past and future of his school, not of his race. Mr. Catto was changing the subject.

How much of the course of this terrible revolution remains yet to be run, or how many political evolutions our Government may yet be forced to make, no man can foresee. But it must be the most superficial view . . . which concludes that any other condition than a total change in the status which the colored man has hitherto had in this country. . . .

There must come a change, one now in process of completion, which shall force upon this nation, not so much for the good of the black man, as for its own political and industrial welfare, that course which Providence seems wisely to be directing for the mutual benefit of both peoples.

Catto then made a call for action, a plea that freedmen's relief groups and abolitionists were making as well. It evoked what people a century later would know as a domestic Peace Corps, though it was not a call to dig wells or help former slaves plant crops. They knew how to do that. But they could not read the Bible or write their own names. Catto was asking for people, educated colored people like himself, to teach the newly freed Americans. The task was immense and there were too few educated Negroes, but it had to be done. The responsibility was theirs.

"Those millions of human beings now scattered through the Southern country must eventually come forth into the sunlight of Freedom," he said.

> Those people will need among them Christian missionaries, intelligent teachers and laborers, to direct them to that course of life and in those modes of industry. . . . It is the duty of every man, to the extent of his interest and means, to provide for the immediate improvement of the four or five millions of ignorant and previously dependent laborers who will be thrown upon society in the reorganization of the Union. . . .
>
> For though born in ignorance and liable to fall in a competition with the intelligent foreigner and migrating Northerner as they go southward, yet he has within him an aspiration and a capability to rise by faith, labor, and perseverance to a respectable place among his competitors.
>
> All that he asks is that there shall be no unmanly quibbles about intrusting to him any position of honor or profit for which his attainments may fit him. And that which is committed to him as a man, he will perform as no other than a man could perform.

A speech that began with an accounting of the history and the schoolhouse of "our alma mater" ended with a call for equal rights. Catto had now taken his place alongside Bassett and Charles Reason, weavers of the strands of education and agitation.

The *Press* said his "ingeniously woven" words stole the show from Bassett and the night's other speakers. Colored teachers who heard the speech set out to reprint it for "widespread circulation." J. W. Cromwell began devising his own plan to go south and teach the millions. Other graduates would follow.

Jake White's journey was shorter. He had just won the principal's job at the colored Vaux School, where forty-nine students learned in a cramped church basement that passed for a public school and had to close for funerals. Years before, Catto had briefly attended Vaux. White and Cordelia Jennings, the public schools' only other colored principal, formally asked Catto's permission to reprint the speech on behalf of all I.C.Y. alumni, for "its literary merits [and] the information it contains."

Obviously pleased, Catto protested that he had not written the speech to be published. But "with the hope, that in a printed form . . . the interest of our Alma Mater may be promoted, a copy is placed at your disposal."

The managers said in their annual report that Catto gave a "pleasant" speech tracing the I.C.Y.'s history and building plans. They did not mention the rest.

★ ★ ★

ROBERT SMALLS, now the captain of the *Planter*, brought the ship into the Navy Yard in Philadelphia for engine repairs. His three-year-old son, Robert Jr., had just died of smallpox. Charlotte Forten had given Smalls letters of introduction to her friends in Philadelphia's abolition circles. A naval commander who befriended Smalls fretted that Northerners would "ruin him" with celebrity and apply "the Barnum principle etc."

Charlotte's friends embraced this curio, a Negro war hero, from the moment he stepped off his ship. Smalls lectured for the Anti-Slavery Society; he told the story of the *Planter* to the Colored Union League and a packed house at Mother Bethel for the A.M.E. General Conference. He implored audiences to send the freedmen money, clothing, books. He paid Bassett and another colored teacher to tutor him day and night because, as one of his children said later, Smalls could not yet spell his name.

On an evening in June, the city's colored South Carolina expatriates held a dinner. The menu for the Fraternal Association, as they dubbed themselves, reflected the skills of the caterers among them: beef and turkey, boiled tongue, four chicken dishes, asparagus and mashed potatoes, lobster salad and terrapin, and a low-country specialty, rice *purleau*. After pies and punch, men lit "segars" and raised glasses—to Woman (" The boon companion of our youth, our greatest solace in affliction. May we ever cherish her virtues, and extend to her our dearest sympathies and manly protection"); the press ("their zeal in the cause of our down-trodden race"); the Fraternal itself; the guests, who included "the brave and noble Captain Smalls . . . and a friend of ours, Mr. O.V. Catto."

As spring mingled with summer in this election year, the Democrats chose General George McClellan to run against Lincoln. McMullen and his supporters in Moyamensing strongly supported the military leader, whose campaign slogan was, "The Constitution as it is, and the Union as it was."

In Washington, Congress defeated a Constitutional amendment ending slavery, approved equal pay for white and colored soldiers, and repealed the Fugitive Slave Act. The epitaph for the act could now be written. A compromise intended to put the slavery issue back to sleep had backfired utterly, sending thousands of Negroes into exile while hardly stanching the flow of fugitives. And it sparked in many an otherwise indifferent white Northerner's heart a new-found emotion: sympathy for the hunted Negro.

Fanny Jackson, a student at Oberlin, and Caroline Langston, wife of colored recruiter John Mercer Langston, were raising money so that colored regiments could have their own flags. In Philadelphia, broadsides went up calling on "Colored Citizens" to attend a July 26 meeting on the subject of streetcars.

The meeting gave the audience a chance to angrily tell of the wrongs they had suffered, including not being able to visit their wounded soldier sons, brothers, and husbands in the hospital. It was resolved that public opinion must be changed and that money be raised to influence white people. It was also resolved that the Christian churches needed to be advocates for Negroes being allowed on the streetcars.

The war sent prices rising in the North—butter was sixty-five to seventy cents a pound, eggs twenty-eight to thirty cents a dozen and chicken twenty to twenty-five cents a pound. Despite the new pay equity law, George Stephens of the Massachusetts Fifty-fourth complained that colored troops were still not getting the same compensation as whites.

In September, Atlanta fell, giving a boost to Lincoln's reelection chances. Later in the month, Alfred Green was attacked—in Philadelphia.

On a Saturday afternoon, Green, who had gone to jail trying to rescue Moses Horner, was set upon by three "roughs" as he walked on South Street, west of Eleventh. A quartermaster at Camp William Penn, he was not crossing a "dead line" into a different neighborhood, one of the geographical realities so common in Northern cities. Never a man to walk away from a confrontation, Green nevertheless told his assailants to let him be. They persisted. When he tried to get away, they struck him with bricks. That was enough of a show of patience for him. Green pulled out his gun and made it clear that he would use it if they did not leave him alone. Not the smartest white ruffians, they would not stop and threw brickbats at Green. So he fired his gun twice, hitting one of them in the leg. The wounded man was taken to Pennsylvania Hospital; his confederates were arrested.

★ ★ ★

OPTIMISM AND REALITY were embraced together by the Negro community in the autumn of 1864; things were better but not nearly good enough. The wounds from the New York riots were just beginning to heal when Secretary of State Seward said that all war measures, including the end of slavery, might be revoked when the war ended.

So 144 Negro men from the North and South came together for four days in Wesleyan Methodist Church in Syracuse in early October to organize and spread the message of suffrage, abolition, and equality before the law. Douglass was there along with Garnet and Bassett and Rock and John Mercer Langston and Catto in the most geographically representative convention of Negroes ever held.

The participants formed the National Equal Rights League, which historians identify as the first national organization "devoted solely to promoting black equality." Seven years after the Dred Scott decision and less than fifteen after the Fugitive Slave Act, 144 colored Americans decided they had waited long enough. Neither the white populace nor its government was going to give them equality. Douglass wrote the convention's major address, stressing the mission of achieving "full rights as citizens."

The convention lashed out at slavery, the denial of suffrage, colonization, and antiliteracy laws. "We have been taunted with our inferiority by people whose statute books contain laws indicting the severest penalties on whomsoever dared teach us God's Word." And the convention also lashed out at the lack of action on the part of Negroes: "Nor can we hope for a change unless we ourselves arise in the dignity of our manhood."

Rock said, "All we ask is equal opportunities and equal rights. This is what our brave men are fighting for. They have not gone to the battlefield for the sake of killing and being killed; but they are fighting for liberty and equality. We ask the same for the black man that is asked of the white man; nothing more, nothing less."

★ ★ ★

MAYOR HENRY was scared. He had received a telegram from Secretary of State Seward: "This Department has received information from the British provinces to the effect that there is a conspiracy on foot to set fire to the principal cities in the Northern states on the day of the presidential election. It is my duty to communicate this information."

It was Wednesday, November 2. The election was the next day.

Lincoln won easily. He won the city but lost badly in McMullen's ward, 2,268 to 972. Republicans controlled the city's election board. Many polls were flooded with "repeaters and outsiders," but this time they were mostly Republicans voting against the Democrats.

Lincoln had a new vice president, selected by his political advisers. Andrew Johnson had not only served in the Senate; he was the military governor of Tennessee, a Democrat, and a rarity, a Unionist from the South.

Mayor Henry woke the day after the election to see the balloting over, his city intact, and his heart calm once more.

Catto was elected a secretary of the new Pennsylvania State Equal Rights League.

On Thanksgiving Day, Equal Rights League chapters formed in the city of Philadelphia and in the state of Tennessee. Colored men a thousand miles apart were giving thanks and organizing under the same banner of equal rights even as the war raged on.

The president of the national Equal Rights League, John Mercer Langston, had bustled into Philadelphia for the first board meeting. Langston was the light-skinned Oberlin man who had won a town clerkship and whose brother Charles had gone to prison for his role in a fugitive rescue. Mercer Langston was more known for "literary distinction" and a Purvis-like partiality to satin vests and doeskin pants. He and a dozen Equal Rights League men from Philadelphia dined aboard the *Planter* with the roughest, toughest, least "literary" figure in this a-borning national movement. They were guests of Captain Smalls.

As the year was ending, Martin Delany, now fifty-two, moved his family to a home at Rev. Daniel Payne's Wilberforce College in Ohio. Supreme Court Chief Justice Roger Taney's death prompted John Rock to write Charles Sumner, asking for the senator's help in easing the way for Rock to be the first colored lawyer permitted to appear before the court. With Taney gone, now there was a chance.

Carrie Le Count and other colored women parishioners at St. Thomas raised twelve hundred dollars at fairs to aid sick and wounded soldiers. The women held fair after fair as the ranks of wounded in city hospitals swelled to the tens of thousands.

As the temperature dipped, Philadelphians skated on frozen ponds at Thirty-fourth and Chestnut and Fourth and Diamond, cheered the fall of Savannah, and chopped ice blocks from the frozen Schuylkill.

★ ★ ★

IN THE EARLY WINTER of 1865, colored Philadelphians celebrated the second anniversary of the Emancipation Proclamation in a hall on Market Street. In an event sponsored by the Banneker Society, they heard Catto deliver the opening address. He was described as a young man with considerable oratorical ability. Senator Sumner could not attend, but he wrote a letter that Jacob White Jr. read aloud. It said, in part, "The astronomer Banneker, whose honored name you bear, would be shut out of the street cars in some of our cities, but such a petty meanness cannot last long."

A few days later, Democrats in town held their own big meeting. The Keystone Club was again celebrating the capture of New Orleans. The city's native son, General George McClellan, was there. It was an evening of verbal tip-toeing, of not criticizing Lincoln even though the Keystone Club had a goal of defending the "Constitutional rights of white men against Republicans and Negro equality."

And a few days after that, Catto joined white and Negro abolitionists in a local Equal Rights League fund-raiser. The speaker was Calvin Fairbank of Kentucky, an Underground Railroad leader who during seventeen years in prison was whipped 150 times for helping slaves escape.

The next day, January 12, colored leaders again met at National Hall on Market Street, but this time to continue planning for a home for the elderly. They had already raised thirty-nine hundred dollars.

Five days later, there was news in the papers that Wilmington, North Carolina, had been captured and that Junius Booth, of the famous acting family, was appearing at the New Chestnut Street Theater in a play called *Retribution*.

On the twenty-fourth, the Philadelphia Female Anti-Slavery Society wrote to the owners of the streetcar companies, protesting their segregation policy.

"You are aware that we have a large and respectable class of colored people in our city, who own property, pay taxes, furnish soldiers and seamen for the army & navy, support churches & schools, charitable & literary institutions, & perform the general duty of citizens. Scarcely a week passes without witnessing the insult offered. . . .

"Delicate women, with young children in their arms, invalids unable to take a long walk, persons enfeebled by age, are refused entrance or compelled to stand upon the front platform—a part of the car regarded generally, and by yourselves, as an unsafe place. Inoffensive men and women have been insolently ordered to leave a car, and have been thrust out by the conductor, sometimes with violence."

The streetcar companies took no action.

At 4:00 P.M. on January 31, on its second try, Congress before packed galleries finally abolished slavery in the United States by passing the Thirteenth Amendment to the Constitution. The vote in the House was 119 to 56, barely the two-thirds needed for passage.

On February 1, Rock became the first Negro lawyer admitted to the bar of the Supreme Court. Eight years earlier, this court under Chief Justice Taney had said no Negro could be a U.S. citizen.

Pennsylvania ratified the amendment on February 3, the seventh state to do so. Catto, writing for the Equal Rights League, sent notice to the state House and Senate criticizing the disenfranchisement of blacks. The war might be ending soon, but the fight for equal rights was heating up.

On February 12, Garnet became the first Negro to deliver a sermon to the U.S. House of Representatives. The hall was packed, the crowd spellbound. The National Equal Rights League had demanded that Congress listen and now one of their own was doing the talking. Garnet talked of slavery to men who had once been its biggest supporters.

"It is the highly concentrated essence of all conceivable wickedness. Theft, robbery, pollution, unbridled passion, incest, cruelty, cold-blooded murder, blasphemy and defiance of the laws of God. It teaches children to disregard parental authority. It tears down the marriage altar. . . . It feeds and pampers its hateful handmaid, prejudice.

"It has divided our national councils. . . . It has wasted the treasure of the Commonwealth, and the lives of thousands of brave men. . . . It has caused the bloodiest civil war ever recorded in the book of time. It has shorn this nation of its locks of strength that was rising as a young lion in the Western world. . . .

"Moses, the greatest of all lawgivers and legislators, said, . . . 'Whoso stealeth a man and selleth him, . . . he shall surely be put to death.' The destroying angel has gone forth through this land to execute the fearful penalties of God's broken law.

"The Representatives of the nation have bowed with reverence to the Divine edict, and laid the axe to the root of the tree, and thus saved succeeding generations from the guilt of oppression, and from the wrath of God."

★   ★   ★

CHARLESTON WAS EVACUATED on February 20, the rebel government in Richmond a week later.

In the first week of March, Lincoln and Johnson were sworn in, with eight-six Philadelphia firemen marching in the inauguration parade. Also there, at Lincoln's invitation, was Frederick Douglass, one of the first Negroes to attend an inauguration as a guest rather than a servant. With him was Louise Dorsey, wife of the caterer. He had once entrusted his daughter to her watchfulness; now he entrusted himself. Douglass knew everyone would be looking at him. Having Louise Dorsey at his side put him more at ease.

He saw Lincoln talking with the vice president and then pointing to his colored guest. Johnson, realizing who Douglass was, made a face of "bitter contempt and aversion."

Douglass saw the face and Johnson knew it. So, Douglass said, the vice president quickly tried to make his countenance look kinder, "the bland and sickly smile of the demagogue." At that point, Douglass turned to Mrs. Dorsey: "Whatever Andrew Johnson may be, he is certainly no friend of our race."

Richmond fell on April 1. The next day, bells tolled from Harrisburg to West Chester, from Massachusetts to Michigan. It was a "Grand carnival of rejoicing" one newspaper said. After seventeen paragraphs describing that rejoicing, there came a heading, "The Colored People," and one paragraph: "On the reception of the news of the capture of Richmond, the colored people of the city turned out in large numbers. They could be seen traversing the different streets carrying with them small flags and emblems of their different lodges. They congregated in the evening at their Lodge rooms, when short addresses were made respecting the events which had transpired during the past day."

Lee surrendered April 9, and by April 14 Philadelphia newspapers were filled with advertisements for illuminating candles, and a caution—"Illuminate your house or your loyalty will be questioned." The oldest colored Philadelphians must have smiled at these notices, recalling how, thirty years ago, a candle in the window signaled the Flying Horses rioters, *Spare this house, whites live here.*

There were no candles in the seven Philadelphia-area cemeteries that held the city's Negro war dead—1,903 bodies, more than one in six of every Philadelphian killed in the war. At Lebanon, a large cemetery owned by the Jacob White Sr. and his son in a rural area of South Philadelphia, 339 Negro soldiers were buried in a site "not presenting a handsome appearance. . . . [T]he land is low and flat, . . . the soldier's plot is not enclosed," and no trees, shrubs, or headstones offered a sign to what the ground held.

Not only had Lee surrendered but Lincoln, in an impromptu victory speech at dusk from the north portico of the White House on April 11, had nudged open another door. For the first time in his presidency—or in anyone's presidency—he spoke openly about limited Negro suffrage. Though some oppose it, "I would myself prefer that it were now conferred upon the very intelligent, and those who serve our cause as soldiers."

Standing in the rain listening was a Confederate sympathizer. Hearing Lincoln talk about extending the vote to Negroes, he told a friend, "That means nigger citizenship. That is the last speech he will ever make."

With those words, John Wilkes Booth walked out of the crowd.

★ ★ ★

THEY BEGAN WALKING up from houses on Lombard and Rodman, South and Shippen streets early on that April day. Mothers dressed children in Sunday finery on a Friday. Fathers formed ranks beneath the banners of their societies and lodges, the Odd Fellows, the Statistical Association, and the Colored Union League. Colored Masons, the Philomathians, the Delmonico Assembly No. 1 brass band, bootblacks, waiters, scrubbed-up scavengers, and men who carried hod; preachers, schoolteachers, undertakers, housepainters, former contrabands and runaways, servant girls in their teens—"a holiday for all," young Emilie Davis wrote in pencil in her pocket diary. A long line of colored soldiers and civilians was parading across the city to the State House steps, black men in uniform, swathed in pride and marching without fear.

Carriages and grand barouches were in the procession as well. It was Good Friday in the city's churches and it was a good Friday for these people as they came by dozens, hundreds, and finally thousands, till the square before Independence Hall overflowed with colored faces. The Twenty-fourth U.S. Colored Troop, trained at Camp William Penn, was about to receive its regimental flag.

The older people could be forgiven if they stepped onto this square with a certain trepidation. Scarcely a decade had passed since black families arriving here on July 4 had been driven off with insults, fists, and stones. (The Democratic Party still met here regularly to talk of restoring a "white man's government" and making peace with the slaveholders.) And it had been scarcely more than a generation since a mob of well-dressed whites had stormed the abolition hall less than three blocks north, "pommeling Negroes" and setting the building ablaze, so close that the dome and spire of the Hall of Independence had glowed red against the night.

Atop the worn marble steps, Garnet was offering the prayer and the much younger Catto was about to speak. The sun glinted off the Delmonico band's trombones, the buttons on the uniforms of the new troops, and Garnet's bald pate. The minister struggled with his cane but stood erect on the very step where only months before Lincoln had addressed a great throng and asked for reelection.

Jacob White Jr. announced they were assembled "to give a God speed to the noble men of this regiment" and to present them with a flag paid for by the Bannekers. He introduced Catto to do the presenting.

The vast silk flag was brilliant blue. The artist Bowser had designed it. At the center, a colored soldier stood atop a craggy peak and looked out on a sweet land of liberty that floated as if in a dream.

As Catto rose to speak, telegraph wires crackled with news from the city of his birth, where an even larger crowd was assembled to see the Union flag hoisted above Fort Sumter's ramparts.

Robert Smalls piloted his ship, the old *Planter*, its deck jammed with colored Americans, into Charleston harbor. What a sight! On the *Planter* were William Lloyd Garrison; the son of Denmark Vesey; and Martin Delany and his son, Toussaint, a veteran of the Fifty-fourth. The deck groaned with the weight of giants and the people they had liberated.

Delany had also helped stage another event—likely the first free and open political meeting of Negroes in Charleston—and it drew so many thousands that men had to hoist Garrison to their shoulders and pass him forward to give his speech. But first a large, dignified man walked up the aisle; with him were two girls carrying a wreath. The man was a slave preacher and he began addressing Garrison.

"I have read of your mighty labors," Samuel Dickerson said, "and here is your handiwork." The girls were his daughters, taken from him in slavery, and now he thanked God and Garrison, for "you have restored them to me."

Garrison's eyes became wet. He quoted a Psalm ("Not unto us, but unto God be all the glory") and said to Dickerson, "I never expected to look you in the face; never supposed you would hear of anything I might do in your behalf."

The flag was about to be raised at Fort Sumter. Daniel Payne, who had fled Charleston thirty years earlier when the state closed his school, had come back. He was about to meet black children—thousands of them—in a makeshift Charleston schoolhouse run by Northern Negro scholars and guarded by colored Union soldiers. No one had ever heard so many Negroes cheer and clap as the *Planter* tied up at the harbor.

In front of Independence Hall, Catto presented the ceremonial battle flag to the 250 men of the Twenty-fourth U.S. Colored Troops and spoke the words of its motto, "Let Soldiers in War Be Citizens in Peace." The wisdom of those words seems self-evident; in 1865, they were revolutionary. Catto even used that word. He said: "De Tocqueville prophesied that if ever America underwent Revolution, it would be brought about by the presence of the black race, and that it would result from the inequality of their condition." If the Frenchman's words seemed too lofty for a thousand freshly trained soldiers, one needed only to consider that the speaker had been teacher to a few dozen of them.

The Twenty-fourth U.S. Colored Troops was heading south to occupy Richmond, a tricky task. What better targets for the wrath of that city's defeated white populace than Negroes in Union blue? Enforcing the peace would be complicated.

This prospect did not faze the regiment's white commander. Lieutenant Colonel James Trippe had drawn up figures: of 987 colored men on his rolls, 780 could read, 457 could write. He commanded 4 college graduates, 3 licensed preachers, a reporter, 18 teachers, 57 clerks, and 47 former students of the I.C.Y. Three of the clerks, detailed to his office, had shown skills worthy of "any first class mercantile establishment in New York or Philadelphia." Trippe wondered whether any rebel colonel had led a regiment this intelligent.

Catto took the occasion of presenting the flag to herald a hopeful world. He paid tribute to colored soldiers who, despite the "old bane of prejudice, have been nobly fighting our battles, trusting to a redeemed country for the full recognition of their manhoods in the future."

"Freedom has rapidly advanced since the firing on Sumter," Catto said. "We have gone from victory to victory. Soldiers! accept this flag on

behalf of the citizens of Philadelphia. I know too well . . . that you will
not dishonor it. Keep before your eyes the noble deeds of your fellows at
Port Hudson, Fort Wagner, and on other historic fields. Desert them not.
Accept, Colonel, this flag on behalf of the regiment, and may God bless
you and them." Catto pressed the banner into Colonel Trippe's hands.

Ceremonies were now over. The people assembled in Philadelphia and
in Charleston would remember this day for a lifetime. The country had
been redeemed, hadn't it?

But that night, at Bloodgood's restaurant in Philadelphia, General
Grant's dinner with his wife was interrupted by a messenger with an
urgent telegram from Washington D.C.—a telegram that would change
everything.

★　★　★

THE NEWS of Lincoln's murder set off storms of grief and anger. Mobs
shouted, "Kill the Copperhead!" at the offices of the *Age*, the anti-Lincoln
paper. Police had to rescue a man overheard saying he was glad Lincoln
had died. Carrie Le Count and the other Ladies Union Association officers cancelled a fair to raise funds for colored troops and published a poem
mourning "the Chief of our holy cause."

In colored America, one bit of news added insult to injury. On the
night of the assassination, the main buildings at Wilberforce College in
Ohio burned. School records, A.M.E. papers, and artifacts from Delany's
Africa trek, all gone. Arson was suspected.

The arrival of Lincoln's funeral train in Philadelphia brought together
more than a hundred fraternal and religious bodies of both races, from the
Moyamensing Hose to the Banneker Institute. McMullen and Catto, stalwarts of their separate worlds, shared a march of mourning.

The president's body lay in state at Independence Hall. The line of
mourners stretched three miles, from the Schuylkill to the Delaware.

In New York, at Irish and Masonic groups' insistence, the Common
Council barred Negroes from the procession. The War Department inter-
vened, but city officials put the Negroes so far back in line that Lincoln's
casket had left the city by the time they began walking.

CHAPTER 12

The Battle for the Streetcars

*Even an army of occupation here could not put
the Negro into the street cars.*

—Henry Peterson, *Saturday Evening Post*
editor, addressing the Pennsylvania
Anti-Slavery Society

REV. WILLIAM JOHNSON ALSTON, Octavius Catto's minister and friend, had not expected to rush home that day. The point of his leisurely eastward walk had been to get his sickly son out to the Delaware, to breathe the river's therapeutic drafts, away from the odors and illnesses of the city. Cholera contagions had come and gone, always taking hundreds of the youngest and the oldest. No matter that the minister's rectory was in a fine neighborhood, barely a square from Independence Hall, or that his African Episcopal Church of St. Thomas was favored by the better colored families, the Fortens, Dorseys, and Le Counts. It was July, and pigs and chickens were underfoot. The cobblestone streets were puddled with the midsummer muck of fish bones and horse droppings. And some people, too, used the alleyways for a privy. The odors clung like a cloak too small. Disease floated in the gutters and buzzed in the air.

So he had walked his son, not yet two years old, down to the ferry that crossed hourly to the Jersey side. It was a fine place for diversion. Alston, an inquisitive, scholarly man of thirty-seven years, could point out cannons on Union steamships and ironclads convalescing in the Navy Yard; or sleek-hulled clippers, their sails furled, disgorging cargoes of tea and silk from India and China. But suddenly James, the only child of William and Annie, stopped drawing breath.

Panic overtook the minister. "I held my ear to his mouth . . . several times to ascertain whether he was still alive. Such a death-like appearance came over him, I felt the necessity of reaching home as soon as possible." To Alston's relief, he saw a yellow streetcar approaching.

It was one of the popular horse-drawn cars, that useful hybrid of horse and rail begun a half-dozen years earlier and now stitching back and forth across the city's fabric. This particular line clip-clopped past the nicer brick homes on Lombard Street and the colored and Irish sections on South, where Catto lived in a boardinghouse across from the Adgers' store. This car would just take minutes to get Alston and his boy home.

Alston flagged down the streetcar. He was lifting James aboard "when the conductor arrested my progress by informing me that I could not enter—being colored," Alston wrote. "I referred him to the condition of my child, but all to no purpose."

Nor was that the most insulting part.

Alston understood the streetcar companies' reasoning even as he despised it. The owners said they were not prejudiced; they were merely sparing the feelings of white passengers. The daily *Age* expounded in scientific tones about the "bodily odors of Negroes" and repeatedly warned that if colored men sat beside white ladies in the cars, the inevitable result would be rape.

But there were no white ladies aboard this Lombard–South Street car. Other than the customary two-man crew—the conductor at the back door, the driver up front with the horses—Alston found himself staring in at empty seats.

He was a rare bird for the 1860s, a free-born Southern Negro who had gone to college in Ohio. At Oberlin and Kenyon, he had studied scripture and elocution. He was no stranger to the cruelties—Kenyon students so shunned the divinity school's first Negro that he took to conversing with cattle. (A favorite Alston reminiscence ended, "Good morning, Mrs. Cow.") The school chaplain made Alston wait alone to take communion after the whites. But a bishop, discovering this, made a point of sitting with Alston, sharing his prayer book, and kneeling with him for communion—thus ending the practice and showing what could be achieved by the mere act of whites and Negroes sitting together.

Alston told the streetcar conductor he'd lived in the South and the Midwest and added, "Never before have I met with a barbarity so satanical." The conductor answered by telling the driver to start the horses. The car began to move. Alston was thrown off so hard that his head nearly struck the pavement.

He managed to carry little James home to his mother. As the boy's fever cooled, Alston prepared a letter describing the encounter. Negroes owned property along the streetcar line and paid taxes, he wrote. And what of the price paid by colored soldiers? "Is it humane to exclude respectable colored citizens from your street cars when so many of our brave and vigorous young men have been and are enlisting to take part in this heavenly ordained slavery extermination?" His own two "brawny-armed and battle-tried brothers" were in the army; his church's women were caring for the wounded. Lastly, he brought up Jesus: "We beg you to remember the words of Him, by whom soon you and I are to be judged. . . . 'Verily, I say unto you, in as much as ye have done it unto one of the least of these, my brethren, ye have done it unto me.'" Alston sent the letter to the *Philadelphia Press*, which published it July 21, 1864.

The issue of the exclusion of the North's largest colored community from the comfort and convenience of the brightly painted cars had simmered and smoldered through the early years of the war. Alston's letter helped bring it to a boil.

Within a week, sixty-five Negro men had put their names to a published notice. "Colored citizens," it began, "The undersigned call upon you to attend a public meeting . . . to give an expression touching our exclusion from the city passenger cars." The words brought to mind the "Now or Never" call for colored enlistment in 1863. Alston was one of sixteen men who signed both. So were the Cattos, father and son. Past meetings had gone all but unnoticed in the white press, but by purchasing space in the newspaper, young Catto and his allies were announcing themselves.

At these meetings, colored residents grappled with the tactics to achieve streetcar equality: Raise money, file suit, persuade newspaper editors and clerics to support their cause. But there was also a tilt in tactics for some, a slap in the face to those who would protest by writing letters. John Oliver, who attended the Alston meeting and organized another one with Catto, accused older leaders of "abominable sycophancy." He said they were afraid to agitate too loudly lest white prejudice increase. He accused those men of believing "it is best to wait until [whites] see fit to treat us better."

The generations were drifting apart. Venerated leaders such as William Still and Robert Purvis had come up as nonviolent Garrisonians and had waged their battles arm in arm with Quaker whites. Less so the younger men who had begun signing the notices and drafting the resolutions. They had taken to the streets to try to free Daniel Webster and Moses Horner. Alfred Green had gone to jail in the abortive rescue of Horner. Then he had gone to war. Oliver had seen white Virginians burn a church he wanted to use as a school for freedmen's children. Catto had led a fledgling army of ninety west to draw swords against the enemy. Now they were impatient to scrub the stink of discrimination from the cars.

Rather than working so hard to persuade the companies to voluntarily change, they planned to persuade the legislators to legislate the change. They were taking a page from Senator Sumner, who was pressing Congress to end the District of Columbia's streetcar ban. Catto and Oliver wanted that pressure to come from the Negro on the street. The issue, once again, was manhood.

William Still had first written to the newspapers in 1859 of "the sore grievance of genteel people . . . excluded from the city passenger railroad cars." He had kept "petitioning and remonstrating," through the early 1860s, and with old allies such as Miller McKim and James Mott, had persuaded a number of white business and civic leaders to sign entreaties to the car companies. These pleas were politely ignored.

But that was before colored soldiers were allowed to fight. Now, Catto and other young men grabbed hold of the car grievance and reshaped it till it sprang less from the needs of "genteel" colored passengers and more the testimonials of their "battle-tried brothers." Men deemed citizen enough to fight for the nation but not to sit inside its streetcars? *That* was an argument. In car after car, riders saw conductors unseat Negroes visiting relative who were drilling at Camp William Penn or convalescing at army hospitals. Speeches and petitions on this and every other equal-rights issue now included a litany: Fort Wagner, Port Hudson, Olustee, and Fort Pillow, where the wounded Negroes had been set on fire.

★ ★ ★

THE MURMUR AND SCREECH of iron wheels in city streets was the sound of fortunes in the making. The first streetcar line had opened in 1858; by the war's start, Philadelphia was a veritable gridiron. Nineteen companies operated lines, and each reported profits. Some owned dozens of cars and hundreds of horses; on the busiest lines, the "headway" between the last car and the next was only a matter of minutes.

The cars were ten to twenty feet long. In winter, they were snug and sealed, little wooden cabin-boats with side windows and cast-iron keels. Some had stoves. Summer cars were open-air and a fine way to ride to the rivers. Blue paint and white lamps adorned the Mount Moriah line, yellow and red for Lombard-South and Frankford-Southwark—each line sported colors like a company coat of arms.

The proprietors had talked the city into selling rights to put rails in the busiest streets. The fare was five cents, and some lines took in ten thousand fares a day. Owners added a trick of the scavengers' trade: gathering up the horse manure to sell as fertilizer to farmers. For companies with a hundred horses or more, this brought a tidy sum.

Merchants with shops on streetcar lines saw their trade increase. Distant villages became near. The well-to-do still rode carriages, but as the city reshaped its body around factories, arsenals, and workshops, the streetcar lines became arteries and veins, ferrying workers out in the morning and back at night; on a summer Saturday, delivering them to the Athletics Base Ball Club's field on Jefferson Street; on a winter's night, to the illuminated Union Skating Park. The rink stayed open till ten, when the last cars ran.

Sledgehammer crews were laying new rail so fast it seemed they must be flinging it down—up to three hundred feet in a day. One line crossed the Schuylkill's new suspension bridge, said to be the first of its kind. As Mayor Henry had said, nothing had ever come along looking better for the city than these new streetcars.

When the war came, the cars carried women and children to loved ones in the city's nine military hospitals. A man could ride down to his ten-hour shift at the Navy Yard repairing paddle-wheelers, to Cramp's Ship with its contract to turn out ironclads, or up to the Baldwin Works, forging its hundred locomotives annually. His long day done, he could ease toward home in Southwark, Frankford, or Moyamensing with his boots resting on the wooden slats of a little streetcar, breezing through the city in a certain amount of style, providing that man was white.

When Alston attempted to ride, he knew the odds were against him. Conductors used their discretion, but every one of the lines had a rule against permitting Negroes inside the cars. Eight lines allowed them on the front platform, the narrow crescent of iron and wood where the driver directed the horses. The platform was a bitter bargain—besides rain and snow, a rider caught his share of muck kicked up by the horses. For safety, he could cling to the finger-thin grilles on the streetcar's front windows, and stand there, visible to passengers within and passersby without, a picture of what Catto had called the white "fantasy of our inferiority."

Some conductors and drivers underlined this point by shouting a certain term when Negroes signaled them to stop. It was as if some Copperhead linotypist had printed the rulebook for all nineteen companies, and had set one sentence in 40-point type: "We don't allow niggers to ride!"

A Philadelphia judge considered the rule in an 1861 streetcar ejection suit brought by a man of color. The learned jurist decided that a "long-civilized" people could not be expected to travel with a race "emerging from the shades of barbarism."

That failed suit had prompted a vitriolic screed in the *Christian Recorder* from a writer who signed "W.S." William Still, now a coal merchant as well as a landlord, had come to believe that few Negroes in the city could match the tactical wisdom he had gained in years of Underground Railroad work. "I deem it highly important in a case that affects the entire colored community, as this case does, to bring to bear all the influence imaginable, to win the day," Still huffed. The plaintiff should have sought support of "leading" citizens. "This, I regret to say, was neglected. . . . Railroads and public places will feel now, that they can reject us by law." The man who had brought the suit retorted: "It was mismanaged, I suppose, because W.S. was not at the head, and consulted on every occasion. . . . If W.S. thought this, why did he not attend the many meetings that were called to raise money to defray the expense of said suit?"

But that was before the Union began enlisting Negroes. Recruits and their families needed to ride the cars. Soldiers, mothers, ministers— the next lawsuit could be brought by any of these. Still was ordered off a car returning from Camp William Penn. Frederick Douglass was twice ejected in Philadelphia—once while accompanying a white Rochester abolitionist, Amy Post, to an antislavery meeting ("Lady," the conductor asked, "does he belong to you?"). Later, when Douglass saw a conductor pushing a Negro off a car, he shouted in his best imitation-white voice, "Let the gentleman alone! No one objects to his riding!"—whereupon Douglass, too, was ordered off.

And one conductor delivered a lesson to the new teacher in the I.C.Y.'s Girls Department, Fanny Jackson.

She had won such praise for her teaching that the I.C.Y. managers recruited her from Oberlin College before her graduation. "I had been so long in Oberlin that I had forgotten about my color," she wrote. "I was sharply reminded of it when, in a storm of rain, a Philadelphia street car conductor forbid my entering a car that did not have on it 'for colored people.'" So skinny that she barely took up a seat ("slim as two matches," as she put it), Jackson nonetheless had to wait "in the storm until one came in which colored people could ride. This was my first unpleasant experience in Philadelphia."

★ ★ ★

IT WAS LIKE the pigs' snouts and offal that graced the Schuylkill after any substantial rain, floating down from the houses and butcher shops of Francisville and lingering there by the swimmers and picnickers. Gentlemen did not mention the thoughts that flared in a white man's mind when he saw a black man near a white woman. Much less, sitting beside her in a horse-drawn car.

Mayor Henry had blurted it out. A delegation of Quakers and businessmen went to him with a grievance: Police were taking sides, helping car conductors remove obstinate colored riders. Could the mayor put a stop to this? Henry, who had so impressed abolitionists by having policemen protect their meetings, refused. Furthermore, he said, "I do not wish the ladies of my family to ride in the car with colored people."

Even Still seemed to apologize for his race. "We make no advocacy for the filthy," he assured the car companies, proposing that "respectable" blacks be let in the cars. Those words so angered younger Negroes that Still eventually amended them, noting that some of his filthier brethren had been forced to live in filth.

The companies made no distinction between clean and filthy. Colored soldiers on leave were forced to ride on platforms; some were removed altogether. Rev. Richard Roberson was riding out on the front platform of a Frankford-Southwark car when a cart crashed nearby, fatally hurling a heavy wheel onto the aging preacher. Hundreds attended his funeral and heard speakers decry the streetcar rule.

Lucretia Mott saw a chance to raise the issue on a cold and rainy ride to her house north of Philadelphia, near Camp William Penn. She saw an old colored woman out on the platform. Mott, seventy-two years old and "all eyes and chin," as a biographer put it, insisted on riding outside with the Negro in the rain. Other passengers protested. The conductor sputtered and swore and shooed both women inside.

And everyone in colored Philadelphia knew the story of Robert Smalls, who liberated a rebel steamship. Then he had helped a cowering Union skipper win a desperate sea battle; now he was Captain Smalls and the toast of the North. Congress voted him a fifteen-hundred-dollar prize. He lectured and learned to read and write as workers at the Navy Yard repaired his ship. When Smalls and the *Planter*'s pilot, a white sailor, climbed into a streetcar to ride to the yard, the conductor asked him to leave.

"Is this the law?" Smalls asked, and the conductor said it was. "Then I'll obey the law," Smalls said.

The white sailor spoke up. You don't understand, he told the conductor. This is the Captain Smalls who stole the ship from the rebs.

"Company regulations," the conductor replied. "We don't allow niggers to ride!"

The sailor left with Smalls, "indignant at the insult to his captain."

Daily newspapers carried that report—along with news from cities where courts and companies had begun integrating the cars. Readers of the *Philadelphia Press* learned that a San Francisco judge had opened up that city's steep railways to Negroes even as colored Californians read in the *Pacific Appeal* of protests in Philadelphia. Still went to Miller McKim and suggested an unusual meeting. Bring in the biggest names, white and colored, and speak to the companies in unison. McKim sent word along the abolition grapevine, inveigling sixty-three sponsors to sign on.

On the night of January 13, 1865, the stories of Smalls and Alston were told in the vastness of Concert Hall, where Catto had delivered his "There must come a change" speech less than a year before. Colored people were not confined to the balcony but were seated downstairs as well, with "the most respectable ladies and gentlemen that our city can boast," a newspaper reported. Prominent whites were in the hall—Rev. Phillips Brooks (who left so inspired that he wrote to his father, saying streetcar reform was at hand); the locomotive king Matthias Baldwin, the I.C.Y. board member Marmaduke Cope, and the long-bearded financier Jay Cooke, who had backed the Union cause with his bonds.

Alston looked across the sea of friendly faces, colored and white, and said he was "so accustomed to being looked upon contemptuously" that he had learned to read white faces. He directed words at employers in the room. "The colored man is proscribed in workshops, and he is denied an opportunity of earning an honest livelihood, and every means is taken to degrade him, and when all these succeed, the colored man is taunted with being 'lazy.'" Then he told the story about his son and the streetcar.

Robert Purvis told his tale of the voyage in which a slaveholder mistook him for white. "We ask no favors," Purvis roared. "But in the name of the living God, we ask, 'Give us justice!'"

The Concert Hall group sought audiences with the mayor and the streetcar owners. The antislavery societies vowed to boycott the cars if the rule remained. Some companies began designating every fourth car for the Negroes—a "Jim Crow" car, Alston lamented. Then the companies made an announcement: They would ask white passengers how they felt about colored riders. Having no illusions about how most white riders felt, the Concert Hall men tried to prevent this poll. The companies ignored them again and began printing ballots.

Abolitionists pointed to the "opprobrious coincidence" of the poll's timing. As the Congress was voting to amend the Constitution to abolish slavery for all time, the city of that document's birth was taking a vote of its own.

The poll also drew attention in Moyamensing.

★ ★ ★

NIGHTMEN. **THEY WERE** called this because, in warmer seasons, their work was too foul for the daytime. Nightmen cleaned the cesspools, the brick cylinders six feet wide and twelve feet deep, vaults that collected waste from the privies in many of the city's buildings. The vaults would fill, slowly but surely, till the nightmen arrived with buckets and rags. They dipped their pails, poured the waste into barrels, and carted the barrels to pits at the city's edge. The stench wormed into clothes, mustaches, all a man's pores and possessions. A nightman might don dark coveralls to mask the stains of his labor but nothing concealed the smell.

On a January day two weeks before the passenger poll, Alexander Till and Lewis Gibson had finished cleaning a cesspool when a large white man approached. The two colored men recognized him. He was Alderman McMullen.

The Squire, whose territory was bisected by the Lombard–South Street railway, knew that Negroes gaining power would sap his political strength. If they ever got the ballot, they would vote for the party of Lincoln, the party of those Concert Hall amalgamators, not McMullen's Democrats. And if they rode the cars, then Irish jobs at the Navy Yard and

the machine shops would be endangered. The workers themselves signed
a petition to keep colored riders off the line that served the yard.

The alderman proceeded to make the two nightmen a sweet-sounding
offer.

Cash money for collecting a box from an address up on Brown Street.
It was a mile north of McMullen's ground, in the residential section called
the Liberties. No buckets to lower, no carts to haul, just fetch the box.

Ride in a streetcar up and back, he said. I will send a fellow along.
Take the Fifth and Sixth Street line.

So Till and Gibson went with McMullen's man, climbing onto one of
the yellow coaches with red lamps. The line ran north on Fifth, past St.
Thomas and its walled churchyard, past Independence Hall, past the oyster sellers and newspaper hawkers in Market Street, ten squares north to
Brown Street's brick homes, and back on Sixth again.

The interior of this car was just twelve feet long. No more than twenty-
two passengers could sit on the seats that ran front to back. Smells were
squeezed in by the glass windows and sliding doors pulled shut against the
January weather.

McMullen's man paid their fare. Till and Gibson sat down in the car
and saw the white passengers react. It was as if they were all sealed in a
tin together. The two colored men got to their feet and tried to step out to
the platform. McMullen's man stopped them. He made them sit as the car
continued on its way to Fifth and Brown.

They went to the address McMullen had given but could find no box.
They were riding back when a streetcar company supervisor climbed aboard.
Something was amiss—two Negroes sitting there at a white man's behest.
He took the colored men before a magistrate, who listened to their story,
observed that they had committed no crime, and sent them on their way.

Their errand stoked the fires.

"Underhand means are being used to prevent a reform," the daily *Bulletin* reported. "One of the lines now carries colored people, and some
of the vulgarest negrophobists have hired the dirtiest negroes they could
find, to ride up and down all day, in order to stir up feeling. . . . Such mean
tricks as these can only further injure the bad cause in aid of which they
are perpetrated." But the Squire paid no penalty for his mean trick.

The two days of polling began January 30. As riders paid their fares,
conductors handed out ballots. Nothing prevented a rider who boarded
two cars that day from voting twice. The question was printed on slips no

bigger than playing cards—"Shall colored persons be allowed to ride in all the cars?" There were boxes marked *for* and *against*.

Newspapers sent reporters onto the cars. They recorded an occurrence as rare as a solar eclipse: a spontaneous public discourse on race. Riders "commenced to discuss the questions," the *Inquirer's* man reported. "In this way much exciting debate was kept up throughout the day in the cars."

Much interest centered on the Fifth and Sixth Street line. The company had recently broken ranks to announce it would experiment with admitting colored passengers. A *Bulletin* editor riding the line "discovered that two well-dressed and well-behaved females who sat immediately beside us wore dusky skins." At his other side sat an "ill-bred" white man, who remarked that "niggers should be put in their proper place on the front platform."

A letter writer who signed as "Justice" told *Bulletin* readers of having congratulated a conductor for the new policy. The conductor said the policy was already driving away white clientele, and "if he had his way he would not stop the car for any nigger."

Passengers scribbled comments on the ballots. "Decidedly against." "Gold down, nigger up." Someone scrawled a phrase from the *Negro-Mania* book: "Never! Never! Never!"

Another rider wrote, "Equal rights the world over." And another: "All men are born free and equal."

McMullen's side won the poll hands-down. One company reported more than four thousand "against" votes to fewer than two hundred in favor. The owners of the Fifth and Sixth Street line announced a few weeks later that the experiment was ending and that Negroes would be allowed only in cars emblazoned *Colored*.

★ ★ ★

A FEW DAYS LATER, Octavius Catto packed his starched shirtfronts and rode a train west to Harrisburg as a snowstorm came east. He was two weeks away from his twenty-sixth birthday and helping lead a movement that was sputtering and stalling. The state Equal Rights League was holding three days of meetings. Catto and the other Philadelphia delegates arrived on a segregated train.

Catto's speechmaking had served him well enough on friendly ground. A month earlier, his words about equality had been "frequently interrupted by loud applause." But that was a Banneker Institute event in Philadelphia. Most people at Banneker commemorations and I.C.Y. commencements were of the same color and city as Catto. The streetcar campaign and the parallel rise of the Equal Rights League required him to prove himself before wider and more skeptical audiences.

The car companies had not bowed to persuasion. Neither had editorial pages at five of the city's seven dailies. Grand juries refused to indict conductors for throwing colored passengers from the cars. Police sided with the conductors. When Negroes insisted on riding, white toughs were punishing them by hoisting cars off tracks. Only three of some two hundred white ministers in the city supported colored riders.

Churches were preoccupied with their own campaign—to stop streetcar operations on the Sabbath. In her thirty-second annual report for the Philadelphia Female Anti-Slavery Society, Mary Grew lambasted the clergy: "Eager, zealous, prompt to do battle against the running of our city cars on Sunday, they have scarcely been disturbed by this wicked and cruel practice of excluding their fellow-citizens and fellow-Christians from those cars on account of their complexion."

Another veteran abolitionist, Benjamin P. Hunt of the Concert Hall committee, wearied of "the weakness" of his erstwhile comrades-in-arms. He aimed a twenty-seven-page missile their way, a pamphlet that singed white clergy for not siding with Alston, excoriated Republican leaders for not making the streetcars a campaign issue, and blamed "our able and leading private men of business" for paying only lip service to this cause.

"The abolition of Slavery away in the South was all very well," he wrote, but the streetcar issue "is a matter of personal contact. They are not opposed, themselves, to riding with colored people—certainly not. . . . But they do wish there were baths furnished . . . in order that they might be made thereby less offensive to ladies."

A student of Ralph Waldo Emerson, Hunt wrote about race with a humor and sarcasm rare for his time. He mocked Mayor Henry, quoted *King Lear*, and observed that there was a "very illogical" fear of amalgamation. He said white Americans outnumbered blacks 6 to 1; thus, "if by an irrepressible orgasm, they should rush together," most whites would mate with whites, and begat more whites, while the black race turned evermore mulatto and vanished altogether in a generation or so. Hunt urged Democrats to consider this scheme: "With patience, they can have a white man's government yet."

So Catto and the other colored delegates gathering in Harrisburg were setting out to make bricks without straw. They needed to persuade the legislature to pass a law for constituents who could not vote—a legislature that had recently considered creating a registry to track the state's Negroes and had allotted monies for shipping them to Liberia.

The delegates headed for a church in Harrisburg's colored section, on a street called Tanner's Alley within sight of the State House. The first three pews of Wesley Union A.M.E. were filled with seventy-one colored men from across the state. Tanner's Alley had been a beehive of activity in Underground Railroad days; Douglass and Garrison had spoken here. In those days, such gatherings had begun with prayers and ended with "Praise God from Whom All Blessings Flow." The league's meetings, too, began with prayers—Alston serving as chaplain—and ended with a melodeon playing, the assembly on its feet, and David Bowser leading the singing of "John Brown's Body."

These meetings were the progeny of the larger convention Douglass had led in Syracuse the previous October. Catto and many of the other Pennsylvania men had been there and had heard Douglass, towering and silver-maned, exhort them to go home and begin their own league branches.

By now, Pennsylvania had emerged as the league's strongest branch. Its leaders, having tramped through the blizzard without, now attended to the blizzard of minutiae within. William Forten, a rich man's son, spoke at length on questions about league travel costs and dues; delegates debated which colored women's groups had done more for the wounded. (Alston defended the exertions of the St. Thomas women.) No one debated the broader purpose: to fight "the cruel prejudice that now meets us at every step . . . barring against us the doors of your public libraries, of your colleges of science, of your popular lecture rooms, of your military academies, of your jury boxes, of your ballot boxes, of your churches, of your theatres, and even of your common street cars."

Downstairs, women prepared hot dishes and sweets; upstairs, as speeches rumbled into the night, Catto was named to the three-man Car Committee. The league needed to act swiftly—an Erie abolitionist was sponsoring a bill to integrate the cars. The bill's chances were slim, but three cheers went up when its author, state senator Morrow B. Lowry, was introduced.

By the next afternoon, internal conflicts threatened to fracture the newborn league.

The state had decreed that separate schools be opened wherever twenty or more colored children resided. Should the league call for those pupils to be "under the charge of colored teachers?"

Alston spoke in favor, telling what he'd seen of teachers black and white. Others demanded to know how such words could come from a league begun "to protest against proscription and prejudice?" Accusations resounded in the room. Alfred Green said it was "disgraceful" that any other delegate from Philadelphia, with its public schools so indifferent to colored needs, could oppose this call for colored teachers. Bowser said he and his neighbors had tried for nine years "to secure a colored teacher for a colored school." The session ran to nearly four hours as the delegates grappled with an educational controversy that would outlive them all.

Catto spoke. He said Negro teachers brought a life experience to the classroom that no white teacher could provide, that they "had the welfare of the race more at heart, knowing that they rose or fell together." But he warned about public perceptions—that the league's "phraseology . . . might be quoted as a document based on preferences for certain teachers merely on account of their color."

One point he repeated, like a schoolteacher hammering home a lesson: "He did not wish his to turn his back on the fact that the colored man was the best teacher for colored children."

He offered an amendment—that if colored and white teachers were similarly educated and trained, colored teachers should be preferred "not by reason of their complexion, but because they are better qualified by conventional circumstances outside of the school-house."

Delegates exchanged glances and nodded in agreement. On a motion from Robert Adger, the amendment passed unanimously. Catto had crafted a challenge to the public schools' and had led the room to a consensus.

But the consensus was fragile. Within hours, Pennsylvania State Equal Rights League delegates from Pittsburgh and Philadelphia moved to reprimand any colored barber or restaurateur who ran a Jim Crow business, serving whites only. Upstate delegates protested. They said a colored barber who shaved colored as well as white in smaller towns—"Copperhead towns," as one man put it—risked seeing his business destroyed.

Jake White Jr.'s brother George, a barber, disputed this. He said he'd shaved black and white chins alike for years and never lost business because of it. The upstate men rolled their eyes—George White's barbershop was in Philadelphia.

Then came a resolution to gently but firmly condemn "our long tried friend," William Lloyd Garrison. The greatest white abolitionist of all had turned strangely quiet on colored suffrage, the right that the league saw as the key to unlock all other rights. Some men in the room said you can't condemn him; others shouted back, *But we must.*

Older delegates offered gentler language on barbershops and Garrison and won unanimous if grudging approval—much as Catto had done on the colored-teachers issue.

He was voted the conference's secretary. He was responsible for the writing-down and printing-up of the proceedings, along with the league's new constitution and its messages to the legislature and the people of the state. These writings were an organizing and fund-raising tool. The league sold copies of *Proceedings* for twenty-five cents, constitutions for five.

The same argument that Alston had made in his letter of protest over the streetcars ran through the league's texts: The price of citizenship had been paid in soldiers' blood. Entwined with this message was another: Unblock our path to the ballot box, and all else becomes possible.

Catto and the two other men on the publications committee began drafting. They wrote 4,014 words in all, displaying the depths of their education and the extent of their culture. They cited the prose of Alexander Hamilton and the poetry of John Greenleaf Whittier. They reminded readers of "the horrid massacre" of Negroes in Detroit and New York and the patriotism of the ninety who went to Harrisburg to fight, only to be turned away. They quoted the words on the Liberty Bell. The sentences and images were the sinews of the causes that Catto would speak about for the rest of his life.

First they addressed the legislature.

"Gentlemen, do not say that years must intervene before the wrong in question can be redressed. . . . Remember, your memorialists do not ask for favors. They claim rights. For conferring of benefits, there may be another, and more convenient time, but 'for justice, All place a temple and all seasons summer.'"

Then they wrote to the people of Pennsylvania.

"Is it not our duty to ask in the name of justice, in the name of humanity, in the name of those whose bones whiten the battle-fields of the South, that every bar to our political enfranchisement be now and forever removed? Do this, and all other evils and outrages will disappear as the dews of morning melt before the morning sun."

On the last night of meetings, Rev. William Alston sent up a prayer for the league and "the achievement of its aims." The last major speech was Catto's. It fell to him to send the seventy-one men off into the February night with breath steaming and hearts ablaze. As colored men in Charleston had chosen his father to speak for them thirty years earlier, colored men in Harrisburg were calling upon the son.

Catto seemed to revel in these moments. He pulled on history, current events, and his own vision for the future. "In the midst of these wildly excited times," he began, there were "thoughts crowding upon us . . . like the flashes in the dark sky."

He held up "the assertion of our inferiority" for rebuke. He said black America had "as many Frederick Douglasses as the whites had Sumners, as many Bannekers as they had Mitchells, as many Vashons as they had Anthons."

Catto was assembling the intellectual pillars of both races, shoulder to shoulder. Benjamin Banneker was the colored pioneer of eighteenth-century astronomy; Maria Mitchell, a renowned white astronomer. Charles Anthon's texts on classics were required in schools; George Vashon, educator and poet, was Oberlin's first Negro graduate.

He said a Union Army in which German-born officers commanded Germans and Irish commanded Irish must allow colored officers to lead colored troops. The league must "call without ceasing upon the clergy and all who follow them in communion; . . . upon the Bench and Bar; . . . upon the Press with its great influence; and upon Congress and the Administration to lend us their aid in a cause so just, so reasonable and so necessary, as the possession of equal rights without regard to color."

Winning the war was only a beginning, Catto said. He predicted "that while our great armies moved on to victory, the nation would move on to justice."

The league men applauded hard, made their way downstairs for the hot foods, and buttoned their coats to head across the fallen snow. The final paragraph of the league's fifty-one-page *Proceedings* described what a legislator would have seen that Friday night in Tanner's Alley, across from the Capitol's dome: "The vast assembly slowly, and with evident feelings and demonstrations of the deep interest which had been awakened in their minds, wended their way from the Church, presenting an . . . encouraging spectacle."

★ ★ ★

AN EQUALLY ENCOURAGING SPECTACLE was just then revealing itself, pearl-like, in the unlikely oyster of a Philadelphia courtroom. The latest streetcar case had landed by marvelous happenstance in the lap of a Republican judge who favored Negro rights.

The aggrieved party was Mrs. Derry, a colored woman who had sat down in a Lombard–South Street car one night on her way home from church work in aid of wounded soldiers. She was asked to leave but she stayed in her seat, pleading the hour and the lack of complaints from the few white passengers. The conductor ordered her out. She refused. He called for assistance from two chums on the corner. Then he took his coat off. The three men grabbed, kicked, and hurled Mrs. Derry to the pavement "with great violence, tearing her clothes" and injuring her.

Judge Joseph Allison noted that past courts had upheld the right of railway companies to eject Negroes. He observed that the world had changed. "The logic of the past four years has in many respects cleared our vision and corrected our judgment," he told the jury. Citizens "deemed worthy . . . to wear the uniform of the soldier of the United States, should not be denied the rights common to humanity." The jury awarded her fifty dollars.

As cheering as his words were to the Equal Rights League, Allison was just one judge and a Republican at that. A poem in the *Inquirer* described how railway companies reacted to his ruling:

> The late decision of the Judge
> (Which railroad men think utter fudge)
> Says that we shan't assault and batter
> Either the black man or the mulatto,

> Nevertheless we'll let you ride
> Upon the platform, not inside.

The Negro passenger in the poem refused to move. The car was run off the track, but as night fell,

> The colored person kept his seat,
> And black folks brought him things to eat.

★ ★ ★

BY THE FALL of 1865, the Equal Rights League was capturing the attention of colored Pennsylvanians from the biggest cities to the smallest "Copperhead towns." Delegates met in Cleveland, approved a constitution, declared Philadelphia the permanent headquarters, and chose a list of officers with Douglass as one of ten vice presidents and Catto as one of two recording secretaries. The state league's agent in Altoona reported: "I have visited the following localities, and in all of them the people are alive to the enterprise, and have interesting and increasing auxiliaries at Lewistown, Huntingdon, Bedford, Williamsport, Lock Haven, Bellefonte, Phillipsburg, Johnstown, Blairsville, Indiana, Hollidaysburg, and this place." The number of chapters in Pennsylvania grew to forty-three. League members took to signing themselves, "Yours for Equal Rights."

Concordville, close to the Delaware state line, sent for copies of the constitution. The chapter in nearby Downingtown begged the leaders to come and speak; so did the league's man in Greencastle, 170 miles west of Philadelphia. In the winter, Catto and another league member rode the farm lanes of eastern Bucks County to churches in Bensalem and Attleborough, where chapters were forming. A colored outpost on the road to Trenton, Attleborough had been an Underground Railroad station and home to an early A.M.E. church.

The little churches in Bucks County offered a respite from the stares a colored lobbyist encountered on the steps to the Capitol's white-columned portico in Harrisburg. One listener told of more than forty colored men and women braving roads rutted by a New Year's thaw. They had come to sing and pray in their "neat and warm little place of worship" and to hear the young man from Philadelphia with the drooping mustache.

The farmers had work to do; cows needed milking, hogs needed slopping. But first the men and women needed to look in the eyes of this city

Negro they had heard about. Their faces were weathered and their boots muddy, but their eyes were sharp. They saw his purposeful stride as he came to the front of the church. And he saw their faces, curious, expectant, taking his measure, wondering whether he and his league could open doors that had been closed to them all their lives. He didn't talk down to them, they saw that right away. Here he was, an educated man but also a millwright's son. He did not quote Aristotle this time. He was at ease in front of students, Equal Rights League delegates, and raucous audiences at streetcar meetings. And he was at ease as well in front of this rural audience; he even told jokes.

"Mr. Catto then made a spirited appeal to the people; urged the importance of immediate action, and read and explained at length the constitution." *At length!* God help the farmers if he plodded through all eighteen sections on credentials and quorums, duties and dues, and the league's Banneker-like powers to have errant members "suspended, reproved or expelled."

But this was not a Banneker debate or a commencement exercise with ranks of white dignitaries needing to be impressed. This was a recruitment meeting. Catto could tick off the league's goals—"morality, education, temperance, frugality, industry"—and then reveal the knife-edge, the vow to achieve "by a union of all our energies . . . a recognition of the rights of the colored people of the nation as American citizens."

His speech "drew frequent exclamations of the audience," and "prolonged laughter at the anecdotes with which his remarks were interspersed."

"I wish I could describe to you the great waking-up, the interest and enthusiasm manifested by those broad-chested, grave, solid-looking farmers," the listener wrote. "These gatherings are a very blessing to those who live in the rural districts; shut out from much that is going on in the busy town, and debarred from most that would interest or improve them . . . but joined to the State League, they can be readily informed of every passing event. Papers containing the speeches of our best men may then reach them: they can be party to all that occurs in Congress and familiar with all the reforms of the day."

The league sent Catto to meet with Congressmen Thaddeus Stevens and William Kelley, and Lucretia Mott's antislavery group. On suffrage as well as streetcars, he could offer rural league audiences the latest wisdom from Philadelphia, Harrisburg, and Washington.

Those audiences "were so roused and inspired by the practical advice, and eloquent arguments of the gentlemen from Philadelphia, whose province it is to inaugurate these auxiliary Leagues, that they have established night schools, reading circles, and debating societies," the same listener wrote. "The desire for improvement and elevation has come upon them like an avalanche."

One of the new Bucks County chapters named itself the Catto League.

★ ★ ★

THE HALL on Spring Garden Street was filling up with learned men. The annual December meeting of the Philadelphia City-Wide Congress of Literary Societies was getting under way, and high on the agenda was an application for admission by the Banneker Institute. The renewed application.

Scarcely seven years had passed since George Stephens and Jake White had submitted the Banneker books, rules, and regimens to inspection by men from the citywide group, only to be voted down on the closest of votes, and only because of color. The Bannekers were reapplying because during those seven years, the world had been turned on its head. Catto made the main speech. One of the white men in the hall, Samuel Pennypacker, a delegate from one of the literary clubs, found himself enthralled by the "very light and very bright Negro" and the audience's reaction.

"It was like casting a firebrand," Pennypacker, a Gettysburg veteran, wrote. "In the midst of a fierce discussion the convention adjourned." In the recess, he polled his society's delegates. Most were ready to vote for the Bannekers. But the society's top brass sent instructions to vote no. Pennypacker was defiant—"We informed the society we would not so vote." Confusion reigned. The majority called for Banneker admission.

"Gone up another step!" the *Christian Recorder* exulted prematurely. The Bannekers had finally been "after a powerful address from our esteemed friend, Mr O. V. Cato, one of the teachers of the High School for colored youth. . . . Onward still moves the world."

Onward, indeed. Pennypacker recounted what happened next: Albert Sloanaker, a local officeholder, went about "organizing literary societies" to set the stage for another vote. Sloanaker was, in Pennypacker's view, "a fat, oily politician" seeking a federal tax-collector's post from Andrew Johnson; legend had it that he had given the president an ornate basket of wax flowers, winning him the sobriquet "Wax Work Sloany." Sloanaker got the post he wanted—and the roster of literary societies revamped. At the next meeting of the societies, the colored men and their allies were stopped at the door.

★ ★ ★

THE WINDS BLEW IN from the northwest on a March morning in 1866. The temperatures hovered above freezing and a light snow carpeted the paving stones as the 900 block of Shippen in Philadelphia filled with people. Orations were applauded; children recited and parents cheered. The Institute for Colored Youth was moving into its new home.

The three-story brick building featured a lyceum, laboratory, reading room, elegant stairwells, and ample latrines. In all, twelve thousand square feet, "a most beautiful structure," according to one newspaper. The building rose above the rooftops in McMullen's Fourth Ward—and it was serving colored children.

(Ebenezer Bassett, ever needful of a few extra dollars, had agreed to be janitor as well as principal. The board was paying him two hundred dollars more a year to sweep the stairs and shovel the snow; "the seats of the privies are to be scrubbed once a week.")

The old I.C.Y. building on Lombard was being purchased by nine of the wealthiest colored men in town, a partnership led by William Still. As the hub of colored learning moved to Shippen Street, its former home was refitted as street-level stores, a chandeliered assembly hall on the second floor, and smaller offices for rent on the third. They renamed it Liberty Hall.

On Shippen, the shivering crowd heard Principal Bassett, Fanny Jackson, the Girls Department head, Catto, Marmaduke Cope, a board officer, and one I.C.Y. senior, one junior, and the scholarly sensation of the class of 1863, Caroline Rebecca Le Count.

Finding fault with Carrie Le Count at age twenty was difficult. She had not achieved a perfect 10 in Latin or trigonometry—only a 9.40—and favored the poetry of Longfellow and other romantics and reformers when she read at public recitals. She mesmerized listeners, particularly men. "She reads with perfect ease, and evinces none of that timidity so usual to those who are not accustomed to reciting in public," a critic who heard her recite "Bingen on the Rhine," a poem about the last words of a young man wounded in battle, wrote. "One . . . could almost fancy he heard the words from the very lips of the dying soldier."

She addressed younger audiences during the day. In a public school system that had hired its first colored teacher just two years before, Le Count was an assistant principal to I.C.Y. graduate Cordelia Jennings at the Ohio School, where 148 colored boys and 97 colored girls attended. Le Count's salary was $340 a year.

Lately, she was noticed at the same events as Catto.

Their lives ran parallel in many ways. Both had been born free to colored tradesmen, a carpenter and a millwright; both excelled in schoolrooms that had not existed for their parents. Both were hired as assistants to principals within months of graduating from the I.C.Y., both became teachers. Both grew up hearing, often in whispers, the words they now said aloud: *antislavery, Underground Railroad, suffrage, equal rights.* Both worshipped at Alston's Episcopal church, a place of prayer for the "better class." Both shone when all eyes were on them.

Both had been chosen by their peers to serve as officers of new colored organizations, he of the Equal Rights League, she of the Ladies Union Association. In that capacity, Le Count wrote on December 11, 1865, to General Butler. The Ladies Union Association had taken a poll at its fair and voted him the favorite of all the Union generals. His 450 votes outdistanced Sherman, Sheridan, even Ulysses Grant.

Butler's conversion to the cause of colored enlistment and his coining of the Unions' "contrabands" rationale for taking in runaway slaves had made him a hero in colored America. People would not forget "your kind and impartial deeds to our unfortunate race . . . performed at a time when the public sentiment was so decidedly unfavorable to our interests," Le Count wrote.

The group wanted the general to sleep well. They sent a gift of a black velvet dressing gown, cap, and slippers.

"Mesdames," he wrote back, "your beautiful presents, forwarded to me by your Corresponding Secretary, Carrie R. Le Count, . . . have given me the liveliest satisfaction." Butler, about to run for Congress, wrote, too, of the valor of colored soldiers he had seen in battle. "Who shall say that such men, so willingly periling their lives to save the country, are not fit to take part in choosing their own rulers and in enacting their own laws?"

The velvet nightwear came from daughters of respectable families with impeccable manners and sophisticated politics—Adgers, Iredells, Millses, and Le Counts. They differed little from legions of women who had fed and bandaged Union soldiers beneath the vast umbrella of the

U.S. Sanitary Commission and its affiliates—except in complexion. Just as the army had initially rejected Negro enlistees, the Sanitary Commission had turned away women of color. So they had formed their own organizations. In Philadelphia, the Ladies Union Association launched itself two weeks after Gettysburg, with a stated purpose of delivering aid to the bedsides of wounded and ailing colored soldiers. Like their white counterparts, they staged fairs and concerts and made bandages and ministered to thousands in the hospitals; they brought farina, baskets of peaches and melons, jellies, pickles, and condensed milk to the fighting men; once they lugged in fifty pounds of tobacco and a legion of clay pipes.

As the war was ending, they turned their efforts to the freedmen's needs—shoes and clothing, soaps and medicines, and above all books, pencils, and chalk for the tens of thousands attending school for the first time. The largest donation on a list Carrie Le Count prepared for shipment to Charleston was twelve hundred school slates.

Another mission loomed as well. "We hope that our friends will make some efforts to gain us admission to the city cars," a Ladies Union Association annual report said, "as we find great difficulty in reaching the Hospitals." But their male friends' efforts were mired in arguments over strategy, and perhaps that was why, one by one, the association's colored officers and supporters began boarding cars in defiance of the rule. Judith Giesberg identified ten Negro women "forcibly ejected" from cars as they traveled to and from volunteer work at Philadelphia's war hospitals or relief societies. Three were officers of the Ladies Union Association.

★ ★ ★

THE NEGROES' BEST ALLY in Harrisburg was the state senator from the farthest corner of the state. Morrow Lowry of Erie had been an abolitionist before he was a Lincoln man, a Republican unafraid of taking on faraway Philadelphia's streetcar companies and "political hucksters," as he called them. He had written a bill to integrate the railways as early as 1861, knowing it would die a quick death in committee. By the war's end, he was in the faction clamoring for power from the State House to the White House, the Radical Republicans. Led by Charles Sumner, Thaddeus Stevens, and a handful of others, including Congressman Kelley of Philadelphia, they believed nothing was more important than extending voting rights to Negroes, who, not incidentally, would vote Republican.

Lowry's second streetcar bill had narrowly passed the state Senate in 1865, after he told of having personally seen a colored veteran barred from a car and "forced to plod his weary way through storm and darkness" on one leg, "the other having been given to his country."

But this bill, too, died in a House committee. The Republicans sympathized but said supporting the bill would cost them a fatal number of votes in the next election. Some Democrats disparaged the bill as a rich man's toy, saying its Concert Hall supporters would never deign to sit in streetcars since they could afford to ride in carriages. Legislators repeated old claims—that abolitionists wanted "amalgamation of the races," that Negroes were happier as slaves.

Several officeholders endeavored to get the bill stolen from a committee chairman's file, so that it could be said that no such measure was actually under consideration.

In 1866, the league's Car Committee—Catto, Forten, and Bowser—revised the old bill. Their draft went further, awarding damages of five hundred dollars per passenger against any streetcar company or employee that barred or helped bar passengers "on account of color, or race, or who shall refuse to carry such person . . . or who shall throw any car, or cars, from the track, thereby preventing persons from riding." Violations were a criminal misdemeanor, punishable by fines of one hundred to five hundred dollars, or thirty to ninety days' imprisonment.

Senator Lowry accepted this draft and promised this session would be different from the last. The timing seemed right. In Washington, the Radical Republicans were poised to get the Fourteenth Amendment passed over Andrew Johnson's veto. The amendment was not everything that Stevens and the others wanted, but it granted citizenship and equality before the law and was the last stepping stone before giving colored men the vote.

In their new offices on Liberty Hall's third floor, Catto and the little knot of league board members were like telegraphers, sending and receiving messages on two causes that fueled each other—the battles for the streetcars and the ballot.

A message went out to state legislators from the Car Committee: support our bill, and we will support our friends. Men elected from across the rich alluvial farm basins and rolling Alleghenies—the Hollidaysburgs and the Huntingdons—needed convincing that a vote for the Negroes' bill would someday win them Negro votes back home.

* * *

THE BILL ADVANCED in fits and starts. Catto, Forten, and Bowser reported to the league's next convention, in Pittsburgh, that their efforts had been stymied by a turncoat Philadelphia senator "who pretended to be friend of the bill."

Some whites and blacks suggested it was time to stop devoting energy to a cause so heroic and hopeless. Rev. Stephen Smith—a colored leader since before Catto was born—professed "an entire lack of confidence" that enough white minds could be changed. In the fall of 1866, Henry Peterson, editor of the *Saturday Evening Post,* told fellow Anti-Slavery Society members in Philadelphia that "even an army of occupation" could not integrate the cars.

At that same meeting, Lucretia Mott spoke up. No one needed reminding that she had been at the barricades for half a century. She had defied a mayor's warning against "unnecessary walking" with Negro men; she had defied a mob that vowed to put the match to her house; and now she defied the pragmatism of her allies. She exhorted the group to keep agitating as the new streetcar bill moved slowly through the State House. "The hour has come to demand it now!" she said.

Harriet Forten Purvis agreed. Robert's wife had never been so public and recognizable as Mrs. Mott, but she had been at all the same barricades, and at greater peril, being colored. She was "very lady-like in manners and conversation," not a shouter like her husband. But nearly two years had elapsed since her own ejection from a car, and the rule still had not changed. At a meeting of the female antislavery society, Mrs. Purvis, now fifty-six years old, all but flew into a rage.

She echoed John Oliver's rant against "sycophancy" and Benjamin Hunt's indictment of weak-willed abolitionists. She said the city's leading antislavery men had done little about the streetcars, "for fear of injuring the Republican party." She told of a lecture she'd attended. Applause had thundered down on the white Republican speaker when he professed to believe that the only way to truly save the Union was to give Negroes equal rights. Equal rights? Three generations of Fortens and Purvises knew better. She described how hollow she felt beneath that thunder— "how useless was all this applause when she could not . . . take a seat in the cars."

★ ★ ★

MORE POETS GAVE VOICE to the streetcar movement. Unsigned verses asked readers to consider the acts of a conductor who had forced a mother and her children out of a car. She had lost her husband to the war:

> He for Freedom, Equality, Suffrage, gave life,
> At Fort Pillow he fell, when the merciless foe,
> With cowardly hate gave the cruel deathblow.

But the conductor in the poem saw one thing only.

> "What! What!" he exclaimed. "Have we niggers in here?"
> "We are tired and sick, sir, Oh pray let me ride,
> I'm a poor soldier's widow, for our country he died. . . ."
> Do you think he was right?
> This manly conductor, who said, "Niggers shan't
> Ride with white!"

The protests became rhythmic: Defy the rule. Tell the newspapers. Speak at the meetings. Go to court.

Men and women—even pregnant women—intermingled into white throngs and made their way to a seat in a car before a conductor noticed. "They made organized effort to appear on every car that was on the street," a white eyewitness wrote. "They could not be excluded, as the cars were compelled to stop because white passengers were waiting." Another writer said confrontations on the cars "are almost of daily occurrence."

Two colored women, one from Baltimore and one "very distinguished lady" from Philadelphia, entered a Spruce–Pine Street car and paid their fares. When the conductor saw them, he ordered them "to quit the car, but [they] declined doing so," a newspaper reported. "The car was then driven off at a furious rate. Upon desiring to get out, the ladies were not allowed to do so" but were told they would be taken "out to the depot and be whitewashed."

Miles Robinson, who had escaped slavery by hiding in a ship's pots-and-pans closet and now ran a dining saloon, set out to "test the prejudices of the cars." He and two friends clung to seats in a Walnut Street car until police yanked them out, breaking lamps in the process. On a winter's night, Robinson's light-skinned wife boarded the Pine Street line; Robinson was barred. But my wife is inside, he said—"all eyes gazed around to see who his wife was." Both Robinsons were ordered off. They refused. The conductor ran the car off the rails, removed the cushions, doused the lamps, and opened the windows, "the other shivering passengers all leaving." A crowd of colored sympathizers formed, and the Robinsons weathered the night, "as immovable as the Rock of Gibraltar." Their tale flew across the nation on the pages of the *National Anti-Slavery Standard* and the *Christian Recorder.*

In June 1866, newly graduated men from colored Lincoln University, in the countryside west of Philadelphia, rushed aboard en masse and filled all the seats of a car bound for the city. When the conductor ordered them to the back, they, too, refused. Three dozen strong, they prevailed.

Tactics risking injury and imprisonment did not lend themselves to broadsides or other forms of public declarations. Perhaps the closest anyone came to such a declaration was a speech delivered on a summer night in 1866. A colored audience had gathered to decry the "shameful" streetcar ejections of four women. The main speaker was Catto.

The ejected women were in his circle. One was Robert Adger's sister, Elizabeth. Another was Amelia Mills, who served with Carrie Le Count as an officer of the Ladies Union Association. They were among nine Negroes who had testified to grand juries about their ejections, to little avail. The league had financed a civil suit by one of its officers, the ever-combative Alfred Green, but the only victory in court had been Mrs. Derry's.

The meeting was on June 21 at Sansom Street Hall, where Fenian Irish nationalists had met; where Susan B. Anthony and the ubiquitous Mrs. Mott had led a women's rights convention, and where a white mob had stormed the celebration of Daniel Webster's freedom. Now the front of the hall was filling up with colored leaders young and old—the Adgers, White Jr., William Whipper, and Stephen Smith.

Rev. William Alston offered a few words, and the audience thundered for him. Then came Catto's turn.

He was twenty-seven now, part educator and part agitator, possessing the elements that his teachers, Reason and Bassett, had compounded in the classrooms of the I.C.Y. Like his father, he threw himself into more than one cause and committee. The night before, he had been at his weekly St. Thomas vestry meeting. If he had not had a streetcar meeting on this night, he would have walked to Liberty Hall for a Banneker meeting. Next Tuesday, he needed to return to Liberty Hall to take minutes at the national Equal Rights League board meeting. The state Equal Rights League had its own meetings. Evening lectures at the I.C.Y. required his attendance. He moved about from one end of the state to the other on behalf of the league, typically accompanied by any number of his "band of brothers," White, Adger, Minton, Green, Bowser, Forten. And in their leisure time, they were starting a local Negro baseball team. You can guess who was captain.

In Sansom Street Hall, he methodically drew together the threads of the car campaign. He called for bodily defiance of the streetcar rule. In another time, that defiance would be described as civil disobedience.

"He recommended the gentlemen to vindicate their manhood," the *Christian Recorder* said, "and no longer suffer defenseless women and children to be assaulted or insulted with impunity by ruffianly conductors and drivers."

He condemned the companies for ejecting soldiers' loved ones and "delicate women," the Victorian way of saying *pregnant*. He offered resolutions—"That we earnestly and unitedly protest against the proscription which excludes us from the city cars, as an outrage against the enlightened civilization of the age." He named the U.S. cities that had already opened their streetcars to Negroes.

> Resolved, That while men and women of a Christian community can sit unmoved and in silence, and see women barbarously thrown from the cars—and while our courts of justice fail to grant us redress . . . we shall never rest at ease, but will agitate and work, by our means and by our influence, in court and out of court, asking aid of the press, calling upon Christians to vindicate their Christianity, and the members of the law . . . by granting us justice and right, until these invidious and unjust usages shall have ceased.

Then he addressed the problem that perplexed Harriet Purvis, Lucretia Mott, and Benjamin Hunt: "We respectfully call upon our liberal-minded and friendly white fellow-citizens to cease to remain silent witnesses of the grievance of which we complain."

★ ★ ★

BY THE END of the year, a few legislators who had opposed the old bill were coming around for the new one. In Washington, Congress was on the brink of granting votes to Negroes in the reconstructed South. Everyone saw that it was only a matter of time before Negroes would vote in Scranton and Altoona. The *Age* warned that black voters would turn Philadelphia into another Haiti.

Citizenship was in hand, the ballot box within sight. A colored writer contemplated the moment.

> Never before in the history of our race or nation has there been a time when the ear of the American people was so open to the hearing of our many sad tales of wrongs and outrages endured as at present. . . . The American people with all their faults and shortcomings seem at last disposed to have their government divided upon the basis of eternal justice. The terrible lessons of the war have not altogether been lost. True, reforms move slowly, and it will require time and patience for the people who have been cradled in oppression and prejudice to become educated out of their false views. But there is no mistaking the fact that there is a better feeling and understanding existing between the white and colored people of this country than ever before.

In Harrisburg on February 5, 1867, Lowry formally introduced the tougher bill drafted by the league's Car Committee. "The prospects for its passage are cheering," Catto, Bowser, and Forten reported to the league. "It will be brought up at the earliest possible moment. . . . [We] are sanguine that the governor will sign it without hesitancy."

Republicans who had balked at the previous bill signed on this time. But one more battle had to be fought, in the middle of the night: Democrats attempted once again to poison the bill with parliamentary maneuvers. Finally, the Republican majority forced a call of the roll—and by a party-line vote of 50 to 27, the streetcars of Pennsylvania were opened to passengers of color.

Saturday's *Philadelphia Press* reported that Republican governor John W. Geary signed the bill on Friday, March 22. All that remained was to test the law in the streets.

This was no routine matter. Men as old as Purvis and Whipper remembered when state law had granted them the vote but gave no shield against white men's blows at the polls. Someone respectable should test the law, someone like Mrs. Derry. Better a minister or teacher than a washer or a maid; better a woman than a man. Someone to stand straight in a rain of words or blows.

★ ★ ★

ON THE FIRST MONDAY of spring, young women in Philadelphia were trying the new styles—the straw bonnets, chintzes, plaid silks from India, and the new hoopskirts, only three yards 'round and more flexible, suited to modern times, to sitting at a teacher's desk or riding a crowded car.

Under a cloudless noontime sky, the Ohio School's young principal and her assistant walked to Eleventh and Lombard streets, where the Tenth and Eleventh Street Railway ran. The assistant, Alice Gordon, stood by as the principal flagged down the yellow car. Carrie Le Count caught the attention of the conductor.

His name was Edwin F. Thompson, and he looked right back at Le Count. He "sneered at her," as a newspaper put it, and kept the car moving. He uttered the same words heard by the war hero, the poet, the colored soldiers and their loved ones, the minister with his ailing boy: "We don't allow niggers to ride!"

Just a month past her twenty-first birthday, Le Count was prepared. She promptly filed a complaint. In court, she held up a copy of the *Press* with the news that the governor had signed the law.

I know nothing of a new law, the magistrate said, and I do not trust that paper.

Le Count went to a state office and returned to the magistrate with a certified copy of the law. Thompson and his company paid a hundred-dollar fine.

★ ★ ★

A LETTER FROM HARRISBURG was read out loud at a meeting in Liberty Hall, the old school building that had been turned into a kind of politics house.

The letter was from Lowry and fourteen other legislators who had supported the car bill. Theirs was the sort of correspondence that might be pasted in a scrapbook or framed upon a wall. "We have found you here every week from [the bill's] presentation to its final passage, earnestly and persistently working for it," the legislators wrote. "This bill is essentially your own."

There would ensue some fussing over who deserved credit. William Still called a separate meeting, gave a two-hour speech on the car campaign and his role in it, and published all this in a pamphlet. He said the young men at Liberty Hall had it all wrong—they had wrongly accused him of judging the bill too all-inclusive; had falsely charged "that I wrote to Governor Geary urging him not to sign it." Still said the tide of public opinion in the streetcar fight had turned mainly because of colored valor in the war, and not any lobbying by the Liberty Hall crowd—"the men who stayed at home and smoked their cigars, and indulged in their sports and other sensual pleasures."

Those men hissed and hooted Still in his own building; someone shouted, "There will be a funeral at the coal yard now!" They also took exception to the advertising of that coal yard on the back cover of his pamphlet. They did agree with him on one point: The bill's passage was, in Still's words, "abundant cause for rejoicing." The *Christian Recorder* imagined Democrats sulking in their dens, castigating one another, and cursing the day "that a bill drafted by colored men passed the Legislature of the Keystone State."

The *Press* reprinted the Lowry letter on the same page as news of the law's first test, a complaint filed by "a mulatto woman named Caroline R. LeCount." An editorial said her case showed that the law would be "vigorously enforced." The *National Anti-Slavery Standard* went further: " Henceforward, the wearied school-teacher, returning from her arduous day's labor, shall not be condemned to walk . . . through cold and heat and storm; henceforward invalid women and aged men shall be permitted to avail themselves of a public conveyance, even though their complexion may not be white."

At the victory meeting, resolutions of thanks were moved and voted for the three lobbyists. They had trundled off a year ago to lay siege to the state capital, a fortress of political hocus-pocus, with no more ammunition than a stack of Equal Rights League pamphlets and an argument that in Harrisburg, in Washington, in America, the time was right. Now they'd come home victors.

The meeting also voted a resolution of gratitude to Lucretia Mott. Then, one by one, Forten, Bowser, and Catto stood, and cheers went up for each of them.

Commentators agreed on the reasons for this victory: Certain legislators had been convinced that the only way to win Negro votes in the future was to pass a bill in the present. The league's trio, the artistic Bowser, the persnickety Forten, and the "rising" Catto, were credited with the final bit of convincing. The various organizations—young and old, colored and white, deferential and defiant—had quelled their inner turmoils long enough to address the State House in one voice. In the Concert Hall Committee's final report, Benjamin Hunt concluded that "love to the Lord and the neighbor" did less to change legislators' minds than "the near approach of negro suffrage in the State." Catto's forces had managed to harness the ballot's power without yet possessing the ballot.

"And even better than this," Hunt wrote, white riders "who, within the last few weeks, have found themselves seated for the first time beside decent and well-behaved colored people . . . without harm or annoyance from the so much dreaded contact, have also found stirring in their hearts, in consequence, a new influx of Christian charity."

Now the victors in this fight could wonder: What might they achieve with the vote? Would all the outrages begin to fade away, as the league had once predicted, to "disappear as the dews of morning before the morning sun?"

As the huzzahs for Catto, Forten, Bowser, and Mott shook the chandeliers of Liberty Hall, that day drew nearer.

CHAPTER 13

Baseball

PERHAPS HIS FIRST TIME batting a ball was with Rev. Thomas Smyth's son Adger in Charleston, playing where no one would see a white boy playing with a colored boy. Or as an eleven-year-old in Allentown, New Jersey, where his father preached and he attended a boys' academy.

Back then, when his skin was still soft and his legs could run all day, he picked up a bat, hit a ball as hard as he could, and watched it touch the sky. The bat was a stick or a piece of a lumber; the ball a cork or a used bullet wrapped in an old sock, sometimes covered snugly with rubber strips from an ancient overshoe. Young Octavius had the hand-eye coordination. He could hit a ball far. His hands were five-fingered baskets where the ball always landed. He could throw a ball clothesline straight. The white boys saw what he could do. He could play.

★ ★ ★

NEGRO BASEBALL EXPLODED after the war. Much more than just a growth in exercise or leisure, the tradition of fraternal, social, and service organizations was stretched now to include baseball clubs with their own officers, dues, meetings, and rules of conduct—one more example of the nation within a nation trying to catch onto an outcropping of white America. Baseball was a public exhibition of Negro equality in a time of optimism, a time of Reconstruction. Just watch. They could play the same game as white men.

And baseball was another way they could establish themselves without whites. They were catching on to a white activity and creating a black one as well.

Clubs formed in Newark, New Jersey, Albany, New York. and Rockford, Illinois, and in cities and town large and small. The Excelsior club was Philadelphia's first, coming together early in 1866. As the weather cooled, another local club formed.

The first full season of the Pythian Base Ball Club was marked with a ceremony on New Year's Day 1867. Catto was the club's captain.

St. Thomas Church, the place of prayer for Catto and many of the best-educated and wealthiest colored families, including families of the Pythians, presented the team a gift to honor the launching of this new club and the high hopes of everyone involved. The gift was unlike any other that Rev. William Alston had ever bequeathed, but it was fitting for the occasion. One can imagine Catto with a surprised smile when he saw what it was: a ceremonial wooden baseball bat in a glass case inscribed to the "Pythian BBC." It remains a cherished church possession to this day.

★ ★ ★

BOYS PLAYED MANY GAMES in the 1840s and 1850s—bass ball, town ball, goal ball, two old cat, or base ball, spelled always as two words. They played English games as well, rounders and cricket.

The games involved bats, balls, and bases. Team size varied as did the shape of the field. Geography was an influence as well. Town ball was popular in Boston but not so much in Manhattan. And town ball in Philadelphia varied from town ball in Indianapolis. Game names changed from place to place.

No one knows exactly when a particular game began, in part because bat and ball games were played in ancient times. Cultures in Mexico, Egypt, Greece, and Persia played them. One Egyptian tomb drawing from 2400 B.C. shows a pharaoh playing a game called *seker-hemat*, or "batting the ball."

A game called baseball was played in the United States and in England in the 1700s. A German book published in 1796 featured seven pages on the rules of "*das englische Base-ball.*" The rules included: a bat two feet long with a four-inch flat face; a changing number of bases depending on the number of players, and just one out for the team batting. Some of the rules do not sound more than two centuries old—the pitcher "served the ball" to the batter, who had three opportunities to put the ball in play.

By the 1820s, young white men were playing baseball in Philadelphia and New York City. One New York observer gave the sport one of its earliest reviews: "It is surprising, and to be regretted that the young men of our city do not engage more in this manual sport; it is innocent amusement, and healthy exercise, attended with but little expense, and has no demoralizing tendency."

Baseball grew quickly in Philadelphia. In the 1830s, in the generation of ball players before Catto, players brought bats and balls to parklands in the south and west ends of the city and onto the ferry to a nearby field in Camden on the Delaware. The games were less about competition than recreation and were, more often than not, games of town ball.

Players heard some criticism for "indulging in such childhood amusement" but that carping was the exception. In 1833, without any fanfare, a group of young "Philadelphia gentlemen" formalized their ball playing and started a team, the Olympic Ball Club. They opened a club headquarters on Broad Street five blocks north of Market Street, the city's east-west spine.

This coming together of white merchants and businesspeople into a team that later memorialized its rules and wrote a constitution was new for the city. In fact, ballplayers had never done that before anywhere. The Olympic club kept records and statistics. Regular practices were scheduled. Umpires were chosen. Dues were paid. Players had uniforms—dark blue pants, white shirts edged in scarlet, and white caps with blue trim.

The Olympics were the nation's first bona fide, official team in any sport. No rejoicing was heard in the halls of sport nor was there any puffing out of the city's municipal chest to embrace this American first.

To be sure, bases, balls, bats, and innings linked baseball and town ball. But the two games had many differences.

Eleven players usually made up a town ball team. The "ball-giver" and the "behind" corresponded to baseball's pitcher and catcher. The other nine players did not have specified positions. The bases—actually stakes—were less than twenty feet apart. There were five of them. After a batter hit the ball, he ran to first base—and then, if he was safe, never stopped. One way fielders could make an out was by hitting the runner with the ball, causing hitters to run with their heads always turning. Every hit ball resulted in either an out or a run.

The Olympics' formation would ultimately mean a great deal to Catto.

★   ★   ★

THE BOOK OF SPORTS, published in Boston in 1834, was one of the first books to look at sports in the United States and Europe. The book spelled out the rules for baseball and described for the first time a playing field shaped like a diamond. In Canada and New Orleans, players were soon hitting balls on fields diamond and square. The New York Knickerbockers, the nation's first team to play nine-man baseball, introduced an innovation in the 1840s—foul lines.

By the 1850s, college and universities were fielding teams, including clubs at Princeton, Harvard, and Williams. Pitchers threw overhand and fast in Boston town ball. In New York baseball, they threw underhand and not so fast. Players in both games fielded barehanded, hurting palms and gnarling fingers. The two games clashed throughout the decade, fighting for supremacy.

The National Association of Base Ball Players, the game's first governing body, formed in New York in 1857. The word *National* expressed more hope than reality. For the first few years, all of its members clubs hailed from the New York City area. The association changed baseball from a recreational outlet to a competitive endeavor with strict rules. Town ball clubs were not permitted to join. A year later, crowds of ten thousand attended a series of three all-star games between Brooklyn and New York. Double plays were made in the field. Runners stole bases. Umpires called strikes. And fans paid an admission fee for the first time.

Newspapers touted one game in the summer of 1859 as the first baseball game between colored teams, the Unknown club of Weeksville pitted against the Monitor club. One paper described the match between the two New York–area teams: "The dusky contestants enjoyed the game hugely, and to use a common phrase, they 'did the thing genteely.' . . . All appeared to have a very jolly time, and the little pickanninies laughed with the rest." That was when the farm boy congressman from Ohio, Joshua Giddings, showed off both his ball field skills and equal rights beliefs by playing with colored men. The game also made the Unknowns known with their 41–15 win.

By the time of Lincoln, the New York game with its nine players on a team, nine innings, and three outs to a side, triumphed over town ball. Its rules were easier to understand. The symmetrical foul lines let spectators crowd closer to the players. The game was simpler to follow. And baseball had evangelists in a way that town ball never did. New Yorkers moved away and started baseball teams in town ball territory, such as Boston. Teams sprang up in Baltimore and San Francisco. Philadelphia, a town ball city, switched as well in the 1860s. Even the Olympics changed over and became a baseball club, prompting many of its veteran town ball players to retire.

A growing array of baseball teams in Philadelphia joined the Olympics in the 1860s, with many forming during the war years. Clubs formed in the New York and New Jersey area, as well as in Denver, Detroit, and Washington, D.C.

The first active baseball season in Philadelphia was 1860, with the first game between two opposing teams played June 11. The Winona club, led by town ball star Elias Hicks Hayhurst, defeated the Equity team 39 to 21. Also in 1860, a group of well-off young music lovers who belonged to the Handel and Haydn Society formed a team, the Athletics. (So today's Oakland Athletics team were born to the sounds of violins in Philadelphia.) As baseball interest grew, fewer men played cricket, once Philadelphia's most popular team game.

Thanksgiving was the unofficial end of the baseball season. Just before that, a newspaper wrote: "This game is deservedly attracting a great deal of attention in this country. Scores of clubs are springing up, and thousands are engaging in it. Some, because it is a wholesome, physical exercise, and others because of its highly exhilarating and fascinating influence. . . . The rules were perfected, and the game clothed with scientific beauty and importance. . . . Time is a precious element in the game, and has been calculated and applied with mathematical precision."

Even as players traded bats for the muskets of war, baseball's popularity soared. The game had been a decidedly middle- and upper-class pursuit because those men could afford to leave work to play. But the war introduced baseball to soldiers who were poor and working class. Prisoner-of-war camps on both sides let the captured men play baseball. For Confederate troops, who had no equipment of their own, a slat from a farmer's fence was now a bat and a walnut wrapped in yarn or bandages became a ball. A few Union troops carried baseballs and bats in their knapsacks.

During a game that Northern troops were playing in Texas, rebels attacked and the game quickly ended, causing one player to lament "we not only lost our centerfielder but . . . the only baseball in Alexandria."

In the midst of the war, about forty thousand troops massed for the most watched sporting event of the time—a baseball game behind Union lines in South Carolina, between the 165th New York Infantry and a regimental all-star nine.

Back home, fewer young men were available to play. Fields at Eleventh and Wharton streets in McMullen's bailiwick and at Camac Woods in North Philadelphia lay empty. A fall game was promoted in the papers to be "between the first eighteen players on the ground." The Brooklyn Atlantics, a team comprising mostly butchers, was considered the best team in the Northeast.

But by 1863, players were coming home from the war and newspapers began hiring men to write about baseball. They were called *sports writers*. People began wagering on games. Other sports vied for people's attention—thoroughbred racing, cock fighting, boxing—but Americans were besotted with baseball. Many cities, such as Boston, New York, Philadelphia, Brooklyn, and Newark, had more than one good team. Soon those clubs began traveling, with New York, Brooklyn, and New Jersey teams coming to Philadelphia, and Philadelphia teams returning the visit in road trips that writers called "invasions," as the language of war and baseball intertwined. Rivalries grew between New York and Philadelphia clubs.

In the summer of 1864, the Olympic club (this was a time when most team names were singular, so it was usually the Olympic Base Ball Club or the Olympic BBC) leased space from the city at Twenty-fifth and Jefferson streets in North Philadelphia, created a field, built a clubhouse, put up a fence, and charged admission of fifteen to fifty cents, depending on who they were playing. The new Union Ball Grounds of Philadelphia raised money for the war effort by hosting a battle between Pennsylvania and New Jersey all-stars—Jersey won 18 to 10. Two thousand spectators arrived on foot and by carriage, encircling the field of green to see the game. Baseball was becoming a social outing.

The Athletics took competitiveness up a notch that year when it stole a player from the feared Eckford club in Brooklyn by offering him money. His name was Alfred James Reach and his price was twenty-five dollars a week. The National Association of Base Ball Players prohibited paying players, but other teams had begun to flout that rule. Reach, a left-handed second baseman, was the first player to switch cities and teams because of salary. (His economic acumen matched his athletic skill. He would become wealthy as a baseball-guide publisher, manufacturer of sporting goods, and first president of another Philadelphia team, the Phillies.)

After the war, President Andrew Johnson showed how important the game was by inviting the champion Brooklyn Atlantics to the White House, a moment in American history when two *isms* came together— nationalism and athleticism. Johnson made their joining official by putting his presidential seal of approval on this new national game.

★   ★   ★

A MIDWEST COLORED TEAM of hotel and restaurant waiters would call itself the Blue Stockings for the color of their leggings. The champion Brooklyn Atlantic took their name from the ocean closest to them. But the new colored team in Philadelphia took a scholarly leap back to ancient Greece and adorned themselves with name of the games that led to the modern Olympics. Enter the Pythian Base Ball Club.

The Pythian leaders were players who understood Greek history. Catto and Jake White were the captain and secretary, respectively, of the team that had a lineup full of their Banneker and I.C.Y. friends. Four lineups, actually—O.V. was on the starting nine while Jake was third string.

The Pythian's maiden voyage was a 70–15 clubbing by the Albany Bachelor in 1866. By the following spring, the team was becoming widely known and highly regarded. "Scrub nine" practice games against other colored clubs may have played a part. And the roster of the Pythian boosted its renown before a ball was struck.

In a colored community overwhelmingly poor, Pythian players were relatively well-off. They could afford the club's annual five-dollar dues and met in a room at Liberty Hall on the same floor as the Equal Rights League. Many players belonged to the state Equal Rights League and other fraternal, civic, and civil rights groups. They worshipped at the best churches. They were whiter than the rest of city's Negro populace—more than two-thirds were mulatto compared with the 25 percent mulatto in Philadelphia. More of them were Pennsylvania born; fewer had come from the South than the rest of the state's Negroes. Most of the city's colored men worked as laborers or porters or in unskilled or semi-skilled jobs, while just one in four Pythian members had such jobs. The players had the leisure time. They could afford to play.

If you were erecting the structure that resembled the best of the colored community after the war, the men who played for the Pythian club were standing on the roof.

And now the season was finally ready to begin. The Pythian club was ready. They had not paid anyone to play, but they had persuaded some Excelsior players to switch allegiances, including Pliny Locke, whose father had been Catto's father's good friend. On June 28, the opponent was the Excelsiors and bad blood was a mild description of the relationship between the two clubs. Catto batted second and played second base. Leading off was John Cannon, the pitcher and the team's best player. Cannon's skills were recognized immediately by the city's white baseball clubs, who called him a "baseball wonder." The Excelsiors went down easily, 35–16, as did the L'Ouverture club in another June contest, 62–7. Out of the gate, the team was 2–0.

Secretaries of the Mutual and Alert baseball clubs in Washington corresponded with the Pythian to set up games in the summer. The time, place, date, and accommodations for the visiting team and umpires for the games were not the only important issues agreed on. These three colored clubs were polite and competitive with one another and shared a sense of what was really important—what happened after the contest. Catto's team could hit, field, *and* throw a soiree.

The first correspondence had come in April and was initiated by George Johnson, the secretary of the Mutual Base Ball Club in the nation's capital. He wrote of the "high position you, as an organization, have attained in our National Game." The letter was written before the win against the Excelsiors, but after the Bachelors had crushed the Pythians.

Johnson asked whether the Pythians would entertain "a friendly competition." He and Jake White arranged summer games in Philadelphia and Washington, a home-and-home series where the Mutual club would also play the Excelsiors while in Philadelphia and the Pythians would also play the Alert club while in Washington. The Alerts were a more experienced and talented squad than the Mutuals.

White wrote most of the letters responding to or offering challenges. But on June 30, still exultant after the game against the Excelsiors, Catto wrote a letter to the Alert club captain in Washington to tie up loose ends for their forthcoming July 6 game in Philadelphia. The letter shows that the new colored Pythian club and white veteran Athletic club already had a relationship. In keeping with the style of the times, the message was delivered formally. In keeping with the author's personal style, the words reflected a swagger.

"As captain of the Pythian's Nine, it falls as my duty to address you this communication in reference to two points touching our forthcoming match. We have secured the grounds of the Athletic, and all of its conveniences (the best in the city) have been put at our disposal. I took the liberty . . . of securing the services of Mr. E. Hicks Hayhurst Esq of the Athletics' First Nine to act as umpire on the occasion."

Catto explained, "Mr. Hayhurst is considered the best umpire . . . and I'm sure, though I met him for the first time a few minutes yesterday that he will satisfy both parties. Secondly, we have on our club a member who has not been in the club thirty days. It is our desire to have him play in the game and we thought it wise . . . to mention the fact and receive your concurrence. . . . There is considerable interest and no little anxiety among the white fraternity—concerning the game. . . . Yours Very truly, O.V.C."

The Alert center fielder was Catto's old friend Billy Wormley, now a rising figure among Washington's colored Republicans. Charles Remond Douglass, Frederick's son, played second base. These two teams were more than a collection of good ball players—they were elite young leaders of a race.

The Pythians won their third game, 23–21, with Catto scoring five times. The home team hosted the party and dinner afterward, providing thirty pounds of ham, claret by the gallon, ice cream, and a box of "segars." Jake White paid $78.26 from the team treasury for the feast, or about $1,200 in today's dollars.

In the fourth game, the Mutuals surprised the Pythians by winning a nail biter, 44–43. The soiree after this game included ham *and* tongue.

The Pythians returned to Washington in the August heat for rematches with both teams. The scheduling included a picnic planned by the ladies on the thirtieth, the day after the game with the Alerts and the day before the Mutuals' match. These Philadelphia-Washington games were spectacles for all to see, examples of a community bettering itself and of the pride felt for its young lions. Big crowds watched. White baseball players came to see. Colored leaders from each city attended. White reporters wrote that the teams were "a well-behaved, gentlemanly set of young fellows." Frederick Douglass sat in the stands and watched his son field *bounders*, the term used then for ground balls.

The Pythians won both games, clobbering the Alerts 52 to 25 and paying back the Mutuals for the loss in Philadelphia with a 50–43 win that saw the Alerts' Charles Douglass serve as umpire. After the Alerts game, the losing team presented the winners with a game ball and an American flag.

From there on out, the 1867 club beat all comers, including the Resolute from Camden and the Monrovia club from Harrisburg.

If anyone doubted the drive and single-mindedness of the team's captain, consider what happened on October 2. Daniel Adger, brother of Robert and son of the store owner, wrote a resignation letter. He was considered a scrub player, relegated to the fourth nine even though his relatives were neighbors and good friends of Catto's. Adger complained that he did not share "his colleagues' opinion of himself as a player lacking in talent." His resignation was accepted.

The year ended with a 9–1 record and the acclaim as the best colored team in the city and perhaps the nation. What more could the Pythians accomplish after one season?

★ ★ ★

THE PYTHIANS HIERARCHY, in addition to fielding a nine, had committees laboring on everything from securing fields and umpires to choosing prizes for opposing teams. Monthly meetings and twice-a-week practices were held. The leadership—White, Catto, the club president, James W. Purnell, and the vice president, Raymond W. Burr—all came out of abolition and Underground Railroad families. Purnell, who was thirty-four, had talked equal rights with his uncle, William Whipper, and with John Brown and Martin Delany.

Raymond Burr, a player on the second nine, was a man possessed of a most impressive political and civil rights pedigree.

His father was John P. Burr, believed to be the son of Aaron Burr, the former vice president of the United States, and a Haitian-born family governess. John Burr, a barber, was among the Negro spectators cleared from the gallery when white state legislators cast ballots in 1838 to take away the vote. He co-authored the *Appeal of 40,000* pamphlet to protest that loss of Negro suffrage. Burr sheltered fugitive slaves in hidden rooms in his home. He began the Demosthenian Institute, a literary society, and was an early Banneker and St. Thomas member. He rallied against the Fugitive Slave Act with Rev. William Catto and signed the "Men of

Color!" broadside. He helped found the Special Vigilance Committee in the 1850s. His wife, Hetty, was at Pennsylvania Hall in 1838 and joined the Female Anti-Slavery Society. Their son, Raymond, a graduate of the I.C.Y., followed Catto to Harrisburg as one of the ninety colored troops seeking to enlist.

Catto, now twenty-eight, had never been better known and had never felt more accomplished. Because of his status as a baseball player and captain, his name was familiar to Negroes throughout the Northeast. He had grabbed onto a handhold of justice by opening the streetcars. He had tried to do the same when he and his band of brothers sought to join the army and when the Bannekers sought to integrate the literary societies.

But he kept reaching for another handhold. The Pythians had displayed their abilities by playing baseball as well as any white team. The next step was to play against white teams. To do that, the club had to do something no colored club had ever done—apply for membership in a state chapter of the National Amateur Association of Base Ball Players, the former National Association of Base Ball Players with the word *Amateur* added because of the paying-for-players controversy. The Pennsylvania association was about to have its annual meeting in Harrisburg.

Colored teams were not welcome on some fields. In deep South Philadelphia, on the Wharton Street field near the Moyamensing Prison, acolytes of McMullen had lined Shippen Street to keep them out. The Pythians played there once in the 1867 season, but the trip was never made without anxiety and rarely without all four nines in attendance.

But now was the time to seek a change. It was October 1867. Negroes were being elected to office in the South. The Pythians had played on the field of the Athletics, an association member and the top team in the state. Catto had come to know the Athletics' Hayhurst. The Pythians had confided to him what they were going to do in Harrisburg. Hayhurst and several more white ballplayers said they were on board. Catto asked Raymond Burr to be the club's man at the meeting.

★ ★ ★

WHEN BURR ARRIVED the night before the convention's opening, bad news greeted him. Hayhurst and D. D. Domer, the convention secretary, told him that they had informally polled the delegates and the result was not good. White teams did not want the Pythians in their association. "The majority of the delegates were opposed to it," Burr said.

Hayhurst and Domer said they didn't want a no vote on the record and asked Burr to withdraw the request so that the team wouldn't be "blackballed."

Burr refused. The credentials committee would spend the next day voting yea or nay on all the clubs seeking to join—including the Pythian request. But there was still a chance for the colored club because Hayhurst was a committee member.

While the credentials committee deliberated, white delegates sat in bunches talking about what the Pythians were trying to do. Burr, the only colored man in the room, listened, but the voices were too low to make out what they said.

The committee voted yea on 265 of 266 applications from clubs around the state and never voted nay. They chose not to vote on the Pythian request, perhaps out of courtesy to Hayhurst. That vote was moved to the next day.

Delegates went to Burr and assured him that the voting results were not their fault. They supported the Pythians, but they had to abide by their clubs' instructions—to vote nay on a colored team's admission. They may have spoken the truth about how they felt. Or they may have just been acting politely. Burr reported he was "treated with courtesy and respect." Someone gave him a free ticket to a baseball game the next day.

After Burr heard about the vote, delegates asked him once more to withdraw the application. He refused again. He said he "did not feel at liberty to do this whilst there was any hope what ever of admission."

He telegraphed home for instructions. Catto replied: "Fight if there was a chance."

Hayhurst arranged for the vote to be taken in the evening because he thought there would be more delegates then and a better chance for a Pythian victory. But once again, the committee chose to ignore the request rather than vote on it. In the end, Burr withdrew the request and went home, having been given a free train ticket by one of the delegates.

A few days later, the Pythians played the Monrovians from Harrisburg and whipped them 59–27. Catto, whose team had lost at the convention, hit a home run.

★　★　★

WHAT HAD HAPPENED in Harrisburg was more significant than the unfulfilled aspirations of a colored baseball team from Philadelphia.

On the blackboard of American team sport, a line of white chalk had been drawn that would not be erased until well into the next century. To be sure, the line had long existed but had never been put to a test. The delegates had mightily tried to avoid that by not taking a vote, but they drew the line just the same. Was it an emotional choice, anger and retribution to Catto, the equal rights agitator? Or was it simply a display of how white men felt? Playing baseball with *them* was more than they were ready to do.

But the wearying refusal of white organizations to admit black members did not tire Catto.

The national association of baseball players rotated the site of its meeting each year. Philadelphia in December at the Chestnut Street Theater was the 1867 destination.

Ten years after its formation, the term *national* remained an overstatement. The association had grown from a New York–area group to a conglomeration of hundreds of teams in the Northeast. Its president was baseball booster and Philadelphia newspaper owner Thomas Fitzgerald, a Republican known as the Colonel. He had been the association's ceremonial head since 1862, when he owned the Athletics. Now he owned the Equity club in Philadelphia as well as the *City Item*, a weekly and the only paper in town that covered baseball regularly. Players and fans turned to page 3 for their baseball news, some of which Fitzgerald wrote himself.

Chances that the national association would permit the Pythians to become a member after the state association deemed them unworthy was the longest of long shots. But Catto was nothing if not persistent, and what did he or his team have to lose?

So the Pythians tendered a formal application. That membership effort promptly became known within the convention as "Catto's proposal."

Unlike the delegates in Harrisburg, these delegates did not avoid voting no.

Led by James Whyte Davis, a New York Knickerbocker and head of the nominating committee, the convention ruled overwhelmingly against the Pythians. This was the official explanation: "If colored clubs were admitted there would be, in all probability, some division of feeling, whereas, by excluding them no injury could result to anyone." Also the recommendation to "exclude colored clubs" was the best way "to keep out of the Convention the discussion of any subject having a political bearing."

Davis and his committee explained what they meant by colored clubs: any club "which may be composed of one or more colored persons."

A number of newspapers criticized the decision. The *New York Times*, a Republican paper, said that the prohibition was "inconsistent with the events of the past decade." The *New York Daily Tribune* called the action "cowardly." The *Wilkes Spirit of the Times* said that the United States was the only nation that had erected a color barrier in sports. The Democrat-leaning *Brooklyn Eagle* agreed with the ruling. In Philadelphia, Fitzgerald's *City Item* labeled it "a lamentable failure," adding: "The principal business seemed to be opposition to the colored man. . . . Baseball is in serious decline hereabouts."

The unwritten rule of baseball was now written nationwide. The glorious opening season of Catto's Pythians had ended in defeat.

★ ★ ★

CATTO'S DISAPPOINTMENT was swallowed up by the day-to-day routine in the new year. The I.C.Y. was bustling, with its students now numbering 232, a 16 percent increase from the year before. The state Equal Rights League kept him on the lecture circuit advocating Negro suffrage. He went to the usual meetings at St. Thomas and at the Bannekers. Also, the meetings were less formal, like those with his friends at the New Jersey shore.

And there was, of course, preparation for the Pythians' second full season.

In late April, Henry Boyer resigned from the club. A member of the third nine, Boyer was a *muffin*, a player with little skill. The season began in August with a 26–12 win against the Blue Sky club of Camden. Three days later, the Active club from Chester lost to the Pythians, 31 to 9.

On the white side of the game, the Athletics dominated the region. Jacob White sent them a note of congratulations after a "brilliant victory" upholding "the pride of Philadelphia on the base-ball field." The club's secretary wrote back a thank you for "these manifestations of confidence from our brethren in the city that have met with us on all sides."

Baseball was changing into a money-making business. Each contest brought in anywhere from one thousand to five thousand dollars at the gate. The fans' "entrance fees" had made baseball America's most lucrative field sport. A writer for the *City Item*, most likely Fitzgerald, wrote presciently about the future of the game: "The result will be the formation of firms with capital, who will employ nines and play them against opponents, the firms paying the nines and giving them at the rate of $1,000 to

$3,000 per annum, according to their value. Two such nines as the Athletics or Atlantics, ought to bring in $50,000, if ably managed. Give half of that sum to the players and a good round $25,000 will remain to the capitalists or managers."

In October, the Mutuals and Alerts of Washington fell to the Pythians. Just as they had the year before, these matches between teams from the two cities drew attention far and wide. This year, there were also accolades. Caroline Le Count, "on behalf of ladies," awarded handsome silk American flags to Catto and White for the wins over the Washington clubs.

Seeing Catto and Le Count together was nothing new by now. She had once favored an audience with a Longfellow poem that sounded as if she was talking about her beau.

> Ah, how skilful grows the hand
> That obeyeth Love's command!
> It is the heart, and not the brain,
> That to the highest doth attain,
> And he who followeth Love's behest
> Far excelleth all the rest!

The talk now was that his "gallant heart" was hers alone. She rarely lost her composure and he rarely misspoke, whether it was making promises, poetry, or a proposal. Nothing was made formal, but the talk was that the two were romantically one. She added his name to her prayers.

The Pythians' winning streak continued. They sank the Monitor club 27–9. They subjugated Monrovia 71–16 on their field in Harrisburg. During the year, the Pythians scored in swarms, averaging more than 39 runs a game while their opponents scored fewer than 21, numbers courtesy of club secretary Jacob C. White Jr.

In the club's annual report, White described the extraordinary baseball year of 1868. Early on, the plans were for a ten-game season, but three challenges never came to pass. It was rare, he wrote, "that a Base Ball Club passes an entire season, contending with other clubs indiscriminately—challenging as well as being challenged—without, in a single instance, meeting with defeat. Such, however, has been the history of the Pythian Base Ball Club this season, and when we take in connection with this the fact that during last season. . . . the club was defeated in but one single instance and by a single run in nine games, it is a record which we may feel proud."

Catto had played in fifteen of the sixteen games in the first two seasons, scoring 59 runs, third highest on the team. White, on the third nine, had played in nine games and scored 21 runs.

In the report, White also complimented the Pythian organization for the way it conducted itself. The clubs' committees "performed their labors with zeal and with an ardent desire to do all in their power to sustain our character and reputation as a base ball club and as an association of gentlemen."

Not only were the Pythians a good team; its players were always respectable.

★　★　★

WILLIAM STILL was a bitter man.

At forty-seven, he was the embodiment of heroism, a tireless Underground Railroad leader who had helped save the lives of hundreds of runaway slaves. He was the Philadelphian who had sounded the early alarm bells about the inequity of the city's horse-drawn streetcars. He was happily married with three children. He had a successful business.

But like fingertips burned on a hot stove, the end of the streetcar campaign still stung. His contributions had been ignored and his anger had flashed when he chastised "the men who . . . smoked their cigars, and indulged in their sports and other sensual pleasures" for getting credit not due them.

And now, nearly two years later, his anger had barely cooled.

As a sponsor of the Pythian baseball club, he committed to paying a dollar in annual dues. In late January 1869, his contempt for the men who played games boiled over when Jake White dunned him for the dues.

"Our kin in the South, famishing for knowledge, have claims so great and pressing that I feel bound to give of my means in this direction . . . in preference to giving for frivolous amusements," Still wrote to White.

White's response was cool, dismissive, and slow in coming. He wrote on March 1 that the club would be happy to accept Still's resignation as a sponsor after he paid his dollar in dues. Otherwise, "neither the acquisition nor the disposition of your means is of interest to us as an organization."

As the weather grew warmer, the business side of baseball took on a public face. The Cincinnati Red Stockings, the nation's first paid, professional team, drew a crowd of fifteen thousand for a game in Philadelphia in the midst of a national tour that saw them go undefeated, 57–0. Only one of the starting nine was from Cincinnati; the rest were recruited stars from around the country. The players earned from $600 to $1,400 for the eight-month season, compared with a typical annual pay of $525 to $750 for a skilled white tradesman.

Now everyone could see that baseball was becoming an occupation, and a lucrative one at that.

On June 24, a letter to the editor of the *City Item* rekindled the light that had been snuffed out at the two baseball conventions in 1867.

The writer raised the possibility of "a game between one of our white clubs and the Pythian, a colored organization of this city." "According to the laws of our last Convention," he explained, "no association game could be played between such clubs; but, in view of the fact that our most prominent clubs are now frequently playing sociable and friendly games, and in view also of the serviceable practice the Pythians may afford, I have no doubt that such a game would be interesting and well patronized. I learn that the Pythians are composed of the most worthy young men among our colored population. Who will put the ball in motion? *A Lover of the Game*."

Who was this *Lover of the Game*? He sounded a great deal like Fitzgerald, a man perhaps disheartened for what he did not do at the national convention. Fitzgerald was also a playwright with the skill and craft to shape words into skillful sentences and the understanding to manipulate the prejudices of the white baseball clubs. His letter deftly dismissed the Pythians as the equals of white teams by referring to a game against them as a "serviceable practice." But the letter also lifted the worth of playing against the Pythian players because they were "the most worthy young men among our colored population." Playing them would be a good deed.

On July 31, another letter to the editor appeared on page 3 with the baseball news. Again, no name was given, but this letter sounded more like Catto than Fitzgerald.

"Why is it that the Athletics will not play the colored baseball club called the Pythians? Are they afraid of them? As I hear the Pythians are very strong. I think it is quite possible that the *apprehension of being beaten by them* is the real cause. Fie, fie! I call on the Athletics Club to play the Pythians forthwith! *A Member*."

That made two writers trying to push back the walls of baseball convention.

The *Item*'s baseball page all but dared the white clubs. "We advise the Pythians to send a polite request to the Athletic, Keystone and Olympic clubs to play them at an early day. It is everywhere understood that the Pythians are very strong, and able to contend successfully with any first-class organization. Only three of the Athletic nine object, and they are afraid of the black balltossers."

The captain of the black "balltossers" did not seem a man to be feared at that moment, lying as he was on a blanket in the beach town of Cape May, New Jersey, easily accessible from Philadelphia by steamship and rail and one of the rare summer destinations welcoming to colored tourists. Harriet Tubman used to work in hotels there to finance her Underground Railroad forays South. Catto and friends vacationed in a rooming house outfitted with a piano and a ten-pin bowling alley.

In an August 12 letter to fellow Pythian Charles McCullough, Catto shook off the formality seen in previous letters. At ease on the sand with friends, he had his mind on the baseball diamond as he wrote about teammates Thomas Charnock, Jefferson Cavens, John Cannon, James Sparrow, and Joshua Atkins.

He was also planning a strategy for playing a white team.

"Charnock and myself think that we had better accept the West Chester boys' invitation, but I do not see how we can play them on Monday the 16th," he wrote. "We would need the grounds of the Athletic—and if you fellows can secure those grounds for that day—and Cavens will hunt up—or get Cannon or someone else to hunt up Adkins and Sparrow—and at the same time secure the services of Clark & Wilson of New Jersey, we can put a conquering nine in the field and some money in our treasury. Let some of them make the effort and the thing will be done.

"I am in practice—we have a bat and ball and I have distinguished myself as a left fielder. With proper precaution and advances,—Clark and Wilson could be obtained to play on our nine—as corresponding members—without touching or in any way affecting their membership of the Excelsior club. It needs good management—and if you can get anyone to attempt it—with the good promises of success—it had best be done immediately—especially in view of the probability of our meeting our white brotherhood—and the additional strength these two men would give our nine. Speak to Cavens—White—Jones & Doc about the matter. Bolivar is awake to it and has written me concerning what ought to be done. There need be much care . . . and it must not be presented as our *necessity*.

"My boy, you made a great mistake in not coming down—we are having a high season and blankets are plenty in Room No. 8—Banneker House, Cape May. We have many things to say but. . . . Let the musicians discourse! Yours truly, O.V.C."

Getting "Clark and Wilson" of the Excelsiors to play would strengthen the club in anticipation of playing white opponents. Jones was likely a reference to Frank Jones, the left fielder on the starting nine. Bolivar was Billy Bolivar, a muffin on the fourth nine. An old friend of Catto's, Bolivar was a Le Count cousin who lived with the family on Rodman Street. Doc? It's not clear whose nickname that was.

Fans were now paying admission to see some colored baseball games. Some contests were even touted as championship games. The Fearless club of Utica crushed the Invincibles of Buffalo 88 to 18 to win the New York State championship. The Unique Club of Williamsport, Pennsylvania, claimed it was the colored champion, because it had never lost two games to the same club since its 1865 inception. However, that streak ended in the summer with a loss to the Lone Stars of Philadelphia.

Two days after Catto's letter from Cape May, a white Philadelphia club agreed to play the Pythians.

In the *City Item*, the four-year-old Masonic club said they'd play as soon as the Pythians formally issued a challenge. The men of the Masonic said, "There is a desire on the part of a great majority of the admirers of the game of base ball to have some club, composed of players of the Caucasian race, play a game with the famous Pythian club, composed of colored gentlemen."

The Masonics opened the floodgates and suddenly *everyone* was talking about playing against the Pythians. The Athletics. The Keystones. The Experts. The Olympics. The Franklins.

But it was just talk. The momentum was there, but a colored-white game was a giant step for baseball. Equality was implied if the two races competed against each other. Besides, no white club wanted to take the chance of being the first to lose to a colored team. Fitzgerald began twisting some arms and cajoling some of his fellow owners. He wanted his former team, the Athletics, to play but they refused. Finally, he found a club to accept the challenge of playing in the first interracial contest.

It would be the Olympic club, the nation's first team, formed before Catto was born. The Olympics and Pythians would compete on Friday, September 3, in Philadelphia. Fitzgerald, whose son once played for the Olympics, would serve as umpire.

★ ★ ★

THE TEAMS were handsomely outfitted. The Pythians wore dark blue pants, white shirts, and a "neat cap."

The crowd was excited and anxious, Negro and white, about four thousand present to witness the unthinkable. Unlike other collections of fans that had, on occasion, been heard to holler a raucous or profane word, this crowd minded its manners and showed its emotion with applause and hurrahs.

Each team scored in the first inning, with the Pythians taking a 3–1 lead. But their star pitcher was injured early in the game and could not carry on with his usual skill. And the club had made a conscious decision not to argue the umpire's decisions.

That made a difference. In 1869, one umpire patrolled all four bases and decided balls and strikes. The clubs made the calls on the bases unless the decision was disputed. Then, and only then, could clubs appeal to the umpire for a final decision. The umpire was prohibited from making a call unless an appeal was made.

Any such appeal by the Pythians would amount to a colored man's challenging a white man's word—in front of four thousand people? Or they could look the other way, keep swinging, and hope for a better day.

Catto and his club decided to look the other way.

The game's umpire concluded a few days later that the Pythians had been too polite for their own good. They had left the Olympics' decisions unchallenged even when those calls were in the wrong.

"An umpire cannot voluntarily interfere between two clubs [and] . . . therefore the judgment must be demanded. However the Pythians, we suppose, were not disposed to be critical or captious under the circumstances. They had made their point in securing a meeting with a good white club, and they would not complain. . . . Their conduct in the field was most gentlemanly. . . .

"The Pythians are a fine body of men, and are superior players generally; their fly catching and throwing being first class; but they are not accustomed to bat swift pitching, (The Olympics making 52 bases on hits; the Pythians only thirty); here they showed their weaknesses; besides, there was a little nervousness perceptible in the early part of the game, owing to the novelty of their situation and surroundings.

"This will account for their failure to note certain important points in the game. For instance, they allowed two Olympics to score who neglected to touch the home-plate on running in. . . . Again—they did not call judgment on Mr. Lovett, whose pitching more than half the time was a swift under-hand throw. If judgment had been called, the umpire would have ruled him out, or compelled him to pitch regularly, with a straight arm. If these points had been noticed by the Pythians, and judgment called on them, the scores must have been very close."

The game lasted nearly three hours. The Olympics scored 8 runs in the second and 14 in the third to capture a lead they would never relinquish, winning 44 to 23.

The *New York Times* carried a short story two days later on page 1. The headline: "A Novel Game in Philadelphia." The story reported that the crowd was "immense" as it witnessed "the first game played between a white and colored club."

The game drew attention across the nation. The *Deseret News* in Utah wrote: "Philadelphia—The Pythian base ball club, colored, after repeated unsuccessful attempts to get white clubs to play them, yesterday had a challenge and accepted it from the Olympic club, white. The novelty of the affair drew an immense crowd, being the first game played between white and colored clubs. The Os defeated the Ps 44–23."

Other interracial matches quickly followed. The colored Resolutes of Boston defeated the white Resolutes of Boston 25 to 15 and also won the right to retain their name. The colored Alerts lost to the white Olympics of Washington, D.C., on a field across from the White House. Good feelings fostered by this spate of white-versus-colored games were not entirely shared. The Maryland Base Ball Club, a white team, refused to play the Olympics in late September because they had played the Alerts—who were not a "conventional organization," a nineteenth-century euphemism for a colored team.

Two weeks after the Pythian loss to the Olympics, Fitzgerald set up another game against a white team—his white team. The City Items, a baseball club of newspapermen, were nevertheless a bona fide team with a 5–3 record against state association teams.

Catto and the Pythians played better and must have appealed more often. The final score for the September 16 contest was Pythians 27, Items 17.

After that, unofficial games between colored and white teams became quite ordinary. Colored clubs would remain banned from state and national baseball organizations for decades. And from tournaments, even though it became common for white teams to sneak light-skinned colored players on their teams.

What happened to the Pythians in Harrisburg was a missed opportunity—for the game of baseball, for the nation. Perhaps something durable and important would have happened if baseball had opened itself up at that moment.

What remained was the gentlemanly persistence of Catto and his team. The Pythians persuaded, forced, and shamed white baseball into sharing a playing field with a colored team. In dark blue pants and white shirts, the colored nine on the field did not just say they were equal, they showed it. As for the color line in baseball, it would remain for another persistent second baseman to cross.

CHAPTER 14

The Hide of the Rhinoceros

THE LAST TIME Frederick Douglass had set foot inside the White House, Abraham Lincoln famously strode to his side, sought his opinion, and greeted him as "my friend." This time, Douglass arrived to find Lincoln's successor slouching in a chair.

Andrew Johnson troubled himself to stand up and greet his colored visitors. The dozen men at this February 1866 session ranged in attainment and age from the coal broker William Whipper to Douglass's son Lewis, fresh from service in the fabled Fifty-fourth. They had been chosen at meetings in Illinois, New York, Pennsylvania, even Florida and South Carolina, to call on the new president. He had vilified the slave-holding "aristocracy" of his native Tennessee and promised Negroes that he would be "your Moses." But now he balked at the Red Sea's banks.

Douglass broached the issue: Lincoln had entrusted colored men with "the sword to assist in saving the nation, and we do hope that you, his able successor, will favorably regard the placing in our hands the ballot, with which to save ourselves."

Johnson repeated his "Moses" pledge but then began a discourse on the enmity of poor whites toward former slaves. He predicted "a war of races" if black and white were too suddenly "thrown together at the ballot box."

He leaned close to Douglass and asked whether he had ever lived on a plantation.

"I have, your Excellency," Douglass replied.

Johnson had grown up poor. Surely, he said, you plantation Negroes sneered at the penniless white family in the hut down the road? Held them in lower regard than your master? "Not I," Douglass said.

And what of majority rule? Johnson asked. How did men as well-informed as Douglass and Whipper think the majority in, say, Ohio, would vote on a question of Negro suffrage?

Mr. President, one of the visitors said, in South Carolina we *are* the majority.

No matter, Johnson said, let each state decide. You acknowledge the enmity in the South; "hence I suggest emigration." The room grew cold, as if someone had thrown the White House windows open to the February air. Johnson was using the new word for the old colonization argument. Would every president make them hear this tired speech?

The man that Catto and a half-dozen other Philadelphia colored leaders had sent was William Whipper. He was no "flippant babbler," an admirer wrote; they picked him because few Negroes commanded as much respect. He had nurtured his lumber-and-coal concern into a small fortune, smuggled slaves to freedom in his freight cars, led temperance and literacy drives, and championed army enlistment. Childless, he had propelled his nephews into business pursuits and to equal-rights conventions. Now, a whiskey-drinking president was lecturing him on Negro prospects and the need for Negro patience. *Patience!* He was turning sixty-two.

As Johnson spoke, Whipper sat in silent contemplation of the world his nephews were inheriting. Perhaps they would live long enough to win the right to vote.

★　★　★

NEWS OF THE president's 1866 meeting appeared in papers across the North. Suffrage now emerged, in the words of the Equal Rights League, as "the all important subject."

The league began circulating new petitions, even as Radical Republicans in Congress defied Johnson and enacted the Reconstruction measures that upended the old order in the South. Under the watchful eyes of soldiers and the federal Freedmen's Bureau, Southern colored men were voting. Could Northerners be far behind?

In Pennsylvania, league officers crafted a two-fold message, saying they had built bridges to their white allies in Congress; "poured in petitions; [and] sent their agents to Washington" but had also determined that "they must not depend solely on the philanthropist or statesman. They must plead their own cause."

As proof of this allied-and-alone philosophy, the league trumpeted the streetcar law. "Messrs. [Forten], Catto and Bowser, prepared, word for word, as it now stands on the statute books, the act passed by the legislature . . . and then ably assisted in securing its passage."

From time to time, Catto and Jake White served as the Pennsylvania State Equal Rights League's liaisons to its two best friends in Congress, Thaddeus Stevens and William Kelley. Both had had successful careers, Kelley as a judge and Stevens as a lawyer. Yet both had an affinity for the oppressed. Stevens was born with a club foot and a withered leg. Kelley had played with colored boys and taught his own daughter to think of the boys and girls "sold away from their parents to grow up in distant states, far from their brothers and sisters."

Catto and White also used their Banneker affiliation to pass the hat for suffrage. Salaried teachers, they each put in ten dollars of their own. The Bustills, Adgers, and Millses gave, along with Sarah Mapps Douglass of the I.C.Y. faculty. Rev. Redman Fauset, an Equal Rights League delegate and a lion of the A.M.E., added his ten dollars; Emilie Davis, the young domestic servant, contributed a dollar. Within weeks they had $221.

Money issues gnawed at the state league. Boasting to Congress of fifty-one Pennsylvania chapters belied the fact that many in those chapters could barely afford the eight-cent copies of the suffrage petitions, much less a dollar donation. Catto sent a plea to colored ministers: Please save us rent. He dressed it in the usual lofty prose, asking leaders of "our several denominations" "to lend us their aid and influence, and to grant us the use of their churches in advancing a cause so Christian-like, so humane, so just."

Churches were relatively safe havens in "copperhead towns," as upstate league men said. Catto argued that the flowering of interest in equal-rights efforts had fueled a rise in church membership. But like the Philadelphia pastors who had dodged antislavery events before the war, upstate colored preachers had reason to tiptoe. The same month as Catto's request, whites stormed a Methodist camp meeting in a Maryland meadow. Though the war had been over for a year and a half, the invaders yelled anti-Union words as they tore apart the tents and trunks of hundreds of colored attendees, robbing them of clothes, bedding, utensils, and china and shooting a young white worshipper as he knelt in prayer.

League petition writers wrapped their case in the Constitution even as they strove to amend it. Denial of suffrage betrayed "the letter and spirit of moral law, the right of protection of life and liberty, and the principle of no taxation without representation." They tried also to lance the persistent boil, the fear of "contact," as Benjamin Hunt had said in his streetcar pamphlet. "Hate us as you will, turn from us at your pleasure," the petition said—but first grant to loyal colored men the same rights that "new immigrants enjoyed and former rebels might well regain."

Meanwhile, the oratorical giants of old, backs creaking but energies a-kindle, returned to the hustings in the name of voting rights. Henry Highland Garnet led colored veterans in a prayer for Andrew Johnson: "May the Lord open the eyes of his understanding." Martin Delany—now Major Delany, encamped with colored troops at Port Royal, South Carolina—sent Johnson advice on national security: Suffrage would secure the loyalty and bravery of colored men, leaving "no earthly power able to cope with the United States, as a military power." The commander-in-chief did not write back.

Charles Remond, now in his late fifties, spoke for suffrage at meeting after meeting in New York's central Mohawk Valley. The bumpy roads and baleful stares primed Remond's inner pump. "They can curse us and call us by all manner of names on the sidewalks, upon the corner of the streets, and in the bar-rooms," he wrote, "but in the meeting we pay them off with both principle and compound interest." As for Douglass, a conductor warned him of "an old-fashioned 'drag-out'" if he refused to exit the whites-only sleeping car en route from Buffalo to Cleveland. He tensed "for the bruising in store," but other riders rose to his defense, he got his berth, and now he was crisscrossing Ohio, "speaking [e]very night and traveling every day."

The Equal Rights League's national president, John Mercer Langston, took a job as a Freedmen's Bureau schools inspector, enabling him to travel the South and give speeches. In Georgia's state constitutional convention, Negroes and whites in the same hall heard him argue for universal suffrage, North and South. Someone shouted a question: Wasn't the newly freed slave too ignorant to vote?

Langston folded his arms and peered at the questioner. "Your slavery has been very hard upon us; it was a fearful thing; it has terribly scarred our backs and limbs; it has kept us in ignorance," he said. "But it taught us to think, and to catch the words that fell from the white man's lips."

Even Catto's father was back on the battlements. Rev. William Catto's latest pulpit-switching had taken him to A.M.E. posts in Newark, Orange, and Jersey City. There he campaigned for voting rights, as he had in New Jersey nearly two decades before, placing him and his son nearly side by side. At one point, the Pennsylvania State Equal Rights League even sent the younger Catto and two other men to confer with counterparts in Camden about joining in a lawsuit for voting rights. But no such joint effort resulted, and if father and son met or spoke about the suffrage effort, records do not reflect it.

They worked alongside many of the same people. A person could hardly attend the meetings without encountering a Langston or a Vashon, a Whipper nephew or a son of Jacob White Sr., a Bustill-Bowser relative, a Minton, a Dorsey, an Adger, a Purvis, or a Forten. People saw each other at Sunday services, Banneker debates, I.C.Y. evening lectures, equal-rights conventions, Odd Fellows meetings, and Pythian games. Yet in records of those events, the names of William and Octavius Catto rarely turn up together. They are both "Undersigned" on the streetcar and enlistment broadsides, but their names are far apart, as if they had walked in separately. Though Octavius had friends in his father's various congregations, on Sundays he climbed St. Thomas's seven marble steps to sit in its high-backed pews and hear its young pastor, Alston.

William Catto's restless nature did not lend itself to home and hearth. He married Mary Anderson after the death of Catto's mother, and by 1870 was sharing his home with a much younger woman. During most of the years when I.C.Y. teaching duties anchored his son in Philadelphia, William Catto lived in other states.

★ ★ ★

ON A MAY EVENING in 1866, the rafters of an old Richmond church rang with the new language of equal rights. Someone had persuaded hundreds of colored Virginians to pack this place and debate resolutions demanding "enfranchisement and protection." A Northern agitator had slipped into the former Confederate capital to encourage such audacity.

John Oliver, Catto's caustic ally in the streetcar fight, had come to Richmond soon after Union soldiers arrived. The burning of his schoolhouse had hardly slowed him. By day, he helped people argue cases in the temporary "freedmen's court"; by night he ran meetings in churches. The "enfranchisement and protection" resolution passed unanimously—along with a call for repeal of Virginia's Jim Crow laws.

New branches of the Union League, the Equal Rights League, and similar groups sprang to life and printed broadsides in Georgia, Virginia, Louisiana—places where mere receipt of the Ram's *Horn* or the *Liberator* had been cause a few years before to arrest the subscriber. Equal Rights Leaguers in the North took inspiration from Southern counterparts. "Rapturous applause" rose from delegates in Pittsburgh when Catto introduced a former slave who had risked his life to start five league chapters in North Carolina. A colored veterans' convention in Philadelphia cheered a letter of support, "name withheld for fear of assassination," from New Orleans—where whites had attacked a colored political parade, killing thirty-four Negroes and three white sympathizers. This news came just weeks after a white Memphis mob killed forty-eight; police joined in both attacks.

New Orleans and Memphis were a long way from Philadelphia; people at Pennsylvania State Equal Rights League meetings could take some comfort in a belief that such bloodletting did not happen in the North—at least, not since the draft riots.

Reports from the once-censored South now shaped and shook Octavius Catto's world. In Eric Foner's words, the 1866 New Orleans slaughter "did more than any other single event" to sour Northerners on Andrew Johnson; the caricaturist Thomas Nast depicted the president smirking in a doorway, the words *your Moses* fading on the wall as whites killed Negroes in the street.

Violence on a lesser scale filled reports to the Freedmen's Bureau and fueled angry speeches at equal-rights meetings. Pennsylvania's league protested "the case of whipping and burning the Colored women nearly to death" in a Virginia county. From Galveston, the Philadelphia man heading up the Texas Freedmen's Bureau reported that the high price of cotton was improving the lot of former slaves—but that attacks on freedmen were "still not infrequent."

"These cases almost defy any attempt to record them, and are reckoned by hundreds, ranging from downright murder, savage beatings, merciless whippings, hunting men with trained bloodhounds, through all the lesser degrees of cruelty and crime," Edgar M. Gregory, a Union brigadier general who had been wounded in the war, wrote.

Gregory made a point of prosecuting the attackers; he was even said to have arrested a Texas judge in "a certain bloodhound case." Planters complained to Andrew Johnson's administration—and Gregory was reassigned to oversee freedmen's schools in Maryland.

There were cheerful reports as well—especially regarding children. "The future to them is radiant with new hopes," a Freedmen's Bureau agent wrote from Montgomery, Alabama. "Children of color walk our streets with books under their arm, and notwithstanding it is contrary to the statute laws of the State to teach a colored child to read."

The teacher of freedmen in Portsmouth, Virginia, was "of dark complexion, of ordinary intelligence," his white supervisor wrote. He identifies "with the people and has their confidence, and is very well liked." Or as a freedman father put it, J. W. Cromwell was "a young man, very smart, and the only 'live' one in the place." Cromwell had heeded Prof. Catto's advice to go South, and teach "the four or five millions"; he had persuaded a white charity to send him to Portsmouth, his birthplace, when he was nineteen.

He made the walls of his schoolroom ring with the same textbook-thumping expectations he had known from Catto and Ebenezer Bassett. "Mr. Cromwell taught us to read widely, to interrogate, to think," a former pupil remembered. "The language of the book, the author's meaning or intentions were never enough. We ourselves had to have opinions. . . . [W]e went afield and developed breadth and the power of initiative."

Like John Oliver or Charlotte Forten, Cromwell described his work with an evangelical zeal. "It is not my purpose to be South . . . to satisfy a romantic, roaming poetic sentiment, but to assist in the elevation of my own down-trodden, unfortunate, illiterate yet not God-forsaken people."

Other I.C.Y. graduates followed. Pliny Locke, Class of 1867, headed for a Tennessee freedmen's school. Two women in the 1870 class scored perfect 100s on city teacher tests in Darien, Georgia. (The astonished mayor demanded proof that the women's diplomas were real.) Other graduates taught freedmen in the District of Columbia, Delaware, Maryland, Kentucky, and both Carolinas. Frances Rollin quit the Class of 1868 a year early to teach in her birthplace, Charleston. She had grown up in the demi-monde of free mulattoes; her father had bundled her off to Philadelphia on the eve of the war.

The young teachers faced no end of tests in "circumstances outside of the school-house," as Catto had said. White Southerners might curse them, white teachers shun them. A Charleston-to-Beaufort steamboat barred Rollin for her color in 1867. So Rollin did what Carrie Le Count had done a few months earlier in Philadelphia: She sued. The Union military commander of the Carolinas had decreed all races welcome on public conveyances; a magistrate fined the steamboat pilot $250. Rollin had free legal advice—from Martin Delany, who regaled her with so many of his triumphs and travails on three continents that she set out to write his biography.

A North-South grapevine of educators, churches, and charities kept the teachers supplied. Harrisburg's Pennsylvania State Equal Rights League branch, known as the Garnet League, raised money to put up a building, part church, part schoolhouse, for freedmen in Clinton, Tennessee. The new teacher there was Sallie L. Daffin, I.C.Y. Class of 1860.

Daffin had already taught in Norfolk and was, in Catto's words, "the pioneer in our ranks." Soon after she started at the Tennessee school, visitors reported "bright, attentive faces, and . . . perfect order." The pupils were young and old; a few were elderly. "Though deprived of the benefits of education while young, they do not think it too late even at the eleventh hour, to endeavor to make up as far as possible for lost time."

Some white Tennesseans could not stomach this sight. As Andrew Johnson often pointed out, many had never owned a slave; they had survived hard childhoods and poor schools. Now they saw former slaves lining up for lessons from well-attired mulattoes, in schools built with Northern money, using textbooks donated by Northern children.

A report to the Tennessee legislature warned of "an eternal hatred" directed against persons "engaged in giving instruction to the humbler class of their fellow men." The report was on a new organization, the Ku Klux Klan, led by the same Confederate general who had presided at Fort Pillow. But some whites in the border states had been Union loyalists all along and now wore Republican ribbons at election time.

A message went up the grapevine: Daffin's school needed Christmas gifts. Pupils in Massachusetts filled a box and shipped it. The holiday was long gone when the box arrived, but Daffin did what teachers do—she improvised. The school in Clinton would celebrate Christmas in April.

Townspeople of both races became caught up in this project. Men cut down a cedar tree and propped it in Daffin's schoolhouse. By the time the children surged in, "the presents were conspicuously displayed on its boughs, to the great delight of the youngsters, to most of whom this was their first sight of a Christmas tree."

Young Northern teachers at the freedmen's schools typically stayed two years before resuming easier, safer lives back home. Clinton parents wrote to Daffin, saluting her "untiring efforts . . . in diffusing education among, not only the children, but among persons of adult age." They begged her to teach in Clinton for at least another year.

Daffin had stopped noticing how much darker and less refined her Clinton pupils were than her I.C.Y. peers. At times she used first-person plural, as if she and her students were allied in some larger purpose. "I feel that I cannot do too much or work too constantly for the elevation of my race and for the banishment of those prejudices which have so long formed a barrier to our rise."

She agreed to return to the Clinton school in the fall of 1868.

★ ★ ★

IN HIS LATEST Freedmen's Bureau post, Edgar Gregory thought he would need to tour Maryland and talk its Negroes into going to school. Instead he found cheering crowds at every stop—a thousand in Centreville and Prince Frederick, two thousand in Havre de Grace, and a procession of colored Union veterans marching to greet him on the road. At a waterfront town, a band struck up for Gregory as his steamboat touched the dock.

Some Maryland freedmen schools added evening classes for men and women. Many, having worked all day, "come in and study so attentively," a teacher reported, "and not infrequently the nodding head falls involuntarily on the desk before it."

Washington schools struggled to accommodate a colored population of 38,000, more than twice what it was before the war. Freedmen had poured into the capital and lived in temporary shanties, or in the bureau's "Freedmen's Village," on the confiscated land of Robert E. Lee. The city had a corps of colored teachers—generations of Wormleys and other free families had been, in effect, rehearsing for this moment. Now I.C.Y. graduates and other Northerners arrived. By the decade's end, Washington counted some 60 colored teachers, including Billy Wormley's sister Anna—and 9,327 school-age colored children. One Washington teacher gave this assignment to pupils born in slavery: Write me a letter saying what work or trade you should like to do when you are grown.

"I think I should like to be a lawyer or a President," a boy wrote, "for I think they are both very useful trades."

★ ★ ★

FROM BEAUFORT, South Carolina, the once-illiterate Robert Smalls gave his Philadelphia tutors cause for cheering. He purchased space in the *Christian Recorder* to herald the convening of an all-colored school board to "promote the general education of the children." Board members—a former Pennsylvania State Equal Rights League officer, a Whipper nephew, and Smalls himself—hoped their Philadelphia friends would donate to this cause. (The *Recorder*'s editor seconded this hope.) Smalls advertised a new business venture with a man who had come to Beaufort by way of Cape May—Richard Gleaves, former operator of the Banneker House.

FREEDMAN'S CHEAP STORE

Wholesale and Retail Dealers in provisions and Groceries,
Dry goods, Trimmings, Hoop Skirts and Notions,
Boots, Shoes and Hats of the latest styles.
Highest price paid for Sea Island cotton.
SMALLS & GLEAVES, Beaufort, S.C.

All told, the advertisements, articles, and commentaries in that March 6, 1867, issue of the *Recorder* presented a mosaic of a revolution in progress: Negro tobacco hands in Petersburg, Virginia, were striking for a raise. The Indiana Equal Rights League. needed "public speakers, poets and singers." Over Johnson's veto, Congress was giving Southern Negroes the vote—a giant step that, all sides agreed, would beg the question of suffrage in the North. Thousands met in Memphis "in celebration of their enfranchisement." The editor saluted their "manly" protest at still being barred from Tennessee juries and high office. An anonymous Bostonian offered twenty thousand dollars to Wilberforce College; in Pittsburgh, little Avery College raised a big banner by hiring as its president Henry Highland Garnet—and charging no tuition. The twenty-five-cent tickets for the next Banneker Institute lecture were worth every penny, the editor assured his readers, not only because the Bannekers included some of "the most intelligent and prominent young gentlemen of this city" but because the lecturer was the new head of the I.C.Y. Girls Department, Fanny Jackson. "Her devotedness to the cause of intellectual and moral improvement, deep as her own soul and her great natural endowments, eminently fit her to instruct from the platform."

Near the bottom of a column of advertising, this small notice appeared:

INFORMATION WANTED

of my children,
Harris, Mary Ann, Joseph, Charles and Enos Dickerson,
who were sold in Virginia in 1852.

Mrs. Mary Dickerson of Philadelphia asked Southern ministers to read this from the pulpit, and if anyone knew of her children, to write her, care of the *Recorder*. Two similar notices ran under hers, and more in the next editions. The paper charged these customers a reduced rate, twelve and a half cents a line, for notices "of a private nature."

Lucinda Johnson hoped to find her mother, sold away in Missouri "when I was eight years old."

The smallest stones in the *Recorder*'s mosaic depicted broken hearts. Ephraim Allen of Philadelphia sought word of his mother, brother, aunt, and cousins, sold to various buyers in Tennessee and Louisiana. Melinda Smith of Millville, New Jersey, listed her five children, "sold in Richmond at different times. Ministers will confer a favor upon a sorrowing mother by reading this notice in their congregations."

Some notices ran for months. Some never reached the intended locales—many Southern postmasters would not deliver the *Recorder*.

★ ★ ★

THE GRIMKÉ SISTERS and Theodore Weld had all gone gray. They had lived for a time in North Jersey and run their little school for both races. They staged school dances on Saturday nights—a woman visitor reported "dancing with old Mr. Weld till the gunpowder ran out of the heels of my boots."

By the war's end, they had moved to Massachusetts; they dined with the Garrisons and raised money for the freedmen. Once in a while, Angelina Grimké Weld appeared at conventions as an honored guest. She would smile as others recalled how she had renounced her Charleston slaveholding roots, invited Negroes to her wedding, and defied the mob at Pennsylvania Hall.

On a February night in 1868, she was reading an article in the *National Anti-Slavery Standard* about a speech by a colored student at Lincoln University, west of Philadelphia, and was startled to see that the speaker's last name was Grimké.

Her hands trembling, she wrote to him. "Mr. Grimke," she began, and while noting that she and her sister had devoted their lives to abolitionism, she asked gently whether he might have been a Grimké family slave. The answer was yes.

"Dear Madam," Archie Grimké wrote back. I know of your "anti slavery celebrity." My brother Frank and I were children of your brother. Our mother was his slave.

A visit was arranged. Angelina, now sixty-three, listened wet-eyed as Archibald and Francis Grimké, both undergraduates at Lincoln, related a Dickensian tale. Their father was Henry—the brother Angelina had persuaded, long ago, to show mercy on one slave; that was the moment that had changed her life.

Henry, a widower, had had three sons by a slave woman and had decreed on his deathbed that she and they be treated as family—but his white heirs had other ideas. Archie and Frank were taken from their mother, "a defenceless woman, crippled in one arm . . . with no one to care for her in the world." After that, their Charleston childhoods had consisted of mistreatment, escape, capture, re-enslavement, a near-fatal term in the workhouse, intervals as Confederate officers' valets, and finally, a lucky friendship with a Northern teacher in Charleston after the war. The teacher found a way to enroll the boys in Lincoln University. They were bright, penniless, and hoping to graduate two years later, with the Class of 1870.

More visits followed. Sarah Grimké, now seventy-five, began a savings account she called her "Archie-fund." And the white Grimké aunts began putting the mulatto Grimké nephews through college.

★ ★ ★

A GREAT NATIONAL PARADOX surfaced in the elections of 1867 and 1868.

Southern Negroes, newly equipped with voting rights, sent delegates to state constitutional conventions, massed at the polls, even elected colored Republicans to state and local office. This new political class included local-born freedmen, "carpetbaggers" from the North, and men like Robert Smalls who were a bit of both.

Smalls bought up property at tax sales in Beaufort—including his master's old house. He convened meetings there and handpicked delegates to the state convention. He won a legal battle over Negro landowning rights. Laura Towne, Charlotte Forten's old teaching colleague at nearby Port Royal, said, "The men, women and children seem to regard him with a feeling akin to worship." He soon began runs for office; his campaigns included torchlight parades, a brass band, and doling-out of favors to both races—even to relatives of his former owners. A Charleston paper remarked at "the kindness of Smalls."

Whipper's nephew, W. J. Whipper, served on the school board in Beaufort, studied law, became a rice planter, helped start South Carolina's Republican Party, and went to the constitutional convention. He truly embodied the marriage of academics and agitation: He married Frances Rollin.

William Catto's old Charleston mulatto friend Richard Holloway ran for alderman as a Republican in 1867 and won. So did the patriarch of Sarah Catto's family, the former slaveholder Richard Dereef—but he ran as a Democrat.

Henry, Robert Purvis's Oberlin-trained son, moved to Columbia, South Carolina, organized colored voters for the Union League, and won a seat in the legislature. The District of Columbia extended suffrage to its colored men in 1866; this move so changed the city's electorate that by 1867 the First Ward Republican Club elected an all-Negro slate of officers, including Billy Wormley. John Oliver was on the grand jury that indicted Jefferson Davis for treason.

At the same time, the party that had legislated suffrage in the South was paying a price in the North.

Thaddeus Stevens's communistic-sounding land scheme was the last straw for many whites. Upholding a freedman's right to a wage was one thing, but redistributing white-owned land was another.

In local elections across the North, disaffected white Republicans voted Democratic. Senator Edgar Cowan of Pennsylvania was among the disaffected. A boat builder and lawyer from near Pittsburgh, he said pandering to the blacks in the South was causing the party to implode in the North and Midwest. "I almost pity the Radicals; after giving 10 states to

the negroes . . . they will have lost the rest," Cowan said. "Any party with
an abolition head and a nigger tail will soon find itself with nothing left
but the head and tail."

Democrats printed badges that said, "OUR MOTTO: This is a White
Man's Country; Let White Men Rule." Andrew Johnson was right about
one thing: In nine Northern states, majorities turned down referendums
on colored voting rights. A move to delete the word *white* from the Pennsylvania constitution's suffrage section failed, 68 to 14, in the same chamber that had passed the streetcar bill. The Democrats' elder statesman,
ever shy about exploiting white prejudices, saw new vigor in his party's
ranks. "Hostility to negro suffrage has been the most powerful cause of
this great change," James Buchanan said.

In Philadelphia, the Democrat who kept Buchanan's portrait on his
wall was trying to elect a new mayor in 1868. Alderman McMullen's candidate was Daniel Fox, who had built an earlier campaign around his
stance on the streetcar issue. Fox had warned that letting Negroes into the
cars would lead to "demands for political equality including the right to
vote and hold office"; now he could say, *I told you so.*

McMullen needed this victory. The city's Select Council had voted in
1867 to create a municipal fire department, aiming to close down the private companies and their periodic street battles. This change had come at
a memorable meeting of the council. Its president, a big, bluff former fireman named William Stokley, made the case for a fire department as "catcalls and curses . . . growls and yells" rained on him from supporters of the
old system. The new law would surely dissolve the Moyamensing Hose.

The mayor's race was hard fought and close. Late on election day, voters in line at a polling place at Eighth and Lombard saw a cluster of men
approach. Shots rang out and people ran in every direction. A Republican
tavern keeper fell, wounded. Witnesses described men standing over him
and firing more shots. Morris Brown Jr.'s cigar store, a popular evening
stop for Pythian and Banneker men, was a few yards away. Billy Bolivar
wrote that the shots narrowly missed Catto.

A policeman ran to the scene—and was shot. A second officer rushed
to his aid. It was too late; Officer James Young was dying. The other policeman testified: Before Young died, he named his killers. "He said they were
a crowd of Moyamensing Hose fellows."

Fox won the mayor's race. Soon after his swearing-in, he began filling
police department posts with men recommended by McMullen.

★ ★ ★

IN SHEER NUMBERS, the "great change" celebrated by Buchanan, McMullen, and other Democrats was not so great. Republican operatives noted the explosion of new Republican votes in the South and made a calculation: If colored men could vote in every state, the party of Lincoln and Grant might enjoy lasting majorities. Fox's Philadelphia election told the tale. He won the mayoralty by fewer than two thousand votes; the city's voting-age colored men numbered at least five thousand.

Grant narrowly won the presidency in 1868 by banking on his hero status and saying little about race. The election returns showed that without the South's newly enfranchised colored men, he would have lost the popular vote. Soon after, the Republican publisher of the *Philadelphia Press* and the *Washington Chronicle*, John W. Forney, stood before a colored audience in Washington and spelled out a new Republican rationale.

"Why, my friends," Forney said, "you know if the Republicans could have settled this thing in the North, as a Republican Congress did in the South, there would not be a disfranchised citizen in the republic." His papers covered Negro events; he had even hired a colored correspondent to ride with the army and send dispatches from Virginia. Colored Philadelphians had paid him a compliment second only to a ceremonial silk flag: When he was about to sail to Europe, Catto and others marched to Forney's house and serenaded him.

But now Forney skipped past the pleasantries. He said the party must get colored men the vote for one reason—to beat the Democrats. "Let the present Congress close the gap by a comprehensive amendment, so as to make suffrage wholly impartial, and the Northern Democracy will be stopped forever." That assumed colored men would vote Republican forever.

★ ★ ★

"HALT! HALT! You damned black son of a bitch, halt!"

In the darkness of a dirt road on Maryland's Eastern Shore, J. W. Cromwell saw too late that five white men with rifles were encircling him. He had just finished his day at the church that housed his freedmen's school. He had heard the talk of white resentment in the county, but being twenty and full of himself he had ignored it. This was not Louisiana; he was barely a hundred miles from Philadelphia.

The shouting white man put the muzzle of his rifle to Cromwell's chest.

Cromwell took a breath and sprinted for the woods.

The silence lasted an instant—long enough to think of his father, who had toiled for years to purchase the family's freedom, or Catto slapping him down from his "pedestals"; long enough to hear the twigs snapping underfoot and the pounding of his heart.

Then the white men began firing. Cromwell heard bullets "whining all around me" as he ran. His dark skin, for once, was a blessing. He credited his survival to "crooked road, dark night, and dense woods alone."

By the next morning, he had recovered himself somewhat. He began a letter to the missionary group that had sent him to this spit of land in the Chesapeake known as Spanish Neck. "The crisis of affairs has at last arrived," Cromwell wrote.

Negroes were teaching Negroes in the same places that had outlawed such activity in dread of equipping the next Nat Turner or Denmark Vesey with the "dangerous instrument of learning." Colored men in Southern states were becoming jurors, sheriffs, school board members, tax assessors, and legislators.

"Violent threats are made to blow us up, to drive us out of the State, etc.," Robert Purvis's son Henry wrote home from his Union League post in Columbia, South Carolina. "We are obliged to go armed, and keep close to our rooms at night." He, at least, was not injured. By Eric Foner's count, 10 percent of colored participants in Southern state constitutional conventions were violently attacked; seven were murdered.

The violence stiffened congressional spines. Hundreds of Klansmen were eventually rounded up and prosecuted. A new Enforcement Act empowered the government to use soldiers to prevent attacks on people trying to vote. But there would never be enough troops in the South to put a soldier at every polling place, or every school.

John Oliver's first Virginia schoolhouse was burned; so was J. W. Cromwell's in Spanish Neck. So was "nearly every colored church and school-house" in the vicinity of Tuskegee, Alabama, in the fall of 1870; and in Monroe County, Mississippi, where the Klan made a resurgence, burning twenty-six freedmen schools in a stretch of five months.

So was Sallie Daffin's school in Clinton, Tennessee. White men burned it down just days after the nation's new president was sworn in. Daffin would forever link the two events in her memory.

Yes, she wrote bitterly, we brought it on ourselves. She slipped into her first-person plural. On the Thursday before the fire, "we hoisted the U.S. flag . . . in honor of the inauguration." She had also written on the blackboard, "Three Cheers for U.S. Grant, President of the U. States."

★ ★ ★

A FINAL, SUSTAINED PUSH for Congress to enact universal suffrage was under way by then. A fifteenth amendment to the Constitution was proposed, disputed, redrafted. Radical Republicans debated how far the amendment should go. Democrats pondered whether they should, in the words of U.S. senator Willard Saulsbury of Delaware, simply concede "the nigger vote." Democrats in other states reprinted his speech.

Colored leaders aimed for one more show of future electoral force, in the form of mass meetings across the nation and thick petitions of Negroes' signatures arriving on Capitol Hill. One of the Pennsylvania State Equal Rights League's sharpest speakers, the dark, diminutive Isaiah Wears, called it "another war."

At the same time, the real war had left people weary. The ailing Thaddeus Stevens received a get-well letter from a Pittsburgh veterans' convention where "a third of the delegates are one armed one leged or maimed soldiers." Some Northerners said it was time to change the subject; the great moral battles had been fought and men needed to make money again. The *New York Tribune* said of Reconstruction, "The country is sick and tired of it. . . . LET US HAVE PEACE."

Richard Gleaves left Cape May for Beaufort less to rally the freedmen than to see whether he and his friend Smalls could sell them hats and hoopskirts. I.C.Y. graduate Theophilus Minton—whose sparkling Latin salutatory speech at commencement had caused people to throw bouquets—grabbed a chance to practice law in Columbia, South Carolina. Even Congressman Kelley found time to dabble in Southern investments. In Baltimore, a Yankee-designed mill hired former rebels to forge twenty-five thousand tons of rail a year. In Philadelphia, onetime streetcar campaign supporter Matthias Baldwin set out to eclipse his company's wartime pace of 100 locomotives a year; by 1869, the Baldwin Works' annual orders from North, Central, and South America were said to reach 228.

In the hub of the colored North, the rising generation was now risen. Catto, Jake White, Charlotte Forten, Fanny Jackson—all would turn thirty before 1870. Students who had become teachers had gone on to become principals.

Forten survived another illness—smallpox—moved to Boston, worked for a freedmen's relief organization, and began writing for the *National Anti-Slavery Standard*. (In a book review, she panned a white novelist's obsequious portrayal of a colored scholar; such a man "is not cowed before a white skin," she wrote, "even if his own be black.") Scribner's published her translation of a popular French novel; by the decade's end she was back in Philadelphia and listed in the census as "authoress."

When not handling Pennsylvania State Equal Rights League or Pythian business, White seemed to glide through his rounds as the first colored principal of the Vaux School with the ease of a figure skater on the nearby Berks Street rink. The school had grown to 101 boys and 64 girls and had moved out of the basement. A recent arrival was Rev. Benjamin Tanner's son, Henry. The Tanners had moved from Pittsburgh for the minister's A.M.E. posting at Mother Bethel. Henry had inherited his father's tiny frame and was said to be "exceedingly shy and retiring." He loved drawing pictures on his slate.

The principal asked to see his drawings. One, a pencil sketch dubbed "The Evening Tea," depicted a cup, saucer, teapot, and tray. White praised the picture and mounted it on his wall. Looking back, people said that was when Henry Ossawa Tanner, barely eleven, began to emerge from his shell.

Le Count's Ohio Street Colored Unclassified school had grown, too. By 1868, she was overseeing 283 students—more than in Vaux, more than at the I.C.Y. White was allowed to hire one "assistant" teacher, Le Count, three—and each of these was, as Catto put it, "a product of our Institute." The city was paying White $770; Le Count, only $480. Some barriers had to wait. She and White still represented the school district's gamble of placing colored principals in charge of colored public schools.

Le Count was a few years younger than White, Catto, and the others and still lived in her parents' narrow house on Rodman Street, just above Ninth, walking distance from her school and from Catto's boardinghouse at Eighth and South.

Her beau, meanwhile, had become one of the best-paid Negroes in the city. By dint of seniority, celebrity, and widely praised teaching skills—along with his frequent applications to the managers for raises—Catto was earning eight hundred dollars a year by the spring of 1868.

He now faced a curious situation: He had become known—known to allies and enemies, known to influential men of both races, who offered opportunities and excitements. From Allegheny City, just outside Pittsburgh, came an entreaty from Garnet. Would Catto consider a teaching post at Avery? The colored college was welcoming students as young as fourteen and charging a modest tuition. No dormitories yet; undergraduates were told to "board in respectable families of Pittsburgh and Allegheny cities." Still, Garnet had grandiose visions and no time to spare. Besides president, he was "Professor of History, Rhetoric, Logic, Mental, and Moral Philosophy, and Political Economy." He offered Catto eleven hundred dollars a year and asked for a quick reply.

For Catto, that would mean a job with a much higher salary, within the Pennsylvania State Equal Rights League's territory, and a chance to work for Garnet. "Esteemed friend," he wrote back. Catto liked the offer, liked Garnet's willingness to let him "freely manage" his teaching duties and believed Avery could be "an honor to our people."

An I.C.Y. board member, Benjamin Coates, wanted Garnet to delay any decision for a few days. That aside, Catto wrote, "you may *use my name as you desire.* . . . I am pretty well satisfied that there will be nothing in the way of my accepting the position if I am appointed."

Garnet replied by Western Union. "Do not resign yet. Write immediately and fully what you can teach say nothing about salary. Send testimonials."

Why did Coates want to slow things down? Perhaps to see whether the I.C.Y. could persuade Catto to stay. But Coates was not a simple man. He was an oddity, a wealthy Quaker dry-goods merchant who cultivated friendships with colored firebrands such as Garnet and Douglass. He had served at the I.C.Y. for years and took great interest in its students. He had financed Robert Campbell's trip to the Niger Valley and Jesse Glasgow's tuition in Edinburgh; he considered Catto "one of the most talented + promising colored men we have among us." Coates was also an unrelenting colonizationist.

Like Garnet, he had a grandiose vision, and a place in it for Catto. Coates confided his idea to an officer of the American Colonization Society—the parent of all state colonization societies, the bane of generations of colored leaders, the hated A.C.S.

A back-to-Africa movement was still possible, Coates insisted. The key, he said, was recruiting popular Negroes to lead the way. "Two or three intelligent + educated Negro gentlemen, in the boards of each state society would have the effect of interesting our colored population very much in the work, such men for instance as William Whipper, ED Bassett, + O.V. Catto in Philadelphia."

Coates believed a booklet of testimonials the A.C.S. had compiled for its fiftieth anniversary made the case well. He said he was donating a copy to the I.C.Y. library, and one each to Whipper, Bassett, and Catto—"all in the *very best* hands, + where they will be appreciated, + most likely to *tell*."

Within a few days of Garnet's telegram, the situation changed. Something *was* said about salary, and the I.C.Y. managers found themselves offering their top male teacher more money. Avery College had been ready to pay Catto $1,100, but he was "willing to remain with us at a salary of $1,000 per annum," the board noted.

So Catto stayed put, accepted a raise, and remained within Ben Coates's reach.

★　★　★

IN ALTOONA, PENNSYLVANIA, the top officer of the strongest state chapter of the national Equal Rights League was becoming frantic. Only six weeks remained before the state league's annual convention, and from William Nesbit's vantage point, everyone looked distracted. As another upstate Pennsylvania State Equal Rights League man put it, men were too busy to pass petitions but would "give there [sic] life for a ball game or a parade."

The timing was critical—as Congress moved closer to considering the suffrage question, every colored political meeting needed to be a mass meeting—a portrait of future votes. Furthermore, the August convention was in Williamsport, a long way from the big cities. People needed to plan. Nesbit sent a note to Jake White at the Liberty Hall office. "It is of so much importance that due notice be given and a stirring appeal made," Nesbit wrote. "I sincerely trust that yourself and Mr Catto will no longer delay."

Nesbit was older than some of the Equal Rights League men in Philadelphia. A western chapter named itself for him. He had been to Liberia in the 1850s and come back a permanent foe of colonization; like William Catto, Robert Purvis, and others of his generation, Nesbit had signed the suffrage petitions that had died in State House dustbins. He wished this to be the last great push. He described the proposed Fifteenth Amendment as "the prize for which we aim . . . the turning point in our destiny, then we will have a fair chance in the race of life, then every man will stand on his own individual merits."

The appeal went out from Philadelphia three weeks later, inviting to Williamsport "every lover of complete enfranchisement," regardless of race or gender. Railroad schedules were provided. Catto, White, and Nesbit wrote: "Fifty thousand of our brothers sleep in death, and thousands walk about maimed and crippled in defense of our country and its flag, and still we are disfranchised."

One officer used a popular tactic: Get hold of the best speeches and pass them around. William Forten wrote to Congressman Leonard Myers of Philadelphia for copies of his and other Radicals' orations, promising to "send them just where the doubting are to be found and where Copperheads may be influenced."

Delegates arrived from Reading, Altoona, Harrisburg, Pittsburgh, and Philadelphia. They cheered for suffrage resolutions. Forten warned Southern delegates to keep voting Republican or risk seeing progress halted. Big-city delegates chided a Reading man for sounding too much like a Democrat. A Williamsport paper seized on this skirmish, portraying the convention as "cheese-colored" young mulattoes versus "a pure Congo."

Neither the state nor the national Equal Rights League went long without ad hominem strife. When Langston, the league's law-trained national president, questioned the legal underpinnings of some Reconstruction measures, Nesbit suspected him of "secret treachery"—and told Thaddeus Stevens. (Stevens, losing weight and strength to illness, said he liked Langston fine but thought his views "very bad.") Douglass attacked Langston, too—though as Delany, Purvis, and Garrison could attest, Douglass had a habit of stepping on his friends.

On certain occasions, the factions quieted and marched as one—to mark a great victory, or mourn a great loss.

Within days of the Williamsport meetings, word went out that sixty-seven-year-old Thaddeus Stevens, known as "The Great Commoner," had finally succumbed to illness.

The Banneker Institute quickly convened a Saturday-night meeting. Fifteen men agreed to don black coats, white gloves, and black-ribbon badges and march "under Marshal O. V. Catto" in the line of fifteen hundred citizens taking Stevens to his rest in Lancaster County. Having lived what preachers called a "useful" life, Stevens even concocted a useful death—he was to be buried in a colored cemetery, lest he lie unprotesting for eternity in a field closed to Negroes.

Catto, White, and a Whipper nephew, James Purnell, drafted a bereavement message on behalf of colored Philadelphia. They lamented the silencing of a voice "eloquent and uncompromising in behalf of equal rights," and the dying of a hope that Stevens "might live to see [us] entirely free." They resolved to grieve him "as a band of brothers."

* * *

THREE WEEKS after Ulysses Grant's election in 1868, Nesbit panicked again. He asked White to circulate another suffrage petition in vote-rich Philadelphia and put it "in the hands of friendly Congressmen." In Nesbit's phrase, Grant's win, however narrow, made the chances for "a suffrage Constitutional Amendment . . . so popular and so plausible that we should do all that is in our power."

One more thing, Nesbit said. This was not the streetcar bill; no votes in Congress could be gained by boasting that colored men wrote the words. He told White, "Let our friendly statesmen supply the form or wording of the Amendment."

Nesbit's letter arrived in November. White went to work. By December 7, the new petitions were in Washington and thank-you letters were arriving at Liberty Hall from Charles Sumner in the Senate and William Kelley in the House.

Congressman Kelley added flair to his note. He claimed to have personally sent the proposed wording for the Fifteenth Amendment that morning. Even as he was scribbling this note, he assured White, a single sentence was headed to the House printer: "The right of citizens of the United States to vote shall not be abridged on account of race, color, or previous condition of servitude."

Furthermore, Kelley had canvassed the corridors and believed the requisite two-thirds vote of the House and Senate was at last within reach.

Send more names when able, he wrote White. Send addresses. Kelley was coming up for reelection in 1870. Associating himself with Negro rights had already hurt him with white Philadelphia workingmen; he could only hope his colored friends would be voting soon. "I look to the proscribed citizens of my state to help me fight the battle," Kelley wrote to White, "and will, so far as I can, provide them with arms and ammunition."

As the amendment worked its way toward a vote, the National Convention of Colored Men met in Washington. Equal Rights Leaguers and others attended; New Jersey's contingent included William Catto; Pennsylvania sent Garnet, Nesbit, Bassett, Wears, Whipper, and Green. They heard Southern delegates admit that linking themselves to Northern Negroes might increase their perils back home; they wrangled over women's participation (a female delegate was seated amid loud hisses), and whether the word *colored* belonged in an organization's name, until Rev. Jabez Campbell of Philadelphia demanded to know why "a hundred subjects" were debated when he had come to Washington solely "to agitate the question of suffrage." Finally, they picked a man to address that issue with the House Judiciary Committee.

The man was Isaiah Wears—the short, intense barber who, by Bolivar's count, had never lost a debate. Wears spoke to the congressmen on a Saturday. He mentioned the founding fathers and the valor at Fort Wagner and Olustee. Then he took a new tack. Let there be "no more of this senseless twaddle" about Negroes being too ignorant to vote, when whites had "stupidly" elected men whose decisions had sparked the rebellion that nearly destroyed the nation. Nor about "giving" the right to vote; "as well might you propose to give us the right to the pavement or highway, to come or to go. . . . It is ours because it is yours. . . . It is one of the pursuits of happiness."

This was a bipartisan audience and Wears could hardly tout Republicans' interest in future votes from grateful Negroes. So he closed by observing that the country was moving, however slowly, toward rights for all, and as a consequence, no party could ever again claim power without embracing the promise of "political equality."

The congressmen lined up to wring his hand.

★ ★ ★

A FEW DAYS LATER, a last-minute disagreement flared in the Capitol. The Senate version said voting rights could not be denied on the basis of "race, color, nativity, property, education or creed." Without these specifics, the Radical essayist Theodore Tilton warned, poll taxes and literacy tests would proliferate. He predicted, "Southern States may invent a dozen cunning schemes to deny the Negro his franchise."

But the Senate's version rattled the House. California congressmen read the words as enfranchising sixty thousand immigrant Chinese laborers. If a man was not barred by "nativity . . . or creed," yellow and red men might vote. A newspaper predicted that every Indian in Oregon would vote Republican. In a Democrats' cartoon, a pigtailed Asian said, "chinaman vot-tee same as melican man"; an Indian shouted, "Ingen vote! plenty whiskey all time"—as a Negro lugged them both, muttering, "I 'spose we'se obliged to carry dese brudders." A Nevada congressman proposed language denying the ballot to pagans.

Colored leaders saw other holes in the amendment. There was no guarantee of a colored man's right to hold office. And the phrase "previous condition of servitude" stuck in craws. William Forten wrote to Sumner, "We cannot have this thrust to endless days in our faces that We are a *Race of Slaves*."

The splintering came at the worst possible time. Many Democrats had won congressional seats on a White-Man's Government pledge even as Grant took the presidency. The new Congress would take the oath in less than two weeks.

At this moment, the hottest of the hotheads stepped forward. Wendell Phillips, writing in the *National Anti-Slavery Standard*, said the Senate's Radicals needed to cool off. Concerns about poll taxes, literacy tests, and nativity were legitimate, he said, but would have to wait for another day. So would Chinese and Indian men.

So would women. When women's suffrage petitions bearing thousands of names landed in the Capitol, one congressman set off laughter on the House floor by suggesting the Post Office Committee handle it, since the matter involved "males."

Confining the amendment to race infuriated women's suffrage leaders. Elizabeth Cady Stanton envisioned white women pushed aside by the lowly. "Think of Patrick and Sambo and Hans and Ung Tung," she wrote, "who do not know the difference between a Monarchy and a Republic, who never read the Declaration of Independence . . . making laws for Lydia Maria Child, Lucretia Mott, or Fanny Kemble."

But time was running out. If the Senate's version was accepted, Wendell Phillips said, legislators in California and Nevada would never vote for it, ruining its chances for ratification. Senators would have their highminded wording—and the Fifteenth Amendment would die. "For the first time in our lives," Phillips wrote, "we beseech them to be a little more *politicians*—and a little less reformers."

His essay was published February 20, 1869. Six days later, the House and Senate approved the shorter, simpler version. A Senate leader told Phillips: "Men thought that if you, the extremest Radical, could support the House proposition, then they might do the same."

William Kelley smiled beneath his lustrous mustache. "Party expediency and exact justice coincide," he said, "for once."

* * *

ALL THAT REMAINED was for three-fourths of state legislatures to ratify. Grant helped by announcing at his inauguration that he was all for ratification. New England states ratified; then New York. Pennsylvania, home to Charles Buckalew, William McMullen, and Samuel Randall, was seen as a more difficult proposition.

In Philadelphia, Catto read Wears's "no more twaddle" speech. Wears had done well, leaving congressmen with a memorable example of a discerning Negro voter. Catto and Henry Minton asked Wears to put the speech in the hands of their old Erie friend.

Wears sent the speech to Morrow Lowry, the legislator whose emotional speeches and steadfast support had been crucial to the streetcar bill. Wears added a note saying he had done so at the urging of Catto and Minton, "fellow sufferers with me in oppression." By the middle of March, the excitable Lowry was reading Wears's speech aloud to the state Senate. The more Lowry read, the more he became enthralled with the moment. He described it to Wears as the first time that "your race had had an opportunity to be heard . . . on the floor of the Pennsylvania Senate."

Ten days later, the legislature voted to ratify the Fifteenth Amendment. Democrats denounced the outcome as an intrusion on states rights, "an outrage upon every citizen."

* * *

A NOVEL TASK confronted Grant in his first months in office—encourage an entire race to get in the Republican fold and stay there. He wanted to give a prominent post to a Negro. This was a tricky business; indeed, Robert Purvis had decided a "trick" was afoot when Andrew Johnson's aide asked Purvis whether he wanted a federal post. But that was Johnson; Grant was different. The ambassadorship to Haiti needed filling. There was talk that the president would ask Frederick Douglass.

Douglass had led Union enlistment drives and enjoyed transatlantic renown. But he had risked Republican fortunes by stubbornly parading to the 1866 convention against party elders' wishes. Nominating him would thrill Negroes—and cost Grant white votes. Meanwhile, Martin Delany was angling for an embassy. He wanted to go to Liberia.

For the Haitian post, Grant looked instead to a lesser-known Negro, with credentials as an equal-rights man and educator. Not to mention, ties in states the party needed, Pennsylvania and Connecticut. And West Indian roots—that would go over well.

★ ★ ★

THE I.C.Y.'S MANAGERS had just heard the latest statistics about the student body (218) and average daily attendance (198.87) when Principal Bassett ignited his bombshell.

Grant was nominating him ambassador to Haiti, Bassett reported, and "from information received from Washington," the Senate was likely to confirm him. He was about to become the first man of color to represent the United States abroad.

Bassett had led the school since the bleak midpoint of the 1850s when, in the managers' euphemistic words, "there existed . . . a strong prejudice against the intellectual and material improvement of the Negro Race and it was necessary in the management of the work to avoid as much as possible giving offence to those who might by their factious opposition have rendered the prosecution of the undertaking more difficult."

To be sure, Bassett had regularly unnerved the managers by inviting a Douglass or a Garnet to deliver a fiery lecture. But under his care the Negroes-teaching-Negroes experiment had grown into a triumph. Alumni taught in New York, New Jersey, and Pennsylvania and in the "freedom schools" of the South. On Shippen Street, visitors streamed through classrooms at the rate of thirty a week. After a two-day visit, a New York reporter described boys and girls ages twelve to nineteen "rigidly examined" in Greek and geometry, Virgil and Horace; he heard them discuss Congress and the Caesars and concluded that they "understood and knew what they recited" and that "they had not been drilled parrot-like for a public show." The school, he wrote, proved the Negro's case for "complete political enfranchisement."

Now, the school needed a new leader. The two top teachers applied. Fanny Jackson, head of the Girls Department, had impressed the board since her arrival. She visited "Normal Schools" that trained teachers and launched special lessons for I.C.Y. pupils aspiring to teach. She had a college degree. She did not pester the managers periodically for raises. Her name was in the newspapers now and again, but for accomplishments in the classroom. Catto tended to turn up in news of extracurricular causes, however noble-minded, such as the Banneker Institute or the Equal Rights League. Or baseball.

The managers chose Jackson.

The ailing chairman, Alfred Cope, wrote to Catto in a shaky hand. "My esteemed friend," he began and proceeded to offer a devout Quaker's version of a dressing-down. Consider our situation, he wrote. You are our assistant principal these past ten years. What if, "at any time within the period of thy engagement," Bassett had taken ill or died suddenly? "I feel a good deal of regret that . . . thou has not kept thyself somewhat fresh in all those branches which are allotted to the station of Principal."

Furthermore, he said, the school had climbed so far uphill that the slim credentials a young Bassett or Catto presented in the 1850s no longer sufficed. "I think thou will see on reflection, that if the school had occupied its present advanced position at the time when EDB became Principal we could not have placed him at the head of the Institute."

His letter to Catto ended: "We all I believe have a high appreciation of thy services to the Instn & shall be glad to do whatever we can to promote thy welfare."

The managers liked orderly transitions and even devised a rule: minimum three months' notice for such exits by the school's leaders. But Bassett would be leaving soon. The board had to act. They made the choice of Fanny Jackson official on May 11, 1869.

That day, Catto began drafting a letter of his own. He wrote to the head of public schools of Brooklyn, twice using the word *immediately*. He mentioned having applied for a job there in 1862. "You may not have entirely forgotten me," Catto wrote.

He had heard that a colored Brooklyn school needed a "Principal Teacher" at a salary of sixteen hundred dollars; "Please consider me an applicant and let me know if I should come on immediately."

What survives is merely a draft and gives no clue whether Catto ever mailed it. The managers raised his pay again, to twelve hundred dollars, the same as Jackson's. His new title was head of the Boys Department. He stayed at the I.C.Y.

Within a month he was back on familiar subjects—addressing a colored audience after a Memorial Day parade, honoring the 339 colored war dead in the low flat earth of Lebanon Cemetery. He and two other speakers reminded everyone that the soldiers had died not only for the Union but for "citizenship," and that fight was raging yet.

★ ★ ★

RATIFYING A CONSTITUTIONAL AMENDMENT was long and slow. Anticipation grew. The *Christian Recorder* led colored readers in a national debate about how to mark the event. "Our Jubilee," a headline said. "What Shall It Be?"

Cornets should sound in each state and territory "at the same hour, so that it will be a united thing," an Indianapolis reader wrote. He suggested fall or spring, since Western farmers were in their fields all summer, and in winter hated leaving home. But rice and cotton growers were busy planting in spring, a man in Georgetown, South Carolina, replied. "Numbers of us, carpet baggers, have long since cast our votes in the legislative halls of the South, for the ratification of the 15th Amendment" and ought to be included.

Before signing "Yours for Equal Rights," the writer offered an intelligence report. "In the old Palmetto State we are enjoying some of the blessing of Reconstruction. Politics at present with us, are somewhat easy; but the under current has its regular tide."

John W. Alvord, head of education for the Freedmen's Bureau, was inspecting Kentucky schools when a rumor flew that the amendment had finally become law. Alvord had other concerns just then.

"The past twenty-four hours have been in the midst of 'ku-klux,'" he wrote on January 31, 1870. "They were out in force on the road as we returned from Berea to Richmond. Three colored men were taken from their beds, cruelly whipped, dragged over the flinty road, until, with bodies lacerated and torn, it is doubtful if they can recover. These were leading men, and the outrage evidently was to deter them and friends from any attempt at political effort or influence."

With each "outrage," Alvord, who was white, grew more convinced of the need for federal protections of colored rights. In one hotel, a man demanded of him, "Is Congress going to set the niggers to voting?"

Why, yes, Alvord thought to himself. And not a minute too soon.

* * *

IN PHILADELPHIA, the Fifteenth Amendment added to McMullen's wagonload of woes. Reformers were prying into his political organization. The new fire department was squashing the volunteer companies. A federal agent was sniffing around the operations of the "Whiskey Ring." The state's new voter registry law was aimed, daggerlike, at his Democrats. And now the Negroes would be lining up to vote Republican.

McMullen began addressing these concerns.

The notion of "bosses" ruling the cities was just then rearing its head in newspapers, magazines, and the national imagination. Readers clucked their tongues at stories of grafters in the gas rings and whiskey rings, of Boss Tweed in New York or the Squire in Philadelphia. "Alderman McMullin and His Operations; 'Repeaters,'" a headline in the *Chicago Daily Tribune* announced. The reporter saw men sneak from poll to poll, offer bogus proofs of domicile, and vote again and again. To get this story he had made a beeline to the Fourth Ward, "knowing Alderman McMullin to be a ruling power in the ward." And that was in 1869, one of the quieter elections.

For its annual banquet, the Moyamensing Hose rented the Academy of Music and sold tickets for a staggering five dollars. Politicians and lawyers crammed the hall. They gave McMullen a jeweled pin worth twenty-five hundred dollars, and a gold tobacco box inlaid with diamonds. His sometimes-rival, Lewis Cassidy, said English was "too poor to give utterance to the deep emotions" the city held in its heart for the Squire. Glasses were lifted, anthems sung, and the stage cleared for the entertainment. *No. 27 Promenade L'Africaine* was a skit about the Negroes; actors strutted in high hats, fancy dress, and blackface.

In an era of curvaceous language, McMullen wrote in straight lines. In letters to Samuel Randall, his man in Congress, he would "coraspond" about "wholes" that needed filling, or "Constituants" who were "sorly" in need of "Publick" work. But he made himself clear. "Fix this for me" or, "We had it fixed" or, "We have enemies to punish." People rarely mistook his intentions.

* * *

AT MIDDAY on a Monday in September 1869, U.S. revenue agent James J. Brooks was examining records in a liquor store on Front Street, near the Delaware River. He was easy to spot by his short stature and prematurely white hair. Three young men ambled in and nonchalantly stood around. One pulled out a pistol, another a blackjack. Passersby heard gunfire. Brooks fell, bleeding from a bruise on his temple and a bullet in his lungs.

His attackers ran to a waiting carriage. Detective Edward K. Tryon saw them. Traffic stopped as the big policeman barreled after the would-be assassins. But Tryon had put on weight since his army days and the carriage rushed off, its curtains drawn.

Americans had heard of notorious men running "whiskey rings," but as Brooks put it, few realized "that *murder* was a word in their vocabulary." Mayor Fox posted a thousand-dollar reward for information in the case. An additional five thousand dollars was posted by the new U.S. marshal in town—Edgar Gregory, coming off his stormy Southern tenure as a Freedmen's Bureau official.

The case Brooks had been investigating was rife with politics and lucre. Grant's Republican administration was intent on paying down the war debt, in part by taxing unlicensed liquor. In Philadelphia this trade was mostly in Democratic hands and relied on outlaw distilleries in Kensington. Temperance drives had hardly dented demand; when a nighttime fire engulfed a six-story whiskey warehouse in 1869, people told of seeing fellow Philadelphians scoop liquor from the gutters with every available container.

By Brooks's account, the ring had offered his superior a thousand dollars a week to take him off the case. The ring was said to have friends in the courts and Congress.

Brooks recovered from his wounds, won a promotion, and claimed the distinction of being the first federal agent targeted by paid assassins. His chief assailant, Hugh Morrow, eventually confessed, insisting he had meant only to injure Brooks. Morrow said he had received only five dollars of the two hundred dollars he had been promised. He and a second man were sentenced to seven years but were freed after two and a half with McMullen's aid. He had also testified at their trials, claiming neither defendant was anywhere near the scene of Brooks's shooting.

Both men were members of the Moya Hose. Morrow said he was recruited for the Brooks attempt at Devitt's, the tavern next door to the hose company and the regular haunt of its men. A young Moya member, Frank Kelly, tended bar there; so did Morrow. Morrow said the shooters had help—the carriage driver, the resident who hid them on Eighth Street, others who helped them slip away to New York under assumed names.

He kept dropping hints about who had ordered the shooting. Brooks secured a prison-cell interview and asked, blandly, why Morrow had shot him.

Morrow said someone had threatened him with jail—which in Philadelphia was a prerogative of aldermen. "With that threat hanging over me and maddened by rum, I would do anything I was told to," he said. He mentioned "the Squire" twice without saying his name. ("I asked the Squire to get me a job.")

Brooks asked where he had gone to school. Morrow said the public school at Tenth and Fitzwater, two blocks south of South Street. Then he added, with no prompting: "Many is the time that I have heard that old Moyamensing Hose bell ring there, and when that rang the boys all scampered out of school. . . . That hose company has been the ruin of a good many." The stenographer noted that Morrow said this with "emphasis."

The other Moya Hose man implicated in the Brooks shooting had been stabbed to death—disemboweled, actually, with a straight razor soon after coming out of prison. Brooks asked whether Morrow wasn't risking the same fate by talking.

Morrow smiled. "With a club in my hand I will go among the whole gang armed with pistols. There is not one of them that dare fire." He seemed to enjoy this idea the more he spoke of it. "With a good club in my hand, I would go."

* * *

THE NEW REGISTRY LAW allotted three "canvassers" to each of the myriad voting districts in each Philadelphia ward. The canvassers could make all the difference: They registered new voters. Who would choose these choosers? The aldermen. McMullen was an alderman, but most aldermen were Republicans. Even reformers suspected the registry law was a Trojan horse filled with Republican loyalists.

A different man might have filed suit. McMullen spoke a warning. Any effort to march an all-Republican column of canvassers into the Fourth Ward would encounter physical force at the polls. "We will crowd the place with men," McMullen promised; "you will have club law there on Election Day."

The Republicans compromised. The three canvassers in each district would include at least one Democrat. With that deal done, only one item on McMullen's list of headaches stood unresolved. That was the Fifteenth Amendment.

★ ★ ★

ON A FRIDAY NIGHT in April 1870, Negro men and women from the northern wards filled the Berks Street ice rink. The weather was warm and they were not there for skating. Ten days remained before the parade to celebrate the Fifteenth Amendment. People needed to go over the order of march. No one knew how whites would react to a colored voting-rights parade in Philadelphia; there had never been one before.

The meeting's leaders, Catto and Wears, also spoke of an event months away, the October 1870 elections. People heard the urgency in their voices. "... *impress upon you the necessity of casting your votes on the Republican side.*" They said it more than once.

They read a letter from Congressman Myers, congratulating them on winning the ballot, and not incidentally congratulating himself and other Radical Republicans for getting the amendment pushed through Congress. Myers was up for reelection.

This was new territory for everyone. Decades of petitions and prayers were giving way, in a flash, to colder considerations about wielding power. Little wonder Nesbit and White were convening a Pennsylvania State Equal Rights League meeting in May on the topic "Changing the Character of the League . . . for political purposes." Republicans in Congress had delivered. On election day, the party would see if these new voters returned the favor.

Other wards met over the next few nights. Liberty Hall thumped with traffic; Catto led a meeting of his Fourth Ward colored political club in one room while the Seventh Ward met in another. The parade was to begin at one o'clock on a Tuesday afternoon. Planners asked merchants to close shops, ministers to open doors for an "appropriate" 9:00 A.M. sermon. Tickets for the evening gala at Horticultural Hall went on sale at Morris Brown Jr.'s cigar store, Bolivar's mother's house, and David Bowser's studio.

At the I.C.Y., Fanny Jackson persuaded the managers to cancel classes on April 26, "that being the day appointed to all the colored people of this city for a public celebration of the ratification of the 15th Amendment."

Three thousand Negroes marched in Boston, led by veterans of the Fifty-fourth Massachusetts regiment. Detroit marchers carried portraits of Lincoln, Grant, and John Brown and sang, "The ballot box has come, now let us all prepare to vote, with the party that made us free." In Baltimore, a wagon was fitted out with a printing press that continually inked fresh copies of the amendment as the procession moved through the streets.

In Philadelphia, people gathered at the stepping-off point at Race Street. New Jerseyans and New Yorkers arrived on the Camden-Amboy ferry and rode streetcars to Broad Street stops. Contingents formed— Odd Fellows, temperance clubs, Bannekers. Frederick Douglass rode in a barouche. Twelve bands' cornets twinkled in the sun. A wagon bore a banner recalling Fort Pillow. The Hod Carriers and Laborers Association, one of the nation's first colored unions, hoisted a pennant that pointed ahead—"U.S. Grant, Our Choice for President in 1872."

Another banner said, "BABYLON IS FALLEN TO RISE NO MORE—Catto Equal Rights League of Bridgeton, N.J." The Fourteenth Ward colored club lugged a giant portrait of William Kelley, "Friend of the Colored Man." Others hoisted pictures of Douglass, Lincoln, Wendell Phillips, John Brown, and Thaddeus Stevens. Five men walked abreast, each holding a shield with a large letter on it. The letters were G-R-A-N-T.

On Broad Street, white Republican dignitaries lined the balustrades of the Union League's new home. The lawyer Charles Gibbons welcomed colored men into the electorate by presenting Catto with a ceremonial silk flag showing a Negro soldier, hand in hand with a white man.

Catto spoke briefly. "The black man knows on which side of the line to vote. He not only reads, but he remembers; and, what is better still— He *thinks*."

One sentence was widely quoted—"The black man knows on which side . . ." Taken alone, the words sounded as if colored men were doing as they were told. But Catto laid down conditions: *So long as* the party upholds certain principles, we will stand for the party "that has throttled slavery; crushed the rebellion [and] reconstructed the South . . . so long as it is true to those principles which know no East, no West, no North, no South; no white man's government nor black man's country—but one destiny for all."

By then, thousands of people, white and black, lined the parade route. Along Lombard, colored homes "looked lively," a white witness said. Residents were "out of doors looking happy and important, and displaying rosettes and miniature flags."

At Ninth Street, the procession passed under an arch of evergreens fashioned by neighborhood women. Moving close to Moyamensing, the parade passed a tavern pointedly draped in mourning. Young colored men greeted it with razzing, mocking shouts. Epithets rained down from windows. As the parade turned north on Fifth, things got worse.

Knots of white boys and men shouted curses and slurs. Some threw stones. Rotten vegetables began to fly. "A crowd of roughs" opened up with a supply of putrid eggs, aiming at the portrait of William Kelley. They kept throwing "till the banner was ruined," the *Press* said, "and not a policeman was about to prevent such outrageous proceedings."

Marchers heard shots. People gasped and looked about but marched on to Horticultural Hall. Inside, Rev. William Alston led prayers. Jake White read President Grant's congratulatory letter. Seats on the speaker's platform filled with dignitaries and old-timers, colored and white—Passmore Williamson, David Bowser, Rev. Benjamin Tanner, Stephen Smith, and William Whipper, who could now look forward to voting with his nephews.

Catto stood up and read off the resolutions of thanks that he and White and Tanner had prepared, thanking the "martyrs and apostles," as well as God and the Republicans, for their contributions to the struggle for suffrage.

Purvis, raspy-voiced after five hours' parading, worked his way around the edges of saying whom to vote for and against. "I know you will never forget the bridge that has carried you over to freedom, and as a fitting corollary, you will never forget your enemies—those who prate of this as a white man's government."

He said, "My voice has broken" and closed by asking that the salute to antislavery societies, equal rights leagues, and other "apostles of liberty" be amended to honor the bonneted figure on the platform. Applause erupted at this mention of Lucretia Mott.

Shouts went up—*Douglass! Douglass!*—and the best-known colored man in America was borne forth to the platform as if by ocean wave. Douglass made his usual lament about having no speech prepared and then launched an oration. How many times, he said, had they heard predictions that the race would founder in freedom, thin out, die off? That was now disproven. Douglass looked at packed galleries and said, "I never saw so many Negroes in my life." Men laughed and cheered.

He inflicted the usual hurts on his fellow speakers—dismissing the "hackneyed cant about thanking God for this deliverance," deriding calls for loyalty to the party he had campaigned for. "Each voter must decide what men and measures will be best."

Douglass said he, too, had heard the usual insults and epithets along the parade. But he said an unfamiliar feeling had overtaken him. He felt safe. The Fifteenth Amendment "seemed to shield me," Douglass said, "as the hide of a rhinoceros."

Beneath the din, men nodded at each other as if to say *He's right,* and *That's it.*

* * *

AT THAT HOUR, the rhinoceros hide was being tested in another part of town. Colored marchers who had not bought tickets to the ball were heading home. The Twenty-fourth and Twenty-seventh ward clubs were trudging toward the Schuylkill's Chestnut Street bridge when whites came after them. The *Public Ledger* described "stones and bricks thrown in profusion." A colored woman was hit as she stepped from a streetcar. So was a little boy.

Someone ran to the nearest station house. Newspapers said the worst violence was imminent when the chief of police arrived with fifty officers and began making arrests.

Meanwhile, an army from Francis P. Henry, Caterer, invaded Horticultural Hall. Waiters offered baked shad and halibut, oysters fried or "stewed & pann'd," beef, chicken, corned beef, lamb with mint sauce, chicken salad, sweet potatoes, white potatoes, spinach and boiled onions; cake and ice cream—chocolate, vanilla, strawberry, lemon—macaroons, lady fingers, pound cake, calf's-foot jelly, raisins, apples and nuts. Diners needed strength. They had marched five miles, and the dancing had not begun yet.

The Excelsior Orchestra struck its first notes at midnight. The last dancers were still on their feet at twenty minutes to four.

* * *

WITH THE FIFTEENTH AMENDMENT'S ratification, some longtime allies decided the work was done. Old abolition groups dissolved; the *National Anti-Slavery Standard* changed its name to the *Standard*. The Philadelphia Female Anti-Slavery Society convened a final meeting. Mary Grew read her thirty-sixth annual report, reciting the rescue of Jane Johnson, the jailing of Passmore Williamson, the fugitive trial of Daniel Webster, the burning of Pennsylvania Hall. Now was the final triumph, the amending of the Constitution to give "equal rights to all." Amid applause, the meeting approved a motion to disband.

For some colored leaders, the temptation to swagger was almost irresistible. High Republican priests were beating a path to their door, offering silk flags and federal appointments. John Mercer Langston accepted a seat on the Washington board of health—and a law professorship at Howard University, the Negro college Congress had chartered. President Grant was said to be considering Catto for a diplomatic post.

Catto embarked on a splurge in the months after the parade. He put down $500 on a $950 share of Liberty Hall, making him a partner with Whipper, Stephen Smith, and others. He ran up a bill of $113.75 for a jacket, shirt, pants, gloves, vest, and overcoat at the popular new clothier on Chestnut Street, John Wanamaker. He sat for a photograph.

In the photograph, Catto wears a white shirt, bow tie and vest, and a dark coat with an elegant lapel. He appears to sit up straight for the camera and looks a few degrees to one side, as if focused on a visitor or the horizon. His hair is neatly cropped and starting to recede. He looks into the distance with a resolute, almost somber gaze, belied ever so slightly by a turning-up at the corners of his mouth, which, were it not for the mustache's downward droop, might evince mirth. It is possible to imagine that a friend, keeping Catto company at the sitting, was trying hard not to make him laugh.

Catto paid for a membership in the Franklin Institute—signaling the end of the rule that had stopped Charlotte Forten's father (but not his telescope) and every other Negro who tried to enter the museum in its first half-century. A public stir ensued. The dean of Jefferson Medical College, the chemist B. Howard Rand, said he would cancel his lecture at the museum if Negroes were admitted. The museum board stood firm. Rand canceled.

Other cultural institutions kept old rules. The Academy of Music barred a colored lecturer—Hiram R. Revels of Mississippi, the first Negro in the U.S. Senate. The academy board deemed it "inexpedient" to let a Negro speak there.

★ ★ ★

THE SEATS in the main second-floor I.C.Y. lecture room faced North. In the summer of 1870, the man who had fallen short in his bid to run the school was looking South.

Catto had called on pupils to go South and teach the freedmen. He had yet to do it himself. He was said to have made a summer trip across Virginia at Republicans' request, stumping for the state's belated ratification of the Fourteenth Amendment and its guarantees of citizenship. He stayed in touch with Wormley in Washington, where the population of freedmen's school-age children was approaching ten thousand. Wormley, rising in the ranks of colored Republicans, served on the board for the district's struggling colored schools.

Those schools were in need of a superintendent and a new curriculum. Wormley and other men on the board beseeched Catto to apply.

Superintendent. Catto dipped pen in ink and wrote the word out. He would be in charge of educating thousands born—as he was—in states that outlawed colored learning.

He asked the I.C.Y. managers to let him resign and go to Washington. He needed them to waive the three-months'-notice rule. His query triggered two meetings in August, a time when anyone with the means left the sweltering city. The managers began looking for a replacement but said if no one suitable was found, Catto's request would be denied.

Just then, he received mail from Washington. The letter threatened harm to him if he took the job. Catto asked for advice from John T. Johnson, a Wormley ally and long-time colored Washington leader.

Johnson said the threats came from colored men who had "sold themselves body and soul to the Devil & the Democratic party." He described them as "desperate" to stop Catto and others from taking over the schools. Johnson begged Catto to take the job and vowed that Catto's Washington allies would protect him in any "wars."

The I.C.Y. fall semester had nearly arrived and Catto's future lingered unresolved. Finally, he relented—and trimmed his request to a leave of absence. If the managers gave him thirty days in Washington, he would endeavor to write a curriculum there. He assured them he had never intended to cause problems for the school he'd been associated with, as student and teacher, for more than half his life.

The managers gave him the thirty days and named a temporary replacement. The new man brought a luster of his own—Richard Greener was Harvard's first Negro graduate.

Great enthusiasm greeted Catto's arrival in Washington—helped, no doubt, by the presence of at least five I.C.Y. alumni among the city's colored teachers. They included recent graduates as well as experienced educators such as Sallie Daffin. The burning of her Tennessee school had not caused her to stop teaching freedmen.

In thirty days, Catto assembled a new curriculum that went on for a dozen pages. He itemized the textbooks to use in each grade and broke down topics into segments for every age. His curriculum included reading, writing, arithmetic, history, and government. There was sowing, planting, and harvesting as well as "bill-making and receipt-writing." In geography class, students would learn "Asia, Africa and Oceanica," as well as the "solar system." Also to be taught were "morals and manner" for younger children, including teaching "Gratitude, truthfulness, kindness, neatness, politeness."

One clue to his brief tenure in Washington was a letter sent home to Jake White, begging White to advance him a few dollars and to see a certain tailor about a desperately needed jacket and a pair of pants. Catto added: Give my love "to the fellows."

His curriculum was still in place a few years later. School officials called it a life raft that carried them from years of chaos to the arrival of a permanent superintendent.

★   ★   ★

BY ELECTION DAY in 1870, Theodore Tilton's prediction about Southern states blocking the path to the polls was proven wrong in one regard: He did not include the North.

The Democratic newspaper in Newark, New Jersey, asked able-bodied party men to stand at polls and demand Negroes' identity papers. In California, the Los Angeles county clerk simply refused to register Negroes. Maryland Democrats drafted an elaborate registration law that would, "if passed, greatly hinder" colored voting. "All that can will be done to keep them from the polls or from voting, unless they can be induced to go with the Democracy," a Baltimore correspondent wrote. "Trouble looms ahead in this matter."

Tennessee enacted a poll tax. Virginia enforced a poll tax and trimmed the number of polls in colored precincts. In Delaware, the New Castle County tax collector stopped collecting Negroes' taxes, depriving men of the tax bill they needed to register as voters. When men tried to stop him in the street to pay their taxes, he walked away.

The Democratic daily in Chambersburg, Pennsylvania, warned that Negroes "emboldened" by the ballot would invade the legislature, the jury box, the judiciary, and inevitably, the bedroom. "They will demand entrance into your family circles. Amalgamation will be written on Radical banners. . . . Now is the time to frustrate their plans. As white men, cast your votes with the White Man's Party for the White Man's ticket."

California's Democratic former lieutenant governor wrote an editorial predicting that the Fifteenth Amendment would give Republicans "one darkey vote for every ten decent Republicans that will leave it forever." At the other end of the country, McMullen let it be known that Philadelphia Negroes could be turned Democratic by "a drink of rum."

McMullen's organization exuded a smacking confidence as election day approached. Sam Randall needed to be reelected to Congress; a Democratic loyalist told him the Republican challenger "labors under the hallucination that the Nigger vote will give his party a chance in the first district." Another party man wrote, "If it were not for the Negroes, we would have everything our way."

★ ★ ★

A WEEK BEFORE the October election, the Pennsylvania State Equal Rights League issued a broadside. Remember those who "mobbed us" and tried to ship us to tropic climes, Jake White and the other officers implored. Remember those who took away our fragile franchise in 1838, and those who helped us get it back. VOTE EARLY, the broadside shouted.

Isaiah Wears had made it simple at a William Kelley campaign meeting three days later: "Go to the polls on Tuesday next and vote the Republican ticket."

White Democrats awoke to discover colored men in line at the polls. Many had stood since four in the morning. In the block-long line at Sixth and Lombard, "Every one was elated" and many clutched Republican tickets. But as the poll opened at seven, a dozen policemen arrived. A lieutenant named Haggerty led them. Some removed the identifying numbers from their cylinder-shaped City of Philadelphia caps.

The police began challenging colored men or shoving them aside while whites voted. One officer, "a big, burly fellow," blocked the way like a stingy doorman. Those who complained were arrested, as was a white Republican poll watcher. Billy clubs came out.

A few blocks away, McMullen nudged a colored man in line at a Fourth Ward poll. The man, Thomas Hall, stood fast. McMullen pushed again. Hall punched him. Then, realizing the gravity of what he had done and whom he had hit, Hall bolted to a police station in another ward. His encounter with the famous alderman was astonishing enough to land in the *New York Times.* McMullen saw him later and said, "Give me your hand, because I respect you as the first black man not to show fear in my presence." Hall was said to reply that he was defending "a principle," even if it cost him his life.

By midday, people were pouring into U.S. Marshal Gregory's office and describing the scene at Sixth and Lombard. One witness counted a half-dozen heads cut open, one by "four different clubs." A newspaper said the police "were actually rioting." Gregory sent word to Mayor Fox, who assured him the city was at peace. But more reports reached Gregory—police were arresting his deputy marshals.

Using the Enforcement Act as his authority for protecting voters, he summoned fifty marines from the Navy Yard. Fox cabled the governor to report an unlawful army, "muskets and bayonets fixed, parading our streets." He demanded "instant disbandment of this armed force." He was too late. The marines were already taking up positions at the voting window to the roll of drums and the cheers of colored onlookers.

The votes were tallied: Congressman Randall survived a scare, Congressman Kelley won, and McMullen's Democrats found themselves in an unusual position at the end of an election day—out-organized and outgunned.

But not outflanked. Across the Delaware, in New Jersey's election four weeks later, white "roughs" swarmed Negroes who had lined up early to vote in Camden County. A constable who led this mob shouted at mid-morning that "the damned niggers" had voted long enough. Truncheons swung, pistols fired, and a chair came down on the head of a Negro; he died ten days later. At nightfall the mob smashed the ballot box.

Colored voters in Camden also found Philadelphia police "crowded around the polls"—and at the ferries, arresting "unoffending colored men" as if commuting to Camden on election day were a crime in itself. One of those arrested was a young Camden teacher, William Armstead, a recent graduate of the I.C.Y.

Two policemen seized Armstead on a Philadelphia wharf for possessing a deadly weapon—a penknife. At a station house, as police stood about, someone clubbed him so hard that he fell to the floor and "blood flowed freely" from his head.

Federal authorities charged twenty-three men with violating the Fifteenth Amendment. No one was shocked that four were identified in court as Philadelphia policemen, including a lieutenant. The *Press* headline was "The Police Again."

*   *   *

IN LATE NOVEMBER, a state senator named W. W. Watt sickened and died. His district included the Fourth Ward and most of the city's colored population. Republicans doubly lamented Watt's demise because it jeopardized the party's one-vote edge in the state senate. Having barely caught their breaths from the drama of the October vote, both parties tensed for a December 20 special election to fill Watt's seat.

Getting him elected had been traumatic enough. A judge heard evidence that twenty-six "repeaters" from the Tweed organization in New York City had slipped into town to vote for his Democratic opponent. Watt had won—and that was before the Fifteenth Amendment changed the arithmetic. Several thousand voting-age colored men of Watt's district had had their mettle tested in the October election. They felt their oats.

The city Republican Committee had a man in mind for Watt's seat—former city controller Joseph R. Lyndall.

Some colored voters wanted a colored candidate—Catto. Newspapers reported that colored Republicans met and voted a resolution calling for his candidacy. But some Republicans said that was a lie, another Democratic plot to divide the party. One black Republican wrote a letter to the editor saying the meeting never happened, the Catto push was not real, and colored men should vote for Lyndall.

Catto put a statement in the newspaper. His name, he said, "to a greater extent than I either desired or expected," was being touted as a candidate, and "[I must] disavow all participation in . . . such an unwise and impolitic step. I understand that some of my friends have been led to believe that my name will be presented for their suffrages.

"On the contrary, I would urge every friend of mine . . . to work diligently and persistently" to elect the party's chosen nominee. He had helped lead a Lyndall rally at Liberty Hall and called him "a true and tried friend" of the race whose election would "secure the district and control the legislature."

Lyndall lost, but no could blame Catto. He had put the party's interest first. They would remember such a thing if, say, a man ran for office later in his life.

Steps Catto took in the next few months had that feel—the feel of a public man, building up his credentials. He joined the Fifth Brigade, a new National Guard unit comprised of colored men—mostly men he knew, such as the Pythian Raymond Burr—and led by Louis Wagner, the former commander of Camp William Penn. The brigade's peacetime duties were chiefly ceremonial, but they drilled to be ready for civil disorders. Serving in the Guard was prestigious. Men were outfitted in Union blue and had to get their own guns. Ranks and titles were assigned. The *New York Times*' "Military Affairs" column mentioned the formation of the brigade and Catto's being named a major.

★ ★ ★

SOME DEMOCRATS made overtures to the Negroes. School officials were about to rename the Bird school for a white party elder, Lewis Cassidy. Colored residents objected. Cassidy took their side, and the school was renamed for James Forten.

Other Democrats could not stomach this new arrangement. Colored voting, colored men clamoring for office; Republicans at every level, from the station house to the White House, groveling before "this black God of their idolatry," as a Democratic legislator said. Men talked of Frederick Douglass's getting a federal post. William G. Armstrong, a Philadelphia bank-note engraver, tried to digest a lesser morsel of Washington news: Congress had fired a white messenger "to give a *nigger* his place."

A mayoral election was approaching, a bigger contest for the city's fortunes than the 1870 races. Daniel Fox declined to run again. Democrats nominated an unexciting party man, James Biddle; Republicans rallied behind the leader of the fight for a modernized fire department—City Council president William Stokley. This large man had made his living selling candy, causing people to dub him Sweet William. He had appealed to new Negro voters by promising to strip the police force of Mayor Fox's rogues. For this, Sweet William had the enmity of the Squire.

The stakes were clear. More than five thousand colored men of voting age lived in the city. If Stokley could capture their votes, he would probably win.

McMullen sent out fresh signals. He announced a Moyamensing Hose parade, and led 250 men across South Philadelphia. Though it did not match the five-mile route of the colored voting-rights parade, bands played, children cheered, and everyone behaved as if the move to a modern fire department were a nonbinding resolution, not a city law. The men of Company No. 27 marched in newly purchased scarlet shirts and black pantaloons.

Armstrong, the Democratic bank note engraver, was privy to talk within the party as the election drew near. "The Fourth Ward ring," he wrote cryptically, had come up with a plan to deal with the "Nigger vote."

★ ★ ★

CATTO NARROWED his attentions in September to the I.C.Y. and the election. The only exception was the dedication of the Lincoln statue on a hill in Fairmount Park. He led Fifth Brigade members in the long line of march, sporting crisp blue uniforms in a bright sun. The Pythians played twice that month and Catto missed both games.

At 5:30 P.M. on Monday of the week before election day, clerks and canvassers at ward offices across the city were poring over the voter registry books when dozens of men burst in, shouting orders and waving weapons. They wrestled the stiff-backed books away from the clerks. Some intruders were recognized as the same men who had shoved Negroes out of voting lines the year before; others were policemen "in citizens' clothes," including a lieutenant. A clerk who resisted them was arrested for assault; another was cut on the stomach and arms. Newspapers decried the hijacking of voter lists amid "the click of pistols and the gleam of knives."

Colored ward clubs met at night to go over instructions. At Liberty Hall, Purvis pointed out that Democrats had made themselves "the white man's party"; Wears reminded everyone that Republicans, however flawed, had emancipated the slaves. At nearby Union Hall, a meeting of white and colored Republicans ended early when rock-throwing whites broke windows and barged in. Police took no action.

Between seven and eight on the night before the election, a colored stevedore left his home on Russell Street, just below Shippen. Jacob Gordon was said to have headed out to buy, of all things, a pair of shoes. At Eighth and Shippen, a hatless white man in dark clothes stepped from the shadows, chased Gordon for a few steps, and shot him twice. Witnesses said the white man fired once more at Gordon as he lay in the street. One witness got a look at the assailant in the light of a gas lamp.

Within an hour, whites set upon another Negro, a thirty-year-old Maryland laborer named Moses Wright, at the same spot. He, too, was shot as he lay in the street, suffering a flesh wound above the eye. He was expected to survive; Jacob Gordon was not. Thomas Fitzgerald's *Item* claimed one of Wright's attackers was heard moments earlier saying, "Let's shoot the first nigger that comes along. That will be one vote less."

Catto and other Banneker men gathered two blocks away in Brown's cigar store. Bolivar came in. The news of the shootings had flown from house to house like an electric current. Men spoke in lowered voices.

McMullen's people had warned for weeks of a "free fight" at the polls. The colored men knew better than to expect much from the mayor. Even the publisher Fitzgerald had given speeches decrying "the worst caprices of a ruffianly police force." And witnesses were saying Jacob Gordon's attacker was a policeman out of uniform.

Nor could they expect marines to safeguard them this time. U.S. Marshal Gregory had run afoul of the governor by sending soldiers to the polls the year before. And Gregory, at age sixty-seven, was dying. An illness of the kidneys had put him in bed since September.

That left the all-colored Fifth Brigade—parade-trained but not accustomed to facing live ammunition or a mob. Catto possessed a rank, a uniform, and a saddle, but he had not yet purchased the requisite sidearm.

Catto looked at the other men and they at him. They had been friends since the Bird School and the "broils," the pews of First African Presbyterian, Mother Bethel, and St. Thomas, the complicated fortunes of the Pennsylvania State Equal Rights League. How many battles had they witnessed or waged together? The fugitive trials, the war, Emancipation, the literary congress, the Franklin Institute, the baseball leagues, the Army, the streetcars, the vote.

Now a battle was engulfing them.

The hour grew late. Catto announced that he was walking home. Directly home—notwithstanding the talk of danger along that short route. Tomorrow would be a long day if the most respected men showed fear.

Catto got a bit theatrical. Bolivar remembered his saying, "I would not stultify my manhood by going to my home in a roundabout way."

Then he said good night to his friends and headed for South Street.

CHAPTER 15

Election Day

THE SUN BEGAN climbing the sky at 6:07 A.M. Within twenty-five minutes, William McMullen was at the polls. They had not opened, but he had much to do. Things had not worked out so well last year.

For more than two decades, he had shinnied up the pole of political power, supporting those above him and holding onto those below. The Squire was still the one Democrat in the city who could get things done. But on this voting day he knew he was slipping. The accursed Republicans were pushing him down and the coloreds were adding the grease. The only way he could take care of Moyamensing was not to fall any farther. A shivering early-morning chill kept him awake. Yes, he had much to do.

McMullen commanded respect through political clout, swagger, and fear. He controlled jobs and he sold whiskey. The night before election day he saw the bartender, Frank Kelly. McMullen's biographer suspects a meeting took place during which the Squire liquored up the boys of Moya Hose and went over a plan, as William Armstrong had put it, to control "the Nigger vote." Fourth Ward men knew what to do. Every colored with a Republican ticket in his pocket was a vote against Democrats and against *our* police.

The violence had already begun with the shootings of Jacob Gordon and Moses Wright, a few dozen feet from McMullen's door. The men of Moyamensing had used this tactic against black voters the year before in Philadelphia and Camden.

Catto had breakfast at eight thirty in his boarding house on South Street above Eighth. For the most part, what he did on election day is known, but less apparent is the when, the timing and order of his activities. He was at school about a block away by nine.

He had much to do as well on this October 10. Make sure Negro voters got to the polls and voted Republican. Teach at the boys' school and keep an eye out that his students were safe. He had seen the thunderclouds forming the night before.

The Fourth and Fifth wards were side by side. The trouble began soon after nine in the morning at a polling place in the Fifth Ward, just where U.S. Marshal Gregory had sent troops to protect colored voters the year before. Negro throngs were already at the poll, having streamed through the gates of suffrage the year before. With the opportunity now to vote for a new mayor, their numbers and anticipation filled the street. White voters were there too, all of these men waiting on a narrow sidewalk, men bent on a mission—some to change the elected officials running the city and others to protect them.

More than a few voters had liquor, not coffee, with their breakfast, so it was not just the expectations of the day that were intoxicating. Missing was "the best of feeling," according to one polite description of the day's mood. White policemen arrived and made things worse. They herded voters into a line, but the line was too big to handle. So they created two lines, one white and one Negro, each approaching the poll from a different direction. As the lines met at the election window, threats and maledictions hung in the din accompanying the votes cast.

The pushing of minutes before became noisy affrays. Policemen, looking to shut the suffrage gate, fought with Negro voters. They bloodied colored men, yanked them out of line, and then replaced them with whites. These new Republican voters complained officially about the treatment they were getting.

About six squares away, Richard Greener, the Harvard grad and I.C.Y. teacher, could not believe what he was seeing—a white man shooting at an unarmed colored man at Tenth and Bainbridge. Greener immediately reported the incident to police but was told that the white man in everyday clothes was Thomas Moran, a "special policeman." Police offered no other explanation.

In addition to intimidation and assaults, Democrats were also using another tried and true method of securing an election-day win—"repeaters" voting again and again.

Between eleven o'clock and noon, Albert Bickley was working as an election-day window inspector at the Sixth and Bainbridge polling place in McMullen's ward. He knew Frank Kelly from the neighborhood and was surprised when he came to the window to vote under the name *Dunn*. He told Kelly that his ruse wouldn't work and was fortunate to quickly duck when Kelly threw a blackjack at him.

At one o'clock, Mayor Fox came to the Fifth Ward polling place on the east side of Sixth Street, just below Lombard, two squares away from Bickley's voting window. Fox made the same plea that a mayor had made outside Pennsylvania Hall in 1838. "I want one and all of you to aid me in maintaining the peace," he told the crowd. "Let each one try now to evade any show of anger or any disposition to quarrel. . . . If you do this, all will have a chance to get in their votes, and each will have the proud satisfaction of knowing that his side is bound to win. Will you help?"

The crowd shouted "We will" and gave the mayor three cheers. He ordered ropes drawn around the two lines so that none but voters could pass. He told unhappy colored voters that he had no control over the formation of separate lines. Then he left. As disgruntled as everyone had been, the scene quieted.

Not for long.

The complaints of the day led to court hearings. Judges sent for the mayor, who defended the fair play of his police force. In the early afternoon, Sixth and Lombard erupted once more as the judges heard more complaints: police again forcing Negroes out of line and white voters put in their stead. Fox vowed to replace the police officials at the poll and said he would return to the troubled street corner. Minutes after he had gone, a crowd came into the courthouse and begged the judges to stop police from "clubbing and shooting" colored men. Judge Joseph Allison saw a civil emergency evolving before his eyes. One complainant's face was badly bruised. He and other judges issued arrest warrants for the policemen who had been obstructing the polls.

In the words of a white onlooker, Hiram Jackson, one of eleven people to describe the events at Sixth and Lombard, a policeman "said that no black sons of bitches should vote there without" a challenge. That policeman, Jackson said, was pulling black voters out of line and passing them to a policeman Jackson knew, Officer Gorman.

He saw Gorman strike a black voter on the head and then saw another policeman with a big mustache hit the same man in the face, knocking him to the gutter. The policeman with the mustache shot the fallen man. "The policemen then commenced shooting and calling out 'Shoot the black sons of bitches,' and I run up Lombard Street to Seventh."

Mayor Fox telegraphed Lieutenant Haggerty, in charge of Third District police, to come to his office. Then they both went to the courthouse. Judge Allison, who had written the Derry streetcar opinion, made it clear to the mayor that police must protect colored voters. White residents who voted at Sixth and Lombard had come into court to support the claims of police violence. One of the officers cited for his brutality toward Negro voters was a lieutenant named Haggerty.

Eli Pickle said he was at Sixth and Lombard that morning after ten and saw a policeman push away a black man trying to vote, then club the man two or three times. In front of a crowd, the officer drew his revolver and fired.

Pickle said Lieutenant Haggerty stood no more than ten feet away and watched the assault. Pickle saw that the black man had a ballot in his hand.

Haggerty was the same lieutenant who had more than a dozen policemen block and bludgeon colored voters at the same poll a year earlier until Gregory sent in the marines.

Upon hearing his name and the accusations against him, Lieutenant Haggerty denied he had done anything improper. He denied that there had been disturbances at all. The skeptical judges arrested and held him on ten thousand dollars' bail. The mayor said nothing. One man told the judges that some police breaking the law at Sixth and Lombard were not in uniform.

Chief of Police St. Clair Mulholland ordered all the officers at the Eleventh Division polls replaced. Bail was posted for Lieutenant Haggerty. Then a new band of frantic voters hastened into the courtroom with news—colored women and children were fleeing a riot that had erupted along Lombard from Sixth to Eleventh streets. Police from across the city were quickly reassigned to the scene. Judges ordered that the arrest warrants issued earlier in the day for the police officers at the Lombard poll be ignored. Every man was needed.

They instructed the mayor to contact the military authorities.

★ ★ ★

SOON THE RIOT was five blocks in one direction, three in the other. The storm kept spreading. A fight on a corner became a brawl along a block. Victims were targeted and chased. A distinct sound of the city was heard throughout the riot area: the popping of pistol balls striking brick. Businesses closed. Colored residents shut their doors, shuttered their windows, though some cautiously peeked. Most did not know in which direction to escape, so they stayed in place. And there was murmuring that it was going to get worse when the sun fell. *Massacre.*

Riots lack order and definition, so eyewitness accounts differ. Yet two things were clear: Panic soaked the streets like Indian summer humidity, and white men, often policemen, chased and shot down Negroes, even pursuing them into their houses. Older colored men like Stephen Smith had not seen this kind of violence since the 1840s.

Four colored men charged with riotous conduct at Sixth and Lombard went before the court. The judge said from the evidence he had seen in this and previous cases on this day, "the riot had been fermented by the police." He freed each man on bail.

In the early afternoon, Levi Bolden, age twenty-two, a childhood playmate of Bolivar's, was standing on Seventh Street, thirty paces north of South Street, when he was shot by a man in a police uniform coat and a white hat. He was carried to Pennsylvania Hospital three blocks away. The hospital treated his wound, but Bolden died three weeks later. Mary Ann Bolden told friends her husband said the shooter was police sergeant John Duffy.

Bolden's shooting happened about two blocks from the shootings the night before of Gordon and Wright. Isaac Chase, a colored waiter, lived in the midst of these two sites, in the rear of 811 Emeline Street, behind Catto's boardinghouse. Chase had come home in the early afternoon after seeing the violence drawing closer to his alley and to his children. His wife, Sarah, was away from the house, but his eleven-year-old daughter, Julia, was upstairs taking care of the younger children.

White rioters invaded Eighth Street and neared Emeline, a street as wide as a man's outstretched arms. Mothers bundled their children and took them upstairs, away from the dangers of the first floor. Chase heard squalls of violence, men running and cursing, the sound of pistols firing and brickbats landing. Could his wife be in trouble? Chase walked out of his house and listened. When it quieted, he walked down the alley to his gate, unbolted it, and looked out.

His timing could not have been worse. He saw two white roughs outside. One had a pistol. Some witnesses say the other had a hatchet and that policemen were with them. He could not lock the gate and ran back toward his front door. They forced the gate open. "Kill him!" one shouted. Chase ran back toward his house when suddenly there were gunshots in the alley. Two shots, then a third. Chase fell just a couple of feet from his door and, somehow with two bullets in his back, got inside. His daughter came down a few steps and saw him struggle to shut the door behind him and then fall, splayed on the floor. She ran upstairs, opened a window and shouted to the crowd that had formed below: "Oh, you have killed my father!"

A man with a pistol pointed it at her, cursed her race, and ordered her back inside. She shut the window. She had seen the man with the pistol before. A teenaged boy said the man with the pistol had a 27 tattooed on his hand.

Not long after the Chase murder, a gunshot glanced off the side of the head of Frank Kelly. He was bleeding. As many white and colored victims of the riot were doing, he went to Pennsylvania Hospital to have his wound treated. His head was bandaged. He walked out of the hospital that same afternoon.

Residents didn't know how widespread the riot was. Negroes were terrorized, suspecting they were being targeted by police or by the scowling drunken roughs walking in packs through the streets—or both. The storm spread south to Fitzwater Street and north to Lombard, twenty-four city blocks in all.

The policemen who were trying to make arrests found themselves in the moving melee of blacks and whites "jammed in together pell-mell." Fights raged on. Housetops were crowded with gawkers hollering and troublemakers pitching rocks and brickbats on the multitude. Down below, paving stones were thrown furiously. Balls of shot thwacked against walls. One nearly hit John Fawcett.

Fawcett, a forty-year-old hod carrier from the Frankford neighborhood, found himself running for his life from a man he would later identify as Frank Kelly of Moya Hose.

Standing at Eighth and South streets after two o'clock, Fawcett didn't know the name of the white man on Eighth Street with the pistol and the bandage around his head when he saw him raise his pistol at him and fire. That first shot missed. Despite the presence of a police station at Eighth and South streets, the bandaged man had not hesitated to shoot at an unarmed colored man. No one in the police station, known as the "Farm" because of the long ago use of the land it was on, paid him any mind. Fawcett ran up South to escape the bandaged man and the crowd running with him. The bandaged man fired again.

Fawcett needed to escape. The shooter and the mob were gaining. He saw a cellar door in front of a stove store in the middle of the block not far from the Adgers' store. Before he could dive in, a white boy stuck out a foot and tripped him. Fawcett scrambled to his feet, and the bandaged man fired again. This time he did not miss.

★ ★ ★

DURING THE TWELVE THIRTY school recess, Catto left the institute, walked home, and saw the crowds and the fear in people's eyes. The "mobocracy" had returned, as Bolivar would describe it, and colored men were "the object of its spleen."

Catto had lunch and was back in school about one o'clock. Fearing for the safety of their students, he and Jackson closed the school early. After two, James Milliken, the assistant adjutant of the Fifth Brigade, told Major Catto to arm himself and report to headquarters at Broad and Race streets at 6:00 P.M. Their unit was officially on active duty with a mission to protect the city and its inhabitants as night fell.

As a major and brigade inspector, he was required to have a sidearm and a sword. The brigade provided him with a horse. Catto had the sword.

He went to the bank at 919 Lombard and withdrew twenty dollars. Then he walked quickly north—away from the riot—and east to meet his friend Cyrus Miller and to purchase a pistol. Along the way, he was accosted by a white man with a gun on Chestnut Street. He got away from his persecutor and must have thought how fortuitous it was that he was on his way to buy a sidearm for protection.

He and Miller met at Third and Walnut. They walked along Third, found a pawnshop, and soon a revolver capable of firing six shots was in Catto's possession. He had some cartridges at home.

The two men said their good-byes at Sixth and Chestnut. It was about three o'clock.

At some point in his day, Catto beseeched the mayor to better protect the city's Negro residents. The mayor said adequate steps would be taken.

Catto began walking home. Some say he was on his way to vote; Bolivar said he had voted that morning. Republican election tickets were in his pocket to give to voters. Tickets were the ballots of the day and where the term "vote the ticket" came from.

Rather than going over to South Street, Catto walked only to Lombard. Because of the riot, that was the safer route. He was acting more prudently than he had the night before. He bumped into Jake White and they spoke, but White was in a hurry. He needed to eat something before going on duty at six. And he had to get his blue uniform ready.

Catto walked up Lombard toward Ninth, stopping for a minute to talk with a woman he knew, Rosa Ingram, in front of her house at 802. Continuing up Lombard, he turned south at Ninth and walked the one more square to South Street. His home at 814 was now a minute away. The street was becoming more crowded.

He passed 825 South and nodded to his neighbor Thomas Bolling, who had been his pupil at the I.C.Y. and who had heard the 1864 "Alma Mater" speech. Bolling saluted his teacher. It was a little past three thirty.

As Catto walked east on South Street, a white man with a bandaged head and a Kossuth hat was walking west. They were both on the south side of the street. No sign of recognition was apparent as they passed each other in front of Annie Howard's house at 822. Just a few more strides.

A moment after they passed each other, the man with the bandage stopped and turned as if he suddenly realized whom he had just walked by. *The damned colored Republican.*

The man crouched, pulled out a pistol, and pointed it at Catto. Annie Howard hallooed a warning to the man she knew as Professor: "Look out for that man!"

The clip-clop of a horse drawing a streetcar west on South Street at Eighth did not drown out the sound of the pistol firing.

The first shot struck Catto as he was retreating, his arms "spread out and shaking." Then Bolling's father saw him cross his arms and squeeze himself. He said to his attacker, who was about to shoot again, "What are you doing?"

He ran injured toward the cover of the rear of the streetcar as it pulled to a stop. The conductor Theodore Stratton had heard that first shot. He saw the bandaged man follow behind the car.

Onlookers on the sidewalk gaped. Streetcar passengers looked on aghast. Despite the witnesses, despite the police station at the corner, the bandaged man proceeded with no haste, as if his task were yet undone. Catto turned and faced him. The man fired again at close range. And again. And again. Catto staggered, turned, and fell into the arms of a police officer who arrived on the scene.

Five years before he had led the efforts to open up the streetcars. Now, as he lay bloodied in the middle of the tracks, Octavius Valentine Catto saw white and colored riders staring at him from a car.

★ ★ ★

THE BANDAGED MAN put the pistol in the pocket of his long dark coat and stepped back onto the sidewalk. No onlooker tried to grab him. Samuel Wanamaker, who had witnessed the shooting from the rear of the streetcar, jumped off and shouted, "Stop that man!" The bandaged man began to run. Wanamaker ran after him. At Ninth Street, a constable joined the chase.

Isaac Barr was with a friend at Ninth and South when he heard shots to his east. A man ran past and turned south on Ninth. A policeman and a crowd followed and someone cried, "Stop that man. He's killed a man."

The chase ended one square away at a Bainbridge Street tavern. Barr got there ahead of the policeman and went in after the bandaged man. He readjusted his eyes to the dark interior when he saw the man breathing hard and sitting in the far end of the room. Behind him, he heard the policeman and some of the crowd arriving and someone saying, "Come in, here he is."

That declaration alerted the suspect, who ran into the yard. Barr followed, corralled him, and brought him back into the bar. He handed him over to two officers who been part of the chase. "There's your man," Barr said. Then he walked outside, his civic deed done.

Moments later, the sound of feet shuffling in the bar unnerved the constable and he went back inside. He could see that the two officers, one short and stout and the other tall, were in the yard. But the bandaged man was not there. Barr ran outside to Bainbridge Street, but there was no sign of Catto's shooter. He was gone.

★ ★ ★

GREENER WAS THE FIRST I.C.Y. colleague to reach the shooting scene and saw the hole on the left side of Catto's chest. Bad news spreads fast and soon Banneker, Pythian, and Institute friends arrived. His body was carried half a block to the police station and his pockets emptied of $15.10, several letters, an empty revolver, and Republican election tickets.

Police kept Catto's friends out of the station as they waited for the coroner. Caroline Le Count arrived and began sobbing inconsolably. Her "piteous cries and pleadings" caused the men to weep. Newspaper accounts identified her as Catto's "betrothed." A block away, the I.C.Y. began to fill with wet-eyed students and teachers.

A telegram went out to Rev. William Catto, now sixty-one, an A.M.E. pastor in Morristown, New Jersey, and confined to a sick bed. He left his bed to come to Philadelphia.

That night the rioting city "settled down into an opposite state of almost painful calmness," Bolivar remembered. In colored homes, "strong men wept like children" at Catto's death. At Pennsylvania Hospital, the night saw no diminishing of patients as they came in wounded on wagons, carried in on settees, or walking in bloody and bruised from the riot. Nor was there a lessening of emotion when the polls closed as crowds through the night talked about the killings of Chase and Catto, and the injuries to so many more. Doctors removed a bullet from Fawcett's hip.

At 10:00 P.M., the publisher John Forney opened the window of the *Philadelphia Press* office and spoke to the crowd gathered outside awaiting election results. Forney announced that Stokley had won the mayor's race and the Republican ticket had swept other offices as well. He praised Negro voters for what they had accomplished on this historic day and said the Democratic loss meant that the "day of prejudice is gone." The applause stopped when Forney told the crowd news of Catto's murder.

In the newspapers the next day, the major front-page story was about a terrible conflagration in a Midwest city. The Chicago Fire, not the Philadelphia election violence, was the big news.

The *Public Ledger* said that at most polling places "the election passed off yesterday in perfect quiet. At a few of them, however, there was a great deal of disorder and turbulence." Then came a full page on the riot and

Catto's murder. The *New York Times* reported the killings in its election day story on Philadelphia. The *Inquirer* had a large story on page 2 about the rioting, including the news that Catto was among ten colored men shot that day.

One of the *Inquirer* stories said: "Every few moments there would be a report of a pistol, a shout or a yell. . . . It is doubtful whether many of those who were most active in using the revolver and the brickbat, and in instigating the riot, can ever be brought to justice. Murders were perpetrated and people were wounded by the dozen."

The story also said that in the riot's aftermath, many men walked the streets with "bandaged heads and bullet-torn clothing."

Nine of the Quaker managers of the institute met informally in the morning. They chose two members to attend the coroner's inquest to learn everything they could about Catto's murder. They decided to close the school until after the funeral and to name Greener, who had headed the boy's school while Catto was in Washington, to step in again. The board also talked of having two members assist in bringing the murderer to justice—but before long, their zeal cooled and they played no role in searching for the bandaged man.

That same morning, colored men and women began to gather at Catto's boardinghouse. Inside, the physicians from the city conducted their post-mortem. The coroner, Dr. E. B. Shapleigh, found bullet wounds in Catto's right arm, left shoulder, left thigh, and left breast, which punctured the right ventricle and killed him. Outside the crowd grew, as if to hold their hero Octavius's body in a protective embrace.

The frail Rev. William Catto, suffering from heart disease, saw the lifeless body of his murdered son. He had reared and nurtured him in the loam of responsibility and education and stiffened his back with expectations. He had sent him on this path of bettering the lives of his people, and now this. *Oh my Lord, my savior, what have I done?*

He "appeared overwhelmed with grief, and . . . wept as though his heart would break."

The news of his son's murder was reverberating across the colored nation by that night. In New York, Rev. Henry Highland Garnet made plans to come to the funeral. In Washington, John Mercer Langston called together the other faculty members of the law department at Howard University to issue a statement: "Yet we cannot but express the hope that out of the life-blood of O.V. CATTO (another of our martyrs) a holier and better civilization may spring, that shall hate no man on account of his creed and color."

By the next day, the *Inquirer* decided to find out what colored Philadelphia thought and had a reporter see the richest colored citizen in town. The aging coal broker Stephen Smith had the presence of mind to say: See Jacob White Jr.

The reporter sat down with White and St. George Taylor. Both had seen Catto the day he died.

Two strange and terrible duties now fell to Jake White. As manager of his father's cemetery, he was preparing for the burial of his best friend. Now he was being asked, in addition, to serve as the calm and reasoned spokesman of the colored city.

Jake and Octavius had been inseparable. They had led the ill-fated journey to Harrisburg to enlist in the war and the against-all-odds campaign to open up the cars. They had played ball together, marched together, made the "marathon sprints" to school together. White had been the manager, the secretary, the third-string Pythian, the friend who went to the tailor when Catto was too busy to buy pants. He could always count on Catto to be the firebrand, the star. But now his friend was gone.

White tried to control his emotions and began speaking to the reporter.

He said the mayor's police caused the riot and that the mayor never controlled "his officers here." "We consider them as ignorant and low-lived set of men as ever trod the soil."

"All of the trouble at Sixth and Lombard was caused by the police. Fifty of them interfered with the electors at the polls in the morning, and when they heard the mayor was coming they all dropped away to the other side of the street. As soon as he was gone, they crowded up again and commenced to interfere. We have been subjected to outrages of all kinds at their hands for a long time."

★ ★ ★

SAMUEL WANAMAKER offered a description of the shooter. "Short, thick set, with a round, smooth face. He wore a darkish coat, light pantaloons, and a kind of dark felt hat, low crowned. The murderer also had a bandage on his head, and answers the description of a man who participated in several of the disturbances previous to the shooting of Mr. Catto, and was supposed to be a ringleader all throughout the early stages of the riot."

One newspaper reported that the shooter was about twenty-two years old and had been treated at Pennsylvania Hospital earlier on election day.

Rewards were offered. The chairman of the city Republican Party put up a thousand dollars. So did the sheriff, who offered the money for the "arrest of the murderers of Professor Catto and Jacob Gordon."

Sheriff William Leeds said he was acquainted with Catto. "Yes, I knew him well. He was intelligent, amiable, honorable, gentle and modest." He described the others who died as "peaceful, respectable, useful," adding, "They deserved commendation, rather than death. They are widely regretted. But they will be avenged. The murderers will be arrested, and retribution will fall heavily on that plague spot of the city, the corrupt, filthy, depraved Fourth Ward."

The *Bulletin* publicized the sheriff's reward in an editorial that also said: "Catto and his fellow-martyrs were murdered in a section of the city which is ruled by a gang of Democrats who have long been a terror to the honest citizens of Philadelphia. That these crimes were committed by the retainers of that gang there is very little reason to doubt."

The *Inquirer* called on the mayor to offer his own reward as well: "The killing in cold blood of this estimable citizen is something more serious than a murder ordinarily is, Professor Catto being a representative man among his people, and, at the time of his death, was using all the power he possessed to protect them in their newly guaranteed rights as citizens. He was murdered because of his prominence and by reason of the cause he espoused."

Fitzgerald's *City Item* noted the rewards in its own lyrical way:

> We suppose the mayor will also offer a reward.
> These murderers are wanted in the other world,
> Let us expedite their journey.

At the African Episcopal Church of St. Thomas, the vestrymen met "to consider the death by assassination of Octavius V. Catto, a member of this vestry." Committees formed to draft and have printed "suitable resolutions" regarding the life of their esteemed brother. The meeting also learned of William Catto's wish to have his son buried at Mother Bethel A.M.E. If there were hurt feelings or complaints, the vestry minutes say only that two of its members would call "on the father and represent the views of this body."

The next day the bandaged man had a name.

The *Bulletin* reported that the alleged shooter was Frank Kelly and that another Moya Hose member, Edward "Reddy" Dever, was wanted as well. The newspaper described Dever as "about 5 feet 7 inches high, 160 pounds weight, 25 years of age, light red hair, smooth full face, rather stoutly built." Kelly was said to be "about 5 feet 6 inches tall, 140 pounds weight, 22 years of age, dark hair, medium build, has a fresh pistol scalp wound on side of his head, hair clipped around the wound."

Chief Mulholland said Kelly had killed Isaac Chase as well. He said that on October 10, both Kelly and Dever "were dressed in blue blouses, and wore police shields," though neither was a policeman. He said Mrs. Chase had been home that day and opened the door to Kelly and Dever, believing them to be police. That was when Kelly shot Chase, the police chief said.

His words suggested that the murder investigation was off to a bumpy start. Mulholland's description was a measure of how much confusion existed. He also said his men had searched already for Kelly and Dever in South Philadelphia. Nothing was said about Kelly's extraordinary escape from police in the bar at Ninth and Bainbridge.

At a large meeting at National Hall, an audience of more whites than Negroes heard the police blamed for the "wanton violence" on election day.

Robert Purvis said that the blood of black men had been shed in the Revolution and Rebellion, "and now let us hope that the blood of our friend will be the end of resistance to the right." He was followed by a prominent Republican, Colonel Alexander McClure. He recalled the *Dred Scott* ruling.

"This murder grew out of sentiment among certain people that the black man has no rights which a white man is bound to respect," McClure said. "This sentiment has been encouraged by white men who dare not shoot. The remedy for this is not written. It is to be found in public opinion and an expression by every honest and enlightened citizen against this sentiment." The audience applauded.

"If the black man can be murdered today with impunity, the white man can be murdered tomorrow."

Isaiah Wears said the assassination of Lincoln "was the instrument of a dying rebellion," while the assassin who murdered Catto "was the instrument of a dying Democracy," by which he meant the Democratic Party.

Rev. J. Walker Jackson, a white Methodist clergyman, said the death of Catto on election day made him feel that he would "never be satisfied" until he had the opportunity "to vote for a colored man for some office." The audience applauded.

"The great men of any race or any age are the educators of the people. Catto was the educator of his people, and his people became the better for his example. He was murdered because of this prejudice against color . . . and if Catto's death wipes this away, thank God that he permitted him to die."

Then the minister from Harrisburg asked a question: "Could it have been because of his erudition and eloquence that his life was taken?"

Audience members responded, "That's it!" and "That's right!"

The coroner conducted an inquest into the murders of Catto, Chase, and Jacob Gordon, who was shot the day before the election and who died the day after.

Among those testifying was Samuel Wanamaker, who witnessed the shooting from the streetcar. He termed the killing "a cold-blooded assassination of a peaceful, inoffensive man." He criticized the "bystanders" on the sidewalk for not capturing the shooter.

Constable Barr, Annie Howard, and Sarah and Julia Chase told their stories. A man named Jacob Helmstadt testified that he was standing in the 700 block of South Street when the Catto shooting occurred and he ran toward the shots. At Eighth and South, he saw two men on the corner and heard one of them ask who did it and the other man replied, "Frank Kelly did it." Helmstadt said soon after he heard young men at a different corner "blowing" about the murder and saying that Frank Kelly did it.

The *New York Times* reported the news of the inquest, writing that "the evidence is conclusive that Frank Kelly was the murderer." The *Inquirer* editorialized how "indignant" Mayor Fox was at the reward posted by the sheriff for Catto's killer because his police were "diligently seeking" the killer. The newspaper chided the mayor: "Mayor Fox ought to know by this time that his police are not under his control" and went on to say that the police "encouraged" the election-day killings. The *Philadelphia Press* stated that both Kelly and Dever were killers. And the *Bulletin* said it expected the new mayor "to destroy the power of the Fourth Ward crowd of bullies."

McMullen, the head of that crowd, had not seen things go his way in the election. Despite the bloodshed, enough Negroes had managed to vote to help elect Stokley, the Republican. The civic outcry against him and his supporters in Moyamensing worsened daily. The alleged killer of Catto was one of his, a Moya Hose man. The other killer was, too. Once more, the Squire's power was threatened. He took pains to assure his ally in Congress that he had everything under control.

McMullen wrote to Sam Randall that after the riot he had spent a few nights quieting the braggarts in his ranks, putting the "blowers back in their wholes."

And before the day ended, the Democratic mayor—McMullen's man—did, in fact, offer his own thousand-dollar reward for the killer of Catto. The rewards now totaled three thousand dollars.

* * *

A COLORED MAN led Catto's horse in the funeral procession on October 16. He also carried the sword of the brigade major.

The funeral began in a light rain. The dead man's body lay in the military armory at Broad Street just below Race. The doors opened at 7:00 A.M. and the long line of mourners stretched down Race Street. Buildings nearby were adorned with American flags and draped in ebony. Negroes and whites shuffled slowly between a double line of colored regimental guards at the armory entrance, walked upstairs and then past the casket in single file to view the body of the man people were calling a martyr. The crowds were so large and emotions so high that the guards "crossed muskets" to maintain order.

Catto was clothed in a dress military uniform. Flowers, wreaths, and bouquets lay on his body, their fragrance filling the large second-story drill room. The casket was trimmed in silver and covered in black cloth. On the lid was an inscription:

Major O.V. Catto
Died October 10, 1871
Aged 32 years

At the head and foot of the bier was a stack of four muskets on which rested the colors of the Fifth Brigade draped in mourning. A brigade guard of honor stood in silent watch. Most of those in line passed by quietly, but a good many shed tears and a contingent of students and teachers from the I.C.Y. sobbed and shuddered at the sight they saw. One colored girl looking at the inscription and the word "Died" on the coffin lid said it should have read "Murdered."

The mourners' line inched past for four hours. William Catto had requested no religious service at the armory. As the clock struck ten, the military and civic organizations that were part of the procession began to take their places on Broad Street.

By eleven, as many as five thousand people had walked past Catto's remains. Billy Wormley had come from Washington, Garnet from New York. Prominent Negroes from across the North were there, joining thousands of whites and blacks who lined Broad Street in what was the largest funeral ever for a Negro in Philadelphia. One account described the street as "a wilderness of umbrellas, carriages, military companies and bands of music."

On this day, in a riot-torn city where a parade of blacks led to rock and egg throwing, where the public streets had been dangerous thoroughfares, there would be no epithets or brickbats hurled. For the first time ever, they could, in their sadness, walk the streets without fear to mourn their hero.

And that was a victory, of sorts.

The hearse, with its six black plumes, was driven to the armory door. The sound of muffled drums presaged the coffin's approach, and twelve pall bearers placed the casket in the hearse. The men bearing the casket were soldiers, Banneker members and Pythians, including Captain Raymond J. Burr. Brigadier General Louis Wagner, who commanded Camp William Penn, led four colored regiments and a detachment of cavalry. The vestry from St. Thomas rode in carriages. Robert M. Adger served as chief marshal of this civilian segment of the procession. He had named one of his sons Octavius.

Mourners walked four abreast. Two hundred pupils came from colored schools and colleges. A double column of carriages, more than 125 in all, carried the funeral's Committee of Arrangements—Greener, William Dorsey, and William Minton; Pythians and Bannekers; a delegation of Congressmen from Washington; state legislators, and members of the Philadelphia Select and Common Councils, but no Democratic members.

The Colored Odd Fellows marched, as did the Colored Coachmen's Association. The Elephant Club kept up. Walking, too were the Clergymen of Philadelphia and the highway department clerks. The ward representatives of the Republican Executive Committee proceeded in lock step.

Alumni and students representing the I.C.Y. marched. Graduates came from as far away as Mississippi and New York.

Hundreds marched on the sidewalk—the Unconditional Republican Club headed by the sheriff, the John F. Hartranft Association, the Tiger Club, and the Abraham Lincoln Literary Society in Wilmington, Delaware. Bands marched and played on the sidewalk, too.

Homes were draped in mourning. The large crowds on the sidewalk slowed the movement south. Police at street corners kept things moving. As bands played dirges, spectators walked south too, adding to the sad thread of mourners and carriages accompanying the dead man on his three-mile journey to Lebanon Cemetery.

★ ★ ★

EULOGIES WOULD ELEVATE his memory and enumerate his deeds. In New York City, A.M.E. clergyman Benjamin Tucker Tanner, who had marched with Catto in celebration of the Fifteenth Amendment, now sought to place his friend in historical context.

Tanner, thirty-six years old, evoking the Israelites and Philistines, likened Catto's struggles to the biblical battles fought in the name of the Lord. And, speaking to the filled pews in New York's Shiloh Presbyterian Church, he likened his friend to the fallen Saul.

> Only when war had fully done its work,
> Could the Hebrew king lay him down to die. . . .
> Yet scaled the king . . .
> And high above the din, he slept in blood.
> So climbed Octavius and all our race.
> The glorious mount to which we long aspired,
> And long essayed by peaceful means to scale
> Was only reached through war more terrible
> Than that which made to shake the Hebrew land.
> But then, the prize was gained, the top was reached,
> And on its summit Catto sleeps his sleep. . . .
> The mount of glorious citizenship,
> Whereupon he fell, there he shall sleep secure. . . .
> Upon the granite of the nation's faith,
> The martyr rests, and we, a million strong,
> Backed by a million more . . .

Do swear that not a rock from out his mount
Shall ever be removed.

Three colored leaders in three cities likened the election day killers to the best known and most feared white terror group of the Reconstruction South.

The New York audience also heard a eulogy delivered by Rev. Henry Highland Garnet, offering his second elegy to Catto.

He compared the murderers to the "Kuklux" and called Democrats "the party that prompted the assassination of Catto." Garnet, who had known the Catto family for more than twenty years, told the audience that no amount of "bribes and threats" could shake his friend's resolve. Therefore, "they resorted to the cowardly weapon of the assassin."

At Union Bethel A.M.E. Church in Washington, the eulogy, entitled "What We Hoped For," was delivered by Rev. Daniel P. Seaton, who had been with Catto in 1864 at the Equal Rights League convention in Syracuse.

"It was hoped by many of his friends," he said, "that the day was not far distant when his name would be enrolled among the noblest of our land in the Legislative halls and Senate chambers of this great Union."

The clergyman noted how well-known Catto was in Washington and added his name to a list with Abraham Lincoln's and John Brown's. And he said that while the Klans of South and North Carolina "mask themselves and commit their cruel depredations in the woods at night, but the unmasked Ku-Klux of Philadelphia, the City of Brotherly Love, have the daring to do theirs in the blaze of the noonday sun."

In Philadelphia, Wears said people erred in believing the Klan consisted of only poor whites. He said merchants, ministers, and mayors shared in the blame. Wears declared, "The same may be said of the Kuklux of the North."

An upstate Pennsylvania newspaper, of all voices, praised Catto and echoed Wears's indictment of the city's elite.

Lashing out at the "aristocratic Philadelphians," who mourned "a martyr they did so little to protect," the *Tioga County Agitator* wrote that the killer was a wolf whose "wolfish spirit came to him . . . from the very men who hold meetings to denounce him." The newspaper said that Catto was seen as an enemy "to the roughs simply because he had devoted himself to the amelioration and elevation of the condition of his race."

Not every Pennsylvania newspaper shared that view. The *Bellefonte Democratic Watchman* wrote: "Considering the fact that thousands of people are homeless and starving in Chicago and the West, a little less display over the funeral of the darkey CATO, in Philadelphia, the other day, would have been in good taste."

On October 23, Levi Bolden succumbed to the gun shots he received on election day.

On December 7, about seven weeks after his son's death, Rev. William T. Catto, who had evaded slavery in the South, avoided colonization, and escaped Maryland marshals, could no longer survive in a failing body weakened by inconsolable grief. He died and was buried in the same cemetery as his son Octavius.

★ ★ ★

THE FUNERAL PROCESSION finally reached its destination just before 2:00 P.M. Lebanon Cemetery was a low tract of land in the city's rural southern end, resting place for 339 soldiers of the U.S. Colored Troops.

Men of the Fifth Brigade formed a line at the grave. Three leaders of colored churches conducted the service—St. Thomas's Alston, A.M.E. bishop Jabez Campbell, and Garnet. Garnet offered up a hymn: "How short the race our friend has run, cut down in all his bloom. The course he yesterday begun, now finished in the tomb."

Each clergyman scattered a handful of dust on the grave. As the last of the rites were intoned, Caroline Le Count stepped forward.

"Frantic with grief," she grasped a clod of earth "from the sexton's shovel and cast it into the tomb, wailing as she did so." Neither soft words nor reassuring hands could calm her. An honor guard discharged three volleys over the grave. The funeral was over and the assemblage began to leave. Mourners heard Caroline's cries.

"Octavius, Octavius! Take me with you."

CHAPTER 16

The Venus
of the High Trapeze

THE JANUARY SUN had fled by the time Detective Edward Tryon's entourage settled into the stuffed seats of the palace car for the long ride east. As the swamp-green locomotive huffed across the frozen flats of northern Indiana, Tryon sized up his prisoner in the gas lamp's light.

The man was half Tryon's age and looked younger. He was slight, nimble, well-attired, and clean-shaven except for a tuft of mustache. By various accounts, he had crisscrossed the country for five years, fleeing charges in two cities, surfacing as far south as New Orleans and finally in Chicago. He had a dark intensity to his eyes, "in which the devil can be found lurking," a newspaper said. Even so, Tryon saw none of the footsoreness or desperation he associated with men on the lam. If anything, the prisoner looked fresher than his handlers.

Tryon had brought along a second policeman, a streetcar conductor and a colored Republican—William Forten, traveling "unofficially," as Tryon put it. They had been riding trains for the better part of three days. Tryon could have used a night in Chicago and a hot bath. But his handlers wanted this long-simmering, foul-smelling case brought quickly to a boil. Tryon's orders were to get the prisoner identified and back to Philadelphia at once.

The man had told police in Cincinnati that his name was Charles Young. But sometime around Thanksgiving of 1876, a clue to the contrary had surfaced. Versions varied—Young had said too much or a Cincinnati police inspector had alerted Philadelphia's police chief or the chief had acted on intelligence already in hand. One newspaper said the tip began with a citizen's query: Was the City of Philadelphia still offering a reward for the capture of Frank Kelly?

★ ★ ★

IN THE FIVE YEARS since Catto's killing, the wind had come out of the sails of Reconstruction.

The Panic of 1873 had thrown nearly one man in three out of work in the cities and visited ruin on farmers and sharecroppers. Voters blamed Grant's scandal-wracked Republican administration and elected Democrats. Across the South, "white-liners" and White Leagues vowed to retake power from colored Republicans "peaceably if we can, forcibly if we must."

Colored Americans had just tasted the fruits of that power—fruits that ranged from William Forten becoming a presidential elector to Robert Smalls and fifteen other Negroes filling Southern seats in Congress. A bill authored by Forten's favorite senator, Charles Sumner, outlasted a filibuster by its fiercest foe, Samuel Randall, and became the 1875 Civil Rights Act, decreeing that no one could be denied a ticket, a table, a hotel room, or a steamship berth on account of race. Test cases bloomed. An aptly named couple, the Peers, won eleven hundred dollars from the Arch Street Theatre's manager, Louisa Drew, for ejecting them amid shouts of "get those niggers out of line." (Perhaps Drew was distracted; her daughter was about to marry a British actor named Barrymore.)

But death, disease, and defeat eliminated all-important allies. Sumner and Thaddeus Stevens had died; their counterpart in Harrisburg, Morrow Lowry, lost his mind and entered an asylum. Southern Democrats, grateful for Randall's filibustering, helped elect him House Speaker. Grant wearily confided to his cabinet that he'd come to consider the Fifteenth Amendment a mistake.

Soldiers were redeploying from the South to the West. *Little Big Horn* entered the national consciousness; massacres of seventy Negroes in Colfax, Louisiana, and as many as three hundred near Vicksburg, Mississippi, did not. On July 4, 1876, as Mayor William Stokley held aloft the glass-encased Declaration of Independence to the roar of Centennial crowds in Philadelphia, a black-white standoff was starting in Hamburg, South

Carolina, that ended with five colored militiamen executed. When Smalls read a colored witness's account of that episode in Congress, a Pittsburgh Democrat demanded the witness's name.

"I will say to the gentleman," Smalls replied, "that if he is desirous that the name shall be given in order to have another Negro killed, he will not get it from me."

But the Pittsburgh congressman spoke for many Northern whites. In Boston, a mass meeting of "highly respectable citizens" likened Louisiana's White League to the founding fathers and protested military intervention. When Wendell Phillips rose to disagree, people hissed the aging abolitionist and shouted, "Played out, sit down."

For better or worse, most of Catto's "band of brothers" had clung to the party of Grant and Stokley. The state Equal Rights League began making members "earnestly pledge" to help Republican campaigns. William Forten, Frederick Douglass, and others supported the party's nominee, Rutherford Hayes, in 1876. The Ohio governor favored equal rights and Southern "self government"—an ominous hint—but Negroes could hardly vote for a Democratic party that called for restoring white rule.

And now, as Detective Tryon's contingent took its prisoner east, an electoral stalemate gripped the nation. With the presidential inauguration seven weeks away, no one knew whether the hand on the Bible would be Hayes's or Samuel Tilden's.

★　★　★

SINCE CATTO'S DEATH, his admirers had affixed his name to a temperance society, an Odd Fellows club, a medal awarded by the Pennsylvania National Guard, and a lodge of the Independent Order of Good Templars. His photograph was reproduced on a carte-de-visite over the inscription, "One more Martyr to the cause of Constitutional Liberty." Jake White sent out solicitations for a Catto monument fund. The Board of Education prepared to move the Ohio Street Colored School to a bigger building and to rename the school for its principal's murdered fiancé.

In Delaware, an A.M.E. minister and his wife named their baby boy Octavius Catto Coppin. Caroline Le Count's brother and his wife named a baby girl Octavia.

Le Count and her three assistants presided over 284 colored boys and girls at the soon-to-be-renamed Ohio School. She routinely pestered the school district to expand its narrow roster of colored teachers. Her dra-

matic readings were a headlined attraction at "literary and musical enter-
tainments" to benefit churches and charities.

At the I.C.Y., Fanny Jackson groomed aspiring teachers, gave political
speeches, and otherwise carried on the traditions of Reason, Bassett, and
Catto with such zeal that the managers felt the need to deliver one of their
trademark admonitions. "A fine voice and a free manner of speaking often
captivates the popular ear and make success in these pursuits compara-
tively easy to a race gifted in these physical qualities," they warned Jackson in an annual report. "But a political life is far from desirable on many
accounts, and is often corrupting to those who engage in it." Jackson further honored Catto's memory by politely ignoring this advice.

But other organizations Catto had shaped or led fell prey to lean times,
disagreement, and despair. The state Equal Rights League moved its
headquarters from the city and lost members because of its Republican
loyalty rule. The Banneker Institute shrank from sixty dues-paying members to fewer than two dozen. The Pythians played their last game.

The monument fund struggled. The Coppin and Le Count babies
named for Octavius died in infancy. And in five years, no one had been
punished for the two-day siege that left Catto and three other Negroes
slain, dozens wounded, and hundreds beaten, terrorized, or sent to jail for
trying to cast their votes.

A police sergeant and a former policeman had been cleared in the
two of the killings; Alderman McMullen was said to have influenced both
outcomes. Levi Bolden's deathbed identification of Sergeant John Duffy
meant less, in the end, than testimony by Duffy's wife that the sergeant
had been home asleep when Bolden was shot. And a court ruled that
Bolden was already dying of Bright's disease, hence the bullet had merely
hastened, not caused, his death. Two eyewitnesses said Edward McNulty
was the man who chased down and shot Jacob Gordon on the eve of the
election, but a jury deadlocked and the former officer walked free.

The memory of the Catto riot, as people called it, lay upon the city
like a low, unyielding fog. Known men had killed Catto and Chase in
"unblushing daylight," as William Forten said; numerous witnesses, colored and white, had identified them to inquests and grand juries. Indictments were returned, rewards posted. Yet two years, three years, four
years hence, they remained at large, as if all officialdom were stymied.

Suspicion filled the vacuum created by the absence of arrests. Kelly
was said to have turned up in Pittsburgh or Richmond and, most disturb-

ingly, in Philadelphia. An editorial writer later claimed police had passed up "a dozen opportunities . . . to arrest him quietly."

Forten, the Mintons, and Le Count's old admirer, Robert Jones, pressed authorities to keep the investigation alive. Justice for Catto's killer—that would be a memorial.

The police department, at least, was better behaved for Stokley's having swept aside the army of McMullen men appointed by his predecessor. The new mayor also led a public-works boom, and in May 1876 opened the Centennial exposition in Fairmount Park. Ten million visitors gazed at the three-story Corliss steam engine and explored the twenty-one-acre main hall, temporarily the world's biggest building. (White men built it; the only Negroes the Centennial employed were dining-room waiters and banjo-picking "darkies" for the exhibit on the South.) Stokley hired three hundred extra police. District Attorney Furman Sheppard put a magistrate's court on the fairgrounds. The Republican mayor and Democratic D.A. were credited with subduing the inevitable wave of pickpockets, prostitutes, thieves, and confidence men. People dubbed the court Sheppard's Rail Road and Stokley the Centennial Mayor. The timing was good: Thanks to a change in the law, Stokley was facing reelection in February 1877.

The fairgrounds closed November 10, 1876. A few weeks later, a tip came in about Kelly.

★ ★ ★

THE INFORMER SAID Kelly might turn up in Chicago as Charles Young. Philadelphia's police chief telegraphed Chicago's chief, who assigned his premiere plainclothesman, the hulking E. J. Steele, who by Christmas 1876 had traced Young to a rented room and by New Year's was ready to pounce.

Young was living with a woman—but on a January evening, as police prepared to make the arrest, he suddenly moved out. Steele kept tailing him and in a few days, the charms of another woman caused Young to drop his guard.

The world-renowned aerialist Emma Jutau, "Venus of the High Trapeze," was drawing crowds to Chicago's Coliseum with her daring leaps, "her Shapely and Bewitching Loveliness," and her death-defying ride down a two-hundred-foot wire, "suspended by her pearly teeth alone." Young was in the ticket line when Steele made his move.

Surrounded by policemen, Young gave up serenely. But Steele discovered "a long and murderous-looking clasp-knife clutched tightly in his right hand and covered from sight in his overcoat pocket." Newspapers said he might have bolted but for his captor's "imposing build."

Chicago police put Young in a cell until Tryon's contingent arrived. The streetcar conductor—Theodore Stratton, who had seen the Catto murder from the platform of his car—took one look at a group of prisoners in Chicago's Central Station and came back to Tryon. That's him, Stratton said, wide-eyed.

Now it was Philadelphia policeman Albert Bickley's turn. He, too, eyed the prisoners and recognized the man who had tried to brain him with a blackjack five years earlier, when Bickley caught him "repeating."

Chicago police had accomplished in five weeks what Philadelphia's much larger force had not achieved in five years. The colored man in Tryon's party, Forten, could not contain himself. Justice in the Catto killing loomed at last. Forten talked excitedly. Stratton, who aspired to become a policeman himself, was struck by one thing Forten said. He said the arrest would be good for Mayor Stokley.

Tryon telegraphed his superiors and prepared to take a handcuffed Frank Kelly to the 5:15 P.M. train.

★   ★   ★

THE WAITERS in the palace car were preparing to serve dinner. Tryon reached for a dog-eared page in the ancient book of detective tricks and made an announcement.

He told Bickley that the handcuffs were unnecessary during the meal. "We can watch this man well enough without keeping him in irons all the time."

Then he turned to the prisoner. "Frank," Tryon said, "one of us will have to sit at your side all the time and we can't let you attempt to get out of our sight. . . . We will have a long ride together, probably 40 hours, and in all that I say to you, I don't want you to say anything that will commit you."

He began asking about family. Kelly mentioned his father and a sister. His father was said to be a barber who, once upon a time, had hoped what many an Irish father hoped, that his son would aspire to the priesthood. Kelly had even received some schooling in that regard, once upon a time.

Tryon turned the subject to "your travels." The train would be cross-ing into Ohio soon, taking on fresh coal and passengers in Toledo, clat-tering past little towns with grand names, Defiance, Napoleon, Elyria, Marseilles. The detective asked what sort of life Kelly had lived in the lus-ter of the so-called Queen City, Cincinnati.

Kelly volunteered that he had lived there as Charles Young.

The conversation ebbed and flowed. Passengers squeezed past, clutch-ing glasses of amber-colored liquor against the bump and sway of the ride. Tryon offered to buy drinks.

"No, for drinking rum has been the cause of all my trouble," Kelly said. "I would not be in the trouble I am arrested for if it hadn't been for rum."

Tryon and Bickley exchanged a glance. Kelly was giving them an open-ing. They started asking him about October 10, 1871.

★ ★ ★

THE TRAIN pulled into Philadelphia at 4:00 A.M. on January 15. John Fawcett, the colored hod-carrier, came in and identified the man who, along with a mob, had chased him to a cellar door and wounded him in the hip.

Two dramas now riveted the attention of colored and white Philadel-phians. One was the arraigning of Kelly for trials in the Catto and Chase killings and the wounding of Fawcett. The other was the nation's larger struggle to resolve the Hayes-Tilden election stalemate. Occasionally, the casts of characters overlapped.

Newspapers rushed to publish pictures of Kelly in his neat cravat, wavy hair, and wispy mustache. At his first court appearances he was strikingly calm—"an attractive man . . . a boyish appearance," the daily *North American* reported. "Yesterday he was well dressed, and shows the sign of good fare."

Reports promptly surfaced in Philadelphia, New York, and Chicago about his secret life as Charles Young.

In that life, federal authorities had charged him with leading a gang of repeaters in a nationally watched congressional race in Cincinnati in 1876. Some repeaters confessed and claimed to have generated several hundred bogus Democratic ballots. The Democratic candidate, an ally of Samuel Randall's, had won his seat by just seventy-five votes.

Then there was the Tilden factor. A notorious gambler and election-fixer named Ephraim Holland, arrested in New York City, confessed to bringing squads of repeaters to Cincinnati that fall. Samuel Tilden, who had made his name as the crusading prosecutor who slew the Tweed ring's dragons, was not accustomed to hearing criminals profess a link to him. But Eph Holland, as he as known, did just that. He claimed that he had been promised thousands of dollars from a Tilden campaign fund—and had not been fully paid.

Holland also said Charles Young had run a gang of repeaters for him.

No doubt remained about Young's true identity. Details of Kelly's statements to Tryon and Bickley began to trickle out. He was said to have admitted to making up the name, to hiding out for a time with an uncle in Williamsport, Pennsylvania, and then with another relative in New Orleans. One published account said he had also stayed in Richmond, Virginia, and was a suspect in a murder there.

Charles Young's life in Cincinnati seemed to more or less parallel Kelly's life in Philadelphia—from his bartending and election work to the story witnesses had told years ago at the Catto inquest about his escape. Police had him in their grip one minute and let him go the next.

He had eased into the back rooms of Cincinnati politics, tending bar at a saloon in a section of the Queen City so known for brawlers, gamblers, and murderous gangs that its nickname was Dead Man's Corner. The election case suggested he had helped import a tactic better known in Philadelphia and New York than in Ohio: leading gangs of repeaters from poll to poll to tilt the result.

"Frank Kelly a Ballot-Box Stuffer," a Philadelphia headline said. The *New York Times* titled its story, "TILDEN'S VOTING MACHINES." John Forney's pro-Republican *Press* attributed Tilden's totals and Democrats' gains in the House to "the Frank Kellys of the United States, acting either as he acted in our streets in October 1871; or as he acted in Cincinnati in October, 1876."

Kelly had been in custody and about to appear before an Ohio judge on the repeating charges when a carriage driver pulled up outside the courthouse. Somehow, the prisoner was spirited into the carriage and out of town. Suspicion fell instantly on the sheriff and the deputies. One newspaper said Young was plucked from the courthouse because he knew the whole Democratic repeating scheme and was threatening to tell.

At his arraignment in Philadelphia, an energetic young lawyer stepped forward to run Kelly's defense. Benjamin L. Temple was a McMullen ally and chairman of the city's Democratic Party. But then, people on both sides of Kelly's case had been Democratic regulars—the defendant, the D.A., the chief defense lawyer.

Kelly pleaded not guilty to all charges. The judge asked how he wished to be tried. "By God and my country," he replied. What the judge meant was, did Kelly want a jury? Temple said yes, the defense requested a jury of Mr. Kelly's peers.

The case promptly became part of the mayoral campaign. Stokley met with Catto's older brother, a caterer from Bordentown, and took pains to assure him "that Mr. Sheppard would prosecute the case in a proper manner." William S. Catto, "an upright and intelligent young man," was quoted as putting his trust in both Stokley and Sheppard and appealing "to the Christian part of the community for justice." He said the bullets killed three of his family, for the loss of Octavius had hastened the deaths of his father and his sister.

On Valentine's Day, William Forten, Isaiah Wears, and Benjamin Tanner led thirty-five hundred people in a Stokley rally at Horticultural Hall. Democrats "drove us from the polls," Wears reminded the audience. "The police not protecting us, the Marines did. Octavius V. Catto, Chase, and others, were murdered, and the murderers allowed to escape. Local Republicanism has in custody the principal one today—although it had to climb the Alleghenies to capture him." Bands played and speakers read a letter from Robert Smalls and two other colored Southern congressmen endorsing Stokley. Forten called him "the great Centennial mayor."

No one could say exactly how important Kelly's arrest was to colored voters' decisions. But on February 21, they voted for Stokley in sufficient numbers to help him win reelection in a squeaker. They went to the polls at a time when the Republican ticket still seemed like the only safe haven for a colored man's vote.

For many, that time was about to end.

On February 26, a special panel of four Southern Democrats and five Northern Republicans met in the Washington hotel owned and operated by Billy Wormley's father and resolved the Hayes-Tilden stalemate. The meeting was so secret that historians still do not know what was said. But things happened afterward. Samuel Randall, who had led the "Tilden or War" Democrats' battle for disputed electoral votes in three Southern states, abruptly changed his tune. He began treating Hayes's election as a fait accompli. He cut off House Democrats' shouted objections and was credited with staving off chaos. With the crucial electoral votes finally in hand, Hayes was sworn in—at a private White House ceremony, lest violence erupt.

Seven weeks later, the new president ordered the last army units out of Southern capitals.

Dissension arose at colored meetings. In Philadelphia, people demanded answers from Wears, who along with Forten, had come to be seen as the party's apologist. J. W. Cromwell, Robert Purvis's son, Charles, and a half-dozen other men in various states sent an open letter to another Hayes defender, John Mercer Langston. "Our people are alarmed and dismayed at the seeming indifference of the President," they wrote. Black voters had been the margin of Republican victory in New York, New Jersey, Ohio, and Pennsylvania. "Shall we tell the colored people of these States that the new Administration is friendly to the interest of the colored people of the country? If so upon what shall we base our argument?"

In reply, Langston pointed to patronage positions Hayes was promising to men of color and made the same suggestion white officeholders would make for the next century or so. "Let us cultivate patience," Langston wrote.

Colored Republicans in the South could only shake their heads. Power was reverting into "the hands of the very men that held us as slaves," a leader of Louisiana freedmen remarked. A South Carolina Negro wrote, "To think that Hayes could go back on us, when we had to wade through blood to help place him where he now is."

A cruel irony attached itself to the Wormley name. The well-to-do Wormleys had always done right by race and country—building schoolhouses only to see them burned, volunteering for the navy in the war's first months, aiding contrabands, teaching freedmen. Now they heard people saying colored rights were bargained away at the "Wormley Conference."

The situation called for words from Frederick Douglass. In good times and bad, he had become the reliable battery, ever able to fire perfect verbal torpedoes into the hull of the white republic. Yet this time Douglass was silent.

He had just received a lucrative appointment from the new president. Douglass was said to have sulked over Grant's not naming him an ambassador. Within weeks of being sworn in, Hayes appointed him the U.S. marshal for the District of Columbia.

Douglass seemed nearly "oblivious to the concessions to white supremacists in the South that had put [Hayes] into office," his biographer wrote.

"[H]e did not see what was happening—did not allow himself to see it. And he accepted with great pride the presidential appointment that had so long eluded him."

Allies chided him. The *Nation* magazine said Hayes was giving him a powerless post, "a sort of vicarious atonement for the abandonment of the 15th Amendment."

One voice in the colored intelligentsia cheered—but for reasons having little to do with Hayes's Southern policy. Where others saw a sinecure, Fanny Jackson saw pupils' upturned faces. "You cannot tell what an inspiration your appointment has been to the School," she wrote to Douglass from the I.C.Y. "The boys are diving into their studies more earnestly than ever. I was very much pleased with your picture in *Harper's* last week. How proud I am of you!"

Perhaps things would work out. The new president professed hope that in return for removing the last army units, Southern governors and legislators would keep their word to him and defend the Negro rights delineated in the Thirteenth, Fourteenth, and Fifteenth Amendments.

"At any rate, the troops are ordered away," Hayes wrote in his diary on April 22, 1877. "Time will tell."

★ ★ ★

THE TRIAL of Frank Kelly began the next morning.

A spacious new Common Pleas courtroom at Sixth and Chestnut streets, the product of Stokley's building boom, filled quickly. A squad of court officers—tipstaves, they were called—combed the crowd for troublemakers and waited on the judge.

From the first morning of the first day, *Commonwealth of Pennsylvania vs. Frank Kelly* achieved something unusual and noteworthy for 1877—an audience of both races, crammed together on narrow seats, for sessions the judge allowed to run as late as 7:00 P.M. They were not a quiet assembly; one account described a constant hubbub in the room. A newspaper came up with a word for the look of the crowd: "piebald."

The same word did not apply to the men in the jury box. They ran a gamut of trades—carpenter, tinsmith, cabinetmaker, moulder, confectioner, "agent," laborer, gardener, salesman, cigar maker, and two well-off "gentlemen"—but not of color. In a city that had barely begun letting Negroes onto juries, clues in various records suggest all twelve men were white.

On the bench sat a compact, gray-bearded man, the son of a prominent chemist. Judge John Innis Clark Hare had trained in the sciences,
too, until a laboratory experiment exploded in his face. He had helped
found the Union League and had argued for admitting Democrats to its
ranks. On the bench, he was "conciliating" and "attentive" and steered
clear of volatile situations. Older Negroes remembered his 1861 ruling—
that streetcar companies need not force "long-civilized" white riders to
share the cars with a race "emerging from the shades of barbarism."

The Kelly trial turned volatile before the judge could raise his gavel.
A witness vanished—Theodore Stratton, the streetcar conductor. Hare
delayed the trial a week. Police found Stratton alive and well and cured
his reluctance to testify by locking him up to await his turn on the stand.
None of this was announced to the jurors, but they had their own concerns. On the trial's opening day, two jurors tensely announced that they'd
received anonymous notes about the case. Hare asked whether the notes
would cloud their judgment. One juror said perhaps and was replaced. The
other said no.

The clock was striking four by the time District Attorney Sheppard's
first assistant, Henry Hagert, opened the prosecution's case. Hagert kept
things simple, almost bland. Terming Catto "a colored man, and a teacher
of a school for colored youth," he sketched the scene, omitting the attacks
on Negro voters, except to say authorities had mobilized the Fifth Brigade
because of "fighting at the polls that day, and being fearful of disorders
at night."

He mentioned the neighbors' warning shouts to Catto, the moves of
the killer ("whom the Commonwealth says was Frank Kelly"), the streetcar, the shots, the sprint to the tavern "where he disappeared." Hagert said
police searched Kelly's home and haunts but found him only after learning
he was "in Chicago under the name of Charles Young."

Hagert's dry outline made the witnesses' words more dramatic.

South Street merchants testified to cowering in their shuttered stores
as the white mob raged outside. Two witnesses told of seeing a man who
fit Kelly's description shooting at a minister and other colored men in St.
Mary Street, a half hour before the murder. William St. Clair remembered
hearing "a shot and a scream . . . and saw a colored man reeling towards
me behind a car." The Negro beseeched a policeman for aid, then "reeled
and fell." W. H. Mullen, perched on a box at Eighth and South, saw the
policeman catch Catto, only to "let him drop."

Thomas Higgins said he and his friends at Eighth and South saw a man turn the corner "with a bandage on his head." Higgins, a white man who had since joined the police force, said the man was five feet five, with "a smooth face and a slight mustache, and good color in his cheeks" and that "[t]here is an expression in his eyes that I carry in my mind yet." He said the man was Kelly.

When Kelly's lawyer, Temple, questioned Higgins's certainty, the policeman raised his voice in court and said, "*I swear he is the man.*"

Charles P. Brown, a white printer, testified to seeing the entire scene, from the moment of the shooting to Constable Barr's sprint down Ninth Street in pursuit of the killer. Brown looked over at Kelly and said, "I recognize the man in the dock as the person who did that shooting."

The thump of those words at the end of the trial's first day would have been a fine place for prosecutors to lay the bookmark for the night, letting jurors sleep on the words of a sturdy witness. But Hare wanted to keep working. As the sun sank, the judge let cross-examination begin.

Temple went to work, moving monklike up and down the rows of evidence, pausing every few feet to plant seeds of doubt. He asked Brown why he hadn't told police all this in 1871. Brown said he assumed his testimony wouldn't matter until there was an arrest. Why hadn't Brown come forward at the coroner's inquest five years ago? Because, he said, "I thought I had better be out of the case." Hadn't he talked to authorities about the reward? He admitted that he had.

Brown also admitted that he'd seen the shooting from as far as a hundred feet away, that he'd never known Kelly and hadn't seen him again until the day the trial was to start. On that day, Brown testified, he'd gone to court and learned of the postponement—and to his surprise saw Kelly being brought upstairs. Brown said he got a front and side view of the defendant's face. "I said to myself, that's the man, sure."

Then Brown blurted out what he'd heard that day. He said the chief of police told him the trial was delayed because a witness "had been spirited away or bought off."

Spirited away. Bought off. Spectators whispered to each other. The state's own witness had not only struggled to explain his long silence and crystal-clear memory; he had struck a fresh blow to the trial's equilibrium, the apple cart of evidence and argument that prosecutors tried to steady and defense lawyers to upset.

So ended the first day.

★ ★ ★

BOTH SIDES SAW where the case was headed. Prosecutors would need every credible witness they had. Temple would use as his personal hammer the five years authorities had taken to drag Kelly to trial, years in which memories should have dimmed, not sharpened. Detective Tryon, perhaps anticipating his own turn as a witness, greeted Brown at court the next morning by saying, "I suppose they will give you a sweating today."

Temple put Brown back on the stand and got him to admit that he'd been so far from the shooting that he was not sure whether the murdered man was colored or white. Temple even got him to admit Tryon's "sweating" remark.

The jury heard from three of the men who had gone to Chicago. Officer Bickley recalled confronting Kelly in 1871 for repeating, then ducking Kelly's blackjack.

Tryon described the conversations with the prisoner over the course of many hours in the eastbound train. He told of ordering Bickley to unlock Kelly's handcuffs in the palace car. He brushed aside defense suggestions that the handcuffs-off, easy-does-it speech had been an old detective's even older game of seduction. Temple demanded to know: Just before that first meal, hadn't Tryon buttered up Kelly by saying, "Be easy with Frank, he won't try to take advantage of us?" Tryon denied using those words.

At that, Kelly went flush-faced in the courtroom and leaped to his feet. "It is false!" he shouted. The judge frowned at him and he sat down.

Tryon recalled Kelly chatting on the train about his father and sister, about living in Cincinnati as Charles Young, about rum's role in his legal troubles, and about October 10—especially after Tryon mentioned the other wanted man in the case. He asked Kelly if he'd seen Reddy Dever in his travels. Tryon said the conversation went like this:

   Kelly: I haven't seen him since the shooting.
   Tryon: Do you mean the shooting of Catto?
   Kelly: Yes.
   Tryon: Did you see him that day?
   Kelly: In the early part of it.
   Tryon: Was he with you when Catto was shot?

To that question, Tryon said, Kelly's answer was: "No, I was alone."

In the dock, Kelly turned beet-red again. He leaped up and repeated, "It is false!"

For the defense's purposes, Tryon's story had to be false. Because if it were true, it would mean Kelly had almost confessed.

★ ★ ★

THEODORE STRATTON'S TESTIMONY began with 1871. He had been at his post on the rear platform of Lombard–South Street Car No. 8 when he saw "a colored man standing with his arms spread out, and shaking or trembling, and a white man in the act of firing."

Stratton said the Negro shouted, "What are you doing?" and ran behind the car. The white man chased him and kept firing. "The colored man turned and faced him, and the white man fired two shots in quick succession. The colored man staggered and fell."

The next thing he knew, people were running and screaming. One of his four passengers, Samuel Wanamaker, was pushing Stratton aside and leaping from the car, pointing at the bandaged man and shouting, "This is an outrage! That is the man who did the shooting!"

Only then, Stratton said, did the bandaged man trouble himself to run.

He described the man much as other witnesses had: dark Kossuth hat, dark coat, slight build, five feet six, smooth face, twenty or twenty-one years. He said he'd seen him before but could not remember where—perhaps in Devitt's Tavern, where Stratton often drank.

Temple asked how he could remember the killer's clothing but not what Catto or anyone else wore that day. Stratton said the killer had stood practically under his nose.

He pointed across the courtroom at Kelly and said, "The man who sits there was in the track about fifteen feet away from me."

No one asked Stratton why he'd disappeared before the trial.

Temple pestered him about the Chicago trip. Hadn't police all but pointed him to Kelly? Stratton denied this. Temple asked about the fourth man, the Negro who'd gone out there with him and Tryon and Bickley.

Stratton remembered William Forten's excitement over Kelly's arrest. "Mr. Forten said, 'If we can catch this man it will be one of the best things for our present mayor.'"

Forten did not testify. But Temple now had fresh seeds to plant and began demanding of colored witnesses: Had Forten spoken to them? Advised them on what to say? Had Robert Adger offered them twenty-five dollars to incriminate Kelly? Annie Howard and Elizabeth Hill denied all these charges on the stand. Adger testified about the rioting at Eighth and South, outside his father's store—and was not asked about offering witnesses money.

★ ★ ★

ISAAC BARR told the jury of his Election Day sprint—how he had been at Ninth and South when shots rang out and people shouted, "Stop that man," how he found himself outrunning a tall policeman, Officer McKnight, in pursuit of a bandaged man.

Someone yelled, "He's run through the tavern!" and in Barr went. He testified to seeing the bandaged man seated calmly at the end of the bar and of shouting to the arriving McKnight—"There's your man!" But the man in the Kossuth hat was instantly on his feet and bolting for the tavern's back door.

Barr remembered catching him in the yard out back—where the bandaged man turned nonchalant again. "He asked me what I wanted with him," Barr testified. As Barr began to answer, the man reached into his coat. The constable grabbed him and held on until McKnight and a shorter policeman arrived.

Then he handed his prisoner over. He even remembered one policeman clapping a hand on the prisoner's shoulder and another on his right arm. That was that, Barr thought. But as he caught his breath outside, heard "a shuffle," dashed back, and saw that the prisoner was gone.

Barr testified that he'd never seen the man before and couldn't say for certain that the accused was Kelly. But of one thing the constable was sure: He'd handed the bandaged man to two policemen and one of them was McKnight.

★ ★ ★

COLORED MEN AND WOMEN who had never faced a white audience of any sort testified to a white judge and twelve white men. The jurors likewise undertook the novelty of weighing colored witnesses' words.

Testimony came from I.C.Y. colleagues and colored friends who had known Catto since grammar school. Robert Allen remembered breakfasting with him at the boardinghouse at eight thirty. Fanny Jackson—no stranger to white men's skeptical stares—walked the jury through the classes and recesses of Catto's final, riot-shortened day at the I.C.Y.

Cyrus Miller told of helping Catto to buy the pistol, but no bullets, at the pawn shop in Walnut Street. St. George Taylor remembered last seeing his friend in Lombard Street around three o'clock, heading west to take Ninth Street instead of Eighth, farther from the danger.

Annie Howard was seventeen when Catto was killed. She described peering from her alley and seeing a young white man in a bandage run up behind Catto. "I hallooed, 'Look out for that man!'" and Catto turned— but the man was already firing. She said she was sure he was Kelly. So did the older woman at her side that day, Elizabeth Hill. Mary Kane, Catto's neighbor at 822 South, remembered hearing Annie Howard shout, "Look out, Professor, that man's going to shoot!" Thomas H. Bolling, with his father at 825 South, remembered saluting Catto. Then he heard the shots.

No one disputed the killer's general appearance, or the time or place or circumstance of Catto's death. Witnesses had more to do with adding a stone of credibility here or there to the prosecutors' mosaic; defense witnesses, to pulling the stones away. In the course of a trial that lasted ten days—not to mention Kelly's two forthcoming trials, for the killing of Chase and the wounding of Fawcett—there was ample room for lesser mysteries, oddities, and revelations.

Revealed, for instance, was the era's laissez-faire approach to safekeeping of evidence in general and bullets in particular. When John Fawcett, the colored hod-carrier, testified to being chased by a mob, tripped by a boy, and wounded by Kelly, he got jurors' attention by showing them the bullet, which, five years earlier, a surgeon in Pennsylvania Hospital had scissored from his hip. Fawcett kept it on his watch chain.

Fawcett was the second witness to display a souvenir bullet. The coroner, describing the bullet wounds he'd found in Catto—arm, thigh, shoulder, heart—said he had given away the fatal ball he'd extracted from the pericardium ("the heart-sack," he explained helpfully). He gave it to a brewery representative who, for reasons unexplained, attended Catto's post-mortem. The brewery man, in turn, testified that *he'd* given the ball in 1872 to a colored saloonkeeper he knew—William Minton, Catto's old friend.

Minton took the stand and verified this testimony by reaching into his pocket and producing the deadly bullet. He also tried to set the record straight—he was a caterer, not a tavern keeper. Older generations of "better class" colored families were usually temperancers; a Minton son could ill afford to be portrayed otherwise.

He said he kept the bullet under lock and key, fending off Temple's suggestions that he'd lent it out and shown it off in Wilmington and Washington. Minton said he'd accepted the bullet on behalf of a group of men "all friendly to Mr. Catto"—the Banneker Literary Institute.

"A memento," Minton testified.

★　★　★

FOR ONE TENSE MOMENT the courtroom was poised to consider a larger mystery—the inner workings of the hose company whose members had included Frank Kelly, Reddy Dever, and Frank Devitt, the tavern keeper who had paid Kelly to tend his bar. That was how Stratton and other witnesses claimed to recognize Kelly—they knew him from Devitt's Tavern. So did John Gregory, who told of getting slugged by Kelly in a past election brawl. "I saw him once in a while tending bar there," Gregory said. "He was generally very genteelly fixed up." So prosecutors needed Devitt to make the link—to confirm that his former employee and the defendant were one and the same.

Devitt had been an alderman and a McMullen ally for years. He had marched as assistant marshal to Grand Marshal McMullen, leading hundreds of red-shirted firemen strutting the streets in one of the grand, defiant parades. Prosecutors, knowing Devitt might not be the most helpful witness, had met with him the night before and came away assured that he would not dispute that the man picked up in Chicago was Kelly, his old employee. That was all they needed.

Instead, his testimony was laden with trip wires. He said a Frank Kelly had tended his bar in 1871 and was at work at nine on the morning of October 10—but that was the last Devitt had ever seen of him. Devitt testified that he "really couldn't say that the prisoner is the man."

Devitt had probably known Kelly longer than any other witness. Yet he was saying he wasn't sure the man in the dock was Kelly. As Tryon testified, even Kelly had admitted that much at arraignment. Devitt was also brazenly rejiggering the story he had told the night before. Jurors needed to see why Devitt and perhaps other witnesses might be protecting Kelly. Hagert asked Devitt: Was the defendant "a member of any company or association to which you belonged?"

Defense lawyers objected—the Commonwealth was attacking its own witness. Judge Hare sustained the objection. The mystery remained a mystery.

★ ★ ★

THE JURORS heard from forty-two prosecution witnesses in four and a half days. Last-minute additions trickled in with various explanations for surfacing so late. One old colored woman said she'd known Frank Kelly since he was a boy, saw him kill Catto, and came forward only now because "the Lord told me to come."

Temple called a dozen defense witnesses. He built his case around questioning motives and memories—especially of the prosecution's colored witnesses—and convincing the jury that whatever else had happened on October 10, 1871, the streets of South Philadelphia had become a convention of young white men with Kossuth hats pulled low and bandages on their foreheads.

How many men had had one eye on a job in Stokley's administration when they swore to give impartial testimony? Several—such as Stratton, who admitted hoping for a harbor police post. How many Negroes had waited till Kelly's arrest to announce that they'd seen him kill Catto or Chase, or wound John Fawcett? Several. And how, Temple demanded to know, could colored Philadelphians claim five years hence to remember the face of a white stranger?

That question prompted some witnesses to give the jury an impromptu seminar on alley life. The races in the "infected region" might not vote the same ticket or prefer each other's company, but neither were they strangers. Kelly had lived at his aunt's house, no more than a hundred feet from Adger's corner store and Catto's boardinghouse. A colored laundress in the neighborhood explained that until the election riot, she'd regularly done Kelly's shirts. A colored man testified, "I used to black his boots."

Several defense witnesses suggested the killer was probably Frank Reilly, a former Third Ward constable who looked a bit like Kelly. In rebuttal, Furman Sheppard called witnesses who said Reilly wasn't bandaged. Reilly couldn't testify—he was dead.

Robert McKnight, the tall policeman—now a former policeman—testified to catching Catto as he fell. He said the colored man called out to him, "Mac, give me your protection"—and that McKnight, seeing a gun, replied, "I will, why don't you protect yourself with that in your hand?" He denied dropping Catto on the pavement, admitted following Barr into the tavern on Bainbridge Street, and denied Barr had ever corralled the suspect in the yard, handed him over to McKnight, or shouted, "Here's your man." McKnight said he, too, had known Kelly, "and I do not believe he is the man."

Now it fell to Kelly's lawyers to leave the jury with one final, memorable impression. They chose not to have their client testify. The last witness they called was William McMullen.

In the years since 1871, other men had launched attempts to curb the Squire's aldermanic powers, his hose company, his police appointees, even his life. With the possible exception of Stokley's having fired McMullen's police hirees, the Squire had not only prevailed in each of these matters, but his reach and resilience had grown. He had even made a secret pact with Stokley and delivered him enough Fourth Ward votes to claim some credit for the mayor's close reelection.

He had seen reformers gunning for the alderman system. So he quit and won a seat on the Common Council by a large majority. He still communicated regularly with his ascending star in Washington, the Speaker of the House. He even seemed at times to order Sam Randall around—"Fix this thing for me," he wrote on notes.

He had been shot in the chest from inches away by the redoubtable but ill-starred Hughy Morrow, a shooting that laid McMullen so low that Randall and other dignitaries came to pay their last respects. But he left the hospital three weeks later, after newspapers ran his obituary.

Indeed, the papers seemed overeager to predict his demise. When Morrow was put on trial in 1872, a lawyer named Swope called the Moyamensing Hose Company "the school for scoundrels and the refuge for thieves." Then Swope pointed at McMullen and called him president of that school. He offered to prove that McMullen had "secreted" the would-be assassins of Agent Brooks in his own home. Suddenly, the Morrow trial courtroom had gone suspiciously dark, its lamps failing and flaring "like the dying spasms of a breathing creature," wrote the *Inquirer*, a paper that credited McMullen with corruptly influencing national elections. But the gas came back, the judge barred the testimony, and McMullen had fended off another inquisition.

Nor had he lost his gift for sending a clear signal. Exercising his influence over Fourth Ward liquor trade, he had had the site of Kelly's purported escape renamed Samuel Randall's Tavern.

In Kelly's trial, McMullen wrapped a ribbon around Temple's defense. He offered names of three men he'd seen in the riot, all more or less resembling Kelly, all bandaged. One was Reilly, the late constable—"I saw that he had a revolver in his pocket."

McMullen portrayed the riot in a way no one else had: He omitted the white attacks on colored voters. "There was fighting going on all that day. There were hundreds of people on the street; colored people got to quarreling on Lisle Street [and] . . . later there was fighting on Emeline street." He helped his friend Sergeant Duffy drive back the crowds.

He said he knew Frank Kelly only as a red-haired boy who tended bar at Devitt's. On cross-examination, McMullen admitted having seen Kelly on the night of October 9—in the hours before all hell broke loose on colored voters.

"There was a lot of voting going on there that day," the Squire protested, "and if strangers had kept away there wouldn't have been any trouble."

★ ★ ★

BY FURMAN SHEPPARD'S COUNT, twenty-eight witnesses described the killer as matching Kelly "as respects age, height, bulk, hat, bandaged, clothing, and sort of face," and six had sworn flat-out that Kelly was the man. Furthermore, the D.A. said in his closing speech, the defendant had chosen to flee to other states, forsake his family and friends, and "to seek to obliterate the very name by which he was known." Were those the acts of the innocent? "Flight," Sheppard said, "is the cheap resource of conscious guilt."

Temple spoke for an hour; then Hare recessed court for an hour; then Temple rose and spoke again for three hours. He hammered once again on the late-discovered memories and inconsistencies. He portrayed Kelly's identification in Chicago a fiction of "so-called detective work." He said Stratton had admitted pining for the harbor police job that the mayor could deliver. He said that the three thousand dollars of reward money explained a lot of the testimony. Temple said the defense's eyewitnesses were just as sure the killer wasn't Kelly as the prosecutors' were sure he was. And he pounded on Forten's comment about "a good thing for our mayor."

Judge Hare's charge to the jury, by one account, sounded as if he wanted a conviction; he observed that some defendants who "escaped justice" and went on to commit "further depredations."

The jurors went upstairs to deliberate and were sequestered overnight.

A few moments after Hare gaveled the courtroom to order the next morning, people heard footsteps from the stairwell. The jurors had reached a verdict. One writer said, "The usual noise of this most disorderly of court rooms hushed of itself into the most profound silence" as twelve men, flanked by tipstaves, walked up the center aisle. Some jurors looked over at Kelly and smiled.

The audience was a "mob of blacks and whites," according to one onlooker, and "the same piebald mob that has attended the Kelly trial from the beginning," according to another. Hare scolded them in advance that he would imprison anyone who tried to spark disorder. He ordered the tipstaves to take up positions in the aisles. Then he told the clerk, "Take the verdict."

At this point, the *Philadelphia Times* reported, Frank Kelly "was as pale as the sheeted dead . . . and his hands, those tell-tales of fear, worked nervously." His sister sat near him. The paper said the defendant had displayed "marvelous self possession" all through the trial. Now, "he did not know what to do with those hands." Prosecutor Hagert played with a pencil. At the defense table, Temple rested his head on his forearms.

The judge told Kelly and the jurors to stand and look at each other. Kelly was already "devouring them with his eyes."

Spectators leaned forward. Five years of waiting and ten days of trial were coming to an end. The clerk repeated the murder charge and asked, "How say you?"

The foreman replied, "Not guilty."

A great sigh arose in the room—"a sound of the release of pent-up breath." Kelly sat down "as if the ordeal had never happened." His sister was heard sobbing.

★　★　★

THE JURORS TOLD REPORTERS afterward that the key to the case was time. "We placed no confidence in . . . witnesses who, seeing the man who shot Catto only for a few minutes swore, after a lapse of six years, that they could identify the prisoner as that man," one juror said. Another said, "We did not believe the positive swearers on either side." At first, two jurors had leaned toward convicting. But the next morning's secret ballot—folded paper slips in a cigar box—yielded twelve slips that said "not guilty."

One historian describes the colored community's reaction as "infuriated." An editorial said Kelly could thank "the authorities, who allowed him to wander at large until it had become almost impossible to establish either his guilt or his innocence."

Much was said about the likelihood that one or more of the still-pending charges would send Kelly to prison. Those charges included two from the Catto riot—the killing of Isaac Chase and the wounding of John Fawcett—and the vote-fraud case in Ohio. The *Press* said the Fawcett evidence was so strong that it amounted to "a foregone conclusion." But who knew whether the Ohio charge would stick?

At a routine hearing in late spring, Benjamin Temple asked a judge to set Frank Kelly free. The prosecutors had held him for five months, long enough, Temple argued, to trigger the state's speedy-trial rule against such delays.

Judge James Ludlow said the delays had been lawful. He asked for the commitment papers holding Kelly for trial in Chase's killing. The agent for Moyamensing Prison announced that no such papers existed.

The judge grew incredulous. A grand jury had taken testimony and handed up a widely publicized indictment. And now, five years later, the courts had no record of it? Ludlow called this "a most extraordinary thing."

He began to prepare his own order, committing Kelly for trial. Temple was on his feet in an instant, saying the prisoner was being held unfairly, the prosecutors had had their bite of the apple.

The judge told Temple to sit down and be quiet.

★ ★ ★

THE LITTLEST VOICES carried in Emeline Street, a close-packed canyon of brick and board that narrowed to nine feet across. Young colored mothers in the 800 block learned to distinguish the cries of their children, and of every other child on the row.

Those sounds had been all-important as the Catto riot raged. In the late spring of 1877, colored women of Emeline Street explained this to the jury in the trial of Frank Kelly for the killing of Isaac Chase.

"I heard the screams of the children," Mary Harris, who lived in the rear apartment of 810 Emeline, testified. She and other women described the moment when a torrent of white men crested Eighth Street's banks and sluiced down Emeline, their hands clutching brickbats, revolvers, and a hatchet, their epithets ricocheting up and down the alley.

"There he is!" "Kill the nigger!" Margaret Barrett, a widow, remembered those words. "They were rallying and whooping, and when they got to Number 1, they broke in the door." She described white men storming into houses, a terror rarely seen in the city since the temperance riot and the Red Row mob.

Barrett and other women threw the bolts on their doors. They rushed their children up to second and third floors, peeked out windows, and saw Chase, a friendly, muscular waiter. He and his wife, Sarah, had several young children and an older daughter Julia, eleven years old. He was in the act of locking his gate, ducking his head, then foolishly chancing a look up toward Eighth Street.

"I said, 'Mr. Chase, don't go out there,'" Anna Myers, the Chases' next-door neighbor testified. "He looked out three times and then shut the gate."

Myers ran upstairs to be with her children. From there, she said, she heard "a rush up the alley." Then she heard white voices holler. "That's the man!" "Kill him!"

Margaret Barrett saw the wave coming. "Everybody scattered to get into their houses," she testified. Mothers huddled with their children. But Chase's wife was working and his children were alone. Chase turned and ran for his door.

Barrett saw two men take down Chase's wooden gate with a hatchet. She recognized both of them, but especially Frank Kelly. "I knew him because I washed for him." He'd been in her house once to pick up his shirts. She said the second man was Reddy Dever.

She saw them charge past the ruins of the gate. Kelly was reaching into his pocket, and then he was out of her sight.

The women heard shots then. Myers remembered "two shots and a fall." Barrett saw the two men come back within her view, moving almost at a saunter, returning to the tumult in Eighth Street. Then came sounds she would never forget.

"We heard the screams of Chase's children."

★ ★ ★

JULIA CHASE was not quite seventeen when she climbed to the witness stand and looked across the courtroom at her mother, in the audience, and at Frank Kelly in the dock. "I am a daughter of the man who was killed," she began.

She said there was "considerable excitement" in Emeline Street all morning, and by early afternoon she was upstairs, tending to the other children while her mother was at work and her father was outside. Then she heard two shots.

She ran to the stairs, saw her father in the doorway, and shouted, "Father, come in and shut the door." Then she heard a third shot and saw him fall, lifeless.

She rushed to her brothers and sisters. Now men were outside the door. She remembered looking outside, recognizing Kelly and shouting, "*Oh! You have killed my father!*"

And she testified: "Frank Kelly pointed a pistol at me and said, 'Go in, you . . . or we'll kill you.'"

Temple tried to cross her up. Hadn't Julia told the coroner's jury something different about sequence of events? That she'd seen Kelly and Dever run up the alley? Julia said she was upstairs and, "I didn't look out, because I was afraid." Hadn't she testified to the coroner that the man with the pistol wore black clothes and a black cap and was tall?

"I may have, and I may not." She was sure about his clothing. Then she said yes, she had used the word *tall*.

Two jurors called out to the judge just then. They said the witness's mother was signaling her from across the courtroom by shaking her head. Mother and daughter denied this; Sarah Chase said she was merely wiping her face. The judge admonished her and made her move to a different seat.

Prosecutors might have fared better if they had limited their case to the women's testimony; the only discrepancies were minor. But Temple played havoc with the words of the men. Albert Addison, seventeen at the time of Chase's killing, claimed to know Kelly from the neighborhood and recalled a tattoo on Kelly's left hand—the number 27.

Addison told of climbing up to the rooftops and jumping from one house to the next until he was almost directly over Chase's house. He said he saw the killing from there.

Temple pressed him. Who had told young Addison to see the chief of police and volunteer his testimony? Had he met with William Forten? No, said Addison. But he had met with William Minton, "in a back room in Liberty Hall."

Once again, a state witness was giving Temple free ammunition. Liberty Hall meant colored political meetings and Negro societies with strange names such as Banneker and Pythian. A juror could imagine a Minton or a Forten or some other Catto crony cooking up testimony "in a back room." A colored witness had practically admitted it.

Temple furiously alleged witness tampering. He said the culprit was Detective Miller of the district attorney's office. He accused him in court, pounding his fist on the rail separating him from Miller. The judge ordered Temple removed from the room for a few minutes, saying he was surprised Miller hadn't leapt the rail to "throttle" the lawyer.

The main defense witnesses, Sergeant Duffy and Councilman McMullen, told the same story they had in the Catto case, of quelling a riot in which blacks and whites were evenly matched. McMullen allowed that he and his friend Duffy had, "I may say," acted bravely.

★　★　★

THE QUEST FOR JUSTICE in the Catto riot seemed to dissipate with each new round of testimony. Words that years earlier would have startled or enraged began to lose their sting. Sergeant Duffy remembered the hunt for Kelly as less a gallop than a trot. He didn't think police had sent out Kelly's description until two months after the riot.

Duffy "supposed the authorities made an effort to arrest." But he had not tried personally to capture Kelly—"because he thought that they didn't want him caught."

McMullen cast himself as generous uncle to Fourth Ward residents. He assured the jury he was looking out for both races' welfare, even that of Isaac Chase.

"I knew Chase well," McMullen testified. He claimed to have handed the colored man a Democratic ticket at a poll that day, a story that circulated right after the riot—that black men, not whites, had slain Chase for voting Democratic. After Chase voted, McMullen told the jury that he took the colored voter for a midday drink. He testified that he last saw Chase heading back to Emeline Street, about 1:00 P.M.

Right after that, McMullen heard there'd been a killing in Emeline Street and went there, promptly, and in the last house on the alley, "saw poor Chase lying upon the floor." He promised Chase's widow he'd pay for the burial, "which I did."

The colored witnesses from Emeline Street found themselves shouted at and threatened on their way to and from court. Albert Addison made the mistake of walking home one night with a flower in his lapel. He said two white men asked whether his "fine clothes" came from the prosecutors. When Addison said no, one of the men ripped the flower from his lapel and predicted, "Kelly will be acquitted anyway." Then he slugged Addison.

★ ★ ★

THE PREDICTION was accurate. The Chase jurors took less time than Kelly's first jury.

Between April and July 1877, Kelly had prevailed in trial after trial—acquitted in Catto's killing; then, for Chase's; finally, acquitted even faster in the wounding of John Fawcett, notwithstanding Fawcett's second displaying of the bullet on his watch chain. As one historian points out, it is hard to prove a murderer guilty in the context of a riot. Much less, a white murderer of Negroes, tried by white jurors in a white-ruled city, his chances improved by five years' delay and by his connections to powerful men. Frank Kelly had become the Venus of the High Trapeze.

Newspapers, especially Republican-minded ones, ridiculed the verdicts. A paper in Akron, Ohio, said "the Democratic ward rough, Kelly, . . . has been able through political influence, to get acquitted." A new Philadelphia paper, the *Public Record*, said, "So far as shooting negroes is concerned, Kelly may now be regarded as a licensed killer, [with] the gang behind him and the jury in front of him." The *New York Times* said "the strongest political combinations" helped Kelly win his trials. The front-page headline declared, "A Democratic murderer escapes."

Mayor Stokley took fitful steps to placate colored Philadelphians. He addressed long-standing calls for City Hall jobs by hiring twenty-one colored "turnkeys," whose daily duties mostly involved cleaning up after drunken prisoners in the cells of Central Station. He appointed a man from Catto's old circle as his personal messenger—a post critics derided as "the cleaning of cuspidors and the shining of shoes."

Stokley's appointee was William Dorsey, a man whose homemade scrapbooks reflected the intensity of colored Philadelphia's interest in the trials. Dorsey routinely clipped newspaper items on every aspect of the colored world—history, politics, religion, education, sports, music, the arts. He especially tracked news of victories and setbacks, large or small, in the battle for equal rights. His scrapbook on the trials ran to ninety pages.

By the middle of summer 1877, all that remained of Kelly's cases was for federal authorities to give him a perfunctory hearing and return him to Ohio on the vote-fraud charges. But those indictments had been filed against Charles Young. So, after all that had been said to prove Young was Kelly, his lawyers now argued to a federal commissioner that Kelly was not Young.

The lawyer Wendell Bowman assured the commissioner that he didn't mean to test the court's patience, and that his client believed in justice and the jury system. "Yes," the commissioner said, "he ought to have respect for our juries, especially in this city." Kelly laughed as hard anyone in the room.

A federal agent in the voting case took a good look at Kelly and testified that he and Young were the same man. The commissioner set bail high, at two thousand dollars, to await transport to Cincinnati. Someone promptly put up the money, and Kelly—in custody for the six months since Detective Steele had grabbed him and taken away his knife—walked free.

His Philadelphia friends took him back to the Fourth Ward for a celebration that lasted through the afternoon and evening. They ended up in the Club House, an Eighth Street saloon whose owner had been among those testifying about the high number of young white men with bandaged heads. Sometime after nine the party spilled out into the July night, and a brawl erupted. A policeman waded in, could not quell things, sounded his ear-splitting "rattle," and restored order with the help of reinforcements and the chief of police. No one was arrested.

In December, a Cincinnati jury convicted Kelly of vote fraud. He was sentenced to thirteen months' imprisonment but was pardoned after six. Also pardoned was Eph Holland, the admitted ringleader of the effort to fabricate Democratic votes.

Holland's pardon came from President Hayes. The source of Kelly's pardon is murky. One newspaper credited Ohio's governor; another said the White House. Rutherford Hayes's papers shed little light—except for a letter to the president, in November 1878, from a man in Philadelphia who signed as Francis Kelly.

"Your very kind favor of an unconditional Pardon from the consequence of the one error of my youth is received," the letter said. "It is with the deepest sense of gratitude to you that I make this acknowledgement."

★ ★ ★

AFTER THE COMPROMISE of 1877, colored electoral power wavered in the North and waned in the South. "The glorious mount of citizenship" in

Tanner's eulogy diminished. Southern states repealed bans on Klan activity; new landlord-tenant laws reduced sharecroppers to freedmen in name only. Theodore Tilton's prediction of voting rights undone by "a dozen cunning schemes" became a reality. Alabama diced its "black belt" into six majority-white congressional districts. Mississippi cemented white rule in five districts by squeezing most of its Negro population into one long "shoestring" district along the Mississippi's banks. Richmond and other cities redrew wards to ensure white control. With the departure of federal soldiers, many of the "freedom schools" staffed by I.C.Y. graduates and other colored teachers closed. With the army gone, one freedman said, the South's pledges to honor the Thirteenth, Fourteenth, and Fifteenth Amendments were "like pie-crust, easily broken."

In Philadelphia, some of the men who in younger days had styled themselves a "band of brothers" marked the tenth anniversary of the Fifteenth Amendment's passage by declaring it the product of crass Republican expediency, not principle. Others, such as William Forten, remained loyal to the party. Hayes supporter John Mercer Langston was named ambassador to Haiti. Ebenezer Bassett came home.

Nearly two years after the last of Kelly's acquittals, a door swung open in a magistrate's courtroom on Eighth Street in Philadelphia, and a middle-aged pipe fitter walked in. A larceny case was being heard by the magistrate—they were not called aldermen anymore. The pipe fitter announced that he wished to clear his name on a charge of murdering a colored man, Isaac Chase, in 1871.

The magistrate and the constable looked up, astonished. Testimony halted in the larceny case. The constable asked the visitor to identify himself.

The visitor, "cool as a cucumber," said his name was Edward J. Dever.

Reddy Dever had come back. The magistrate noted his not-guilty plea and whisked him off to a prison cell.

Newspapers said Dever had been living in New Orleans and had gone a bit gray since the days "when he ran with the gang." His surrender after more than seven years' absence was so astounding that for weeks people debated his motivations. Theories were advanced: Dever wanted to regain the affection of his ailing father or was under "religious influences and advice," a plausible guess in a decade when revival meetings drew tens of thousands.

Or—and this was said to be the talk of his closest associates—Dever was "continually haunted" at the prospect of being recognized and arrested, and at the same time harbored little doubt that he'd win his case on the basis of "evidence and influence."

To help him in that regard, Benjamin Temple materialized at his side.

News of his arraignment moved down the telegraph wires to other cities. The last man to face a jury in the Catto riot merited the front page of the *Washington Post*, and a flash of anger on Capitol Hill.

The Congress had been contemplating the various waves of fraud and intimidation in recent elections. House members debated renewing the Force Act, so that at some boiling point, city police and state militias would yield to federal troops' intervention on behalf of voters' rights. Speaker Randall opposed this, as he always had. He said the latest proof was Mayor Stokley's acclaimed use of city police in the railroad strike of 1877.

Congressman Charles O'Neill, a Philadelphia Republican, asked the House to remember that marines had saved an election in 1870, and that in 1871, police stood by as "colored voters were driven about the streets at the mercy of the mob." He said one of the men murdered that day was "Professor Octavius V. Catto, a scholar, a gentleman, and a soldier who had attained the rank of major."

Randall was growing impatient with this speech, but O'Neill was not finished. He had known Catto and likened him to Joseph Rainey, a colored Reconstruction congressman from the South, but said Catto was the greater scholar. He turned to Kelly's trials. "You cannot convict him. Another man . . . is about to be tried, who will very likely escape. His Democratic friends will rush to his assistance, as in the trials of the former." If House members needed particulars, O'Neill said, "I have on my desk a scrapbook, that was compiled by an intelligent man of color." It was the work of William Dorsey.

Randall had had enough. He turned the topic away from 1871, saying, "I do not desire to enter into any of the individualities of the discussion in regard to my city."

In fact, Randall was well apprised of Dever's pending case, which ended in acquittal. The House Speaker's steady source of information was McMullen, his friend, sponsor, and adviser. Negroes, newspapers, and Republicans could speculate about powerful Democrats influencing the trials, but they had no way of knowing with certainty.

They were not privy, for instance, to a message Randall received from McMullen, a note that historian Harry Silcox unearthed a century later in Randall's papers. The note was dated a few days after the jury delivered the last verdict in the violence that ended the life of Octavius Catto.

"All things are quiet here," McMullen wrote. "I have had a hard weeks work getting Dever acquitted."

The Legacy

OCTAVIUS CATTO and his "band of brothers" and sisters were unapologetic young African Americans working to pull down a white lattice of politics and culture built on slavery and discrimination.

Catto's people lived in a time when teachers were whipped for teaching, when some people of color kept slaves of their own, when white mobs burned black churches and schools, and standing in line to cast a vote meant risking life and limb. The stories survive in the unlit cellars of American history.

For them, *civil rights* was newborn.

That these civil rights leaders had accomplishments and improved the lives of African Americans is without question. They opened up Pennsylvania's streetcars to people of color, persuading white legislators to enact the state's first law ever written by African Americans. They helped win the right to vote. They forged a tradition of academic rigor. They proved blacks could teach and sent legions of teachers into the Reconstruction South. They broke the baseball color line, however briefly. They led the black enlistment drives that helped win the Civil War.

What is in question is what role this nineteenth-century generation played for future civil rights generations. What is their legacy?

"Influence is the hardest thing to trace," Eric Foner says. Historical memory is often short-lived. We know of no moment when Rosa Parks's elders told her the story of Caroline Le Count. Nor are we aware of any-one's describing Catto's streetcar tactics to Rev. Martin Luther King Jr., though King may very well have read of him.

Second baseman Jackie Robinson probably never heard of second baseman Octavius Catto.

But there remain intriguing links between the band of brothers and sisters and modern times. Some are apparent and some, again quoting Foner, may be "subterranean," showing up in schools, churches, and move-ments and in the lives of descendants.

★ ★ ★

SOME OF THE LINKS are personal. They begin with W.E.B. Du Bois.

If Dr. King knew the name of Octavius Catto, it is because Du Bois devoted three pages to the murder in his landmark study, *The Philadel-phia Negro.*

A founder of the NAACP, he knew Jake White and William Bolivar and Caroline Le Count because those surviving friends of Catto's assisted him with the research for *The Philadelphia Negro.* Du Bois, in fact, asked White to proofread the chapter on education to "note any errors of fact or judgment into which I have fallen."

It was Du Bois who rescued Bolivar's account of the 1871 riot and kill-ing and presented it to a wider national audience along with Bolivar's bit-ing description of Mayor Daniel Fox: "a mild, easygoing Democrat who seemed a puppet in the hands of astute, conscienceless men."

And it was Du Bois who wrote that the violence on that Election Day reminded black residents of the years before Emancipation: "The mur-der of Catto came at a critical moment; to the Negroes, it seemed a re-vival of the old slavery-time riots in the day when they were first tasting freedom."

Du Bois, who died on the eve of King's March on Washington in 1963, lived well into the modern civil rights movement and was an early archi-tect of that movement.

Other founders of the NAACP could trace their roots to Catto's time. William Lloyd Garrison's grandson was among the civil rights group's ear-liest white stalwarts. So was Florence Kelley, by then a women's rights leader and a champion of child labor laws. She was the daughter of Con-gressman William Kelley and witnessed the travails of her father, the voting-rights champion and Catto ally whose portrait was a target for the hurled rotten eggs of angry whites. On an NAACP statement in 1922 supporting an anti-lynching law, her name was on the letterhead with that of Du Bois and NAACP official Archibald Grimké, one of the slave-born nephews that the Grimké sisters discovered at Lincoln University.

Jacob White Jr., Catto's lifelong friend, remained a school principal until the mid-1890s. He was the leading African American man in public education in Philadelphia and remained a storied educator until his death in 1902. He quietly became the model of what Catto had espoused—black teachers for black students.

He also was board chairman in the 1890s of the Frederick Douglass Clinic at Fifteenth and Lombard, the first medical institution in the North to be staffed and run by blacks. The clinic became one of the nation's most important training centers for black doctors, nurses, and pharmacists.

Jake White, along with Robert Adger, William Dorsey, and William Bolivar, also understood that the activists' lives should be archived and remembered, that their stories "shouldn't be buried with their bodies," as a black journalist wrote in 1939. All four men were collectors and their accumulated books, letters, newspapers, broadsides, and organizational records became the papers of the American Negro Historical Society, now housed in the Historical Society of Pennsylvania. White's widow, Amelia, continued to donate his materials after his death.

In a 1904 speech, Adger explained why the American Negro Historical Society was important: "We want the Newspapers, the Churches and the Parents to tell their Children what our past Condition was, and about those dear people who are dead and gone, of the sacrifices they made in our behalf, and grand opportunities we are now offered." He added later, in a letter, "I am anxious to perpetuate those grand heroes who have espoused our Cause."

The collection includes the records of the Pythian baseball club, from lineups to the menus of postgame feasts. Portions of this book, and many others looking at nineteenth-century American black life, rely on the collection Catto's friends began. Dorsey's hundreds of scrapbooks of newspaper and magazine clippings documenting black life the world over is the highlight of what these men accumulated.

In addition to influencing historical memory, Jake White influenced a pupil—Henry Ossawa Tanner—who, in turn, helped change the art world.

White's effort to create a monument to his friend never quite succeeded. As early as 1872 and as late as 1889, he was meeting, cajoling, and trying to raise money for a memorial. He did not succeed, but his idea lives on in the hands of a white Irishman. In 2003, Philadelphia City Council member James Kenney began working to have a Catto statue erected at the foot of City Hall.

As an adult, Kenney heard about Catto and was startled that he had never heard of him before.

★ ★ ★

CAROLINE REBECCA LE COUNT taught until 1911. In that year, the school district decided to change the name of her Catto school and merge it with two others—and Le Count retired. She moved in with a sister in the Germantown neighborhood. She never married.

We found no photograph of her. We are left with the image of a woman best known for grit and grace in trying to step on a streetcar. The longer-lasting image, however, is that of another black educator and advocate for blacks teaching blacks.

She was the first black woman in Philadelphia to pass the city teacher's examination. When a school board official had the temerity in 1880 to belittle black students' achievements and lay the blame on the inferior abilities of black teachers, Caroline Le Count led the response. She noted in a letter reprinted in the newspapers that white teachers had to pass their certification examination with a 65 average at minimum, while she and other black teachers needed to score a 70. One newspaper described her as "a match for all of the officers and members of the Board of Education combined."

In an 1887 speech about the importance of black teachers, the *Philadelphia Bulletin* reporter John Durham—an I.C.Y. graduate who later became the U.S. minister to Haiti—said Philadelphia needed "no demonstration" of the impact that excellent black teachers had: "The names of Professor Reason—I name them in chronological order—of Professor Bassett, of Mrs. Fanny Jackson-Coppin, of Mr. Catto, Mr. Jacob White, of Miss Caroline Le Count, rank with the best educators that this city has produced."

While education was clearly the fulcrum for her life, it was not the only endeavor in which she excelled. For decades, "Carrie" remained a performer.

In addition to her renown at poetry recitals, "Liney," as she was known to her friends, also sang at concerts and told stories in dialect at church events and fund-raisers throughout her adult life. Her Irish accent was spot-on and crowds would line up to see her perform.

She gave a talk titled "Historical notations on the Institute for Colored Youth, the Ohio Street and the O.V. Catto Schools" to the American Negro Historical Society and reprised this lecture as late as 1913, weaving in anecdotes and leaving her audience "delighted and highly instructed."

In 1899, she celebrated her thirty-second year as Catto School principal, for which occasion her students gave her a turquoise ring. A newspaper story said she had taught "our prominent young Philadelphians, . . . none having failed to do credit to their earlier training."

In 1909, Booker T. Washington saluted her and Catto in his book *The Story of the Negro: The Rise of the Race from Slavery*, which examines the lives of prominent black achievers.

By then, Caroline's friend Lillie Dickerson was seven years old.

On September 13, 2003, we were fortunate enough to visit with Lillie, by then a 101-year-old African American woman who grew up and still lived in South Philadelphia. We sat in her six-bedroom row home on Fitzwater Street and asked about her life and whether she ever had heard her parents or their friends talking about Catto, Bolivar, Le Count, or anyone else of that civil rights generation.

She told us that her grandfather was a runaway slave who worked for a Main Line family, the Wheelers, and that her grandmother from Sierra Leone was taken in by the Biddle family. Lillie's great-aunt was Cordelia Sanders, the young woman to whom Catto wrote the love poem in 1860.

"Catto? He was a fighter for Negro rights" is what Lillie remembered people saying. We asked whether she ever heard of Caroline Le Count.

"Liney," she replied, and her face lit up. "Liney Le Count was a teacher. I remember her. She was in my house all the time."

Lillie explained that she was nine or ten years old and "Liney" was a respected elder, well-known to all. "She was a learned woman, friendly with my grandmother." Lillie remembered meeting "Mr. Billy Bolivar" as well. And back then, she said, when people visited "from Charleston, they either stayed with us or the Adgers."

Her friend Caroline died in 1923, one month before her seventy-seventh birthday. The teacher to as many as eight thousand black students in a forty-seven-year career, she is buried at Eden Cemetery, a historic black burial site in a suburb of Philadelphia that also is the resting place of William Still and Absalom Jones.

* * *

AS WE WRITE nearly a century and a half beyond the Civil War, most Americans would have a difficult time identifying a black civil rights leader in the nineteenth century other than Frederick Douglass.

But there was a time in Philadelphia when those names were not just remembered but revered. The revered name in Pittsburgh was Delany; in Ohio, the Langstons; in Boston, John S. Rock; and in New York, Garnet. As late as the 1930s in Philadelphia, the names of Purvis and Forten, White and Catto, Still and Le Count were invoked as a prideful refrain in the same way black Americans had once spoken of Fort Wagner, Olustee, and Fort Pillow. Newspapers, such as the *Philadelphia Tribune*, were still evoking the heroes of another time. That refrain, on the lips of old men and old women, became a declaration of here's-what-we-built-in-our-day.

From their lives of "simple dignity" with "limited resources and homespun opportunities," the *Tribune* wrote, "sprang the cultural aspirations of a people."

Nothing epitomized those aspirations like the transformative school of the day, the Institute for Colored Youth.

Alumni, teachers, even undergraduates answered Catto's 1864 call to help the millions "come forth into the sunlight of Freedom." One fact bears repeating: The I.C.Y. sent more teachers south to teach freedmen's children than any other educational institution in the North. In addition, many I.C.Y. graduates remained in the North, working in schools in Brooklyn, Princeton, Newark, Camden, and North Woodbury, New Jersey.

Other I.C.Y. alumni became pioneers in nursing, medicine, law, and architecture. Harvard's Widener Library and the soaring columns and sweeping stairwells of the Free Library, the Museum of Art, and other Philadelphia landmarks are the work of Julian Francis Abele, a turn-of-the-century I.C.Y. student. He was the first black graduate of the University of Pennsylvania's architecture program.

I.C.Y. graduates and teachers were role models for black children nationwide and stereotype busters for whites dubious of black educational attainment.

Consider this story, told in 1890 at a conference on "the Negro question" held at Lake Mohonk in New York State: A black woman washing floors at the Academy of Natural Sciences in Philadelphia overheard two white men trying to decipher a Latin inscription. She said to them, "Perhaps I can help you, gentlemen."

The woman, a graduate of the I.C.Y., translated the Latin.

A better-known I.C.Y. student was Herschel V. Cashin. He was a student of Catto's, and his sister married William Dorsey. He moved to Alabama in 1869 where he "could best serve his people" by joining the political struggle of Reconstruction. He became a tax collector and a state legislator and one of the first black lawyers in Alabama.

The Cashin story is told by his great-granddaughter, Sheryll Cashin, who credits Catto for her great-grandfather's resolve and commitment to equal rights. Descendants carried on in his tradition. Cashin's grandson, John Jr., who was a civil rights activist in twentieth-century Alabama, ran for governor against George Wallace.

John Cashin Jr.'s daughter, Sheryll, clerked for Supreme Court Justice Thurgood Marshall, worked in the Clinton administration, and teaches law at Georgetown University. Her 2008 book about four generations of her family is *The Agitator's Daughter*.

Few I.C.Y. people had as much impact as Fanny Jackson. Her acclaim began in one century and continued to another.

In 1881, she married a widower, Rev. Levi Coppin, whose first wife had died along with their baby boy, Octavius. She and her husband lived in different cities for their first four years. Invariably ahead of her time, she urged women to "maintain financial independence from their husbands."

At the turn of the century, a female journalist wrote: "By common consent, Fanny Jackson Coppin ranks first in mental equipment, in natural gifts and achievements among colored teachers."

Coppin resigned from the institute in 1901 as the school turned further away from academics and added more "industrial" courses, moving from applied physics to "bed making."

About that time, the school moved from the city to the countryside to the west. In 1914, the transformation became complete as the I.C.Y. became the Cheyney Training School for Teachers, which in turn became Cheyney University. On Bainbridge Street, the old building became a public school. Its new name would have brought a smile to William McMullen's face and a frown to every black educator's. Carved in the wall above the building's first-floor windows was a tribute to McMullen's ally: the Samuel J. Randall Public School.

A condominium today, the site features dueling historic designations—the prominently featured Randall School name remains and, on the street in front of the building, a blue state of Pennsylvania historical marker announces that this is where the Institute for Colored Youth, led by Principal Fanny J. Coppin, once stood.

★ ★ ★

COPPIN DIED IN 1913—after writing most of a book, doing mission work in Africa, and sharing stages in the United States with the great antilynching crusader of the day, Ida B. Wells. Both women understood that lynchings, which numbered twenty-five hundred between 1885 and 1900, were not an exclusively Southern phenomenon any more than violent attacks on black voters and their leaders were.

Veterans of earlier fights rallied against the lynchings—William Still, Isaiah Wears, Ebenezer Bassett, "the old war horses," as Ida Wells wrote. One old war horse, Robert Smalls, was credited with turning back a lynch mob in the streets of his native Beaufort—at age seventy-four. The hero of the *Planter* died in 1915, in the house where his mother had worked as a slave.

Ebenezer Bassett began another sort of legacy. Naming a Negro to a diplomatic post had been exotic and unprecedented when President Ulysses S. Grant sent Bassett to Haiti in 1869; now it became a routine affair for Republican presidents rewarding black political supporters. Rutherford Hayes sent John Mercer Langston to replace Bassett in Haiti; Benjamin Harrison, in turn, sent Frederick Douglass. Richard Greener, who had taken Catto's place at the I.C.Y., went on to become U.S. consul at Vladivostok. (Greener asked his new friend, Booker T. Washington, to put in "a good word for me" with President William McKinley.) Henry Highland Garnet was named minister to Liberia in 1881.

Each posting was, of course, hailed as an advancement for the race. Even so, as the century rolled to a close and the nation retreated from the equal-rights triumphs of Civil War and Reconstruction days, some of the race's greatest voices were too far away to be heard.

Garnet, having survived amputation, slave catchers, and draft riot mobs, lasted only a year in Liberia before he succumbed to disease at age sixty-seven.

Bassett returned briefly to Haiti as Douglass's assistant, and not a minute too soon: Douglass, then in his seventies, happened to be sitting in

Port-au-Prince as Haitian troops moved in to suppress a rebellion. "The sound of firing was heard . . . from a Gatling gun," Bassett wrote. " I took Mr. Douglass by the arm and said, we will have to get out of here."

Douglass lived until 1895. His last speeches, too, were against the lynchings; his last trip was to a women's rights convention. He gave a friend, Susan B. Anthony, a picture of himself—a daguerreotype from 1848, when he was young, clean-shaven, and full of fire, dodging brickbats with William Lloyd Garrison and saying prayers with William Catto.

One by one, the other "old war horses" passed away: Robert Purvis in 1898, William Still in 1901, Robert M. Adger in 1910. Bolivar died in 1914, after writing his Pencil Pusher column of memories in the *Philadelphia Tribune* for twenty-two years. He outlived his friend Fanny Coppin by just enough to finish the writing of her *Reminiscences of School Life and Hints on Teaching*. The book was her jewelry box of I.C.Y. memories.

She told of Bassett and Reason, of Robert Campbell in his turban, of "very black" Jesse Glasgow solving equations as fast as a white visitor could shout them; of the Le Count sisters, the Minton brothers, and the "pleasing voice, gracious yet forceful manner and persuasive power" of her colleague Octavius Catto.

★ ★ ★

WILLIAM McMULLEN'S OBITUARY begins: "His life was worthy of a book, but not one in all its chapters, fitted for Sunday-school instruction." The Squire was seventy-seven and died on a Sunday in 1901, in his home at Ninth and Bainbridge, in sight of the I.C.Y. and just a brickbat's throw from the house where he was born.

He had been a Common or Select Council member since 1878 and was considered an elder statesman, respected for his ability to develop alliances with his former enemies, most notably Republicans and Negroes. People admired his spunk when he made two hot-air balloon ascents in 1893 and 1895.

When he died, the Moyamensing Legion, the surviving remnant of the Moyamensing Hose Company, put out a flag tied with mourning crepe.

His operative Frank Kelly returned to Cincinnati and set up shop as a bartender and tactical adviser to that city's rising political boss, a Republican, George B. Cox. By 1912, Boss Cox was the bane of a new wave of municipal reformers and muckrakers. One of them wrote about Kelly in an exposé of Cox's regime for *McClure's* magazine: "There was a politician who got into trouble in Philadelphia one election day in the '70s—a sleek, dapper little man, with a soul as cool and hard and shiny as a billiard ball. He came to Cincinnati under a false name and, for a while he tended bar for Cox."

The article said Kelly was often visited there by "Philadelphia politicians—the wise ones of the secret machine."

After 1871, at least, that Democratic machine no longer sponsored wanton attacks on colored voters in Philadelphia.

Whether it was the casting-out by Mayor William Stokley of Mayor Fox's police, or the civic realization that the city could no longer tolerate such public lawlessness, *riot* and *Negro* were coupled no more in the 1800s.

But day-to-day prejudice and less publicized explosions of white hatred did not fade away. In 1898, white workers staged a two-week strike to protest the hiring of two black motormen by the Philadelphia and West Chester Streetcar Company.

As more and more black customers began venturing into restaurants where they once would not have been welcome, a way of discouraging these new customers was seen. As one restaurateur put it: "But once that he has finished, cup, saucer, plate and any other china he may have used for his meal are broken before his face, rapped with a hammer or flipped against a sharp corner of the wall. . . . The guests look up and understand. The Negro seldom returns."

The Civil Rights Act of 1875, the law Charles Sumner authored and the band of brothers advocated, would have clapped a federal lawsuit on the restaurateur for discriminating. But by the end of the century, the Supreme Court had gutted that law along with many of the other guarantees of the Fourteenth and Fifteenth Amendments. Rosa Parks's generation would have to win this battle all over again a half century later.

But some legacies of the band of brothers and sisters had the "hardihood," as William Still would say, to survive into the twentieth century and even the twenty-first.

★ ★ ★

ALAIN LOCKE, born in Philadelphia in 1886, grew up to be the nation's first black Rhodes scholar.

Locke was the son of Pliny Ishmael Locke, the I.C.Y. graduate and Catto teammate on the Pythians. He went to Tennessee to teach at a freedmen's school. His grandfather, Ishmael Locke, was the institute's first principal.

In 1907, Alain Locke graduated magna cum laude in three years from Harvard and received his Ph.D. there. As a writer and philosophy professor, historians credit him with "much of the development of modern black literature."

He was the leading black intellectual of his generation, interpreting and advocating for the cultural and artistic contributions of African Americans. His writing introduced the world to the Harlem Renaissance in the 1920s. He taught at Harvard and Howard and Fisk and the University of Wisconsin and the New School in New York. He lectured widely on black contributions to ancient Egypt wrote scholarly books on topics his father's generation would not have thought scholarly: *The New Negro* in 1925; *The Negro and His Music* in 1936, and *The Negro in Art* in 1940.

Another notable grandson link is Stanton L. Wormley, who called Billy Wormley Granddad. Born in 1909, he attended Howard, earned a Ph.D. from Cornell and came back to teach at Howard, in the city where white mobs in the "Snow Storm" destroyed the school his ancestors built.

He became chair of the German and Russian Department and later president of the university. He awarded Vice President Hubert Humphrey an honorary degree in 1967.

Howard, a college "born in the great rush of hope that emancipation had engendered," as Kevin Boyle writes, was one reason black activists and intellectuals flocked to the nation's capital after Reconstruction. Catto's old student J. W. Cromwell published a black newspaper in Washington and wrote books on black history. Richard Greener taught law at Howard before he voyaged off to Vladivostok; Robert Purvis's physician son Charles taught obstetrics in Howard's medical department. Even Charlotte Forten made her way to Washington, boarding with her Purvis cousins while she taught high school.

Then she got to know the pastor at Fifteenth Street Presbyterian Church, and in 1878, she and Rev. Francis Grimké married. Her marriage to the other slave-born Grimké nephew marked the second time in the century that a Grimké wed an equally devoted advocate of racial justice.

Before long, the Grimké brothers were heading up the Washington branch of the NAACP. The family did not forget Lincoln University, where the white Grimké sisters had discovered their black nephews in 1866. To this day, Lincoln offers aid to needy students who demonstrate literary promise or "courage and ability in striving for the advancement of the Negro race." The scholarships are named after the nephews' mother, Nancy, who was taken from them in slavery; for their aunt Angelina, who fought to end slavery; and for Charlotte Forten Grimké.

Charlotte Forten's legacy was preserved, too, on the South Carolina island where she taught freedmen's children. The old school grounds became a retreat for modern civil rights activists. Beneath the live oaks that once sheltered Charlotte and her pupils, Dr. King worked on a speech best known for the words "I have a dream."

★   ★   ★

THERE WAS A CATTO SCHOOL in Philadelphia until recently, not the one run by Caroline Le Count but a more contemporary one in West Philadelphia that was used for many years as a disciplinary institution for middle-school students. Just a few years ago, the name on the building was changed to the Paul Robeson School.

But this switch from a nineteenth-century civil rights activist to a twentieth-century one is less of a change than many realize. Robeson could trace his ancestry to the Bustill family in eighteenth-century Philadelphia. So, indeed, could Jacob White Jr. and others from the early days—the I.C.Y. teacher Sarah Mapps Douglass, whose activism dated to Pennsylvania Hall; and the painter of John Brown's portrait and the U.S. Colored Troops' ceremonial flags, David Bustill Bowser.

Coppin's name lives on at Coppin State University in Maryland. Bishop Daniel Payne's dream of education lives on at Wilberforce University in Ohio, where the school's theological seminary bears his name. Morris Brown College is in Atlanta; the Octavius V. Catto Community School serves grade-school students in Camden, New Jersey. A Pennsylvania historical marker at 1032 Lombard Street marks the home of Jacob White Jr., the principal at the Vaux School for forty years.

A memorial to Catto was erected in Eden Cemetery in 2007. All the graves in Lebanon Cemetery were dug up in 1903 when the ground was bought for a housing development. The remains of the African Americans buried there were moved to Eden Cemetery, but some of those bodies were dumped in unmarked graves.

For years, Catto's grave was lost. Catto family descendant Leonard Smith looked for it. So did Harry Silcox. When city officials began searching in 2007, the cemetery announced that it had located the body and a memorial was dedicated.

We have written about Frederick Douglass and other black leaders briefly setting foot in the White House in the 1860s. Henry O. Tanner, in a way, is still there.

In 1996, two weeks before the November presidential election, Hillary Rodham Clinton announced that *Sand Dunes at Sunset, Atlantic City*, a painting completed by Henry Ossawa Tanner in 1885, would be the first work by any African American painter the White House acquired and made part of the permanent collection.

In 1999, the state of South Carolina deleted the word *mulatto* from its laws. One hundred and sixty years after a mulatto named Octavius Catto was born, the General Assembly erased an 1895 clause that banned the "marriage of a white person with a Negro or mulatto or a person who shall have one-eighth or more of Negro blood."

★ ★ ★

RETIREE EDGAR CATTO MONTGOMERY is a Catto descendant who moved from Detroit to Spartanburg, South Carolina, in the 1990s and discovered black education in disrepair in the state his ancestors left 150 years earlier. Explaining why he ran for the school board and then pushed to get better books and more black teachers, he said, "I was coming in to make change. Had to be done."

He said he had no idea that Octavius Catto had said, "There must come a change," in a speech in 1864, or that Catto had been a passionate supporter of black teachers.

"We have black principals here now," Montgomery said. "Never had that before."

Catto's great-grandnephew, Leonard Garnet Smith, was in failing health in 2008. He had to retire from his post as a hospital administrator in Alexandria, Virginia. But something stirred Smith's Catto gene, too: an African American candidate who braved the dangers and defied the odds.

By autumn, Smith was urging all of his friends, black and white, to vote for Barack Obama. He worked the polls on Election Day, and by 9:00 P.M. was so excited that he could not speak. When Pennsylvania's electoral votes helped clinch Obama's victory, Smith got his voice back.

"Oh . . . What a Great Day it Was/Is!!!" he wrote. "I could feel the souls of OV Catto and the many others who gave their lives for the cause of freedom whisper a collective 'AMEN'!!!!"

And in that amen, we hear a chorus with familiar strains: that first and foremost, they were all Americans, fighting for their country, tasting freedom and fighting for more, battling for justice and a better life with a faith and reliance on scholarship and hard work. When we reclaim their lives, we reclaim the best of America.

They struggled, lost, but kept struggling. Their tenacity is difficult to fathom, but it bespeaks their legacy. Perhaps Lillie Dickerson said it best: "They were all fighters."

★ ACKNOWLEDGMENTS ★

OUR THANK-YOU LIST is long because there was so much we needed to know. On that list are five people, above all others, who made this book possible: Harry Silcox, Philip Lapsansky, Avery Rome, Roger Lane, and Catto family descendant Leonard Smith.

Harry Silcox, who died in 2009, was a retired high school principal and historian who wrote often about neighborhoods and street life in nineteenth-century Philadelphia. He was the first historian since W.E.B. Du Bois to look closely at the life of Octavius V. Catto. Silcox wrote a scholarly article on Catto in 1977, and his 1989 book on William McMullen is the first on the Democratic power broker. When we began this project, Harry became our biggest supporter and gave us a tour of Catto's South Philadelphia that we will never forget.

Philip Lapsansky is the longtime chief of the African American collections at the Library Company of Philadelphia and a sage of nineteenth-century civil rights history. His name will ring a bell for readers familiar with the acknowledgment page of history books, because so many authors have stood before "Dr. Phil" and asked for help.

And he gives it, with a twinkle in his eye and a suggestion of four or five books to read. He knows the answers to questions on everything from song sheets to funeral practices to what Isaiah Wears was really like. Dr. Phil, we owe you.

Avery Rome is an exquisite editor who has always improved our work. She has been our sage adviser, doing far more than pushing us to use more active verbs. When we were trapped in historical mire, she pulled us out. When we despaired that anyone would care, she assured us they would. She challenged us to use our own voices and kept up a drumbeat of optimism.

Roger Lane, the award-winning author and Haverford College history professor, has assumed the thankless task of being our reader in the early stages of this book. He's scolded us for not telling enough and complimented us when we managed to tell a story right. A scholar on American and Philadelphia history in the 1800s, he barely knew us when he entrusted us with a treasure—all the microfilm reels of the William Dorsey scrapbook collection. Best of all, he's become a friend.

In addition to Silcox, Lapsansky, and Lane, some other Philadelphia-area historians, librarians, and archivists have kept the torch lit for the civil rights generations of the 1800s. Among the ones who have aided us are Margaret Hope Bacon, Laura Blanchard, Charles L. Blockson, V. Chapman-Smith, Christopher Densmore, Emma Jones Lapsansky-Werner, and Arthur Sudler.

Other major historians have given generously of their time and advice—Roy Finkenbine, Eric Foner, Steven Hahn, Richard S. Newman, Julie Winch, and Donald Yacovone. We are neophytes from the newspaper world, and that made their guidance all the more valuable.

Several historians shared with us some of their findings in as-yet unpublished works—Judith Ann Giesberg, who reshaped our thinking about the frontline role of women in the streetcar movement, and Kaye Wise-Whitehead, who opened the diaries of Emilie Davis, a young African American woman in the mid-nineteenth century. Steve Berry's groundbreaking scholarship on Rev. William T. Catto's life as an on-again, off-again Presbyterian minister was invaluable to us, as was his generous guidance on where we should look for information.

Harlan M. Greene, director of archival and reference services at the Avery Research Center for African American History and Culture at the College of Charleston, helped us navigate the black history world of South Carolina. He made the Charleston of Rev. William T. Catto come alive for us. Also generous was W. Marvin Dulaney, the former Avery director.

Greene led us to a community of experts, historians, and archivists throughout South Carolina who kindly assisted two visiting Yankees.

Mentioning his name introduced us to the help of Jane M. Aldrich, Marion Chandler, Roberta Copp, Lisa Hayes, Charles H. Lesser, Daniel Littlefield, Richard D. Porcher, Bernard Powers, Dale Rosengarten, Christina Shedlock, Allen H. Stokes, and Steven D. Tuttle. Another Charlestonian who took an enormous amount of time to make our trip worthwhile was Linda Ramball Jones, who made sure we had a place to stay.

We also must offer our gratitude to Philadelphian Scott Wilds, whose wizardry of Southern genealogy helped us wade through the Catto family history, and Rev. Mark Kelly Tyler, pastor of Mother Bethel A.M.E. Church, who alerted us to little-known attacks on black voters in Camden in 1870.

At the Urban Studies Program of the University of Pennsylvania, co-director Elaine Simon and program administrator Isabel Boston lent us the keys to a gold mine—the Penn libraries.

And so many more helped us. Here they are in alphabetical order, and we hope we have not forgotten anyone. Lloyd R. Applegate, Frank Bearden, Jan Broske, Allison Bruno, Terry Buckalew, Randall K. Burkett, Nan Card, Robert Cassanello, Gerald Casway; Ward J. Childs, Noel Day, Fran Donnelly, John Fabiano, Paul Finkelman, Valerie Gay, Augie Hermann, Linnea Hermanson, Richard Hershberger, Ruthann Hubbert-Kemper, Nicole Joniec, Shira Kamm, Connie King, Danielle Kovacs, Bette Davis Lawrence, David Levering Lewis, Adam Levine, Ana Ramirez Luhrs, Bill Marimow, Louis Massiah, Sarah-Jane Mathieu, and Larry McCray.

Also, Jeremy McInerny, Kristy McShea, Randall Miller, Charlene Mires, James Mundy Jr., Michael Panzer, James Paradis, Stacey Peeples, Alix Quan, James Rahn, Jeffrey Ray, Linda Ries, Beverly Brown Ruggia, Gary Saretsky, Ralph E. Shaffer, David Shayt, Sheila M. Skjeie, Eileen Sklar, David Smith, Debby Smith, Joel Spivak, R. Phillip Stone, Marni Sweet, Joan Vidal, Morris Vogel, Anthony Waskie, Travis Westly, and Lisa Zollinger.

Here is a list of the institutions that opened their doors to us, literally and online. We owe a thank-you to them and to their archivists and librarians: African American Collections at the Robert W. Woodruff Library, Emory University; African Episcopal Church of St. Thomas; Avery Research Center for African American History and Culture, College of Charleston; Charles L. Blockson Collection at Temple University; City of Philadelphia Archives; College of Education, Temple University;

Free Library of Philadelphia; Friends Historical Library at Swarthmore College; Germantown Historical Society; Historical Society of Pennsylvania; Leslie Pickney Hill Library, Cheyney University; Library Company of Philadelphia; Library of Congress; Morris County (New Jersey) Heritage Commission; New Jersey State Vital Records Office; Pennsylvania Hospital; *Philadelphia Inquirer*; Presbyterian Historical Society; Society for American Baseball Research (SABR); South Caroliniana Library, University of South Carolina; Special Collections and Archives, W.E.B. Du Bois Library, University of Massachusetts; State Library of Massachusetts; Union League of Philadelphia; Van Pelt Library at the University of Pennsylvania; Wofford College and South Carolina Conference, United Methodist Church.

Before there was Micah, there was Ike. John Taylor "Ike" Williams and his literary agency, Kneerim & Williams, represented us with great zeal and good humor. Micah Kleit, our editor at Temple University Press, has been exceedingly patient with our less-than-breakneck speed at completing this book.

There is no way to properly thank our spouses, Cindy Roberts and Libby Rosof, for their unwavering support, endless sacrifice, and wise counsel. The same is true for our children, Ellery Roberts Biddle and Alex and Minna Dubin, and our mothers, Fran Biddle and Mary Dubin.

We also must heartily thank two members of the Catto family, Leonard Smith and Edgar Catto Montgomery. We discovered Leonard online as we both searched for historical information. He welcomed our project and shared family lore—stories that invariably proved true. A retired Virginia hospital administrator and a descendant of Catto's brother, William, he gave us one nugget whose importance we did not realize at the time: "There were a hundred O. V. Cattos."

Edgar, whom we interviewed in South Carolina, clearly inherited O. V. Catto genes. Retired after a career as a union and hospital official in Detroit, he moved to Spartanburg, joined his town's school board, and became a leader in desegregating the district's teacher corps—providing black teachers for black students because it was the right thing to do. To Leonard and Edgar, we hope we've done justice to your ancestors' memory.

★ NOTES ★

ABBREVIATIONS

ANHS = American Negro Historical Society/Leon Gardiner Collection, Historical Society of Pennsylvania, Philadelphia

B = *Philadelphia Bulletin* and *Evening Bulletin*

BAP = Black Abolitionist Papers, 5 vols. (1830–1890), Library Company of Philadelphia

BAPM = *Black Abolitionist Papers, 1830–1865,* edited by George E. Carter et al., microfilm edition, 17 reels (Sanford, NC: Microfilm Corporation of America, 1981)

CCPL = Charleston County Public Library, Charleston, SC

CR = *Christian Recorder* newspaper

Dorsey scrapbooks = William H. Dorsey Scrapbook Collection, microfilm, Leslie Pinckney Hill Library, Cheyney University, Cheyney, PA, and Samuel Paley Library, Temple University, Philadelphia

FD = *Frederick Douglass' Paper*

FLS = Friends Historical Library of Swarthmore College, Swarthmore, PA

HSP = Historical Society of Pennsylvania, Philadelphia

I.C.Y. records, FLS = Records of the Institute for Colored Youth, Richard Humphreys Foundation Records, Friends Historical Library of Swarthmore College, Swarthmore, PA

I.C.Y. records, LC = Records of the Institute for Colored Youth, Library Company of Philadelphia, PA

INQ = *Philadelphia Inquirer*

LC = Library Company of Philadelphia

LOC = Library of Congress

NASS = *National Anti-Slavery Standard*

NS = *North Star* newspaper

NYT = *New York Times*

PL = *Philadelphia Public Ledger*

PMHB = *Pennsylvania Magazine of History and Biography*

PP = *Philadelphia Press*

PSERL = Pennsylvania State Equal Rights League Papers, Historical Society of Pennsylvania, Philadelphia

PREFACE

Pages

Except where noted, this Preface draws from the following sources: Griffin, *Trial of Frank Kelly*, 10–13, 23–24; *PP* and *PL*, Oct. 11–14, 1871, Apr.–July 1877; treatment records, Oct. 9–Oct. 14, 1871, Pennsylvania Hospital.

x   **Catto walked with . . . tasting freedom:** Description of Catto's demeanor on Oct. 1, 1871, is based on eyewitness accounts in Griffin, *Trial of Frank Kelly*; his athleticism is detailed in Chapter 13; "tasting freedom" quotation: Du Bois, *Philadelphia Negro*, 39.

CHAPTER 1: CHARLESTON

Pages

5   **On November 24, 1800:** Rosenfeld, *American Aurora*, 882; Hunter, *Thomas Jefferson's Road to the White House.*

5   **Octavius Catto's grandmother was:** Nov. 24, 26, 1800, June 13, 1801, court documents, South Carolina Department of Archives and History; Huff, *Langdon Cheves*, 29–30.

5–7   **Founded in 1670 . . . a fine was paid:** Fraser, *Charleston!* 1–2, 3, 8–9, 13, 15, 17, 28, 450–451.

7   **South Carolina beat back:** Ibid., 18–20, 23–24, 26, 31, 38, 42–47, 53, 64–67, 69, 84–85; Rawick, *American Slave*, 98–100.

7   **There was no sham or pretext . . . Fear drove the attitudes:** Fraser, *Charleston!* 52, 63, 67, 82.

7   **Visitors to the:** Ibid., 54–55, 130, 199–200; Gonaver, "Race Relations," 5, 73–75; Jordan, *White Over Black*, 3.

7–8   **Visiting ministers accused . . . use of his slave girls:** Fraser, *Charleston!* 54, 130; Stuart, *Three Years in North America*, 2:127–128.

8   **Not everyone took . . . of a slave militia:** Fraser, *Charleston!* 199, 154.

8   **The nation's first:** Ibid., 178; Ballard, *One More Day's Journey*, 95–96; Koger, *Black Slaveowners*, 1.

8   **This free population:** Harris, "Charleston's Free Afro-American Elite."

9   **Fanny and Mary Shields . . . declared guardian of Fanny and Mary Shields:** Petition of James Pring, Nov. 26, 1800, South Carolina Department of Archives and History; Clarke, *Wrestlin' Jacob*, ix.

9   **To be sure:** Hyde, *Story of Methodism*, 454; McClintock and Strong, *Cyclopaedia*, 876.

9   **Fanny was free:** 1810 Census; Ballard, *One More Day's Journey*, 30.

9   **By now, South Carolina:** BAP, 3:140; Ballard, *One More Day's Journey*, 76.

9   **Fanny's son:** Poole, "On Borrowed Ground," 2; 1810 Census.

9   **Who was William Catto's father?:** City of Charleston health records, 1800–1840.

10   **Perhaps he bore a scar:** Smith interview, 2003, and e-mail message to the authors, Jan. 28, 2010.

10   **"wagoner":** Moebs, *Black Soldiers*, 237; Newman, *List of Black Servicemen*, 23.

10   **William Catto's last name:** Wills, birth, death, estate, and capitation tax records, including State Free Negro Capitation Tax Books, 1800–1847, and

church records at Avery Research Center for African American History and Culture, College of Charleston, Charleston, SC, and South Carolina Historical Society, Charleston. Capitation books were a record of annual taxes that free blacks in South Carolina had to pay.

10   **Free blacks in:** Powers, *Black Charlestonians*, 44, 61; documents filed by Patrick McGann, Sept. 4, 1819, South Carolina Department of Archives and History.

10   **McGann, born in Ireland:** Greene, Hutchins, and Hutchins, *Slave Badges*, 95–97; Barsheba Cattle will records at CCPL.

10   **Fanny Shields needed:** Greene interview.

10   **So in 1819:** Johnson and Roark, *Black Masters*, xi–xii, xv, 187; Fraser, *Charleston!* 200; Payne, *Recollections*, 14–15.

11   **Nor did being free and brown . . . our shield:** Johnson and Roark, *Black Masters*, 214–218; Poole, "On Borrowed Ground," 1; Drago, *Initiatives*, 36–37.

11   **Perhaps he learned from Thomas:** Johnson and Roark, *Black Masters*, 108–109; Payne, *Recollections*, 15–20.

11   **Payne's boyhood in Charleston:** City directories, CCPL; Fraser, *Charleston!* 197–198; Payne, *Recollections*, 11–20.

11   **But the time of such teaching:** Nash, *Forging Freedom*, 204–205, 241–242; BAP, 3:7, 146–147, 5:259; "Black History and Culture," 101; Newman, *Transformation of American Abolitionism*, 43–44.

12   **What is known has melded:** Gonaver, "Race Relations," 79–82; BAP, 3:412; Fraser, *Charleston!* 187; Koger, *Black Slaveowners*, 30.

12   **What happened next:** Historians debate now whether the Vesey arrests and hangings followed a planned slavery uprising or were more a paranoid overreaction to harsh talk by free Negroes and slaves.

12   **Whichever it was:** Fraser, *Charleston!* 200–202; Payne, *Recollections*, 79–80.

12   **Did young William Catto see:** Adger, *My Life and Times*, 52–53.

12   **On December 25:** Payne, *Recollections*, 83–84; Fraser, *Charleston!* 202; Koger, *Black Slaveowners*, 177–178.

12   **The fears that followed:** Jenkins, "Chaos, Conflict, and Control," 26; Fraser, *Charleston!* 202–203; Harris, "Charleston's Free Afro-American Elite," 292–293; Gray and Oliver, *Memory of Catastrophe*, 40.

13   **Vesey and the men:** Harris, "Charleston's Free Afro-American Elite," 292–293; Fraser, *Charleston!* 202; Koger, *Black Slaveowners*, 181.

13   **Vesey had become:** Kennedy and Parker, *Official Report of the Trials of Sundry Negroes*; Berry, "William Catto's Pursuit," 43.

13   **Three Methodist churches:** Willson, *Sketch of the Methodist Church*, 13–14.

14   **In addition to opening:** Mathews, *Religion in the Old South*, 139.

14   **"This care over:** Willson, *Sketch of the Methodist Church*, 8–9, 21–22.

14   **The missionary work:** Mathews, *Religion in the Old South*, 9, 139–140.

14   **Before the name Vesey:** Fraser, *Charleston!* 203; Woodson, *History of the Negro Church*, 131–134.

15   **The state's lawyer likened:** Whitaker, Clapp, Simms, and Thornwell, *Southern Quarterly Review*, 472.

15   **A federal judge:** McFeely, *Grant*, 301; Hoar and Bellows, *Autobiography*, 25; Fraser, *Charleston!* 224; BAP, 5:97–98.

15   **White men could enter:** Henry, *Police Control of the Slave*, 134–137, 164; Birnie, "Education of the Negro in Charleston."

15   **Free Negroes could not:** Fraser, *Charleston!* 190; Payne, *Recollections*, 35.

15   **By 1830, William Catto:** Berry, "William Catto's Pursuit," 42.

15   **Low-country planters:** Easterby, *South Carolina Rice Plantation*, 254–256; Porcher and Littlefield interviews; Calhoun, *Papers*, 49–50.

16   **Another Negro probably trained:** Delany, *Condition*, chap. 10; Neuffer, *Names in South Carolina*, 15:47.

16   **Because he was a Negro:** Jones, *Religious Instruction of the Negroes*, 115.

16   **A British visitor:** Lyell, *Second Visit*, 1:267.

17   **To the extent:** Holloway, *Why I Am a Methodist*; Constitution and By Laws; State Free Negro Capitation Tax Books, 1832–1833; Jeronimus, *Travels by His Highness*, 270–292; Jenkins, "Chaos, Conflict, and Control," 54–55.

17   **A longer walk from:** Charleston street directories; CCPL; Weld, *American Slavery as It Is*, 53–57.

17   **Catto might have heard:** Fraser, *Charleston!* 208.

17   **The Cumberland Street Sabbath school:** Holloway, *Why I Am a Methodist*, 7–11; Koger, *Black Slaveowners*, 98. Samuel and Anthony Weston were brothers; "Toney" was ten years older.

17   **Some scholars have argued:** Johnson and Roark, *Black Masters*, xv; Koger, *Black Slaveowners*, 81–83.

18   **In 1830, 474 mulattoes:** Wikramanayake, *World in Shadow*, 190; Henry, *Police Control of the Slave*, 180–181.

18   **Some Negro slave owners:** Johnson and Roark, *Black Masters*, 212–213; Harris, "Charleston's Free Afro-American Elite," 289–296; Wikramanayake, *World in Shadow*, 190; Constitution and By Laws, 24.

18   **The societies were hothouses:** Harris, "Charleston's Free Afro-American Elite," 294.

18   **But none of what happened inside:** BAP, 1:34; Wikramanayake, *World in Shadow*, 69; Johnson and Roark, *Black Masters*, 49.

18   **A white man snatched:** CR, Feb. 24, 1887.

19   **Stuart, the Scotsman:** Stuart, *Three Years in North America*, 2:127–128, 141.

19   **In August 1831:** BAP, 3:412; Fraser, *Charleston!* 209, 213.

19–20   **On the morning of July . . . across the Atlantic:** BAP, 3:165; Jervey, *Robert Y. Hayne*, 379–381; Foner, *Forever Free*, 23–24, 29; Jenkins, "Chaos, Conflict, and Control," 26; Gray and Oliver, *Memory of Catastrophe*, 40. See also Mayer, *All on Fire*, 120–124.

20   **William Catto's earliest known:** William Catto to Richard Holloway, Holloway Family Scrapbooks.

20   **Her name was Sarah:** Hagy, *Directories*, 99; Berry, "William Catto's Pursuit," 42; Birnie, "Education of the Negro in Charleston," 13–21; Wikramanayake, *World in Shadow*, 116. Dereef family holdings are described in Johnson and Roark, *Black Masters*, 203.

20–21   **"fervent piety and great nobility:** PP, Oct. 14, 1871; Silcox, "Nineteenth Century Philadelphia Black Militant," 53 (the first scholarly research on O. V. Catto).

21   **A generation later:** Holt, *Black over White*, 63.

21 **William and Sarah:** 1840 Census; Hagy, *Directories*, 35; State Free Negro Capitation Tax Books, 1832–1836; Greene interview.

21 **In those same 1830s:** Mathews, *Religion in the Old South*, 205–207; Woodson, *History of the Negro Church*, 131–134; Willson, *Sketch of the Methodist Church*, 13–21; Minutes for the South Carolina Conference of the Methodist Episcopal Church for the years 1830–1838, Columbia and Charleston, S.C., South Carolina Conference Papers; *Report of the Committee of the South-Carolina Conference*; *Exposition of the Causes and Character* (1833); *Exposition of the Causes and Character* (1834).

22 **Catto was a member:** Wightman, *Life of William Capers*, 11, 52; Fraser, *Charleston!* 207–208; Mathews, *Religion in the Old South*, 139, 205–207; Snay, *Gospel of Disunion*, 90, 107; *Southern Christian Advocate*, various dates in 1838.

22 **Capers showed:** Wightman, *Life of William Capers*, 339; *Exposition of the Causes and Character* (1833 and 1834); Berry, "William Catto's Pursuit," 43–44.

22 **In 1835, the law came crashing:** *Charleston!* 211; Payne, *Recollections*, 27.

22 **Payne, an endlessly curious scholar:** Payne, *Recollections*, 22, 27, 34–35, 51.

23 **A Negro leader in New York City:** BAP, 3:intro., 32–33, 216.

23 **Catto and his mulatto friends:** Johnson and Roark, *Black Masters*, 213–216; Poole, "On Borrowed Ground," 1; Drago, *Initiatives*, 36–37.

23 **On behalf of his fellow:** William Thomas Catto to the South Carolina Conference of the Methodist Church, Feb. 11, 1836, South Carolina Conference Papers.

24 **The clergymen had other concerns:** Report of the Missionary Society, Feb. 15, in Minutes for the South Carolina Conference of the Methodist Episcopal Church, 1836, 15–21, South Carolina Conference Papers.

25 **Catto's 1836 letter:** William Thomas Catto et al. to the South Carolina Conference of the Methodist Church, Feb. 11, 1836, South Carolina Conference Papers.

25 **On February 22, 1839:** 1840 Census; Silcox, "Nineteenth Century Philadelphia Black Militant," 53; Koger, *Black Slaveowners*, 44, 145.

CHAPTER 2: ARM IN ARM

Pages

27 **On a May Monday in 1838:** Letter of May 1838, in Barnes and Dumond, *Letters of Theodore Dwight Weld*, 678–679.

27 **the prince and princess:** See, e.g., "overnight" fame of Angelina Grimké, in Bacon, *Valiant Friend*, 73.

27 **"temple of freedom . . . extraordinary edifice:** See, e.g., Theodore Weld and Thaddeus Stevens letters to hall managers, in Managers of the Pennsylvania Hall Association, *History*, 6, 10.

27 **The splendid gas lamps:** Ibid., 3; hall interior details also in *Pennsylvania Freeman*, May 31, 1838.

28 **"the pretty Quakeress:** Lerner, *Feminist Thought of Sarah Grimké*, 12, quoting the *Detroit Morning Post*.

28   **"in such a hurry:** Barnes and Dumond, *Letters of Theodore Dwight Weld*, 205, 208, 265, 625–626; Lerner, *Grimké Sisters*, 238.

28   **They had toured New England:** Lerner, *Grimké Sisters*, 146, 205, 227.

28   **"19/20 of an abolitionist:** Ibid., 12.

28   **she balanced the pages:** Angelina Grimké to Sarah Douglass, Feb. 25, 1838, in Barnes and Dumond, *Letters of Theodore Dwight Weld*, 572–575.

28   **She wore a simple brown:** Ibid., 661, 668–69.

29   **He explained that:** Angelina Grimké to Jane Smith, Dec. 17, 1836, quoted in Lerner, *Grimké Sisters*, 154.

29   **"most mobbed man":** Ibid., 208, 210, 236.

29   **The couple prepared:** Original draft of Weld-Grimké wedding invitation, Weld collection, HSP.

29   **She had freed her two slaves:** Barnes and Dumond, *Letters of Theodore Dwight Weld*, 679.

29   **preferring the popular sentiment:** Dorsey, "Gendered History of African Colonization."

29   **Presiding was the great abolitionist:** Lerner, *Grimké Sisters*, 240–241.

29   **Hoarse as he was:** Barnes and Dumond, *Letters of Theodore Dwight Weld*, 678–679.

29   **Garrison read the wedding certificate:** Lerner, *Grimké Sisters*, 206, 152; Mayer, *All on Fire*, 196–197.

29   **Then came the names:** BAP, 3:118.

29   **Dawson and her daughter:** Lerner, *Grimké Sisters*, 240.

30   **Her sister's wedding:** Barnes and Dumond, *Letters of Theodore Dwight Weld*, 678–679.

30   **There were "six whites . . . on Chestnut Street":** Lerner, *Grimké Sisters*, 170, quoting the *Emancipator* newspaper, May 17, 1838.

30   **"perched by the parlor window:** Bacon, *Valiant Friend*, 76.

30   **A visiting British abolitionist:** Braithwaite, *Memoirs of Joseph John Gurney*, 116–117.

30   **About nineteen thousand . . . and one library:** Geffen, "Industrial Development," 309; Lane, *Roots of Violence*, chap. 1; Winch, *Elite of Our People*, 84–85. Willson's work was first published in 1841.

30   **The colored population lived:** Winch, *Elite of Our People*, 6.

30–31   **In the past few years . . . as men seized a box:** BAP, 3:165, 5:236–237; Lovejoy, *Elijah Parish Lovejoy*, 10–11; Feldberg, *Turbulent Era*, 111; Richards, *Gentlemen of Property*, 69; Warner, *Private City*, 130–131.

31   **The South "was Philadelphia's best:** Taylor, *Philadelphia in the Civil War*, 9–14; Ignatiev, *How the Irish Became White*, 135.

31   **But even a leading Quaker:** Bacon, *Valiant Friend*, 41–42, 101.

31   **Few of the city's Quakers:** See Barnes and Dumond, *Letters of Theodore Dwight Weld*, 829–832; Mary Grew's final report of the Philadelphia Anti-Slavery Society, 1870, in Stanton, *History of Woman Suffrage*, 327–328.

31   **The schoolteacher Sarah Douglass:** Barnes and Dumond, *Letters of Theodore Dwight Weld*, 830–831; Douglass's Dec. 1837 letter, in Litwack, *North of Slavery*, 207.

31   **When the Grimké sisters:** Lapsansky-Werner and Bacon, *Back to Africa*, 20; Lerner, *Grimké Sisters*, 132–133, 160.

32   **Another woman . . . best-known colored merchant:** Winch, *Gentleman of Color*, 4–5.

32 **"In reply to your question:** Sarah L. Forten to Angelina E. Grimke, Apr. 15, 1837, in BAP, 3:221–223.

32 **Sometimes those enemies came:** Nash, *Forging Freedom*, 227.

33 **It made sense, then:** For a description of the Motts' house, see Warner, *Private City*, 132; Bacon, *Valiant Friend*, 76, and chap. 7.

33 **The mayor commanded 160 police:** Warner, *Private City*, 139, 187.

33 **in the State House:** Mires, *Independence Hall*, 17, 70–72.

33 **Now, the hall's managers:** Managers of the Pennsylvania Hall Association, *History*, 140; Warner, *Private City*, 129, 130, 132.

33 **Sarah Forten and the hall committee:** Managers of the Pennsylvania Hall Association, *History*, 6.

33 **Joseph Eaton . . . dug the cellar:** Names and trades of artisans in Pennsylvania Hall Association, Records, FLS.

33–34 **The result was a . . . letters of gold:** *Pennsylvania Freeman*, May 31, 1838; Managers of the Pennsylvania Hall Association, *History*, 3.

34 **Benjamin Lundy, whose journal was:** Bacon, *Valiant Friend*, 75; Oberholtzer, *Literary History of Philadelphia*, 320; Managers of the Pennsylvania Hall Association, *History*, 59–62; Lerner, *Grimké Sisters*, 248.

34 **The proximity to Independence Hall:** Managers of the Pennsylvania Hall Association, *History*, 6, 10.

34 **On election days . . . the lines:** Silcox, *McMullen*, 18–19; Winch, *Gentleman of Color*, 292–296; Salvatore, *We All Got History*, 13.

34 **The Pennsylvania General Assembly . . . a recent state court decision:** Nash, *Forging Freedom*, 62, 182; BAP, 3:252, 255, 412, 4:262–263.

35 **Gurney, the visiting Briton:** Braithwaite, *Memoirs of Joseph John Gurney*, 116–117.

35 **Much was made of the new hall's:** Managers of the Pennsylvania Hall Association, *History*, 10, 37–51, 137.

35 **"I learnt with great satisfaction . . . renewed its "gag rule:** John Quincy Adams to the Pennsylvania Hall Association, Jan. 19, 1838, in ibid., 11–12; BAP, 3:326; Warner, *Private City*, 132; Managers of the Pennsylvania Hall Association, *History*, 78.

35 **Abolitionists noted that this step:** BAP, 3:326. Whittier's 1839 poem, "The New Year," appears in Whittier, *Complete Poetical Works*, 281–283.

36 **"The Grimkés are doing:** Lucretia Mott to J. Miller McKim, Mar. 15, 1838, in Palmer, *Letters of Lucretia Coffin Mott*, 37–42.

36 **Two black abolitionists:** Winch, *Gentleman of Color*, 299–300; *Pennsylvania Freeman*, Mar. 15, 29, 1838; Brown, "Pennsylvania and the Rights of the Negro," 46.

36 **"We advise our friends:** *Pennsylvania Freeman*, Apr. 5, 1838.

36 **On Monday, May 14:** The two policemen are noted in Warner, *Private City*, 133, and the Managers of the Pennsylvania Hall Association, *History*, 182, which quotes the speech by Brown, 13–35.

36 **The next day, Philadelphians awoke:** Managers of the Pennsylvania Hall Association, *History*, 136, 138.

37 **Tuesday, May 15, was the first day:** *Proceedings of the Anti-Slavery Convention of American Women.*

37 **Harriet Purvis, who helped start:** Winch, *Gentleman of Color*, 257, 262–263; Palmer, *Letters of Lucretia Coffin Mott*, 206; BAP, 3:81; Oberholtzer, *Literary History of Philadelphia*, 328; Payne, *Recollections*, 53–54.

37–38   **The Purvises rode . . . Joan of Arc from Charleston:** Sturge, *Visit to the United States*, 46–47; Managers of the Pennsylvania Hall Association, *History*, 70–72, 137, 147, 181–182.

38   **As the main salon began to fill:** Managers of the Pennsylvania Hall Association, *History*, 147; Birney, *Grimké Sisters*, chap. 15.

38–39   **Juliana Tappan took the floor . . . and that of the slave:** *Proceedings of the Anti-Slavery Convention of American Women*, 5; Managers of the Pennsylvania Hall Association, *History*, 99–100, 130.

39   **Others spoke up for "colonization:** Garrison's comments in Managers of the Pennsylvania Hall Association, *History*, 72; sketch of Purvis, in BAP, 3:81; Mott to George Combe, June 13, 1839, in Palmer, *Letters of Lucretia Coffin Mott*, 51–53.

39   **"The offspring of prejudice:** BAP, 3:221–223.

39   **"Why is colonization necessary?:** *Colored American*, June 2, 1838.

39–40   **In truth, the colonization movement . . . rise of the black church:** Bordewich, *Bound for Canaan*, 82; Winch, *Gentleman of Color*, 191; Bacon, *But One Race*, 93; Appiah and Gates, *Africana*, 28–29; Nash, *Forging Freedom*, 234–240; Litwack, *North of Slavery*, 20–29.

40   **Many a white abolitionist still:** Dorsey, "Gendered History"; sketch of Cresson, in Lapsansky-Werner and Bacon, *Back to Africa*, 5, 8, 10, 69; Brown, "Temple of Amalgamation," 219.

40   **In the hall, Garrison said . . . not an American:** Managers of the Pennsylvania Hall Association, *History*, 72; Lovell, *Report of a Delegate*, 8.

40   **That was true. The shouter was:** Background pamphlet on W. W. Sleigh, "Abolitionism Exposed!" Samuel J. May Anti-Slavery Collection; Managers of the Pennsylvania Hall Association, *History*, 73.

40   **Beneath the much-complimented gas lamps:** Debate minutes, in Managers of the Pennsylvania Hall Association, *History*, 73; *Proceedings of the Anti-Slavery Convention of American Women*; Lovell, *Report of a Delegate*.

40   **But seating them on the . . . three-thousand-person capacity:** Managers' action, in Managers of the Pennsylvania Hall Association, *History*, 96; Ruchames, *Letters of William Lloyd Garrison*, 362–364.

40–41   **"A daughter of Carolina . . . the only ones available:** Managers of the Pennsylvania Hall Association, *History*, 115–117, 137, 147.

41   **Laura H. Lovell, a delegate . . . became very riotous:** Lovell, *Report of a Delegate*, 10–11, 53.

41   **The audience heard rocks . . . of the State House:** Managers of the Pennsylvania Hall Association, *History*, 117–127, 147–148, 183; *Pennsylvania Freeman*, May 17, 1838; Birney, *Grimké Sisters*, chap. 15. Eyewitness accounts by Lovell, in *Report of a Delegate*, 10–13, and by Garrison, in Ruchames, *Letters of William Lloyd Garrison*, 362–364. PL, May 16, 1838.

41–42   **The hall's wooden shutters. . . . "Like some gray rock:** Managers of the Pennsylvania Hall Association, *History*, 148; Neall description, in Whittier, *Works of Whittier*, 73.

42   **A calmness came to her:** Barnes and Dumond, *Letters of Theodore Dwight Weld*, 572–575; Birney, *Grimké Sisters*, 240.

42   **"What is a mob?:** Speech by Angelina Grimké Weld is transcribed in Managers of the Pennsylvania Hall Association, *History*, 124–126.

42   **Pointing to the windows:** "Hear it, hear it," in Lovell, *Report of a Delegate*, 12.

42   **Garrison, too, sat spellbound:** Ruchames, *Letters of William Lloyd Garrison*, 362–364.

43   **"I have seen it . . . like a trumpet:** Wilbanks, *Walking by Faith*, xii, 37–38. See also Weld, *American Slavery as It Is*, 53–57; *Stranger's Guide*, 37–38, 80–82.

43–44 **Before she sat down . . . So said the first reports:** Lovell, *Report of a Delegate*, 12; Birney, *Grimké Sisters*, 240.

44   **On Thursday morning:** Pleasonton Diary, May 7–21, 1838. For more on Pleasonton, see Pleasonton and Others, *Influence of the Blue Ray*, 183–185.

44   **A more complicated picture:** Pleasonton Diary, May 17, 1838; Birney, *Grimké Sisters*, 240; Managers of the Pennsylvania Hall Association, *History*, 148, *Proceedings of the Anti-Slavery Convention of American Women*, 8.

44   **Thursday morning's *Freeman* described . . . in the mob as well:** Lovell, *Report of a Delegate*, 13–15: *Address of John G. Watmough*, 5–6; Birney, *Grimké Sisters*, chap. 15; Managers of the Pennsylvania Hall Association, *History*, 185.

44   **Inside, the women convened:** Lovell, *Report of a Delegate*, 13–14; Managers of the Pennsylvania Hall Association, *History*, 130–135.

45   **But a new rumor:** Managers of the Pennsylvania Hall Association, *History*, 17; Ruchames, *Letters of William Lloyd Garrison*, 362–64; Brown, *Proclaim Liberty!* 214.

45   **Neall and the other managers sent . . . are against you:** *Address of John G. Watmough*, 5–8; Managers of the Pennsylvania Hall Association, *History*, 137–139, 185.

46   **Now a one-day veteran of . . . this one woman had unearthed:** Lovell, *Report of a Delegate*, 16–17.

46   **The anti-slavery men . . . by the arm:** Stanton, *History of Woman Suffrage*, 326–327; Managers of the Pennsylvania Hall Association, *History*, 138–140; Lovell, *Report of a Delegate*, 17; Lerner, *Grimké Sisters*, 247.

47   **The hall committee's report:** Managers of the Pennsylvania Hall Association, *History*, 140, 187.

47   **Women like Thankful Southwick . . . unexpected scene to me:** Lovell, *Report of a Delegate*, 17.

47   **"There will be no meeting . . . the hall's main doors:** Managers of the Pennsylvania Hall Association, *History*, 140–150, 185; Lerner, *Grimké Sisters*, 248; Scharf and Westcott, *History of Philadelphia*, 1:652.

47–48 **"to entertain a lively hope . . . began to give way:** Managers of the Pennsylvania Hall Association, *History*, 150, 175–199; *Address of John G. Watmough*, 7–8.

48   **By now, Laura Lovell:** Lovell on the Buffum story, in *Report of a Delegate*, 18–19.

48–49 **The only man still . . . fires burning:** Managers of the Pennsylvania Hall Association, *History*, 188.

49   **They were playing the hoses:** Ibid., 150; Warner, *Private City*, 134.

49   **White Philadelphia mobs had . . . approbation & encouragement:** Runcie, "Hunting the Nigs"; Nash, *Forging Freedom*, 177; Davis, *Parades and Power*, 46; Ignatiev, *How the Irish Became White*, 220; *Address of John G. Watmough*, 5–6; Diary of Sidney Fisher, May 19, 1838, in Wainwright, *Philadelphia Perspective*, 49–50; Braithwaite, *Memoirs of Joseph John Gurney*, 116–117.

50 **Colonel Pleasonton detected:** Pleasonton Diary, May 17–18, 1838.

50 **Inside the main salon:** Managers of the Pennsylvania Hall Association, *History*, 140, 150.

50 **Whittier was visiting with:** Bacon, *Valiant Friend*, 77–78, Oberholtzer, *Literary History of Philadelphia*, 323.

50 **The fire moved quickly:** Managers of the Pennsylvania Hall Association, *History*, 150.

50–51 **On Friday morning . . . congregations in the cause:** *Proceedings of the Anti-Slavery Convention of American Women*, 6–7; Stanton, *History of Woman Suffrage*, 327; Lovell, *Report of a Delegate*, 20–21.

51 **Sarah Grimké wrote . . . "our beautiful house:** Philadelphia Female Anti-Slavery Society annual report, 1839, Samuel J. May Anti-Slavery Collection.

51 **It might have targeted Garrison, too:** Garrison and Garrison, *William Lloyd Garrison*, 170; Garrison to Mrs. Sarah T. Benson, May 19, 1838, in Ruchames, *Letters of William Lloyd Garrison*, 362–364.

52 **The Friday morning minutes:** Requited Labor Convention records, 8, Samuel J. May Anti-Slavery Collection.

52 **As the sound grew closer:** Lovell, *Report of a Delegate*, 22.

52 **The men ran past:** Bacon, *Valiant Friend*, 78.

52 **The rioters kept going:** Oberholtzer, *Literary History of Philadelphia*, 334; PL, May 19, 1838; Scharf and Westcott, *History of Philadelphia*, 1:652; Warner, *Private City*, 136.

52 **Sheriff Watmough said:** *Address of John G. Watmough*, 7–8.

52 **Crowds formed in the streets**: Pleasonton Diary, May 20–21, 1838.

53 **The sheriff rode north . . . from the state:** *Address of John G. Watmough*, 8–11; Brown, *Proclaim Liberty!* 215; Managers of the Pennsylvania Hall Association, *History*, 140, 195; Pleasonton Diary, May 18–20, 1838.

53 **By Sunday morning:** Warner, *Private City*, 136.

53 **"To be sure there was:** Sidney Fisher's diary entry dated May 19, 1838, in Wainwright, *Philadelphia Perspective*, 49–50.

53 **Evil had come:** From *Sermon Occasioned by the Destruction of Pennsylvania Hall*.

53 **Whittier said the fire would:** Oberholtzer, *Literary History of Philadelphia*, 326; Managers of the Pennsylvania Hall Association, *History*, 167–170.

54 **Lucretia Mott insisted the:** Palmer, *Letters of Lucretia Coffin Mott*, 42–45; Winch, *Gentleman of Color*, 304.

54–55 **The resolution had set off . . . such sympathy say I:** Lucretia Mott to Edward M. Davis, June 18, 1838, in Palmer, *Letters of Lucretia Coffin Mott*, 42–45; "S" [Sarah Douglass] to editor, July 22, 1838, in *Colored American*, Aug. 4, 1838.

55 **The county convened a grand jury:** Brown, *Proclaim Liberty!* 219.

55 **Five days later:** *Proceedings and Debates of the Convention to Amend the Constitution*, 260–261.

55 **The women's antislavery convention:** *Proceedings of the Anti-Slavery Convention of American Women*, second meeting, 6; Stanton, *History of Woman Suffrage*, 327–328.

55 **The new mayor, Isaac Roach:** Brown, *Proclaim Liberty!* 185; Bacon, *Valiant Friend*, 80–81.

55 **The women eventually held:** Stanton, *History of Woman Suffrage*, 327.

55 **Such setbacks, however, became:** Lapsansky, "Feminism, Freedom, and Community."

56 **Sarah Douglass went on to:** Coppin, *Reminiscences*, 146–149; BAP, 3:118; Oberholtzer, *Literary History of Philadelphia*, 323.

56 **Robert Purvis, twenty-seven when the hall burned:** Sturge, *Visit to the United States*, 46–47.

56 **Purvis started spending more time:** BAP, 3:81, 4:188; Dusinberre, *Civil War Issues*, 52–53; Perkins, *Fanny Jackson Coppin*, 108.

56 **For those who had been:** Birney, *Grimké Sisters*, 241–242; Lerner, *Grimké Sisters*, 263.

57 **The book told of men and women whipped:** Weld, *American Slavery as It Is*, 55.

57 **Riots in Philadelphia . . . than pogroms:** BAP, 3:389–391; Lane interviews.

57 **The burning hall thus became:** "from which buck negroes" quotation: Rev. W. G. Brownlow, in *Ought American Slavery to be Perpetuated?* 109.

57 **Later in the nineteenth century:** NS, Mar. 23, 1855; Du Bois, *John Brown*, 41; Du Bois, *Philadelphia Negro*, 29.

58 **A despairing Daniel Neall wrote:** Neall to John Priestly, May 21, 1838, minutes of Pennsylvania Hall Managers, FLS.

58 **The ruins stood:** Oberholtzer, *Literary History of Philadelphia*, 323; Warner, *Private City*, 134.

CHAPTER 3: "KEEP THE FLAME BURNING . . ."

Pages

59 **On a January day in . . . "vice and pauperism:** BAP, 3:430–437; Litwack, *North of Slavery*, 40–46.

59–60 **On January 5, Catto joined . . . present his views was Catto:** Second Presbyterian Church of Charleston records, box 1, pp. 100, 116; Berry, "William Catto's Pursuit," 44; McFeely, *Frederick Douglass*, 129–134; Smyth, *Autobiographical Notes*.

60 **That spring:** *Proceedings of the Meeting in Charleston.*

60 **Charleston church leaders:** Palmer, *Life and Letters of James Henley Thornwell*, 286–288.

61 **While this larger conversation:** Second Presbyterian Church of Charleston records, box 1, pp. 124–125.

61 **The task before them:** Berry, "William Catto's Pursuit," 44; Clarke, *Wrestlin' Jacob*, 171–172.

61 **His wife, Sarah, died in 1845:** Guardianship bond posted by William T. Catto, 1845, South Carolina Department of Archives and History.

61–62 **So now William Catto had . . . a sponsor in Smyth:** Berry, "William Catto's Pursuit," 46; BAP, 3:5, 4:121, 5:109.

62–63 **Just two years older than Catto . . . great instruments of the 19th Century:** Waugh, *Thomas Smyth*; Smyth, *Autobiographical Notes*, 115–131; McFeely, *Frederick Douglass*, 129–134; Soskis, "Heroic Exile," 55; Blackett, *Building an Antislavery Wall*, 85.

63–64 **Trips to Britain . . . "I scarce knew what to say," Douglass wrote:** Smyth, *Autobiographical Notes*, 372–374; McFeely, *Frederick Douglass*,

132–134; Soskis, "Heroic Exile," 55; Foner, *Life and Writings of Frederick Douglass*, 1:181; Douglass to William A. White, July 30, 1846, Gilder Lehrman Center.

64   **O'Connell had shaken:** Quarles, *Black Abolitionists*, 133; Quinn, "Rise and Fall of Repeal," 55–56.

64–65   **Douglass wrote . . . Smyth for libel:** Frederick Douglass to William Lloyd Garrison, Sept. 29, 1845 (from Dublin), in Foner, *Life and Writings of Frederick Douglass*, 1:120 (online at http://www.yale.edu/glc/archive/1089.htm); Douglass, *Life and Times*, 237–238; McFeely, *Frederick Douglass*, 132–134.

65   **Smyth denied calling Douglass:** Smyth, *Autobiographical Notes*, 372–374.

65   **"I am playing mischief:** Douglass to William A. White, July 30, 1846, Gilder Lehrman Center.

65   **The Negro in Smyth's parlor:** Smyth, *Autobiographical Notes*, 115–131, 393–394.

65   **He spoke with Margaret:** Waugh, *Thomas Smyth*. The "Adger's Wharf" section, under heading "Walled City" in Charleston Multimedia Project on CCPL Web site (http://www.ccpl.org/), says James Adger was "allegedly, the richest man in South Carolina"; a review in *South Carolina Historical Magazine* 94, no. 2 (Apr. 1993): 140, calls him "reputedly the fourth richest man in the United States." See also Clarke, *Dwelling Place*, 168.

66–67   **Margaret Smyth's racial views . . . chains to America:** Smyth, *Autobiographical Notes*, 389–390, 393–394; BAP, 3:71; Rev. J. M. Connelly to "Dear Brethren," Feb. 29, 1848, Board of Foreign Missions, Correspondence, letter 52, microfilm roll 63; engraving of a "Liberia packet" in *Fifteenth Report of the Maryland State Colonization Society*.

67   **At the same time, the Smyths:** *Richmond (VA) Watchman and Observer*, Aug. 24, 1848; Charleston Presbytery minutes, 391, 417; *Minutes of the General Assembly of the PCUSA*, vol. 12, 1848, 32–34. For new names of Negro children, see Ullman, *Delany*, 50–51; Painter, "Martin R. Delany," 162; Lane, *William Dorsey's Philadelphia*, 77; *CR*, Oct. 8, 1864. On towns changing names, see "Black History and Culture," 65.

67   **To be a missionary:** Berry, "William Catto's Pursuit," 46.

67   **And on an October day:** Charleston Presbytery minutes, 368, 389–390.

67   **The Presbytery asked:** Berry, "William Catto's Pursuit," 43–46.

68   **But knowing Smyth:** Waugh, *Thomas Smyth*.

68–69   **Catto was sent upstate . . . on that limb:** William T. Catto to Thomas Vardell, May 13, 1847, Board of Foreign Missions, Correspondence, microfilm roll 62; Berry, "William Catto's Pursuit," 47–48; *Proceedings of the Meeting in Charleston*; Jones, *Religious Instruction of the Negroes*, 153; Clarke, *Dwelling Place*, 171–172.

69   **In addition to . . . "probationary" ordination:** Berry, "William Catto's Pursuit," 47–48.

69   **The Catto family would:** Walter Lowrie to William T. Catto, Jan. [28?], 1848, Board of Foreign Missions, Correspondence, microfilm roll 63.

69   **They were probably leaving:** *Charleston Mercury*, 1848 editions; Johnson and Roark, *Black Masters*, 43; Eaton, "Censorship of the Southern Mails"; *NASS*, Aug. 12, 1847; Board of Foreign Missions, Minutes, Nov. 8–9, 1838, microfilm roll 1, pos. 21.

70   **The sound that greeted:** Fields, *Slavery and Freedom*, 42–45. 1840 Census record for Catto children, Beman G. and William S., identify Mary as Catto's second wife; Smith interviews and e-mail messages to authors, 2003–2009; 1850 Census for Spring Garden district of Philadelphia; 1860 Census for New Haven, CT; also marriage and death records in New Jersey State Archives.

70   **But free black voices:** McFeely, *Frederick Douglass*, 46; *Richmond (VA) Watchman and Observer*, Mar. 30, 1848.

70   **Not that Baltimore welcomed:** *NASS*, Aug. 12, 1847 and Dec. 23, 1847, citing article in *Baltimore Patriot*.

70   **Except in parts of its Eastern Shore:** Fields, *Slavery and Freedom*, 15–17, 48.

71   **News of the Cattos' imminent voyage:** Rev. H. W. Ellis to Walter Lowrie, Mar. 24, 1848, Mrs. J. M. [Catherine Sawyer] Connelly to Walter Lowrie, Mar. 26, 1848, and Walter Lowrie to William Catto, Jan. [28?], 1848, in Board of Foreign Missions, Correspondence, microfilm roll 63.

71   **Lowrie had just received:** *Foreign Missionary Chronicle*, Feb. 1848.

71–72   **Walter Lowrie did not mention . . . at either place:** Lowrie to Catto, Jan. [28?], 1848; Mrs. J. M. [Catherine Sawyer] Connelly to Walter Lowrie, Apr. 12, 1848, and May 1, 1848; Rev. J. M. Connelly to Lowrie, Feb. 29, 1848; Board of Foreign Missions Correspondence, microfilm rolls 62 and 63.

72   **On his son Octavius's ninth:** William Catto to Walter Lowrie, Feb. 22, 1848, Board of Foreign Missions, Correspondence, microfilm roll 63.

72   **He turned to what he knew:** Ibid; Dubin, *South Philadelphia*, 16.

72   **"Where a few years ago:** Davis and Haller, *Peoples of Philadelphia*, 117.

72   **This group's efforts:** Campbell, *Maryland in Africa*; *Fifteenth Report of the Maryland State Colonization Society*.

72   **A white man in New York:** Lowrie to William Catto, Jan. [28?], 1848; Payne, *Recollections*, 77–91; "Calhounia," in *NS*, Oct. 12, 1849.

73   **Finally, the near presence:** BAP, 4:253; Bordewich, *Bound for Canaan*, 295, 300–301.

73   **At their monthly meeting:** Charleston Presbytery minutes, 445–446, 450–451; *Richmond (VA) Watchman and Observer*, Apr. 28, 1848; McFeely, *Frederick Douglass*, 172.

73   **My dear friend:** *NS*, Oct. 20, 1848; Board of Foreign Missions, Correspondence, letter 48, microfilm roll 63.

CHAPTER 4: WITH GIANTS

Pages

77   **"contribute our something":** Catto, *Semi-Centenary Discourse*, 7.

77   **willingness to host antislavery meetings:** *NS*, Oct. 13, 1848; Payne, *History*, 237. See also BAP, 4:195; Winch, *Gentleman of Color*, 312–313.

77   **Two days of antislavery strategy meetings . . . crane their necks:** Meetings in Brick Wesley from accounts by Frederick Douglass in *NS*, Oct. 13, 1848, and Martin Delany, *NS*, Oct. 6, 1848, and a formal report, "Proceedings of the Anti-Slavery Convention Held in Philadelphia," *NS*, Nov. 10, 1848. Statements and resolutions are quoted from "Proceedings." See also Catto, *Semi-Centenary Discourse*, 107.

77   **Grownups said the giants:** Gibbs, *Shadows and Light*, 24–25.

77   **Giants! Their names:** "Proceedings," *NS*, Nov. 10, 1848.

78   **At least five:** Quarles, *Black Abolitionists*, 145, 148, 155; Payne, *Recollections*, 72; Bacon, *But One Race*, 75–83, 102; BAP, 3:195–196.

78   **Douglass was due . . . later by train:** Delany in *NS*, Oct. 6, 1848.

78   **They were for whites:** Brown, *American Fugitive*, 312–315.

78   **Douglass, clean-shaven:** Douglass explains his age in Douglass, *Narrative of the Life*, 23–24.

78   **Douglass had learned his ABC's:** Douglass, *My Bondage*, 125.

78   **Delany's mother . . . them at home:** BAP, 4:129–130; Ullman, *Delany*, 3–4.

78   **enrolled at nineteen . . . pulled the school down:** Schor, *Garnet*, 15; Sterling, *Speak Out*, 89–90; Swift, *Black Prophets*, 117–118.

78–79   **Remond, born free . . . problem was her color:** Sterling, *Speak Out*, 380; Hill, *Our Exemplars*, 276–286.

79   **Yet these men were founding . . . petitioning legislatures:** BAP, 3:336–337, 368–373.

79   **to thousands of Americans:** BAP, 3:28; McFeely, *Frederick Douglass*, 99–100, 106; Ullman, *Delany*, 91–106.

79   **Each led a secret second life:** Siebert, *Underground Railroad*, 403–440; Ullman, *Delany*, 27–28; Switala, *Underground Railroad in Pennsylvania*, 85–86.

79   **Garnet got around on a wooden leg:** Pasternak, *Rise Now*, 38; Winkelman, "Rhetoric of Henry Highland Garnet," 13.

79   **Remond's voice rang "like the bugle blast:** Stebbins, *Upward Steps*, 96–98; Woodson, *Negro in Our History*, 178.

79   **Douglass, whose yellow cheekbones . . . "Stand up, Mr. Garnet:** McFeely, *Frederick Douglass*, 8; *NS*, Oct. 6, 13, 1848; Ullman, *Delany*, 7, 26–27; "Black History and Culture," 17; Schor, *Garnet*, 4; Crummell, *Africa and America*, 273; Former U.S. representative John Hickman, *CR*, Sept. 29, 1866.

79   **Octavius's father . . . delivered the prayer:** "Proceedings," *NS*, Nov. 10, 1848.

79   **Dr. Bias . . . a free medical exam:** Quarles, *Black Abolitionists*, 148; Payne, *Recollections*, 72; William Carl Bolivar, Pencil Pusher Points, *Philadelphia Tribune*, Dec. 12, 1912, May 30, 1914.

80   **He and Bias and three other men:** Payne, *History*, 221–222; Wayman, *My Recollections*, 38; Handy, *Scraps of African Methodist Episcopal History*, 182.

80   **the conference needed preachers:** Campbell, *Songs of Zion*, 32–37.

80   **Payne had become the conference's:** Payne, *Recollections*, 85–91.

80   **By September, Catto was pastor:** *NS*, Oct. 20, 1848.

80   **Catto's fifth child . . . Garrison:** 1850 Census for Spring Garden district of Philadelphia reports a mulatto male child, Garrison, age two, born in New Jersey.

80   **or celebrate July 4:** See, e.g., Winch, *Gentleman of Color*, 52.

80   **"a company of degraded creatures:** Purvis's mother-in-law, Charlotte Forten, quoted by H. C. Howells in Armistead, *Tribute for the Negro*, 87.

80   **he placed Octavius in . . . school for Negroes:** Silcox, "Nineteenth Century Philadelphia Black Militant," 55; *PP*, Oct. 14, 1871.

80 **"The Convention was mainly addressed:** "Visit to Philadelphia," *NS*, Oct. 13, 1848.

80 **the *North Star* . . . thunder to derision:** For thunder, *NS*, Mar. 3, 1848; for derision, *NS*, June 22, 1849.

80 **"because it is RIGHT:** Women's Association of Philadelphia, Sarah Mapps Douglass, corresponding secretary, *NS*, July 6 and 13, 1849.

80 ***North Star's* ledger books . . . Wm. T. Catto:** *NS* ledger book, 1847–1849, "Financial Papers," image 76, Frederick Douglass Papers.

80 **one city to another, one pulpit to:** By age fifty, William Catto had lived in at least six cities and towns and worshipped or preached in at least seven churches, switching from Methodist to Presbyterian to A.M.E. and back to Presbyterian.

81 **"contributing his something:** Catto, *Semi-Centenary Discourse*, 7.

81 **fire-breathing broadsides:** Payne, *History*, 250. For a description of the ten resolutions drafted for an 1850 meeting led by Catto and William Still, see Chapter 5.

81 **appeal to white New Jersey:** Aug. 1849 petition, in Wright, "Negro Suffrage in New Jersey," 188.

81 **"fell far short of the realities:** William Catto, in Still, *Underground Railroad*, 49–52, quoted in *New York Tribune*, July 5, 1856.

81 **more quietly and safely in chains:** Payne, *History*, 250.

81 **He exhorted other black ministers:** *Minutes and Sermon of the Second Presbyterian and Congregational Convention*, 10.

81–82 **"unwept" . . . "uncared for, unprayed for:** From a speech by Charles Remond, *NASS*, July 18, 1844.

82 **So Catto placed his entire bet:** According to family lore, William favored Octavius. Smith interviews and e-mail messages to authors, 2003–2004. There is no indication that any of O.V.'s siblings were enrolled at the Bird school or other well-regarded schools.

82 **The white Charleston ministers:** Mathews, *Religion*, 137–148; Clarke, *Dwelling Place*, 251; LaMotte, *Colored Light*, 49–50.

82 **Charles Lenox Remond had . . . from the Union:** BAP, 3:28, 368–373, 442–445.

83 **Hundred Conventions tour . . . loved by Frederick Douglass":** BAP, 3:415–423; McFeely, *Frederick Douglass*, 110–112; Douglass, *Life and Times*, 229–231; Bordewich, *Bound for Canaan*, 229; Douglass to White, July 30, 1846, Gilder Lehrman Center.

84 **names of the leaders . . . bigger newspapers:** Pasternak, *Rise Now*, 59–60.

84 **American workingmen soon began . . . brims:** Lengyel, *Americans from Hungary*, 41.

84 **At the biggest . . . police admonitions:** Gibbs, *Shadows and Light*, 26–28; Mires, *Independence Hall*, 86.

84 **"putting down aristocrats . . . the Jacobins:** Silcox, *McMullen*, 45; Steinberg, *Transformation of Criminal Justice*, 146.

84 **Garnet dared a New York:** *NS*, May 19, 1848.

84 **he had studied scripture:** Swift, *Black Prophets*, 116–118.

84 **"Ye destroyers . . . rise above them all:** *FD*, Oct. 22, 1852.

84 **"Thanks to steam . . . terrified:** *NS*, Apr. 28, 1848.

85   **broke up black Harrisburg church services:** Eggert, *Harrisburg Indus-
      trializes*, 236.

85   **tossing in a hornet's:** Kashatus, *Just Over the Line*, 44–45.

85   **As the Harrisburg meeting . . . the melee ended:** Richards, *Gentlemen
      of Property*, 156; Quarles, *Black Abolitionists*, 57–58; Douglass's account in
      NASS, Aug. 19, 1847.

85   **Instead, some editorials . . . is a darkey:** *NASS*, Sept. 16, 1847, quoting
      Doylestown (PA) Democrat.

85   **Garnet took a trip:** *NS*, June 23, July 7, Aug. 25, 1848.

85   **his bad limb:** Schor, *Garnet*, 9.

85   **His ejection followed a pattern:** Mabee, *Black Freedom*, 113; McFeely,
      Frederick Douglass, 92–93; Douglass, *Life and Times*, 223–225; *NYT* and
      New York Tribune, July 19, 1854, in BAP, 4:230–232; Wallace, *Philadelphia
      Reports*, 6:30–33.

86   **Delany visited Marseilles:** Ullman, *Delany*, 94–95; *NS*, July 14, 1848;
      Rollin, *Life and Public Services*, 56–58.

87   **Langston's future grandson:** Sterling, *Speak Out*, 378; Berry, *Langston
      Hughes*, 2–3.

87   **a rifle on his lap:** Winch, *Gentleman of Color*, 351–352; Lane, *Roots of
      Violence*, 47, 136.

87   **Remond's thin frame:** *NASS*, May 22, 1845, quoting *Newtown (PA) Jour-
      nal*; Nye, *Fettered Freedom*, 168.

87   **"I have been in danger:** Remond speech, *Liberator*, July 9, 1841; Ullman,
      Delany, 51.

87   **Free Soil convention in Buffalo . . . in Cleveland:** McFeely, *Frederick
      Douglass*, 157–158; Ullman, *Delany*, 106; *NS*, Aug. 11, Sept. 29, 1948.

87   **"The Business Committee presented:** *NS*, Sept. 29, 1848.

88   **tutored by two . . . Edinburgh:** McFeely, *Frederick Douglass*, 152–154,
      160–161; Douglass in *NS*, Sept. 22, 1848.

88   **he was becoming known:** Douglass on William Catto, *NS*, Oct. 20,
      1848; *NS*, Oct. 6, 1848; Payne, *History*, 222.

88   **Douglass . . . a shaming tool:** McFeely, *Frederick Douglass*, 161.

88–89 **"Little Wesley, presided over . . . against us:** *NS*, Oct. 13, 1848.

89   **On Remond's motion:** "Proceedings," *NS*, Nov. 10, 1848.

89   **Catto frowned:** *Minutes and Sermon of the Second Presbyterian and Con-
      gregational Convention*, 5–6.

89   **at least two women in the room:** See, e.g., Lapsansky, "World the Agita-
      tors Made."

89   **I hear the cry of millions:** Campbell, *Autobiography*, 288–289; Brown,
      Anti-Slavery Harp, 13–14.

89   **the Biases' white friend . . . in 1844:** Quarles, *Negro in the Civil War*,
      164–165; BAP, 4:253; Bordewich, *Bound for Canaan*, 301.

90   **"the bulwark of American slavery:** See Birney, *American Churches*.

90   **The call for churches . . . outposts of abolition:** BAP, 4:195; Winch,
      Gentleman of Color, 312–313.

91   **And something in Douglass made him lash out:** *NS*, June 22, 1849.

91   **Did the Constitution address:** See, e.g., a Douglass–Remond debate,
      NYT, May 21, 1857.

91   **Was Purvis's vast inheritance:** Winch, *Gentleman of Color*, 119–120;
      Bacon, *But One Race*, 125–126.

91   **He managed to hurt a loyal friend:** BAP, 4:127.

91   **Douglass named a son:** See, e.g., McFeely, *Frederick Douglass*, 224.

91–92 **Delany, who had named his first-born:** Ullman, *Delany*, 50–51.

92   **named one boy Garrison:** 1850 Census reported that William Catto's household included Garrison, age two, born in New Jersey. 1860 Census and other records add Beman Garnet Catto, born in 1855.

92   **Delany was hoarse . . . staggers, and must soon fall:** Delany in *NS*, Oct. 6, 1848.

92   **"to arouse this class . . . and degrade us:** Douglass in *NS*, Oct. 13, 1848.

CHAPTER 5: LESSONS

Pages

93   **When William Catto convened . . . *dis*franchised condition:** William T. Catto and Joseph C. Moore, "The Harrisburg Delegation," *NS*, Feb. 2, 1849; Bolivar, Pencil Pusher Points, *Philadelphia Tribune*, Jan. 18, 1913.

93–94 **Catto had called . . . appeal to Pennsylvania voters:** Catto and Moore, "Harrisburg Delegation"; Adeleke, *Without Regard to Race*, 63–64; Turner, *Negro in Pennsylvania*, 167; Litwack, *North of Slavery*, 91; U.S. Department of State, *Citizenship of the United States*, 71–72; BAP, 5:15, 18. The estimate of fifty thousand voting-age black men in the North is based on 1850 Census, tables for 1840 and 1850, 62–66.

94   **"When the last scroll . . . our oppressors:** "Appeal to the Voters of the Commonwealth . . . ," in Foner and Walker, *Proceedings*, 63–65, 124–125, 131; BAP, 4:242.

94–95 **The Harrisburg convention . . . shook their heads:** "Observer," *NS*, July 6, 1849; *NS*, Feb. 2, 1849.

95   **but he took well . . . *Persuasive*:** Casway, "Octavius Catto and the Pythians of Philadelphia"; Kirsch, *Baseball in Blue and Gray* 70; Coppin, *Reminiscences*, 143–144; Silcox, "Nineteenth Century Philadelphia Black Militant," 57.

95   **"very light and very bright:** Pennypacker, *Autobiography of a Pennsylvanian*, 101–104.

95   **the Indian bloodline:** See discussion of the Dereefs' court case in Chapter 1.

95   **"outstanding scholarly work:** Ebenezer Bassett, quoted in Silcox, "Nineteenth Century Philadelphia Black Militant," 57.

95   **"true poetic fervor:** Octavius Catto to Cordelia Sanders, May 28, 1860, Catto Papers.

95   **William, Mary, and Frances . . . Beman Garnet Catto:** Catto children's names are from U.S. Census records for 1850 and 1860; New Jersey state marriage license records, New Jersey State Archives; Montgomery interview; Smith interviews; *Minutes and Sermon of the Second Presbyterian and Congregational Convention*. See also, e.g., *Contributions to the Ecclesiastical History of Connecticut*, 439. For Beman's jailing in Maryland, see Swift, *Black Prophets*, 302, 325; BAP, 4:253.

95   **People soon took to calling him O.V.:** Catto is referred to as O.V. in roughly half the letters to and from him in ANHS; in Board of Managers,

Minutes, 1855–1866, he is identified sixteen times as "O.V." and twenty times as "Octavius" over a dozen years.

96 **The Lombard Street School . . . 199 pupils:** Winch, *Gentleman of Color*, 231, 325; Lane, *Dorsey's Philadelphia*, 135; *Thirty-first Annual Report of the Controllers of the Public Schools . . . 1849.*

96 **A Forten daughter, Margaretta . . . a tiny school:** Winch, *Gentleman of Color*, 350–351.

96 **Le Count's children all clamored:** Caroline, Ada, and James Le Count Jr. all became schoolteachers or principals. See, e.g., *Annual Report of the Controllers of the Public Schools*, for the years 1864 (*Forty-sixth Annual Report*), 1867 (*Forty-ninth Annual Report*), and 1871 (*Fifty-third Annual Report*); Lane, *Dorsey's Philadelphia*, 155; Coppin, *Reminiscences*, 180–181.

96 **But the school board customarily . . . the Bird school:** *Thirty-first Annual Report of the Controllers of the Public Schools . . . 1849*, 25; Winch, *Gentleman of Color*, 231, 325–326; Lane, *Dorsey's Philadelphia*, 135, 150; Silcox, "Nineteenth Century Philadelphia Black Militant," 55.

96 **the bulky horse-drawn omnibuses:** See, e.g., William Wells Brown's account of visiting Philadelphia in 1854, in Brown, *American Fugitive*, 312–315.

96 **The Cattos rented rooms:** The 1850 Census places the Cattos in the Spring Garden district; *McElroy's Philadelphia City Directory* for 1852 gives their street address as 71 Kessler, identified in records as Kessler Alley, Kessler Street, and Kessler's Court.

96 **Cheap row houses were bunched:** Description of Spring Garden: Davis and Haller, *Peoples of Philadelphia*, 90; Kirkpatrick, *Revenge of Thomas Eakins*, 26–27.

96 **Men carried pistols . . . Flayers:** Kirkpatrick, *Revenge of Thomas Eakins*, 26–27.

96–97 **Among the seven families . . . the races mingled:** Winch, *Elite of Our People*, 49, 66; Silcox, *McMullen*, 30; Sewell, *Sorrows Circuit*, 39; NASS, Jan. 4, 1849; 1850 Census; *McElroy's Philadelphia City Directory*, 1850.

97 **the Baldwin Locomotive . . . Model 4-4-0:** Brown, *Baldwin Locomotive Works*, 8–21; Kirkpatrick, *Revenge of Thomas Eakins*, 26–27; Taylor, *Philadelphia in the Civil War*, 11.

97 **David Bustill Bowser . . . paint their signs:** Lane, *Dorsey's Philadelphia*, 116, 120–121.

97 **In the December suffrage . . . or shut up:** Catto and Moore, "Harrisburg Delegation."

97 **Catto's contact on Fifth Street:** Still, *Underground Railroad*, 34, 82, 612; Weigley, "Border City," 387. Contacts between Rev. William Catto and William Still in articles from Sept. 30, 1859, to Feb. 3, 1860, in the *Liberator* and in *NS*, show they jointly led at least two major antislavery meetings, in 1850 and 1856.

98 **Still's main duty . . . their aging mother:** Bordewich, *Bound for Canaan*, 355–357; BAP, 4:53–60; Brown, *Narrative of the Life of Henry Box Brown*, 50–59; Still, *Underground Railroad*, 81–83.

98 **Other doors opened:** *Philadelphia African-American Census 1847.*

99 **Henry Bibb . . . "concubine:** Bordewich, *Bound for Canaan*, 380–382; "Letters from Negro Leaders to Gerrit Smith," 441.

99 **Box Brown's Virginia . . . 'Father! Father:** Brown, *Narrative of the Life of Henry Box Brown*, 38–46.

99 **That 1835 mob, formed after . . . off the rioters:** Winch, *Gentleman of Color*, 288–292; Ignatiev, *How the Irish Became White*, 125–130; Salvatore, *We All Got History*, 22; Runcie, "Hunting the Nigs."

99–100 **On August 1, 1842, Bias . . . financed out of his pocket:** Winch, *Gentleman of Color*, 351–352; Ignatiev, *How the Irish Became White*, 23, 136–138. Salvatore, *We All Got History*, 22–24; Bolivar, Pencil Pusher Points, *Philadelphia Tribune*, Apr. 6, 1912; Litwack, *North of Slavery*, 159.

100 **Some Negro families fled to New Jersey:** Ballard, *One More Day's Journey*, 77.

100 **"our utter and complete nothingness:** Robert Purvis to the Massachusetts abolitionist Henry Clarke Wright, Aug. 22, 1842, in BAP, 3:389–391.

100 **The banner that triggered:** *PL*, Aug. 4, 1842; quoted in Foner, *Douglass: Selected Speeches*, 48n2.

100 **A witness to the temperance mob:** Ignatiev, *How the Irish Became White*, 137.

100 **The spark for a riot:** See, e.g., these instances in which white violence was sparked by reports, accurate or not, of black men seen with white women: Purvis and his wife "promenading" in Chapter 2, the "Snow Storm" in Chapter 8, and the Detroit events in Chapter 11. See also Lane, *Roots of Violence*, 9.

100 **flaming barrels of tar:** See, e.g., tar prepared for use as a weapon against Daniel Paul Brown in Chapter 2, against Martin Delany and Charles Langston in Chapter 4, and against the abolitionist Daniel Neall, in Bacon, *Valiant Friend*, 85, and Hare, *Greatest American Woman*, 109.

100–101 **the Harrisburg bombardment of Frederick Douglass . . . disfigured the flesh:** Quarles, *Black Abolitionists*, 57–58; Richards, *Gentlemen of Property*, 156; Garrison to Sarah T. Benson, May 19, 1838, in Ruchames, *Letters of William Lloyd Garrison*, 362–364; Von Frank, *Trials of Anthony Burns*, 210–217. For brickbats, see, e.g., Garrison to Sarah T. Benson, May 19, 1838, in Ruchames, *Letters of William Lloyd Garrison*, 362–364.

101 **(Box Brown had sprinkled:** Brown, *Narrative of the Life of Henry Box Brown*, 52–53.

101 **Did you escape . . . Flying Horses riot:** Ignatiev, *How the Irish Became White*, 126; Winch, *Gentleman of Color*, 289.

101 **"gentlemen of property:** See, e.g., Feldberg, *Philadelphia Riots*, 14–15; Sidney Fisher's description of the "mob of well-dressed persons" attacking Pennsylvania Hall in Chapter 2.

101 **city leaders tended to blame Negroes' parading:** See, e.g., the grand jury, in Chapter 2, that probed the 1838 Pennsylvania Hall fire; and a grand jury that blamed the Aug. 1, 1842, riot on the black parade, in Salvatore, *We All Got History*, 24.

101 **Odd Fellows Hall, erected recently:** Lane, *Dorsey's Philadelphia*, xiii; Oberholtzer, *Literary History of Philadelphia*, 325.

101 **Arch Street's tailors:** A store ad, *Friends' Intelligencer*, Sept. 29, 1849.

101 **Jobs at the docks as stevedores:** Bronner, "Village into Town," 34; Geffen, "Industrial Development," 353; Nash, *Forging Freedom*, 253. See also, e.g., Lane, *Dorsey's Philadelphia*, 72; Ignatiev, *How the Irish Became White*,

115–118. See street life descriptions in Bolivar, Pencil Pusher Points, *Philadelphia Tribune*, June 6, July 20, 1912.

101   **"Peppery pot! Smokin' hot:** Lane, *Dorsey's Philadelphia*, 72; Bolivar, Pencil Pusher Points, *Philadelphia Tribune*, July 20, 1912.

101   **A bowl cost a few pennies:** Schenone, *Thousand Years*, 177.

101   **The sturdiest commerce:** See, e.g., Lane, *Roots of Violence*, 21, 23; Lane, *Dorsey's Philadelphia*, 70, 82, 126.

101   **men William Catto saw:** BAP, 4:68–71; Delany, *Condition*, 131–132. Occupations: early city directories and Lane, *Dorsey's Philadelphia*, 107, 112, 149.

101   **went to the Bird school:** *PP*, Oct. 14, 1871; Coppin, *Reminiscences*, 156; Blockson, *African Americans in Pennsylvania*, 68; Lane, *Dorsey's Philadelphia*, 318.

101   **Professional schools were closed:** Lane, *Dorsey's Philadelphia*, 175, 177.

102   **A visiting colored writer . . . Sunday best:** William J. Wilson, writing as "Ethiop" in *FD*, Nov. 9, 1855, in BAP 4:310–322.

102   **Farther south, and closer to the Little Wesley Church:** Nash, *Forging Freedom*, 248; Davis and Haller, *Peoples of Philadelphia*, 91; Geffen, "Industrial Development," 315, 335, 374.

102   **John Wesley Cromwell told of white gangs:** Cromwell, *Unveiled Voices*, 97–98.

102   **Negro children and . . . firemen:** *NS*, July 6, 1849; Bolivar, Pencil Pusher Points, *Philadelphia Tribune*, May 3, 1913, June 22, 1912.

102   **"a nation within a nation:** Ullman, *Delany*, 143.

102   **Philadelphia was its capital:** The 1860 U.S. Census counted 22,185 Negroes in Philadelphia, more than any other Northern city. One in every 24 Philadelphians was black. Boston's ratio was 1 in 77; New York City's black total was 12,472, or 1 in every 63.

102   **Negro intellectuals . . . and confer:** See, e.g., *FD*, Oct. 26, 1855.

102   **An industry of caterers and cooks:** Lane, *Dorsey's Philadelphia*, 111–114; Nash, *Forging Freedom*, 150; Wainwright, "Age of Nicholas Biddle," 264.

102   **Queen Victoria:** White and White, *Styling*, 101; Nash, *Forging Freedom*, 151; Dudgeon, *Keyed Bugle*, 67.

103   **The city was to some degree:** Bordewich, *Bound for Canaan*, 4–5, 46–50.

103   **The Pennsylvania Abolition . . . Benjamin Franklin:** Newman, "Pennsylvania Abolition Society," 7.

103   **the line drawn in a South Street office:** Dubin, *South Philadelphia*, 207.

103   **Negroes had become joiners . . . for burial:** Lane, *Dorsey's Philadelphia*, 73–74, 108, 279–308.

103   **grown in three decades from:** Davis and Haller, *Peoples of Philadelphia*, 121–122; Geffen, "Industrial Development."

103   **Philadelphia . . . the destiny of our people:** Nash, *Forging Freedom*, 6, citing *NASS*, Oct. 19, 1848.

103   **the sight a young Sarah Grimké . . . slaves a lesson:** Weld, *American Slavery as It Is*, 23.

103   **Morris Brown, banished . . . flourish:** BAP, 3:196.

103   **lining the windowsills with paving stones:** Gibbs, *Shadows and Light*, 19–20.

103   **clamoring to see an 1848 exhibit . . . degradation:** NS, Oct. 6, 1848; Mabee, *Black Freedom*, 102–103.

104   **William Wells Brown:** Brown, *American Fugitive*, 312–315; Bordewich, *Bound for Canaan*, 21; BAP, 4:254.

104   **Amos Beman . . . "TWELVE OF US:** Letter to Beman, Oct. 5, 1833, quoted in *FD*, Oct. 13, 1854 ; Warner, "Amos Gerry Beman," 200–221.

104–105   **Beman left Wesleyan . . . Negroes in Connecticut:** BAP, 4:1–12; *FD*, May 4, 1855.

105   **"Of the wooly haired Africans:** Noah Webster to Amos Beman, 1843, in Sterling, *Speak Out*, 291.

105   **Many of the movement's staunchest:** For Levi Coffin, see, e.g., Bordewich, *Bound for Canaan*, 65–66.

105   **Walt Whitman . . . of antislavery verse:** Kaplan, *Walt Whitman*, 137–139, 145, 162–163.

105   **Le Count was a . . . an undertaker:** CR, Dec. 11, 1865; Lane, *Dorsey's Philadelphia*, 126.

105   **Jacob White Sr.'s house:** *Philadelphia African-American Census 1847*; Bolivar, Pencil Pusher Points, *Philadelphia Tribune*, Sept. 13, 1913; Winch, *Elite of Our People*, 163–164; Vigilance Committee of Philadelphia, *Journal C of Station No. 2.*

105   **A little Le Count cousin . . . hide-and-seek:** Lawrence interviews.

105   **Purvis provided many threads:** See, e.g., Purvis's oft-repeated story of the voyage with the Virginian, in Chapter 2, and his meeting with Daniel O'Connell in Chapter 3; Holley, *Life for Liberty*, 102.

106   **"mingled without question:** Purvis letter, quoted in Winch, *Gentleman of Color*, 261.

106   **portrait of Cinque:** Powell, "Cinqué," 68; BAP, 3:381–382; Winch, *Gentleman of Color*, 324–325; Bacon, *But One Race*, 84–85.

106   **the Negro telescope:** Forten: *New York Colored American*, Apr. 3, 1841; Payne, *Recollections*, 51; Winch, *Gentleman of Color*, 278; Winch, *Elite of Our People*, 121n4; BAP, 5:281.

106   **Fortens and Purvises and their allies:** See, e.g., Lapsansky, "World the Agitators Made"; Lapsansky, "Feminism, Freedom, and Community"; Winch, *Gentleman of Color*, 113, 169–170; BAP, 4:262–263.

106–107   **a Purvis boy and a Remond girl . . . sued the museum:** Bacon, *But One Race*, 111.

107   **On the long list . . . "R. B. Forten—Telescope:** Fox, "John Scott Medal," 422.

107   **The same December week . . . How long:** NS, Feb. 2, 1849.

107–108   **The Pennsylvania suffrage drive . . . but every day reality:** "Observer," NS, July 6, 1849; BAP, 3:252.

108–109   **A white writer . . . gotten on earth:** NASS, Jan. 4, 1849.

109   **Pennsylvania Hall—people assured each other:** See, e.g., in Chapter 9, the paid notice in *New York Weekly Anglo-African*, Feb. 4, 1860, quoting Banneker members trying to persuade a landlord that "burning down halls in Philadelphia" was over.

110   **Steps had been taken:** Ignatiev, *How the Irish Became White*, 154.

110   **"wounds & bruises the consequences:** Thomas P. Cope diary entry, May 2, 1849, in Cope and Harrison, *Philadelphia Merchant*, 576; [Hunt], *Why Colored People*, 23–24.

110   **In 1849, a young congressman . . . slave hound from Illinois:** Goodwin, *Team of Rivals*, 128.

110–111   **Lucretia Mott . . . walked from the room:** NASS, Mar. 29, 1849.

111   **Now the Negro suffrage drive:** Except where noted, our account of the campaign relies on Wright, "Negro Suffrage in New Jersey," 184–195.

111   **Catto was becoming . . . bringing his family:** Ibid.; Morgan, *Morgan's History*, 94; undated, handwritten *North Star* records at LOC place him in Camden; 1850 Census suggests the Cattos lived mostly in Philadelphia from mid-1848 to the early 1850s.

111   **Smallpox, yellow fever . . . took five hundred:** Geffen, "Industrial Development," 317–319; Sewell, *Sorrows Circuit*, 53–54.

111   **He preached once in Camden . . . or Buffalo, New York:** *CR*, June 28, 1883, July 6, 21, 1866; Morgan, *Morgan's History*, 67.

111   **At the church's annual conference:** Payne, *History*, 250.

111   **The A.M.E. was still years away:** BAP, 3:37, 4:195.

112   **A series of anonymous . . . minstrel shows:** Dorsey, "Gendered History."

112   **"I charge it back upon . . . Thos. Jefferson:** *Colored American*, July 3, 1841.

112–113   **On the evening of October 10, 1849 . . . Killers:** Ignatiev, *How the Irish Became White*, 155–156; *Washington (DC) National Era*, Oct. 18, 1849; Cope and Harrison, *Philadelphia Merchant*, 581; NS, Oct. 19, 1849, quoting *INQ*; *PL*, Oct. 11, 1849, 3.

CHAPTER 6: THE IRISH, THE KILLERS, AND SQUIRE McMULLEN

Pages

115   **The Killers' tale starts with:** Boston, "Bible Riots"; Feldberg, *Philadelphia Riots*; Warner, *Private City*, 142–153; Geffen, "Industrial Development," 357–358; Silcox, *McMullen*, 36; Ignatiev, *How the Irish Became White*, 34–36.

115   **Irish-born Protestant Edmund Burke:** Walsh, "Penal Laws Era."

115   **That sentiment accompanied Irish immigrants:** "Berkeley the Philosopher."

116   **In 1797, the year John Adams came:** Dubin, *South Philadelphia*, 15.

116   **From 1790 to 1840, 70 percent:** Silcox, *McMullen*, 28.

116   **In the 1790s, the Congress declared . . . a common Irishman:** Ignatiev, *How the Irish Became White*, 41–42.

116–117   **So the Irish went from a people . . . for their livelihoods:** Ibid., 38, 76, 96; Davis, *Parades and Power*, 34–35; Dubin, *South Philadelphia*, 16.

117   **By 1811, Negroes lived among:** Lapsansky, "Since They Got Those Separate Black Churches"; Ignatiev, *How the Irish Became White*, 125, 129, 156; Silcox, *McMullen*, 32–33.

117   **the historian Noel Ignatiev notes:** Ignatiev, *How the Irish Became White*, 130.

117–118   **Negroes trying to take jobs away . . . from public office:** Ibid., 76, 87, 149, 157; Feldberg, *Philadelphia Riots*, 3, 90–91; Davis, *Parades and Power*, 150. See also Dubin, *South Philadelphia*, 17; Ignatiev, *How the Irish Became White*, 75–76.

118–119   **While Quakers, few in number . . . public office:** Ignatiev, *How the Irish Became White*, 6–7, 68–69.

119   **By the 1840s, O'Connell saw:** Gibbs, *Shadows and Light*, 21–24; BAP, 3:intro., 13; Ignatiev, *How the Irish Became White*, 42, 97–99.

119   **O'Connell, who had ardently supported:** Quinn, "Rise and Fall of Repeal," 46–47, 50–52; Ignatiev, *How the Irish Became White*, 13–14.

119–120   **The address appealed to the . . . foolish "niggerology:** Quinn, "Rise and Fall of Repeal," 55–56; Ignatiev, *How the Irish Became White*, 9, 12–14. For more on "niggerology," see Roediger, *Wages of Whiteness*, 136.

120   **In 1842:** 1842 temperance parade riot: Salvatore, *We All Got History*, 22–24; Winch, *Gentleman of Color*, 351–352, Foner, *Douglass: Selected Speeches*, 48; Quinn, "Rise and Fall of Repeal," 61.

120–121   **Three weeks after the August . . . just like white folks:** Ignatiev, *How the Irish Became White*, 136–137.

121   **By now, Philadelphia was more:** Quinn, "Rise and Fall of Repeal," 59.

121–122   **The friction was apparent to . . . star-spangled banner:** Ignatiev, *How the Irish Became White*, 23–25, 99, 137–138; Quinn, "Rise and Fall of Repeal," 64, 68.

122   **Years later, Frederick Douglass:** Rice and Crawford, *Liberating Sojourn*, 131.

122   **The Irishman Douglass admired . . . and mournful keen:** Keneally, *Great Shame*, 132–133.

122–123   **More than a million . . . nearly fifty thousand came:** The Irish famine and exodus: the Irish Memorial, a large statue with informational displays at Front and Chestnut streets, Philadelphia. Also, Geffen, "Industrial Development," 309; Feldberg, *Philadelphia Riots*, 21, 37; Ignatiev, *How the Irish Became White*, 39–40, 45.

123   **Philadelphia by 1844 . . . of fundamentalism:** On wages, Geffen, "Industrial Development," 308, 318–319, 321, 335.

124   **This was also a time:** Silcox, *McMullen*, 18–20.

124   **White men's attacks on Negroes:** Lane, *Roots of Violence*, 9; Ignatiev, *How the Irish Became White*, 157; Dennis J. Clark, "The Philadelphia Irish: Persistent Presence," in Davis and Haller, *Peoples of Philadelphia*, 74.

124–132   **To understand what happened . . . who lost an arm in the riots:** See sources previously cited for the Kensington and South Philadelphia riots and their aftermath: Feldberg, *Philadelphia Riots*; Ignatiev, *How the Irish Became White*; Boston, *Bible Riots*. On the creation of public schools in 1834, see BAP, 4:188.

132   **As for the city's Negroes:** Ignatiev, *How the Irish Became White*, 153.

133   **The Killers were:** Bruce Laurie, "Fire Companies and Gangs in Southwark: The 1840s," in Davis and Haller, *Peoples of Philadelphia*, 79; Dubin, *South Philadelphia*, 161–163; Kirkpatrick, *Revenge of Thomas Eakins*, 26–27; Lane, *Roots of Violence*, 9–12, 18.

133   **The gang became the:** The novel about the Killers, *The Life and Adventures of Charles Anderson Chester, the Notorious Leader of the Philadelphia 'Killers,'* published in Philadelphia in 1850, with no author listed (though

historians speculate that George Lippard wrote it), is discussed in David R. Johnson, "Crime Patterns in Philadelphia, 1840–70," in Davis and Haller, *Peoples of Philadelphia*, 98.

134   **A pamphleteer romanticized:** Silcox, *McMullen*, 45–46; Ignatiev, *How the Irish Became White*, 155.

134   **One Sunday afternoon on Spafford Street:** Sewell, *Sorrows Circuit*, 335.

134   **The Killers had connections:** Thomas P. Cope diary entry, Oct. 10, 1849, in Cope and Harrison, *Philadelphia Merchant*, 581.

134   **As the violence of the gangs:** Laurie, "Fire Companies," 71, 78–79; Ignatiev, *How the Irish Became White*, 143; Silcox, *McMullen*, 35–36.

135   **Engine companies . . . the United States:** Laurie, "Fire Companies," 75–81; Scharf and Westcott, *History of Philadelphia*, vol. 3.

135   **Success was measured in:** Dubin, *South Philadelphia*, 7.

135   **"A dangerous body of men," . . . taken it over:** Silcox, *McMullen*, 21; Ignatiev, *How the Irish Became White*, 143.

136   **Matthias Baldwin knew it, too:** Brown, *Baldwin Locomotive Works*, 136–137.

136   **The company that attracted:** Silcox, *McMullen*, 36; "Old Vol. Fire Ladies" in Frank H. Schell Collection.

136   **Firemen were seen by:** Laurie, "Fire Companies," 76–77; Geffen, "Industrial Development," 348; Silcox, *McMullen*, 37–38

136–137   **McMullen. His name was a synonym . . . country England lost:** Silcox, *McMullen*, 35–38; Ignatiev, *How the Irish Became White*, 160–161; Quinn, "Rise and Fall of Repeal," 77.

137   **In late 1845, McMullen was served:** Silcox, *McMullen*, 39–42, 44; Ignatiev, *How the Irish Became White*, 161.

CHAPTER 7: "ARISE, YOUNG NORTH"

Pages

139   **The report from Trenton . . . "laid on the table":** Wright, "Negro Suffrage in New Jersey," 192–195.

139   **Frederick Douglass . . . pathway to duty:** Martin, *Mind of Frederick Douglass*, 38; Mayer, *All on Fire*, 428–434.

139   **their votes could tip the scales:** Litwack, *North of Slavery*, 90.

140   **there was not much progress . . . white backlash:** Ibid., 75–91, 176–77; BAP, 3:43, 252, 4:11–12, 5:259; *Christian Freeman*, May 22, 1845.

140   **On a brutally hot July:** Fraser, *Charleston!* 228; Cornelius, *Slave Missions*, 121–123.

140   **(Rev. Thomas Smyth's wife . . . "the insurrection:** Margaret Smyth to Janey Adger, July 23, 1849, in Flinn Papers.

140   **more owners were freeing:** Mitchell, *Maryland Voices*, 5.

140   **Illinois, Indiana, and Iowa banned:** BAP, 5:56; Foner, *Reconstruction*, 26.

140   **The District of Columbia strengthened:** Brown and Lewis, *Washington from Banneker to Douglass*, 9.

140   **Maryland considered enslaving . . . a crime:** Fields, *Slavery and Freedom*, 70–80.

140   **The Oregon Territory banned:** BAP, 4:102.

140–141 **A religious journal . . . among you:** *Richmond (VA) Watchman and Observer*, Jan. 11, 1849, Jan. 18, May 3, May 5, 1849.

141 **Citizens of Mercer County:** Lomax, *Black Baseball Entrepreneurs*, 3.

141 **The Pennsylvania legislature . . . remonstrances:** *FD*, Apr. 29, 1852; Ullman, *Delany*, 152; BAP, 3:252.

141 **"the removal & transportation:** Turner, *Negro in Pennsylvania*, 167.

141 **"My first impulse:** Angle, *Complete Lincoln-Douglas Debates*, 116.

141 **In Philadelphia, a typographers union:** Foner, "Blacks and the Labor Movement," 35.

142 **Brigham Young, kept a copy:** Bush, "Mormonism's Negro Doctrine," 73–74.

142 **the chairman of the New Jersey . . . duties as ministers, teachers:** Wright, "Negro Suffrage in New Jersey," 187–190, 192–195.

142 **Another Catto baby:** The youngest child was Erskine or "Earskine," four months old, 1850 Census.

142 **Ishmael Locke's wife . . . Pliny:** Buck, *Alain Locke*, 11; Coppin, *Reminiscences*, 144.

142 **Locke had new duties . . . by colored teachers:** Lane, *Dorsey's Philadelphia*, 136–137; Perkins, *Fanny Jackson Coppin*, 64–65.

142–145 **Californians, their ranks . . . Star Spangled Banner:** Bordewich, *Bound for Canaan*, 312–318; Goodwin, *Team of Rivals*, 140–149; *History of the Trial of Castner Hanway*, 31; Winston, "Howard University Department of History"; Coppin, *Reminiscences*, 19; Ferris, *Alexander Crummell*, 11; Gates, *Loose Canons*, 72–73.

145 **The first arrest . . . People cheered:** *NASS*, Oct. 10, 1850, 2; Quarles, *Black Abolitionists*, 197–198; Bordewich, *Bound for Canaan*, 323; Yellin, *Harriet Jacobs*, 108.

145 **Hired slave catchers . . . fake name:** Bordewich, *Bound for Canaan*, 324; May, *Fugitive Slave Law*, 14, 18, 21–22.

145 **Philadelphia's most notorious:** Wilson, *Freedom at Risk*, 50–53; Alberti obituary, *Philadelphia Telegraph*, reprinted in *NYT*, July 27, 1869.

145 **A colored church in Rochester . . . months of the law:** Bordewich, *Bound for Canaan*, 319, 324.

146 **Poems called "Blood Money" . . . of cowards:** Kaplan, *Walt Whitman*, 137–139, 162–163; Murphy, *Walt Whitman*, 663.

146 **The law instantly imperiled:** See, e.g., Litwack, *North of Slavery*, 248–249.

146 **Catto and William Still convened:** *Liberator*, Nov. 1850; BAP, 4:68–71.

147 **Liberator . . . subscribers in California:** Bordewich, *Bound for Canaan*, 313.

147 **An antislavery mob:** *NASS*, Nov. 21, 1850, 3, citing *Cincinnati Gazette*, Nov. 11, 1850.

147 **At Chardon, Ohio . . . force of arms:** *NASS*, Nov. 21, 1850, citing *Boston Journal*.

147 **At a Boston rally, the former slave . . . never be taken alive:** Foner and Branham, *Lift Every Voice*, 217–220, quoting *Liberator*, Apr. 5, 1850.

147 **Martin Delany picked up this cry . . . both live:** Ullman, *Delany*, 112.

148 **when a kidnap ring . . . New Orleans:** Bordewich, *Bound for Canaan*, 135–136; Winch, *Gentleman of Color*, 232–233.

148 **Two Forten relatives . . . Mississippi:** Winch, *Gentleman of Color*, 122–124.

148   **Octavius Catto . . . of Charleston:** For the taking of Robert M. Adger's grandmother, see his father's 1896 obituary, in Du Bois, *Philadelphia Negro*, 121–122.

148   **Kidnapping had faded:** Salvatore, *We All Got History*, 12–14.

148   **The Fugitive Slave . . . was the wiser:** See, e.g., Mayer, *All on Fire*, 406–407, 409; Litwack, *North of Slavery*, 248–249.

148   **In the Lancaster County:** Katz, *Resistance at Christiana*, 268–272; Bordewich, *Bound for Canaan*, 325–333; Mires, *Independence Hall*, 96–98.

148   **the "estimable" . . . "daily diminishing:** *Senate Journal*, 32nd Cong., 1st sess., Dec. 2, 1851, 29–30.

148   **At Rochester, Douglass . . . sheltered them:** Douglass, *Life and Times*, 245.

148   **Rosetta remembered . . . fleeing humanity:** "My Mother as I Recall Her," May 1900, in Sterling, *Speak Out*, 180–182.

149   **Bibb's newspaper . . . "The Christiana Hero:** Bordewich, *Bound for Canaan*, 380–388; Katz, *Resistance at Christiana*, 268–272.

149   **dog pound in the basement:** Mires, *Independence Hall*, 101–102.

149   **His childhood friend was Robert Bridges Forten:** BAP, 5:281–282.

149–150   **Samuel Ringgold Ward . . . "go to Canada:** Ward, *Autobiography of a Fugitive Negro*, 116–117.

150   **Austin Bearse . . . taken his own life:** Stowe, *Key to Uncle Tom's Cabin*, 154.

150–151   **The author who interviewed . . . *Uncle Tom's Cabin*:** BAP, 4:125; Stowe, *Uncle Tom's Cabin*, xii, xxii, xxiii; McCray, *Life-Work of the Author*, 105–106.

151   **a who's-who of 161:** Delany, *Condition*, 113–160.

151   **if only for their children's . . . himself more useful":** Ibid., 7, 108, 125, 127–128, 208; Ullman, *Delany*, 141–145.

151   **A.M.E. Church had made him steward . . . matter of months:** Payne, *Recollections*, 109–110; Wayman, *My Recollections*, 51; Wright, *Centennial Encyclopaedia*, 62, 293–294.

151   **A minister who had signed:.** Peterson, *Looking-Glass*, 98–99.

152   **The Purvises . . . another home:** Winch, *Gentleman of Color*, 353.

152   **Her brother, Robert Forten . . . Charlotte behind:** Stevenson, "Charlotte Forten"; Sterling, *We Are Your Sisters*, 188.

152   **Thanks to the underground . . . thirty thousand:** Bordewich, *Bound for Canaan*, 324, 379–380; Litwack, *North of Slavery*, 249.

152   **Farewell old master:** Lyrics in Siebert, "Underground Railroad in Massachusetts," 448.

153   **They lost the writers . . . Liberia:** BAP, 4:33–34, 254, 5:109.

153   **"like a besieged city . . . its gates:** Douglass, *Life and Times*, 279.

153   **Garnet sailed to . . . in [the United States] again:** Swift, *Black Prophets*, 255–257.

153–154   **Daniel Payne went . . . retreat in order:** Douglass, *Life and Times*, 279.

154   **legislators now proposed to enslave:** Fields, *Slavery and Freedom*, 70–80.

154   **birthplace, Nova Scotia:** 1860 Census. See Walker, *Black Loyalists*.

154   **He prepared his family to move . . . Long Branch:** Morgan, *Morgan's History*, 63, 67, 72, 81, 96; PP, Oct. 14, 1871, regarding Octavius's attending the academy in Allentown in 1853.

154   **preached in Trenton in 1849 . . . suffrage effort:** Morgan, *Morgan's History*, 94; Wright, "Negro Suffrage in New Jersey," 184–195.

154   **In June 1850:** *CR*, June 28, 1883.

154   **Camden was a leisure-time:** Kirsch, *Creation of American Team Sports*, 22–23, 53–54; Shiffert, *Baseball in Philadelphia*, 4, 14. See also Lane, *Dorsey's Philadelphia*, chap. 11; Bolivar, Pencil Pusher Points, *Philadelphia Tribune*, May 3, 1913.

155   **One of the A.M.E. pulpits:** Morgan, *Morgan's History*, 63.

155   **Allentown also had . . . at a time:** *PP*, Oct. 14, 1871; Applegate, *Life of Service*, 25, 135–139.

155–156   **Ishmael Locke's night classes . . . no one hired black teachers:** Perkins, *Fanny Jackson Coppin*, 61–67; Lane, *Dorsey's Philadelphia*, 135–139; Silcox, "Nineteenth Century Philadelphia Black Militant," 55; *Forty-sixth Annual Report of the Controllers of the Public Schools . . . 1864*, 192.

156   **TEACHER WANTED . . . being equal:** *Washington (DC) National Era*, May 27, 1852.

156   **That colored man:** BAP, 4:193; Perkins, *Fanny Jackson Coppin*, 66–67; Simmons, *Men of Mark*, 1105–1112.

157   **ten dollars for tuition . . . attend free:** Charles Reason, in *Washington (DC) National Era*, Oct. 7, 1852.

157   **Sarah Mapps Douglass:** Perkins, *Fanny Jackson Coppin*, 66–67, 81; BAP, 3:118, 4:193.

157   **"Composition, History, Algebra:** *Washington (DC) National Era*, Oct. 7, 1852.

157   **In the future . . . six pupils:** Board of Managers, annual reports, I.C.Y. records, FLS and LC; BAP, 4:193.

157   **Enrollment grew pyramid-style:** Lane, *Dorsey's Philadelphia*, 138.

157   **Seniors knew . . . *Christian Recorder*:** See, e.g., "Institute for Colored Youth," in *CR*, May 16, 1863.

157–158   **"Inscribe a regular decagon . . . where I stand:** *CR*, May 21, 1864.

158   **Commencement programs . . . Latin, and Greek:** Program for Dec. 19–20, 1867, commencement, Dorsey scrapbooks.

158   **Each year, as many . . . commonplace:** Lane, *Dorsey's Philadelphia*, 138.

158   **a boy's diary:** Cromwell, *Unveiled Voices*, 97.

158   **Instruction was . . . cities applied:** Lane, *Dorsey's Philadelphia*, 139.

158   **"There were always more pegs:** Bolivar, Pencil Pusher Points, *Philadelphia Tribune*, Mar. 30, 1912.

158   **In three years, enrollment grew:** BAP, 4:193.

158   **William Catto moved back:** *PP*, Oct. 14, 1871.

158   **Jake Jr. in the I.C.Y. . . . boy, Pliny:** Coppin, *Reminiscences*, 144–191, esp. 156–157 on Jacob White Jr.

158   **The ratio of students:** Lane, *Dorsey's Philadelphia*, 139. The maximum student-teacher ratio in the Philadelphia public schools currently runs 33-to-1 in grades 4–12.

166   **Franklin Pierce asked twenty thousand:** Ullman, *Delany*, 151; Holmes, *Parties and Their Principles*, 259. Inaugural details: U.S. Congress, Senate, "I Do Solemnly Swear."

166   **In Philadelphia . . . must become a habit:** *Library of the Institute for Colored Youth*; *Pennsylvania Freeman*, Apr. 7, 1853.

166 **Two springs later . . . promising day:** "Librarians' Second Annual Report," *FD*, Apr. 27, 1855.

166–167 **The news was that on Saturday . . . true to us than these:** BAP, 4:189–193, 205–206; *FD*, Feb. 10, 1854; Lane, *Dorsey's Philadelphia*, 111; Faculty portraits in Coppin, *Reminiscences*, 140–141; Perkins, "Heed Life's Demands"; Still, *Underground Railroad*, 612; Vigilance Committee of Philadelphia, *Journal C of Station No. 2*.

167 **"principle of action:** Foner, *Douglass: Selected Speeches*, 325.

167 **At one meeting, Douglass traded:** Ibid., 173, 174; Litwack, *North of Slavery*, 241.

167 **I stand in relation to him:** Quarles, *Black Abolitionists*, 242.

167 **Garrison told an ally:** Martin, *Mind of Frederick Douglass*, 39.

168 **The governor of Pennsylvania . . . had spoken well:** Perkins, *Fanny Jackson Coppin*, 67–68; Salvatore, *We All Got History*, 81; "Governor Pollock's Visit to the Colored Schools," signed "W.S." (probably William Still), *Provincial Freeman*, June 9, 1855; Silcox, "Philadelphia Negro Educator"; Bowen, *History of Philadelphia*, 167–168.

CHAPTER 8: "HOW MUCH I YEARN TO BE A *MAN*"

Pages

169 **A young Negro schoolteacher sued . . . by ninety-nine years:** *NYT* and *New York Tribune* articles, July 19, 1854; *FD*, Sept. 22, 1854; BAP, 4:230–233, 294.

169 **Charles Langston went to jail . . . efforts of the Court:** Dunbar-Nelson, *Masterpieces of Negro Eloquence*, 49–62; Quarles, *Black Abolitionists*, 213–214.

169 **I hear the voice of Langston:** Unattributed lyrics in Campbell, *Autobiography*, 288–289.

170 **A Syracuse band composed:** Bordewich, *Bound for Canaan*, 412.

170 **Charlotte Forten wrote a . . . Boston and Philadelphia:** Diary entry for Feb. 7, 1858, in Stevenson, *Journals of Charlotte Forten Grimké*, 285; Wesley and Uzelac, *William Cooper Nell*, 298; Johnson, *Autobiography*, 133.

170 **Martin Delany, irked at the meekness:** Adeleke, *Without Regard to Race*, 65–67.

170 **Garrison's *Liberator* published two . . . a dollar:** Stevenson, *Journals of Charlotte Forten Grimké*, 23, 36.

170 **He also helped a former slave:** Coppin, *Reminiscences*, 13.

170 **a Charles Dickens story . . . Douglass's collected speeches:** Diary entries for July 19 and 26, 1857, in Stevenson, *Journals of Charlotte Forten Grimké*, 232–240.

170 **"kind and cordial . . . Liberty and Truth:** Diary entry for Sept. 12, 1855, in ibid., 139–141.

170 **"the talented thousandth:** Lawson and Merrill, "Antebellum 'Talented Thousandth,'" 142–155.

171 **"I never rose to recite:** Coppin, *Reminiscences*, 15.

171 **"preparing to lead the struggle:** Lapsansky, "World the Agitators Made," 95–98.

171 **believing education was their birthright:** See, e.g., "Oberlin" in William Wormley to Octavius Catto, Sept. 11, 1860, ANHS, box 3A; and

Charlotte Forten's musings on schools, classmates and examinations, in Stevenson, *Journals of Charlotte Forten Grimké*, 129–140.

171   **teach the oppressed . . . "hatred of oppression:** Charlotte Forten hymn, in *Provincial Freeman*, Aug. 29, 1855; *Colored American*, Apr. 10, 1841.

171   **Fanny Jackson grew fond . . . is power:** Perkins, "Heed Life's Demands," 181.

171–172   **"For God's sake . . . or missus:** Yetman, *Voices from Slavery*, 147–150.

172   **A slave boy in Richmond:** Von Frank, *Trials of Anthony Burns*, 85–86.

172   **A Philadelphia girl named Cordelia:** *The Friend; a Religious and Literary Journal*, June 20, 1863, FLS; Perkins, *Fanny Jackson Coppin*, 70–71.

172   **A slave mother in Winchester . . . Ossawa:** Bruce, *Henry Ossawa Tanner*, 28; Seraile, *Fire in His Heart*, 5–10.

172   **Colored writers from two generations . . . children:** *Douglass' Monthly*, May 4, 1855.

172   **two books that, she said:** John Wesley Cromwell obituary, in *Journal of Negro History*, "Notes," 566. Also, see Cromwell profile in Simmons, *Men of Mark*, 898–907

172–173   **New York state's . . . He lost:** BAP, 3:322, 367; Ullman, *Delany*, 17, 26–27.

173   **"a dynasty of social activists:** Lapsansky, "World the Agitators Made," 95–98.

173   **In Ohio that year . . . He won:** BAP, 4:281; Foner and Branham, *Lift Every Voice*, 273; Cheek and Cheek, "John Mercer Langston," 226–227, 233–234.

173   **Even the temperance drives:** See BAP, 3:14–15, 20, 129–130, 4:210–211, 242.

173   **welcoming Underground Railroad . . . seamstress:** Winch, *Elite of Our People*, 163–164; Still, *Underground Railroad*, 611–612.

173   **Jake Sr., by turns a barber . . . colored cemeteries:** Lane, *Dorsey's Philadelphia*, 106–108.

173   **His friend, Rev. William Catto . . . directors:** Lapsansky, "Discipline," 404.

173   **The Cattos and the Whites:** Ibid.; old maps show Kessler Street is a block or two from Old York Road, where the Whites lived; Silcox, "Nineteenth Century Philadelphia Black Militant," 56.

173–174   **When Catto left the A.M.E. . . . $1,436.20:** Murphy, Melton, and Ward, *Encyclopedia of African American Religions*, 302; Waters, *We Have This Ministry*, 27; Catto, *Semi-Centenary Discourse*, 91–92, 99, 102.

174   **"deathly silence" . . . the year Jake was born:** William Watkins, Jacob M. Moore, and Jacob C. White Sr., "Address to Colored Churches in the Free States," Nov. 1836, BAP, 3:189–195; Jake's essay was published Dec. 29, 1852, BAP, 4:137.

174   **Jake Jr. was . . . of the past:** Lapsansky, "Discipline," 402; Lane, *Dorsey's Philadelphia*, 107–108.

174   **"quiet, soft spoken . . . patriarchal appearance:** Boyer, *Brief Historic Sketch*, 13.

174   **Rev. William Catto tried to bar them:** *Minutes and Sermon of the Second Presbyterian and Congregational Convention*, 5–6.

174   **she had already walked:** See protests described in Von Frank, *Trials of Anthony Burns*, esp. 175, 217.

174   **She suffered . . . the Remonds:** See, e.g., "Chronology," in Stevenson, *Journals of Charlotte Forten Grimké*, xxxiii–xl, 32, 36.

174–175   **His "gloomy countenance . . . in the world:** Diary entries for Sept. 8, Oct. 25, 1857, in Stevenson, *Journals of Charlotte Forten Grimké*, 164, 166.

175   **Sarah Remond, turning thirty . . . bore were his property:** Haltunnen and Perry, *Moral Problems in American Life*, 134–135.

175   **"might for a time enjoy freedom:** Sarah Remond, in *Derbyshire Courier*, Apr. 13, 1861, *BAPM*, reel 13, frame 452.

175   **thrown down a stairs . . . lecturing experiences:** Wesley and Uzelac, *William Cooper Nell*, 26; diary entry, Apr. 9, 1857, in Stevenson, *Journals of Charlotte Forten Grimké*, 209.

175   **By age seventeen . . . liberty until death:** Stevenson, "Charlotte Forten," 279–297; Von Frank, *Trials of Anthony Burns*, 175–176.

175   **Anthony Burns had been arrested:** Von Frank, *Trials of Anthony Burns*, 210–217; BAP, 4:227–229.

176   **A white abolitionist in the crowd . . . not man enough:** Von Frank, *Trials of Anthony Burns*, 210–217; Quarles, *Black Abolitionists*, 208.

176   **Of course, Burns . . . the offer from P. T. Barnum:** Von Frank, *Trials of Anthony Burns*, 233–236, 287–290, 301–304.

176   **She strolled in Salem's woods . . . Nature's God:** Stevenson, *Journals of Charlotte Forten Grimké*, 62–63.

176   **"fine series of barns" and:** Brown, *Black Man*, 254.

176   **Mott cousins tutored Rosetta Douglass:** McFeely, *Frederick Douglass*, 152–154, 160–161.

176   **Ellen Wright . . . "I am getting old:** Sterling, *We Are Your Sisters*, 187; Sterling, *Speak Out*, 188.

177   **shot through with the word *refused*:** Stevenson, *Journals of Charlotte Forten Grimké*, 22, 98, 232.

177   **In the summer . . . history at her disposal:** Diary entries, June 17–25, 1857, 22–23, 232–240, esp. entry for July 19, 1857, in ibid., 186; Lapsansky, "World the Agitators Made," 95–98; Lapsansky, "Feminism, Freedom, and Community," 10.

177   **She was still in her teens . . . Wendell Phillips thanked her:** Stevenson, *Journals of Charlotte Forten Grimké*, xxxiii, 9; Winch, *Gentleman of Color*, 347.

178   **as if they were old enough:** Lapsansky, "World the Agitators Made," 96n12.

178   **"burning down halls in Philadelphia":** *New York Weekly Anglo-African*, Feb. 4, 1860.

178   **the Fortens had been free . . . Whites nearly as long:** Winch, *Gentleman of Color*, 8–12; Winch, *Elite of Our People*, 163–164.

178   **Rosetta Douglass . . . "Respectable, too:** Sterling, *We Are Your Sisters*, 138–139.

178   **Born in slavery . . . the same year as Jake:** Coppin, *Reminiscences*, 5, 9–11; Perkins, *Fanny Jackson Coppin*, 13–21.

178   **a colored man named Snow . . . for months:** *History of Schools for the Colored Population*, 201, 211–212; Brown and Lewis, *Washington from Banneker to Douglass*, 9.

178-179 **That was the Washington . . . pay her tuition:** Perkins, *Fanny Jackson Coppin*, 13-22; Coppin, *Reminiscences*, 3, 9-11, 16-17, 42-43; Morgan, *Morgan's History*, 113; Sweet, "Fourth of July and Black Americans."

179 **She arrived at the Ohio . . . of what was wrong:** Coppin, *Reminiscences*, 13-14; Perkins, *Fanny Jackson Coppin*, 20; Campbell, *Autobiography*, 288-289.

180 **In colored communities . . . "profane swearing:** Schor, *Garnet*, 11-12; Sterling, *Speak Out*, 76-77.

180 **Would the downfall . . . Sanction Slavery:** Ballard, *One More Day's Journey*, 60; Lapsansky, "Discipline," 410.

180 **The sponsor of both events:** See Lapsansky, "Discipline," and Martin, "Banneker Literary Institute," the two studies on which most of this account of the Banneker group is based.

180 **Toussaint L'Ouverture Martin:** See I.C.Y. students' names in *CR*, Oct. 8, 1864.

180 **Benjamin Banneker . . . by 1856:** Lapsansky, "Discipline," 399-402; Mires, *Independence Hall*, 52.

180 **The organization spent eighty-seven . . . members expelled:** Lapsansky, "Discipline," 405-406.

180 **the annual report for 1857:** ANHS, box 5G, folder 7.

180-181 **When the minister . . . finished high school:** Lapsansky, "Discipline," 402, 404, 410; Martin, *Banneker Literary Institute*, 303, 315.

181 **"quieter and more persuasive way":** Bolivar, Pencil Pusher Points, *Philadelphia Tribune*, Jan. 18, 1913.

181 **"pedestals," as he once said:** Cromwell, *Unveiled Voices*, 97, quoting John W. Cromwell's diary.

181 **visitors from other states:** Perkins, *Fanny Jackson Coppin*, 69; Coppin, *Reminiscences*, 19-22.

181-182 **A white Maryland minister . . . Shore of Maryland:** Long, *Pictures of Slavery*, 301-302.

182 **A new principal . . . raised his hand:** Perkins, *Fanny Jackson Coppin*, 68; the managers advertised the position in several issues of *FD*, starting Sept. 21, 1855.

182 **Bassett was the son . . . for the vote:** Wynes, "Ebenezer Don Carlos Bassett," 232; *FD*, May 19, 1854, May 4, 1855.

182 **In 1854, Bassett wrote . . . from whites:** *FD*, Mar. 16, 1855.

182 **The notice of . . . turned twenty-two:** Perkins, *Fanny Jackson Coppin*, 68; Andrews, *Memorial*, 427.

182 **Bassett added trigonometry:** Perkins, *Fanny Jackson Coppin*, 68.

182-183 **A printer's son, born in Jamaica . . . man in the turban:** BAP, 4:352-355; Blackett, *Beating Against the Barriers*, 139-149; I.C.Y. records, 60; *The Friend; a Religious and Literary Journal*, June 20, 1863; I.C.Y. Board of Managers, annual report, *CR*, Oct. 8, 1864; illustration in Coppin, *Reminiscences*, 140.

183 **Bassett built on . . . to editors:** *CR*, Mar. 21, 1863; Schor, *Garnet*, 141; *PP*, Jan. 23, 1865.

183 **He likened an antislavery oration:** Quarles, *Black Abolitionists*, 246.

183 **to the likes of Remond:** *The Friend; a Religious and Literary Journal*, June 20, 1863; Perkins, *Fanny Jackson Coppin*, 69-70; *Philadelphia Daily Times*,

June 6, 1857, in *Friends' Intelligencer* 14 (1857–1858): 190; Douglass lecture, *CR*, Mar. 21, 1863.

183 **gave Bassett leeway, even lending:** Lane, *Dorsey's Philadelphia*, 306; Board of Managers, minutes, Mar. 12, 1867, June 9, 1868, Jan. 13, 1869, excerpts, I.C.Y. records, FLS.

183 **"peaceable principles . . . black intelligentsia:** Perkins, *Fanny Jackson Coppin*, 69–70.

183 **The principal assigned . . . on their feet:** Mar. 13, 1863, and other diary entries, Cromwell, *Unveiled Voices*, 97; "The Examination of the Pupils . . . ," *CR*, May 11, 1861.

184 **His efforts bore fruit . . . parts of the country:** Perkins, *Fanny Jackson Coppin*, 68–69.

184 **He took to showcasing . . . never published:** Coppin, *Reminiscences*, 21; Lapsansky, "Discipline," 405; *CR*, Jan. 26, 1861.

184 **Jesse Glasgow . . . prize after prize:** *CR*, Jan. 26, 1861; Lane, *Dorsey's Philadelphia*, 140.

184 **Martin Delany, ever more certain . . . and volunteered:** Ullman, *Delany*, 208, 215, 220; Blackett, "Delany and Robert Campbell," 8–12.

184–185 **in Canada West . . . walking the streets:** Bordewich, *Bound for Canaan*, 260.

185 **Two of Robert Adger Sr.'s fourteen . . . slavery illegal:** *CR*, May 7, 1864; Yellin, *Harriet Jacobs*, 113–114.

185 **"the combined anguish:** Blight, *Frederick Douglass' Civil War*, 14.

185 **Most states, North and South . . . discouraging:** Litwack, *North of Slavery*, 93–94; Quarles, *Black Abolitionists*, 72.

185 **Denial of a museum:** Stevenson, *Journals of Charlotte Forten Grimké*, 30–31, also Sept. 5, 1854 and Sept. 12, 1855 diary entries, 98, 140.

185 **A white Cincinnati gang's assault . . . accept the conditions:** BAP, 5:148–150.

186 **Most business at the:** See, e.g., Philadelphia Presbytery minutes, Jan. 2, Mar. 5, July 12, Nov. 12, 1855, Oct. 7, 1857, microfilm roll 2.

186 **announced that the only colored . . . writing a book:** Minutes for July 5, 1857, in ibid.

186 **Catto, in his late forties:** Minutes for Oct. 5, 1854, 328–330, in ibid.

186 **"are addressed . . . sure and steady:** Catto, *Semi-Centenary Discourse*, 60.

186 **He trudged around:** Ibid., 105–111.

186 **he was sending out a letter . . . five for a dollar:** ANHS, microfilm roll 8, frame 1241.

186 **favorable if brief notice:** See, e.g., *Historical Magazine, and Notes and Queries Concerning the Antiquities*, Jan. 1858, 30; *Presbyterian Magazine* 7 (Oct. 1857): 469–470.

187 **"a large brick . . . Daniel Payne:** Catto, *Semi-Centenary Discourse*, 105–106.

187 **switched faiths three times:** William Catto's role at Charleston's Trinity Methodist Church in 1836 and at Second Presbyterian in the mid-1840s are discussed in Chapters 1 and 3; his turn with the A.M.E. Church in Philadelphia and New Jersey, 1848–1853, before rejoining the Presbyterians in 1854, when he came to First African Presbyterian Church in Philadelphia is discussed in Chapters. 4 and 5.

187   **The book began:** Catto, *Semi-Centenary Discourse*, 3–103.

187   **invite his audience to identify . . . the line of march:** Ibid., 5–7.

187   ***Discourse* became Catto's legacy:** Historians who have cited William Catto's book range from W. E. B. Du Bois and Carter G. Woodson to Benjamin Quarles and Gary Nash.

187–188   **Half a block . . . carrying his dagger:** Silcox, *McMullen*, 39, 41, 46, 49; Ignatiev, *How the Irish Became White*, 161, 163; *PP*, Apr. 1, 1901; See 1861 photo of McMullen, in Silcox, *McMullen*, 56.

188   **His "court" consisted of . . . Moyamensing Hose House:** Silcox, *McMullen*, 49; addresses in *McElroy's Philadelphia City Directory, 1856*; Ignatiev, *How the Irish Became White*, 162.

188   **This spot was an easy walk:** 1850 Census found Moyamensing to be 45 percent Irish; *Philadelphia African-American Census 1847* counts 3,391 Negroes in Moyamensing. See also Ignatiev, *How the Irish Became White*, 129.

188   **The police department had:** Weigley, "Border City," 372; Mires, *Independence Hall*, 100; Ignatiev, *How the Irish Became White*, 159.

188   **The Negroes had grown in . . . two cents a night:** *Philadelphia African-American Census 1847*; 1850 Census; Ignatiev, *How the Irish Became White*, 40; Sewell, *Sorrows Circuit*, 323–325; Geffen, "Industrial Development," 335.

188   **He had been accused . . . point of his dirk:** Silcox, *McMullen*, 46; Ignatiev, *How the Irish Became White*, 161–162.

188   **The old time fire companies, too . . . nativists and Negroes:** Ignatiev, *How the Irish Became White*, 143, 155; Geffen, "Industrial Development," 348; Silcox, *McMullen*, 90.

188   **McMullen, in his thirties:** Silcox, *McMullen*, esp. 42–43; Ignatiev, *How the Irish Became White*, 160–169.

189   **Richard Vaux . . . Moyamensing Hose:** Silcox, *McMullen*, 17, 39; Ignatiev, *How the Irish Became White*, 163.

189   **Up and down the ballot, Democrats . . . the white workingman:** Dusinberre, *Civil War Issues*, 27, 42; Whiteman, *Gentlemen in Crisis*, 2; Ignatiev, *How the Irish Became White*, 108, 166.

189   **Slavery was a necessary . . . health & happiness:** *Pennsylvanian*, Jan. 29, 1856, in Dusinberre, *Civil War Issues*, 27.

189   **the newspaper reflected:** Smith, *Press, Politics, and Patronage*, 204; "Philadelphia Correspondent," *NASS*, Mar. 27, 1858.

190   **Buchanan did his best . . . again and again:** Baker, *James Buchanan*, 71.

190   **For their part, Republicans tried . . . mechanics, laboring men:** Foner, *Free Soil*, 62–65; Dusinberre, *Civil War Issues*, 34.

190   **Some Republicans tried . . . 'mudsills of society:** Foner, *Free Soil*, 120.

190   **(Too bad only . . . "Demogoges:** Salvatore, *We All Got History*, 79.

190   **Vaux and Buchanan . . . defeating a rich incumbent:** Ignatiev, *How the Irish Became White*, 163; Silcox, *McMullen*, 20, 39, 49–51; Weigley, "Border City," 370.

190–191   **An alderman was . . . coming to his court:** Ignatiev, *How the Irish Became White*, 71; Sewell, *Sorrows Circuit*, 323–325.

191   **After a while, he decorated:** Silcox, *McMullen*, 66.

191–192   **On March 4, 1857 . . . us like dogs:** Goodwin, *Team of Rivals*, 188–191; Litwack, *North of Slavery*, 59–62; BAP, 3:53–54.

192   **At another meeting in New Bedford . . . do likewise:** Quarles, *Black Abolitionists*, 231–232.

192   **A New Haven speaker . . . people are nothing:** Ullman, *Delany*, 211–213; Bacon, *But One Race*, 128; BAP, 4:304–309.

192   **In Boston, organizers . . . Red, White and Blue:** BAP, 3:308–309; diary entry for Feb. 7, 1858, in Stevenson, *Journals of Charlotte Forten Grimké*, 285; Bethel, *Roots of African-American Identity*, 10–12; lyrics in Wesley and Uzelac, *William Cooper Nell*, 298.

193   **Supreme Court's "slaveholding wing . . . good might come:** Quarles, *Black Abolitionists*, 231, citing *NASS*, Apr. 1857; BAP, 4:33–34.

193   **In Philadelphia, a national conference . . . "recommended it:** White, *Minutes and Sermon of the Second Presbyterian and Congregational Convention*, 8, 10, 20.

193–194   **That same week . . . in good standing with us:** Philadelphia Presbytery minutes, Oct. 29, 1857, microfilm roll 2.

194   **a smaller meeting convened . . . Lombard Street:** Sanborn, *Life and Letters of John Brown*, 451; BAP, 4:317, 380.

194   **"their voices would drop to a whisper:** Douglass, *Life and Times*, 337.

194–195   **Rev. Dudley A. Tyng . . . nine hundred slaves:** BAP, 1:444; *Washington (DC) National Era*, Aug. 6, 1857; Watson, *Annals of Philadelphia*, 325; *NASS*, Dec. 19, 1857, Jan. 30, 1858; Bell, *Major Butler's Legacy*, 319; Foner and Branham, *Lift Every Voice*, 328–331.

195   **A Boston publisher reprinted:** *Our Country's Troubles.*

195   **"there were many signs of hope:** Blight, *Frederick Douglass' Civil War*, 14n22.

196–197   **a letter for Jake White Jr. . . . flogged:** BAP, 4:371–374; Yacovone, *Voice of Thunder*, 6–9; Davis and Haller, *Peoples of Philadelphia*, chap. 6, 118; Farr, "Slow Boat to Nowhere," 170; Johnson and Roark, *Black Masters*, 203.

197   **Another member of the rising . . . "secret societies," as he called them:** See Miller, *Gullah Statesman*, esp. 6–9; Blassingame, *Slave Testimony*, 372–379.

198   **On the thirteenth day . . . laid upon Charleston:** BAP, 4:371.

198   **By the time Stephens . . . against the act:** Lapsansky, "Discipline," 408; Bolivar, in *Philadelphia Sentinel*, May 8, 1886, quoted in Johnson, *Autobiography*, 131–132; Martin, "Banneker Literary Institute," 315.

198   **The prime sponsor . . . Bleeding Kansas:** Johannsen, *Stephen A. Douglas*, esp. 449–452; BAP, 4:389.

199   **George Stephens had . . . excluded by them:** Yacovone, *Voice of Thunder*, 9; Ballard, *One More Day's Journey*, 61.

199   **Octavius graduated . . . named valedictorian:** Board of Managers, minutes, Jan. 17, 1859, excerpts, I.C.Y. records, FLS, and Coppin, *Reminiscences*, 141; Lane, *Dorsey's Philadelphia*, 138.

199   **signed up for . . . Washington, D.C.:** Silcox, "Nineteenth Century Philadelphia Black Militant," 57, citing *PP*, Oct. 14, 1871.

199   **Diploma in hand . . . modern language:** Lapsansky, "Discipline," 404; *PP*, Jan. 13, 1860; Ballard, *One More Day's Journey*, 60–61; *CR*, Mar. 2, 1860.

199–200   **that a well-run colored literary . . . from us:** Martin, "Banneker Literary Institute," 303.

200 **the Industrial Revolution . . . "or to combat:** Lapsansky, "Discipline," 401–402, 406, 411; Martin, "Banneker Literary Institute," 306; Freedley, *Practical Treatise on Business*, 344; Salvatore, *We All Got History*, 64, 165; *CR*, Mar. 9, 1861; Bolivar, Pencil Pusher Points, *Philadelphia Tribune*, Jan. 18, 1913.

200 **Members donated a book:** Banneker Literary Institute, 1857 annual report, ANHS, box 5G, folder 7.

200 **annual two dollars' dues . . . White argued "for:** Lapsansky, "Discipline," 402, 410.

200 **writings and speeches:** See, e.g., White Jr.'s 1852 essay, BAP, 4:137, and his July 4, 1859 speech in *Celebration of the Eighty-third Anniversary*.

200 **Parker T. Smith resigned . . . speak that night:** Lapsansky, "Discipline," 409.

200 **Parker Smith briefly . . . the largest share:** BAP, 2:39.

201 **The death of a beloved . . . "inexpressible grief:** *CR*, Jan. 26, 1861.

201 **When a loyal white ally . . . band of brothers:** *CR*, Aug. 18, 1868.

201 **Octavius's friend Robert Adger:** Lapsansky, "Discipline," 407.

201 **a household steeped:** *PL*, Nov. 2, 1896, in Du Bois, *Philadelphia Negro*, 121–122.

201 **Furniture, china, . . . right to vote:** "The Colored People of This City," *PP*, Sept. 4, 1860. For titles of books on the Adgers' shelves, see Ball and Martin, *Rare Afro-Americana*, esp. 56–71, 84, 172–173, 179.

201 **The sixteen Adgers:** *PP*, Sept. 4, 1860, says fifteen Adger children; other accounts say fourteen.

201 **curators of the colored city:** For a testament to Dorsey's curator role, see, e.g., Lane, *Dorsey's Philadelphia*, 107, 317–318.

201 **"to tell their children:** Ball and Martin, *Rare Afro-Americana*, 5.

201–202 **People spoke of one item . . . saved the banner:** Bolivar, Pencil Pusher Points, *Philadelphia Tribune*, Apr. 6, 1912; *PL*, Aug. 4, 1842, in Foner, *Douglass: Selected Speeches*, 48.

202 **A crowd estimated at . . . the three-hour debate:** Angle, *Complete Lincoln-Douglas Debates*, 102–137. Audience estimates vary; *NYT*, Oct. 8, 1992.

202 **At the end of 1858 . . . earth and the universe:** Blackett, *Beating Against the Barriers*, 149–160.

202 **Campbell's plans appealed:** Lapsansky-Werner and Bacon, *Back to Africa*, ix, xi, 40–41; Blackett, "Delany and Robert Campbell," 8–12.

202–203 **"with a view of interesting . . . Catto had a job:** Saettler, *Evolution of American Educational Technology*, 33–36; Lane, *Dorsey's Philadelphia*, 138; Simmons, *Men of Mark*, 1, 105; Board of Managers, minutes, Jan. 17, 1859, Mar. 12, 1867, June 9, 1868, Jan. 13, 1869, excerpts, I.C.Y. records, FLS.

203 **The *Weekly Anglo-African* . . . spherical trigonometry:** *New York Weekly Anglo-African*, [July 23?], 1859, 332.

203 **taught English and:** Board of Managers, annual report, 1860, I.C.Y. records, FLS; *CR*, May 11, 1861.

203 **said to excel at cricket:** Casway, "Octavius Catto and the Pythians of Philadelphia," 7; Kirsch, *Baseball in Blue and Gray*, 70.

203 **"town ball . . . base ball:** Kirsch, *Baseball in Blue and Gray*, 14–18; Sullivan, *Early Innings*, 59–62; Kirsch, *Creation of American Team Sports*, 65–67; *INQ*, Dec. 13, 1860.

203   **Twice he canceled his:** Hine and Jenkins, *Question of Manhood*, 409.

203   **He believed in corporal . . . my Virginia pedestals:** Cromwell, *Unveiled Voices*, 97; I.C.Y. Board of Managers, minutes, May 10, 1870, FLS.

203–204   **a restlessness began to . . . William Henry Johnson:** Lapsansky, "Discipline," 402–403; Boliver in *Philadelphia Sentinel*, May 8, 1886, quoted in Johnson, *Autobiography*, 132–133; Martin, "Banneker Literary Institute," 311, 316; *PP*, Jan. 13, 1860.

204   **The new mayor, Alexander . . . four hundred thousand people:** Steinberg, *Transformation of Criminal Justice*, 292n5; BAP, 4:358; Chambers, *American Slavery*, 197–199.

CHAPTER 9: A CHANCE ON THE PAVEMENT

Pages

205   **he and five other colored teachers . . . Pierce Butler:** Board of Managers, minutes, annual report, May 21, 1860, excerpts, I.C.Y. records, FLS. Teachers identified in the report were Bassett, Catto, Grace Mapps, Martha Farbeaux, Jacob White Jr., and Sarah M. Douglass. See, e.g., Mayer, *All on Fire*, 455; "Revival of the Slave Trade," *Douglass' Monthly*, Oct. 1859, quoting *PP*.

205   **President James Buchanan had named:** Cohen, *Rittenhouse Square*, 285–288.

205   **"war, hatred and revenge:** Lane, *Dorsey's Philadelphia*, 140.

206   **modern as Douglass . . . in 1859:** See Catto's I.C.Y. commencement address, in Chapter 11, and his speech at an equal-rights meeting in Harrisburg, in Chapter 12; Aristotle, *Politics*, 613.

206   **One assailant all . . . hundred," Alberti said:** NASS, Feb. 19, 1859, in Wilson, *Freedom at Risk*, 51–53; *Philadelphia Telegraph* article reprinted in *NYT*, July 27, 1869.

206   **McKim, who was forty-eight:** Johnson and Brown, *Twentieth Century Biographical Dictionary*, vol. 7, which gives McKim's birth date as Nov. 14, 1810.

206–207   **Alberti had been implicated . . . Fugitive Slave Act:** Wilson, *Freedom at Risk*, 51–53, 55–56, 96; BAP, 4:252; Still, *Underground Railroad*, 111; in [McKim], *Arrest, Trial and Release*, see Brewster comments, 7, and Patton testimony, 12–13; Savidge, *Life of Benjamin Harris Brewster*, 24–25, 73; Scharf and Westcott, *History of Philadelphia*, 2:1550, 1575.

207   **Debates in the city's antislavery . . . in the North:** NASS, Mar. 19, 1859; Goodwin, *Team of Rivals*, 160–161; Gallman, *Mastering Wartime*, 1; NASS, Mar. 19, 1859.

207   **such as the poet Frances Watkins:** Sterling, *We Are Your Sisters*, 162.

208   **He could be sneering . . . and won a hundred dollars:** Lane, *Roots of Violence*, 48; Johnson, *Autobiography*, 125–126.

208   **second only to Harriet Tubman's . . . William Still:** Quarles's finding, cited in Lane, *Dorsey's Philadelphia*, 104, 107–108.

208   **"No public improvement," . . . ten miles an hour:** Speirs, *Street Railway System*, 7; *Medical Times and Gazette*, 2:1861, 167; Timbs, *Year-Book of Facts*, 75–77.

208   **a degree from Princeton . . . Modern City:** Weigley, "Border City," 371, 413; Nash, *First City*, 178; Steinberg, *Transformation of Criminal Justice*, 179, 196; James Forten, quoted in Douty, *Forten the Sailmaker*, 194.

208   **Not everyone favored:** See Chapter 12.

208   **suspected railway owners were corrupting:** White, *Philadelphia Perspective*, 21.

209   **"It spoils the road . . . soared in value:** July 14, 1859, entry, in Wainwright, *Philadelphia Perspective*, 326–328; also Dec. 6, 1858, entry, 310.

209   **The Butler family's roots . . . elect his candidate, Buchanan:** Bell, *Major Butler's Legacy*, esp. the Aaron Burr story, 112–114, 294, and the illustrations and maps identifying the Butlers' Philadelphia mansions and estates, and the fourteen Butler plantations in South Carolina and Georgia; Dusinberre, *Them Dark Days*, 217.

209   **Then the Panic . . . four kings:** Nash, *First City*, 189; Bell, *Major Butler's Legacy*, 312; Wainwright, *Philadelphia Perspective*, 310. The story of this poker game is told in Dusinberre, *Them Dark Days*, 217, which puts the figure at twenty-four thousand dollars; "The Last Slave Auction in the South," a *Kansas City Future State* article reprinted in *NYT* on Dec. 25, 1895; and Haley, *Afro American Encyclopaedia*, 345–347, which says another player, the card-saloon's proprietor, warned Butler against such heavy bets "but Butler laughed at him." The proprietor's hand had the four kings.

209   **"Pierce Butler has gone:** Wainwright, *Philadelphia Perspective*, 317.

210   **a "kind master" who kept families intact:** Bell, *Major Butler's Legacy*, 315. See the plantation visit by Robert Gould Shaw in Chapter 11 for some views of Butler from people he owned.

210   **a Maryland slave's letter:** Bob Butt to editor, *NASS*, Feb. 5, 1859, quoted in Blassingame, *Slave Testimony*, 112–113.

210–211 **Philander Doesticks . . . from the back river:** See *Great Auction Sale of Slaves* for the entire text of the "Doesticks" article. Most of the story of Doesticks that follows is from Bell, *Major Butler's Legacy*, 330–339.

211   **Sarah Remond cited:** Foner and Branham, *Lift Every Voice*, 328–331.

211   **"tho doubtless exaggerated:** Sidney Fisher diary, Mar. 11, 1859, in Wainwright, *Philadelphia Perspective*, 319.

211   **Fisher personified the ambivalence . . . "the northernmost city:** Barnes and Dumond, *Letters of Theodore Dwight Weld*, 726–729; lecture by Roger Lane, Bates Seminar Series on the History of Nursing, University of Pennsylvania, Philadelphia, Mar. 5, 2008.

211   **His friend George . . . almighty howling:** Wainwright, *Philadelphia Perspective*, 343–344, and Dec. 30, 1858 entry, 312–313.

211   **Fisher's essays . . . McKim:** Ibid., 459, 511, 526–527.

211   **"For the sake of preserving:** Jan. 2, 1860, entry, in ibid., 343–344.

212   **a message reached the Vigilance . . . secret meeting:** Still, *Underground Railroad*, 112.

212   **Three days later, a telegram arrived:** May, *Fugitive Slave Law*, 116–118; [McKim], *Arrest, Trial and Release*, 3. The pamphlet is signed "M." Lapsansky (interview, 2006) says McKim surely wrote it.

212   **Harrisburg's Vigilance . . . was well liked:** [McKim], *Arrest, Trial and Release*, 116–118; *Washington (DC) National Era*, Apr. 7, 14, 1859; Ray Allen Billington, notes in Forten, *Journals*, 230–231.

213   **Previous commissioners had . . . my missing Negro:** [McKim], *Arrest, Trial and Release*, 7–8; Bacon, *But One Race*, 134; Wilson, *Freedom at Risk*, 52–53.

213–214   **McKim and the Vigilance . . . muster its witnesses:** [McKim], *Arrest, Trial and Release*, 3–7; BAP, 4:58–59; Weigley, "Border City," 387; Dusinberre, *Civil War Issues*, 48–50; Johnson and Brown, *Twentieth Century Biographical Dictionary*, vol. 7. See also Mott to McKim, July 19, 1839, in Palmer, *Letters of Lucretia Coffin Mott*, 55.

214   **"Miller feared there was:** Martha Coffin Wright to David Wright, Apr. 7, 1859, in Garrison Family Papers.

214   **"The Saturday . . . of his children:** [McKim], *Arrest, Trial and Release*, 7; *Washington (DC) National Era*, Apr. 7, 1859, quoting B.

214   **a less visible drama:** Still, *Underground Railroad*, 112–117.

215   **Entourages from the South . . . white gals:** Taylor, *Philadelphia in the Civil War*, 10; Kilbride, *American Aristocracy*, 79–98, 91–92, 98, and chap. 6, esp. 127–129.

215   **Many tourists brought . . . just a few days:** See, e.g., Still, *Underground Railroad*, 88–97, 112–113, 539–540; Finkel, *Legacy in Light*, 36.

215   **This anonymous network . . . Vigilance Committee:** BAP, 3:38–39; Ignatiev, *How the Irish Became White*, 141, 156; Lapsansky interview, 2008; Webb, *Garies and Their Friends*, 37; Ignatiev, *How the Irish Became White*, 156; Gardner, "Gentleman of Superior Cultivation," 297.

216   **1847 Personal Liberty Law . . . havoc with such laws:** Dusinberre, *Civil War Issues*, 56–57; *Narrative of Facts in the Case of Passmore Williamson*, 6–7.

216   **By the time Commissioner Longstreth's:** Webster trial events: [McKim], *Arrest, Trial and Release*; Savidge, *Life of Benjamin Harris Brewster*, 82–91; Mabee, *Black Freedom*, 314–315; Martha C. Wright to David Wright, Apr. 7, 1859, and Martha C. Wright to Eliza Osborne, Apr. 9, 1859, in Garrison Family Papers (available at http://womhist.alexanderstreet.com/mcw/doclist.htm); diary entries for Apr. 4–23, 1859, in Stevenson, *Journals of Charlotte Forten Grimké*, 356–358. Also, Bolivar, Pencil Pusher Points, *Philadelphia Tribune*, July 4, 1914.

216   **"an immence throng of negroes:** Savidge, *Life of Benjamin Harris Brewster*, 86.

216   **McKim was impressed at how many . . . public's perception:** McKim, "Philadelphia Correspondence," *NASS*, Apr. 23, 1859.

217   **Another illness had forced:** "Chronology," in Stevenson, *Journals of Charlotte Forten Grimké*, xxxiii–xl.

217   **Thus ensconced, Lucretia . . . dare to face anything:** [McKim], *Arrest, Trial and Release*, 10–13; Mabee, *Black Freedom*, 314; Hare, *Greatest American Woman*, 230.

217   **Brewster had already . . . please the masses:** Scharf and Westcott, *History of Philadelphia*, 2:1550, 1575; Savidge, *Life of Benjamin Harris Brewster*, 17, 24–25, 73, 86–87.

217   **vaunted gentlemanly bearing . . . what is law:** [McKim], *Arrest, Trial and Release*, 17, 25.

217–218   **His opponents knew . . . opportunity evaporated:** *NASS*, Apr. 23, 1859.

218 **The throng grew, filling . . . evening papers:** [McKim], *Arrest, Trial and Release*, 8–12; Martha Wright to David Wright, Apr. 7, 1859, Garrison Family Papers, http://womhist.alexanderstreet.com/mcw/doc3.htm.

218 **William Furness . . . out of place:** Powell, *Personal Reminiscences*, 152–153.

218 **During a recess . . . traitor most accurst":** Hallowell, *James and Lucretia Mott*, 388–389.

218–220 **In court, the . . . answered with a roar:** [McKim], *Arrest, Trial and Release*, 12–15, 22–24, 25–27.

220 **some white citizens . . . pressed forward:** Mabee, *Black Freedom*, 314–315; Hare, *Greatest American Woman*, 231.

220 **She hooked her arm through Webster's:** MacDonell, "Lucretia Mott," 452–460.

220 **Colored men hoisted . . . to go there:** [McKim], *Arrest, Trial and Release*, 27–28; Martha Wright to David Wright, Apr. 7, 1859.

221 **Sansom Street Hall, with its frescoed:** Description of hall: *Stranger's Guide*, 50.

221 **Webster and his wife stayed:** Bacon, *But One Race*, 134.

221 **Whites were overheard vowing:** Whites outside the courthouse were heard threatening to "deliver up Dangerfield to his alleged master." Hare, *Greatest American Woman*, 231.

221 **Though Longstreth had . . . even for Philadelphia:** Stevenson, Apr. 6, 1859, *Journals of Charlotte Forten Grimké*, 357.

221 **Mary Grew, who had been preparing . . . and sentiments:** Brown, *Mary Grew*, 64–65.

221 **Webster's young . . . and dispersed:** State University of New York database, Martha Wright to David Wright, Apr. 7, 1859; Savidge, *Life of Benjamin Harris Brewster*, 90.

221 **At the victory meeting . . . was mobbed:** Martha Wright to Eliza Osborne, Apr. 9, 1859; Billington, notes in Forten, *Journal*, 112–113.

221–222 **Martha Wright, sitting . . . had often done:** Martha Wright to Eliza Osborne, Apr. 9, 1859; *NASS*, Apr. 23, 1859; Billington, notes in Forten, *Journal*, 112–113.

222 **"Their enemies" were surging . . . did their duty:** Martha Wright to Eliza Osborne, Apr. 9, 1859; Ignatiev, *How the Irish Became White*, 32.

222–223 **As the Webster trial was . . . safely in Canada:** Still, *Underground Railroad*, 116–117; Lane, *Dorsey's Philadelphia*, 2, 44, 77, 232; Sterling, *We Are Your Sisters*, 138–139; BAP, 2:409–411; Stevenson, Apr. 1859, *Journals of Charlotte Forten Grimké*, 358.

224 **Managers went . . . to $200:** Board of Managers, minutes, May 16, 1859, I.C.Y. records, FLS.

224 **Commencement was . . . deafening cheers:** See, e.g., reprint of *Philadelphia Daily Times*, June 6, 1857, in *Friends' Intelligencer* 14 (1857–1858); CR, May 11, 1861; Lane, *Dorsey's Philadelphia*, 139–140.

224–225 **Catto and Jake White Jr. focused . . . Charlotte Forten's lyrics:** *Celebration of the Eighty-third Anniversary*; Quarles, *Black Abolitionists*, 122–123; PP, July 5, 1859; Bolivar, in *Philadelphia Sentinel*, May 8, 1886, reprinted in Johnson, *Autobiography*, 132; Nash, *Forging Freedom*, 176–177; Mires, *Independence Hall* 54; [Hunt], *Why Colored People*, 23; Sweet,

"Fourth of July and Black Americans," 256–275; Davis, *Parades and Power*, 43–46; Martin, "Banneker Literary Institute," 311–313; *FD*, July 27, 1855. For boys hawking peanuts and other typical July 4 details, see *PP*, July 5, 1864.

225   **From his first youthful essay:** BAP, 4:137, 210–211; Martin, "Banneker Literary Institute," 303.

226   **The *Weekly Anglo African* reported . . . Monitor 15:** Sullivan, *Early Innings*, 34–36; Goodwin, *Team of Rivals*, 129–130; Julian, *Life of Joshua R Giddings*, 399.

226   **Thomas Hamilton's black publications:** BAP, 5:27.

226   **Now came his rejoinder:** Ullman, *Delany*, 200–201; Floyd J. Miller, preface to Delany, *Blake*.

226–227   **The hero of the novel is Jamaican-born . . . a penny by it:** Delany, *Blake*, xi; BAP, 4:29–130.

227   **"a violence of gestures . . . after that:** Quarles, *Allies for Freedom*, 50; Ullman, *Delany*, 146; Floyd J. Miller, editor's note and introduction to Delany, *Blake*.

227   **He was in some ways . . . that continent's "heathens:** See, e.g., Ullman, *Delany*, ix, 516; BAP, 4:127.

227   **Even Garnet was tilling . . . the Gospel in Africa:** Blackett, "Delany and Robert Campbell," 8–12.

227   **"He stands up so straight:** "Dr. M. R. Delany," *Douglass' Monthly*, Aug. 1862.

227–228   **Daniel Payne, . . . by the thousands:** Payne, *Recollections*, 93–94, 160–166.

228   **Delany, perhaps more . . . to experiments:** Ullman, *Delany*, ix, 220; BAP, 4:129–130; Blackett, *Beating Against the Barriers*, 164.

228   **While he was . . . "Uncle" was John Brown:** Quarles, *Allies for Freedom*, 47–49, 74.

228–229   **Frederick Douglass never forgot . . . take him seriously:** Douglass, *Life and Times*, 271–273, 314.

229   **In the 1850s, however, Brown had:** Various accounts, e.g., Bordewich, *Bound for Canaan*, 414–415.

229   **He had staged a . . . "Secretary of War:** Quarles, *Allies for Freedom*, 37–51.

229   **Brown's footprints were all over . . . Bowser's shabby studio:** See Brown's clandestine Mar. 1858 meeting at Stephen Smith's house in Chapter 8; BAP 4:317, 380; Henry Minton obituary [*Globe?*], June 2, 1883, in Dorsey scrapbooks, microfilm roll 4; Okur, "Underground Railroad in Philadelphia," 541.

229   **Robert Adger, close . . . Bassett of the I.C.Y.:** Ball and Martin, *Rare Afro-Americana*, 4, 39, 41nn6, 27.

229   **In September a group . . . Douglass declined:** Sanborn, *Life and Letters of John Brown*, 153–154, 541.

229–230   **He had already . . . "*God dam em*":** Douglass, *Life and Times*, 317–320; Sanborn, *Life and Letters of John Brown*, 540–543; Quarles, *Allies for Freedom*, 80.

230   **Douglass was speaking . . . hold his breath:** Douglass, *Life and Times*, 220.

230   **"All of our men became . . . convert to abolition:** Bolivar, Pencil
Pusher Points, *Philadelphia Tribune*, Dec. 13, 1913.

230   **Within thirty-six hours . . . north to Canada:** Dusinberre, *Civil
War Issues*, 83–84; Quarles, *Allies for Freedom*, 96; Bordewich, *Bound for
Canaan*, 425.

231   **Brown's captors found . . . finally to Britain:** McFeely, *Frederick Douglass*, 198–203; Douglass, *Life and Times*, 307–310; Quarles, *Allies for Freedom*, 114; Gregory, *Frederick Douglass*, 46–48.

231   **The extent of his involvement:** Quarles, *Allies for Freedom*, 76–80.

231   **Even so . . . perhaps for life:** Douglass, *Life and Times*, 321.

231   **Legislators drafted bills . . . "cut his throat:** BAP, 5:54, 56; *Anti-Slavery History of the John Brown Year*, 167–168, 210–218; Still, *Underground Railroad*, 593–594.

231   **"I do not exaggerate . . . penalty of expulsion:** Goodwin, *Team of Rivals*, 227.

231–232   **Some colored leaders chided . . . every slave:** Quarles, *Allies for Freedom*, 114–115, 117–118.

232   **In Hartford . . . the Marseillaise:** BAP, 5:51.

232   **I hear the voice of John Brown:** Campbell, *Autobiography*, 288–289.

232   **a counter-chorus of white lawyers:** *Grand Union Meeting*, 10–12.

232   **The Banneker Institute planned:** *New York Weekly Anglo-African*, Feb. 4, 1860, in *BAPM*, roll 12, frame 0473.

232   **Mayor Alexander Henry flooded:** Dusinberre, *Civil War Issues*, 85; *PP*, Nov. 29, 1859; Isaac Clothier's reminiscences, *PL*, Dec. 14, 1902.

232   **By late November, the forlorn . . . began crying:** Ames, *Life and Letters of Peter and Susan Lesley*, 379; Lane, *Dorsey's Philadelphia*, 105; Mabee, *Black Freedom*, 314–350, esp. 326.

232–233   **Wendell Phillips came down . . . leader of riots:** Martyn, *Wendell Phillips*, 296n; *PP*, Nov. 29, 1859; Fisher and Mellen, *Builder of the West*, 62–64; *Grand Union Meeting*, 24–28.

233   **abolitionists wore black and draped:** Bacon, *But One Race*, 135; Weigley, "Border City," 390.

233   **The city's Southern medical students . . . owned:** Ames, *Life and Letters of Peter and Susan Lesley*, 382.

233   **six hundred Negroes and sixteen white . . . "So is mine:** Salvatore, *We All Got History*, 89; *PP*, Dec. 3, 1859; Dusinberre, *Civil War Issues*, 86; Catto, *Semi-Centenary Discourse.*

233   **Henry David Thoreau . . . an angel of light:** Renehan, *Secret Six*, 230.

233   **Purvis, addressing a . . . out the window:** Ibid.; Jackson, *America's Most Historic Highway*, 274; Redpath, *Echoes of Harpers Ferry*, 95; *PP*, Sept. 4, 1860.

233   **"so extraordinary":** Dusinberre, *Civil War Issues*, 86.

234   **A thicket of policemen:** Efforts to move Brown's casket: Weigley, "Border City," 389–390.

234   **The Great Union Meeting of December 7:** The meeting is described in detail in the fifty-eight-page pamphlet *Grand Union Meeting.*

234   **a confidant of President Buchanan's:** Silcox, *McMullen*, 114.

235   **All sang a song . . . from the gallows swing:** *Grand Union Meeting*, 6.

235–236   **One week after . . . & a great crowd.":** *PL*, Dec. 14, 1902, in Dorsey scrapbooks, microfilm roll 15. See also *PP*, Dec. 17, 1859; Young, *Memorial*

History, 515n1; Cary, *George William Curtis,* 126–129; Row, *Masonic Biography and Dictionary,* 232–237; Dusinberre, *Civil War Issues,* 90; Phillips, *Speeches, Lectures, and Letters,* 336.

236 **Kelley was a new father:** Summary, Kelley Collection.

236 **rotten eggs at his portrait:** *PP,* Apr. 27, 1870.

236 **he took aside Clothier . . . night of his life:** Dorsey scrapbooks, microfilm roll 15.

236–237 **Another was said . . . Mott herself:** MacDonell, "Lucretia Mott," 457.

237 **The vitriol burned Emma . . . riddled with holes:** Smedley, *History of the Underground Railroad,* 188–189.

237 **The arrested men . . . disorder in the hall:** *PP,* Dec. 17, 1859. See also Palmer, *Letters of Lucretia Coffin Mott,* 290–293, esp. 293n.

237–238 **Hundreds of colored . . . Masons would not relent:** *New York Weekly Anglo-African,* Feb 4, 1860; BAPM, roll 12, frame 0473; Quarles, *Allies for Freedom,* 138–139; Yacovone, *Voice of Thunder,* 116.

238 **The diarist Sidney Fisher:** Wainwright, *Philadelphia Perspective,* 343–344.

238–239 **"Notwithstanding our . . . not overtasked:** *Senate Journal,* 36th Cong., 1st. sess., Dec. 27, 1859, 29–53.

239 **By then, many . . . see it staged:** Lerner, *Grimké Sisters,* 266; BAP, 4:125; Geffen, "Industrial Development," 355.

239 **David Bowser began painting:** Bowser's portrait of John Brown, available at www.explorepahistory.com.

239 **In Edinburgh, the . . . manhood in America:** Quarles, *Allies for Freedom,* 166; Dorsey scrapbooks, microfilm roll 141.

239–240 **A letter in Brown's . . . place to go for help:** Sanborn, *Life and Letters of John Brown,* 521–522; Quarles, *Allies for Freedom,* 73, citing *New York Herald,* Oct. 25, 1859.

240 **"I remember the . . . slaves cases, etc.:** Ball and Martin, *Rare Afro-Americana,* 4.

240 **One "broil" involved . . . to be seen again:** Johnson, *Autobiography,* 125–126; Bolivar, Pencil Pusher Points, *Philadelphia Tribune,* Feb. 15, 1913.

241 **In 1860, Marshal Jenkins:** Quarles, *Black Abolitionists,* 214–215; Cadwalader, *Cadwalader's Cases,* 311–235; Bacon, *But One Race,* 136–137; Dusinberre, *Civil War Issues,* 60.

241 **A Virginia slaveholder . . . shoulders:** "Deposition of Charles T. Butler and other witnesses."

241 **"demonstrations of joy" . . . "King Cotton:** *Harrisburg Telegraph,* Mar. 4, 1860.

242 **Charges were dismissed against five:** Quarles, *Black Abolitionists,* 214.

242 **Purvis went to the courtroom . . . indignation:** Foner and Branham, *Lift Every Voice,* 331–339.

242 **Cadwalader ruled that the marshals:** Cadwalader, *Cadwalader's Cases,* 311–325.

243 **Catto and the Bannekers . . . lover of freedom:** *New York Weekly Anglo-African,* Apr. 7, 1860; BAPM, roll 12, frame 0621.

243 **The poet Frances Watkins . . . inactivity:** "An Appeal for the Philadelphia Rescuers," *New York Weekly Anglo-African,* June 23, 1860.

243 **Alfred Green's term . . . ungodly nation:** Quarles, *Black Abolitionists,* 214–215; Cayley, *Expanding Prison,* 259–260.

243 **"On the whole:** *Anti-Slavery History of the John Brown Year,* 58–61.

244 **The city's Democrats . . . white Democrats cheered:** *PP,* Aug. 30, Sept. 13, 1860; Silcox, *McMullen,* 46, 113 (photo), 114–115, 150; Ignatiev, *How the Irish Became White,* 160–163; *PP,* Oct. 25, 1858.

245 **As for the other Douglass . . . fifty lectures:** Quarles, *Allies for Freedom,* 163–164.

245 **she decried the "unspeakable":** Stanley, "Right to Possess All the Faculties," 134–135.

245 **She repeated . . .** *Uncle Tom's Cabin:* Foner and Branham, *Lift Every Voice,* 328–331.

245 **In spring, Douglass . . . man for Douglass:** Douglass, *Life and Times,* 314–325. Rosetta's words about her sister are in McFeely, *Frederick Douglass,* 207.

245 **"Presented to S. P. Remond, by:** Midgley, *Women Against Slavery,* 44.

245–246 **They prepared and . . . "your late sudden bereavement:** Lane, *Dorsey's Philadelphia,* 326; invitation in ANHS, microfilm roll 8, frame 1267.

CHAPTER 10: THE WOLF KILLERS

Pages

247 **They were ending a:** BAP, 5:54–56; *Liberator,* Jan. 13, 1860.

248 **At the same time, another:** Kilbride, *American Aristocracy,* 79–98; *Liberator,* Dec. 20, 1859.

248 **Not only did Philadelphia have:** 1860 Census; Lane, *Dorsey's Philadelphia,* 44; Foner, "Battle," 260–291, comments about census validity comes from Lane, interview, Mar. 5, 2008.

248 **The reporter visited:** *PP,* Sept. 4, 1860. Those interviewed are not named, but it appears the reporter talked with Robert Purvis and Robert Adger.

249 **And because they were poor:** Silcox, *McMullen,* 31–32; Sewell, *Sorrows Circuit,* 39, 42, 44, 126–127, 156, 187–188, 194, 237–238, 246, 264, 323–325, 356, 358–359; *INQ,* Aug. 1, 1861. Teacher's tour is in Sewell, *Sorrows Circuit,* 91. Bedford no longer exists. Once located between Seventh and Eighth streets, one block south of South Street, it would be part of Kater Street today.

250 **While Negroes were:** BAP, 5:58–59, 66–67.

251 **Abraham Lincoln, who already:** Goodwin, *Team of Rivals,* 9.

251 **Not as impressed were Negro:** BAP, 5:71–73.

251 **Robert and Joseph Henson held:** Lomax, *Black Baseball Entrepreneurs,* 1.

251 **Amos Webber donned a:** Salvatore, *We All Got History,* 59–63.

252 **It was addressed:** Catto poem, ANHS, microfilm roll 66.

252 **Cordelia, like Octavius, had her roots:** Gonaver, "Race Relations," 41, 66–70, 71–75, 100–106; Stevens-Cogdell and Sanders-Venning Collection.

253 **Catto's life as a young romancer:** William Wormley to Octavius Catto, Sept. 11, 1860, Catto Papers.

253 **Wormley mentioned:** Brown and Lewis, *Washington from Banneker to Douglass.*

253 **In June, another sort of lecture:** Ullman, *Delany,* 237.

254   **Taking the latter first:** Shiffert, *Baseball in Philadelphia*, 17, 26, 22–24, 31; Kirsch, *Baseball in Blue and Gray*, 54–55; Kirsch, *Creation of American Team Sports*, 70.

254   **By summer, the possibility . . . Jayne's Hall:** Ullman, *Delany*, 208; Silcox, *McMullen*, 55. Jayne's Hall rally: *Grand Union Meeting*, 24–28.

254   **Lincoln understood the:** Gallman, *Mastering Wartime*, 2; Ignatiev, *How the Irish Became White*, 165; Weigley, "Border City," 391; Gillette "Corrupt and Contented," chap. 1.

254   **And Lincoln opponents painted him:** "Young America" cartoon, Schoenberg Center.

255   **Fortunately for Mayor Henry:** Ignatiev, *How the Irish Became White*, 167; Weigley, "Border City," 391; Roth, *Mayors of Philadelphia*, vol. 3.

255   **When Lincoln won in November:** Gillette, "Corrupt and Contented," 3, 88; *PP*, Sept. 13, 1860.

255   **Soon after his reelection:** Lane, *Roots of Violence*, 10.

255   **South Carolina passed a resolution:** *INQ*, Nov. 8, 10, 12–13, 1860.

255   **The Banneker Institute:** Blight, *Frederick Douglass' Civil War*, 64; *INQ*, Dec. 4, 1860.

256   **In Philadelphia, skaters dotted the frozen:** *INQ*, Dec. 17, 1860.

256   **Democrats and businessmen met . . . Purvis, Lucretia Mott, and Miller McKim:** Taylor, *Philadelphia in the Civil War*, 11–12.

256   **South Carolina was overreacting:** Yacovone, *Voice of Thunder*, 12–13.

256   **Secession gained momentum:** White, *Philadelphia Perspective*, 71.

256   **State representative Randall:** *INQ*, Jan. 4, 22, 1861; Morris, *Free Men All*, 217.

257   **In the South, many free people of color:** Johnson and Roark, *Black Masters*, 293.

257   **The wind off the Delaware River:** *INQ*, Jan. 19, 28, 1861.

257   **The Banneker member who had spent:** Yacovone, *Voice of Thunder*, 125–128.

258   **The main actor in the living present:** *INQ*, Feb. 21–22, 1861; Mires, *Independence Hall*, 107, 109; Fehrenbacher, *Lincoln*, 211–213; Weigley, "Border, City," 393–394.

258   **Lincoln's stance against:** *INQ*, Mar. 12, 1861.

259   **Tents held busy recruiting:** Gallman, *Mastering Wartime*, 4–5; Mires, *Independence Hall*, 107–108, 110; BAP, 5:140–141.

259   **In Philadelphia, the kind of violence:** Weigley, "Border City," 394.

260   **And Sidney Fisher's diary:** Wainwright, *Philadelphia Perspective*, 400; Bell, *Major Butler's Legacy*, 347–350.

260   **Actually, the whole issue:** Scott, *War of the Rebellion*, 749–820.

260   **Congress declared that returning:** *Chiriqui Improvement Co.* (pamphlet), Aug. 9, 1861, Lincoln Papers, ser. 1, General Correspondence, 1833–1916.

261   **Lincoln was so enamored:** BAP, 5:155; Fehrenbacher, *Lincoln*, 353–357.

261   **It couldn't be a very long war:** McDowell, "Civil War."

261   **But with each passing month:** BAP, 5:117, 121–122.

262   **The *Weekly Anglo-African* called:** BAP, 3:intro., 58.

262   **The Lincoln administration said no:** McPherson, *Struggle for Equality*, 266.

262   **Frederick Douglass was not satisfied:** Foner, *Reconstruction*, 4–5.

263   **In April, McMullen volunteered:** Ignatiev, *How the Irish Became White*, 167; Silcox, *McMullen*, 56–59; *INQ*, Apr. 20, 22–24, May 3, 7, June 1, 10, 12, 19, 22, July 1, 3, 20, 30. Also, Gallman, *Mastering Wartime*, 12.

263   **Our Country is now in great danger:** Frank Whitaker wrote "Independent Rangers Song"; it is part of an unnamed collection of songs, poems, and pamphlets at LC.

264   **A special summer session:** Foner, *Reconstruction*, 4–5; *INQ*, Aug. 13, 1861.

264   **Just three blocks north:** Documentation of Sanders marriage in the Stevens-Cogdell and Sanders-Venning Collection; Catto's address that year is in *McElroy's Philadelphia City Directory*; Bolivar, Pencil Pusher Points, *Philadelphia Tribune*, Sept. 13, 1913.

264   **Newspaper advertisements showed:** Advertisements appeared in *INQ*, Oct. 24, 1861.

264   **In September, graduates of:** *CR*, Sept. 28, 1861.

264   **One of the institute's favorite:** Sterling, *Speak Out*, 219–220.

265   **Lincoln proclaimed September 26:** *New York Weekly Anglo-African*, Oct. 10, 1861.

265   **A month later, the Pennsylvania:** *INQ*, Oct. 28, 1861.

265   **In an effort to show:** Weigley, "Border City," 405.

266   **Along the Schuylkill's east bank, 609:** Ibid., 398–399; *INQ*, Nov. 27, 1861.

266   **Shortly before Thanksgiving:** William Wormley to Octavius Catto, Nov. 7, 1861, ANHS, folder 8.

266   **The battle was brief:** Burton, *Siege of Charleston*, 28, 71–73; Rose, *Rehearsal for Reconstruction*, 11–12.

267   **On a Tuesday evening six days:** *INQ*, Dec. 21, 1861.

267   **In 1860, Mayor Henry had:** *PL*, Dec. 14, 1902; Dorsey scrapbooks, microfilm roll 15.

267   **Doubts arose about the celebrated:** U.S. Congress, Senate, *Reports of the Committees*, 1863.

267   **Northern teachers and missionaries:** BAP, 5:134–136; Wainwright, *Philadelphia Perspective*, 459.

268   **Miller McKim quit the:** BAP, 5:259; *INQ*, July 10, 1862; Port Royal Relief Commission, *Freedmen of South Carolina*, 19–20; Rose, *Rehearsal for Reconstruction*, 41, 161–162.

268   **Charlotte Forten, too, was drawn:** Aug. 17, 1862, Stevenson, *Journals of Charlotte Forten Grimké*, 376; *Atlantic Monthly*, May 1864, June 1864.

268   **Edward Pierce, a government agent:** *INQ*, Feb. 20, 1862.

269   **The Tammany Hall Young Men's:** McPherson, *Negro's Civil War*, 87.

269   **Union general William T. Sherman:** Robertson, "Negro Soldiers in the Civil War."

269   **Some tell me 'tis a burnin' shame:** Miller and Lanier, *Photographic History of the Civil War*, 9–10:176.

269   **Negroes were already finding ways:** Quarles, *Negro in the Civil War*, 81; Rose, "Civil War."

269   **In April, General Benjamin:** Foner, *Reconstruction*, 5, 45–48; Yacavone, *Voice of Thunder*, 130, 158–159; Scott et al., *War of the Rebellion*, 749–754; Hahn, *Nation Under Our Feet*, 69.

270   **On April 16, Lincoln signed a bill:** *INQ*, Apr. 17, 1862; also, Brown and Lewis, *Washington from Banneker to Douglass*.

270–271   **The South, too, pressed Negroes . . . Fort Sumter:** Simmons, *Men of Mark*, 165–167; Miller and Turkel, *Heroes of the American Reconstruction*, 134–138.

271   **Early in the year:** McPherson, *Negro's Civil War*, 264; BAP, 3:259.

271   **Rev. William Catto left Washington:** BAP, 4:164; Sterling, *We Are Your Sisters*, 139.

271   **Her father had other:** BAP, 5:152.

271   **Alston, the minister:** *INQ*, Dec. 1; Kirsch, *Creation of American Team Sports*, 83.

271   **But barely moving at all:** Quarles, *Negro in the Civil War*, 155–156; *INQ*, Dec. 2, 1861; Ulmann, 263.

272   **The war had not changed the racism:** McPherson, *Negro's Civil War*, 89.

272   **Negroes had new enemies:** Salvatore, *We All Got History*, 112; Klement, *Limits of Dissent*, 108; Ullman, *Delany*, 279; Ignatiev, *How the Irish Became White*, 119; McPherson, *Negro's Civil War*, 70.

272   **A Philadelphia man "discharged an Irish:** Ignatiev, *How the Irish Became White*, 165.

272   **Prejudice did not drape:** Board of Managers, annual report, 1862, I.C.Y. records, FLS.

273   **Walking those streets was a:** *INQ*, Mar. 12, June 12, 1862.

273   **Despite the law, three Union military leaders:** The story is told in Robertson, "Negro Soldiers in the Civil War."

273   **General David Hunter put:** Colored Kansas Volunteers into battle: BAP, 5:203.

274   **Colored military units had been:** BAP, 5:125; *PP*, May 25, 1861.

274   **And when the War Department changed:** See Robertson, "Negro Soldiers in the Civil War."

275   **On September 22, President Lincoln:** Quarles, *Negro in the Civil War*, 159, 164.

275   **It was as if every bell in every tower:** Emerson's reaction: ibid., 162.

275   **Colored men began enlisting:** Lane, *Dorsey's Philadelphia*, 286.

275   **Near Butler, Missouri, the colored unit from:** First black war fatalities: Paradis, *African Americans and the Gettysburg Campaign*, 20. Return of Smalls to South Carolina: Miller, *Gullah Statesman*, 132–133; Billington, notes in Forten, *Journal*, 137–138. Song lyrics can be found in the Barker Papers. Barker was chairman of the camp's finance committee.

275   **She was teaching the story:** Forten teaching: Forten, *Journal*, 137–138.

275   **Even so, a fear of a forced exodus:** *NYT*, Oct. 3, 1862; Saxton, *Rise and Fall of the White Republic*, 265; *INQ*, Dec. 2, 1862.

276   **Back in Philadelphia, black leaders:** Newman, Rael, and Lapsansky, *Pamphlets of Protest*, 308.

276–277   **The Chiriqui colony idea . . . shores of Île à Vache:** Guelzo, *Lincoln's Emancipation Proclamation*, 252–253; Dennett, *Lincoln and the Civil War*, 203; *Chiriqui Improvement Co.*; BAP, 5, 155; Vorenberg, "Abraham Lincoln and the Politics of Black Colonization," 28–34.

277   **Emancipation eve, and the:** BAP, 5:184.

277   **"They sang and shouted:** Benjamin Rush Plumly to Abraham Lincoln, Jan. 1, 1863, Lincoln Papers.

277   **In snow-bound Boston:** Goodwin, *Team of Rivals*, 497–501.

277   **At a military encampment near:** Yacavone, *Voice of Thunder*, 216–220.

278   **Lost in the joy was the fact:** Foner, *Reconstruction*, 30.

278   **Lincoln, the orator:** "Emancipation Proclamation Background Information," Smith, *Trial by Fire*, chap. 18.

278   **In New York, Rev. Henry Highland Garnet knelt:** Garnet, *Memorial Discourse*, 54.

278   **At Port Royal, Charlotte Forten:** Looby, *Complete Civil War Journal*, 76.

CHAPTER 11: MANHOOD

Pages

281   **On January 8, 1863:** *INQ*, Jan. 9, 1863; Weigley, "Border City," 405.

282   **The Republican nominee:** Gillette, "Corrupt and Contented"; Silcox, *McMullen*, 59–60.

282   **On the morning of:** Blankenburg, "Forty Years in the Wilderness," 7–8; McClure, *Old Time Notes*, 35–38.

282   **Just days before, local Democrats:** Ignatiev, *How the Irish Became White*, 172.

282   **The tactics of intimidation:** White, *Philadelphia Perspective*, 445–446.

283   **When two *Philadelphia Press* reporters:** *PP*, Feb. 4, 1863.

283   **"What we endeavored to do:** *INQ*, Jan. 12, 1863.

283   **For many, the Proclamation was a call:** BAP, 5:175–177.

283   **Bishop Daniel Payne of:** Payne, *Recollections*, 34; Lane, *Dorsey's Philadelphia*, 237.

283   **A Pennsylvania legislative committee:** *INQ*, Apr. 3, 1862, Mar. 19, 1863.

283   **The A.M.E. Church now urged:** Gallman, *Mastering Wartime*, 48; Hine and Jenkins, *Question of Manhood*, 382–398; Horton and Horton, "Violence, Protest, and Identity."

283   **One Negro soldier:** BAP, 5:187–192.

284   **The governor of Massachusetts:** Ullman, *Delany*, 283–284; *INQ*, Mar. 19, 1863.

284   **Douglass had learned to sing:** Douglass, *Narrative*, 76; McFeely, *Frederick Douglass*, 140.

284   **As at every important meeting:** *CR*, Mar. 21, 1863.

284   **The opposing wind still roared:** Ignatiev, *How the Irish Became White*, 88.

285   **The fact that Amelia Howard:** "Activities of Business," *INQ*, Feb. 9, 1863.

285   **A month later:** BAP, 5:202; *INQ*, Mar. 10, 1863; McPherson, *Negro's Civil War*, 71.

285   **The same month, Harriet Jacobs:** BAP, 5:193–194.

286   **The war made its appearance:** *INQ*, May 22, 1863; Paradis, *African Americans and the Gettysburg Campaign*, 36–37.

286   **The rolls of the Fifty-fourth were now:** BAP, 3:intro., 59; Salvatore, *We All Got History*, 118; BAP, 5:216–219, 239; see also Robertson, "Negro Soldiers in the Civil War."

286   **Their mettle was proven:** Paradis, *African Americans and the Gettysburg Campaign*, 17–19.

287   **By June, the advancing Southern:** *INQ,* May 22, June 12, 1863;
Weigley, "Border City," 407–409; Kirsh, *Baseball in Blue and Gray,* 57; *INQ,*
June 6, 16, 1863.

287   **Rachel Cormany of Chambersburg . . . Tillie Pierce:** Paradis, *African
Americans and the Gettysburg Campaign,* 30–31.

287   **In the nation's capital:** Terry, "Brief Moment in the Sun"; Hudson, "Fort
Pocahontas."

288   **Aside from Chestnut Street:** Weigley, "Border City," 408.

288   **So whites went about:** Ibid., 409; *INQ,* June 1, 1863.

288   **At the commencement ceremonies:** *CR,* May 16, 1863; *PP,* May 11,
1863.

288   **The *Christian Recorder* also:** CR, May 30, 1863.

289   **The I.C.Y. had become:** *Douglass' Monthly,* Feb. 1862: Lane, *Dorsey's
Philadelphia,* 135; Perkins, *Fanny Jackson Coppin,* 70–71.

290   **Catto was eager for tomorrow:** Lapsansky, "Friends, Wives, and Strivings"; Taylor, *Philadelphia in the Civil War,* 188; "Men of Color, To Arms"
(broadside), American Time Capsule.

291   **Catto was just twenty-four:** Bolivar, Pencil Pusher Points, *Philadelphia
Tribune,* Aug. 30, 1913, Jan. 3, 1914; *INQ,* June 12–13, 1863; for Bassett's
meeting with mayor, see Ebenezer Bassett to Alexander Henry, June 16,
1863, and Henry's reply, June 16, in Henry Papers; Paradis, *African Americans and the Gettysburg Campaign,* 37–38; Taylor, *Philadelphia in the Civil
War,* 188.

293   **Catto's company may have:** Bell, *Major Butler's Legacy,* 366; Post, *Soldiers' Letters,* 252–253, 254–257.

293   **Trains to Harrisburg:** Brainerd, *Life of Rev. Thomas Brainerd D.D.,* 303.

294   **Negro and white leaders wrote:** *PL,* June 18, 1863; *INQ,* July 6, 1863;
Gallman, *Mastering Wartime,* 47–48.

294   **The day after Catto's return:** *INQ,* June 19, 1863; Leigh, "Chronicle of
the Union League of Philadelphia," 94 (a stamp in the book shows Harvard
College Library received it May 9, 1902).

294   **The next day was Saturday:** *INQ,* June 20, 27, 1863; Gallman, *Mastering
Wartime,* 47.

294   **The recruits were greeted:** Text of greeting in Barker Papers.

295   **In a preview of the expected July 6:** *INQ* and *PP,* June 24, 1863.

295   **George Gordon Meade, commander of:** Weigley, "Border City," 410;
INQ, June 29, 1863.

295   **The battle at Gettysburg began:** For a biography of Pleasonton,
visit the Famous Americans Web site at http://famousamericans.net/
augustusjamespleasonton. See also Pleasonton and Others, *Influence of
the Blue Ray,* 185; Gallman, *Mastering Wartime,* 16–17; Weigley, "Border City," 409; Desjardin, *These Honored Dead,* 201. Equine deaths: "The
Price in Blood: Casualties in the Civil War," in Davis, *Civil War,* http://
www.civilwarhome.com/casualties.htm.

296   **As the news of the success at Gettysburg:** Gallman, *Mastering Wartime,* 7, 184; Weigley, "Border City," 413.

296   **Catto and his friends Jake White:** *PP,* June 24, July 7, 1863; *INQ,* July
7, 1863.

296   **Kelley, the first white elected:** "Addresses of the Hon. W. D. Kelley,"
Schoenberg Center; *PP,* July 7, 1863.

296 **On that same July 6 day:** Billington, notes in Forten, *Journal*, 213–214.
297 **The Civil War was the largest:** Foner, *Reconstruction*, 32; *INQ*, July 14–17, 1863; Swift, *Black Prophets*, 326–328; Schecter, *Devil's Own Work*, 14–16, 252, 280–282; McPherson, *Negro's Civil War*, 72–73; *National Cyclopaedia of American Biography*, 414; Litwack, *North of Slavery*, 78.
297 **Colored New Yorkers were afraid:** *INQ*, July 17, 1863; Gallman, *Mastering Wartime*, 185.
299 **local Republican leader John Read:** Read to Lincoln, July 16, 1863, Lincoln Papers.
299 **If there had been a riot:** Sidney Fisher diary, July 19, 1863, in Wainwright, *Philadelphia Perspective*, 457–458; Weigley, "Border City," 390, 411.
299 **While Negroes were the victims:** McPherson, *Negro's Civil War*, 72–73.
299 **The day after the riots in New York ended:** Robertson, "Negro Soldiers in the Civil War"; Salvatore, *We All Got History*, 119.
300 **One of the dead was a corporal named Holloway:** *CR*, Aug. 22, 1863.
300 **The failed attack on Fort Wagner:** Billington, notes in Forten, *Journals*, 213–214; *INQ*, July 30, 1863.
300 **Federal interviewers in Union-occupied:** Blassingame, *Slave Testimony*, 372–379; Billingsley, *Yearning to Breathe Free*, 108–109.
301 **Miller McKim, too, had recently returned:** Sidney Fisher diary, Aug. 31, 1863, in Wainwright, *Philadelphia Perspective*, 459.
302 **Philadelphians read *A Tale of Two Cities*:** *INQ*, July 22, Aug. 11, 26, Sept. 22, 1863; BAP, 5:256.
302 **On September 1, trainloads of spectators:** *INQ*, Sept. 1, 1863.
302 **Two days later, passengers:** *INQ*, Sept. 3, 1863.
302 **In the fall, voters in the local:** *PP*, Oct. 12, 1863.
303 **In late November, President Lincoln:** White, *Philadelphia Perspective*, 208–209; *INQ*, Nov. 20, 1863.
303 **On February 19, 1864:** Winch, *Gentleman of Color*, 345.
303 **A day later and seven months:** Yacovone, *Voice of Thunder*, 66–69, 372–379; Robertson, "Negro Soldiers in the Civil War"; see also *Battle of Olustee*, http://battleofolustee.org/.
304 **Despite the continued unequal treatment:** Foner, *Reconstruction*, 8.
304 **Not everyone in government took notice:** Saxton, *Rise and Fall of the White Republic*, 255.
304 **As Johnson was offering his view:** *PP*, Oct. 12, 1863; *FD*, May 16, 1863; *McElroy's Philadelphia City Directory*, 1864; Foner, "Battle."
304 **In a time when the names of phony:** *INQ*, Mar. 18, 1864.
305 **With a name that sounded:** Fuchs, *Unerring Fire*, 23; Cimprich, *Fort Pillow*, 80; *Reports of Committees of the Senate* (Report 63), 15–16, 50–53; *Report of the Joint Commission on the Conduct of the War* (Report 65), 1–128.
306 **Robert B. Forten, father of:** *INQ* and *PP*, Apr. 28, 1864; BAP, 5:281–282.
307 **The twelfth annual commencement:** For Institute stories, see *PP*, May 10, 1864, and *INQ*, May 3, 1864; Coppin, *Reminiscences*, 143; Guelzo, *Lincoln's Emancipation Proclamation*, 252–253; Dennett, *Lincoln and the Civil War*, 203; McPherson, *Political History of the United States of America*, 212.
312 **Robert Smalls, now the captain:** Miller, *Gullah Statesman*, 15, 20–23; Uya, *From Slavery to Public Service*, 25; Billingsley, *Yearning to Breathe Free*, 87; *CR*, June 25, 1864.

312   **As spring mingled with summer:** BAP, 5:278; Silcox, *McMullen*, 61–62.

313   **In Washington, Congress defeated:** BAP, 5:115, 280; *INQ*, Apr. 25, June 17, 1864; Salvatore, *We All Got History*, 129; Lane interview, Oct. 2008.

313   **Fanny Jackson, a student at Oberlin:** *NASS*, July 9, 1864; *INQ*, July 25, 1864.

313   **The meeting gave the audience:** *INQ*, July 27, 1864.

313   **The war sent prices:** *INQ*, Aug. 22, 1864; BAP, 5:296–298.

313   **In September, Atlanta fell:** BAP, 5:278; *INQ*, Sept. 26, 1864.

314   **Optimism and reality were embraced:** Brawley, *Early Negro American Writers*, 16.

314   **So 144 Negro men from:** Davis, "Pennsylvania State Equal Rights League"; BAP, 5:304–305; Brawley, *Early Negro American Writers*, 16; Lane, *Roots of Violence*, 49–55; Foner, *Reconstruction*, 27.

314   **Mayor Henry was scared:** Henry Papers.

315   **Lincoln won easily:** *INQ*, Nov. 9, 1864.

315   **"repeaters and outsiders:** Beers, "Centennial City," 437.

315   **On Thanksgiving Day, Equal Rights League:** *CR*, Dec. 3, 24, 1864; Cheek and Cheek, "John Mercer Langston," 437.

315   **As the year was ending:** Ullman, *Delany*, 291–292; BAP, 5:308–310.

315   **Carrie Le Count and other:** BAP, 5:313; Weigley, "Border City," 399, 402.

315   **As the temperature dipped:** *INQ*, Dec. 24, 26, 1864, Jan. 3, 21, 1865.

316   **In the early winter of 1865:** *CR*, Jan. 7, 1865; *PP* and *INQ*, Jan. 3, 1865.

316   **A few days later, Democrats in town:** Silcox, *McMullen*, 66.

316   **And a few days after:** *INQ*, Jan. 11, 1865; *CR*, Jan. 7, 17, Feb. 1, 1865; PSERL minutes.

316   **The next day, January 12:** *PP*, Jan. 13, 1865.

316   **Five days later, there was news:** *PP*, Jan. 17–18, 1865.

316   **On the twenty-fourth, the Philadelphia Female Anti-Slavery:** *PP*, Jan. 24, 1865.

317   **At 4:00 P.M. on January 31:** BAP, 5:344; *INQ*, Feb. 1, 1865.

317   **On February 1, Rock became the:** BAP, 5:308; Foner, *Reconstruction*, 28.

317   **On February 12, Garnet:** Garnet, *Memorial Discourse*.

318   **Charleston was evacuated:** *INQ*, Feb. 21, 1865.

318   **In the first week:** *INQ*, Mar. 1, 1865; Douglass, *Life and Times*, 364–365; Lane, *Dorsey's Philadelphia*, 113.

318   **Richmond fell on April 1:** *INQ*, Apr. 4, 1865.

318   **Lee surrendered April 9:** *PP* and *INQ*, Apr. 11, 1865.

319   **Not only had Lee:** Kauffman, *American Brutus*, 209–210; Goodwin, *Team of Rivals*, 728.

319   **They began walking up:** Apr. 14, 1865, entry from Davis Diary; *CR*, Apr. 22, 1865.

320   **Atop the worn marble steps:** *CR*, Apr. 22, 1865; *PP*, Apr. 15, 1865; Miller, *Gullah Statesman*, 24–25.

320   **As Catto rose to:** Fraser, *Charleston!* 173; Ullman, *Delany*, 307; Rollin, *Life and Public Services*, 193–199; Rose, *Rehearsal for Reconstruction*, 342–344.

320   **Delany had also helped stage:** Mayer, *All on Fire*, 578–584.

321   **The flag was about to be raised:** Payne, *Recollections*, 161–165; *INQ*, Apr. 18, 1865.

321   **No one had ever heard:** *PP* and *INQ*, Apr. 15, 1865; *CR*, Apr. 22, 1865.

322   **Ceremonies were now over:** Kauffman, *American Brutus*, 38–39.

322   **The news of Lincoln's murder:** *PP* and *INQ*, Apr. 17, 1865; *CR*, Apr. 22, 1865.

322   **In colored America, one bit:** Payne, *Recollections*, 153–154; Ullman, *Delany*, 309–310.

322   **The arrival of Lincoln's funeral train:** Sauers, *Guide to Civil War Philadelphia*, 84; Lewis, *Assassination of Lincoln*, 118.

322   **The president's body lay:** *PP*, Apr. 21–24; *INQ*, Apr. 22; Beers, "Centennial City," 417–419; Mires, *Independence Hall*, 110–111.

322   **In New York, at Irish:** Foner, *Reconstruction*, 75; BAP, 5:317–319.

CHAPTER 12: THE BATTLE FOR THE STREETCARS

Pages

323   **Even an army of occupation:** Foner, "Battle," 367.

323   **Rev. William Johnson Alston:** *PP*, July 21, 1864, Apr. 21, 1865; *CR*, July 23, 1864.

323   **Catto's minister and friend:** African Episcopal Church of St. Thomas vestry minutes; *Proceedings of the States Equal Rights Convention; CR*, June 30, 1866.

323   **the river's therapeutic drafts:** Vogel interview.

323   **Cholera contagions:** Walther; *CR*, Dec. 23, 1865.

323   **the better colored families . . . Le Counts:** Winch, *Gentleman of Color*, 161–162; Du Bois, *Philadelphia Negro*, 198–199; African Episcopal Church of St. Thomas vestry minutes.

323   **pigs and chickens . . . a privy:** Salvatore, *We All Got History*, 19; Levine interview; *INQ*, July 18, 1861; Gillette, "Corrupt and Contented," chap. 2.

323   **So he had walked:** 1870 and 1880 Census; Coppin, *Reminiscences*, 182.

323   **inquisitive, scholarly:** Bragg, *History of the Afro-American Group*, 87, 198; *CR*, Feb. 6, July 5, 1862, Apr. 4, 1863, Jan. 2, 1864; *NYT*, May 31, 1874.

323   **cannons . . . clippers:** Winch, *Gentleman of Color*, 338; Weigley, "Border City"; Taylor, *Philadelphia in the Civil War*, 202; 1863–1864 advertisements and shipping information, *PP*.

324   **yellow streetcar:** Joel Spivak private papers; Spivak interview.

324   **begun a half-dozen years . . . just take minutes:** Speirs, *Street Railway System*, 11; Meyers and Spivak, *Philadelphia Trolleys*, 9.

324   **where Catto lived:** McElroy's *Philadelphia City Directory*, 1864; 1870 Census.

324   **"bodily odors of Negroes":** Foner, "Battle," 357.

324   **He was a rare bird . . . "Good morning, Mrs. Cow:** Bragg, *History of the Afro-American Group*, 87, 197; Green, *Fact Stranger Than Fiction*, 15–16; *PP*, Jan. 14, 1865.

324   **The school chaplain made Alston . . . sitting together:** Carus, *Memorials*, 257–258.

325   **Alston was thrown off so hard:** [Hunt], *Why Colored People*; "The Passenger Cars," *PP*, Jan. 14, 1865.

325 **Within a week, sixty-five Negro men . . . father and son:** *INQ* advertisement, July 25, 1864; "Men of Color, To Arms" (broadside), American Time Capsule; Foner, "Battle," 281–282.

325 **At these meetings:** See, e.g., Still, *Brief Narrative*; "The Cars and Our People," *CR*, June 30, 1866.

325 **But there was . . . generations were drifting apart:** Foner, "Battle," 280–281; Lane, *Roots of Violence*, 49.

326 **Alfred Green . . . had gone to war:** BAP, 5:125–126.

326 **Oliver had seen:** Jan. 14, 1863, letter Oliver wrote, BAP, 5:172–173.

326 **They were taking a page from . . . was manhood:** Foner, "Battle," 280–281; *INQ*, Feb. 8, 1865; McPherson, *Negro's Civil War*, 262; "Appeal to the Colored People of Pennsylvania," *CR*, Dec. 24, 1864; "The Cars," *CR*, June 30, 1866.

326 **William Still had first written . . . politely ignored:** Hunt, *Report of the Committee*, 1–2.; Still, *Brief Narrative*, 2–4; Foner, "Battle," 275–277.

326 **Speeches and petitions . . . litany:** See, e.g., Still, *Brief Narrative*, 16; Catto's speech, *CR*, Apr. 22, 1865; *Proceedings of the States Equal Rights Convention*, 51; Langston, "Citizenship and the Ballot."

326 **The murmur and screech:** Streetcar background: Meyers and Spivak, *Philadelphia Trolleys*; McClure, *Old Time Notes*; Speirs, *Street Railway System*; Foner, "Battle," pts. 1 and 2; Spivak private papers and interview.

327 **The cars were ten:** Spivak papers; car description based, in part, on J. G. Brill Co. streetcar, Museum of the Historical Society of Berks County, Reading, PA.

327 **The fare was five cents . . . a tidy sum:** *INQ*, Jan. 23, 1861; *Reports of the Several Railroad Companies*, 302–305.

327 **Merchants with shops . . . back at night:** See, e.g., Wainwright, *Philadelphia Perspective*, 326–328.

327 **on a summer Saturday . . . on Jefferson:** *INQ*, July 28, 1864; Kirsch, *Blue and Gray*, 110.

327 **Sledgehammer crews . . . of its kind:** Spivak interview.

327 **As Mayor Henry:** Speirs, *Street Railway System*, 7.

327 **ten-hour shift at the Navy Yard:** Lapsansky interviews.

327 **paddle-wheelers . . . Cramp's Ship:** Taylor, *Philadelphia in the Civil War*, 201–202.

327–328 **Eight lines allowed . . . of our inferiority:** Foner, "Battle," 268; *CR*, Apr. 22, 1865.

328 **Some conductors and drivers . . . to ride:** Foner, "Battle," 273; Judge Allison's ruling in *Derry vs. Lowry*, quoted later in this chapter.

328 **A Philadelphia judge . . . barbarism:** Foner, "Battle," 268–269.

328 **That failed suit . . . us by law:** *CR*, Jan. 26, 1861; Still, *Brief Narrative*, 4, 11–12.

328 **"It was mismanaged . . . said suit:** *CR*, Feb. 2, 1861; *Washington (DC) National Era*, Sept. 29, 1859.

328 **Still was ordered off . . . Camp William Penn:** *CR*, Dec. 27, 1863.

328 **Frederick Douglass was twice ejected . . . ordered off:** Douglass, *Life and Times*, 459.

328–329 **And one conductor . . . experience in Philadelphia:** Coppin, *Reminiscences*, 13–15; Perkins, *Fanny Jackson Coppin*, 80–84.

329 **pigs' snouts and offal . . . horse-drawn car:** *PP* articles, 1864–1865; Foner, "Battle," 265; [Hunt], *Why Colored People*, 16–17, 24.

329 **Mayor Henry had . . . with colored people:** [Hunt], *Why Colored People*, 3–4; Foner, "Battle," 357.

329 **Even Still seemed . . . in filth:** Foner, "Battle," 279.

329 **Colored soldiers . . . decry the streetcar rule:** For examples, see Foner, "Battle," 269–272; *CR*, Nov. 15, 29, 1862.

329 **Lucretia Mott saw . . . both women inside:** Bacon, *Valiant Friend*, 187; Bolton, *Lives*, 6; Sterling, *Lucretia Mott*, 201.

330 **And everyone in colored . . . carried that report:** Foner, "Battle," 272–273; *CR*, July 30, 1864.

330 **news from cities:** *CR*, Nov. 11, 1863, July 9, 1864; Foner, "Battle," 282–284; Giesberg, *Army at Home*, 123, 131.

330 **Still went to Miller McKim:** Giesberg, *Army at Home*, 11–12; Foner, "Battle," 286.

330–331 **On the night of January 13 . . . 'Give us justice:** Foner, "Battle," 286–289; *PP* and *B,* Jan. 14–15, 1865; Speirs, *Street Railway System*, 24.

331 **antislavery societies vowed:** Bacon, *But One Race*, 150–151; Still, *Brief Narrative*, 14–15.

331 **a "Jim Crow" car, Alston lamented:** *PP,* Jan. 23, 1865.

331 **Having no illusions:** Speirs, *Street Railway System*, 25; Foner, "Battle," 289.

331 **As the Congress . . . vote of its own:** Foner, "Battle," 355; Still, *Brief Narrative*, 16.

331 **Nightmen cleaned . . . concealed the smell:** Levine interview.

331–332 **On a January day two weeks . . . his mean trick:** *PP,* Jan. 17, 23, 1865; Foner, "Battle," 289–290; Silcox, *McMullen*, 62; [Hunt], *Why Colored People*, 5; *B,* Jan. 18, 1865.

332–333 **The two days of . . . *for* and *against*:** *INQ,* Jan. 31, 1865; Foner, "Battle," 355.

333 **Newspapers sent reporters . . . car for any nigger:** *PP, B, INQ,* Jan. 31, Feb. 1, 1865.

333 **experiment with admitting:** Speirs, *Street Railway System*, 25; Foner, "Battle," 285, 355–356.

333 **Passengers scribbled comments . . . free and equal:** *INQ,* Jan. 31, 1865.

333 **McMullen's side won:** Foner, "Battle," 355; Speirs, *Street Railway System*, 25.

333 **One company reported more:** *INQ,* Jan. 31, 1865.

333 **rode a train west:** Executive board minutes, 1864–1872, PSERL; weather records, Feb. 8, 1865, Pennsylvania Hospital; *CR*, Feb. 4, 18, 25, 1865.

333 **sputtering and stalling:** Giesberg, *Army at Home*, 126.

333 **The state Equal Rights . . . meetings:** *Proceedings of the State Equal Rights Convention*.

333 **on a segregated train:** Ray interview.

333–334 **"frequently interrupted by loud applause:** *PP,* Jan. 3, 1865.

334 **Neither had editorial pages . . . the conductors:** Hunt, *Report of the Committee*, 2, 5; Speirs, *Street Railway System*, 26–27.

334 **hoisting cars off tracks:** Lane, *Roots of Violence*, 50; Foner, "Battle," 369.

334   **Only three of some two hundred:** [Hunt], *Why Colored People*, 10–11; *McElroy's Philadelphia Directory*, 1850s and 1860s.

334   **In her thirty-second annual report . . . complexion:** Grew quoted in Brown, *Mary Grew*, 114.

334–335   **Another veteran . . . white man's government yet:** [Hunt], *Why Colored People*, 13–17, 25; Auge, *Lives of the Eminent Dead*, 629.

335   **recently considered creating a registry:** *INQ*, Mar. 3, 1862.

335   **and had allotted monies . . . Liberia:** *Laws Enacted in the General Assembly of the Commonwealth of Pennsylvania*, 700–701.

335   **on a street called Tanner's Alley:** Houts, "Black Harrisburg's Resistance to Slavery."

335   **The first three pews . . . own league branches:** *Proceedings of the State Equal Rights Convention*, 13, 24; *CR*, Dec. 17, 1864, Feb. 4, 7, 18, 25, 1865; Davis, "Pennsylvania State Equal Rights League," 613.

335   **emerged as the league's strongest:** Lane, *Roots of Violence*, 49; McPherson, *Struggle for Equality*, 234.

335   **William Forten, a rich man's son:** Winch, *Gentleman of Color*, 333.

335   **(Alston defended the exertions:** *Proceedings of the State Equal Rights Convention*, 15–17, 19–21, 40; Lane, *Dorsey's Philadelphia*, 134–136.

336–337   **But the consensus was fragile . . . grudging approval:** *Proceedings of the State Equal Rights Convention*, 8, 9, 31–35.

337   ***Proceedings* for twenty-five cents, constitutions for:** Executive board minutes, 1865–1866, PSERL.

337–338   **Catto and the two other men . . . the morning sun:** *Proceedings of the State Equal Rights Convention*, 43, 48–51.

338   **On the last night of meetings, Rev. William . . . had Anthons:** Ibid., 37.

338   **Maria Mitchell . . . George Vashon:** Ibid.; executive board minutes, 1864–1872, PSERL. See, e.g., Bergland, *Maria*; Reinhold, "Charles Anthon," 19–20. George Vashon (1824–1878): BAP, 3:322.

338–339   **He said a Union Army . . . encouraging spectacle.":** *Proceedings of the State Equal Rights Convention*, 37–38.

339   **The aggrieved party . . . awarded her fifty dollars:** Wallace, *Philadelphia Reports*, 6:30–33; *PP*, Apr. 27, 1865.

339–340   **A poem in the *Inquirer* described . . . him things to eat:** *INQ*, June 3, 1865.

340   **Delegates met in Cleveland . . . secretaries:** *Proceedings of the First Annual Convention of the National Equal Rights League*, 24–25, 32–36.

340   **"I have visited the following localities . . . "Yours for Equal Rights:** *CR*, Nov. 4, 1865, Mar. 31, 1866, and state president, William Nesbit, Nov. 4, Dec. 23, 30, 1865.

340   **Concordville . . . man in Greencastle:** Executive board minutes, 1866, PSERL.

340–342   **In the winter, Catto . . . like an avalanche:** *CR*, Dec. 30, 1865, Feb. 17, 1866; Charles W. Lauble Jr., Historic Langhorne Association, e-mail messages to authors, Jan. 2009; Salvatore, *We All Got History*, 9–11; *INQ*, Feb. 8, 1865, 4; Hubbert-Kemper interview; "Preamble and Constitution of the National Equal Rights League," in *Proceedings of the First Annual Meeting of the National Equal Rights League*, 33–36; executive board min-

utes, 1865–1866, PSERL. For a photograph of the old Capitol, visit http://
cpc.state.pa.us/cpcweb/history/hillscapbwlg.jpg.

342 **One of the new . . . Catto league:** Ibid., including minutes of the
league's Aug. 1866 convention.

342–343 **The hall on . . . at the door:** Pennypacker, *Autobiography of a Pennsylvanian*, 101–104; *CR*, Dec. 9, 1865; "Pennypacker, Samuel Whitaker," in
Encyclopedia Americana, 1919, 21:539–540.

343 **The winds blew in from the northwest:** Weather records, Mar. 9, 1866,
Pennsylvania Hospital.

343 **The Institute for Colored Youth was moving:** Board of Managers, minutes, Jan. 16 and Mar. 13, 1866, excerpts, I.C.Y. records, FLS; *CR*, Mar. 17,
1866.

343 **"a most beautiful structure:** *CR*, Mar. 17, 1866.

343 **(Ebenezer Bassett, ever needful . . . once a week:** Board of Managers,
minutes, Mar. 13, 1866, excerpts, I.C.Y. records, FLS.

343 **The old I.C.Y. building on Lombard . . . Liberty Hall:** Lane, *Dorsey's
Philadelphia*, 111–112.

343 **only a 9.40 . . . dying soldier:** *CR*, May 16, 1863, Feb. 4, 1865.

344 **Le Count was an assistant . . . $340 a year:** *Forty-sixth Annual Report
of the Controllers of the Public Schools . . . 1864*, 101.

344 **the same events as Catto:** Lane, *Roots of Violence*, 52.

344 **she of the Ladies Union Association:** *Report of the Ladies Union Association*, 6–8; *CR*, Aug. 5, 1865, Apr. 14, 1866.

344 **daughters of respectable families:** Giesberg, *Army at Home*, 126–127.
The Iredells: Board of Managers, annual report, 1866, I.C.Y. records, FLS;
Coppin, *Reminiscences*, 147.

345 **Sanitary Commission had turned away:** *Report of the Ladies Union
Association*, intro.

345 **In Philadelphia, the Ladies Union . . . "forcibly ejected":** Ibid.; Giesberg, *Army at Home*, 126–128; *CR*, June 30, 1866; *PP*, Mar. 28, 1867.

345 **The Negroes' best ally in Harrisburg:** Foner, "Battle," 362–365;
McPherson, *Struggle for Equality*, 235–236; see also Lowry speech, and
salutes to him in *Proceedings of the State Equal Rights Convention*, 12–13,
17, 19, 32.

346 **Lowry's second streetcar . . . the next election:** Foner, "Battle," 363–365.

346 **afford to ride in carriages:** See Lane, *Roots of Violence*, 51.

346 **happier as slaves:** *INQ*, Feb. 7, 1865.

346 **Several officeholders . . . under consideration:** [Hunt], *Why Colored
People*, 4; Foner, "Battle," 365; Hunt, *Report of the Committee*, 2.

346 **different from the last:** Foner, "Battle," 369.

346 **The timing seemed . . . colored men the vote:** Ibid.; Foner, *Reconstruction*, 228–261.

346 **Catto and the little knot:** Executive board minutes, 1866–1867, PSERL.

346 **A message went out:** Foner, "Battle," 369.

347 **The bill advanced in fits . . . friend of the bill:** Executive board minutes, 1866, PSERL.

347 **Some whites and . . . demand it now:** Foner, "Battle," 366–367.

347 **Harriet Forten Purvis agreed . . . seat in the cars:** Winch, *Gentleman
of Color*, 354, 112.

347　**She was "very lady-like:** Bacon, *But One Race*, 102–103.

348　**More poets:** *CR*, Nov. 10, Dec. 15, 1866.

348　**Men and . . . daily occurrence:** Lane, *Roots of Violence*, 50; *CR*, June 30, 1866, Feb. 9, 1867; McClure, *Old Time Notes*, 596.

348　**Two colored women, . . . whitewashed:** *CR*, Sept. 23, 1865; Lane, *Roots of Violence*, 50.

348　**Miles Robinson, who had escaped:** Lane, *Roots of Violence*, 50; Still, *Underground Railroad*, 539–541; Foner, "Battle," 359, 366.

349　**In June 1866, newly . . . speaker was Catto:** *CR*, June 30, 1866; Lane, *Roots of Violence*, 50.

349　**These women were in . . . Alfred Green:** Hunt, *Report of the Committee*, 2; executive board minutes, Jan.–Feb. 1866, PSERL.

349　**Fenian Irish nationalists had met:** Independence Hall Association of Philadelphia, "Philadelphia Timeline, 1866."

349　**a women's rights convention:** For a description of this event, see U.S. Department of the Interior, National Park Service, "More Women's Rights Conventions."

350　**from one end of the state to the other:** PSERL and *CR* articles, 1865–1867.

350　**of his "band of brothers:** See Banneker, PSERL, and other records, such as the "undersigned" of the July 1864 streetcar meeting notice.

350　**And in their leisure time:** Bolivar, Pencil Pusher Points, *Philadelphia Tribune*, Aug. 24, 1912, May 3, 1913.

350　**He called for bodily defiance . . . civil disobedience:** Nash, *First City*, 252–253; Lane, *Roots of Violence*, 49–50; Silcox interview, 2003; Giesberg, *Army at Home*, 130n49.

350–351　**By the end of the year, a few legislators . . . in Scranton and Altoona:** Hunt, *Report of the Committee*, 3; Speirs, *Street Railway System*, 26; Foner, "Battle," 368–369, 372.

351　**"Never before in the history . . . ever before:** *CR*, Dec. 14, 1866.

351　**In Harrisburg on February 5, 1867:** Foner, "Battle," 369; *PP*, Mar. 28, 1867.

351　**"The prospects for its passage . . . without hesitancy:** Executive board minutes, Feb. 1867, PSERL; Foner, "Battle," 371.

351　**Republicans who had balked . . . Friday, March 22:** Foner, "Battle," 371, 373; Speirs, *Street Railway System*, 26.

352　**On the first Monday of spring:** Advertisements in *PP* and *B*, Mar. 1867.

352　**Under a cloudless noontime sky:** Weather records, Mar. 1867, Pennsylvania Hospital.

352　**the Ohio School's young principal . . . hundred-dollar fine:** *PP*, Mar. 28–29, 1867; Westcott, *Official Guide Book to Philadelphia*, 79.

352　**A letter from Harrisburg . . . essentially your own:** *PP*, Mar. 28, 1867; Still, *Brief Narrative*, 2–3, 21–23.

353　**There would ensue some fussing . . . pleasures:** Foner, "Battle," 374–376; Still, *Brief Narrative*, 1–2, 16, 23.

353　**Those men hissed . . . the Keystone State:** Still, *Brief Narrative*, 2, 23, 374.

353　**The *Press* reprinted the Lowry . . . "vigorously enforced:** *PP*, Mar. 28, 1867.

353 The *National Anti-Slavery Standard* . . . not be white: NASS, Mar. 30, 1867; Giesberg, *Army at Home*, 130.

353 At the victory meeting, . . . up for each of them: PP, Mar. 28, 1867.

353–354 Commentators agreed . . . possessing the ballot: Ibid.; Hunt, *Report of the Committee*, 3, 5; Foner, "Battle," 376–377; Speirs, *Street Railway System*, 26.

354 "And even better . . . of Christian charity: Hunt, *Report of the Committee*, 6.

354 chandeliers of Liberty Hall: CR, Nov. 17, 1866.

CHAPTER 13: BASEBALL

Pages

355 Negro baseball exploded: Lomax, *Black Baseball Entrepreneurs*, 1; Bolivar, Pencil Pusher Points, *Philadelphia Tribune*, Aug. 24, 1912, May 3, 1913.

356 The first full season of: Authors examined the bat, courtesy of Arthur Sudler, African Episcopal Church of St. Thomas archivist.

356 Boys played many games: Shiffert, *Baseball in Philadelphia*, 4, 13–14; Voigt, *Remarks*; Kirsch, *Baseball in Blue and Gray*, 2; Block, *Baseball Before We Knew It*, 230–232. For illustrations of Egyptian bat and ball games, see Peter A. Piccione, *Batting the Ball*, http://www.cofc.edu/~piccione/sekerhemat.html.

356 A game called baseball: Block, *Baseball Before We Knew It*, 25, 67–73; Goldstein, *Playing for Keeps*, 10.

357 By the 1820s, young white men: Kirsch, *Baseball in Blue and Gray*, 2; *National Advocate*, Apr. 25, 1823; see Protoball Chronologies at Project Protoball.

357 Baseball grew quickly in: Kirsch, *Creation of American Team Sports*, 53–54; Shiffert, *Baseball in Philadelphia*, 4, 14.

357 In 1833, without: Kirsch, *Baseball in Blue and Gray*, 2–3; Shiffert, *Baseball in Philadelphia*, 13–19; Lomax, *Black Baseball Entrepreneurs*, 5–8.

357 Eleven players usually: Hershberger, "Reconstruction of Philadelphia Town Ball."

358 *The Book of Sports*: Block, *Baseball Before We Knew It*, 80, 224, 281; Sullivan, *Early Innings*, 9–10, 13–15; Kirsch, *American Team Sports*, 3, 58–59, 71, 95.

358 By the 1850s: Kirsch, *Baseball in Blue and Gray*, 3, 4, 18, 73. Sullivan, *Early Innings*, 32–33; Kirsch, *Creation of American Team Sports*, 84; Block, *Baseball Before We Knew It*, 83–84; Goldstein, *Playing for Keeps*, 13; for more nineteenth-century baseball history, see Protoball Chronologies at Project Protoball.

358 The National Association of Base Ball Players: Kirsch, *Baseball in Blue and Gray*, 14; Kirsch, *Creation of American Team Sports*, 65–67; Sullivan, *Early Innings*, 22, 27–29, 43; Lomax, *Black Baseball Entrepreneurs*, 21–22.

358 Newspapers touted one game: Sullivan, *Early Innings*, 34–36; Julian, *Life of Joshua R Giddings*, 399.

359 By the time of Lincoln: Goldstein, *Playing for Keeps*, 12–14; Kirsch, *Baseball in Blue and Gray*, 2–3, 21; Kirsch, *Creation of American Team Sports*, 58–59, 71, 95; Shiffert, *Baseball in Philadelphia*, 18.

359   **A growing array of baseball . . . mathematical precision:** Kirsch, *Baseball in Blue and Gray*, 21, 70–71; Kirsch, *Creation of American Team Sports*, 22–23, 43, 54–56, 85–86; Shiffert, *Baseball in Philadelphia*, 18–26, 31.

359   **Even as players traded:** Aubrecht, "Civil War Baseball"; Kirsch, *Baseball in Blue and Gray*, 28–29, 39–40, 42, 47; Kirsch, *Creation of American Team Sports*, 80–81.

360   **Back home, fewer young men:** *INQ*, Oct. 26, 1861, May 22, 1862; Kirsch, *Baseball in Blue and Gray*, 11–12, 95; Goldstein, *Playing for Keeps*, 24; Shiffert, *Baseball in Philadelphia*, 34.

360   **But by 1863, players were coming home:** Kirsch, *Baseball in Blue and Gray*, 50–51; Shiffert, *Baseball in Philadelphia*, 32–33; Kirsch, *Creation of American Team Sports*, 83.

360   **In the summer of:** Kirsch, *Baseball in Blue and Gray*, 60, 110; *INQ*, May 23, 26, 1864.

360   **The Athletics took:** For more on the team's history, visit the Philadelphia Athletics Historical Society Web site, http://www.philadelphiaathletics.org/; *NYT*, Jan. 14, 1929.

361   **After the war, President Andrew Johnson:** Kirsch, *Baseball in Blue and Gray*, 115.

361   **A Midwest colored team:** Ibid., 122.

361   **The Pythian leaders were:** Pilkington, "Bringing the Fight to the Diamond"; Lane, *Dorsey's Philadelphia*, 323; Kirsch, *Creation of American Team Sports*, 126–127, 150–152; Bolivar, Pencil Pusher Points, *Philadelphia Tribune*, Aug. 24, 1912; Lomax, *Black Baseball Entrepreneurs*, 16, 28; see also early Pythian Base Ball Club records on microfilm at ANHS.

363   **"As captain of the Pythian's Nine:** Lane, *Roots of Violence*, 54.

363   **The Alert center fielder was Catto's:** Terry, "Brief Moment in the Sun," 86.

363   **The Pythians won their third game:** Menu in Pythian Base Ball Club records on microfilm at ANHS.

363   **The Pythians returned to:** Kirsch, *Baseball in Blue and Gray*, 123–126.

364   **Raymond Burr, a player on the second nine:** BAP, 3:195–196; *Pennsylvania Freeman*, Mar. 15, 1838; Coppin, *Reminiscences*, 183; Winch, *Elite of Our People*, 167–170.

365   **Colored teams were not welcome:** Bolivar, Pencil Pusher Points, *Philadelphia Tribune*, May 13, 1913.

365   **When Burr arrived the night:** Pythian Base Ball Club records on microfilm, ANHS. See also Pilkington, "Bringing the Fight to the Diamond"; Lomax, *Black Baseball Entrepreneurs*, 23; Shiffert, *Baseball in Philadelphia*, 55–56; Kirsch, *Baseball in Blue and Gray*, 128.

367   **The national association of baseball players:** Lomax, *Black Baseball Entrepreneurs*, 24, 57.

367   **Ten years after its formation:** Feeney, "Power of One"; Lomax, *Black Baseball Entrepreneurs*, 24–25, 57; Shiffert, *Baseball in Philadelphia*, 57–58; Threston, *Integration of Baseball in Philadelphia*, 9.

368   **Catto's disappointment was swallowed:** Board of Managers, annual report, 1868, I.C.Y. records, FLS; African Episcopal Church of St. Thomas vestry minutes; *CR*, June 3, 1865.

368 **On the white side of:** Kirsch, *Baseball in Blue and Gray*, 126; *City Item*, Oct. 3, 1868.

369 **In October, the Mutuals and:** Pythian Base Ball Club records, ANHS

369 **Seeing Catto and Le Count:** *CR*, Feb. 4, 1865.

369 **The Pythians' winning streak:** Pythian Base Ball Club records, ANHS.

370 **As a sponsor of the Pythian:** Lomax, *Black Baseball Entrepreneurs*, 18–19; Lane, *Roots of Violence*, 52.

370 **As the weather grew warmer:** Beers, "Centennial City," 458; Goldstein, *Playing for Keeps*, 114.

371 **On June 24, a letter to the:** *City Item*, June 24, 1869.

371 **Who was this *Lover of the Game*:** Feeney, "Power of One."

371 **On July 31, another letter:** *City Item*, July 31, 1969.

372 **The *Item's* baseball page all but dared:** *City Item*, Aug. 7, 1869.

372 **The captain of the black:** *CR*, June 3, Sept. 2, 1865; *INQ*, July 14, Aug. 13, 1863; Geffen, "Industrial Development," 332; Bolivar, Pencil Pusher Points, *Philadelphia Tribune*, June 6, 1912.

372 **In an August 12 letter:** Pythian Base Ball Club records, ANHS.

373 **Getting "Clark and Wilson":** *McElroy's Philadelphia City Directory*, 1870.

373 **Fans were now paying admission:** Lomax, *Black Baseball Entrepreneurs*, 27; *City Item*, Aug. 21, 1869.

373 **Two days after Catto's letter:** *City Item*, Aug. 14, 1869.

373 **The Masonics opened the floodgates:** *City Item*, Aug. 28, 1869.

373 **But it was:** Kirsch, *Baseball in Blue and Gray*, 126–127; Feeney, "Power of One."

374 **It would be the Olympic club:** Shiffert, *Baseball in Philadelphia*, 25, 61; Voigt, Remarks, 7–8.

374 **The teams were handsomely:** *City Item*, Sept. 11, 1969; Hershberger, "Reconstruction of Philadelphia Town Ball."

375 **The *New York Times* carried a short story:** *NYT*, Sept. 5, 1869; Ryczek, *When Johnny Came Sliding Home*, 100–108.

375 **The game drew attention:** *Deseret News*, Sept. 7, 1869.

375 **Other interracial matches quickly followed:** Kirsch, *Baseball in Blue and Gray*, 126–127; *Washington, D.C., Critic*, Sept. 20, 1869.

375 **Two weeks after the:** Shiffert, *Baseball in Philadelphia*, 60.

376 **After that, unofficial games:** Kirsch, *Baseball in Blue and Gray*, 127; Shiffert, *Baseball in Philadelphia*, 61.

CHAPTER 14: THE HIDE OF THE RHINOCEROS

Pages

377 **The last time Frederick Douglass:** See, e.g., *Huntington (PA) Globe*, Feb. 14, 1866; *Gettysburg Compiler*, Feb. 19, 1866; McFeely, *Frederick Douglass*, 246–248; Douglass, *Life and Times*, 382–385.

377 **"my friend:** Goodwin, *Team of Rivals*, 700.

377 **slouching in a chair:** Quarles, *Frederick Douglass*, 226.

377 **He had vilified . . . "your Moses:** Schroeder-Lein and Zuczek, *Andrew Johnson*, 329; Du Bois, *Black Reconstruction in America*, 237–247.

378 **The man that Catto and . . . Whipper:** *CR*, Jan. 6, 1866.

378 **He was no "flippant babbler," . . . a whiskey-drinking president:** *CR*, Mar. 30, 1876; Bordewich, *Bound for Canaan*, 186, 409; BAP 3:129–130; Schroeder-Lein and Zuczek, *Andrew Johnson*, 88–89.

378 **Suffrage now emerged . . . "the all important subject:** Douglass, *Life and Times*, 385; Lane, *Dorsey's Philadelphia*, 141: William Nesbit in *Proceedings of the First Annual Convention of the National Equal Rights League*, 52; Davis, "Pennsylvania State Equal Rights League," 621.

378 **The league began . . . colored men:** Davis, "Pennsylvania State Equal Rights League," 621.

378–379 **In Pennsylvania, league . . . securing its passage:** "Address of Penna. State Equal Rights League," *Chambersburg (PA) Franklin Repository*, June 5, 1867.

379 **Catto and Jake White . . . and William Kelley:** Davis, "Pennsylvania State Equal Rights League," 615.

379 **Yet both had an . . . and sisters:** Trefousse, *Thaddeus Stevens*, preface and 1–3, 214–215; Sklar, *Florence Kelley and the Nation's Work*, 3–30; Winch, *Gentleman of Color*, 115–116.

379 **Catto and White also used . . . had $221:** *CR*, Apr. 28, 1866.

379 **Money issues gnawed . . . in church membership:** Davis, "Pennsylvania State Equal Rights League," 617; Nesbit, Bustill, and Forten, "To the honorable the Senate and House"; various PSERL records, folder 8, box 2G, ANHS.

379 **upstate colored preachers . . . in a Maryland meadow:** Davis, "Pennsylvania State Equal Rights League," 617; Fields, *Slavery and Freedom*, 143.

380 **"the letter and spirit . . . might well regain:** Davis, "Pennsylvania States Equal Rights League," 624.

380 **Henry Highland Garnet . . . his understanding:** *CR*, Jan. 12, 1867.

380 **Martin Delany . . . did not write back:** Levine, *Martin R. Delany*, 406–408.

380 **Charles Remond, now . . . compound interest:** Yellin, *Harriet Jacobs*, 203.

380 **As for Douglass, a conductor . . . every day:** Frederick Douglass to Amy Kirby Post, Jan. 26, 1868, Post Family Papers.

380–381 **John Mercer Langston . . . white man's lips:** Cheek and Cheek, "John Mercer Langston," 113–120.

381 **Even Catto's father . . . decades before:** For some of Rev. W. T. Catto's church postings, see Morgan, *Morgan's History*, 63, 67, 72, 80, 81, 83, 84; and *CR*, Apr. 4, July 18, 1868.

381 **There he campaigned for voting:** CR, Dec. 1, 1868.

381 **At one point, the Pennsylvania State Equal Rights League . . . voting rights:** Davis, "Pennsylvania State Equal Rights League," 615, 623; PSERL executive board minutes, 1865–1867.

381 **They worked alongside . . . Forten:** See, e.g., *Proceedings of the State Equal Rights Convention*; *Proceedings of the First Annual Meeting of the National Equal Rights League*; many references to Whites, Bustills, and Mintons in Lane, *Dorsey's Philadelphia*; Winch, *Gentleman of Color*; reports from Equal Rights League conventions in CR; African Episcopal Church of St. Thomas vestry minutes.

381 **St. Thomas's seven marble . . . high-backed pews:** Douglass, *Annals of the First African Church*, 135–137.

381 **and by 1870 was:** 1870 Census.

381 **lived in other states:** 1860 Census, street directories, newspaper articles, Morgan, *Morgan's History*, and other records show William Catto living in Washington, DC, New Haven, CT, Buffalo, NY, and Morristown, NJ, during and after 1859.

381 **On a May evening:** "General Intelligence," *CR*, June 9, 1866; BAP, 5:134–136.

382 **New branches of the Union League:** Foner, *Forever Free*, 4, 160; league's branches begun in North Carolina: Foner, *Reconstruction*, 64, 283, 305.

382 **"Rapturous applause":** Pennsylvania State Equal Rights League Pittsburgh convention, ANHS, microfilm roll 9; Foner, *Reconstruction*, 305; David S. Cecelski, "Abraham Galloway: Prophet of Biracial America," in Glisson, *Human Tradition*, 3–30.

382 **"name withheld for fear:** *CR*, Jan. 12, 1867.

382 **New Orleans and Memphis . . . in the street:** Foner, *Forever Free*, 118–121; Lane, *Roots of Violence*, 52–53.

382 **"the case of whipping and burning:** Ball and Martin, *Rare Afro-Americana*, 10.

382 **From Galveston . . . cruelty and crime:** Freedmen's Bureau, *Executive Documents*, 304–313.

382–383 **a Union brigadier . . . in Maryland:** *INQ*, Nov. 8, 1871; Skinner, *After the Storm*, 99–101; Crouch, *Freedmen's Bureau and Black Texans*, 6–21.

383 **"The future to them is radiant:** Conway, *Final Report of the Bureau of Free Labor*, 32.

383 **"of dark complexion . . . intelligence:** Cromwell, *Unveiled Voices*, 11.

383 **the only 'live' one in the place:** *Freedman's Record* (Boston) 1, no. 12 (Dec. 1865), quoted in American Antiquarian Society, "Freedmen's Teachers."

383 **"Mr. Cromwell taught . . . initiative:** John Wesley Cromwell obituary, *Journal of Negro History*, "Notes," 566.

383 **"It is not my purpose . . . God-forsaken people:** Cromwell, *Unveiled Voices*, 12.

383 **Pliny Locke, Class of 1867:** Foner, *Freedom's Lawmakers*, 135; Coppin, *Reminiscences*, 144; Board of Managers, annual report, 1868, I.C.Y. records, FLS.

383 **Two women in the 1870 class . . . diplomas were real:** Perkins, *Fanny Jackson Coppin*, 101; Evans, "Nineteenth Annual Report of the Board of Managers, Institute for Colored Youth."

383 **Other graduates taught freedmen:** Board of Managers, annual reports and minutes, 1868–1872, I.C.Y. records, FLS; Catto's 1864 commencement speech; teachers' postings reported in *CR* and other newspapers; list of teachers in *Report of the Board of Trustees of Colored Schools*, 54–56; Coppin, *Reminiscences*, 144–181.

383 **Frances Rollin:** Coppin, *Reminiscences*, 157.

383 **White Southerners might curse . . . white teachers shun them:** Phillips, "White Reaction to the Freedmen's Bureau in Tennessee"; Weisenfeld, "Who Is Sufficient for These Things?" 209.

383 **A Charleston-to-Beaufort steamboat:** Powers, *Black Charlestonians*, 180–184, 236, 340n12; Koger, *Black Slaveowners*, 157, 198.

384–385 **A North-South grapevine . . . school in the fall:** Jones, *Soldiers of Light*, 14–48; *CR*, Apr. 25, Oct. 3, 1868; *NYT*, Feb. 8, 1866; Hahn, *Nation Under Our Feet*, 276; Foner, *Forever Free*, 136; Sterling, *We Are Your Sisters*, 269–270.

385 **Edgar Gregory thought . . . the desk before it:** Richard Paul Fuke, "Land, Lumber and Learning: The Freedmen's Bureau, Education, and the Black Community in Post-Emancipation Maryland," in Cimbala and Miller, *Freedmen's Bureau and Reconstruction*, 304–305.

385 **Washington schools . . . Robert E. Lee:** Washington's African American population "increased from 14,316 in 1860 to 38,663 in 1867." Harrison, "Welfare and Employment Policies."

385 **generations of Wormley . . . colored children:** Guide to the Wormley Family Papers; Brown and Lewis, *Washington from Banneker to Douglas*; *Report of the Board of Trustees of Colored Schools*.

385 **"I think I should like . . . useful trades:** "Editor's Drawer," *Harper's New Monthly Magazine*, May 1867, 813. Available at harpers.org/.

386–387 **From Beaufort, South Carolina, . . . care of the *Recorder*:** *CR*, Mar. 6, 1867.

387 **The paper . . . private nature:** Johnson, "Looking for Lost Kin."

387 **Lucinda Johnson hoped:** *CR*, July 20, Aug. 3, 1867.

387 **Ephraim Allen of . . . in their congregations:** *CR*, May 4, 1867, Nov. 21, 1868.

387 **Some notices ran for:** Emeline Hodges sought her father in *CR* notices that ran in July and Aug. 1870; Mary Long ran an advertisement in *CR* from Dec. 1873 through Feb. 1874.

387 **many Southern postmasters would not:** Seraile, *Fire in His Heart*, 28.

387 **The Grimké sisters and:** Lerner, *Grimké Sisters*, 358–366; Lerner, *Feminist Thought*, 40, 170–172.

387 **"dancing with old Mr. Weld:** Ames, *Life and Letters of Peter and Susan Lesley*, 357.

388 **A great national paradox:** Foner, *Forever Free*, 142–143.

389 **Smalls bought up property . . . kindness of Smalls:** Uya, *Black Politicians During Reconstruction*, 383–388.

389 **Whipper's nephew, W. J. . . . married Frances Rollin:** Powers, *Black Charlestonians* 180–184, 236n12; Coppin, *Reminiscences*, 157; Foner, *Reconstruction*, 327, 360–361, 378.

389 **Richard Holloway ran for . . . as a Democrat:** Koger, *Black Slaveowners*, 273n47.

389 **Robert Purvis's Oberlin-trained . . . legislature:** Bacon, *But One Race*, 168–169; Winch, *Gentleman of Color*, 361.

389 **The District of Columbia extended . . . Billy Wormley:** Terry, "Brief Moment in the Sun," 86.

389 **John Oliver was on . . . treason:** BAP, 5:134–136.

389 **At the same time, . . . land was another:** Foner, *Forever Free*, 142–143.

389–390 **Senator Edgar Cowan . . . head and tail:** Brown, "Pennsylvania and the Rights of the Negro," 51; *American National Biography, Dictionary of American Biography*, for "Cowan, Edgar (Senator)," available at http://bioguide.congress.gov/.

390 **"OUR MOTTO . . . White Men Rule:** Foner, *Reconstruction*, drawings after 386.

390   **In nine Northern states:** Harrell et al., *Unto a Good Land*, 524.

390   **A move to delete the word . . . Buchanan said:** Davis, "Pennsylvania State Equal Rights League," 627; Brown, "Pennsylvania and the Rights of the Negro," 51–52.

390   **Daniel Fox, who had built . . . and hold office":** Silcox, *McMullen*, 62.

390   **a memorable meeting . . . growls and yells":** Sprogle, *Philadelphia Police*, 151–152; *Report of a Committee of One*, 7–8.

390   **Late on election day . . . Moyamensing Hose fellows:** *INQ*, Oct. 20, 22, 1868; Du Bois, *Philadelphia Negro*, 40.

390   **men recommended by McMullen:** Silcox, *McMullen*, 74.

391   **Republican operatives . . . lasting majorities:** Foner, *Forever Free*, 146–147; Foner, *Reconstruction*, 337–343; Harrell et al., *Unto a Good Land*, 524; Saxton, *Rise and Fall of the White Republic*, 266.

391   **by fewer than two thousand votes . . . at least five thousand:** Silcox, "Black Better Class," 46; Ignatiev, *How the Irish Became White*, 170.

391   **John W. Forney, stood before . . . stopped forever:** *Proceedings of the National Convention . . . in Washington, D. C.*, 15–16; Nash, *First City*, 236; "Serenade to Hon. John W. Forney," *CR*, Mar. 4, 1867.

391–392   **"Halt! Halt! You . . . at last arrived," Cromwell wrote:** Fuke, *Imperfect Equality*, 105.

392   **Negroes were teaching . . . and legislators:** Foner, *Forever Free*, 159–160.

392   **"Violent threats are made . . . rooms at night:** Bacon, *But One Race*, 168.

392   **By Eric Foner's . . . murdered:** Foner, *Reconstruction*, 426.

392   **The violence stiffened . . . trying to vote:** Foner, *Forever Free*, 171–177; Foner, *Reconstruction*, chap. 9.

392   **John Oliver's first . . . burned:** BAP, 5:172–173.

392   **so was J. W. Cromwell's:** Cromwell, *Unveiled Voices*, 10–12, 98–100; Simmons, *Men of Mark*, 900.

392   **"nearly every colored church:** Foner, *Reconstruction*, 428.

392   **burning twenty-six freedmen schools:** Hahn, *Nation Under Our Feet*, 276.

392–393   **So was Sallie Daffin's school . . . President of the U. States:** Phillips, "White Reaction," 55.

393   **words of U.S. senator Willard Saulsbury . . . reprinted his speech:** Shaffer, "At Last, the Ballot," n31.

393   **Colored leaders . . . "another war:** PP, Sept. 26, 1869; *Senate Journal*, 40th Cong., 3rd sess., Jan. 15, 1869, 105–106.

393   **"a third of the delegates are:** Palmer and Ochoa, *Selected Papers of Thaddeus Stevens*, 152–154.

393   **Some Northerners said it was time . . . LET US HAVE PEACE:** Furness, *Records of a Lifelong Friendship*, 145–146; Harrell et al., *Unto a Good Land*, 524.

393   **Even Congressman Kelley:** Foner, *Reconstruction*, 310.

393   **In Baltimore, a Yankee-designed . . . to reach 228:** *Van Nostrand's Eclectic Engineering Magazine*, 1869, 95–96.

394   **Forten survived . . . "authoress:** Winch, *Gentleman of Color*, 348; Stevenson, *Journals of Charlotte Forten Grimké*, preface; Karcher, *First Woman in the Republic*, 737n124.

394 **White seemed to glide:** Lane, *Dorsey's Philadelphia*, 147–152; *CR*, Feb. 24, 1876.

394 **The Tanners had moved . . . Mother Bethel:** Lane, *Dorsey's Philadelphia*, 121.

394 **his father's tiny frame . . . from his shell:** *CR*, Nov. 6, 1873; *Philadelphia Tribune*, Aug. 19, 1937.

394 **she was overseeing 283 students . . . only $480:** *Forty-ninth Annual Report of the Controllers of the Public Schools . . . 1867*, 120, 135.

394 **She and White still represented:** Lane, *Dorsey's Philadelphia*, 147–152.

394 **still lived in her parents':** *McElroy's Philadelphia City Directory*, 1868.

394 **one of the best-paid Negroes:** Lane, *Dorsey's Philadelphia*, 305.

394 **frequent applications . . . eight hundred dollars a year:** Board of Managers, minutes, Mar. 12, 1867, excerpts, I.C.Y. records, FLS; Lane, *Dorsey's Philadelphia*, 305.

395 **From Allegheny City:** Catto to Garnet, Mar. 11, 1868, and Garnet to Catto, telegram, Mar. 14, 1868, ANHS; Board of Managers, minutes, Mar. 27, 1868, excerpts, I.C.Y. records, FLS.

395 **welcoming students as young as . . . Political Economy:** *CR*, Nov. 14, 1868.

395–396 **He was an oddity . . . most likely to *tell*:** Lapsansky-Werner and Bacon, *Back to Africa*, 2–53, 181, 249–250, 269–273; *CR*, Mar. 9, 1867; executive board minutes, 1868, PSERL.

396 **everyone looked distracted . . . or a parade:** Davis, "Pennsylvania State Equal Rights League," 617.

396 **Nesbit was older . . . foe of colonization:** Palmer and Ochoa, *Selected Papers of Thaddeus Stevens*, 345n1; Blockson, *African Americans in Pennsylvania*, 165; Ullman, *Delany*, 174; *CR*, Nov. 18, 1865.

396 **Nesbit had signed the suffrage petitions:** See, e.g., Nesbit, Bustill, and Forten, "To the Honorable the Senate and House."

396 **He wished this to be:** *CR*, Dec. 12, 1868.

397 **The appeal went out:** *CR*, July 25, 1868.

397 **William Forten wrote to . . . influenced:** Winch, *Gentleman of Color*, 369.

397 **Delegates arrived:** *CR*, Aug. 29, 1868; *Williamsport Standard*, Aug. 1868 (day illegible), ANHS.

397 **When Langston, the league's . . . "very bad:** Palmer and Ochoa, *Selected Papers of Thaddeus Stevens*, 345–347.

397 **Douglass attacked Langston, too:** Wright, *Negro in Pennsylvania*, 38.

397–398 **The Banneker Institute . . . of brothers:** *CR*, Aug. 22, 1868; Foner, *Reconstruction*, 344; *PP*, Aug. 18, 1868.

398 **Three weeks after . . . arrived in November:** William Nesbit to Jacob White Jr., Nov. 25, 1868, PSERL.

398 **By December 7, the new petitions . . . arms and ammunition:** William Kelley to White Jr., Dec. 7, 1868, and Charles Sumner to White Jr., Dec. 7, 1868, PSERL.

399 **the National Convention of Colored Men:** *Proceedings of the National Convention . . . in Washington, D.C.*

399 **Isaiah Wears—the short, intense barber . . . never lost a debate:** Brown, *Rising Son*, 513; Bolivar, Pencil Pusher Points, *Philadelphia Tribune*, Jan. 18, 1913.

399–401   **A few days later . . . do the same:** McPherson, *Struggle for Equality*, 425–428; Shaffer, "At Last, the Ballot," esp. 260n; Winch, *Gentleman of Color*, 368–369; *NYT*, Feb. 8, 1866; Foner, *Reconstruction*, 448; Yellin, *Harriet Jacobs*, 208. For "dese brudders" cartoon, see Foner, *Reconstruction*, 312.

401   **"Party expediency . . . for once:** Gillette, *Retreat from Reconstruction*, 19.

401   **Grant helped by . . . New England states:** McFeely, *Frederick Douglass*, 270; Litwack, *North of Slavery*, 91.

401   **In Philadelphia, Catto read . . . "fellow sufferers:** *Philadelphia Sunday Republic*, Mar. 21, 1868, clipping in Dorsey scrapbooks; Silcox, "Black Better Class," 48.

401   **Democrats denounced . . . citizen:** "Democratic Platform," *Chambersburg (PA) Franklin Repository*, July 21, 1869.

401   **Robert Purvis had decided a "trick":** Bacon, *But One Race*, 169–170.

401   **There was talk . . . Frederick Douglass:** McFeely, *Frederick Douglass*, 270; Douglass, *Life and Times*, 417–418.

402   **stubbornly parading to the 1866 convention:** Douglass, *Life and Times*, 387–391; Palmer and Ochoa, *Selected Papers of Thaddeus Stevens*, 192.

402   **Meanwhile, Martin Delany . . . Liberia:** Ullman, *Delany*, 412–413.

402   **The I.C.Y.'s managers:** Board of Managers, minutes, Apr. 13, 1869, I.C.Y. records, FLS.

402   **the first man of color to represent:** See, e.g., Wynes, "Ebenezer Don Carlos Bassett," 232–240.

402   **"there existed . . . a strong prejudice:** Perkins, *Fanny Jackson Coppin*, 99.

402   **Alumni taught in New York, New Jersey:** See, e.g., Coppin, *Reminiscences*, 144–181.

402   **visitors streamed . . . thirty a week:** Perkins, *Fanny Jackson Coppin*, 99.

402   **After a two-day visit, . . . enfranchisement:** "H. H.," "The Education of Our Colored Population."

402–403   **Now, the school . . . at the I.C.Y.:** Perkins, *Fanny Jackson Coppin*, 84–88; Board of Managers, minutes, Apr. 13, May 11, 1869, I.C.Y. records, FLS; Cope to Catto, Apr. 23, 1869, Catto to John W. Buckley, May 11, 1869, Catto Papers.

404   **addressing a colored audience . . . raging yet:** Faehtz, *National Memorial Day*, 888.

404   **"Our Jubilee:** *CR* editorial and letters, July 3, Aug. 14, Sept. 4, 1869.

404   **John W. Alvord, head of . . . not a minute too soon:** Alvord, *Letters from the South*, 33–41.

405   **McMullen's wagonload of woes:** Ignatiev, *How the Irish Became White*, 169–170; Silcox, *McMullen*, 75–76, 53–54.

405   **The state's new voter registry law:** Silcox, *McMullen*, 72–73; Steinberg, *Transformation of Criminal Justice*, 205–206.

405   **clucked their tongues . . . McMullin and His Operations:** Wainwright, *Philadelphia Perspective*, 520; *Chicago Daily Tribune*, Oct. 16, 1869.

405   **For its annual . . . dress, and blackface:** Silcox, *McMullen*, 68; Ignatiev, *How the Irish Became White*, 168.

405   **In letters to Samuel Randall . . . enemies to punish:** Silcox, *McMullen*, 76, 81, 112–128, 150–151.

405   **At midday on a:** Brooks, *Whiskey Drips*, 298–345; Vidocq, *Secrets of Internal Revenue*, 29–44; Silcox, *McMullen*, 71–72; Davis and Haller, *Peoples of Philadelphia*, 106; Sprogle, *Philadelphia Police*, 251–252; *PL*, Sept. 8, 1869; "Hugh Mara—An Interview with Him," *INQ*, Sept. 4, 1872.

406   **when a nighttime fire . . . container:** Hines, Marshall, and Weaver, *Larder Invaded*, illustration and caption, 96.

407   **He kept dropping . . . I would go:** "Hugh Mara—An Interview with Him."

407   **The new registry law . . . The Republicans compromised:** Ignatiev, *How the Irish Became White*, 169; Silcox, *McMullen*, 72–73; Steinberg, *Transformation of Criminal Justice*, 205–206.

408   **On a Friday night in April 1870 . . . was up for reelection:** *INQ*, Apr. 16, 1870.

408   **Nesbit and White . . . for political purposes:** "To the Colored People of Pennsylvania," Mar. 31, 1870, PSERL.

408   **Other wards met over . . . Bowser's studio:** *PL*, Apr. 22, 1870; *PP*, Apr. 23, 1870; Silcox, *McMullen*, 74; *Celebration in Honor of the Ratification of the Fifteenth Constitutional Amendment*.

408   **the managers to cancel:** Board of Managers, minutes, Apr. 12, 1870, I.C.Y. records, FLS.

408   **Three thousand Negroes marched:** Wang, *Trial of Democracy*, 50–51.

409   **In Philadelphia, people gathered:** *PP*, *PL*, and *B*, Apr. 26–27, 1870. Douglass in barouche: *INQ*, Apr. 27, 1870. Catto Equal Rights League of Bridgeton, N.J.: *PP*, Apr. 27, 1870.

409   **He *thinks*:** *PL*, Apr. 27, 1870.

409   **One sentence was widely quoted:** See, e.g., Blockson, "African Americans in Pennsylvania," 26; Silcox, "Nineteenth Century Philadelphia Black Militant," 71; Lane, *Roots of Violence*, 57; Biddle and Dubin, "Forgotten Hero."

411   **hide of a rhinoceros:** *PP*, Apr. 27, 1870.

411   **baked shad:** "Celebration Ball, in Honor of the Ratification of the Fifteenth Amendment, at Horticultural Hall . . . April 26th, 1870," ANHS.

411   **some longtime allies . . . its name to the *Standard*:** Foner, *Reconstruction*, 448. Karcher, *First Woman in the Republic*, xxv.

411–412   **The Philadelphia Female . . . motion to disband:** *INQ*, Mar. 25, 1870.

412   **High Republican priests:** Lapsansky-Werner and Bacon, *Back to Africa*, 269–273.

412   **Langston accepted a seat . . . board of health:** Cheek and Cheek, "John Mercer Langston," 113–120.

412   **said to be considering Catto:** *PP*, Oct. 11,1871.

412   **Catto embarked on a splurge:** Folder 5, box 3A, ANHS.

412   **Catto paid for a membership . . . Rand canceled:** *PP*, Oct. 14, 1871; Silcox, "Nineteenth Century Philadelphia Black Militant," 72; Perkins, *Fanny Jackson Coppin*, 106–107.

412   **The academy board deemed it "inexpedient":** Foner, "Battle," 377.

412   **The seats . . . faced North:** Evans, "Nineteenth Annual Report of the Board of Managers of the Institute for Colored Youth."

413   **He was said to have . . . citizenship:** *PP*, Oct. 14, 1871.

413   **He stayed in touch with Wormley:** Baseball scorecard showing Wormley playing for Washington Alerts against Pythians and Catto, July 6,

1867, in Pythian Base Ball Club records, ANHS; Wormley to Catto, Sept. 11, 1860, and Nov. 7, 1861, and John T. Johnson to Catto, Aug. 14, 1870, in which he calls Wormley one of "your friends" on a Washington school board, all in box 3A, folder 5, ANHS.

413   **approaching ten thousand:** 9,327 school-age black children is noted in *Report of the Board of Trustees of Colored Schools.*

413   **Wormley, rising in the:** For more on Wormley, see ibid, and *Republican ticket. First ward . . .* (Washington, D.C., 1870), American Time Capsule, portfolio 206, folder 13.

413   **beseeched Catto to apply:** Silcox, "Nineteenth Century Philadelphia Black Militant," 71; Johnson to Catto, Aug. 14, 1870.

413   ***Superintendent.* Catto dipped pen:** "Superintendant," "Superind," and "Supt." appear on a sheet of scratch paper in Catto Papers.

413   **Just then, he . . . any "wars:** Johnson to Catto, Aug. 14, 1870; *History of Schools for the Colored Population,* 214; Bryan, *History of the National Capital,* 559–560.

413   **The I.C.Y. fall . . . gave him thirty days:** Board of Managers, minutes, "Special Meeting," Aug. 17, 1870, "Special Meeting," Aug. 29, 1870, I.C.Y. records, FLS; Perkins, *Fanny Jackson Coppin,* 104–105; Coppin, *Reminiscences,* 142.

413   **Great enthusiasm greeted . . . five I.C.Y. alumni:** *Report of the Board of Trustees of Colored Schools,* 42, 54–55; Coppin, *Reminiscences,* 151–152.

414   **In thirty days, Catto . . . politeness:** *Report of the Board of Trustees of Colored Schools,* 42–53.

414   **a letter sent home to Jake . . . the fellows:** Catto to Jake White, Oct. 2, 1870, Catto Papers.

414   **still in place . . . a life raft:** *Report of the Board of Trustees of Colored Schools,* 4.

414   **Democratic newspaper in Newark . . . in this matter:** Shaffer, "At Last, the Ballot"; *INQ,* Apr. 4, 1870.

414   **Tennessee enacted a poll tax . . . colored precincts:** Foner, *Reconstruction,* 422.

414   **New Castle County . . . walked away:** Shaffer, "At Last, the Ballot."

414–415   **The Democratic daily . . . White Man's ticket:** *Chambersburg [PA] Valley Spirit,* Oct. 5, 1870.

415   **California's Democratic . . . leave it forever:** *Auburn [CA] Placer Herald,* Apr. 30, 1870.

415   **McMullen let it . . . "a drink of rum:** Silcox, "Black Better Class," 50.

415   **McMullen's organization . . . our way:** Silcox, *McMullen,* 75; *NYT,* Oct. 12, 1870.

415   **the Pennsylvania State Equal Rights League . . . VOTE EARLY:** Broadside, Oct. 4, 1870, in roll no. 3 of microfilm edition, Woodson Collection.

415   **Isaiah Wears made it . . . the Republican ticket:** Silcox, "Black Better Class," 49.

415   **Many had stood since . . . Haggerty led them:** *PP,* Oct. 12, 1870, 6; *NYT,* Oct. 12, 1870; *PL,* Oct. 12, 1870.

415   **"a big, burly fellow," . . . Billy clubs came out:** *NYT,* Oct. 12, 1870; *INQ,* Oct. 13, 1870.

415 **McMullen nudged a:** Silcox, *McMullen*, 74–75; *NYT*, Oct. 12, 1870.

416 **By midday, people were . . . cheers of colored onlookers:** *PP* and *NYT*, Oct. 12, 1870; *Chicago Daily Tribune*, Oct. 20, 1870; *INQ*, Oct. 12–13, 1870; Lane, *Roots of Violence*, 54; *PP*, Oct. 12, 1870.

416–417 **in New Jersey's election . . . "The Police Again:** *NYT*, Nov. 22, 1870, Jan. 18, Feb. 11, 13, 1871; *INQ*, Nov. 9, 1870; *PP*, Nov. 29, Dec. 9, 1870; *PL*, Nov. 17, 1870.

417 **In late November:** *Lancaster Intelligencer*, Nov. 30, 1870; *PP*, Dec. 8, 19, 1870; *INQ*, Nov. 23, 24, Dec. 19, 1870.

417 **A judge heard evidence:** *Huntingdon Globe*, Mar. 30, 1870.

417 **The city Republican Committee had:** *PP*, Dec. 8, 1870.

417 **Some colored voters . . . vote for Lyndall:** *PP*, Dec. 1, 1870.

417 **Catto put a statement . . . control the legislature:** *INQ*, Dec. 19, 1870.

417 **Lyndall lost:** *NYT*, Dec. 23, 1870.

418 **He joined the Fifth Brigade:** "Military Affairs," *NYT*, May 14, June 11, 1871.

418 **Some Democrats . . . James Forten:** Silcox, *McMullen*, 73; Winch, *Gentleman of Color*, 355.

418 **Other Democrats could not:** *Huntingdon Globe*, Mar. 30, 1870.

418 **"this black God of their idolatry:** W. H. McCandless, quoted in Brown, "Pennsylvania and the Rights of the Negro," 49.

418 **Men talked of Frederick . . . federal post:** McFeely, *Frederick Douglass*, 270; Douglass, *Life and Times*, 417–418; Bacon, *But One Race*, 169–170.

418 **William G. Armstrong . . . a *nigger* his place:** Armstrong diary, Mar. 31, 1871.

418 **Daniel Fox declined . . . of the Squire:** Silcox, *McMullen*, 78; Lane, *Dorsey's Philadelphia*, 199–201; Beers, "Centennial City," 440; *INQ*, Sept. 29, 1871.

418 **More than five thousand colored:** *INQ*, Apr. 16, 1870; Ignatiev, *How the Irish Became White*, 170.

418–419 **He announced a . . . black pantaloons:** Silcox, *McMullen*, 70.

419 **Armstrong, the Democratic:** Armstrong diaries, May 28, 1871.

419 **dedication of the Lincoln statue:** *PP*, Sept. 23, 1871.

419 **The Pythians played . . . missed both games:** *NYT*, Sept. 17, 1871; *PP*, Sept. 20, 1871.

419 **At 5:30 P.M. on Monday . . . the gleam of knives:** *PP*, *INQ*, and *B,* Oct. 3, 1871.

419 **At Liberty Hall, . . . emancipated the slaves:** *INQ*, Oct. 9, 1871.

419 **At nearby Union . . . no action:** Silcox, *McMullen*, 78; Ignatiev, *How the Irish Became White*, 70; *INQ*, Oct. 12, 1871.

419 **Between seven and eight . . . gas lamp:** *PP*, Oct. 18, 1871; Silcox, *McMullen*, 78; Lane, *Dorsey's Philadelphia*, 200; *McElroy's Philadelphia City Directory*, 1870.

419–420 **Within an hour, . . . one vote less:** *Evening City Item* and *B,* Oct. 10, 1871; *PP*, Sept. 23, 30, Oct. 9, 18, 1871; *INQ*, Oct. 12, 18, Nov. 8 ("Obituary"), 1871; *PL*, Apr. 27, 1877; Du Bois, *Philadelphia Negro*, 40; Lane, *Roots of Violence*, 54; inventory of Catto's estate, Department of Records, City of Philadelphia. For black views of Mayor Fox's police, see *Penn Monthly*, 174; Bolivar, Pencil Pusher Points, *Philadelphia Tribune*, June 6, 1912.

CHAPTER 15: ELECTION DAY

Pages

Except where noted, this chapter draws from two sources: Dorsey scrapbooks and Griffin, *Trial of Frank Kelly*, for which page numbers include the preface, 8–18, 21–27, 30, 45.

The Dorsey scrapbooks include dated newspaper clippings, some of which, alas, lack a date, newspaper name, or both. All clippings, however, are numbered. The identified clippings with dates in 1877 all come from *PL*: Apr. 25, no. 23; Apr. 27, nos. 36–37, 39, 42; May 1, nos. 56, 58, 60; June 19–22, nos. 76–84. Also, nos. 44–45, with dates uncertain, but *PL* is the likely newspaper.

421   **The sun began climbing:** Weather records, Oct. 10, 1871, Pennsylvania Hospital.

421   **McMullen commanded respect:** Silcox, *McMullen*, 77–82; Silcox interviews.

422   **The violence had already begun:** Bolivar, Pencil Pusher Points, *Philadelphia Tribune*, July 12, 1912.

422   **The Fourth and Fifth wards:** Ward map in Du Bois, *Philadelphia Negro*, 59; Lane, *Dorsey's Philadelphia*, 299.

422   **About six squares away, Richard Greener:** *PP*, Oct. 11, 1871.

423–424   **At one o'clock, Mayor Fox . . . anything improper:** *INQ*, Oct. 11, 1871; *PP*, Oct. 14, 1871.

425   **In the early afternoon:** *PP*, Oct. 26, 1871; *INQ*, Oct. 11, 1871; Silcox, *McMullen*, 80.

425   **Bolden's shooting happened about:** *INQ*, Oct. 11, 1871; Bolivar, Pencil Pusher Points, *Philadelphia Tribune*, July 22, 1912; Lane, *Dorsey's Philadelphia*, 200; Silcox, *McMullen*, 80–81.

426   **Residents didn't know:** Lane, *Dorsey's Philadelphia*, 200; *INQ*, Oct. 11, 1871.

427   **Fawcett, a forty-year-old hod carrier:** *NYT*, July 11, 1877.

427   **He went to the bank:** *INQ*, Oct. 12, 1871.

428   **Catto began walking home:** *INQ*, Oct. 12, 1871; Du Bois, *Philadelphia Negro*, 41; *INQ*, Oct. 11, 1871; "vote the ticket" remark: Lapsansky interviews.

428   **Rather than going over to South Street:** Silcox, *McMullen*, 80.

428   **He passed 825 South:** Thomas Boling earning an I.C.Y. diploma: *PP*, May 10, 1864.

428   **As Catto walked:** Silcox, *McMullen*, 81; *INQ*, Oct. 12, 1871; Lane, *Dorsey's Philadelphia*, 200.

428   **The man crouched:** Silcox, *McMullen*, 81; *PL*, Apr. 25, 1877; Ballard, *One More Day's Journey*, 81–82.

429   **The bandaged man put the pistol:** *INQ*, Oct. 12–13, 1871; *PL*, Oct. 14, 1871.

430   **Greener was the first I.C.Y.:** Simmons, *Men of Mark*, 328; *PP* and *INQ*, Oct. 11, 1871.

430   **A telegram went out to:** *INQ*, Oct. 12, 1871.

430   **That night the rioting city:** Du Bois, *Philadelphia Negro*, 41; Fawcett's wound: *INQ*, Oct. 11, 1871.

430   **At 10:00 P.M., the publisher:** *PP*, Oct. 11, 1871.
430   **In the newspapers the next day . . . The *Public Ledger* said:** Front pages of *INQ, PL, PP,* and *NYT*, Oct. 11, 1871.
431   **Nine of the Quaker managers:** Board of Managers, minutes, Oct. 11, 1871, I.C.Y. records, FLS.
431   **That same morning, colored men and:** *INQ* and *PP*, Oct. 12, 1871.
431   **The news of his son's murder:** *PP*, Oct. 17, 1871.
432   **By the next day, the *Inquirer* decided . . . of the riot:** *INQ*, Oct. 12, 1871.
433   **One newspaper reported that:** *INQ*, Oct. 11, 1871.
433   **Rewards were offered:** *B* and *INQ*, Oct. 12–13, 1871; verse in *City Item*, Oct. 12, 1871.
433   **At the African Episcopal:** African Episcopal Church of St. Thomas vestry minutes, Oct. 12, 1871.
434   **The *Bulletin* reported that . . . South Philadelphia:** *B*, Oct. 13, 1871.
434–435 **At a large meeting at National . . . "That's right:** *PL* and *PP*, Oct. 14, 1871.
435   **The coroner conducted an inquest:** *PL* and *PP*, Oct. 14, 1871.
435   **The *New York Times*:** *NYT* and *INQ*, Oct. 14, 1871; *PP* and *B*, Oct. 14–15, 1871.
435   **McMullen, the head of:** *B*, Oct. 13–14, 1871; Silcox, *McMullen*, 81–82.
436   **A colored man led:** Silcox, *McMullen*, 81–82; *PP* and *INQ*, Oct. 16–17, 1871.
438   **Eulogies would elevate his:** Tanner, "To the Memory of Professor O. V. Catto."
439   **Three colored leaders in:** *NYT*, Oct. 30, 1871; Seaton, *Eulogy on the Life and Death of Prof. Octavius V. Catto.*
439   **In Philadelphia, Wears said:** Foner and Branham, *Lift Every Voice*, 512.
439   **Lashing out at the:** *Tioga County Agitator* (Wellsborough, PA), Oct. 25, 1871.
440   **On October 23:** Treatment records, Oct. 23, 1871, Pennsylvania Hospital.
440   **On December 7, about seven weeks:** *PP*, Dec. 8, 1871; *New York Evangelist*, Dec. 21, 1871.
440   **The funeral procession finally reached:** *PP* and *INQ*, Oct. 17, 1871.

CHAPTER 16: THE VENUS OF THE HIGH TRAPEZE

Pages
441   **The January sun had fled:** Griffin, *Trial of Frank Kelly*, 3–15, 21, 24; *PL*, Apr. 25, 27, 1877; *Chicago Daily Tribune*, Jan. 12, 1877; "Prof. Catto," *North American*, Jan. 17, 1877.
441   **a dark intensity to his eyes:** Griffin, *Trial of Frank Kelly*, 16, 19.
441   **William Forten, traveling "unofficially:** *PL*, Apr. 27, 1877.
441–442 **The man had told . . . capture of Frank Kelly:** *INQ*, Jan. 17, 1877; *PP*, Jan. 24, 1877; *Washington Evening Star*, Jan. 24, 1877; *North American*, Jan. 17, 1877; *Chicago Daily Tribune*, Jan. 12, 1877.
442   **The Panic of 1873 had . . . forcibly if we must:** Foner, *Forever Free*, 190; Harrell et al., *Unto a Good Land*, 528–540; Beers, "Centennial City."
442   **Forten becoming a:** Winch, *Gentleman of Color*, 369–370; Lane, *Dorsey's Philadelphia*, 218.

442 **Robert Smalls and fifteen other Negroes:** Foner, *Reconstruction*, chap. 8.

442 **Forten's favorite senator:** See, e.g., Winch, *Gentleman of Color*, 369–370.

442 **filibuster by its fiercest foe, Samuel Randall:** Ignatiev, *How the Irish Became White*, 173–174.

442 **An aptly named couple:** Lane, *Dorsey's Philadelphia*, 170; Hoffman, *Barrymores*, 15.

442 **Morrow Lowry, lost his mind:** *NYT* obituary, Jan. 24, 1885.

442 **Southern Democrats, grateful for Randall's:** Ignatiev, *How the Irish Became White*, 173–174.

442 **Grant wearily confided to his cabinet:** Foner, *Reconstruction*, 577.

442 **Soldiers were redeploying . . . consciousness:** Harrell et al., *Unto a Good Land*, 534, 557–558.

442 **massacres of seventy Negroes . . . Vicksburg, Mississippi:** Foner, *Forever Free*, 151; Foner, *Reconstruction*, 558.

442 **Mayor William Stokley held aloft:** *Godey's Lady's Book* 93 (Nov. 1876): 191.

442–443 **a black-white standoff . . . get it from me:** Billingsley, *Yearning to Breathe Free*, 126–128; Foner, *Reconstruction*, 570–571; Saxton, *Rise and Fall of the White Republic*, 259, 267n.

443 **But the Pittsburgh congressman . . . "Played out, sit down:** Foner, *Reconstruction*, 554; Foner, *Short History*, 234.

443 **For better or worse:** Lane, *Dorsey's Philadelphia*, 209–210, 218; Winch, *Gentleman of Color*, 369–370.

443 **The state Equal Rights . . . "earnestly pledge:** Winch, *Gentleman of Color*, 369–370; Ball and Martin, *Rare Afro-Americana*, 12l; Blight, *Jubilee*, 217.

443 **and Southern "self government":** Foner, *Forever Free*, 197; Blight, *Race and Reunion*, 135.

443 **Since Catto's death, . . . temperance society:** *CR*, Feb. 26, 1874.

443 **Odd Fellows club:** Brooks, *Official History and Manual*, 118;

443 **a medal awarded:** *PP*, Oct. 14, 1871.

443 **Good Templars:** *CR*, Aug. 29, 1878.

443 **His photograph:** A portrait of Octavius Catto appears in "Let Your Motto Be Resistance: African American Portraits," online version of the National Gallery, Smithsonian Institution exhibition held Oct. 19, 2007–Mar. 2, 2008 in Washington, DC, http://www.npg.si.edu/exhibit/motto/.

443 **Jake White sent out solicitations:** "Catto Monument Association" letter, Feb. 27, 1872, White Papers.

443 **The Board of Education prepared:** Coppin, *Reminiscences*, 181.

443 **In Delaware, an A.M.E.:** Coppin, *Unwritten History*, 346–347.

443 **a baby girl Octavia:** Death certificate for Octavia Le Count, "Date of Death: Feb. 7, 1874," Philadelphia City Archives. Octavius Catto Coppin's death at age nine months, in 1877: Coppin, *Unwritten History*, 346–347.

443–444 **Le Count and her three . . . charities:** See, e.g., *Fifty-third Annual Report of the Board of Public Education*, 148, 166; Lane, *Dorsey's Philadelphia*, 149–150, 155, 312.

444 **At the I.C.Y., . . . ignoring this advice:** Lane, *Dorsey's Philadelphia*, 143–145; Coppin, *Reminiscences*, 22–23; Perkins, *Fanny Jackson Coppin*, 97, 113–114.

444   **But other organizations Catto had:** Lane, *Dorsey's Philadelphia*, 218;
Lane, *Roots of Violence*, 55; Winch, *Gentleman of Color*, 370; *CR*, July
20, 1872; Davis, "Pennsylvania State Equal Rights League," 632; Lomax,
Black Baseball Entrepreneurs, 31; final game records are from 1871, ANHS;
Lapsansky, "Discipline," 85, 102.

444   **The monument fund struggled:** Ball and Martin, *Rare Afro-Americana*,
16.

444   **The Coppin . . . died in infancy:** Coppin, *Unwritten*, 346–347; death
certificate for Octavia Le Count, age two, City of Philadelphia.

444   **A police sergeant and . . . walked free:** *PP* and *INQ*, Oct. 18, 1871;
Griffin, *Trial of Frank Kelly*, 45; Silcox, *McMullen*, 82.

444   **The memory of the Catto riot:** Silcox, *McMullen*, 86; Scharf and Westcott, *History of Philadelphia*, 1:837.

444   **"unblushing daylight":** *PP* [Feb. 15, 1877?], Dorsey scrapbooks, no. 22.

444   **turned up in Pittsburgh or Richmond:** Griffin, *Trial of Frank Kelly*,
44; *Philadelphia Day*, June 2, 1877; "Matters in the Courts," *INQ*, June 4,
1877.

445   **"a dozen opportunities . . . to arrest him quietly:** Editorial, Dorsey
scrapbooks, no. 22, pp. 70–71, probably from *Philadelphia Times*, May 5,
1877.

445   **Forten, the Mintons:** Lane, *Dorsey's Philadelphia*, 227; *PL*, Apr. 27, 1877.

445   **The police department, at least:** Lane, *Dorsey's Philadelphia*, 200–201;
INQ, Feb. 10, 19, 1877; Steinberg, *Transformation of Criminal Justice*, 172.

445   **The new mayor also led . . . November 10, 1876:** Gillette, "Corrupt and Contented," 136–137; Beers, "Centennial City," 462–467; Foner,
Reconstruction, 564–565; see also "Exhibition Facts," in Centennial Exhibition; Sprogle, *Philadelphia Police*, 155–157.

445   **Sheppard's Rail Road:** Scharf and Westcott, *History of Philadelphia, vol.*
3, 1552.

445   **Centennial Mayor:** *CR*, Feb. 22, 1877.

445–446   **The informer said Kelly . . . "imposing build:** *Chicago Daily Tribune*,
Jan. 12, 1877; Flinn and Wilkie, *History of the Chicago Police*, 374–375.

445   **The world-renowned aerialist:** Tait, *Circus Bodies*, 37–40, 48–49. *Chicago Daily Tribune*, mid-Jan. 1877, reported "rushing crowds" for per-
formances by Jutau and her trapeze partner, George Brown; "Circuses" column, *New York Clipper*, Mar. 3, 1876.

447   **John Fawcett, the colored hod-carrier:** Griffin, *Trial of Frank Kelly*, 23;
INQ, July 11, 1877.

447   **Newspapers rushed to:** *Philadelphia Day*, Jan. 16, 1877, in Dorsey scrapbook no. 22, microfilm roll no. 2.

447   **"an attractive man . . . a boyish appearance:** *North American*, Jan. 17,
1877.

447   **Reports promptly surfaced in Philadelphia:** *Philadelphia Day*, Jan. 16,
1877; *North American*, Jan. 29, 1877; *NYT*, Feb. 17, 19, 1877; *INQ*, Feb. 19,
1877.

448   **"the Frank Kellys of the United States:** Editorial, *PP*, Jan. 24, 1877.

448   **Benjamin L. Temple:** Silcox, *McMullen*, 76, 78, 87; *INQ*, Sept. 5, 1873,
Jan. 28, Sept. 29, 1880.

448   **But then, people on:** *North American and U.S. Gazette*, Sept. 21, 1871.

449 **"By God and my country:** *PP*, Feb. 3, 1877.

449 **Stokley met with Catto's older . . . and his sister:** *Philadelphia Day* [Feb. 1, 1877?], in Dorsey scrapbooks.

449 **On Valentine's Day, William Forten . . . Centennial mayor:** *CR*, Feb. 22, 1877; *PP* [Feb. 15?] 1877, Dorsey scrapbooks.

449 **help him win reelection in:** *Mayors of the City of Philadelphia.*

449 **For many, that time was:** Lane, *Dorsey's Philadelphia*, 203, 217.

449–450 **On February 26, a special panel . . . out of Southern capitals:** Foner, *Reconstruction*, 580–582; Hoogenboom, "Inaugurating a 'Most Successful Administration'"; Blight, *Race and Reunion*, 134–139.

450 **Dissension arose . . . patience," Langston wrote:** Lane, *Dorsey's Philadelphia*, 203; *CR*, June 21, 1877.

450 **"the hands of the very men:** Foner, *Reconstruction*, 582.

450 **"To think that Hayes:** Kantrowitz, *Ben Tillman*, 67.

450–451 **Yet this time Douglass was . . . long eluded him:** McFeely, *Frederick Douglass*, 289.

451 **"a sort of vicarious atonement:** Yellin, *Harriet Jacobs*, 232–233.

451 **"You cannot tell what an inspiration:** Sterling, *We Are Your Sisters*, 409–410.

451 **"At any rate, . . . "Time will tell:** Rutherford B. Hayes, diary entry for Apr. 22, 1877, Hayes diary and letters.

451 **The trial of Frank Kelly:** In addition to Griffin, *Trial of Frank Kelly*, 5–39, the trial account is from Apr. and May 1877 newspaper clippings in the Dorsey scrapbooks: *B*, May 4; *PP*, May 5; *PL*, Apr. 24, 27, 30, May 1, 2, 3; *Philadelphia Public Record*, Apr. 25, 26, May 4; *Philadelphia Times*, May 3, 5. One unlabeled clipping is probably *PL*, Apr. 28.

451 **A spacious new Common Pleas courtroom:** *McElroy's Philadelphia City Directory*, 1877; Westcott, *Historic Mansions and Buildings of Philadelphia*, 113.

451 **"piebald:** *Philadelphia Times*, May 5, 1877.

452 **On the bench sat a compact:** Johnson and Brown, *Twentieth Century Biographical Dictionary*, vol. 5, entry for "J. I. Clark Hare L.L.D."; Brown, *Forum*, 165–168.

452–457 **A witness vanished . . . a Minton son could ill afford:** *PL*, Apr. 24, 1877; Lane, *Dorsey's Philadelphia*, 226.

458 **Devitt had been an alderman . . . defiant parades:** *INQ*, Oct. 20, 22, 1868; "Fireman's Parade," *Delaware County* [Chester, PA] *Republican*, July 23, 1869.

459 **A colored laundress . . . black his boots:** *PL*, June 19–21, 1877.

460 **In the years since . . . his obituary:** Ignatiev, *How the Irish Became White*, 170–175; Silcox, *McMullen*, 71, 83, 85.

460 **A lawyer named Swope called . . . another inquisition:** *INQ*, Oct. 24, 1872.

460 **renamed Samuel Randall's Tavern:** Silcox, *McMullen*, 84.

463 **One historian . . . "infuriated:** Lane, *Dorsey's Philadelphia*, 203.

463 **An editorial said Kelly:** Dorsey scrapbook, 22, pp. 70–71, likely *Philadelphia Times*, May 5, 1877.

463 **The *Press* said . . . "a foregone conclusion:** *Philadelphia Times*, May 5, 1877.

463   **At a routine hearing in . . . sit down and be quiet:** *Philadelphia Day,*
       June 2, 1877; *INQ,* June 4, 1877.

463–467 **The littlest voices carried . . . Then he slugged Addison:** Newspaper
       articles from 1877 in Dorsey scrapbook no. 22, including: *PL,* June 19, 21;
       PP, June 22; *Philadelphia Public Record,* June 23, 25. Two undated articles
       are probably *PL,* June 20 and 23. Emeline Street width estimated by stand-
       ing in the street, now Kater Street, in 2004. The judge wondering whether a
       detective would "throttle" Benjamin Temple: *INQ,* June 26, 1877.

467   **acquitted even faster . . . watch chain:** *PP,* July 10, 11, 1877.

467   **hard to prove a murderer . . . years' delay:** Lane, *Dorsey's Philadel-*
       phia, 203.

467   **"the Democratic ward rough:** *Summit County Beacon* (Akron, OH), July
       25, 1877, supplement; editorial, *Philadelphia Public Record,* June 25, 1877;
       NYT, July 11, 1877.

467   **Mayor Stokley took fitful . . . ran to ninety pages:** Lane, *Dorsey's Phil-*
       adelphia, esp. xii–xiv, 209–210; Dorsey scrapbook no. 22.

467–468 **By the middle of . . . No one was arrested:** *INQ,* July 11, 12, 20, 1877;
       Summit County Beacon, July 25, 1877, supplement.

468   **a Cincinnati jury convicted . . . thirteen months' imprisonment:**
       Philadelphia Evening Express, Dec. 13, 1877.

468   **but was pardoned after six:** Frank Kelly's pardon is mentioned in an
       unlabeled, undated clipping, Dorsey scrapbooks, no. 22, p. 98.

468   **Holland's pardon . . . make this acknowledgement:** Hayes pardoned
       Holland on Feb. 6, 1878, according to a letter to Congress from the attor-
       ney general's office. This, and the letter from Francis Kelley of Philadelphia
       to Hayes, Nov. 7, 1878, are courtesy of Nan Card, curator of manuscripts,
       Rutherford B. Hayes Presidential Center, Fremont, OH.

468   **One newspaper credited:** *Philadelphia Public Record,* Oct. 1, 1880.

468   **another said the White House:** *New York Daily Tribune,* Aug, 3, 1878;
       Georgia Weekly Telegraph, Aug. 6, 1878.

468   **After the Compromise of 1877:** Foner, *Forever Free,* 206–207.

469   **Southern states repealed . . . ensure white control:** Foner, *Reconstruc-*
       tion, 590–595.

469   **many of the "freedom schools" . . . closed:** Bacon, "Pennsylvania Aboli-
       tion Society's Mission," 25.

469   **"like pie-crust, easily broken:** Foner, *Reconstruction,* 590.

469   **In Philadelphia, some . . . to the party:** Lane, *Dorsey's Philadelphia,*
       203–204.

469   **John Mercer Langston . . . Bassett came home:** McFeely, *Frederick*
       Douglass, 335.

469   **Nearly two years after . . . a prison cell:** *INQ,* Feb. 26, 1879.

469–470 **Newspapers said . . . materialized at his side:** *INQ,* Feb. 27, May 20,
       1879.

470   **the front page of the *Washington Post*:** *Washington Post,* Apr. 15, 1879.

470   **a flash of anger on Capitol Hill . . . discussion in regard to my city:**
       Congressional Record, 46th Cong., 1st sess., Apr. 24, 1879, 818–832.

470   **The House Speaker's steady source:** Silcox, *McMullen,* 150–151.

471   **a few days after the jury:** *NYT,* May 24, 1879.

471   **"All things are quiet here:** Silcox, *McMullen,* 88.

EPILOGUE: THE LEGACY

Pages

473–474   **"Influence is the hardest . . . But there remain intriguing:** Eric Foner, e-mail message to authors, May 9, 2009; "subterranean" comment is from the same message.

474   **A founder of the:** For more about Du Bois and NAACP history, see http://www.naacp.org/about/history/index.htm; Lane, *Dorsey's Philadelphia*, 78, 107, 318; Du Bois, *Philadelphia Negro*, 42. Du Bois thanks colored school principals for enrollment figures on 93 and 352.

474   **It was Du Bois:** Du Bois, *Philadelphia Negro*, 39–40.

474   **Du Bois, who died on the eve:** For a biography of Du Bois, see http://www.naacp.org/about/history/dubois/index.htm.

474   **Other founders of the:** For more on Florence Kelley, see Sklar, *Florence Kelley and the Nation's Work*. Letter against lynching on NAACP letterhead with her name and Archibald Grimké's: James Weldon Johnson to Whitefield McKinlay, Mar. [?], 1922, in Woodson Collection, microfilm edition, reel 1.

475   **Jacob White Jr., Catto's lifelong:** *Philadelphia Tribune*, July 14, 1914; Lane, *Dorsey's Philadelphia*, 107, 136, 150.

475   **He was also board chairman:** Lane, *Dorsey's Philadelphia*, 181–182.

475   **Jake White, along with Robert:** Ibid., 317; *Philadelphia Tribune*, Apr. 26, 1913, Nov. 23, 1939.

475   **Adger explained why:** Martin, "Banneker Literary Institute," 303–322.

475   **In addition to influencing:** *Philadelphia Tribune*, Aug. 19, 1837.

475   **White's effort to create:** ANHS; Ball and Martin, *Rare Afro-Americana*, 16; *NYT*, Nov. 12, 1871; Biddle and Dubin, "Forgotten Hero."

476   **Caroline Rebecca Le Count taught:** Coppin, *Reminiscences*, 181; Le Count obituary, *Philadelphia Record*, Jan. 27, 1923.

476   **She was the first black woman:** *Annual Report of the Controllers of the Public Schools . . . 1874*, and reports for the years 1849 (*Thirty-first Annual Report*), 1864 (*Forty-sixth Annual Report*), and 1867 (*Forty-ninth Annual Report*).

476   **When a school board official:** Lane, *Dorsey's Philadelphia*, 155.

476   **In an 1887 speech about:** *CR*, Dec. 22, 1887.

476   **In addition to her renown:** Lane, *Dorsey's Philadelphia*, 25, 312; Lawrence and Dickerson interviews.

477   **She gave a talk:** Bolivar, Pencil Pusher Points, *Philadelphia Tribune*, Apr. 26, 1913.

477   **In 1899, she celebrated:** *Philadelphia Tribune*, Feb. 18, 1899.

477   **In 1909, Booker T. Washington:** Washington, *Story of the Negro*, 306.

477   **On September 13, 2003:** Dickerson interview.

477   **Her friend Caroline died in 1923:** Caroline Le Count obituary, *Philadelphia Record*, Jan. 27, 1923. Estimate of how many students taught is based on school board annual reports spanning two centuries and more than five decades, and calculations of student numbers by Du Bois in *Philadelphia Negro*, 352–353. Authors' visit to Eden Cemetery, Philadelphia, PA, 2003, noted the names.

478   **But there was a time in Philadelphia:** *Philadelphia Tribune*, Nov. 23, 1939.

478   **Nothing epitomized those aspirations:** Ullman, *Delany,* 412–413; Lane, *Dorsey's Philadelphia,* xiii; Lane and Silcox interviews. For schools in the North, see Ballard, *One More Day's Journey,* 57–58.

478   **Other I.C.Y. alumni became:** Julian Francis Abele: for more on Abele and his history in Philadelphia, see Free Library of Philadelphia, "Julian F. Abele, Architect"; Sarah Iredell and nursing: Coppin, *Reminiscences,* 147; Theophilus J. Minton, Dr. Nathan Mossell, and medicine: Lane, *Dorsey's Philadelphia,* 44–45, 174–183.

478   **Consider this story:** Barrows, *Mohonk Conference,* 56.

479   **He was a student of Catto's:** Cashin, *Agitator's Daughter,* 10, 14–15, 26, 29, 31, 33–35, 40, 43–44, 203.

479   **In 1881, she married:** Coppin, *Reminiscences,* 122; Perkins, *Fanny Jackson Coppin,* 7–8.

479   **Coppin resigned from the:** Lane, *Dorsey's Philadelphia,* 141–142, 161–162; Jordan, *History of Delaware County,* 470–472. Washington on I.C.Y. advisory board: see Harris and Molesworth, *Alain L. Locke,* 8.

479   **About that time, the school moved:** Jordan, *History of Delaware County,* 470–472. Renaming of school: see Edmunds, *Public School Buildings of the City of Philadelphia.*

480   **Coppin died in:** Dunster, *Crusade for Justice,* 58–62; Yellin, *Harriet Jacobs,* 256; Lane, *Dorsey's Philadelphia,* 162.

480   **Veterans of earlier fights . . . Wells wrote:** Dunster, *Crusade for Justice,* 78–85.

480–481   **Ebenezer Bassett began another . . . get out of here:** Wynes, "Ebenezer Don Carlos Bassett," 232–240; McFeely, *Frederick Douglass,* 334–352; Washington Papers, 4:269, 291; BAP, 3:336–337.

481   **Douglass lived . . . women's rights convention:** McFeely, *Frederick Douglass,* 381.

481   **He gave a friend, Susan B. Anthony:** Powell interview.

481   **She told of Bassett . . . persuasive power":** Coppin, *Reminiscences,* esp. 21, 139–143.

481   **William McMullen's obituary:** *PP* and *North American* obituaries, Apr. 1, 1901.

481   **His operative Frank Kelly:** Wright, *Bossism in Cincinnati,* 8.

481   **By 1912, Boss Cox was:** Turner, "Thing Above the Law."

482   **After 1871, at least:** Lane, *Dorsey's Philadelphia,* 83, 200.

482   **But day-to-day prejudice:** Lane, *Roots of Violence,* 39; black diners: Lane, *Dorsey's Philadelphia,* 191–192.

482   **The Civil Rights Act of 1875:** Lane, *Roots of Violence,* 54–55.

482   **But some legacies:** Still, *Brief Narrative,* 1.

482   **Alain Locke, born in:** "Black History and Culture," 51; Washington Papers, 7:69n3.

483   **Another notable grandson link:** Guide to the Wormley Family Papers.

483   **Howard, a college "born in the great rush:** Boyle, *Arc of Justice,* 90.

484   **The scholarships:** Yellin, *Harriet Jacobs,* 234–237; Winch, *Gentleman of Color,* 347–350.

484   **Charlotte Forten's legacy:** Bacon, "Pennsylvania Abolition Society's Mission," 25.

484   **But this switch from a:** Bolivar, Pencil Pusher Points, *Philadelphia Tribune,* June 27, 1914; Lawrence interview, 2003.

484 **A memorial to Catto was:** The authors attended the unveiling of the memorial; see Lane, *Dorsey's Philadelphia*, 109.

485 **In 1996, two weeks before:** Hillary Clinton announcement on Oct. 22 that Tanner landscape will be hung in the White House; *Jet Magazine*, Nov. 18, 1996.

485 **In 1999, the state of:** *Washington Post*, Nov. 3, 1998; *NYT*, June 3, 1999.

485 **Retiree Edgar Catto:** Montgomery interview.

485 **Catto's great-grandnephew:** Smith interviews, e-mail messages, 2003–2009.

★ BIBLIOGRAPHY ★

Accessible Archives. Online database of nineteenth-century newspapers. http://www.accessible.com/accessible/.

Address of John G. Watmough, High Sheriff, to His Constituents, in Reference to the Disturbances Which Took Place in the City and County of Philadelphia, During the Summer of 1838. [Philadelphia]: C. Alexander, Printer, 1838. Available at www.loc.gov/.

Address of the Eastern Executive Committee of the State Anti-Slavery Society to the Citizens of Pennsylvania. Philadelphia: Merrihew & Gunn, 1838. Samuel J. May Anti-Slavery Collection. Division of Rare and Manuscript Collections. Cornell University Library, Ithaca, NY. Available at http://digital.library.cornell.edu/m/mayantislavery/.

Adeleke, Tunde. *Without Regard to Race: The Other Martin Robison Delany.* Jackson: University Press of Mississippi, 2003.

Adger, John B. *My Life and Times, 1810–1899.* Philadelphia: Presbyterian Historical Society, 1899.

African Episcopal Church of St. Thomas, Philadelphia, PA. Vestry minutes, 1866–1871.

Albertson, Karla Klein. "The Cadwalader Family: Art and Style in Early Philadelphia." *Antiques and the Arts Online,* 1996. http://antiquesandthearts.com/archive/cadwal.htm.

Alotta, Robert I. *Mermaids, Monasteries, Cherokees, and Custer.* Chicago: Bonus Books, 1990.

Alvord, John W. *Letters from the South, Relating to the Condition of Freedmen, addressed to Major General O. O. Howard.* Washington, DC: Howard University Press, 1870.

American Annual Cyclopedia and Register of Important Events of the Year 1869. New York: D. Appleton, 1870.

American Antiquarian Society. "Freedmen's Teachers." *Northern Visions of Race, Region, and Reform.* American Antiquarian Society Online Resource. Available at http://mac110.assumption.edu/aas/intros/freedteachers.html.

American Periodical Series Online, 1740–1900. ProQuest Information and Learning Company Ann Arbor, MI. http://www.proquest.com/en-US/.

An American Time Capsule: Three Centuries of Broadsides and Other Printed Ephemera. LOC.

Ames, Mary Lesley, ed. *Life and Letters of Peter and Susan Lesley.* New York: G. P. Putnam's Sons, 1909.

Anderson, Jean Bradley, with Historic Preservation Society of Durham. *Durham County: A History of Durham County, North Carolina.* Durham: Duke University Press, 1990.

Andrews, Alfred. *Memorial: Genealogy, and Ecclesiastical History.* Chicago, 1867.

Angle, Paul, M., ed. *The Complete Lincoln-Douglas Debates of 1858.* Chicago: University of Chicago Press, 1991.

Annual Meeting of the American Institute of Instruction. Boston: Committee of Publication, 1866.

Annual Report of the Controllers of the Public Schools of the City and County of Philadelphia . . . for the Year Ending June 30, 1874. Philadelphia: Controllers of the Public Schools, 1875.

The Anti-Slavery History of the John Brown Year; Being the 27th Annual Report of the American Anti-Slavery Society. 1861. Reprint, New York: Negro Universities Press, 1969.

Appiah, Kwame Anthony, and Henry Louis Gates Jr., eds. *Africana: The Encyclopedia of the African and African American Experience.* New York: Basic Civitas Books, 1999.

Applegate, Lloyd R. *A Life of Service: William Augustus Newell.* Toms River, NJ: Ocean County Historical Society, 1994.

Aptheker, Herbert, ed. *The Correspondence of W. E. B. Du Bois.* 3 vols. Amherst: University of Massachusetts Press, 1973–1978.

Aristotle. *Politics.* Translated by H. Rackham. Bk. 7. Cambridge, MA: Harvard University Press, 1959.

Armistead, Wilson. *A Tribute for the Negro: Being a Vindication of the Moral, Intellectual, and Religious Capabilities of the Coloured Portion of Mankind.* London: W. Irwin, 1848.

Armistead, Wilson, and F. G. Gash. *The Garland of Freedom; A Collection of Poems, Chiefly Anti-Slavery.* London, 1853.

Armstrong, William G. Diaries, 1866–1888. HSP.

Asher, Jeremiah. *An Autobiography, with Details of a Visit to England, and Some Account of the History of the Meeting Street Baptist Church, Providence R.I., and of the Shiloh Baptist Church, Philadelphia, Pa.* Philadelphia: Jeremiah Asher, 1862.

Aubrecht, Michael. "Civil War Baseball: Baseball and the Blue and the Gray." *Baseball Almanac,* 2004. http://www.impactprospects.com/bghistory.htm.

Auge, Moses. *Lives of the Eminent Dead: And Biographical Notices of Prominent Living Citizens of Montgomery County, Pa.* Norristown, PA: privately printed, 1879.

Austin, James Trecothick. *Review of the Rev. Dr. Channing's Letter to Jonathan Phillips esq.* Boston: J. H. Eastburn, printer, 1839.

Bacon, Margaret Hope. *But One Race: The Life of Robert Purvis.* Albany: State University of New York Press, 2007.

———. "'One Great Bundle of Humanity': Frances Ellen Watkins Harper (1825–1911)." *PMHB* 113 (Jan. 1989): 21–43.

———. "The Pennsylvania Abolition Society's Mission for Black Education." *Pennsylvania Legacies* (HSP) 6 (Nov. 2005): 21–49.

———. *Valiant Friend: The Life of Lucretia Mott.* New York: Walker, 1980.

Baker, Jean H. *James Buchanan.* American Presidents, Times Books. New York: Henry Holt, 2004.

Ball, Wendy, and Tony Martin. *Rare Afro-Americana: A Reconstruction of the Adger Library*. Boston: G. K. Hall, 1981.

Ballard, Allen B. *One More Day's Journey*. New York: McGraw Hill, 1984.

Baltzell, E. Digby. *Puritan Boston and Quaker Philadelphia*. New York: Free Press, 1979.

Barker, Abraham, Papers, Camp William Penn, 1863. HSP.

Barnard, Henry. *Special Report of the Commissioner of Education on the Condition and Improvement of Public Schools in the District of Columbia*. Washington, DC: Government Printing Office, 1871.

Barnes, Gilbert H., and Dwight L. Dumond, eds. *Letters of Theodore Dwight Weld, Angelina Grimké Weld, and Sarah Grimké, 1822–1844*. Gloucester, MA: American Historical Association, 1934.

Barrows, Isabel C. *Mohonk Conference on the Negro Question*. Boston: G. H. Ellis, 1890–1891.

Bartlett, David W. *Cases of Contested Elections in Congress, from 1834 to 1865*. Washington, DC: Government. Printing Office, 1865.

Baseball Almanac. Online compendium of baseball history, with information from nineteenth-century baseball jargon to the game during the Civil War. http://www.baseball-almanac.com/.

Bateman, Newton. *Sixth Biennial Report of the Superintendent of Public Instruction*. Reports made to the General Assembly of Illinois, 25th sess. Dec. 1866, vol. 2. Springfield, IL: Baker, Bailhache, 1867.

Beecher, Catherine E. *Treatise on Domestic Economy for the Use of Young Ladies at Home and at School*. New York: Harper & Brothers, 1852.

Beers, Dorothy Gondos. "The Centennial City, 1865–1876." In *Philadelphia: A Three-Hundred-Year History*, edited by Russell F. Weigley, 417–470. New York: Norton, 1982.

Bell, Howard H., ed. *Proceedings of the National Negro Conventions, 1830–1864*. New York: Arno Press, 1969.

Bell, Malcolm Jr. *Major Butler's Legacy: Five Generations of a Slaveholding Family*. Athens: University of Georgia Press, 1987.

Bergland, Renee. *Maria Mitchell and the Sexing of Science: An Astronomer Among the American Romantics*. Boston: Beacon Press, 2008.

"Berkeley the Philosopher." In *The Great Irish Famine*. Irish Famine Curriculum by the New Jersey Commission on Holocaust Education. http://www.nde.state.ne.us/ss/irish/irish_pf.html.

Berry, Faith. *Langston Hughes: Before and Beyond Harlem*. Secaucus, NJ: Citadel Press, 1992.

Berry, Stephen R. "William Catto's Pursuit of God's Calling in Slaveholding America." *Journal of Presbyterian History*, Spring–Summer, 2005, 41–53.

Bethel, Elizabeth Rauh. *The Roots of African-American Identity: Memory and History in Antebellum Free Communities*. New York: Palgrave-Macmillan, 1999.

Biddle, Daniel R., and Murray Dubin. "The Forgotten Hero." *Inquirer Sunday Magazine*, July 6, 2003.

Billingsley, Andrew. *Yearning to Breathe Free: Robert Smalls of South Carolina and His Families*. Columbia: University of South Carolina Press, 2007.

Birney, Catherine H. *The Grimké Sisters, Sarah and Angelina Grimké: The First American Women Advocates of Abolition and Woman's Rights*. Boston: Lee & Shepard, 1885.

Birney, James G. *The American Churches, the Bulwarks of American Slavery, by an American*. Concord, N.H.: Parker Pillsbury, 1885.

Birnie, C. W. "Education of the Negro in Charleston, S.C., Prior to the Civil War." *Journal of Negro History* 12 (Jan. 1927): 13–21.

Blackett, R.J.M. *Beating Against the Barriers: Biographical Essays in Nineteenth-Century Afro-American History.* Baton Rouge: Louisiana State University Press, 1986.

———. *Building an Antislavery Wall: Black Americans in the Atlantic Abolitionist Movement, 1830–1860.* Baton Rouge: Louisiana State University Press, 1983.

———. "Martin R. Delany and Robert Campbell: Black Americans in Search of an African Colony." *Journal of Negro History* 62 (Jan. 1977): 1–25.

"Black History and Culture." Special issue, *Pennsylvania Heritage* (Pennsylvania Historical and Museum Commission) 4, no. 1 (Dec. 1977).

Blankenburg, Rudolph. "Forty Years in the Wilderness." In *The Arena,* edited by B. O. Flower, 7–8. Trenton, NJ: Albert Brandt, 1905.

Blassingame, John W. *Slave Testimony: Two Centuries of Letters, Speeches, Interviews, and Autobiographies.* Baton Rouge: Louisiana State University Press, 1977.

———, ed. *The Frederick Douglass Papers.* Series 1, Speeches, Debates, and Interviews. Vol. 2, *1847–54.* New Haven, CT: Yale University Press, 1982.

Blight, David W. *Frederick Douglass' Civil War: Keeping Faith in Jubilee.* Baton Rouge: Louisiana State University Press, 1989.

———. *Race and Reunion: The Civil War in American Memory.* Cambridge, MA: Harvard University Press, Belknap Press, 2001.

Block, David. *Baseball Before We Knew It.* Lincoln: University of Nebraska Press, 2005.

Blockson, Charles, historian. Interview with authors, Dec. 2003.

Blockson, Charles L. *African Americans in Pennsylvania Above Ground and Underground: An Illustrated Guide.* Harrisburg, PA: RB Books, 2001.

Board of Foreign Missions. Presbyterian Church in the U.S.A. Correspondence: Africa. Incoming letters, 1844–1847 and 1847–1853. Presbyterian Historical Society, Philadelphia, PA.

———. Minutes, 1837–1890. Microfilm. Presbyterian Historical Society, Philadelphia, PA.

Bolton, Sarah K. *Lives of Girls Who Became Famous.* New York: Thomas Y. Crowell, 1914. Project Gutenberg, 2004. http://www.gutenberg.org/files/12081/12081-h/12081-h.htm.

The Booker T. Washington Papers. Urbana: University of Illinois Press, 2000. http://www.historycooperative.org/btw/.

Bordewich, Fergus. *Bound for Canaan: The Underground Railroad and the War for the Soul of America.* New York: HarperCollins, 2005.

Boston, Rob. "Bible Riots: When Christians Killed Each Other Over Religion in Public Schools." *Liberty, a Magazine for Religious Liberty,* May–June 1997. http://www.libertymagazine.org/index.php?id=1581.

Bowen, Daniel. *A History of Philadelphia with a Notice of the Villages in the Vicinity.* Philadelphia: privately printed, 1839.

Bowman, John S., ed. *The Civil War Almanac.* New York: World Almanac Publications, Bison Books, 1983.

Boyd, Andrew. *Boyd's Business Directory of over 100 Cities and Villages in New York State.* Albany: Chas van Benthuysen & Sons, 1869. Cornell University Library, Making of America. http://dlxs2.library.cornell.edu/m/moa/help.html.

Boyer, Arthur Truman. *Brief Historic Sketch of the First African Presbyterian Church of Philadelphia, Pa; Along With Rev. Wm. Catto's History and Discourse from 1807 to 1940.* Philadelphia: privately printed, 1944.

Boyle, Kevin. *Arc of Justice: A Saga of Race, Civil Rights, and Murder in the Jazz Age.* New York: Henry Holt, 2004

Bragg, George F. Jr. *History of the Afro-American Group of the Episcopal Church*. Baltimore: Church Advocate Press, 1922. http://docsouth.unc.edu/church/ragg/bragg.html.

Brainerd, Mary. *Life of Rev. Thomas Brainerd D.D.* Philadelphia: J. B. Lippincott, 1870.

Braithwaite, J. Bevan, ed. *Memoirs of Joseph John Gurney, with Selections from His Journal and Correspondence, Part 2*. Philadelphia: Book Association of Friends, 1854.

Branch, Taylor. *At Canaan's Edge: America in the King Years 1965–68*. New York: Simon & Schuster, 2006.

———. *Parting the Waters: America in the King Years, 1954–63*. New York: Simon & Schuster, 1988.

Brawley, Benjamin G. *Early Negro American Writers: Selections. . . .* Chapel Hill: University of North Carolina Press, 1935. Reprint, Salem, NH: Ayer, 1968.

Bremer, Frederika. *Homes of the New World*. New York: Harper Brothers, 1853.

Bronner, Edwin B. "Village into Town, 1741–1746." In *Philadelphia: A Three-Hundred-Year History*, edited by Russell F. Weigley, 33–67. New York: Norton, 1982.

Brooks, Charles H. *The Official History and Manual of the Grand United Order of Odd Fellows in America*. Philadelphia: Odd Fellows Journal Print, 1902.

Brooks, James J. *Whiskey Drips: A Series of Interesting Sketches*. Philadelphia: William B. Evans, 1873.

Brotz, Howard, ed. *Negro Social and Political Thought, 1850–1920*. New York: Basic Books, 1966.

Brown, David Paul. *The Forum; or, Forty Years Full Practice at the Philadelphia Bar*. Philadelphia: R. H. Small, 1856.

Brown, Elsa Barkley. "Negotiating and Transforming the Public Sphere: African American Political Life in the Transition from Slavery to Freedom." *Public Culture* 7 (Feb. 1994).

Brown, Henry. *Narrative of the Life of Henry Box Brown, Written by Himself*. Manchester: Lee & Glynn, 1851.

Brown, Ira V. *Mary Grew: Abolitionist and Feminist, 1813–1896*. Cranbury, NJ: Associated University Presses, 1991.

———. "Pennsylvania and the Rights of the Negro, 1865–1887." *Pennsylvania History: A Journal of Mid-Atlantic Studies* 28 (Jan. 1961): 46–57.

———. *Proclaim Liberty! Antislavery and Civil Rights in Pennsylvania, 1688–1887*. University Park, PA: privately printed, 2000.

Brown, John, Collection. No. 299, box 1, folder 32. Kansas State Historical Society, Topeka. http://www.territorialkansasonline.org/.

Brown, John K. *The Baldwin Locomotive Works, 1831–1915: A Study in American Industrial Practice*. Baltimore: Johns Hopkins University Press, 1995.

Brown, Letitia W., and Elsie M. Lewis. *Washington from Banneker to Douglass, 1791–1870*. Washington, DC: Education Department, National Portrait Gallery, 1971.

Brown, Lloyd L. *The Young Paul Robeson: On My Journey Now*. Boulder, CO: Westview Press, 1997.

Brown, Randall. "Blood and Base Ball." *Base Ball: A Journal of the Early Game*. 3 (Spring 2009).

Brown, William Wells. *The American Fugitive in Europe: Sketches of Places and People Abroad*. Boston, MA: John P. Jewett, 1855.

———. *The Anti-Slavery Harp: Collection of Songs for Anti-Slavery Meetings*. 2nd edition. Boston: Bela Marsh, 1849.

———. *The Black Man: His Antecedents, His Genius, and His Achievements*. 1863. New York: Cosimo, 2007.

————. *The Rising Son; or, The Antecedents and Advancement of the Colored Race.* Boston: A. G. Brown, 1874.

Bruce, Marcus. *Henry Ossawa Tanner: A Spiritual Biography.* New York: Crossroad, 2002.

Bruno, Alison, Adger family descendant. Interview with authors, 2003.

Bryan, Wilhelmus. *A History of the National Capital from Its Foundation Through the Period of the Adoption of the Organic Act.* Vol. 2. New York: Macmillan, 1916.

Buck, Christopher. *Alain Locke: Faith and Philosophy.* Los Angeles: Kalimat Press, 2005.

Burkett, Randall, historian. E-mail interview with authors, 2004.

Burns, Stewart, ed. *Daybreak of Freedom: The Montgomery Bus Boycott.* Chapel Hill: University of North Carolina Press, 1997.

Burton, E. Milby. *The Siege of Charleston, 1861–1865.* Columbia: University of South Carolina Press, 1982.

Burton, Orville Vernon. "Race and Reconstruction: Edgefield County, S.C." In *The Politics of Freedom, African Americans and the Political Process During Reconstruction.* Vol. 5 of *African American Life in the Post Emancipation South, 1861–1900,* edited by Donald G. Nieman. New York: Garland, 1994.

Bush, Lester E. Jr. "Mormonism's Negro Doctrine: An Historical Overview." In *Neither White nor Black: Mormon Scholars Confront the Race Issue in a Universal Church,* edited by Lester E. Bush Jr. and Armand L. Mauss, 11–68. Midvale, UT: Signature Books, 1984.

Butler, Diana Hochstedt. *Standing Against the Whirlwind: Evangelical Episcopalians in Nineteenth-Century America.* New York: Oxford University Press, 1995.

Cadwalader, John Jr. *Cadwalader's Cases: Being Decisions of the Hon. John Cadwalader . . . , 1858–1879.* Vol. 1. Philadelphia: Rees Welsh, 1907.

Calderhead, William L. "Philadelphia in Crisis: June–July, 1863." *Pennsylvania History: A Journal of Mid-Atlantic Studies* 28 (Apr. 1961): 142–155.

Calhoun, John C. *The Papers of John C. Calhoun: Dec. 7, 1846–Dec. 5, 1847.* Edited by Robert Meriwether, Robert, Clyde N. Wilson, and Shirley B. Cook. Columbia: University of South Carolina Press, 1998.

Campbell, Israel. *An Autobiography: Bond and Free; or, Yearnings for Freedom. . . .* Philadelphia: privately printed, 1861. Available at www.docsouth.unc.edu/.

Campbell, James T. *Songs of Zion: The African Methodist Episcopal Church in the United States and South Africa.* Chapel Hill: University of North Carolina Press, 1998.

Campbell, Penelope. *Maryland in Africa: The Maryland State Colonization Society, 1831–1857.* Urbana: University of Illinois Press, 1971.

Campbell, Robert. *A Pilgrimage to My Motherland: An Account of a Journey Among the Egbas.* New York: Thomas Hamilton, 1860.

Capers, William. *Catechism for the Use of Methodist Missions. First Part.* 3rd edition. Charleston, SC: John Early, 1853. E-Edtn: University of North Carolina at Chapel Hill. http://docsouth.unc.edu/church/capers/menu.html.

Carus, William, ed. *Memorials of the Right Reverend Charles Pettit McIlvaine, Bishop of Ohio.* New York: Thomas Whittaker, 1882.

Cary, Edward. *George William Curtis.* Boston: Houghton Mifflin, 1894.

Cashin, Sheryll. *The Agitator's Daughter: A Memoir of Four Generations of One Extraordinary African-American Family.* New York: PublicAffairs, 2008.

Casway, Jerrold. "Octavius Catto and the Pythians of Philadelphia." *Pennsylvania Legacies* (HSP) 7 (May 2007): 5–9.

Catto, Octavius V. *Our Alma Mater: An Address Delivered at Concert Hall on the Occasion of the Twelfth Annual Commencement of the Institute for Colored Youth, May 10th, 1864.* Philadelphia: C. Sherman, Son, 1864.

Catto, William T. *A Semi-Centenary Discourse Delivered in The First African Presbyterian Church, Philadelphia, on the Fourth Sabbath of May, 1857: with A History of the Church from its First Organization: including A Brief Notice of Rev. John Gloucester, Its First Pastor. Also, An Appendix, Containing Sketches of All The Colored Churches in Philadelphia.* Philadelphia: Joseph M. Wilson, 1857.

Catto, William and Octavius. Misc. Papers. ANHS, box 3A, folder 5.

Cayley, David. *The Expanding Prison: The Crisis in Crime and Punishment and the Search for Alternatives.* Toronto: House of Anansi Press, 1998.

Celebration in Honor of the Ratification of the Fifteenth Constitutional Amendment, on Tuesday, April 26th, 1870, in Philadelphia. The Committee of Arrangements, Joseph C. Bustill, Chairman. N.p., n.d.

The Celebration of the Eighty-third Anniversary of the Declaration of American Independence, by the Banneker Institute, Philadelphia, July 4th, 1859. Philadelphia: W. S. Young, Printer, 1859. Daniel A. P. Murray Collection, LOC. Available at http://memory.loc.gov/ammem/murrayquery.html.

Centennial Exhibition. Philadelphia 1976. Free Library of Philadelphia. http://libwww.library.phila.gov/cencol/.

A centennial fourth of July Democratic celebration. The massacre of six colored citizens of the United States at Hamburgh, SC, July 4, 1876. Debate on the Hamburgh massacre, in the U.S. House of Reps, July 15th and 18th, 1876. From Slavery to Freedom, African-American Pamphlet Collection, 1822–1909, LOC. Available at http://memory.loc.gov/ammem/aapchtml/aapchome.html.

Chambers, William. *American Slavery and Colour.* London: W & R Chambers, 1857.

Channing, William Ellery. "Remarks on the Slavery Question in a letter to Jonathan Philips, Esq." Boston, 1839. Samuel J. May Anti-Slavery Collection. Division of Rare and Manuscript Collections. Cornell University Library, Ithaca, NY. Available at http://digital.library.cornell.edu/m/mayantislavery/.

The Charleston (SC) Directory, 1801–1825. CCPL.

Charleston Presbytery. Presbyterian Church (U.S.A.). Minutes, 1839–1861. Microfilm. Presbyterian Historical Society, Philadelphia, PA.

Charleston Union Presbytery. Presbyterian Church (U.S.A.). Minutes, 1823–1839. Microfilm. Presbyterian Historical Society, Philadelphia, PA.

Cheek, William, and Aimee Lee Cheek. "John Mercer Langston: Principle and Politics." In *Black Leaders of the Nineteenth Century,* edited by Leon F. Litwack and August Meier, 103–126.Urbana: University of Illinois Press, 1991.

———. *John Mercer Langston and the Fight for Black Freedom, 1829–65.* Urbana: University of Illinois Press, 1996.

Cimbala, Paul Alan, and Randall M. Miller, eds. *The Freedmen's Bureau and Reconstruction: Reconsiderations.* New York: Fordham University Press, 1999.

Cimprich, John. *Fort Pillow: A Civil War Massacre and a Public Memory.* Baton Rouge: Louisiana State University Press, 2005.

City of Charleston health records.1800–1840. CCPL.

Clark, Dennis. *Erin's Heirs: Irish Bonds of Community.* Lexington: University Press of Kentucky, 1991.

Clarke, Erskine. *Dwelling Place: A Plantation Epic.* New Haven, CT: Yale University Press, 2005.

———. *Wrestlin' Jacob: A Portrait of Religion in the Old South.* Atlanta, GA: John Knox Press, 1999.

Cohen, Charles J. *Rittenhouse Square, Past and Present.* Philadelphia: Charles Cohen, 1922.

Constitution and By Laws of the Friendly Union Society. Friendly Union Society Papers. Avery Research Center for African American History and Culture. College of Charleston, Charleston, SC.

Contributions to the Ecclesiastical History of Connecticut. New Haven, CT: William L. Kingsley, 1861.

Conway, Thomas W., General Superintendent of Freedmen. *Final Report of the Bureau of Free Labor, Department of the Gulf, to Maj. Gen. E.R.S. Canby*. New Orleans: New Orleans Times Book and Job Office, 1865.

Cooper, Thomas, ed. *The Statutes at Large of South Carolina*. 7 vols. Columbia, SC: A. S. Johnston, 1837–1840.

Cope, Thomas Pym and Elizabeth Cope Harrison. *Philadelphia Merchant: The Diary of Thomas P. Cope, 1800–1851*. South Bend, IN: Gateway Editions, 1978.

Coppin, Fanny Jackson. *Reminiscences of School Life, and Hints on Teaching*. Philadelphia: A.M.E. Book Concern, 1913.

Coppin, Levi Jenkins. *Unwritten History*. Philadelphia: A.M.E. Book Concern, 1919.

Cornelius, Janet Duitsman. *Slave Missions and the Black Church in the Antebellum South*. Columbia: University of South Carolina, 1999.

Cromwell, Adelaide M. *Unveiled Voices, Unvarnished Memories: The Cromwell Family in Slavery and Segregation, 1692–1972*. Columbia: University of Missouri Press, 2006.

Cromwell, John Wesley. *The Negro in American History: Men and Women Eminent in the Evolution of the American of African Descent*. Washington: The American Negro Academy, 1914.

Crouch, Barry A. *The Freedmen's Bureau and Black Texans*. Austin: University of Texas Press, 1999.

Crouch, Stanley, and Playthell Benjamin. *Reconsidering the Souls of Black Folk: Thoughts on the Groundbreaking Classic Work of W.E.B. Du Bois*. Philadelphia: Running Press, 2003.

Crummell, Alexander. *Africa and America: Addresses and Discourses*. Springfield, MA: Willey, 1891.

Curtis, James C., Lewis L. Gould, eds. *The Black Experience in America*. Austin: University of Texas Press, 1970.

Custis, John Trevor. *The Public Schools of Philadelphia: Historical, Biographical, Statistical*. Philadelphia: Burke & McFetridge, 1897.

Davis, Allen F., and Mark H. Haller, eds. *The Peoples of Philadelphia: A History of Ethnic Groups and Lower-Class Life, 1790–1940*. Philadelphia: Temple University Press, 1973.

Davis, Burke. *The Civil War: Strange and Fascinating Facts*. New York: Random House, Wing Books, 1960.

Davis, Emilie. Diary, 1863–1865. Collection 3030. HSP.

Davis, Hugh. "The Pennsylvania State Equal Rights League and the Northern Struggle for Legal Equality, 1864–1877." *PMHB* 126 (Oct. 2002): 611–634.

Davis, Susan G. *Parades and Power: Street Theater in Nineteenth-Century Philadelphia*. Berkeley and Los Angeles: University of California Press, 1986.

Delany, Martin R. *Blake; or, The Huts of America*. Edited by Floyd J. Miller. Boston: Beacon Press, 1970.

———. *The Condition, Elevation, Emigration and Destiny of the Colored People of the United States Politically Considered*. Philadelphia, 1852. Reprint, New York: Arno Press, 1968.

Dennett, Tyler, ed. *Lincoln and the Civil War in the Diaries and Letters of John Hay*. New York: Da Capo Press, 1988.

Densmore, Christopher, archivist. Interview with authors, various dates, 2003–2009.

"Deposition of Charles T. Butler and other witnesses in the Matter of Moses Honner [*sic*], Fugitive Slave," Mar, 23, 1860. Records of District Courts of the United States, 1685–2004. National Archives and Records Administration. Available at http://www.archives.gov/education/lessons/fugitive-cases/.

Desjardin, Thomas A. *These Honored Dead: How the Story of Gettysburg Shaped American Memory*. Cambridge, MA: Da Capo Press, 2003.

Dickerson, Lillie. Interview with authors, Sept. 2003.

Dixon, Mark E. "Mary Miles' Long Ride."*Main Line Today* [Newtown Square, PA], June 6, 2007.

Donald, David H. "Why They Impeached Andrew Johnson." *American Heritage Magazine* 8 (Dec. 1956). Available at americanheritage.com.

Dorsey, Bruce, "A Gendered History of African Colonization in the Antebellum United States." *Journal of Social History* 34 (Fall 2000): 77–103.

——. *Reforming Men and Women: Gender in the Antebellum City*. Ithaca, NY: Cornell University Press, 2006.

Douglass, Frederick. *The Life and Times of Frederick Douglass, Written by Himself.* 1892. Reprint with introduction by Rayford W. Logan. London: Collier-Macmillan, 1962.

——. *My Bondage and My Freedom*. New York: Miller, Orton, 1855.

——. *Narrative of the Life of Frederick Douglass, an American Slave: Written by Himself.* Edited by John W. Blassingame, John R. McKivigan, and Peter P. Hinks. 1845. Reprint, with introduction by Benjamin Quarles, Cambridge, MA: Harvard University Press, 1988.

Douglass, Frederick, Papers. American Memory, Manuscript Division, LOC. http://memory.loc.gov/ammem/doughtml/.

Douglass, Rev. William. *Annals of the First African Church*. Philadelphia: King & Baird Printers, 1862.

Douty, Esther M. *Forten the Sailmaker: Champion of Negro Rights*. Chicago: Rand McNally, 1969.

Drago, Edmund L. *Initiatives, Paternalism, and Race Relations*. Athens: University of Georgia Press, 1990.

Dubin, Murray. *South Philadelphia: Mummers, Memories, and the Melrose Diner*. Philadelphia: Temple University Press, 1996.

Du Bois, W.E.B. *Black Reconstruction in America*. 1935. New York: Atheneum, 1972.

——. *John Brown, a Biography*. 1909. Armonk: M. E. Sharpe, 1997.

——. *The Philadelphia Negro*. 1899. Philadelphia: University of Pennsylvania Press, 1996.

Dudgeon, Ralph T. *The Keyed Bugle*. 2nd edition. Lanham, MD: Scarecrow Press, 2004.

Dunbar-Nelson, Alice Moore, ed. *Masterpieces of Negro Eloquence*. New York: Bookery Publishing, 1914.

Dunster, Alfreda M., ed. *Crusade for Justice: The Autobiography of Ida B. Wells*. Chicago: University of Chicago Press, 1970.

Dusinberre, William. *Civil War Issues in Philadelphia, 1856–1865*. Philadelphia: University of Pennsylvania Press, 1965.

——. *Them Dark Days: Slavery in the American Rice Swamps*. Athens: University of Georgia Press, 2000.

Easterby, J. H., ed. *The South Carolina Rice Plantation: As Revealed in the Papers of Robert F. W. Allston*. Columbia: University of South Carolina Press, 2004.

Eaton, Clement. "Censorship of the Southern Mails." *American Historical Review* 48, no. 2 (Jan. 1943): 266–280.

Edmunds, Franklin D. *The Public School Buildings of the City of Philadelphia.* Philadelphia: Board of Public Education, School District of Philadelphia, 1917.

Egerton, Douglas R. *He Shall Go Out Free: The Lives of Denmark Vesey.* Lanham, MD: Rowman & Littlefield, 2004.

Eggert, Gerald G. *Harrisburg Industrializes: The Coming of Factories to an American Community.* University Park: Penn State University Press, 1993.

Encyclopaedia of Contemporary Biography of Penna. Vol. 2. New York: Atlantic Publishing and Engraving, 1889.

Evans, William. "Nineteenth Annual Report of the Board of Managers of the Institute for Colored Youth." *The Friend; a Religious and Literary Journal,* May 1871, 101–102.

Evidence Taken by the Committee of Investigation of the Third Congressional District, under Authority of the General Assembly of the state of South Carolina. Columbia: J. W. Denny, 1870.

Exposition of the Causes and Character of the Difficulties in the Church in Charleston in the Year 1833. Charleston, SC: E. J. Brunt, 1833.

Exposition of the Causes and Character of the Difficulties in the Church in Charleston in the Year 1834. Charleston, SC: E. J. Brunt, 1834.

Faehtz, Ernest F. M. *The National Memorial Day: A Record of Ceremonies over the Graves of the Union Soldiers, May 29 and 30, 1869.* Washington, DC: Grand Army of the Republic, 1870.

Farr, James. "A Slow Boat to Nowhere: The Multi-Racial Crews of the American Whaling Industry." *Journal of Negro History* 68 (Spring 1983): 159–170.

Feeney, Ryan. "The Power of One: Thomas Fitzgerald and the Origin of Interracial Baseball." Race and Sports class paper. Princeton University, 2001. Baseball Hall of Fame library, Cooperstown, NY.

Fehrenbacher, Don E., ed. *Lincoln: Speeches and Writings, 1859–1865.* New York: Library of America, 1989.

Feldberg, Michael. *The Philadelphia Riots of 1844: A Study of Ethnic Conflict.* Contributions in American History. Westport, CT: Greenwood Press, 1975.

———. *The Turbulent Era: Riot and Disorder in Jacksonian America.* New York: Oxford University Press, 1980.

Ferris, William H. *Alexander Crummell: An Apostle of Negro Culture.* American Negro Academy Occasional Papers, no. 20. Washington, DC: American Negro Academy, 1920. Reprint: Salem, NH: Ayer, 1970.

Fields, Barbara Jeanne. *Slavery and Freedom on the Middle Ground: Maryland During the Nineteenth Century.* New Haven, CT: Yale University Press, 1985.

Fifteenth Report of the Maryland State Colonization Society. Baltimore, 1847.

Fifty Years with Passenger Railways of Philadelphia. Philadelphia: New York News Bureau, Philadelphia Local Service, 1904.

Fifty-third Annual Report of the Board of Public Education of the First School District of Pennsylvania . . . for the Year Ending December 31, 1871. Philadelphia: Board of Public Education, 1872.

Finkel, Kenneth, ed. *Legacy in Light: Photographic Treasures from Philadelphia Public Collections.* Philadelphia: LC, 1990.

Fisher, John S., and Chase Mellen. *A Builder of the West: The Life of General William Jackson Palmer.* Manchester, NH: Ayer, 1981.

Fitchett, E. Horace. "The Status of the Free Negro in Charleston, SC, and His Descendants in Modern Society: Statement of the Problem." *Journal of Negro History* 32 (Oct. 1947): 430–451.

Flinn, John J., and John E. Wilkie. *History of the Chicago Police: From the Settlement of the Community to the Present Time.* Chicago: Police Book Fund, 1887.

Flinn, John William, Papers, 1798, 1824–1942. Manuscripts Division. South Caroliniana Library, University of South Carolina, Columbia.

Foner, Eric, historian. Interview with authors, 2005, 2006, 2009.

Foner, Eric. *Forever Free: The Story of Emancipation and Reconstruction.* New York: Alfred A. Knopf, 2005.

———. *Freedom's Lawmakers: A Directory of Black Officeholders During Reconstruction.* Schomburg Center for Research in Black Culture. New York: Oxford University Press, 1993.

———. *Free Soil, Free Labor, Free Men: The Ideology of the Republican Party Before the Civil War.* New York: Oxford University Press, 1970.

———. *Reconstruction: America's Unfinished Revolution, 1863–1877.* New York: Harper & Row, 1988.

———. *A Short History of Reconstruction, 1863–1877.* New York: Harper & Row, 1990.

Foner, Eric, and Olivia Mahoney. *America's Reconstruction.* Baton Rouge: Louisiana State University Press, 1995.

Foner, Philip S. "The Battle to End Discrimination Against Negroes on Philadelphia Streetcars: (Part I) Background and Beginning of Battle." *Pennsylvania History: A Journal of Mid-Atlantic Studies* 40 (July 1973): 260–291.

———. "The Battle to End Discrimination Against Negroes on Philadelphia Streetcars: (Part II) The Victory." *Pennsylvania History: A Journal of Mid-Atlantic Studies* 40 (Oct. 1973): 355–379.

———. "Black Participation in the Centennial of 1876." *Phylon* 39, no. 4 (1978).

———. "Blacks and the Labor Movement in Pennsylvania: The Beginnings." In "Black History and Culture," special issue, *Pennsylvania Heritage* (Pennsylvania Historical and Museum Commission) 4, no. 1 (Dec. 1977): 34–38.

———. *The Voice of Black America: Major Speeches by Negroes in the United States, 1797–1973.* New York: Capricorn Books, 1975.

———, ed. *Frederick Douglass: Selected Speeches and Writings.* Abridged and adapted by Yuval Taylor from Foner's 5-vol. *Life and Writings of Frederick Douglass.* Chicago: Lawrence Hill Books, imprint of Chicago Review Press, 1999.

———, ed. *Life and Writings of Frederick Douglass.* 5 vols. New York: International, 1950.

Foner, Philip S., and Robert J. Branham. *Lift Every Voice: African American Oratory, 1787–1900.* Tuscaloosa: University of Alabama Press, 1998.

Foner, Philip S., and George E. Walker, eds. *Proceedings of the Black State Conventions, 1840–1865.* Philadelphia: Temple University Press, 1979–1980.

Forten, Charlotte E. *The Journal of Charlotte L. Forten: A Free Negro in the Slave Era.* Edited and with an introduction and notes by Ray Allen Billington. New York: Dryden Press, 1953.

Forty-ninth Annual Report of the Controllers of Public Schools of the First School District of Pennsylvania . . . for the Year Ending December 31st 1867. Philadelphia: Board of Controllers, 1868.

Forty-sixth Annual Report of the Controllers of the Public Schools of the First School District of Pennsylvania, for the Year Ending December 31, 1864. Philadelphia: Controllers of the Public Schools, 1865.

Foster, Helen Bradley. *New Raiments of Self: African American Clothing in the Antebellum South.* Oxford: Berg, 1997.

Fox, Robert. "The John Scott Medal." *Proceedings of the American Philosophical Society* 112, no. 6 (Dec. 9, 1968): 416–430.

Franklin, John Hope, and Loren Schweninger. *In Search of the Promised Land: A Slave Family in the Old South.* New York: Oxford University Press, 2006.

Franklin, V. P. "Educational Philosophy." In *W.E.B. Du Bois: An Encyclopedia,* edited by Gerald Horne and Mary Young, 68–73. Westport CT: Greenwood, 2001.

Fraser, Walter J. *Charleston! Charleston! The History of a Southern City,* Columbia: University of South Carolina Press, 1989.

"Frederick Douglass in Ireland." *Journal of Negro History* 8 (Jan. 1923): 102–107.

Fredrickson, George M. *The Black Image in the White Mind: The Debate on Afro-American Character and Destiny, 1817–1914.* Middletown, CT: Wesleyan University Press, 1987.

Freedley, Edwin T. *A Practical Treatise on Business.* Philadelphia: Lippincott, Grambo, 1853.

Freedmen's Bureau. *Executive Documents, Printed by order of the House of Representatives.* 39th Cong., 1st sess., 1865–1866. Serial no. 1238. Washington, DC: Government Printing Office, 1866.

Free Library of Philadelphia. "Julian F. Abele, Architect." http://libwww.freelibrary.org/75th/abele.htm.

Friedman, Lawrence Meir. *A History of American Law.* New York: Simon & Schuster, 1973.

Fuchs, L. Richard. *An Unerring Fire: The Massacre at Fort Pillow.* Mechanicsburg, PA: Stackpole Books, 2002.

Fuke, Richard Paul. *Imperfect Equality: African Americans and the Confines of White Racial Attitudes in Post-Emancipation Maryland.* Reconstructing America. New York: Fordham University Press. 1999.

Furness, Horace H., ed. *Records of a Lifelong Friendship, 1807–1882: Ralph Waldo Emerson and William Henry Furness.* Boston: Houghton Mifflin, 1910.

Gallman, J. Matthew. *Mastering Wartime: A Social History of Philadelphia During the Civil War.* New York: Cambridge University Press, 1990.

Gardner, Eric. "'A Gentleman of Superior Cultivation and Refinement': Recovering the Biography of Frank J. Webb." *African American Review* 35, no. 2 (Summer 2001): 297.

Garnet, Henry Highland, and James McCune Smith. *A Memorial Discourse, by Henry Highland Garnet, delivered in the Hall of the House of Reps . . . , with introduction by James McCune Smith.* Philadelphia: J. M. Wilson, 1865.

Garrison, Wendell Phillips, and Francis Jackson Garrison. *William Lloyd Garrison, 1805–1879: The Story of His Life Told by His Children.* Vol. 2, *1835–1840.* New York: The Century, 1885.

Garrison Family Papers, 1694–2005. Sophia Smith Collection. Smith College, Northampton, MA.

Gates, Henry Louis Jr. *Loose Canons: Notes on the Culture Wars.* New York: Oxford University Press, 1992.

Gatewood, Willard B. *Aristocrats of Color: The Black Elite, 1880–1920.* Fayetteville: University of Arkansas Press, 2000.

Geffen, Elizabeth M. "Industrial Development and Social Crisis, 1841–1854." In *Philadelphia: A Three-Hundred-Year History,* edited by Russell F. Weigley, 307–362. New York: Norton, 1982.

Gibbs, Mifflin Wistar. *Shadows and Light: An Autobiography with Reminiscences of the Last and Present Century.* Washington, DC: M. W. Gibbs, 1902.

Giesberg, Judith, historian. Interview with authors, various dates, 2006–2009.

Giesberg, Judith. *Army at Home: Women and the Civil War on the Northern Home Front.* Chapel Hill: University of North Carolina Press, 2009.

Gilbert, Tom. *Baseball and the Color Line: The African American Experience.* Danbury, CT: Franklin Watts, 1995.

Gilder Lehrman Center for the Study of Slavery, Resistance, and Abolition. Yale University, New Haven, CT. Available at http://www.yale.edu/glc/archive/1099.htm.

Gilder Lehrman Collection. New-York Historical Society. New York, NY.

Gillette, Howard F. Jr. "Corrupt and Contented: Philadelphia's Political Machine, 1865–1887." PhD diss., Yale University, 1970.

Gillette, William. *Retreat from Reconstruction, 1869–1879.* 2nd edition. Baton Rouge: Louisiana State University Press, 1982.

Glisson, Susan M., ed. *The Human Tradition in the Civil Rights Movement.* Lanham, MD: Rowman & Littlefield, 2006.

Goldstein, Warren. *Playing for Keeps: A History of Early Baseball.* Ithaca, NY: Cornell University Press, 1989.

Gonaver, Wendy. "Race Relations: A Family Story, 1765–1867." Master's thesis, College of William and Mary, 2000.

Goodwin, Doris Kearns. *Team of Rivals: The Political Genius of Abraham Lincoln.* New York: Simon & Schuster Paperbacks, 2005.

Gopsill's Philadelphia City and Business Directory, 1867–1868.

Graham, Shirley. *There Was Once a Slave . . . The Heroic Story of Frederick Douglass.* New York: Julian Messner, 1947.

Grand Union Meeting, Philadelphia, Dec. 7, 1859. Philadelphia. HSP.

Gray, Peter, and Kendrick Oliver, eds. *The Memory of Catastrophe.* Manchester: Manchester University Press, 2004.

Great Auction Sale of Slaves, at Savannah, Georgia, March 2d and 3d, 1859. New York: American Anti-Slavery Society. Available at http://antislavery.eserver.org.

Green, John P. *Fact Stranger Than Fiction: Seventy-five Years of a Busy Life with Reminiscences of Many Great and Good Men and Women.* Cleveland: Riehl Printing, 1920. http://docsouth.unc.edu/southlit/greenfact/green.html.

Greene, Harlan, project archivist, Avery Research Center for African American History and Culture, College of Charleston, Charleston, SC. Interview with authors, May 2006.

Greene, Harlan, Harry S. Hutchins Jr., and Brian E. Hutchins. *Slave Badges and the Slave-Hire System in Charleston, South Carolina, 1783–1865.* Jefferson, NC: McFarland, 2004.

Gregory, James M. *Frederick Douglass The Orator.* Springfield, MA: Gregory, Willey, 1893.

Griffin, Henry H. *The Trial of Frank Kelly for the Assassination and Murder of Octavius V. Catto, on October 10, 1871.* Philadelphia: *Philadelphia Daily Tribune,* c. 1877.

Guelzo, Allen C. *Lincoln's Emancipation Proclamation: The End of Slavery in America.* New York: Simon & Schuster, 2004.

A Guide to the Wormley Family Papers, 1773–1991. Richmond: Library of Virginia, 2006. http://ead.lib.virginia.edu/vivaead/published/lva/vi01270.frame.

Gutman, Herbert G. *The Black Family in Slavery and Freedom, 1750–1925.* New York: Vintage Books, 1976.

Guy, Yvette Richardson. *A History of Trinity United Methodist Church: From Dissension to Unity.* Charleston: Trinity United Methodist Church, 1991.

Hagy, James W. *Directories for the City of Charleston, South Carolina, For the Years 1830–31, 1835–36, 1836, 1837–38 and 1840–41.* Baltimore: Clearfield, 1997.

Hahn, Steven, historian. Interview with authors, Jan. 2005.

Hahn, Steven. *A Nation Under Our Feet: Black Political Struggles in the Rural South from Slavery to the Great Migration*. Cambridge, MA: Harvard University Press, 2003.

Haley, James T. *Afro American Encyclopaedia*. Nashville, TN: Haley & Florida, 1895.

Hallowell, Anna, ed. *James and Lucretia Mott, Life and Letters*. Boston: Houghton Mifflin, 1884.

Haltunnen, Karen, and Lewis Perry, eds. *Moral Problems in American Life: New Perspectives in Cultural History*. Ithaca, NY: Cornell University Press, 1998.

Hamersly, Lewis R. *The Records of Living Officers of the U.S. Navy and Marine Corps*. 5th edition. Philadelphia: L. R. Hamersly, 1894.

Handy, James A. *Scraps of African Methodist Episcopal History*. Philadelphia: A.M.E. Book Concern, 1902. Available at www.docsouth.unc.edu/.

Hare, Lloyd C. M. *The Greatest American Woman: Lucretia Mott*. New York: American Historical Society, 1937.

Harrell, David E. Jr., Edwin S. Gaustad, John B. Boles, Sally Foreman Griffith, Randall M. Miller, and Randall B. Woods. *Unto a Good Land: A History of the American People*. Vol. 1, *To 1900*. Grand Rapids, MI: Eerdmans, 2005.

Harris, Leonard, and Charles Molesworth. *Alain L. Locke: The Biography of a Philosopher*. Chicago: University of Chicago Press, 2008.

Harris, Robert L. Jr. "Charleston's Free Afro-American Elite: The Brown Fellowship Society and the Humane Brotherhood." *South Carolina Historical Magazine* 82 (1981): 289–310.

Harrison, Eliza Cope, ed. *Best Companions: Letters of Eliza Middleton Fisher and Her Mother . . . 1839–46*. Columbia: University of South Carolina Press, 2001.

Harrison, Robert. "Welfare and Employment Policies of the Freedmen's Bureau in the District of Columbia." *Journal of Southern History* 72 (Feb. 2006): 75–110.

Hayes, Rutherford B. Diary and letters. Rutherford B. Hayes Presidential Center, Fremont, OH. http://www.ohiohistory.org/onlinedoc/hayes/.

Henry, Alexander, Papers. [1862–1876]. HSP.

Henry, H. M. *The Police Control of the Slave in South Carolina*. New York: Negro Universities Press, 1968.

Hershberger, Richard. "A Reconstruction of Philadelphia Town Ball." *Base Ball: A Journal of the Early Game* 1 (Fall 2007): 31–38.

"H. H." "The Education of Our Colored Population." *Indiana School Journal* 12 (1867): 151–155.

Hildebrand, Reginald F. *The Times Were Strange and Stirring: Methodist Preachers and the Crisis of Emancipation*. Durham, NC: Duke University Press, 1995.

Hill, Matthew Davenport, ed. *Our Exemplars, Poor and Rich. . . .* London: Cassell, Petter & Galpin, 1861.

Hill, Samuel S., Charles H. Lippy, and Charles Reagan Wilson. *Encyclopedia of Religion in the South*. Macon, GA: Mercer University Press, 2005.

Hine, Darlene H., and Earnestine Jenkins, eds. *A Question of Manhood*. Vol. 2, *From Emancipation to Jim Crow*. Bloomington and Indianapolis: Indiana University Press, 1999.

Hine, William C. "The 1867 Charleston Streetcar Sit-Ins: A Case of Successful Black Protest." *South Carolina Historical Magazine* 77 (1976).

Hines, Mary Ann, Gordon Marshall, and William Woys Weaver. *The Larder Invaded: Reflections on Three Centuries of Philadelphia Food and Drink*. Catalogue of a joint exhibition held Nov. 17, 1986–Apr. 25, 1987 in Philadelphia by LC and HSP. http://www.dianepublishing.net/The_Larder_Invaded_p/091407670ll.htm.

Hinks, Peter P. *To Awaken My Afflicted Brethren*. University Park: Penn State University Press, 1997.

History of Schools for the Colored Population. New York: Arno Press, 1969. Original title: *Special Report of the Commissioner of Education on the Condition and Improvement of Public Schools in the District of Columbia, 1871*.

A History of the Trial of Castner Hanway and Others, for Treason . . . by a Member of the Philadelphia Bar. Philadelphia: Uriah Hunt & Sons, 1852.

Hite, Roger W. "Voice of a Fugitive: Henry Bibb and Ante-Bellum Black Separatism." *Journal of Black Studies* 4, no. 3 (Mar. 1974): 269–284.

Hoar, George F., and John Bellows. *Autobiography of Seventy Years*. New York: C. Scribner's & Sons, 1903.

Hochschild, Adam. *Bury the Chains: Prophets and Rebels in the Fight to Free an Empire's Slaves*. Boston: Houghton Mifflin, Mariner Books, 2006.

Hoffman, Carol Stein. *The Barrymores: Hollywood's First Family*. Lexington: University Press of Kentucky, 2001.

Holley, Sallie. *A Life for Liberty: Anti-Slavery and Other Letters of Sallie Holley*. Edited by John W. Chadwick. New York: G. P. Putnam & Sons, 1899.

Holloway, James H. *Why I Am a Methodist: A Historical Sketch of What the Church Has Done for the Colored Children Educationally as Early as 1790 at Charleston S.C.* [Charleston]: H. Wainwright, print., 1909. From Slavery to Freedom: The African-American Pamphlet Collection, 1822–1909, LOC. Available at http://memory.loc.gov/ammem/aapchtml/aapchome.html.

Holloway Family Scrapbooks. Avery Research Center for African American History and Culture. College of Charleston, Charleston, SC.

Holmes, Arthur. *Parties and Their Principles: A Manual of Political Intelligence*. New York: D. Appleton, 1859.

Holt, Thomas. *Black over White: Negro Political Leadership in South Carolina During Reconstruction*. Urbana: University of Illinois, 1977.

Hoogenboom, Ari. "Inaugurating a 'Most Successful Administration.'" Thirteenth Hayes Lecture on the Presidency, Feb. 17, 2002, Hayes Museum, Fremont, OH. Available at http://www.rbhayes.org/hayes/scholarworks/.

Horton, James Oliver, *In Hope of Liberty: Culture, Community and Protest Among Northern Free Blacks, 1700–1860*. New York: Oxford University Press, 1998.

Horton, James Oliver, and Lois E. Horton. "Violence, Protest, and Identity: Black Manhood in Antebellum America." In *"Manhood Rights": The Construction of Black Male History and Manhood, 1750–1870*, 382–398. Vol. 1 of *A Question of Manhood: A Reader in U.S. Black Men's History and Masculinity*, edited by Darlene Clark Hine and Earnestine Jenkins. Bloomington: Indiana University Press, 1999.

Hotchkin, S. F. *Early Clergy of Pennsylvania and Delaware*. Philadelphia: P. W. Ziegler, 1890.

Houts, Mary D. "Black Harrisburg's Resistance to Slavery." In "Black History and Culture," special issue, *Pennsylvania Heritage* (Pennsylvania Historical and Museum Commission) 4, no. 1 (Dec. 1977): 9–13.

Hubbert-Kemper, Ruthann, executive director, Pennsylvania Capitol Preservation Committee. Interview with authors, July 2004.

Hudson, Leonne. "Fort Pocahontas." *Civil War Times Illustrated* (Gettysburg, PA), Mar. 1998. http://www.fortpocahontas.org/CivilWarTimes.html.

Huff, Archie Vernon. *Langdon Cheves of South Carolina*. Columbia: Published for the South Carolina Tricentennial Commission by the University of South Carolina Press, 1977.

Hunt, Benjamin P. *Report of the Committee Appointed for the Purpose of Securing to Colored People in Philadelphia the Right to the Use of the Street-Cars*. Philadelphia: Merrihew & Son, [1867?].

[Hunt, Benjamin P.?]. *Why Colored People in Philadelphia Are Excluded from the Street Cars*. Variously attributed to Hunt, William D. Kelley, and Benjamin Bacon. Philadelphia: Merrihew & Son, 1866.

Hunter, Kathleen. *Thomas Jefferson's Road to the White House: Teaching with Historic Places*. Washington, DC: National Trust Historic Preservation, 1993.

Hyde, A. B. *The Story of Methodism*. New York: M. W. Hazen, 1888.

Ignatiev, Noel. *How the Irish Became White*. New York: Routledge, 1995.

Independence Hall Association of Philadelphia. "Philadelphia Timeline, 1866." *Philadelphia History*. http://www.ushistory.org/philadelphia/timeline/1866.htm.

Jackson, Joseph. *America's Most Historic Highway: Market Street*. Philadelphia: John Wanamaker, 1926. http://www.libraries.psu.edu/do/digitalbookshelf/.

———. *Encyclopedia of Philadelphia*. Vol. 3. Harrisburg, PA: National Historical Association., 1931.

Jeffrey, Julie Roy. *Abolitionists Remember: Antislavery Autobiographies and the Unfinished Work of Emancipation*. Chapel Hill: University of North Carolina Press, 2008.

Jenkins, Wilbert Lee. "Chaos, Conflict, and Control: The Responses of the Newly-Freed Slaves in Charleston South Carolina to Emancipation. and Reconstruction, 1865–1877." PhD diss., Michigan State University, 1991.

———. *Seizing the New Day: African Americans in Post–Civil War Charleston*. Bloomington: Indiana University Press, 1998.

Jeronimus, C. J., ed. *Travels by His Highness Duke Bernhard of Saxe-Weimar-Eisenach Through North America in the Years 1825 and 1826*. Translated by William Jeronimus. Lanham, MD: University Press of America, 2001.

Jervey, Theodore D. *Robert Y. Hayne and His Times*. New York: Macmillan, 1909.

Johannsen, Robert Walter. *Stephen A. Douglas*. Urbana: University of Illinois Press, 1997.

Johnson, Allen, ed. *Dictionary of American Biography*. Vol. 1. New York: Scribner's, 1928.

Johnson, Michael P. "Looking for Lost Kin: Efforts to Reunite Freed Families After Emancipation." In *Southern Families at War: Loyalty and Conflict in the Civil War South*, edited by Catherine Clinton, 15–34. New York: Oxford University Press, 2000.

Johnson, Michael P., and James L. Roark. *Black Masters: A Free Family of Color in the Old South*. New York: Norton, 1984.

———. *No Chariot Let Down: Charleston's Free People of Color on the Eve of the Civil War*. Chapel Hill: University of North Carolina Press, 1984.

Johnson, Rossiter, and John H. Brown, eds. *The Twentieth Century Biographical Dictionary of Notable Americans*. Boston: Biographical Society, 1904.

Johnson, William Henry. *Autobiography of Dr. William Henry Johnson*. Albany, NY: Argus, 1900.

Jones, Charles C. *The Religious Instruction of the Negroes. In The United States*. Savannah, GA: Thomas Purse, 1842. Available at http://docsouth.unc.edu/.

Jones, J. B. *The City Merchant; or, The Mysterious Failure*. Philadelphia: Lippincott, Grambo, 1851.

Jones, Jacqueline. *Soldiers of Light and Love: Northern Teachers and Georgia Blacks, 1865–1873*. Athens: University of Georgia Press, 1992.

Jordan, John W., ed., *History of Delaware County, Pa., and Its People*. Vol. 2. New York: Lewis Historical Publishing, 1914.

Jordan, Winthrop D. *White Over Black: American Attitudes Toward the Negro, 1550–1812.* Chapel Hill: University of North Carolina Press, 1969.

Journal of Common Council. City of Philadelphia. 1863, 1871. Van Pelt Library, University of Pennsylvania.

Journal of Negro History. "Notes." Vol. 12, no. 3 (July 1927): 563–566.

Joyce, John St. George. *Story of Philadelphia.* Philadelphia: Rex Printing House, 1919.

Joyner, Charles. *Down by the Riverside: A South Carolina Slave Community.* Urbana: University of Illinois Press, 1986.

Julian, George W. *The Life of Joshua R Giddings.* Chicago: A. C. McGlurg, 1892.

Kantrowitz, Stephen David. *Ben Tillman and the Reconstruction of White Supremacy.* Chapel Hill: University of North Carolina Press, 2000.

Kaplan, Justin. *Walt Whitman: A Life.* New York: Simon & Schuster, 1980.

Karcher, Carolyn L. *The First Woman in the Republic: A Cultural Biography of Lydia Maria Child.* Durham, NC: Duke University Press, 1994.

Kashatus, William C. *Just Over the Line: Chester County and the Underground Railroad.* University Park: Penn State University Press, 2002.

Katz, Jonathan. *Resistance at Christiana: The Fugitive Slave Rebellion, Christiana, Pa., September 11, 1851: A Documentary Account.* New York: Thomas Y. Crowell, 1974.

Kauffman, Michael W. *American Brutus: John Wilkes Booth and the Lincoln Conspiracies.* New York: Random House, 2004.

Kelley, Florence, Collection. University Library, University of Illinois at Chicago.

Keneally, Thomas. *The Great Shame and the Triumph of the Irish in the English-Speaking World.* New York: Nan A. Talese, 1999.

Kennedy, Lionel H., and Thomas Parker. *An Official Report of the Trials of Sundry Negroes, Charged with an Attempt to Raise an Insurrection in the State of South-Carolina . . . Prepared and Published at the Request of the Court.* Charleston: James R. Schenck, 1822. http://memory.loc.gov/ammem/sthtml/sthome.html.

Kennicott, Patrick C. "Black Persuaders in the Antislavery Movement." *Journal of Black Studies* 1 (Sept. 1970): 5–20.

Khan, Lurey. *One Day, Levin . . . He Be Free: William Still and the Underground Railroad.* Lincoln, NB: Author's Guild BackinPrint.com edition, iUniverse, 2002.

Kilbride, Daniel. *An American Aristocracy: Southern Planters in Antebellum Philadelphia.* Columbia: University of South Carolina Press, 2006.

Kirkpatrick, Sidney D. *The Revenge of Thomas Eakins.* New Haven, CT: Yale University Press, 2006.

Kirsch, George B. *Baseball in Blue and Gray: The National Pastime During the Civil War.* Princeton, NJ: Princeton University Press, 2003.

———. *The Creation of American Team Sports: Baseball and Cricket, 1838–1872.* Urbana: University of Illinois Press, 1989.

Klein, Philip S., and Ari Hoogenboom. *A History of Pennsylvania.* University Park: Penn State University Press, 1980.

Klement, Frank L. *The Limits of Dissent: Clement L. Vallandigham and the Civil War.* New York: Fordham University Press, 1998.

Koger, Larry. *Black Slaveowners: Free Black Slave Masters in South Carolina, 1790–1860.* Columbia: University of South Carolina Press, 1985.

Lagen, Charles A. *Henry S. Hagert Memorial: Poems and Verses, with Sketch of His Life.* Philadelphia: J. B. Lippincott, 1886.

Lake, Obiagele. *Blue Veins and Kinky Hair: Naming and Color Consciousness in African America.* Westport, CT: Praeger, 2003.

LaMotte, Louis C. *Colored Light: The Story of the Influence of Columbia Theological Seminary, 1828–1936.* Richmond, VA: Presbyterian Committee of Publication, 1937.

Lane, Roger, Benjamin R. Collins Professor of Social Sciences, Haverford College. Interview with authors, various dates, 2003–2009.

Lane, Roger. *Roots of Violence in Black Philadelphia, 1860–1900.* Cambridge, MA: Harvard University Press, 1986.

———. *William Dorsey's Philadelphia and Ours.* New York: Oxford University Press, 1991.

Langston, John Mercer. "Citizenship and the Ballot: The Relations of the Colored American to the Government and Its Duty to Him—a Colored American the First Hero of the Revolutionary War." Speech delivered Oct. 25, 1865. Electronic Oberlin Group. Oberlin Through History. http://www.oberlin.edu/external/EOG/LangstonSpeeches/citizenship.htm.

Lapsansky, Emma Jones. "Discipline to the Mind: Philadelphia's Banneker Institute." *PMHB* 97 (Jan. 1993): 83–102.

———. "Feminism, Freedom, and Community: Charlotte Forten and Women Activists in Nineteenth Century Philadelphia." *PMHB* 113 (Jan. 1989): 3–20.

———. "Friends, Wives, and Strivings: Networks and Community Values Among Nineteenth-Century Philadelphia Afro-American Elites." *PMHB* 108 (Jan. 1984): 3–24.

———. "Since They Got Those Separate Black Churches: AfroAmericans and Racism in Jacksonian Philadelphia." *American Quarterly* 32 (Spring 1980): 54–78.

———. "The World the Agitators Made: The Counterculture of Agitation in Urban Philadelphia." In *The Abolitionist Sisterhood: Women's Political Culture in Antebellum America,* edited by Jean Fagan Yellin and John C. Van Horne, 91–99. Ithaca, NY: Cornell University Press, 1994.

Lapsansky, Philip, historian and archivist, LC. Interview with authors, various dates, 2003–2009.

Lapsansky-Werner, Emma J., and Margaret Hope Bacon. *Back to Africa: Benjamin Coates and the Colonization Movement in America, 1848–1880.* With Marc Chalufour, Benjamin B. Miller, and Meenakshi Rajan. University Park: Penn State University Press, 2005.

Lawrence, Bette Davis, Le Count family descendant. Interview with authors, various dates, 2003–2004.

Laws Enacted in the General Assembly of the Commonwealth of Pennsylvania, Passed in the Session of 1854. Harrisburg: A. Boyd Hamilton, 1854.

Lawson, Ellen N., and Marlene Merrill. "The Antebellum 'Talented Thousandth': Black College Students at Oberlin Before the Civil War." *Journal of Negro Education* 52 (1983): 142–155.

Leigh, Oliver H.G. *Chronicle of the Union League of Philadelphia, 1862–1902.* Philadelphia: Wm. F. Fell, 1902.

Lemire, Elise. *Miscegenation: Making Race in America.* Philadelphia: University of Pennsylvania Press, 2002.

Lengyel, Emil. *Americans from Hungary.* Philadelphia: Lippincott, 1948.

Lerner, Gerda. *The Feminist Thought of Sarah Grimké.* New York: Oxford University Press, 1998.

———. *The Grimké Sisters from South Carolina: Rebels Against Slavery.* Boston: Houghton Mifflin, 1967.

"Letters from Negro Leaders to Gerrit Smith." *Journal of Negro History* 27 (Oct. 1942): 432–453.

Letters on the Condition of the African Race in the United States by a Southern Lady. Philadelphia, 1852.

"Letters to Antislavery Workers and Agencies." *Journal of Negro History* 10 (July 1925): 519–543.

Levine, Adam, historian. Interview with authors, June 2004

Levine, Robert S., ed. *Martin R. Delany: A Documentary Reader.* Chapel Hill: University of North Carolina Press, 2003.

Lewis, David Levering. *W.E.B. Du Bois: Biography of a Race, 1868–1919.* New York: Henry Holt, 1993.

Lewis, Elsie M. "The Political Mind of the Negro, 1865–1900." *Journal of Southern History* 21 (May 1955): 189–202.

Lewis, Lloyd. *The Assassination of Lincoln: History and Myth.* Lincoln: University of Nebraska Press, 1994.

Library of the Institute for Colored Youth. Philadelphia: HSP, 1853.

Licht, Walter. *Getting Work: Philadelphia, 1840–1950.* Philadelphia: University of Pennsylvania Press, 2000.

"The Life and Legacy of Francis Johnson: America's First International Superstar." Exhibition at Free Library of Philadelphia, Central Branch May–June 2007.

Lincoln, Abraham, Papers. LOC.

Lippard, George. *The Bank Director's Son.* Philadelphia: E.E. Barclay & A.R. Orton, 1851.

Littlefield, Daniel C., professor of history, University of South Carolina. Interview with authors, 2006.

Litwack, Leon F. *North of Slavery: The Negro in the Free States, 1790–1860.* Chicago: University of Chicago Press, 1961.

Lofgren, Chas A. *The Plessy Case: A Legal-Historical Interpretation.* New York: Oxford University Press, 1987.

Logan, Rayford W. *Howard University: The First Hundred Years, 1867–1967.* New York: New York University Press, 1968.

Lomax, Michael E. *Black Baseball Entrepreneurs, 1860–1901.* Syracuse, NY: Syracuse University Press, 2003.

Long, John Dixon. *Pictures of Slavery in Church and State.* Philadelphia: John Dixon Long, 1857. Available at www.docsouth.unc.edu/.

Looby, Christopher, ed. *The Complete Civil War Journal and Selected Letters of Thomas Wentworth Higginson.* Chicago: University of Chicago Press, 1999. http://www.press.uchicago.edu/Misc/Chicago/333302.html

Lovejoy, Elijah Parish. *Elijah Parish Lovejoy: A Remembrance.* Waterville, ME: Colby College, 1987.

Lovell, Laura. *Report of a Delegate to the Anti-Slavery Convention of American Women, Held in Philadelphia, May, 1838; including an account of other meetings held in Pennsylvania Hall, and of the Riot. Addressed to the Fall River Female Anti-Slavery Society, and published by its request.* Boston, MA: I. Knapp, 1838.

Lyell, Sir Charles. *A Second Visit to the United States of North America.* 2 vols. New York: Harper & Brothers; London: J. Murray, 1849.

Lyman, Joseph B., and Laura E. Lyman. *The Philosophy of Housekeeping.* Pittsburgh: Harford & Goodwin & Betts, 1867.

Mabee, Carleton. *Black Freedom: The Nonviolent Abolitionists from 1830 Through the Civil War.* New York: Macmillan, 1970.

MacDonell, Agnes. "Lucretia Mott." *Macmillan's Magazine,* Nov. 1880–Apr. 1881.

MacManus, Seumas. *The Story of the Irish Race.* 1921. Revised, New York: Devin-Adair, 1977.

Malloy, Jerry. "Early Black Baseball and Charles Douglass." July 2003. Posted to Original Baseball Research, Web site of Clifford Blau, a Society for American Baseball Research member. http://members.dslextreme.com/users/brak2.0/antebell.htm.

Managers of the Pennsylvania Hall Association. *History of Pennsylvania Hall.* Philadelphia: Merrihew & Gunn, 1838. Reprint, New York: Greenwood, Negro Universities Press, 1969.

Martin, Tony. "The Banneker Literary Institute of Phila: African American Intellectual Activism Before the War of the Slaveholders' Rebellion." *Journal of African American History* 87 (Summer 2002): 303–322.

Martin, Waldo E. Jr. *The Mind of Frederick Douglass.* Chapel Hill: University of North Carolina Press, 1985.

Martineau, Harriet. "1802–1876. The Martyr Age of the United States." *London and Westminster Review,* Dec. 1838.

Martyn, Carlos. *Wendell Phillips, The Agitator.* 1890. Reprint, New York: Negro Universities Press, 1969.

Maryland State Archives. Annapolis. http://www.msa.md.gov/.

Mathews, Donald G. *Religion in the Old South.* Chicago: University of Chicago Press, 1977.

Mathews, Marcia M. *Henry Ossawa Tanner: American Artist.* Chicago: University of Chicago Press, 1994.

May, Samuel J. *The Fugitive Slave Law and Its Victims.* New York: American Anti-Slavery Society, 1861.

Mayer, Henry. *All on Fire: William Lloyd Garrison and the Abolition of Slavery.* New York: Norton, 1998.

Mayors of the City of Philadelphia, 1691–2000. Department of Records. City of Philadelphia. http://www.phila.gov/phils/Mayorlst.htm.

McArver, Susan Wilds. "The Salvation of Souls and the Salvation of the Republic of Liberia: Denominational Conflict and Racial Diversity in Antebellum Presbyterian Foreign Missions." In *North American Foreign Missions, 1810–1914: Theology, Theory, and Policy,* edited by Wilbert R. Shenk, 133–162. Grand Rapids MI: Eerdmans, 2004.

McClintock, John, and James Strong. *Cyclopaedia of Biblical, Theological, and Ecclesiastical Literature.* Vol. 2. New York: Harper & Brothers, 1894.

McClure, Alexander K. *Old Time Notes of Pennsylvania.* Philadelphia: John C. Winston, 1905.

McCray, Florine Thayer. *The Life-Work of the Author of "Uncle Tom's Cabin."* New York: Funk & Wagnalls, 1889.

McDowell, Deborah. "The Civil War: Advantages of the North and South, Turning Points, Women, African-Americans, Fighting and Effects." May 14, 2007. http://www.associatedcontent.com/article/239097/the_civil_war_advantages_of_the_north.html?cat=37.

McElroy's Philadelphia City Directory. 1837–1877.

McFeely, William S. *Frederick Douglass.* New York: Norton, 1995.

———. *Grant: A Biography.* New York: Norton, 1982.

McHenry, Elizabeth. *Forgotten Readers: Recovering the Lost History of African American Literary Societies.* Durham, NC: Duke University Press, 2002.

[McKim, James Miller]. *The Arrest, Trial and Release of Daniel Webster, a Fugitive Slave: Correspondence of the Anti-Slavery Standard.* Philadelphia: Pennsylvania Anti-Slavery Society, 1859.

M'Clintock, Elizabeth, to Mary Truman, July 9, 1838. Women's Rights National Historical Park, Seneca Falls, NY.

McPherson, Edward. *The Political History of the United States of America, During the Great Rebellion, Including a Classified Summary of the Legislation of the Second Session of the Thirty-sixth Congress, the Three Sessions of the Thirty-seventh Congress, the First Session of the Thirty-eighth Congress, With the Votes Therein*. Washington, DC: Philip & Solomons, 1865.

McPherson, James M. *The Negro's Civil War*. New York: Pantheon Books, 2003.

———. *The Struggle for Equality: Abolitionists and the Negro in the Civil War and Reconstruction*. Princeton, NJ: Princeton University Press, 1967.

Meffert, John W., and Sherman E. Pyatt. *Charleston South Carolina*. Charleston: Avery Research Center, Arcadia Publishing, c. 2000.

Meier, August. *Negro Thought in America, 1880–1915: Racial Ideologies in the Age of Booker T. Washington*. Ann Arbor: University of Michigan Press, 1988.

Meyers, Allen, and Joel Spivak. *Philadelphia Trolleys*. Portsmouth, NH: Arcadia Publishing, 2003.

Midgley, Clare. *Women Against Slavery: The British Campaigns, 1780–1870*. New York: Routledge, 1992.

Miel, Charles F. B. *A Soul's Pilgrimage*. Philadelphia: Geo. W. Jacobs, 1899.

Miller, Edward A. *Gullah Statesman: Robert Smalls from Slavery to Congress, 1839–1915*. Columbia: University of South Carolina Press, 1995.

Miller, Francis Trevelyan, and Robert Sampson Lanier. *Photographic History of the Civil War*. 10 vols. New York: Reviews of Reviews, 1911–1912.

Minton, Henry M., M.D. "Early History of Negroes in Business in Philadelphia." Paper delivered to the American Negro Historical Society, Philadelphia, Mar. 1913.

The Minutes and Sermon of the Second Presbyterian and Congregational Convention, held in the Central Presbyterian Church, Lombard Street, Philadelphia. . . . New York: Daly, Printer, 1858.

Minutes of the General Assembly of the Presbyterian Church of the United States of America. Vols. 12–16. Philadelphia: Presbyterian Board of Education, 1848–1858. Presbyterian Historical Society.

Mires, Charlene. *Independence Hall in American Memory*. Philadelphia: University of Pennsylvania Press, 2002.

Mitchell, Charles W. *Maryland Voices of the Civil War*. Baltimore: Johns Hopkins University Press, 2007.

Moebs, Thos. T. *Black Soldiers, Black Sailors, Black Ink: Research Guide on African-Americans in U S Military History, 1526–1900*. Chesapeake Bay, MD: Moebs, 1994.

Montgomery, Edgar Catto, Catto family descendant. Interview with authors, May 2006.

Morgan, Joseph H. *Morgan's History of the New Jersey Conference of the AME Church . . . with Biographical Sketches of Members*. Camden: New Jersey State Library, 1887.

Morison, Samuel Eliot. *The Life and Letters of Harrison Gray Otis, Federalist, 1765–1848*. Boston: Houghton Mifflin, 1913.

Morris, Thomas D. *Free Men All: The Personal Liberty Laws of the North, 1780–1861*. Union, NJ: Law Book Exchange, 2001.

Mossell, Mrs. N.F. *The Work of the Afro-American Woman*. 2nd edition. Philadelphia: George S. Ferguson, 1908.

Mother Bethel A.M.E .Church. Records. Microfilm no. 4370. Van Pelt Library, University of Pennsylvania.

Murphy, Francis, ed. *Walt Whitman: The Complete Poems*. London: Penguin Group, 1996.

Murphy, Larry G., J. Gordon Melton, and Gary L. Ward, eds. *Encyclopedia of African American Religions*. New York: Garland, 1993.

Murray, Andrew E. *Presbyterians and the Negro: A History*. Philadelphia: Presbyterian Historical Society, 1966.

The Mysteries and Miseries of Philadelphia, as Exhibited and Illustrated by a Late Presentment of the Grand Jury, and by a Sketch of the Condition of the Most Degraded Classes in the City. N. p., 1853.

Narrative of Facts in the Case of Passmore Williamson. Philadelphia: Pennsylvania Anti-Slavery Society, 1855.

Nash, Gary B. *First City: Philadelphia and the Forging of Historical Memory*. Philadelphia: University of Pennsylvania Press, 2001.

———. *Forging Freedom: The Formation of Philadelphia's Black Community, 1720–1840*. Cambridge, MA: Harvard University Press, 1988.

The National Cyclopaedia of American Biography. Vol. 2. New York: Jas T White & Co, 1895.

"Negroes to ride in city railway passenger cars!" Broadside. Philadelphia, [1866?]. Portfolio 159, folder 26. An American Time Capsule: Three Centuries of Broadsides and Other Printed Ephemera, LOC.

Nesbit, William, Joseph C. Bustill, and William D. Forten. On behalf of the Pennsylvania State Equal Rights League. "To the honorable the Senate and House of Representatives of the United States . . . Feby. 20, 1866." [Pennsylvania, 1866?]. From Slavery to Freedom: The African-American Pamphlet Collection, 1822–1909, LOC. Available at http://memory.loc.gov/ammem/aapchtml/aapchome.html.

Neuffer, Claude H., ed. *Names in South Carolina*. Vols. 13–18. Columbia: State Printing Company, 1966–1971.

Nevin, Alfred. *History of the Presbytery of Philadelphia and of the Philadelphia Central*. Philadelphia: W. S. Fortescue, 1888.

New Jersey State Archives. Trenton.

New Jersey State Library. Trenton. www.njstatelib.org.

Newman, Debra L. *List of Black Servicemen Compiled from the War Department Collection of Revolutionary War Records*. Washington, DC: National Archives and Records Service, 1974.

Newman, Richard, historian. Interview with authors, 2005.

Newman, Richard S. "The Pennsylvania Abolition Society: Restoring a Group to Glory." *Pennsylvania Legacies* (HSP) 6 (Nov. 2005): 6–10.

———. *The Transformation of American Abolitionism*. Chapel Hill: University of North Carolina Press, 2002.

Newman, Richard, Patrick Rael, and Philip Lapsansky. *Pamphlets of Protest: An Anthology of Early African-American Protest*. New York: Routledge, 2000.

Nieman, Donald G., ed. *The Politics of Freedom: African Americans and the Political Process During Reconstruction*. New York: Garland, 1994.

Nye, Russell B. *Fettered Freedom: Civil Liberties and the Slavery Controversy, 1830–1860*. East Lansing: Michigan State College Press, 1949.

Oberholtzer, Ellis Paxson. *The Literary History of Philadelphia*. Philadelphia: George W. Jacobs, 1906.

Oberlin Online. "Oberlin-Wellington Rescuers." http://www.oberlin.edu/colrelat/blackHistory/discovermore.html.

Ochse, Orpha Caroline. *The History of the Organ in the United States.* Bloomington: Indiana University Press, 1988.

O'Donoghue, Jo, and Sean McMahon. *Brewer's Dictionary of Irish Phrase and Fable.* London: Weidenfeld & Nicolson, 2004.

Ohio Historical Society. Columbus. http://www.ohiohistory.org/.

Ohio State Teachers Association. *Ohio Educational Monthly: A Journal of School and Home Education* (Columbus). Vol. 11 (1870).

Okur, Nilgun Anadolu. "Underground Railroad in Philadelphia, 1830–1860." *Journal of Black Studies* 25, no. 5 (May 1995): 537–557.

Oliver Optic's Magazine: Our Boys and Girl (Boston). Vols. 5–6 (1869).

Ought American Slavery to Be Perpetuated? A Debate . . . Phila, Sept. 1858. Philadelphia: J. B. Lippincott, 1858.

Our Country's Troubles: Sermon Preached . . . By Rev. Dudley A. Tyng, Rector. At the Request of Laymen in Boston. Boston: John P. Jewett, 1856.

Painter, Nell Irvin. "Martin R Delany: Elitism and Black Nationalism." In *Black Leaders of the Nineteenth Century,* edited by Leon F. Litwack and August Meier, 149–172. Urbana: University of Illinois Press, 1988.

Palmer, Benjamin Morgan. *The Life and Letters of James Henley Thornwell.* 1875. New York: Arno Press and the *New York Times,* 1969.

Palmer, Beverly Wilson, ed. *Selected Letters of Lucretia Coffin Mott.* Urbana: University of Illinois Press, 2002.

Palmer, Beverly Wilson, and Holly Byers Ochoa, eds. *The Selected Papers of Thaddeus Stevens, April 1865–August 1868.* Pittsburgh: University of Pittsburgh Press, 1997.

Paradis, James, historian. Interview with authors, 2006.

Paradis, James M. *African Americans and the Gettysburg Campaign.* Lanham, MD: Scarecrow Press, 2004.

Pasternak, Martin B. *Rise Now and Fly to Arms: The Life of Henry Highland Garnet.* New York: Garland, 1995.

Payne, Daniel A. *History of the African Methodist Episcopal Church.* Nashville, TN: Publishing House of the A.M.E. Sunday-School Union, 1891. Available at www.docsouth.unc.edu/.

———. *Recollections of Seventy Years.* Nashville, TN: Publishing House of the A.M.E. Sunday-School Union, 1888. Available at www.docsouth.unc.edu/.

Penn Monthly, Devoted to Literature, Science, Art and Politics (Philadelphia). Vol. 8 (Mar. 1877).

Pennsylvania Civil War Era Collection. Pennsylvania State University Libraries, via Olive Activepaper Archive. Aurora CO: Olive Software, 2000–2009. http://digitalnewspapers.libraries.psu.edu/.

Pennsylvania Hall Association. *History of Pennsylvania Hall, Which Was Destroyed by a Mob, on the 17th of May, 1838.* Philadelphia: Merrihew & Gunn, 1838. Reprint, New York: Negro Universities Press, 1969. Available at www.loc.gov/.

Pennsylvania Heritage. Special Edition: Black History and Culture (Pennsylvania Historical and Museum Commission). Vol. 4, no. 1 (Dec. 1977).

Pennsylvania Hospital, Philadelphia. Treatment records and weather records, 1838–1877. PSERL.

Pennypacker, Samuel Whitaker. *The Autobiography of a Pennsylvanian.* Philadelphia: John C. Winston, 1918.

Perkins, Linda M. *Fanny Jackson Coppin and the Institute for Colored Youth, 1865–1902.* New York: Garland, 1987.

———. "Heed Life's Demands: The Educational Philosophy of Fanny Jackson Coppin." *Journal of Negro Education* 51, no. 3 (1982): 181–190.

Perry, Mark. *Lift Up Thy Voice: The Grimké Family's Journey from Slaveholders to Civil Rights Leaders*. New York: Viking, 2001.

Peterson, Daniel H. *The Looking-Glass: Being a True Report and Narrative of the Life . . . of the Rev. Daniel H. Peterson, A Colored Clergyman*. New York: Wright, Printer, 1854.

Philadelphia African-American Census 1847: A Statistical Inquiry into the Condition of the People of Colour of the City and Districts of Philadelphia. Digitized by FLS, 2002. http://www.swarthmore.edu/Library/friends/paac1847/main.html.

Philadelphia African Americans: Color, Class, and Style, 1840–1940. Philadelphia: Balch Institute Press, 1988. Published in conjunction with the exhibition "Philadelphia African Americans: Color, Class, and Style, 1840–1940," at the Balch Institute for Ethnic Studies Museum.

Philadelphia City Archives. Death records, July 1, 1860–June 30, 1915.

Philadelphia Presbytery. Presbyterian Church (U.S.A.). Minutes, 1843–1873. Microfilm. Presbyterian Historical Society.

Phillips, Paul David. "White Reaction to the Freedmen's Bureau in Tennessee." *Tennessee Historical Quarterly* 25 (1966): 50–62.

Phillips, Wendell. *Speeches, Lectures, and Letters*. Boston: Walker Wise, 1864.

Pilkington, Jim. "Bringing the Fight to the Diamond: The Pythians Base Ball Club and the Struggle for Racial Equality." Senior thesis, Swarthmore College, 2007.

Pleasonton, Augustus J., Diary, 1838–1844. HSP.

Pleasonton, General Augustus J., and Others. *The Influence of the Blue Ray of the Sunlight and of the Blue Colour of the Sky. . . .* Philadelphia: Claxton, Haffelfinger, 1876.

Poole, Jason. "On Borrowed Ground: Free African-American Life in Charleston, South Carolina, 1810–61." *Essays in History* (Corcoran Department of History, University of Virginia) 36 (1994).

Porcher, Richard D., professor emeritus, The Citadel. Interview with authors, July 2006.

Port Royal Relief Commission. *The Freedmen of South Carolina: Address Delivered by J. Miller M'Kim*. Philadelphia: Willis P Hazard, 1862.

Post, Lydia M. *Soldiers' Letters, from Camps, Battle-field and Prison. . . .* New York: Bunce & Huntington, 1865.

Post Family Papers. University of Rochester Rare Books and Special Collections. Rochester, NY.

Powell, Aaron M. *Personal Reminiscences of the Anti-Slavery and Other Reforms and Reformers*. Published by Anna Rice Powell, Plainfield, NJ. New York: Caulon Press, 1899.

Powell, Richard J. "Cinqué: Antislavery Portraiture and Patronage in Jacksonian America." *American Art* 11, no. 3 (Fall 1997): 48–73.

Powers, Bernard J., historian, College of Charleston, SC. Interview with authors, 2006.

Powers, Bernard J. *Black Charlestonians: A Social History, 1822–1885*. Fayetteville: University of Arkansas Press, 1994.

Presbyterian Magazine (Philadelphia). Vol. 7 (1857).

"Pring, James, Guardian of Fanny and Mary Shields, Free Blacks, Versus Francis Mulligan." Judgment roll, June 13, 1801. South Carolina Department of Archives and History.

Proceedings and Debates of the Convention to Amend the Constitution of Pennsylvania in 1837. Vol. 13. Harrisburg, 1839.

Proceedings of the Anti-Slavery Convention of American Women, Held in Philadelphia May 15th, 16th, 17th, and 18th, 1838. Philadelphia: Printed by Merrihew & Gunn, 1838. Available at http://memory.loc.gov.

Proceedings of the First Annual Meeting of the National Equal Rights League, held in Cleveland, Ohio, October 19, 20, and 21, 1865. Philadelphia: E. C. Markley & Son, 1865.

Proceedings of the Great Union Meeting, Held in the Large Saloon of the Chinese Museum . . . Nov 21, 1850. Philadelphia: B. Mifflin, Printer, 1850.

Proceedings of the Meeting in Charleston, S.C., May 13–15, 1845, on the Religious Instruction of the Negroes. . . . From Slavery to Freedom: The African-American Pamphlet Collection, 1822–1909, LOC. Available at http://memory.loc.gov/ammem/aapchtml/aapchome.html.

Proceedings of the National Convention of Colored Men, Held in the City of Syracuse, N.Y., October 4, 5, 6, and 7, 1864, with the Bill of Wrongs and Rights, and the Address to the American people. 1864. Philadelphia: Rhistoric Publications, 1969.

Proceedings of the National Convention of the Colored Men of America, Held in Washington, D. C., on January 13, 14, 15, and 16, 1869. Washington, DC: Great Republic Book & Newspaper Printing Establishment, 1869.

Proceedings of the State Equal Rights Convention of the Colored People of Pennsylvania, Held in the City of Harrisburg, February 8th, 9th and 10th, 1865, Together with a Few of the Arguments Suggesting the Necessity for Holding the Convention, and an Address of the Colored State Convention to the People of Pennsylvania. 1865. Philadelphia: Rhistoric Publications, 1974.

Project Protoball. Baseball history archives. http://www.retrosheet.org/Protoball/.

Quarles, Benjamin. *Allies for Freedom and Blacks on John Brown.* New York: Oxford University Press, 1974.

———. *Black Abolitionists.* New York: Oxford University Press, 1969.

———. *Frederick Douglass.* Washington DC: Associated Publishers, 1948.

———. *Lincoln and the Negro.* 1962; reprint, New York: Da Capo Press, 1991.

———. *The Negro in the Civil War.* Boston: Little, Brown, 1969.

———. *Public Life of Frederick Douglass.* Madison: University of Wisconsin Press, 1940.

Quinn, John F. "The Rise and Fall of Repeal: Slavery and Irish Nationalism in Antebellum Philadelphia." *PMHB* 130 (Jan. 2006): 45–78.

Rawick, George P., ed. *The American Slave: A Composite Autobiography.* Westport, CT: Greenwood Press, 1972.

Ray, Jeffrey, curator, Atwater Kent Museum, Philadelphia. Interview with authors, June 2004.

Redpath, James. *Echoes of Harpers Ferry.* Boston: Thayer & Eldridge, 1860.

Reed, Geo. E., ed. *Papers of the Governors, 1871–1883.* Vol. 9 of *Pennsylvania Archives,* Harrisburg: State of Pennsylvania, 1902.

Reinhold, Meyer. "Charles Anthon." In *Biographical Dictionary of North American Classicists,* edited by Ward W. Briggs Jr., 19–20. Westport, CT: Greenwood Press, 1994.

Renehan, Edward J. Jr. *The Secret Six: The True Tale of the Men Who Conspired with John Brown.* Columbia: University of South Carolina Press, 1997.

The Report of a Committee of One, on the Official Life and Administrations of the Hon. William S. Stokley. Philadelphia, 1880.

Report of Special Committee on the Passage by the House of Representatives of the Constitutional Amendment for the Abolition of Slavery, January 31st, 1865. From Slavery to Freedom: The African American Pamphlet Collection, 1822–1909, LOC. Available at http://memory.loc.gov/ammem/aapchtml/aapchome.html.

Report of the Board of Trustees of Colored Schools of Washington and Georgetown, D.C. Washington, DC: M'Gill & Witherow, 1871.

Report of the Committee of the South-Carolina Conference of the Methodist Episcopal Church, on the subject of the Schism in Charleston, with the Accompanying Documents. Published by order of the Conference. Charleston, SC: J. S. Burges, 1835.

Report of the Ladies' Union Association of Philadelphia. Philadelphia: G. T. Stockdale, 1867. Available at www.hsp.org.

Report of the Secretary of War. Washington, DC: Government Printing Office, 1868.

Report of the Secretary of War. Washington, DC: Government Printing Office, 1870.

Reports of the Several Railroad Companies of Pennsylvania, Communicated by the Auditor General, to the Legislature, Jan. 22, 1864. Harrisburg: Singerly & Myers, 1864.

Rhodehamel, John H., and Louise Taper, eds. *Right or Wrong, God Judge Me: The Writings of John Wilkes Booth.* Urbana: University of Illinois Press, 2001.

Ribowsky, Mark. *A Complete History: The Negro Leagues, 1884–1955.* Secaucus, NJ: Citadel Press, Carol Publishing Group, 1995.

Rice, Alan J., and Martin Crawford, eds. *Liberating Sojourn: Frederick Douglass and Transatlantic Reform.* Athens: University of Georgia Press, 1999.

Richards, Leonard. *Gentlemen of Property and Standing: Anti-Abolition Mobs in Jacksonian America.* New York: Oxford University Press, 1970.

Rieder, Jonathan, sociology professor Barnard College. Speech delivered at Friends Select School, Philadelphia, Apr. 30, 2008.

Ripley, C. Peter, ed. *Black Abolitionist Papers.* 5 vols. Chapel Hill: University of North Carolina Press, 1985–1992.

Robertson, James I. Jr. "Negro Soldiers in the Civil War." *Civil War Times Illustrated* (Gettysburg, PA), Oct. 1968.

Roediger, David R. *The Wages of Whiteness: Race and the Making of the White Working Class.* New York: Verso Press, 1991.

Rollin, Frank A. [Frances Anne]. *Life and Public Services of Martin R. Delany.* Boston: Lee & Shepherd, 1868.

Rosa, Todd Anthony. "Negro Leagues." In *St. James Encyclopedia of Pop Culture,* ed. Sara Pendergast and Tom Pendergast. Reading, UK: Gale Group, 2000.

Rose, P. K. "The Civil War: Black American Contributions to Union Intelligence." *Studies in Intelligence,* Winter 1998–1999, 73–80.

Rose, Willie Lee. *Rehearsal for Reconstruction.* Athens: University of Georgia Press, 1999.

Rosenfeld, Richard. *American Aurora: A Democratic-Republican Returns.* New York: St. Martin's Press, 1997.

Roth, Anthony A. *Mayors of Philadelphia, 1691–1972.* Vol. 3. Collections of the Genealogical Society of Pennsylvania, HSP.

Row, Augustus. *Masonic Biography and Dictionary: Comprising the History of Ancient Masonry, Antiquity of Masonry, Written and Unwritten Law, Derivation and Definition of Masonic Terms, Biographies of Eminent Masons, Statistics, List of all Lodges in the United States, etc.* Philadelphia: J. B. Lippincott, 1868.

Ruchames, Louis, ed. *The Letters of William Lloyd Garrison.* Vol. 2, *A House Divided Against Itself, 1836–1840.* Cambridge, MA: Harvard University Press, Belknap Press, 1971.

Runcie, John M. "Hunting the Nigs in Philadelphia: The Race Riot of 1834." *PMHB* 39 (Apr. 1972): 187–218.

Ryczek, William J. *When Johnny Came Sliding Home.* Jefferson, NC: McFarland, 1998.

Rydell, Robert W. *All the World's a Fair: Visions of Empire at American International Expositions, 1876–1916.* Chicago: University of Chicago Press, 1987.

Saettler, Paul. *The Evolution of American Educational Technology.* Englewood, CO: Libraries Unlimited, 1990.

Salvatore, Nick. *We All Got History: The Memory Books of Amos Webber.* New York: Times Books, 1996.

Samuel J. May Anti-Slavery Collection. Division of Rare and Manuscript Collections, Cornell University Library, Ithaca, NY. http://digital.library.cornell.edu/m/mayantislavery.

Sanborn, Franklin B., ed. *The Life and Letters of John Brown, Liberator of Kansas and Martyr of Virginia.* 3rd edition. Cambridge, MA: F. B. Sanborn, 1910.

Sauers, Richard Allen. *Guide to Civil War Philadelphia.* New York: Da Capo Press, 2003.

Savidge, Eugene C. *Life of Benjamin Harris Brewster, with Discourses and Addresses.* Philadelphia: J. B. Lippincott, 1891.

Saxton, Alexander. *The Rise and Fall of the White Republic: Class Politics and Mass Culture in Nineteenth-Century America.* Haymarket. New York: Verso, 1990.

Schankman, Arnold. "William B. Reed and the Civil War." *Pennsylvania History: A Journal of Mid-Atlantic Studies* 39 (Oct. 1972): 455–470.

Scharf, J. Thomas, and Thompson Westcott. *A History of Philadelphia, 1609–1884.* 3 vols. Philadelphia: L. H. Everts, 1884.

Schecter, Barnet. *Devil's Own Work: The Civil War Draft Riots and the Fight to Reconstruct America.* New York: Walker, 2005.

Schell, Frank H., Collection. HSP.

Schenone, Laura. *A Thousand Years over a Hot Stove: A History of American Women Told Through Food, Recipes, and Remembrances.* New York: Norton, 2003.

Schoenberg Center for Electronic Text and Image. Van Pelt Library. University of Pennsylvania, Philadelphia, http://sceti.library.upenn.edu/.

Schor, Joel. *Henry Highland Garnet: A Voice of Black Radicalism in the Nineteenth Century.* Westport, CT: Greenwood Press, 1977.

Schroeder-Lein, Glenna R., and Richard Zuczek. *Andrew Johnson: A Biographical Companion.* Santa Barbara CA: ABC-CLIO, 2001.

Schwartz, Joel. "To Every Man's Door: Railroads and Use of the Streets in Jacksonian Philadelphia." *PMHB* 128 (Jan. 2004): 35–62.

SCIWAY: South Carolina Information Highway. South Carolina: African American History and Resources. http://www.sciway.net/afam/. Time-Line, http://www.usca.edu/aasc/timeline.htm.

Scott, Robert N., et al. *The War of the Rebellion: A Compilation of the Official Records of the Union and Confederate Armies.* U.S. War Department, series 2, vol. 1. Washington, DC: Government Printing Office, 1894.

Seaton, D. P. *An Eulogy on the Life and Death of Prof. Octavius V. Catto.* Washington, DC: R. Beresford, 1871.

Second Presbyterian Church of Charleston. Records, 1809–1981. South Carolina Historical Society, Charleston.

Second Presbyterian Church of Charleston. Sessions Book. c. 1817–1837. Avery Research Center for African American History and Culture. College of Charleston, Charleston, SC.

Seraile, William. *Fire in His Heart: Bishop Benjamin Tucker Tanner and the AME Church.* Knoxville: University of Tennessee Press, 1998.

Sermon Occasioned by the Destruction of Pennsylvania Hall, and Delivered the Lords Day Following, May 20, 1838. . . . Philadelphia: Printed by John C. Clark, 1838. Samuel J. May Anti-Slavery Collection. Division of Rare and Manuscript Collections. Cornell University Library, Ithaca, NY. Available at http://digital.library.cornell.edu/m/mayantislavery/.

Sernett, Milton C., ed., *African American Religious History: A Documentary Witness.* Durham, NC: Duke University Press, 1999.

Sewell, Rev. Benjamin T. *Sorrows Circuit; or, Five Years' Experience in the Bedford Street Mission, Philadelphia.* [Philadelphia]: Young Men's Central Home Mission, published for support of the Gospel in the Bedford Street Mission, 1859.

Shaffer, Ralph E. "At Last, the Ballot." Chap. 3 of *Implementing the Fifteenth Amendment in California: 1870.* Pomona: Ralph E. Shaffer, 2005. Available at http://www.csupomona.edu/~reshaffer/Books/black/amend_xv.htm.

Shapiro, Herbert. *White Violence and Black Response: From Reconstruction to Montgomery.* Amherst: University of Massachusetts Press, 1988.

Shayt, David. "Stairway to Redemption: America's Encounter with the British Prison Treadmill." *Technology and Culture* (Society for the History of Technology) 30, no. 4 (Oct. 1989). 908–938.

———. "Stepping to It: The Prisoner Treadmill at Old Charleston Jail." Paper delivered at Society for Industrial Archeology conference, Savannah, GA, June 4, 1999.

Shiffert, John. *Baseball in Philadelphia: A History of the Early Game, 1831–1900.* Jefferson, NC: McFarland, 2006.

Siebert, Wilbur H. *The Underground Railroad from Slavery to Freedom.* New York: Macmillan, 1898; reprint, Mineola, NY: Dover African-American Books, 1967.

———. "The Underground Railroad in Massachusetts." *New England Quarterly* 9 (Sept. 1936): 447–467.

Silberman, Max. "A Short History of the Philadelphia Athletics." Philadelphia Athletics Historical Society. Available at http://www.philadelphiaathletics.org/. Silcox, Harry, historian. Interview with authors, various dates, 2003–2007.

Silcox, Harry C. "The Black Better Class Political Dilemma: Philadelphia Prototype Isaiah C. Wears." *PMHB*, 113 (Jan. 1989): 45–66.

———. "Nineteenth-Century Philadelphia Black Militant: Octavius V. Catto (1839–1871)." *PMHB* 44 (Jan. 1977): 53–76.

———. "Philadelphia Negro Educator: Jacob C. White, Jr., 1837–1902." *PMHB* 97 (Jan. 1973): 75–98.

———. *Philadelphia Politics from the Bottom Up: The Life of Irishman William McMullen, 1824–1901.* Philadelphia: Balch Institute Press, 1989.

Simmons, Rev. William J. *Men of Mark: Eminent, Progressive, and Rising.* Cleveland: George M. Rewell, 1887.

Skinner, J. E. Hilary. *After the Storm; or, Jonathan and His Neighbours in 1865–6.* Vol. 2. London: Richard Bentley, 1866.

Sklar, Kathryn Kish. *Florence Kelley and the Nation's Work: The Rise of Women's Political Culture, 1830–1900.* New Haven, CT: Yale University Press, 1997.

Smedley, R.C. *History of the Underground Railroad in Chester and the Neighboring Counties.* 1883. Mechanicsburg, PA: Stackpole Books, 2005.

Smith, Culver H. *The Press, Politics, and Patronage: The American Government's Use of Newspapers, 1789–1875.* Athens: University of Georgia Press, 1977.

Smith, J. Clay Jr. *Emancipation: The Making of the Black Lawyer, 1844–1944.* Philadelphia: University of Pennsylvania Press, 1993.

Smith, Leonard Garnet, O. V. Catto's great-great-grandson. Interview with authors, various dates, 2003–2010.

Smith, P. Frazer. *Pa. State Reports.* Vol. 55, *Comprising Cases Adjudged in the Supreme Court of Pennsylvania.* Jan. and May terms, 1867. Philadelphia: Kay & Brother, 1868.

Smith, Page. *Trial by Fire: A People's History of the Civil War and Reconstruction.* New York: McGraw Hill, 1982.

Smyth, Thomas D. D. *Autobiographical Notes, Letters, and Reflections.* Edited by Louise Cheves Stoney. Charleston, SC: Walker, Evans & Cogswell, 1914.

Snay, Mitchell. *Gospel of Disunion: Religion and Separatism in the Antebellum South.* Chapel Hill: University of North Carolina Press, 1997.

Soskis, Benjamin. "Heroic Exile: The Transatlantic Development of Frederick Douglass, 1845–1847." http://www.yale.edu/glc/soskis/index.htm.

South Carolina 1840 Census Index. HSP.

"South Carolina Civil War, 1861–1865." Available at www.sciway.net/hist.

South Carolina Conference Papers, 1834–1843. South Carolina United Methodist Collection. Sandor Teszler Library, Wofford College, Spartanburg, SC.

South Carolina Department of Archives and History, Columbia, SC.

South Carolina History Project. University of South Carolina. http://www.teachingushistory.org/.

South Carolina Synod. Presbyterian Church (U.S.A.). Minutes, 1845–1861. Microfilm. Presbyterian Historical Society.

Speirs, Frederic W. *The Street Railway System of Philadelphia, Its History and Present Condition.* 1897. New York: Johnson Reprint, 1973.

Spivak, Joel, author. Interview with authors, Apr. 2004.

Sprogle, Howard O. *Philadelphia Police, Past and Present.* Philadelphia: self-published, 1887.

Stanley, Amy Dru. "The Right to Possess All the Faculties That God Has Given: Possessive Individualism, Slave Women, and Abolitionist Thought." In *Moral Problems in American Life: New Perspectives on Cultural History,* edited by Karen Halttunen and Lewis Perry, 123–144 Ithaca, NY: Cornell University Press, 1999.

Stanley, Gerald. "Racism and the Early Republican Party: The 1856 Presidential Election in California." *Pacific Historical Review* 43 (1974): 171–187, 1974.

Stanton, Elizabeth Cady, ed. *History of Woman Suffrage.* Vol. 1, *1848–1861.* New York: Fowler & Wells, 1881.

State Free Negro Capitation Tax Books, 1832–1836. CCPL.

State University of New York, Binghamton, Database. Thomas Dublin and Kathryn Kish Sklar, Women and Social Movements in the United States, 1600–2000. http://womhist.alexanderstreet.com/.

Stebbins, Giles B. *Upward Steps of Seventy Years: Autobiographic, Biographic, Historic.* New York: United States Book, 1890.

Steers, Edward Jr. *Blood on the Moon: The Assassination of Abraham Lincoln.* Lexington: University Press of Kentucky, 2001.

Steinberg, Allen. *The Transformation of Criminal Justice in Philadelphia, 1800–1880.* Chapel Hill: University of North Carolina Press, 1989.

Sterling, Dorothy. *Lucretia Mott.* New York: Feminist Press at CUNY, 1999.

———. *The Trouble They Seen: The Story of Reconstruction in the Words of African Americans.* New York: Da Capo Press, 1994.

———. *We Are Your Sisters: Black Women in the Nineteenth Century.* New York: Norton, 1984.

———, ed. *Speak Out in Thunder Tones: Letters and Other Writings of Black Northerners, 1787–1865.* Garden City, NY: Doubleday, 1973.

Stevens-Cogdell and Sanders-Venning Collection. LC.

Stevenson, Brenda E. "Charlotte Forten (1837–1914)." In *Portraits of American Women: From Settlement to the Present,* edited by Catherine Clinton and G. J. Barker-Benfield, 279–297. New York: Oxford University Press, 1998.

———, ed. *The Journals of Charlotte Forten Grimké.* Schomburg Library of Nineteenth-Century Black Women Writers. New York: Oxford University Press, 1988.

Still, William. *A Brief Narrative of the Struggle for the Rights of the Colored people of Philadelphia in the City Railway cars, and a Defence of William Still. . . .* 1867. Philadelphia: Rhistoric Publications, 1969.

———. *The Underground Railroad: A Record of Facts, Authentic Narratives, Letters, &c. Narrating the Hardships, Hairbreadth Escapes, and Death Struggles of the Slaves in Their Efforts for Freedom, as Related by Themselves and Others.* Philadelphia: Porter & Coates, 1872.

Stowe, Harriet Beecher. *A Key to Uncle Tom's Cabin, Presenting the Original Facts and Documents upon Which the Story Is Founded.* Boston: John P. Jewett, 1853.

———. *Uncle Tom's Cabin, or, Life Among the Lowly.* Edited by Jean Fagan Yellin. Oxford: Oxford University Press, 1998.

St. Philip's Protestant Episcopal Church, Charleston SC. Church register, 1823–1940. Caroliniana Collection, University of South Carolina, Columbia.

The Stranger's Guide in Philadelphia and Its Environs. . . . Philadelphia: Lindsay & Blakiston, 1852.

Stuart, James. *Three Years in North America.* 2 vols. London: Whittaker, 1833.

Sturge, Joseph. *A Visit to the United States in 1841.* London: Hamilton, Adams, 1842.

Sudler, Arthur, archivist. Interview with authors, various dates, 2003–2009.

Sullivan, Dean A., ed. *Early Innings: A Documentary History of Baseball, 1825–1908.* Lincoln: University of Nebraska Press, 1995.

Sumner, Charles. *Recent Speeches and Addresses.* Boston: Ticknor & Fields, 1856.

Sweet, Frank W. *Legal History of the Color Line: The Rise and Triumph of the One-Drop Rule.* Palm Coast, FL: BackinTyme Books, 2005.

Sweet, Leonard I. "The Fourth of July and Black Americans in the Nineteenth Century: Northern Leadership Opinion Within the Context of the Black Experience." *Journal of Negro History* 61 (July 1976): 256–275.

Swift, David E. *Black Prophets of Justice: Activist Clergy Before the Civil War.* Baton Rouge: Louisiana State University, 1989.

———. *John Jos Gurney: Banker, Reformer and Quaker.* Middletown, CT: Wesleyan University Press, 1962.

Swift, Lindsay. *William Lloyd Garrison.* Philadelphia: Geo. W. Jacobs, 1911.

Switala, William J. *Underground Railroad in Pennsylvania.* Mechanicsburg, PA: Stackpole Books, 2001.

Tait, Peta. *Circus Bodies: Cultural Identity in Aerial Performance.* London: Routledge, 2005.

Tanner, Benjamin Tucker. "To the Memory of Professor O. V. Catto." Eulogy delivered Oct. 29, 1871.

Taylor, Frances W., Catherine T. Matthews, and J. Tracy Power. *The Leverett Letters: Correspondence of a S. Carolina Family, 1851–1868.* Columbia: University of South Carolina Press, 2000.

Taylor, Frank. *Philadelphia in the Civil War, 1861–1865.* Philadelphia: City of Philadelphia, 1913.

Terry, David Taft. "A Brief Moment in the Sun." In *First Freed: Washington, D.C., in the Emancipation Era,* ed. Elizabeth Clark-Lewis, 71–97. Washington, DC: Howard University Press, 2002.

Thirty-first Annual Report of the Controllers of the Public Schools of the City and County of Philadelphia . . . for the Year Ending June 30, 1849. Philadelphia: Controllers of the Public Schools, 1849.

Threston, Christopher. *The Integration of Baseball in Philadelphia*. Jefferson, NC: McFarlane, 2003.

Tifft, Susan E. "Out of the Shadows." *Smithsonian Magazine*, Feb. 2005. http://www.smithsonianmag.com/history-archaeology/shadow.html.

Timbs, John. *The Year-Book of Facts in Science and Art*. London: Simpkins Marshall, 1861.

Train, George F. *Observations on Horse Railways, Addressed to the Right Hon. Milner Gibson, M. P., President of the Board of Trade, London*. London: Sampson Low, Son, 1860.

Trefousse, Hans Louis. *Thaddeus Stevens, Nineteenth-Century Egalitarian*. Chapel Hill: University of North Carolina Press, 1997.

Trinity Methodist Episcopal Church of Charleston. Records, 1830–1839. South Carolina Historical Society, Charleston.

Turkel, Stanley. *Heroes of the American Reconstruction: Profiles of Sixteen Educators, Politicians, and Activists*. Jefferson, NC: McFarland, 2005

Turner, Edward Raymond. *The Negro in Pennsylvania: Slavery-Servitude-Freedom, 1639–1861*. Washington, DC: American Historical Association, 1911.

Turner, George Kibbe. "The Thing Above the Law: The Rise and Rule of George B Cox and His Overthrow by Young Hunt and the Fighting Idealists of Cincinnati." *McClure's Magazine* 38 (Mar. 1912): 575–591.

Ullman, Victor. *Martin R. Delany: The Beginnings of Black Nationalism*. Boston, MA: Beacon Press, 1971.

University of Rochester Frederick Douglass Project. http://www.lib.rochester.edu/index.cfm?page=2494.

U.S. Congress. *Report of the Joint Commission on the Conduct of the War*. 38th Congress, 1st sess. Report 65, "Fort Pillow Massacre." Washington, DC: Government Printing Office, 1864.

———. Senate. "'I Do Solemnly Swear': A Half Century of Inaugural Images." Available at www.senate.gov.

———. Senate. *Reports of Committees*. Vol. 1 of 4. Washington, DC: Government Printing Office, 1863.

———. Senate. *Reports of Committees of the Senate of the United States, for the First Session of the 38th Congress*. Report 63, "Fort Pillow Massacre." Washington, DC: Government Printing Office, 1864.

———. *Senate Journal*, 32nd Cong., 1st sess., Dec. 2, 1851–40th Cong., 3rd sess., Jan. 15, 1869. Available at http://memory.loc.gov/ammem/amlaw/lwsjlink.html.

U.S. Department of State. *Citizenship of the United States, Expatriation, and Protection Abroad*. Washington, DC: Government Printing Office, 1906.

U.S. Department of the Interior. National Park Service. Women's Rights National Historical Park. "More Women's Rights Conventions." http://www.nps.gov/wori/historyculture/more-womens-rights-conventions.htm.

U.S. Office of Education. *Special Report of the Commissioner of Education on the Condition and Improvement of Public Schools in the District of Columbia*. Washington, DC: Government Printing Office, 1871.

Uya, Okon Edet. *Black Politicians During Reconstruction: A Case Study of Robert Smalls*. New York: Oxford University Press, 1971.

———. *From Slavery to Public Service: Robert Smalls 1839–1915*. New York: Oxford University Press, 1971.

Valley of the Shadow: Two Communities in the American Civil War. Virginia Center for Digital History, University of Virginia database. http://valley.vcdh.virginia.edu/.

Vidocq, U.S. [pseud.] *The Secrets of Internal Revenue: Exposing the Whiskey Ring, Gold Ring, and Drawback Frauds. . . .* Philadelphia: William Flint, 1870.

Vigilance Committee of Philadelphia. Pennsylvania Anti-Slavery Society. *Journal C of Station No. 2 of the Underground Railroad, Agent William Still, 1852–1857.* Pennsylvania Abolition Society Papers, HSP. Available at http://www.hsp.org/default.aspx?id=993.

Villard, Oswald Garrison. *John Brown 1800–1859, A Biography Fifty Years After.* Boston: Houghton Mifflin, 1910.

Vincent's Semi-annual United States Register, Jan.–July, 1860 (Philadelphia).

Vogel, Morris, historian. Interview with authors, 2004.

Voigt, David Q. Remarks. "Philadelphia's Baseball History." HSP symposium, Feb. 24, 1990.

Von Frank, Albert J. *The Trials of Anthony Burns: Freedom and Slavery in Emerson's Boston.* Cambridge, MA: Harvard University Press, 1998.

Vorenberg, Michael. "Abraham Lincoln and the Politics of Black Colonization." *Journal of the Abraham Lincoln Association* 14 (Summer 1993): 23–46.

Wainwright, Nicholas B. "The Age of Nicholas Biddle, 1825–1841." In *Philadelphia: A Three-Hundred-Year History,* edited by Russell F. Weigley, 258–306. New York: Norton, 1982.

———, ed. *A Philadelphia Perspective: The Diary of Sidney George Fisher Covering the Years 1834–1871.* Philadelphia: HSP, 1967.

Walker, James W. St. G. *The Black Loyalists: The Search for a Promised Land in Nova Scotia and Sierra Leone, 1783–1870.* Toronto: University of Toronto Press, 1999.

Wallace, Henry E. *Philadelphia Reports.* Vol. 6. Philadelphia: J. B. Hunter, 1870.

Walsh, John. "The Penal Laws Era." Irish Cultural Society of the Garden City Area, Apr. 2007. http://www.irish-society.org/Hedgemaster%20Archives/Penal_Laws.htm.

Walther, Eric H. *The Shattering of the Union: America in the 1850s.* Lanham, MD: Rowman & Littlefield, 2003.

Walther, Rudolph J. *Happenings in Ye Olde Philadelphia 1680–1900.* Philadelphia: Walther Printing House, 1925.

Wang, Xi. *The Trial of Democracy: Black Suffrage and Northern Republicans, 1860–1910.* Athens: University of Georgia Press, 1997.

Ward, Samuel Ringgold. *Autobiography of a Fugitive Negro: His Anti-Slavery Labours in the United States, Canada, and England.* London: John Snow, 1855.

Ward, William H. ed. *Records of Members of the Grand Army of the Republic.* San Francisco: H. S. Crocker, 1886.

Warner, Robert A. "Amos Gerry Beman—1812–1874: A Memoir on a Forgotten Leader." *Journal of Negro History* 22 (Apr. 1937): 200–221.

Warner, Sam Bass. *The Private City.* Philadelphia: University of Pennsylvania Press, 1968.

Washington, Booker T. *The Story of the Negro: The Rise of the Race from Slavery.* New York: Doubleday, Page, 1909.

Waskie, Anthony. "Forgotten Black Hero of Philadelphia." Biography of O.V. Catto. n.d. http://www.afrolumens.org/rising_free/waskie1.html.

Waters, Sheldon. B. *We Have This Ministry: A History of the First African Presbyterian Church.* Philadelphia: Gloucester Memorial and Historical Society, First African Presbyterian Church, 1994.

Watson, John F. *Annals of Philadelphia and Pennsylvania.* Vol. 1. Philadelphia: J. M. Stoddart, 1877.

Waugh, Barry. *Thomas Smyth (July 14, 1808–August 20, 1873).* Southern Presbyterian Review Digitization Project, PCA Historical Center, St. Louis, 2003. http://www.pcahistory.org/periodicals/spr/bios/smyth.html.

Wayman, Alexander W. *My Recollections of African M. E. Ministers; or, Forty Years' Experience in the African Methodist Episcopal Church.* Philadelphia: A.M.E. Book Rooms, 1881.

Webb, Frank J. *The Garies and Their Friends.* London: G. Routledge, 1857.

Weigley, Russell F. "The Border City in Civil War, 1854–1865." In *Philadelphia: A Three-Hundred-Year History,* edited by Russell F. Weigley, 363–416. New York: Norton, 1982

Weisenfeld, Judith. "Who Is Sufficient for These Things? Sara G. Stanley and the American Missionary Association, 1864–1868." In *This Far by Faith: Readings in African-American Women's Religious Biography,* edited by Judith Weisenfeld and Richard Newman, 203–219. New York: Routledge, 1996.

Weld, Theodore Dwight. *American Slavery as It Is: Testimony of a Thousand Witnesses.* New York: American Anti-Slavery Society, May 1839.

Weldon, Shawn. *Our Faith Filled Heritage: The Archdiocese of Philadelphia, 1808–2008.* Document covering 1808–1861. N.p., 2006.

Wesley, Dorothy Porter, and Constance Porter Uzelac, eds. *William Cooper Nell, Selected Writings, 1832–1874.* Baltimore: Black Classics Press, 2002.

West, Michael Rudolph. *The Education of Booker T. Washington: American Democracy and the Idea of Race Relations.* New York: Columbia University Press, 2006.

Westcott, Thompson. *The Historic Mansions and Buildings of Philadelphia: With Some Notice of Their Owners and Occupants.* Philadelphia: Porter & Coates, 1877.

———. *The Official Guide Book to Philadelphia.* Philadelphia: Porter & Coates, 1875.

Whitaker, David Kimball, Milton Clapp, William Gilmore Simms, and James Henly Thornwell, eds. *Southern Quarterly Review* 7 (1845).

White, Jacob C. Jr., Papers. HSP.

White, Jonathan W., ed. *A Philadelphia Perspective: The Civil War Diary of Sidney George Fisher.* New York: Fordham University Press, 2007.

White, Shane, and Graham White. *Styling: African American Culture from Its Beginnings to the Zoot Suit.* Ithaca, NY: Cornell University Press, 1998.

Whitehead, Karsonya Wise. "Reconstructing Memories: A Case Study of Emilie Davis, a Nineteenth-Century Freeborn Colored Woman." PhD diss., University of Maryland, Baltimore County, 2009.

Whiteman, Maxwell. *Gentlemen in Crisis: The First Century of the Union League of Philadelphia, 1862–1962.* Philadelphia: Union League of Philadelphia, 1975.

Whittier, John Greenleaf. *The Complete Poetical Works of John Greenleaf Whittier.* Boston: Houghton Mifflin, 1892.

———. *The Works of Whittier.* Vol. 3, *Anti-Slavery Poems and Songs of Labor and Reform.* Project Gutenberg, 2005. http://www.gutenberg.org/etext/9576.

Wiggins, David K., and Patrick B. Miller. *The Unlevel Playing Field: A Documentary History of the African American Experience in Sport.* Urbana: University of Illinois Press, 2003.

Wightman, William M. *Life of William Capers.* Nashville, TN: Methodist Episcopal Church South, 1902.

Wikramanayake, Marina. *A World in Shadow: The Free Black in Ante-Bellum South Carolina.* Columbia: University of South Carolina Press, 1973.

Wilbanks, Charles, ed. *Walking by Faith: The Diary of Angelina Grimké, 1828–1835.* Columbia: University of South Carolina Press, 2003.

Wilds, Scott, genealogist. Interview with authors, various dates, 2003–2008.

Willson, Rev. John O. *Sketch of the Methodist Church in Charleston, S.C., 1785–1887.* Charleston: Lucas, Richardson, 1888.

Wilson, Carol. *Freedom at Risk: The Kidnapping of Free Blacks in America, 1780–1865.* Lexington: University Press of Kentucky, 1994.

Winch, Julie, historian. Interview with authors, various dates, 2006–2009.

Winch, Julie. *A Gentleman of Color: The Life of James Forten.* New York: Oxford University Press, 2002.

———, ed. *The Elite of Our People: Joseph Willson's Sketches of Black Upper-Class Life in Antebellum Philadelphia.* University Park: Penn State University Press, 2000.

Winik, Jay. *April 1865: The Month that Saved America.* New York: HarperCollins, 2001.

Winkelman, Diana Michelle. "The Rhetoric of Henry Highland Garnet." Master's thesis, Baylor University, 2007.

Winston, Michael R. "The Howard University Department of History, 1913–1973." *Negro History Bulletin,* July–Dec. 1998.

Wolf, Edwin II. *Negro History: 1553–1903.* Philadelphia: LC, 1969.

Woodson, Carter G. *The History of the Negro Church.* 2nd edition. Washington, DC: Associated Publishers, 1921. DocSouth, University Library, University of North Carolina, Chapel Hill. http://docsouth.unc.edu/.

———. *The Negro in Our History.* Washington, DC: Associated Publishers Inc., 1922.

Woodson, Carter G., Collection of Negro Papers and Related Documents. Manuscript Division. LOC.

Wright, Henry C. *Bossism in Cincinnati.* N.p.: privately printed, 1905.

Wright, Louise Wigfall. *A Southern Girl in '61: The War-Time Memories of a Confederate Senator's Daughter.* New York: Doubleday, Page, 1905.

Wright, Marian Thompson. "Negro Suffrage in New Jersey, 1776–1875." *Journal of Negro History* 33 (Apr. 1948): 168–223.

Wright, Richard R. Jr. *Centennial Encyclopaedia of the African Methodist Episcopal Church.* Philadelphia: A.M.E Book Concern, 1916.

———. *The Negro in Pennsylvania: A Study in Economic History.* Philadelphia: A.M.E. Book Concern, 1912; reprint, New York: Arno Press, 1969.

Wynes, Charles E. "Ebenezer Don Carlos Bassett, America's First Black Diplomat." *Pennsylvania History* 51 (July 1984): 232–240.

Yacovone, Donald, historian. E-mail interview with authors, 2005.

Yacovone, Donald, ed. *A Voice of Thunder: The Civil War Letters of George E. Stephens.* Urbana: University of Illinois Press, 1997.

Yellin, Jean Fagan. *Harriet Jacobs: A Life; The Remarkable Adventures of the Woman Who Wrote "Incidents in the Life of a Slave Girl."* New York: Basic Civitas Books, 2004.

Yetman, Norman R., ed. *Voices from Slavery.* Mineola, NY: Dover, 2000.

Young, John R., ed. *Memorial History of the City of Philadelphia.* Vol. 1. New York: New York History, 1895.

★ INDEX ★

Note: Page numbers in italics refer to illustrations.

Daniel R. Biddle, the *Philadelphia Inquirer*'s former politics editor, has been a journalist for more than four decades. His investigative stories on the courts won a Pulitzer Prize and other national awards. He has been a Nieman Fellow at Harvard University and teaches journalism at the University of Delaware.

Murray Dubin, author of *South Philadelphia: Mummers, Memories and the Melrose Diner*, was a reporter and editor at the *Philadelphia Inquirer* for 34 years before leaving the newspaper in 2005. He lives in Philadelphia with his wife, Libby Rosof.